C O N T E N [_____]

G000275106

ROUTE PLANNING & MOTORING INFORMATION

Key to Map Symbols	iv
Key to Map Pages	v
Route Planner	vi-vii
Mileage Chart Britain	viii
Mileage Map Britain	ix
Radio Station Map	Inside back cover

ROAD MAPS

England, Wales & South Scotland: 4 miles to 1 inch	2-77
North Scotland: 6.25 miles to 1 inch	78-89
Ireland: 9 miles to 1 inch	90-97

LONDON MAPS

M25 London Orbital Motorway	98-99
Greater London - West: 1.25 miles to 1 inch	100-101
Greater London - East: 1.25 miles to 1 inch	102-103
Central London Street Plan: 4 inches to 1 mile	104-105

URBAN AREA MAPS 1.25 miles to 1 inch

Southampton - Portsmouth	106-107
Cardiff	108
Bristol & Bath	109
West Midlands	110-111
Derby & Nottingham	112-113
South Yorkshire	114-115
Merseyside	116-117
Greater Manchester	118-119
West Yorkshire	120-121
Tyne & Wear	122-123
Teesside	123
Greater Glasgow	124-125
Edinburgh	126

CITY & TOWN CENTRE PL[___]

Aberdeen, Bath	127
Belfast	97
Birmingham	110
Blackpool, Bournemouth	127
Bradford	120
Brighton, Bristol	127
Buxton, Cambridge, Canterbury, Cardiff, Cheltenham, Chester	128
Cork	91
Coventry, Derby, Dover	129
Dublin	95
Dundee, Durham, Eastbourne	129
Edinburgh, Exeter, Folkestone	130
Glasgow	124
Gloucester, Harrogate, Hastings	130
Hereford, Inverness, Kingston-upon-Hull	131
Leeds	120
Leicester, Lincoln	131
Liverpool	117
Manchester	118
Middlesbrough, Newcastle upon Tyne	123
Norwich	131
Nottingham, Oxford, Perth, Plymouth, Portsmouth, Reading	132
Salisbury, Scarborough	133
Sheffield	115
Southampton, Stoke-on-Trent, Stafford, Swansea	133
Torbay, Weston-super-Mare, Winchester, Windsor, Worcester, York	134

INDEX

Index to Place Names in Britain	135-166
Index to Place Names in Ireland	167-168

KEY TO MAP SYMBOLS

Road Maps Britain & Ireland

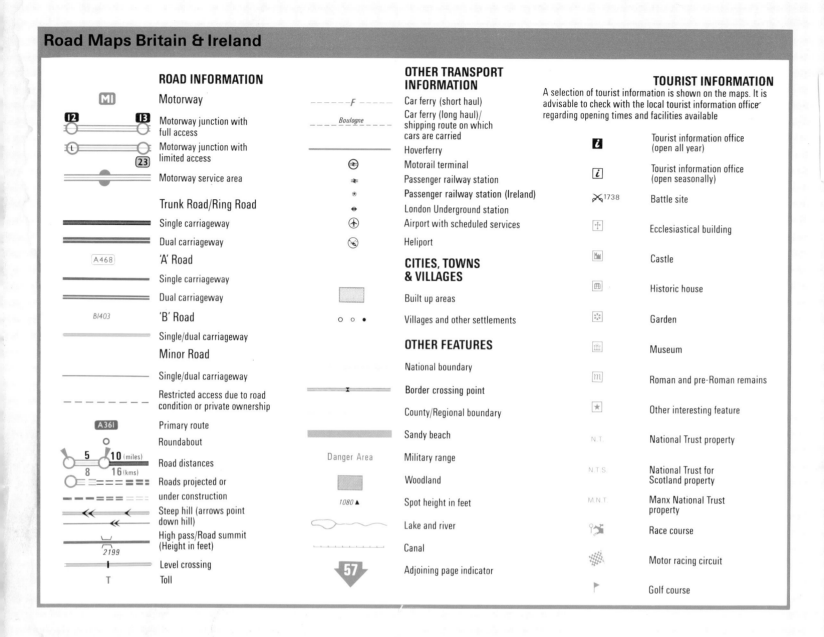

ROAD INFORMATION

MI Motorway

Motorway junction with full access

Motorway junction with limited access

Motorway service area

Trunk Road/Ring Road

Single carriageway

Dual carriageway

'A' Road — A468

Single carriageway

Dual carriageway

'B' Road — B1403

Single/dual carriageway

Minor Road

Single/dual carriageway

Restricted access due to road condition or private ownership

Primary route — A361

Roundabout

5 **10** (miles) / 8 **16** (kms) Road distances

Roads projected or under construction

Steep hill (arrows point down hill)

High pass/Road summit (Height in feet) 2199

Level crossing

T Toll

OTHER TRANSPORT INFORMATION

--- F Car ferry (short haul)

--- Boulogne Car ferry (long haul)/ shipping route on which cars are carried

Hoverferry

Motorail terminal

Passenger railway station

Passenger railway station (Ireland)

London Underground station

Airport with scheduled services

Heliport

CITIES, TOWNS & VILLAGES

Built up areas

o o ● Villages and other settlements

OTHER FEATURES

National boundary

Border crossing point

County/Regional boundary

Sandy beach

Danger Area Military range

Woodland

1080 ▲ Spot height in feet

Lake and river

Canal

57 Adjoining page indicator

TOURIST INFORMATION

A selection of tourist information is shown on the maps. It is advisable to check with the local tourist information office regarding opening times and facilities available

ℓ Tourist information office (open all year)

i Tourist information office (open seasonally)

✕ 1738 Battle site

Ecclesiastical building

Castle

Historic house

Garden

Museum

Roman and pre-Roman remains

★ Other interesting feature

N.T. National Trust property

N.T.S. National Trust for Scotland property

M.N.T. Manx National Trust property

Race course

Motor racing circuit

Golf course

Urban Area Maps

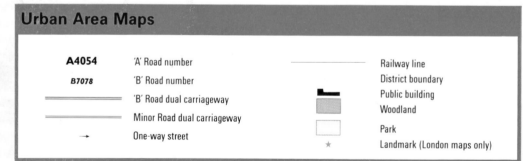

A4054 'A' Road number

B7078 'B' Road number

'B' Road dual carriageway

Minor Road dual carriageway

→ One-way street

Railway line

District boundary

Public building

Woodland

Park

★ Landmark (London maps only)

City & Town Centre Plans

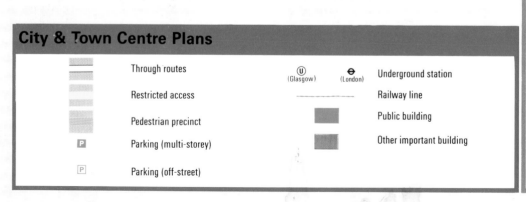

Through routes

Restricted access

Pedestrian precinct

P Parking (multi-storey)

P Parking (off-street)

U (Glasgow) **⊖** (London) Underground station

Railway line

Public building

Other important building

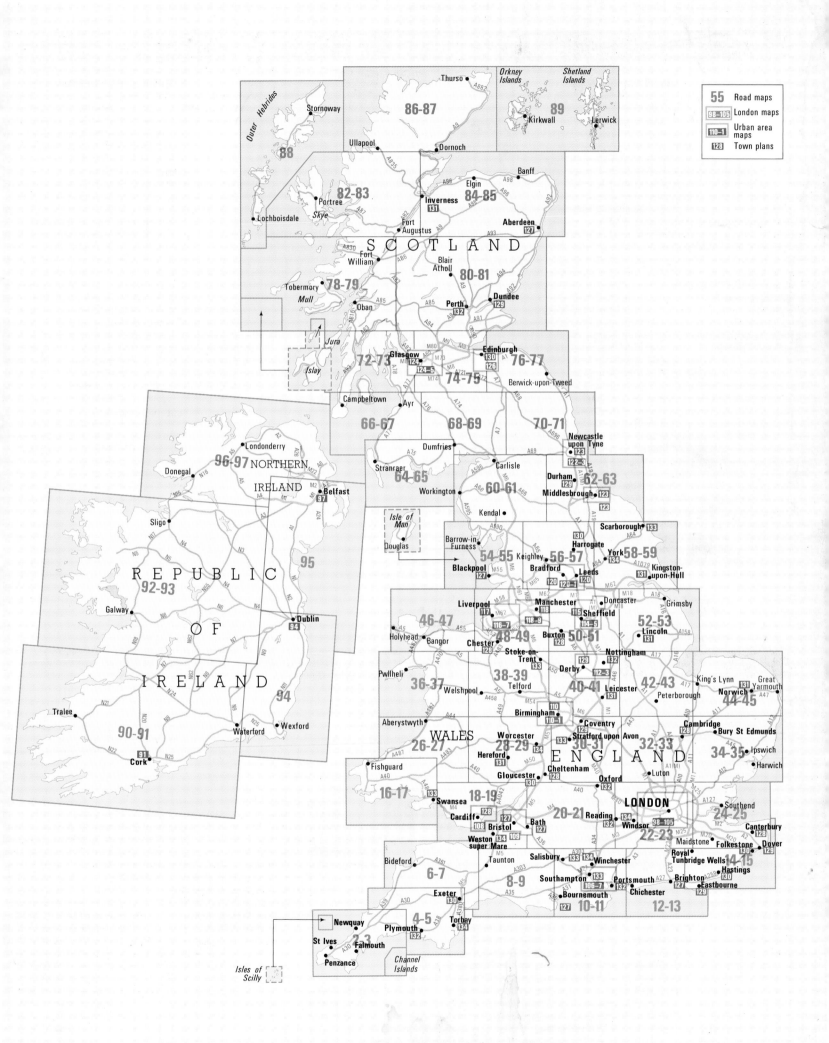

KEY TO MAP PAGES

Road maps 55
London maps 98-105
Urban area maps 110-1
Town plans 128

v

© Collins

ROUTE PLANNER

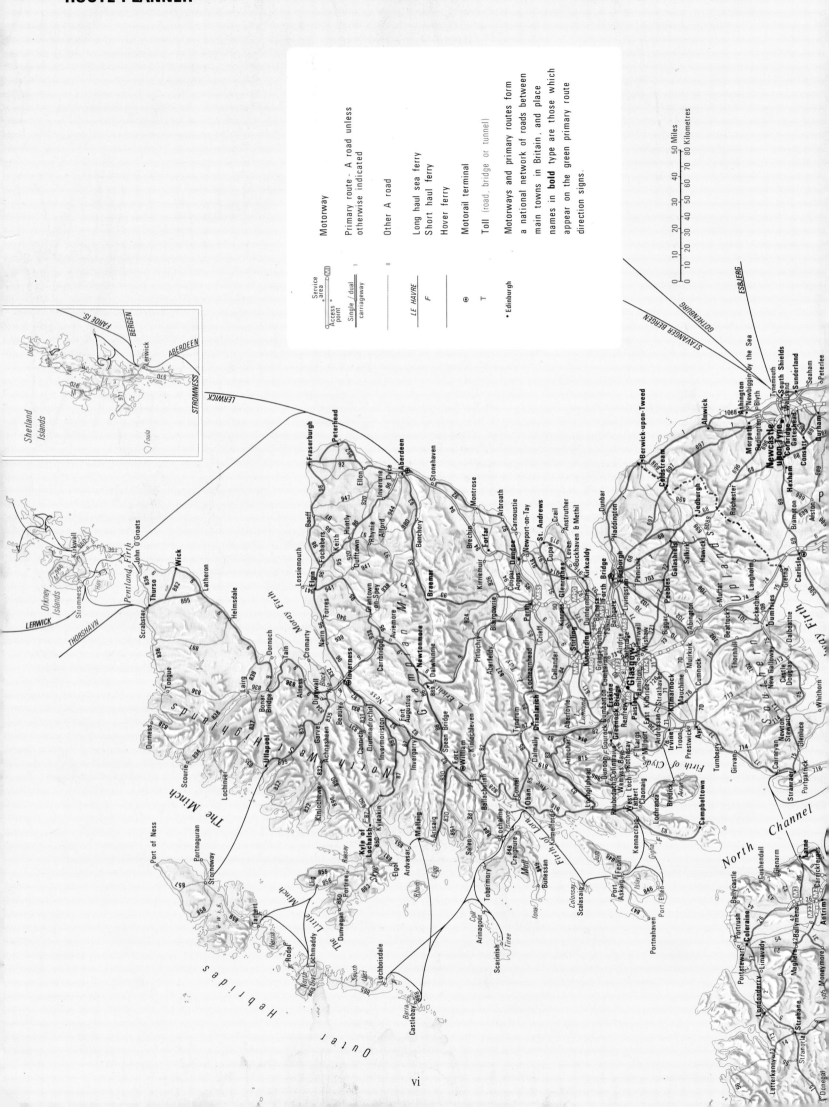

MILEAGE CHART BRITAIN

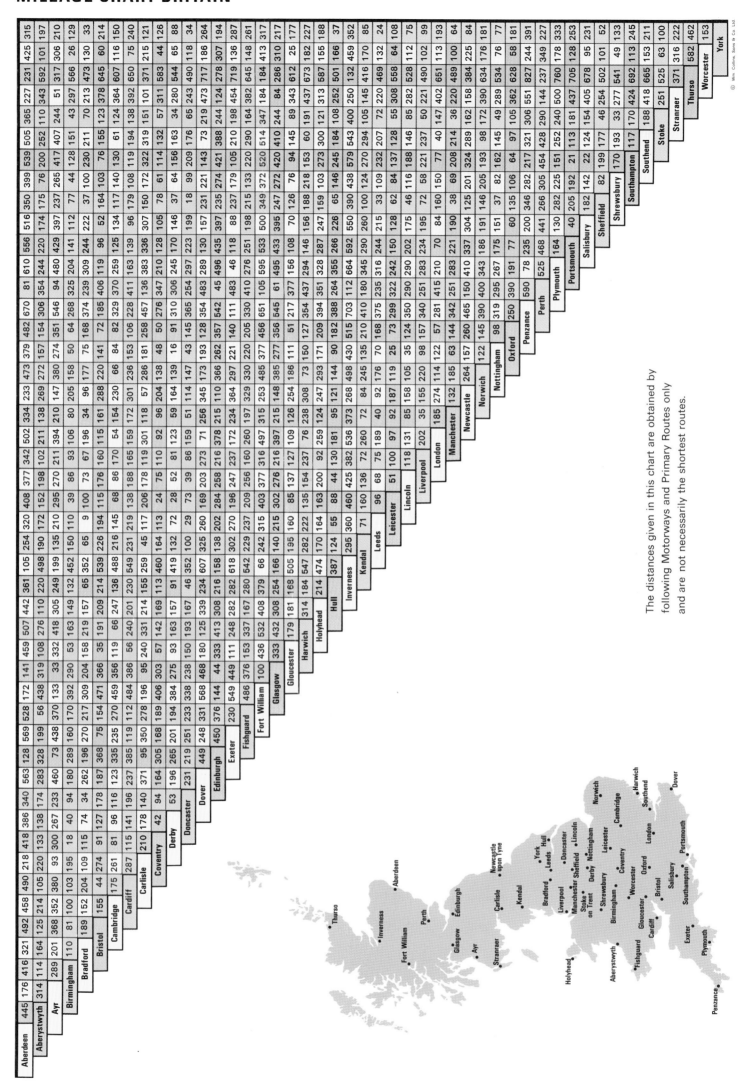

The distances given in this chart are obtained by following Motorways and Primary Routes only and are not necessarily the shortest routes.

© Wm Collins, Sons & Co. Ltd.

MILEAGE MAP BRITAIN

Road distances between centres have been calculated using motorway, primary routes, and principal A roads, and not necessarily by the most direct route. The figures are shown in miles but can be converted to kilometres by multiplying by 1·6.

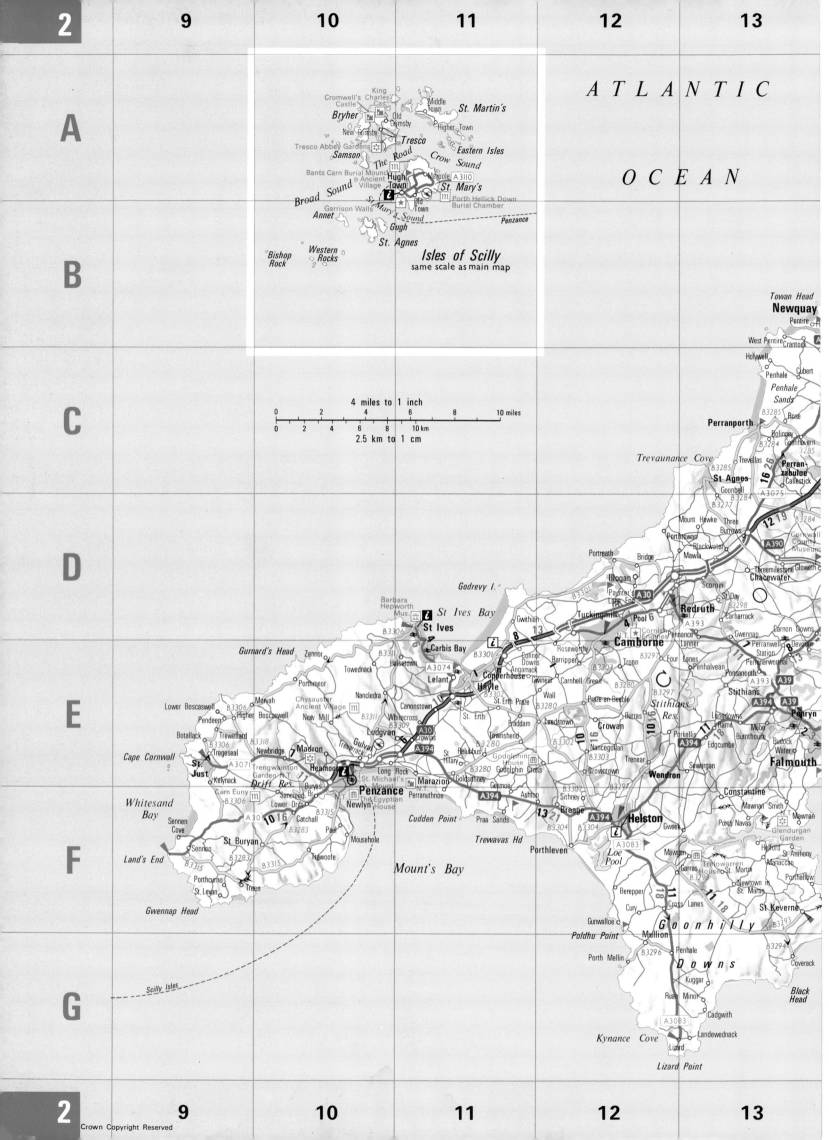

A T L A N T I C

O C E A N

Isles of Scilly
same scale as main map

Cromwell's
Castle
King
Charles
Cas.
Middle
Town
St. Martin's
Bryher
Old
Grimsby
Higher Town
New Grimsby
Tresco
Eastern Isles
Tresco Abbey Gardens
Crow Sound
Samson
The Road
Bants Carn Burial Mound
& Ancient Village
Maypole A3110
Broad Sound
Hugh
Town
St. Mary's
Porth Hellick Down
Burial Chamber
Garrison Walls
Old
Town
St. Mary's Sound
Annet
Gugh
Penzance
St. Agnes
Bishop
Rock
Western
Rocks

4 miles to 1 inch

0   2   4   6   8   10 miles

0 2 4 6 8 10 km

2.5 km to 1 cm

Towan Head
Newquay
Pentire
West Pentire Crantock
Holywell
Cubert
Penhale
*Penhale
Sands*
Perranporth
Rose B3285
Bolingey
Goonhavern
B3284 B3285
Trevaunance Cove Trevellas
**Perran-
zabuloe** Callestick
St Agnes 16 26
Goonbell A3075
B3284
B3277
Mount Hawke Three
Burrows
12 19 B3284
Porthtowan
Blackwater **Cornwall
County
Museum**
A390
Portreath Bridge
Mawla
Godrevy I. Illogan
Threemilestone Gloweth
B3301 St Day Chacewater
Barbara
Hepworth
Mus. Paynter's
Lane End A30 Scorrier
St Ives Bay Tuckingmill **Redruth** Carharrack
B3306 **St Ives** Gwithian Pool 6 Carharrack
4 A393 B3298
Carbis Bay 8 13 Cornish Engines Carn Brea Gwennap
Gurnard's Head Zennor Roseworthy Carnon Downs
B3306 B3331 **Camborne** Lanner 7 Perranwell
Halsetown B3301 Connor
Downs Barripper A39
Towednack A3074 Angarrack Troon B3297 Penhalvean Perranarworthal
Porthmeor Lelant Gwinear Carnhell Green B3280 Stithians
Morvah Nancledra Copperhouse St. Erth Praze Praze-an-Beeble B3297 **Penryn**
Chysauster
Ancient Village Canonstown **Hayle** B3302 Wall Stithians
Res. A394 A39
Lower Boscaswell New Mill Whitecross St. Erth Praddam Leedstown Crowan Burras Longdowns
Higher Boscaswell B3309 B3280 Nancegollan Porkellis Carne Mabe
Pendeen B3311 A30 Townshend B3302 B3303 Burnthouse Budock
Botallack Ludgvan Crowlas B3280 Godolphin
House Trenear Edgcumbe Water
Trewellard Madron 7 Trevarrack St. Hilary Godolphin Cross Wendron Falmouth
B3306 B3318 Gulval Relubbus Crowntown A394
Tregeseal Newbridge Heamoor B3280 Germoe B3302
Cape Cornwall Trengwainton
Garden N.T. Long Rock Marazion Ashton Sithney Constantine
**St.
Just** A3071 St. Michael's
Mount Perranuthnoe A394 Breage B3304 **Helston** Mawnan Smith
Kelynack Drift Res. Buryas **Penzance** N.T. B3307 B3304 Gweek Port Navas
Carn Euny Sancreed Br. Egyptian
House Praa Sands A3083 Mawgan
Whitesand
Bay Lower Drift **Newlyn** Cudden Point B3304 Loe
Pool Trelowarren
House St. Martin Helford
B3306 Paul Trewavas Hd. Garras B3293 Porthallow
Sennen
Cove **St Buryan** Mousehole Porthleven Berepper Newtown in
St. Martin St. Keverne
Sennen B3283 Cury Cross Lanes 11 18 B3293
Land's End B3315 Trewoofe Mount's Bay Gunwalloe Poldhu Point Mullion Glendurgan
Garden
Porthcurno B3315 Trewavas Hd. 18 Goonhilly
St. Levan Treen Porth Mellin B3296 Penhale Downs B3294
Gwennap Head Kuggar Coverack
Ruan Minor
A3083
Cadgwith
Scilly Isles Kynance Cove Landewednack
Lizard Black
Head
Lizard Point

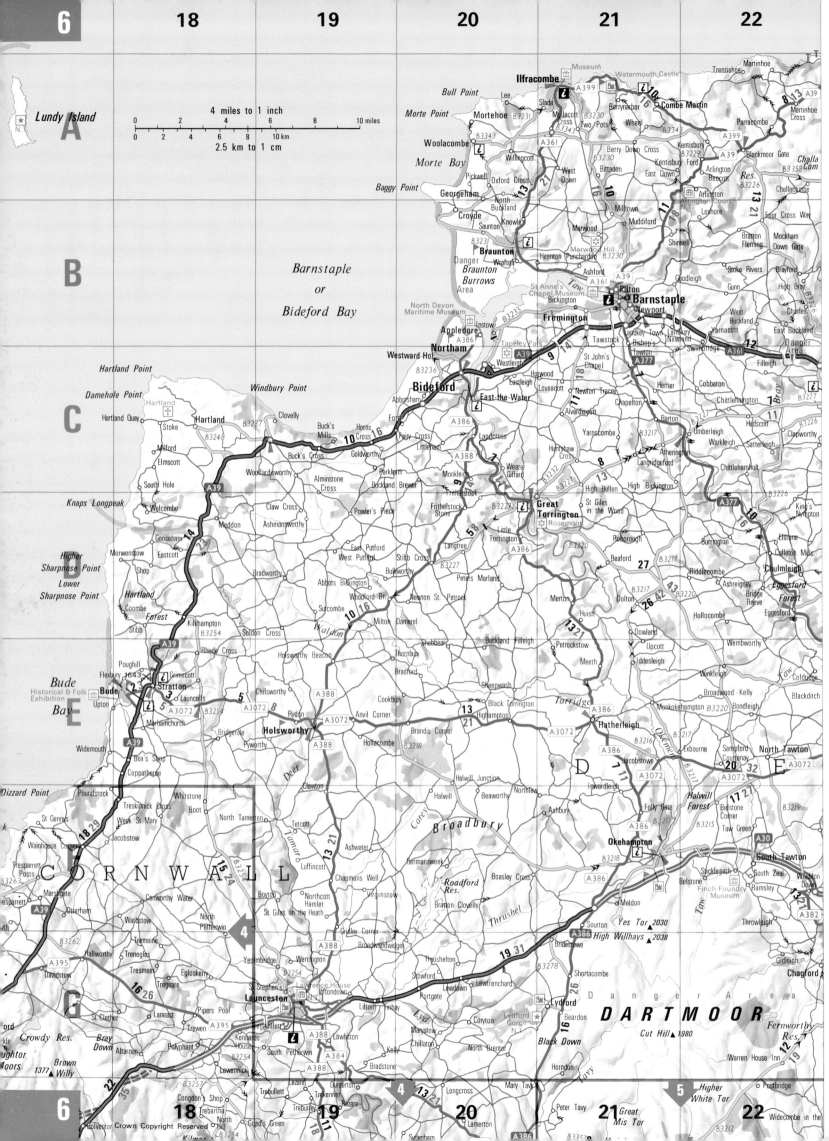

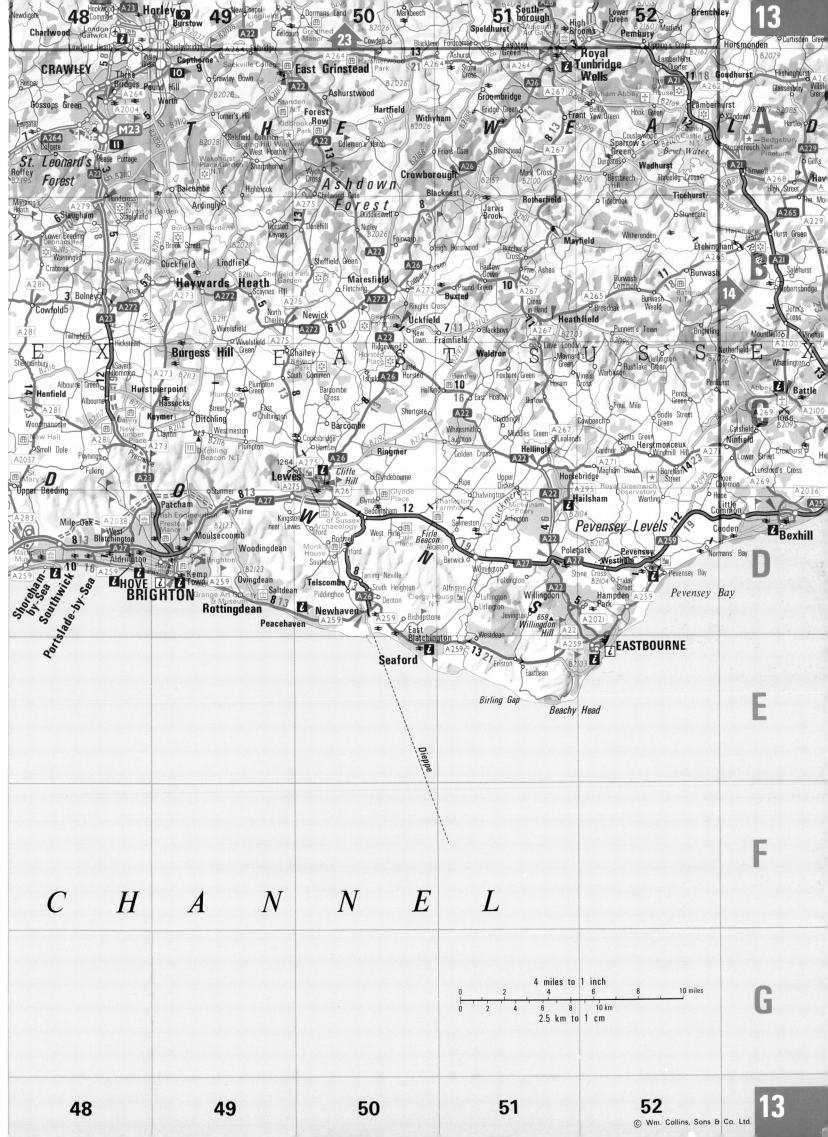

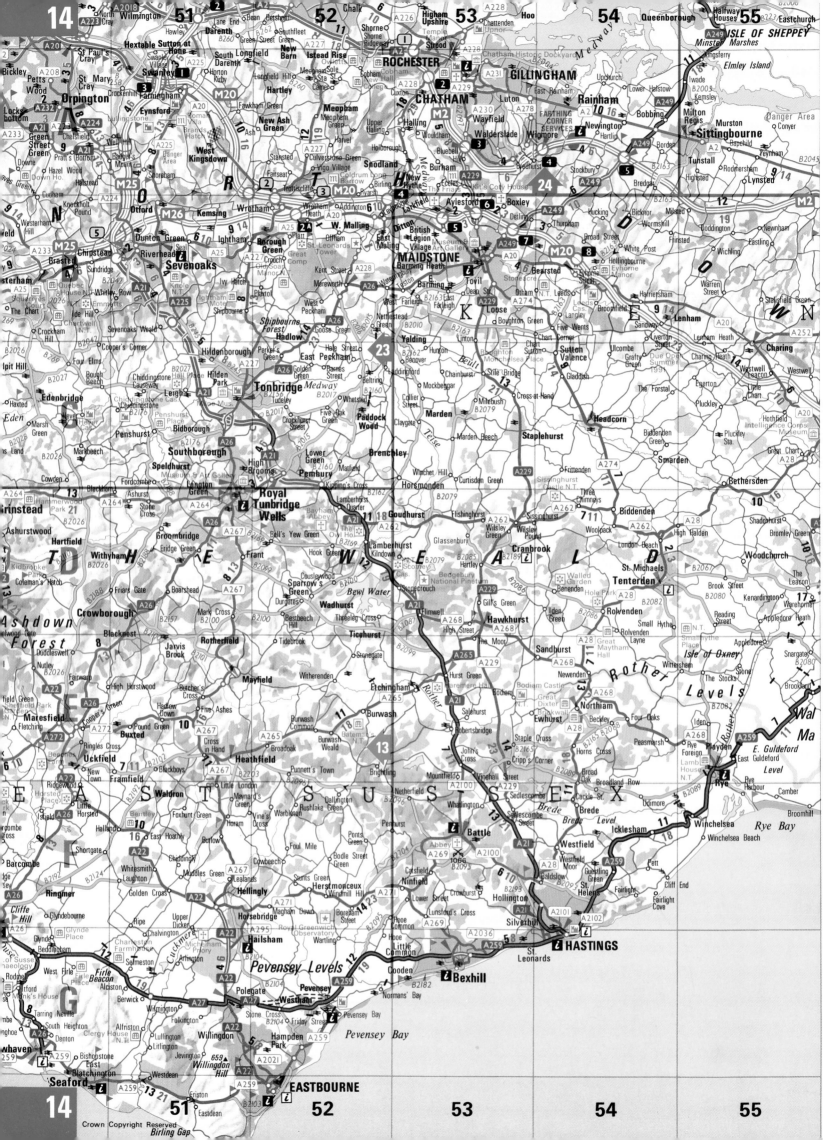

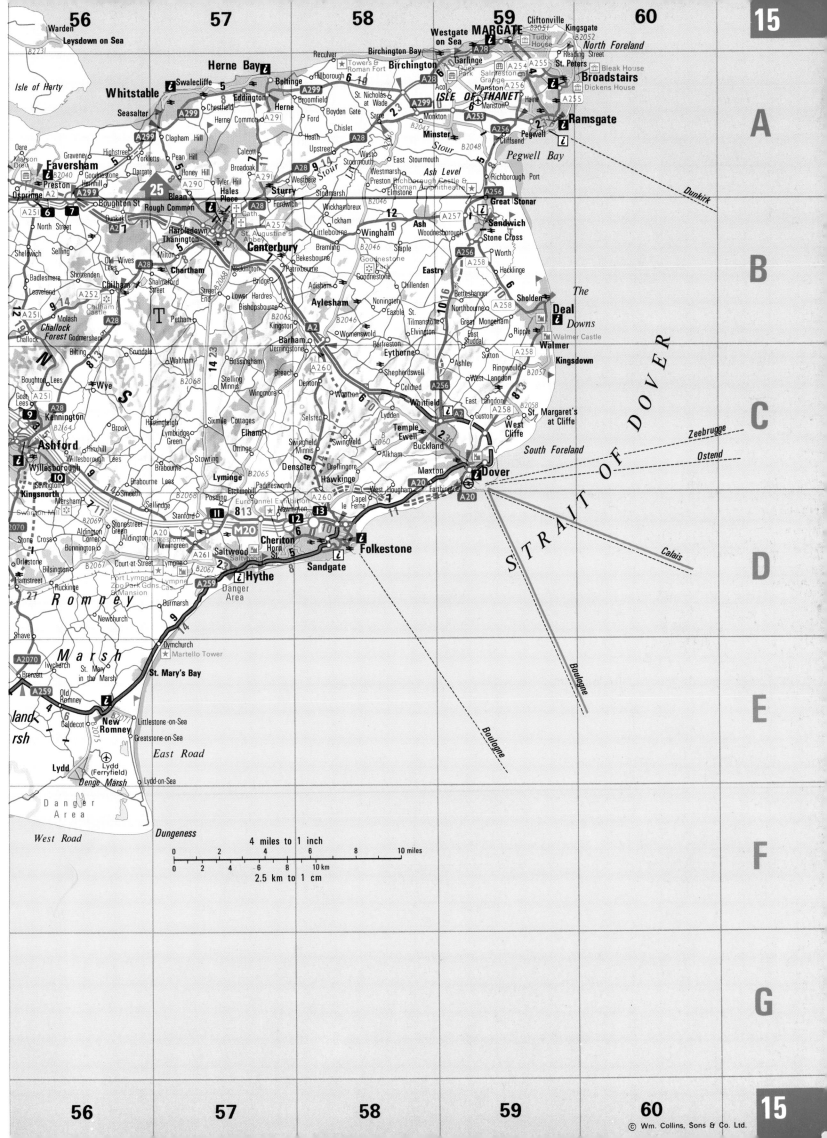

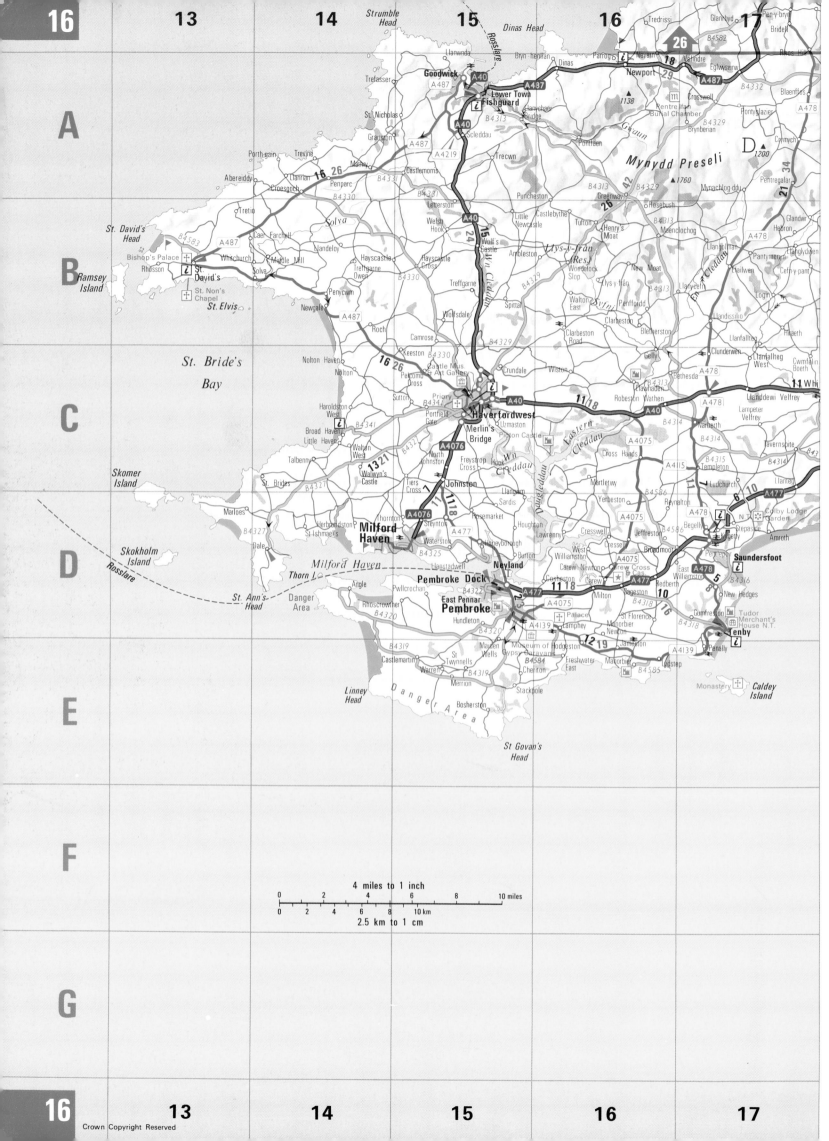

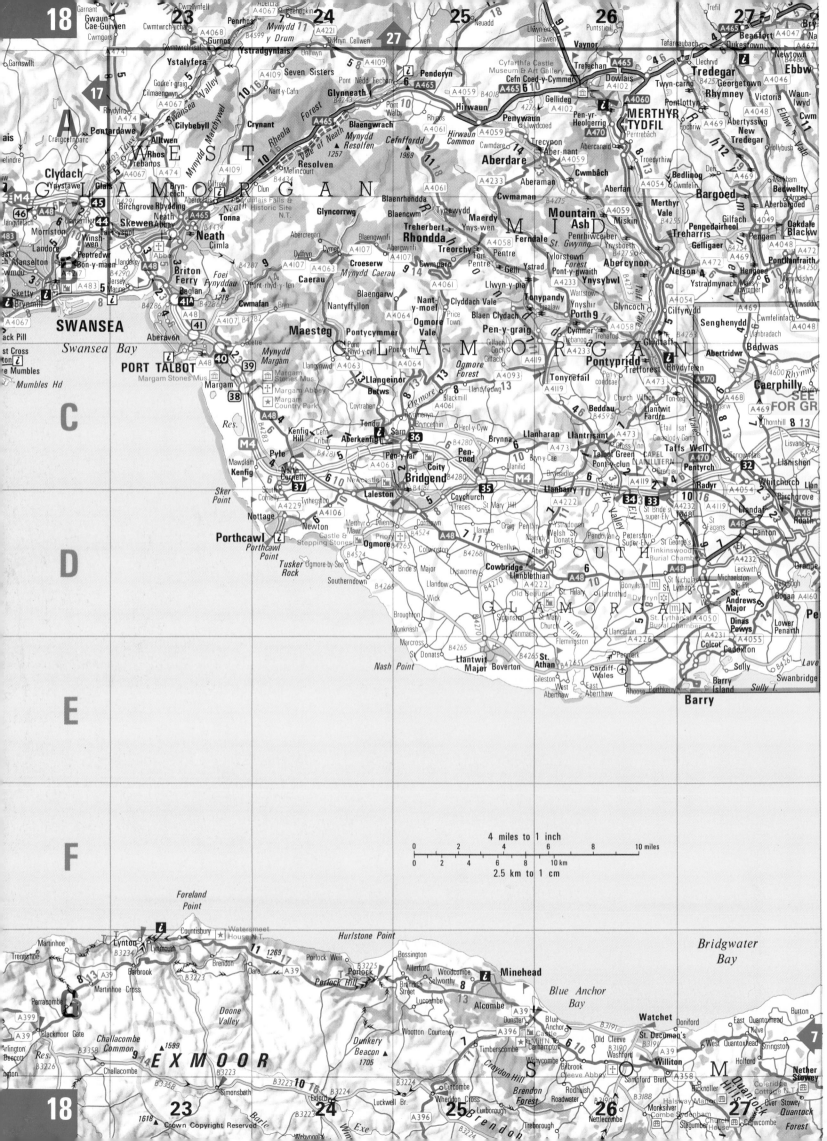

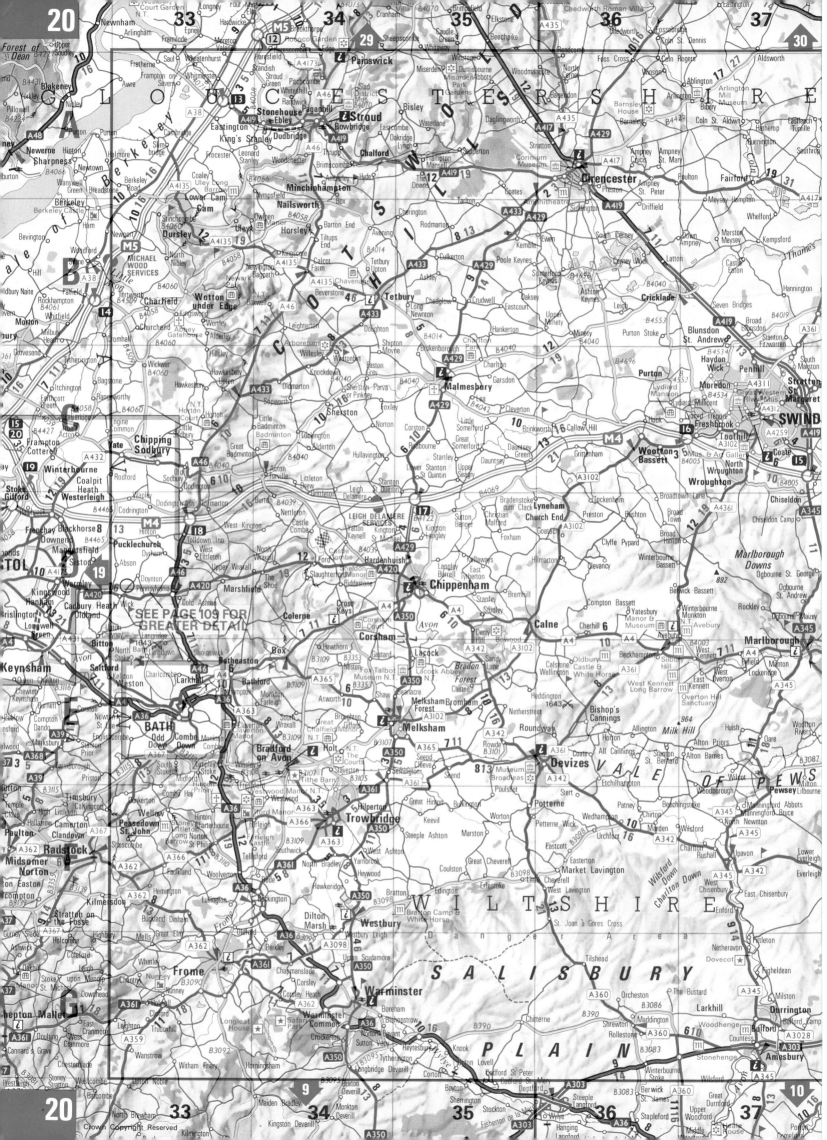

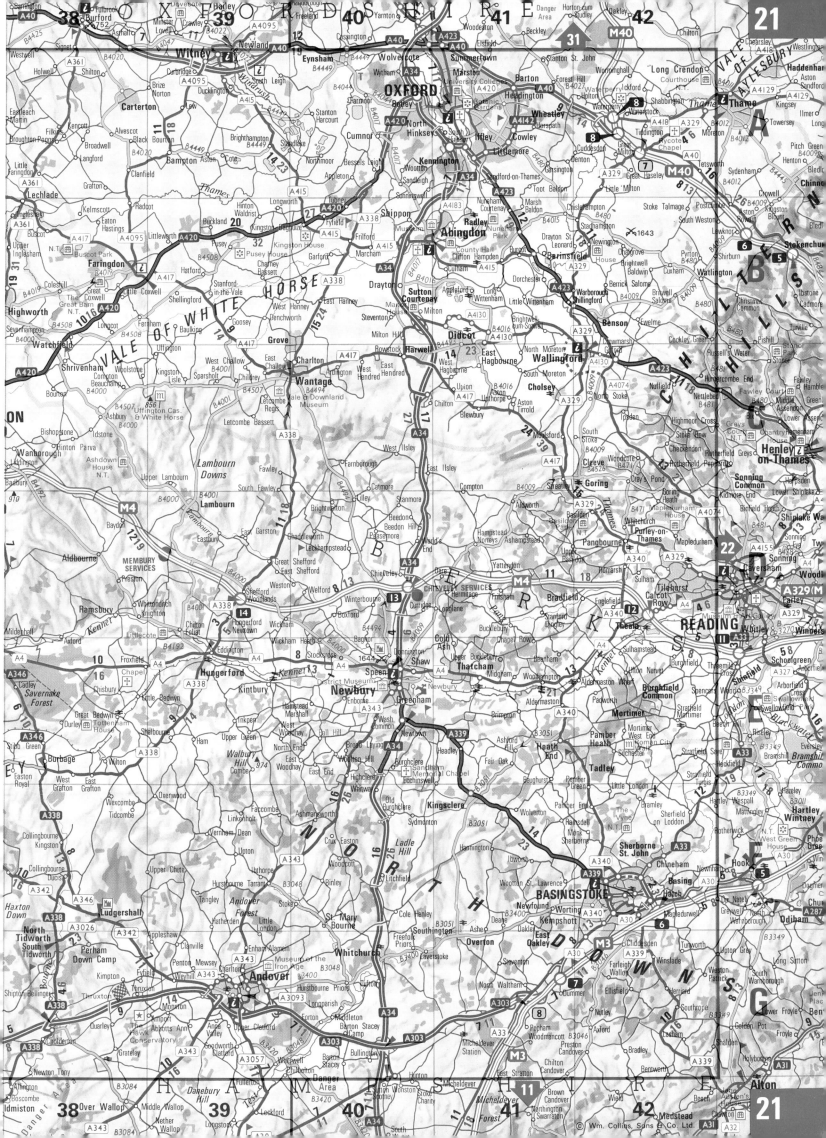

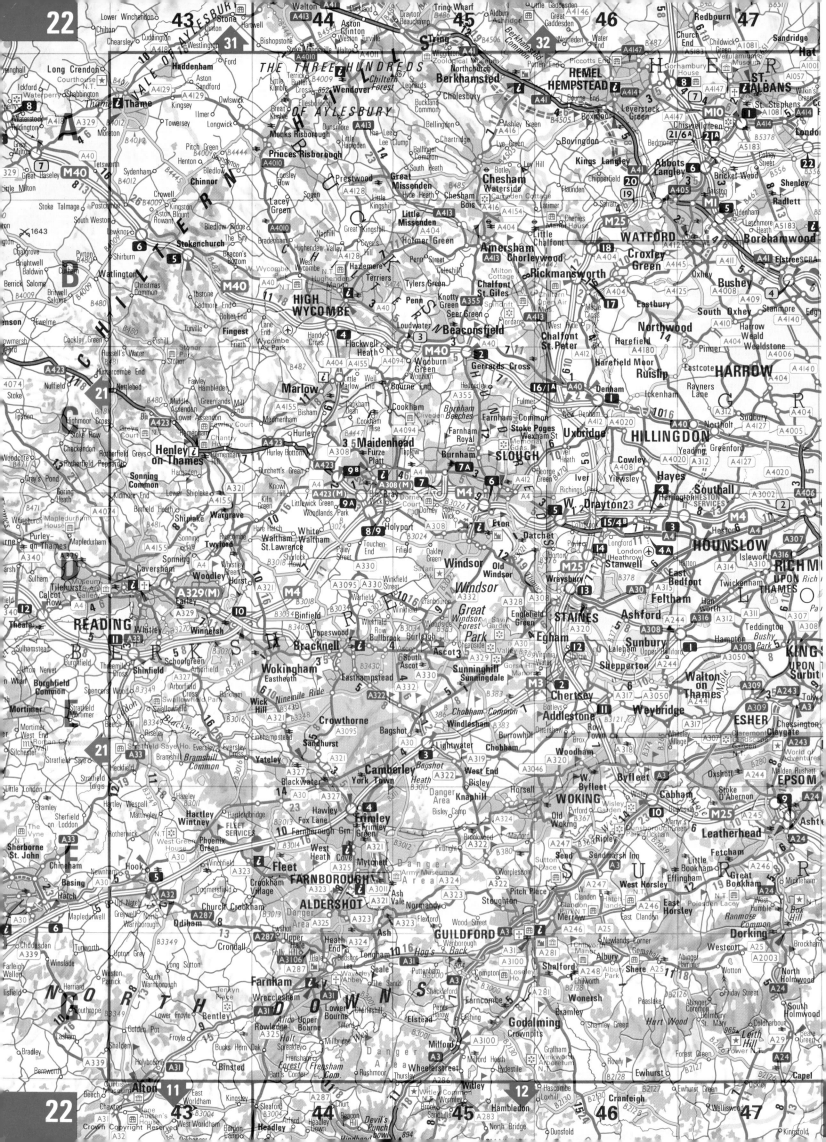

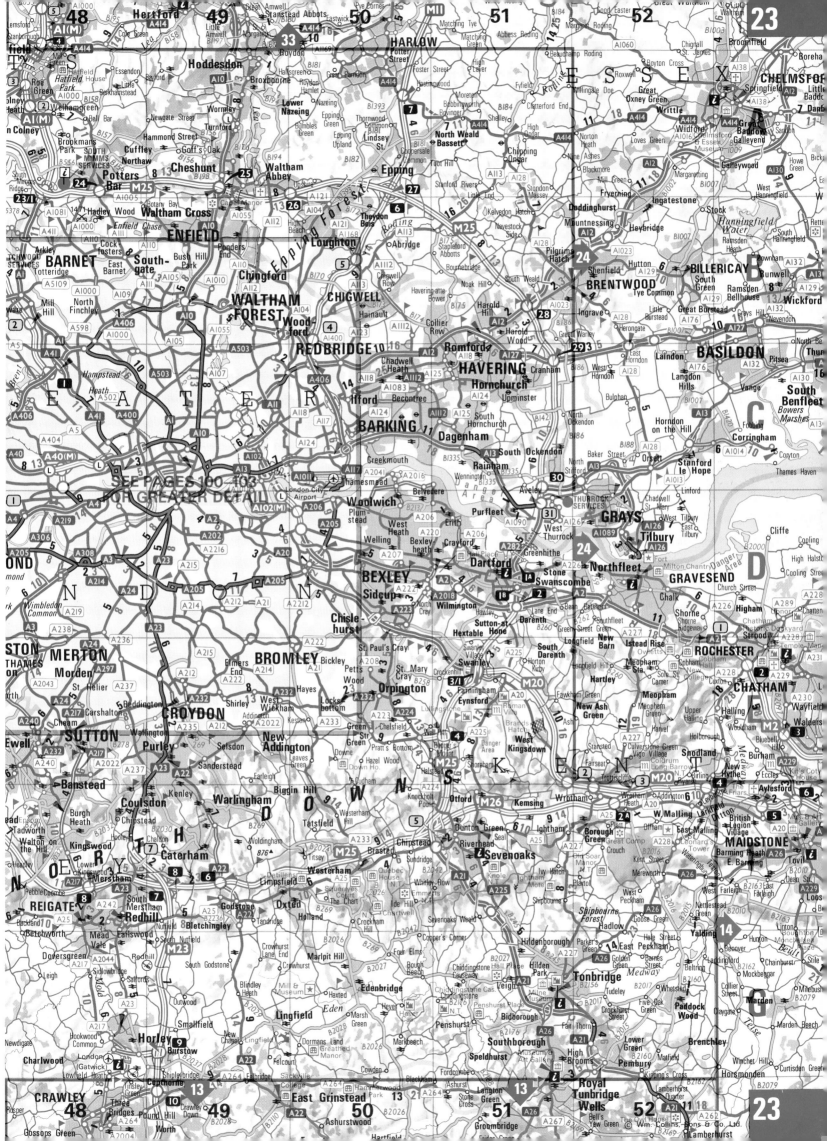

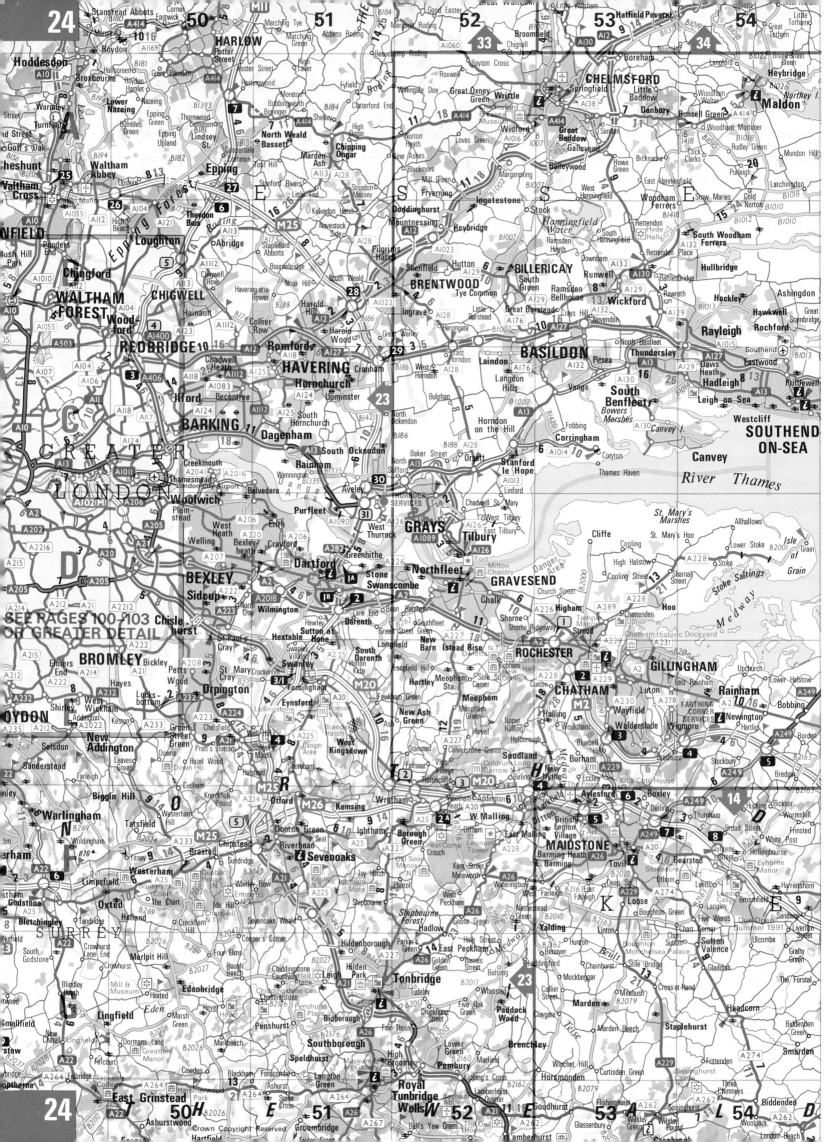

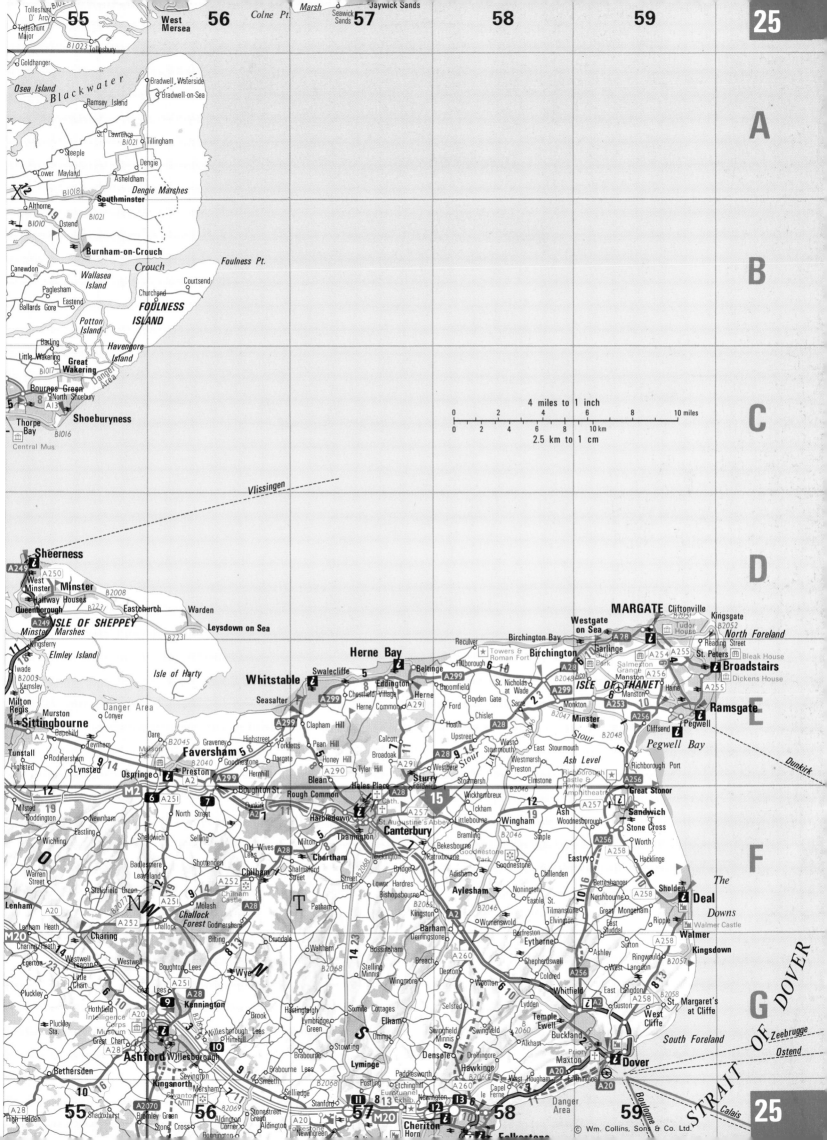

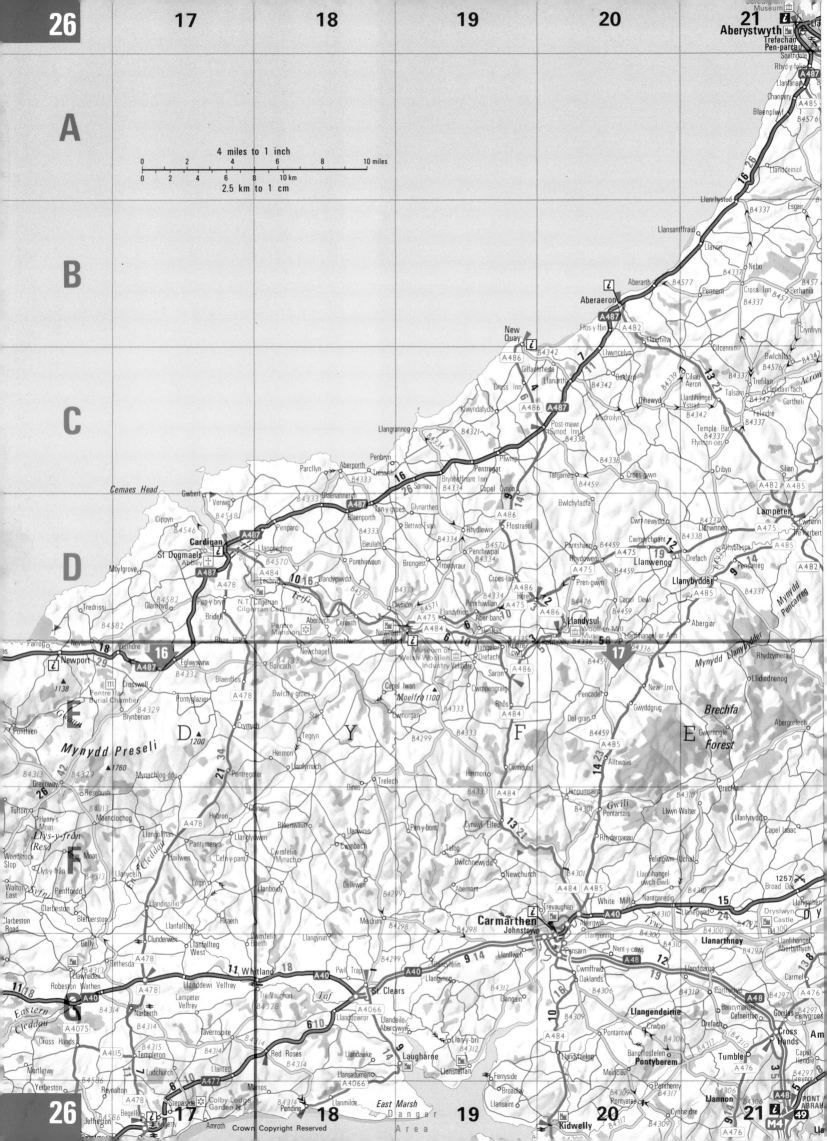

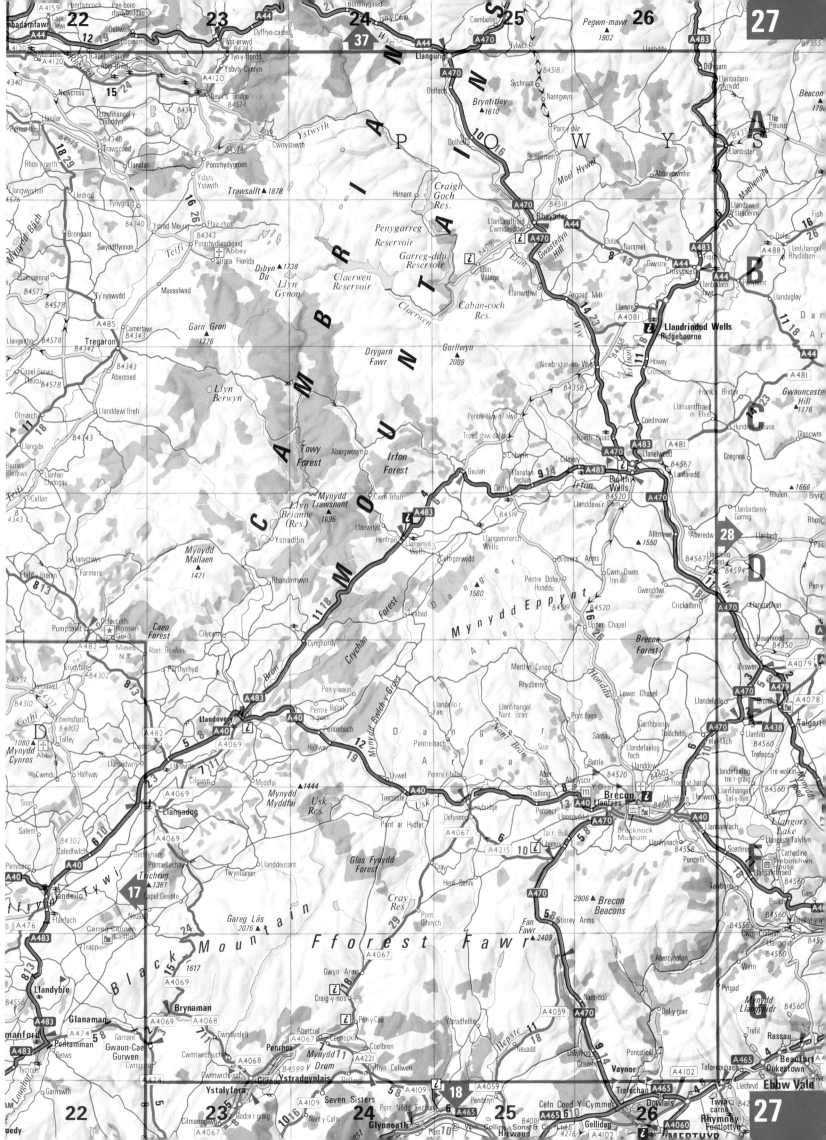

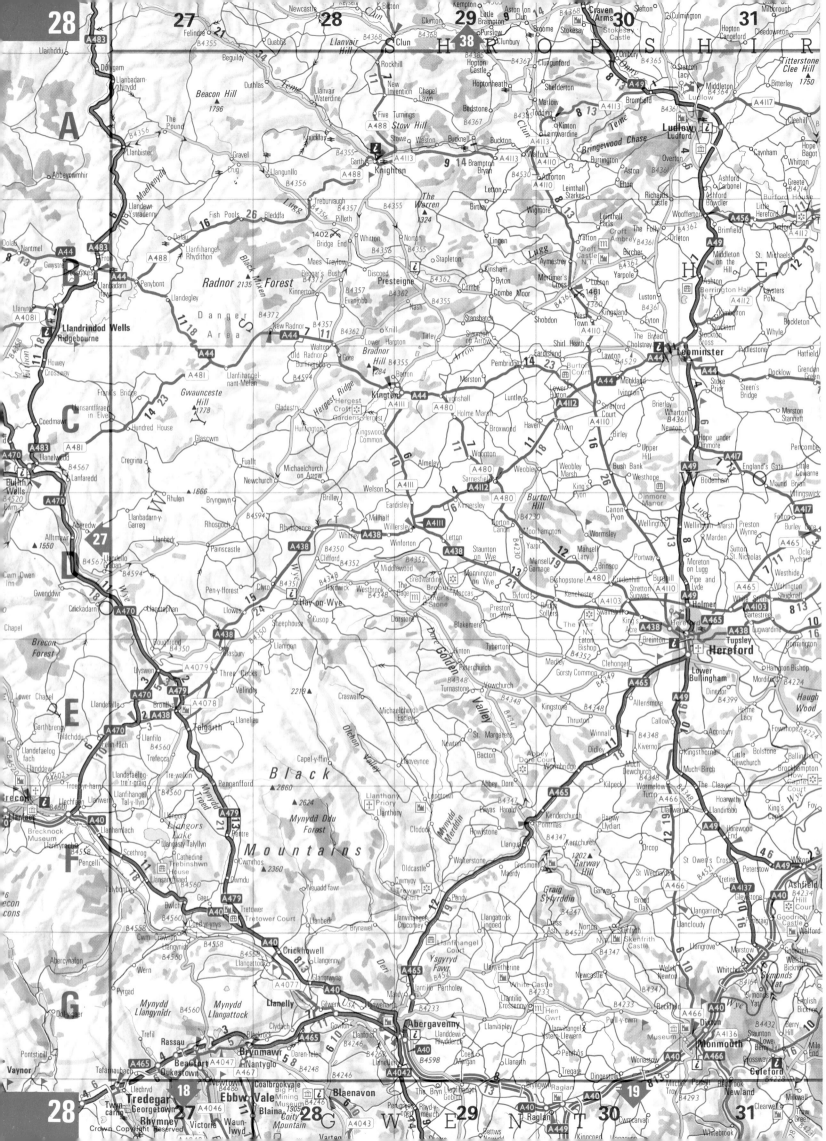

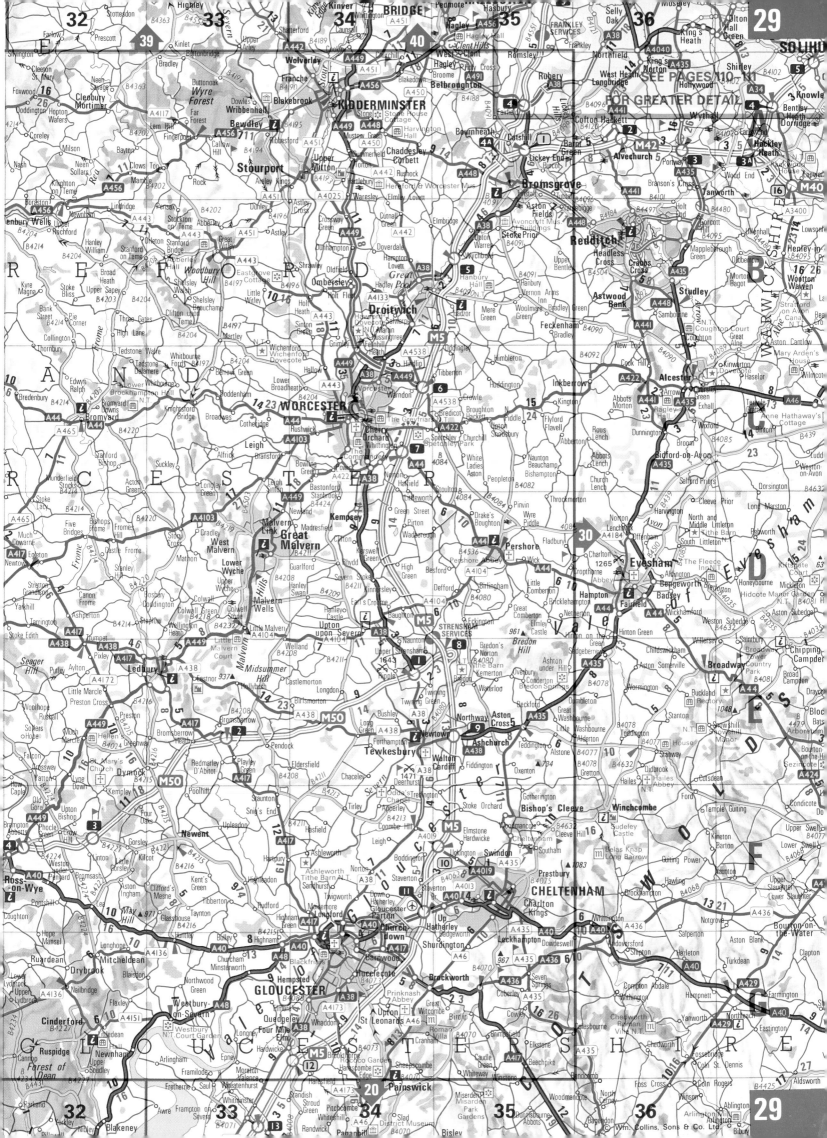

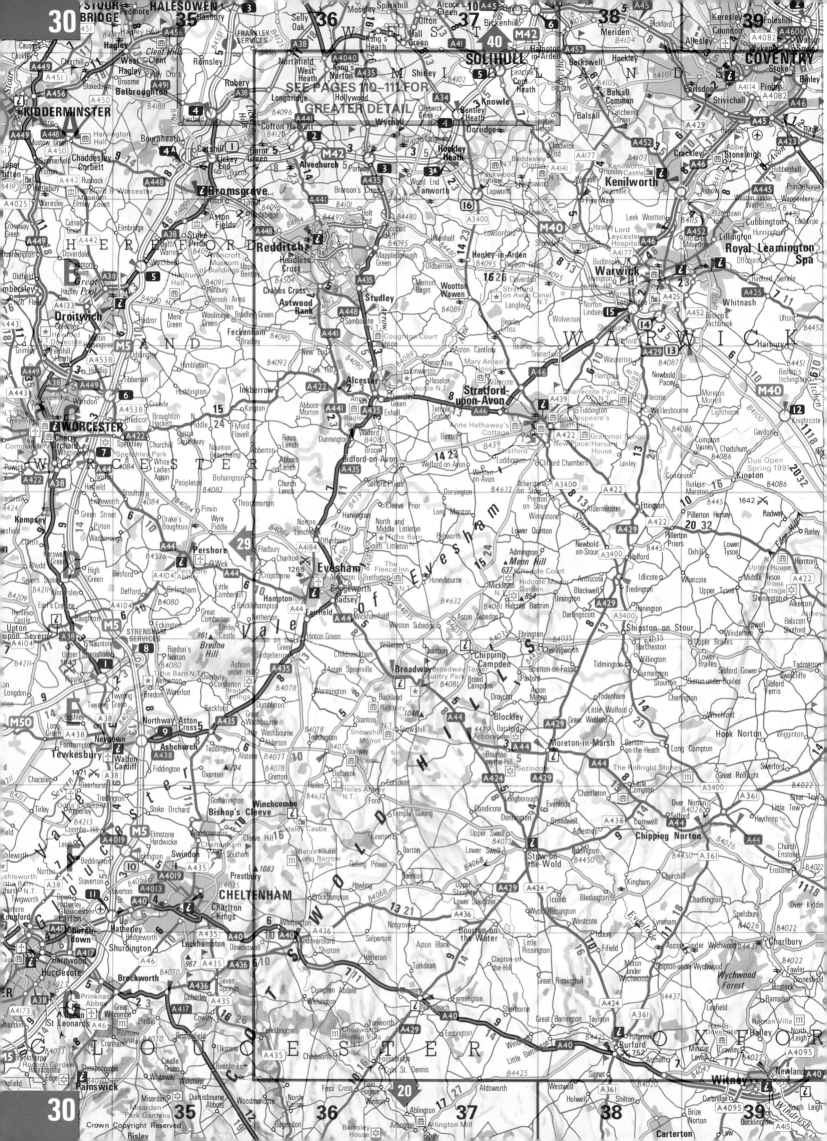

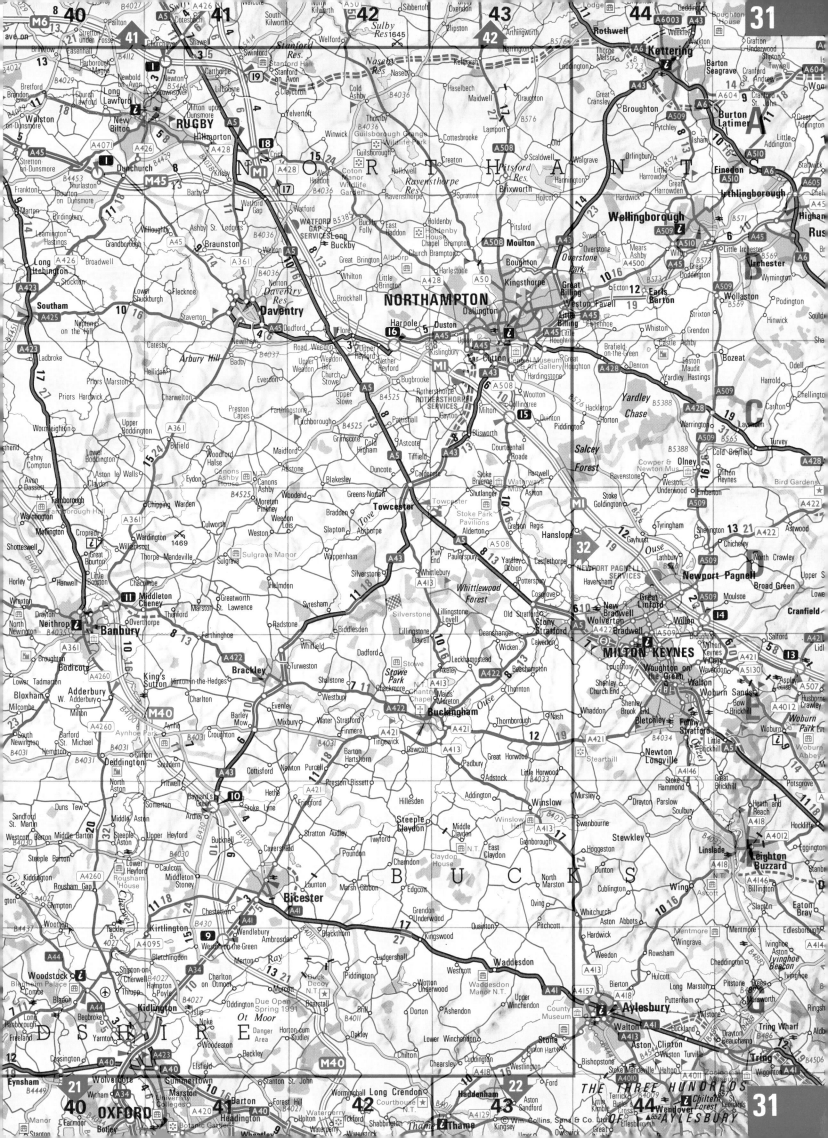

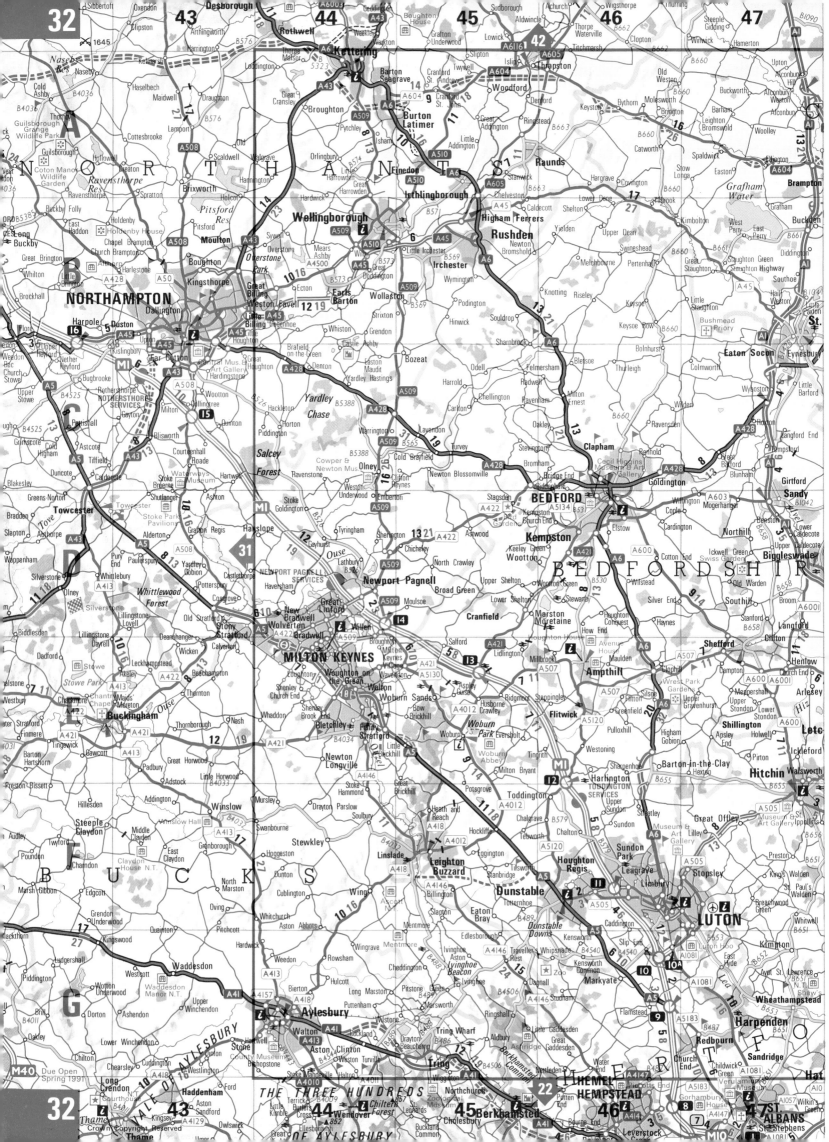

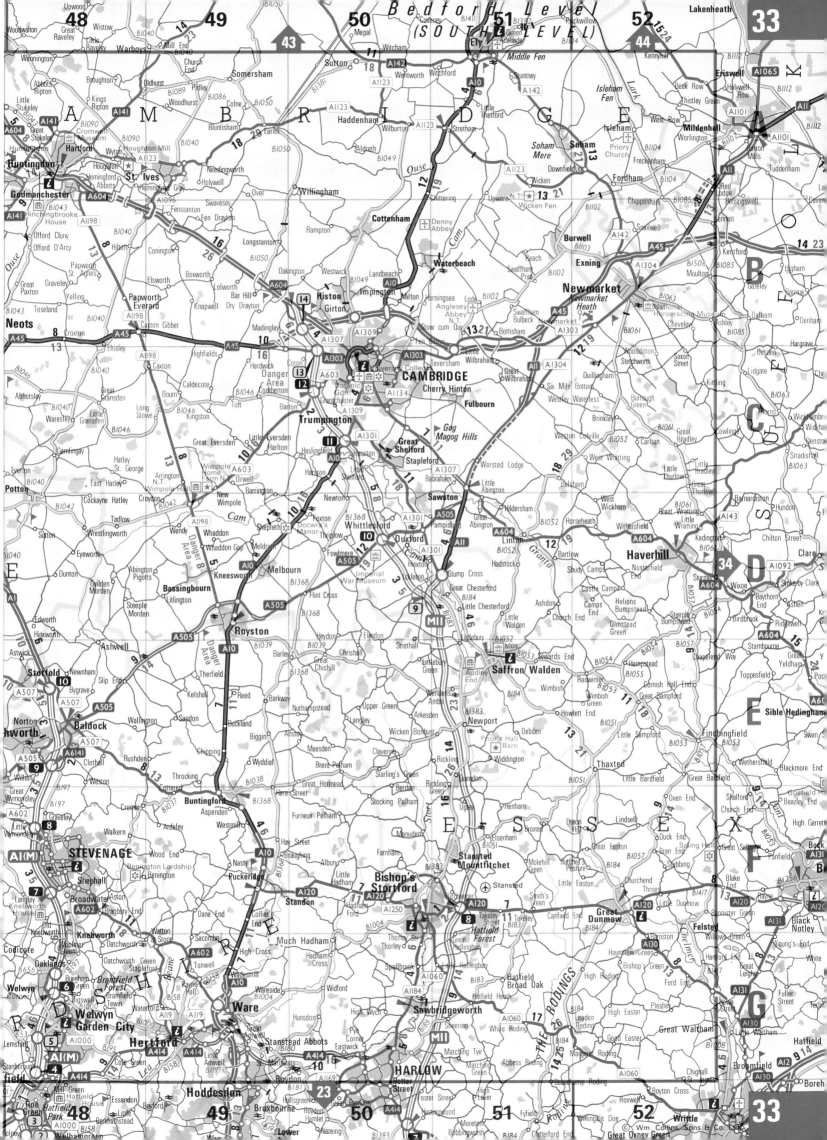

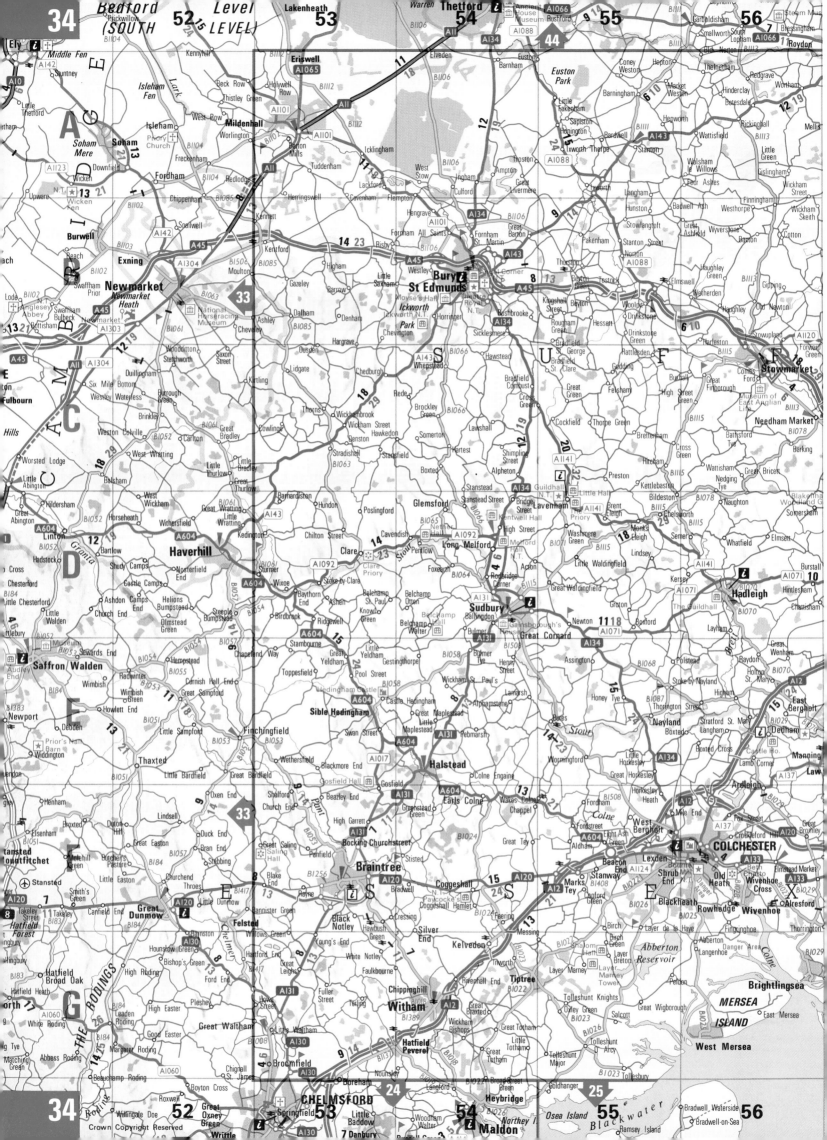

A

B

C

D

E

F

G

LLEYN PENINSULA

Pontllyfni Penygroes
Llanllyfni
Aberdesach
Clynnogfawr Capel-uchaf Nebo
Nasareth
Gyrn-goch
Gurn Ddu Upper Clynnog Pant-glas
Trevor
Yr Eifl 1712 Garn Dolbenmaen Llanfihangel-y-pennant
1849 Llanaelhaearn Bryncir Glan-Dwyfach Dolbenmaen
Llithfaen Golan
Carreg Ddu Pistyll Prenteg
Morfa Nefyn Edern Llangybi St Cybi's Well Rhoslan Pentre'r-felin Criccieth
Nefyn Penarth Fawr Medieval Ho. Llanarmon Moel-y-Gest 861 Porthmadog
Rhos-y-llan Tudweiliog Tan-y-graig Bodffion Y Ffôr Chwilog Morfa Bychan Borth-y-Gêst
Llannor
Penllech Dinas Llaniestyn Efailnewydd Denio Holiday Camp
Llangwnadl Carn Fadryn 1217 Rhyd-y-clafdy Pwllheli West End Pen-ychain
Penrhyn Mawr Meillteyrn Sarn Nanhoron Penrhos Tremadog Bay
Bryncroes Llanbedrog Morfa Harlech
Tŷ-hen Mynydd Rhiw Llandegwning Mynytho
Rhoshirwaun Llangian Abersoch St Tudwal's Road Harlech
Y-Rhiw Plas-yn-Rhiw N.T. Llanbedrog Sarn-bach Bwlch-y-tocyn
Anelog Aberdaron Porth Neigwl or Hell's Mouth
Braich y Pwll Aberdaron Bay Llandanwg
Uwchmynydd Llanenddwyn
Bardsey Sound Pen y Cil Trwyn Cilan Dyffryn Ardudwy
Bardsey Tal-y-bont
Cŵed

Barmouth Bay

Llwyngwril
Llangelynin
Rhoslefain
Tonfanau
Tywyn

4 miles to 1 inch
0   2   4   6   8   10 miles
0 2 4 6 8 10 km
2.5 km to 1 cm

Aberystwyth
Trefechan
Pen-parcau

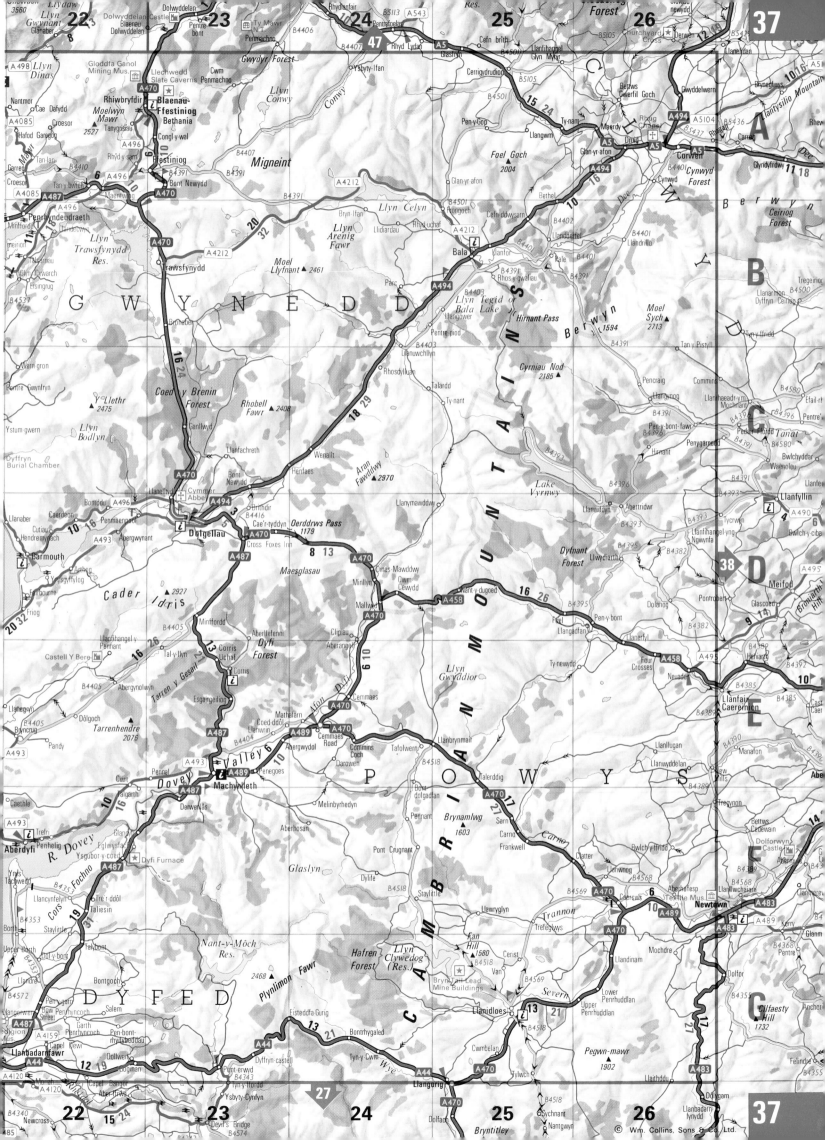

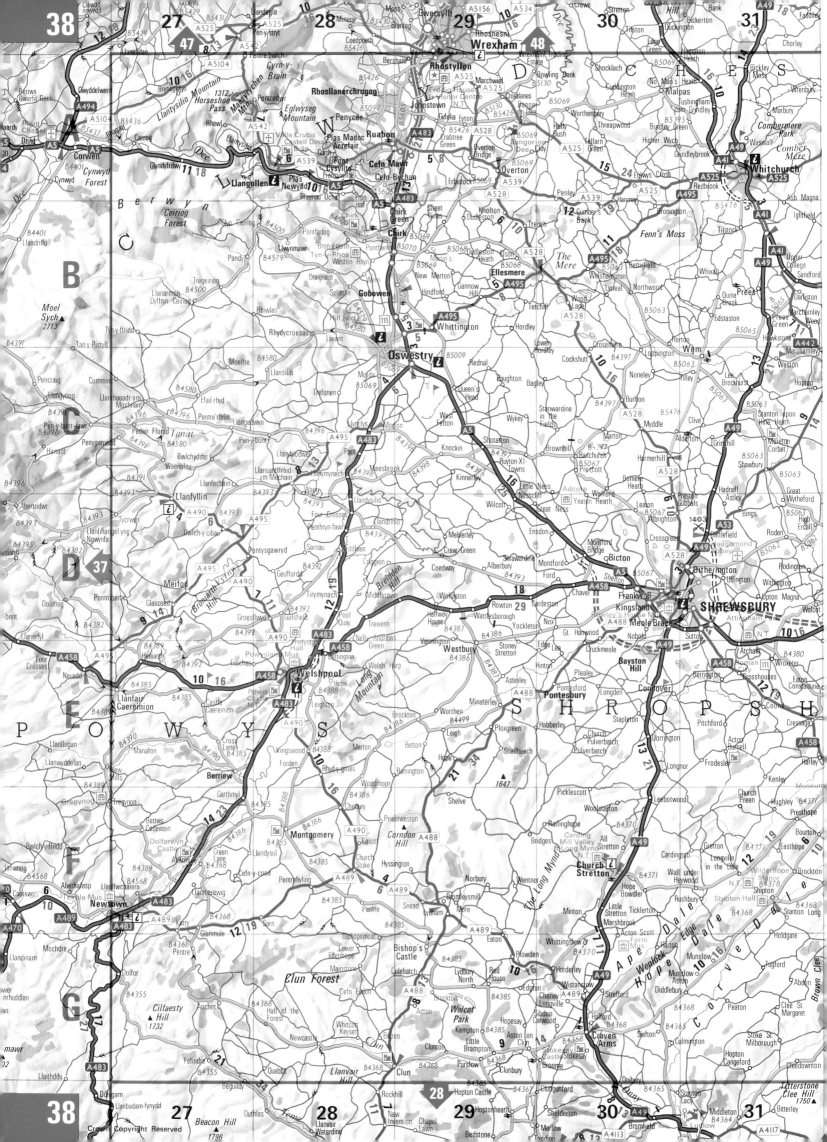

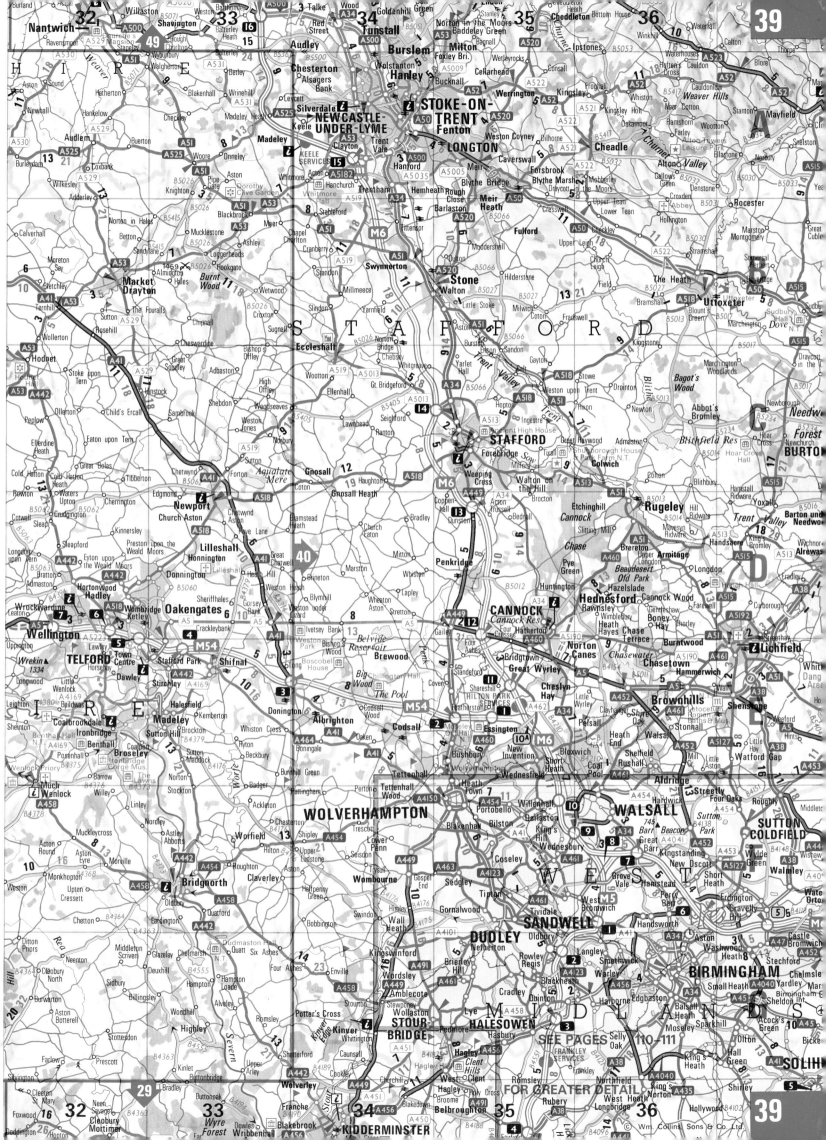

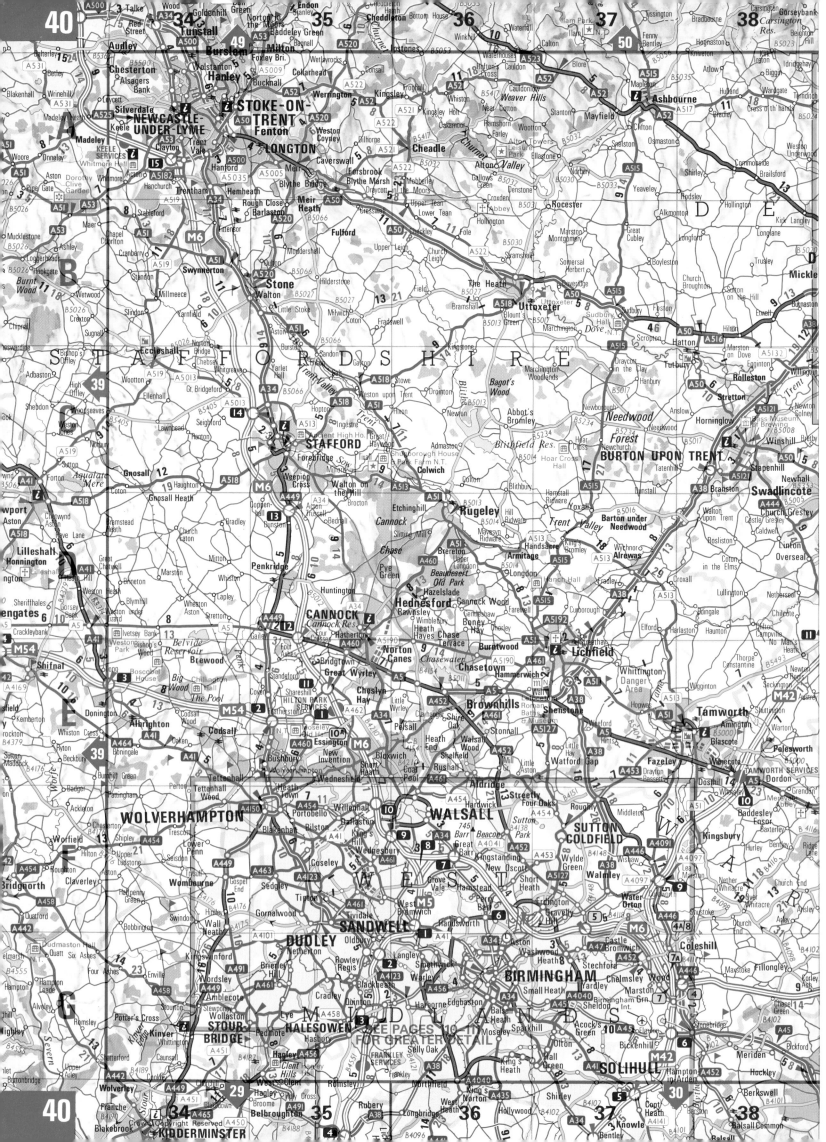

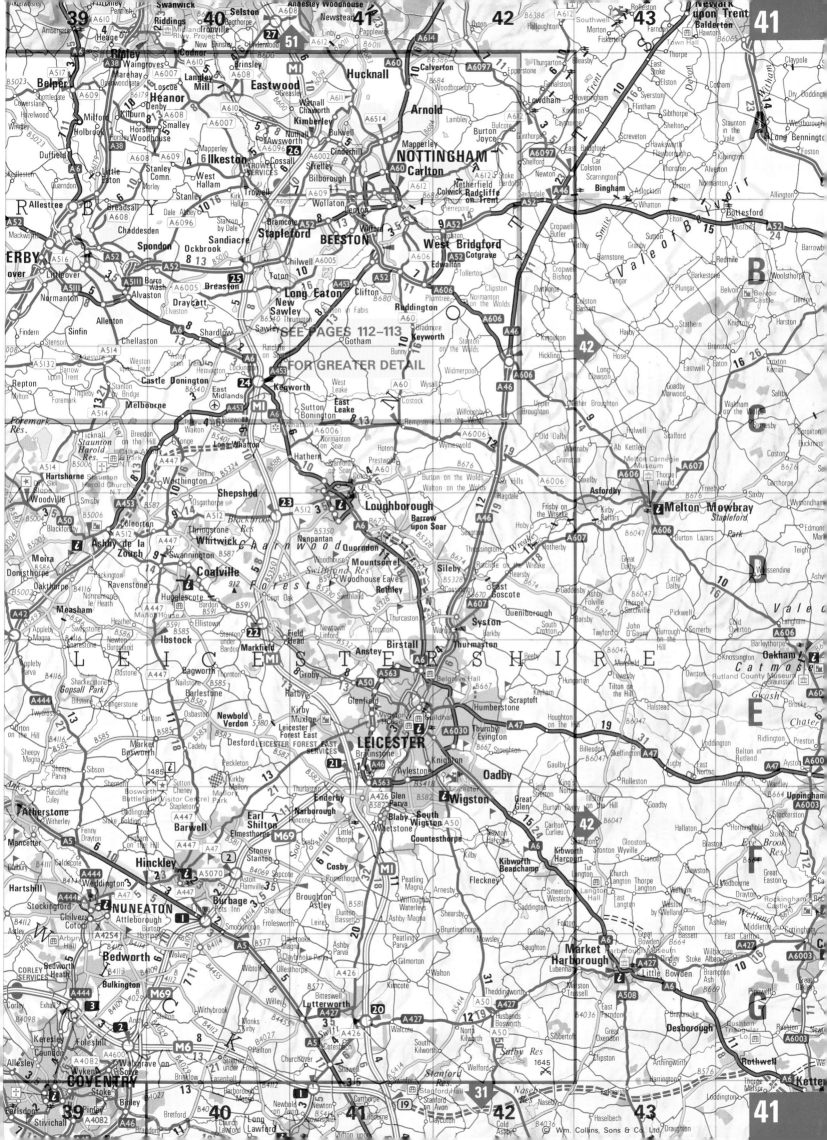

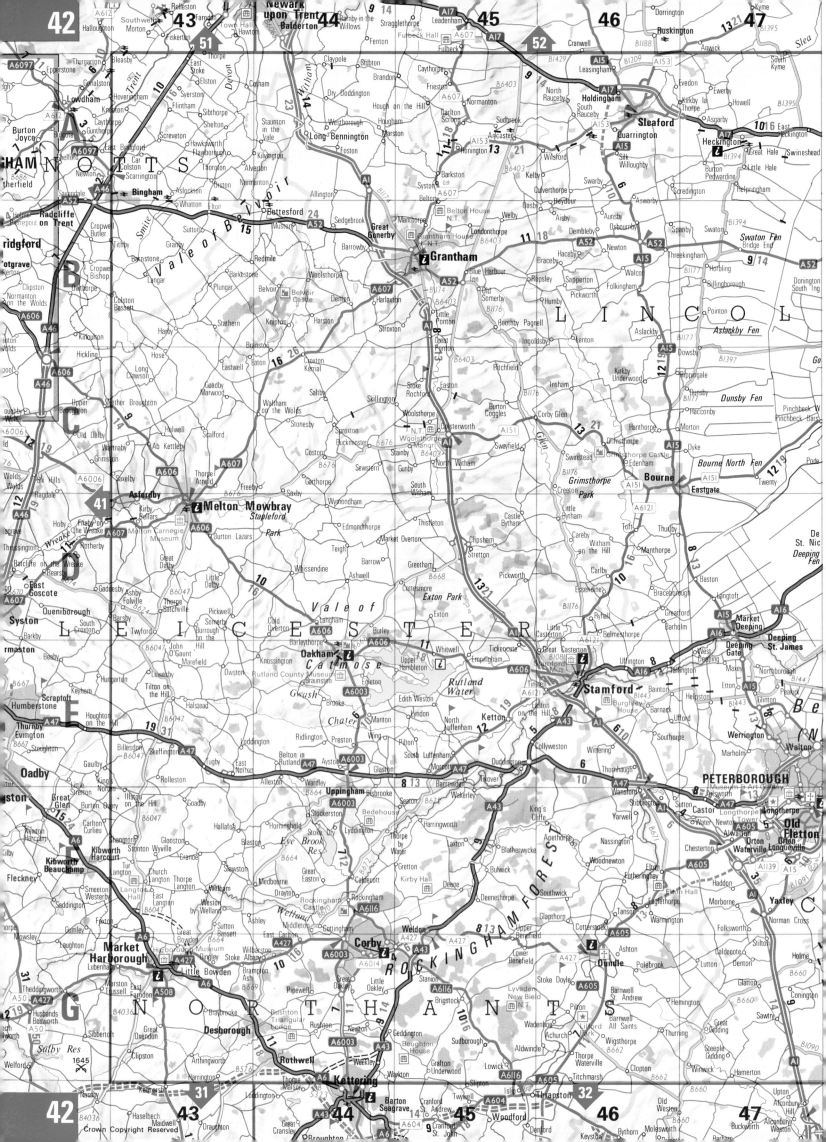

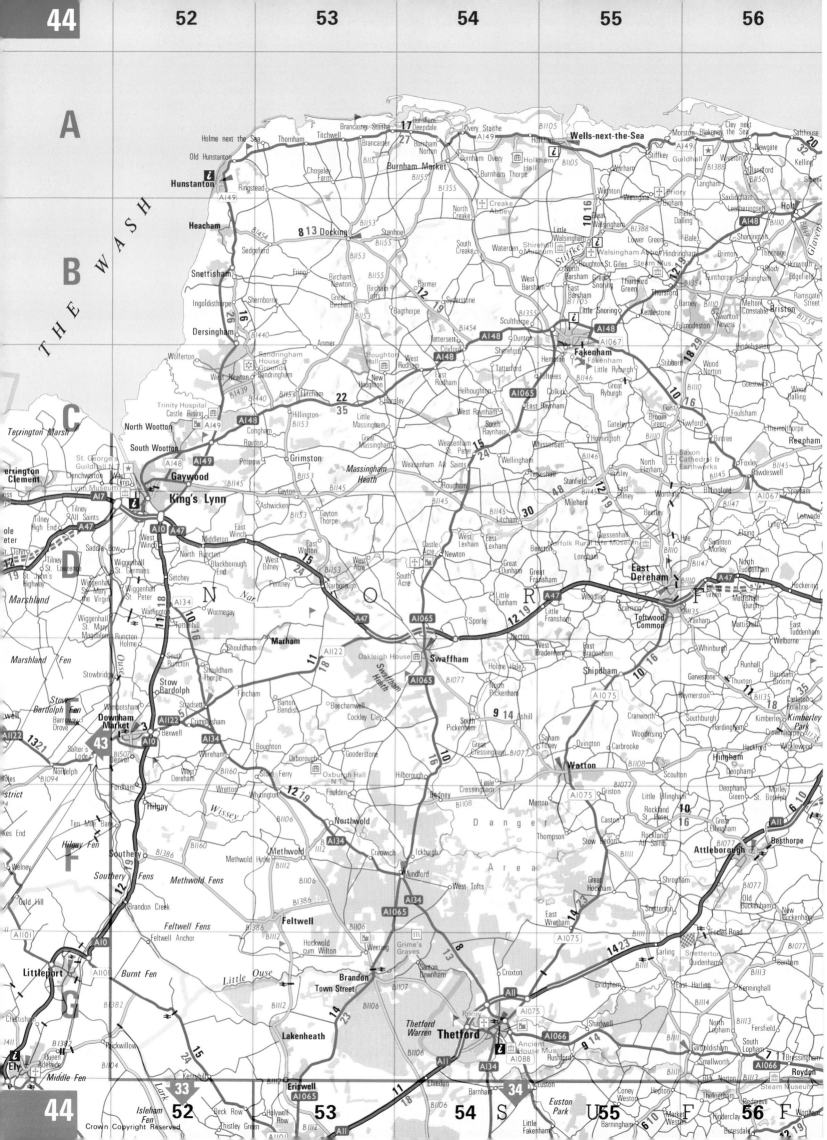

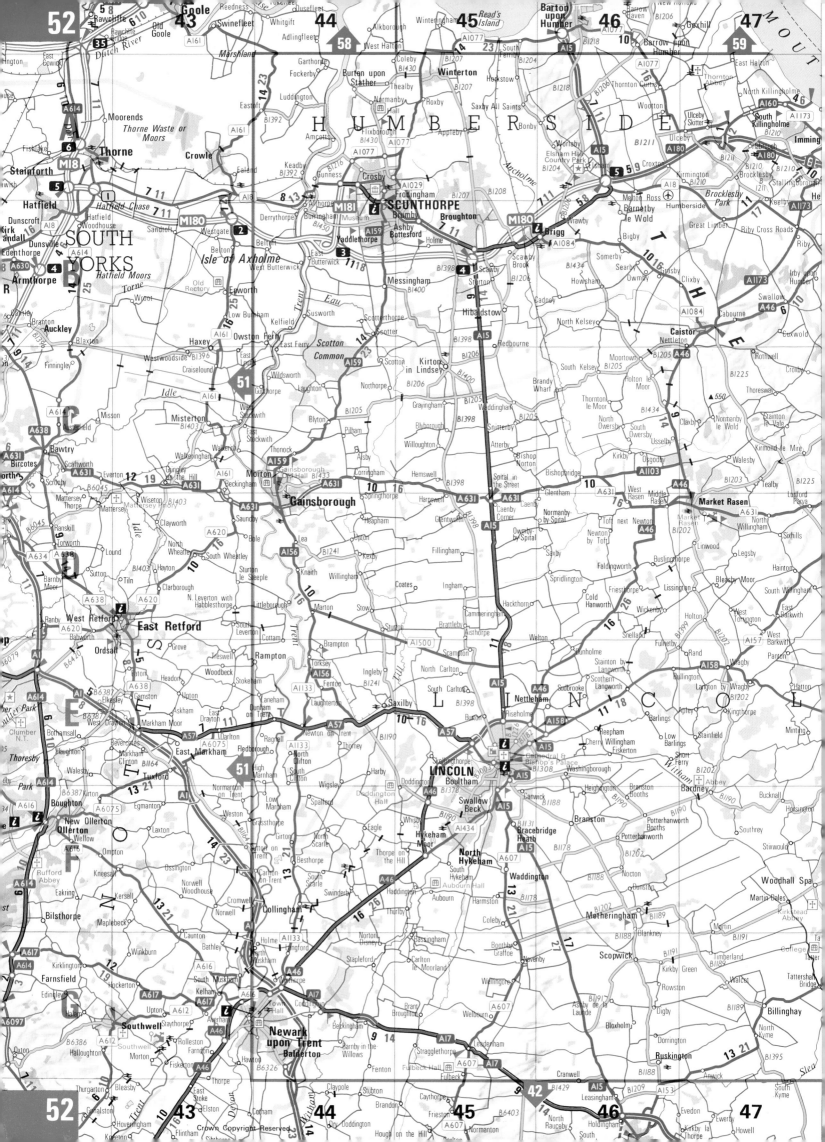

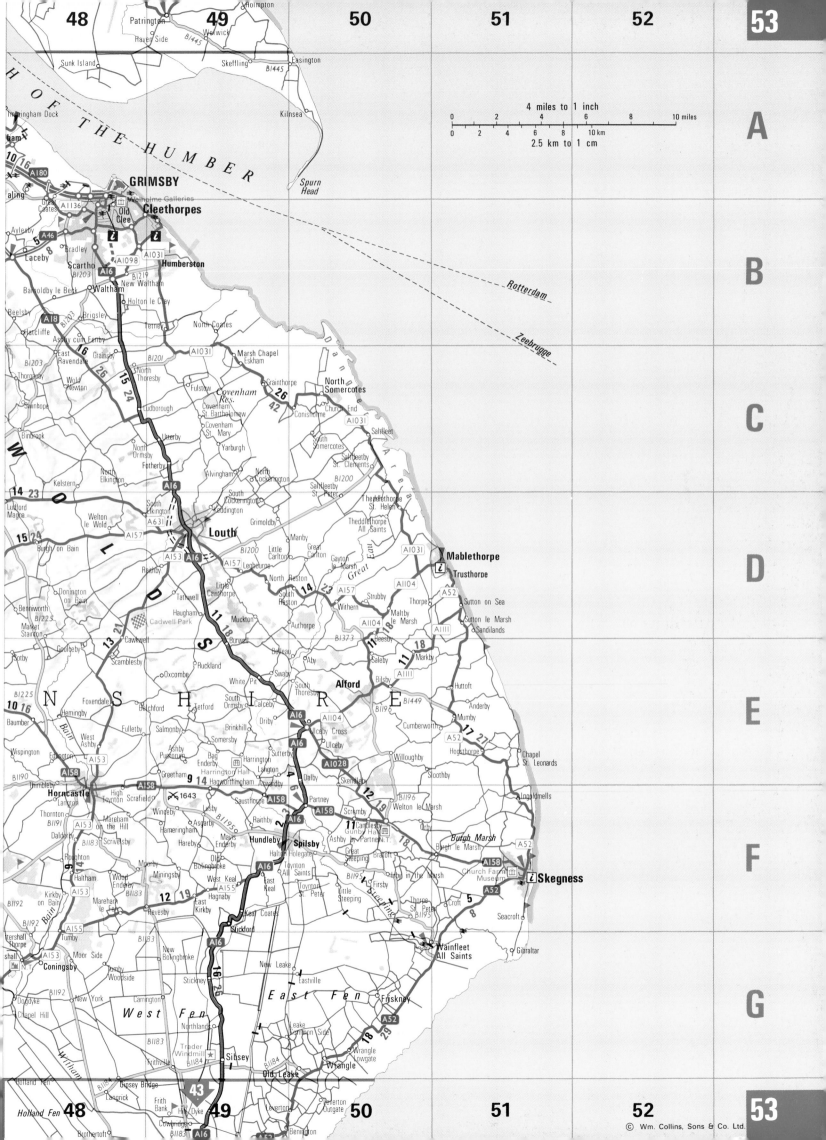

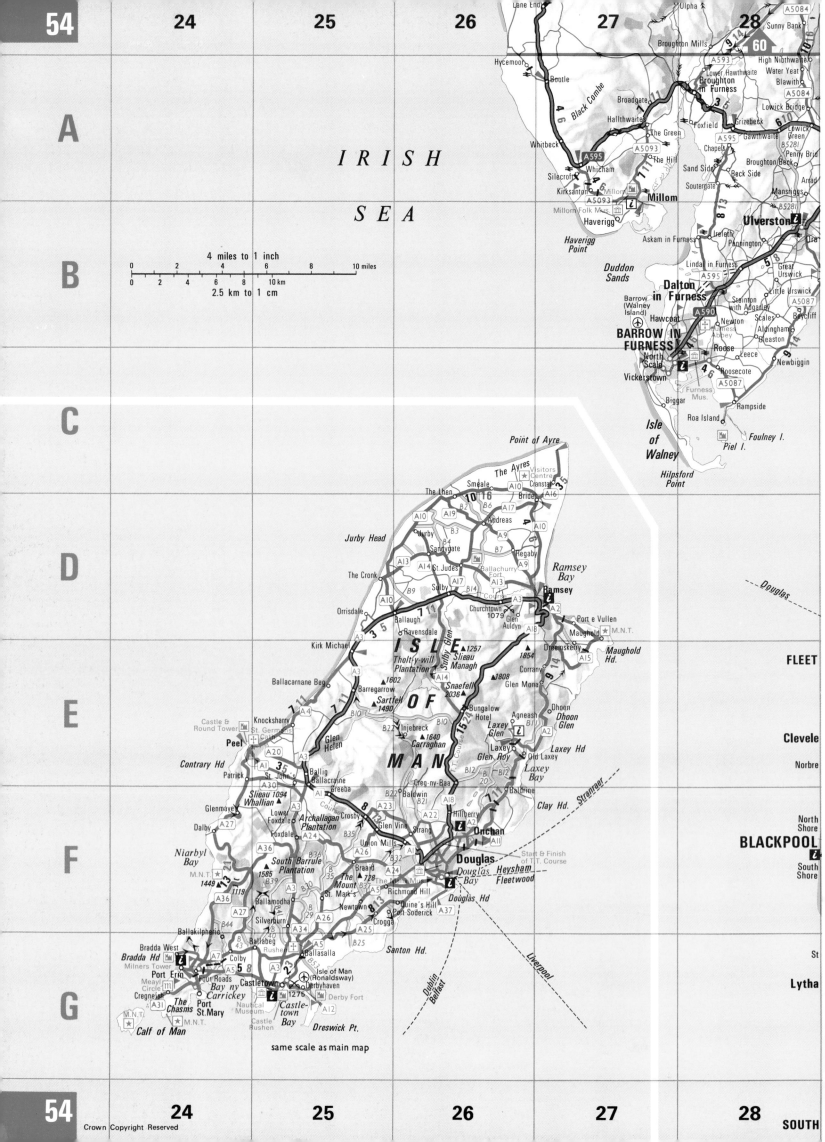

I R I S H

S E A

4 miles to 1 inch

0   2   4   6   8   10 miles

0   2   4   6   8   10 km

2.5 km to 1 cm

Lane End   Ulpha   A5084

Sunny Bank

Broughton Mills

Hycemoor

Bootle

Black Combe

Broadgate

Hallthwaite

Whitbeck

The Green

Foxfield

Grizebeck

Whicham

The Hill

Sand Side

Broughton Beck

Silecroft

Kirksanton

Millom

The Hill

Millom Folk Mus.

Haverigg

Haverigg Point

Duddon Sands

Lindal in Furness

Dalton in Furness

Barrow (Walney Island)

Hawcoat

BARROW IN FURNESS

North Scale

Vickerstown

Biggar

Isle of Walney

Hilpsford Point

Roa Island

Piel I.

Foulney I.

High Nibthwaite

Water Yeat

Blawith

Lowick Bridge

Lowick Green

Gawthwaite

Penny Brid

Arrad

Mansriggs

ULVERSTON

Ireleth

Askam in Furness

Pennington

Great Urswick

Little Urswick

Stainton with Adgarley

Newton

Furness Abbey

Scales

Bardsea

Baycliff

Roose

Leece

Newbiggin

Roosecote

Rampside

Point of Ayre

The Ayres

Visitors Centre

Cranstal

Smeale

Bride

The Lhen

Jurby Head

Jurby

Sandygate

Regaby

Ramsey Bay

St. Judes

Ballachurry Fort

The Cronk

Sulby

T.T. Course

Ramsey

Orrisdale

Ballaugh

Churchtown 1079

Glen Auldyn

Port e Vullen

Maughold M.N.T.

Ravensdale

Maughold Hd.

Kirk Michael

I S L E

1257 Slieau Managh

1854 Dreemskerry

Corrany

Tholt-y-will Plantation

Ballacarnane Beg

1602

O F

1808

Glen Mona

Barregarrow

Sartfell 1490

Snaefell 2036

Bungalow Hotel

Agneash

Dhoon Glen

Dhoon

Castle & Round Tower

Knocksharry

St. Germains St. Germans Cath.

M A N

1640 Carraghan

Injebreck

Laxey Glen

Laxey Hd.

Peel

Glen Helen

Laxey

Contrary Hd.

Patrick

St. John's

Ballig

Ballacraine

Greeba

Creg-ny-Baa

Old Laxey

Laxey Bay

Baldwin

Glenmaye

Slieau Whallian 1094

Lower Foxdale

Archallagan Plantation

Crosby

Glen Vine

Strang

Baldrine

Dalby

Foxdale

Hillberry

Niarbyl Bay

M.N.T. 1449

South Barrule Plantation

1585

Union Mills

Braaid

The Mount 728

Onchan

Douglas

Douglas Bay

1119

Ballamodha

St. Mark's

Richmond Hill

The Manx Mus.

Ballakilpheric

Silverburn

Newtown

Quine's Hill

Port Soderick

Douglas Hd.

Bradda West

Bradda Hd.

Milners Tower

Meayll Circle

Cregneish

Four Roads

Colby

Ballabeg

Rushen

Ballasalla

Santon Hd.

Port Erin

Bay ny Carrickey

Castletown

Derbyhaven

Isle of Man (Ronaldsway)

The Chasms

Port St. Mary

Nautical Museum

Castle Rushen

Castletown Bay

Derby Fort

Dreswick Pt.

M.N.T.

Calf of Man

same scale as main map

Heysham

Fleetwood

Liverpool

Stranraer

Dublin Belfast

FLEET

Clevele

BLACKPOOL

North Shore

South Shore

Lytha

FLEET

Clevele

Norbre

SOUTH

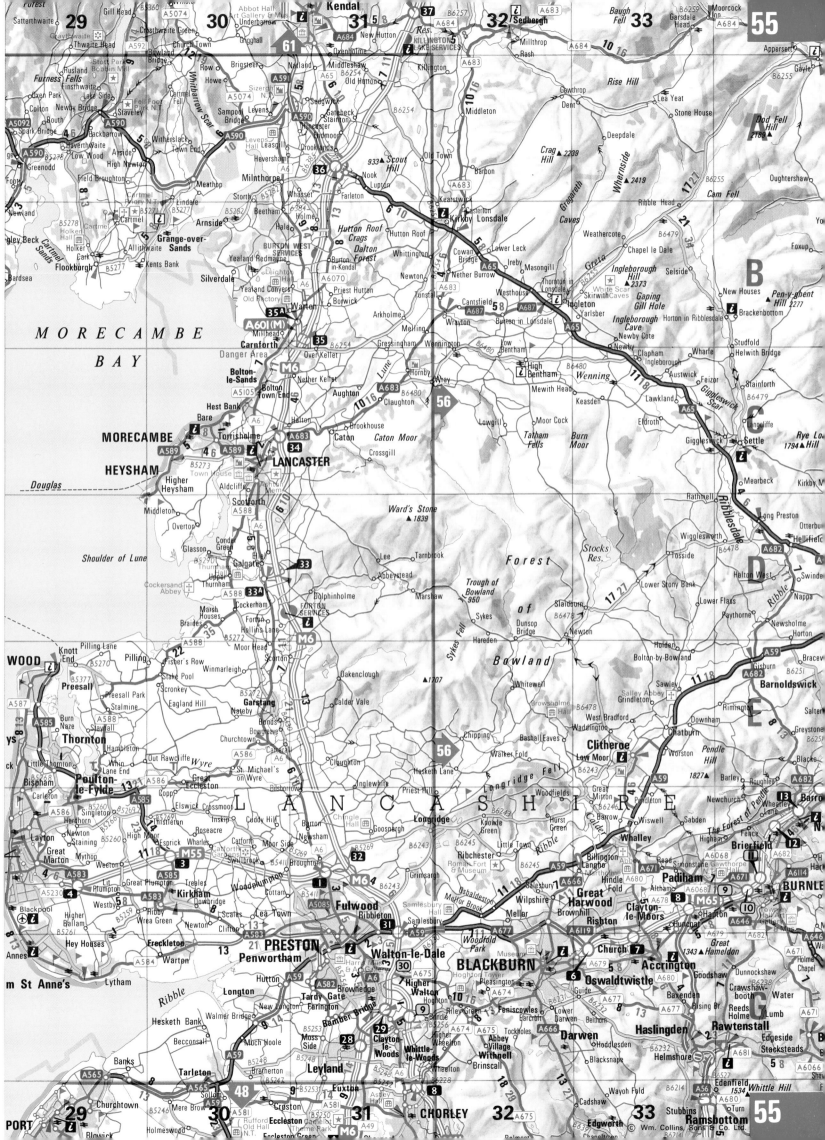

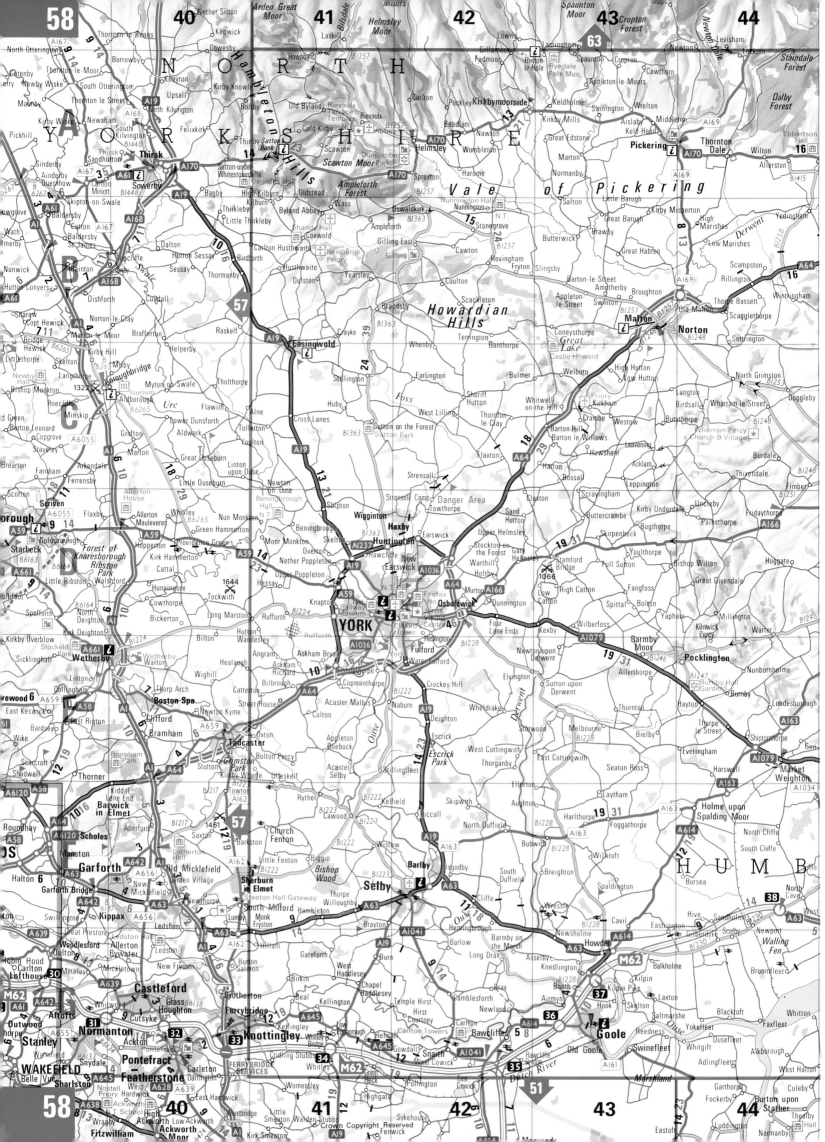

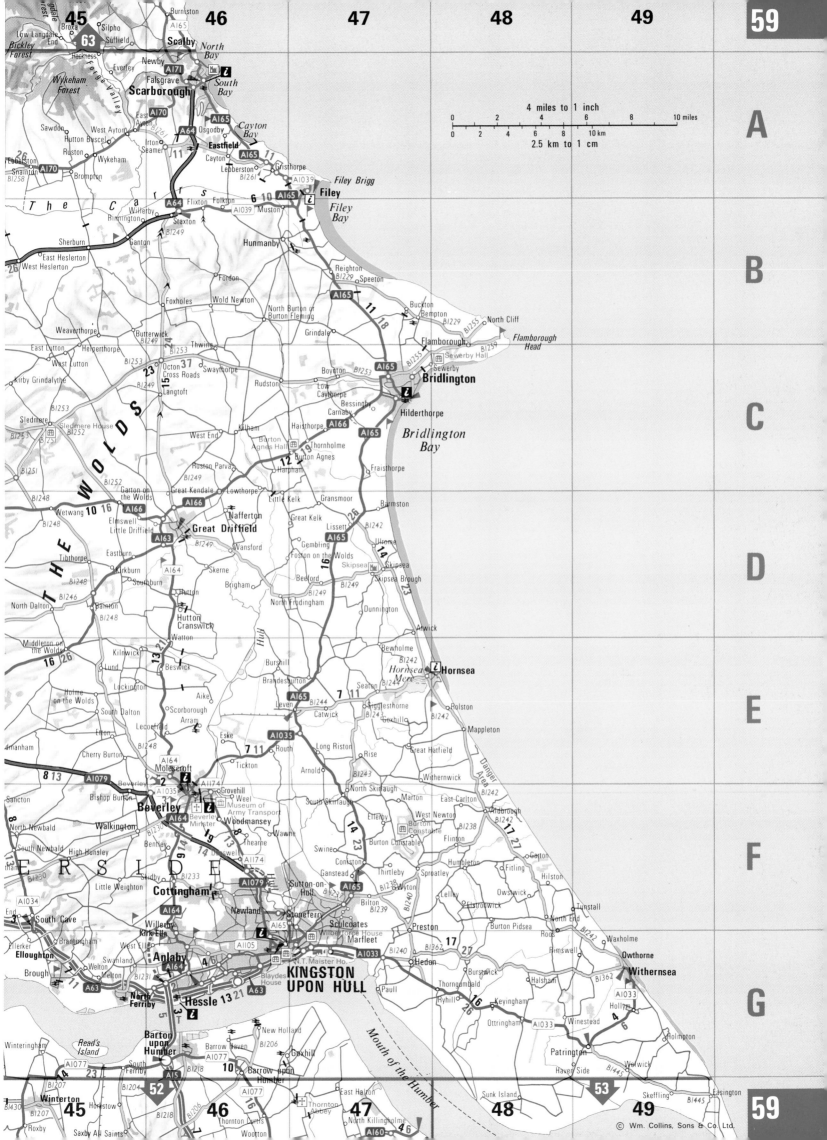

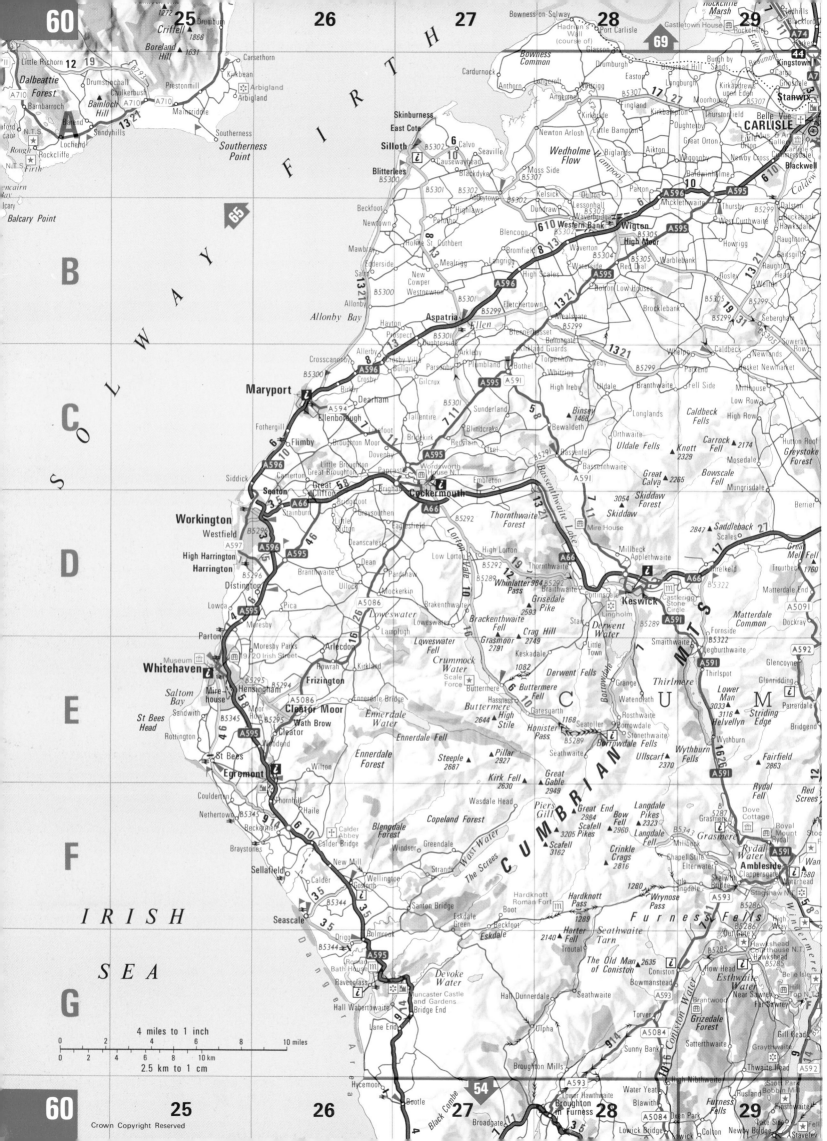

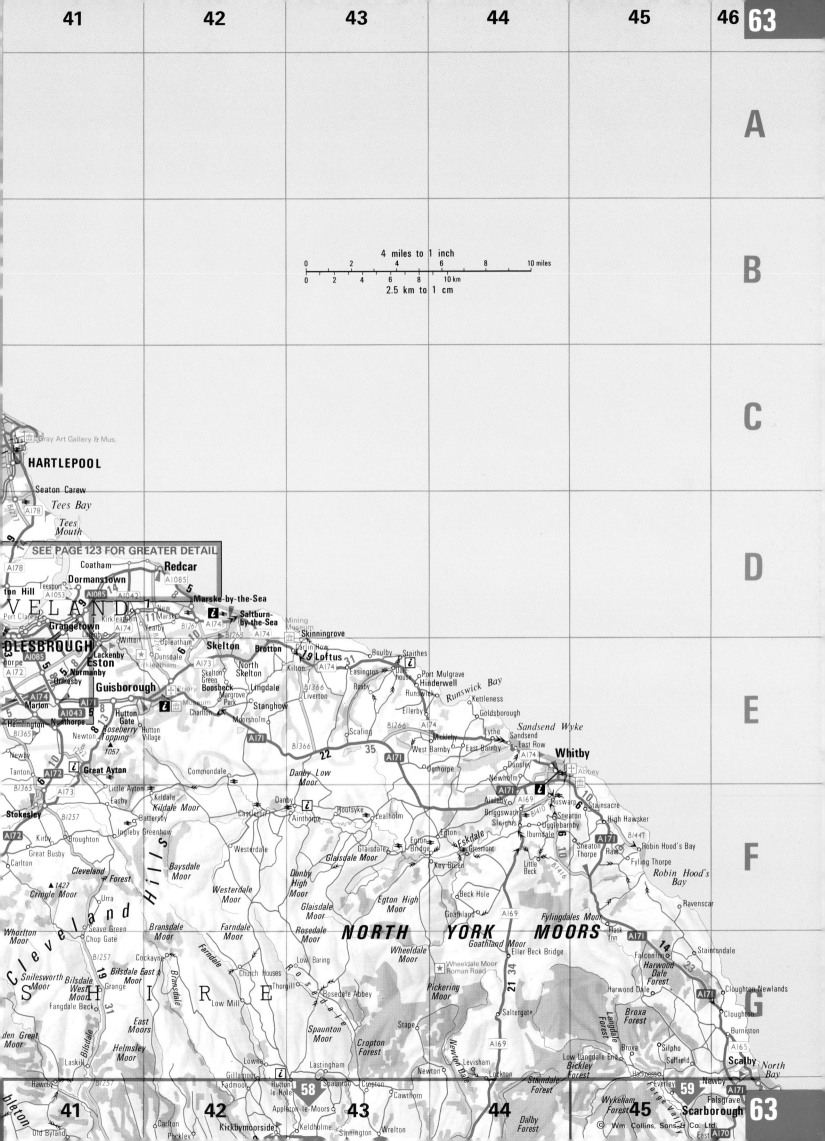

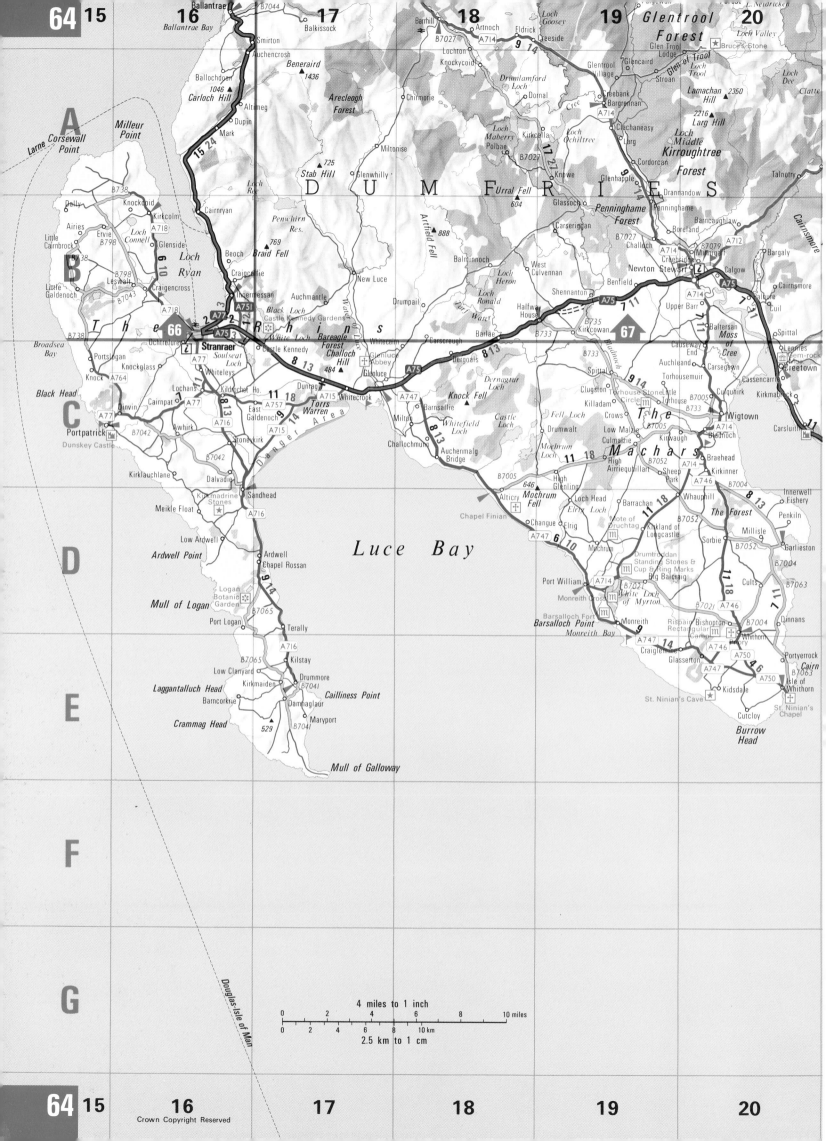

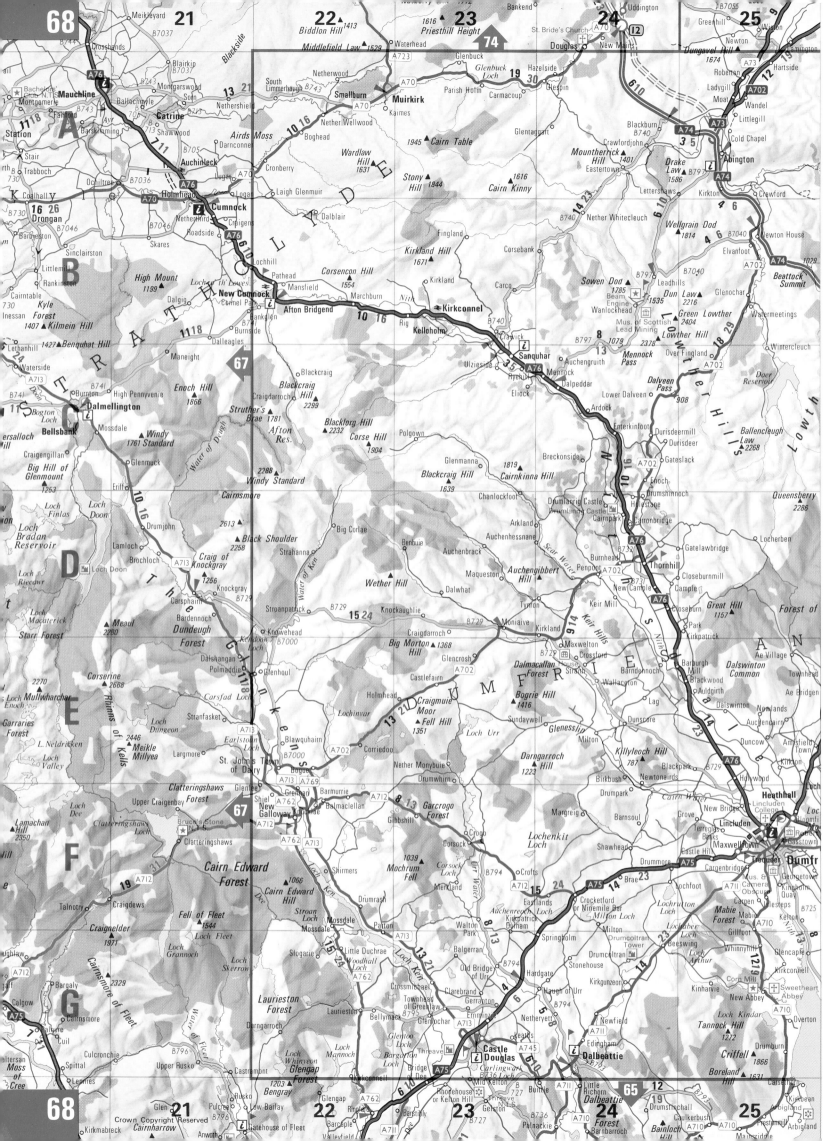

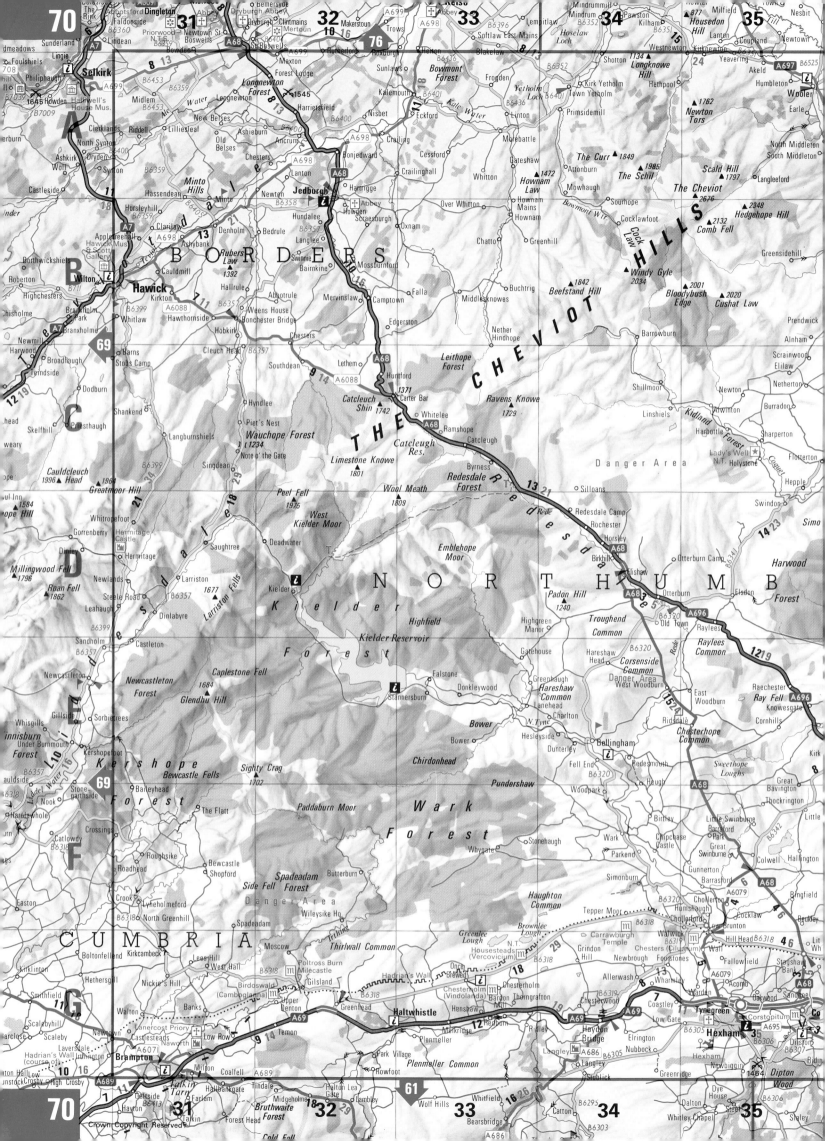

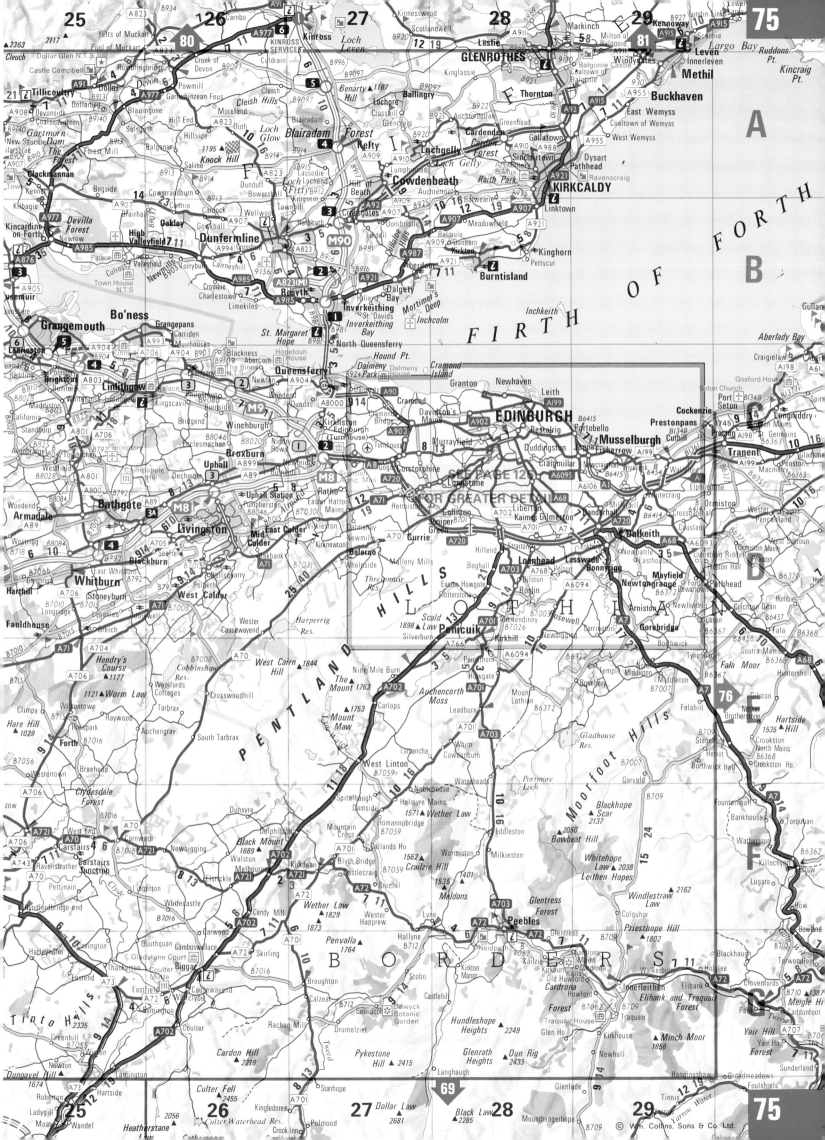

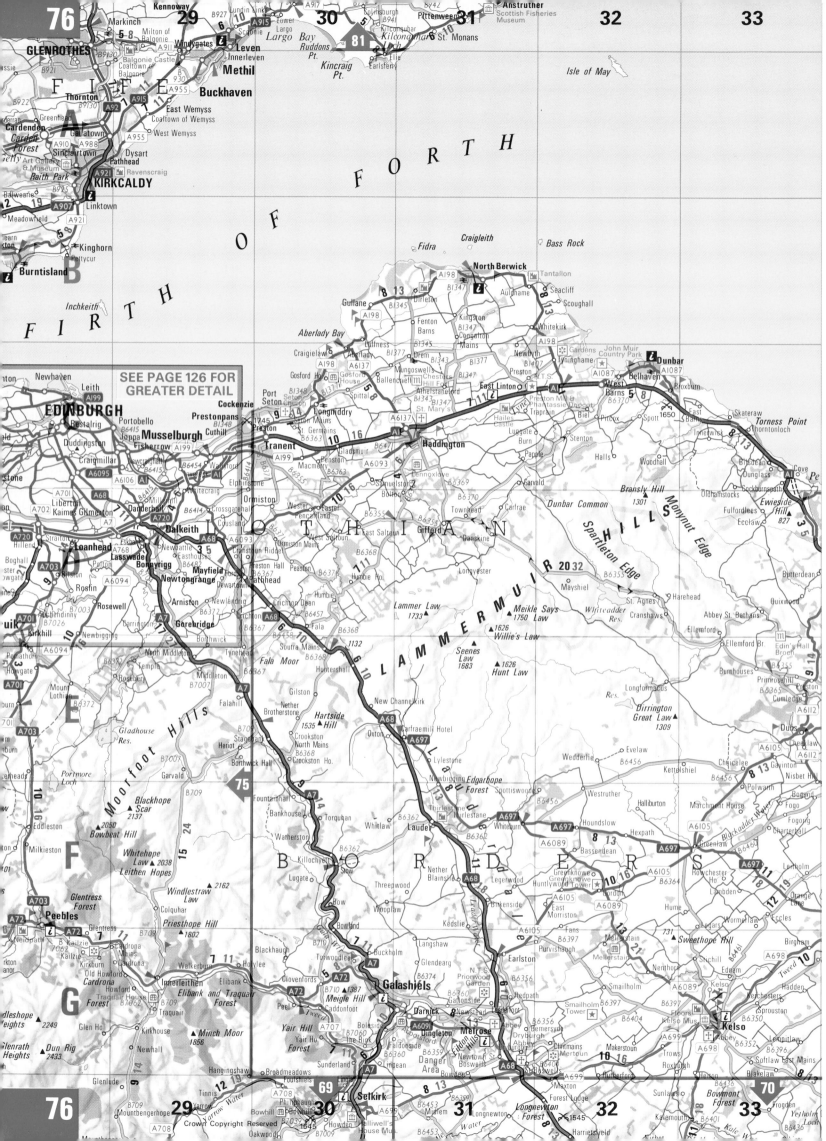

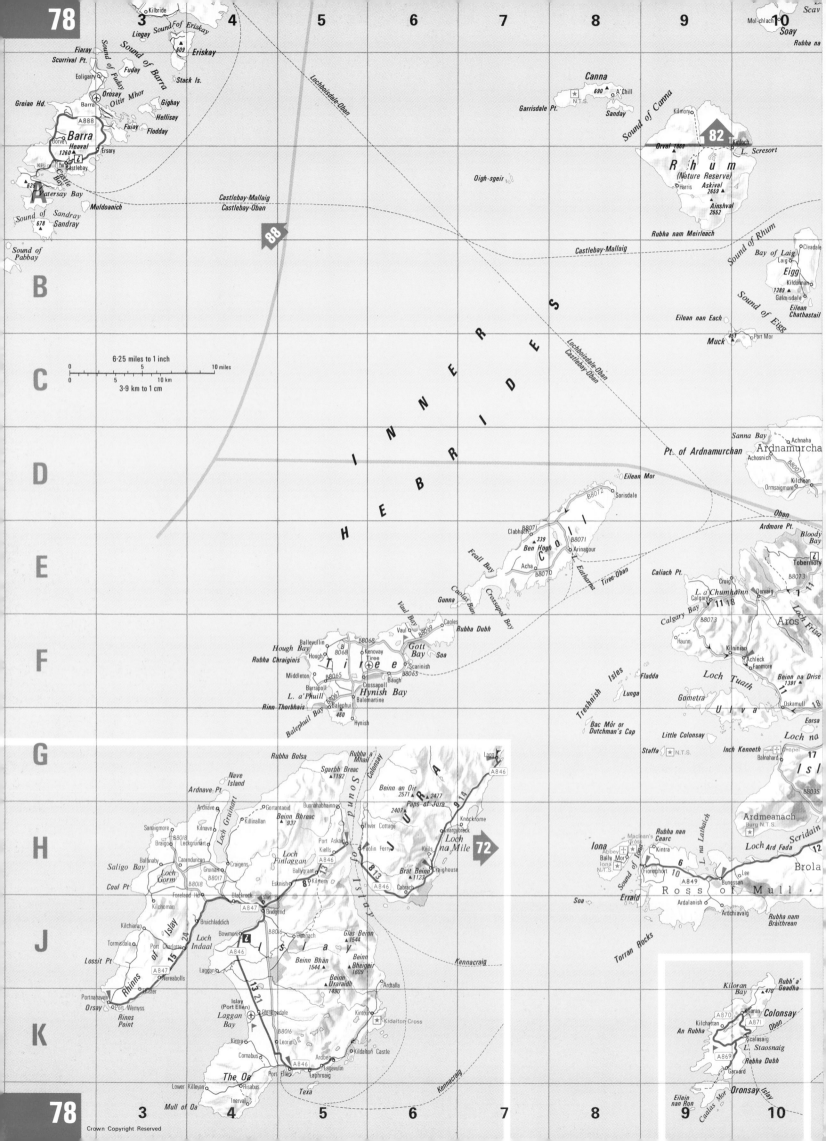

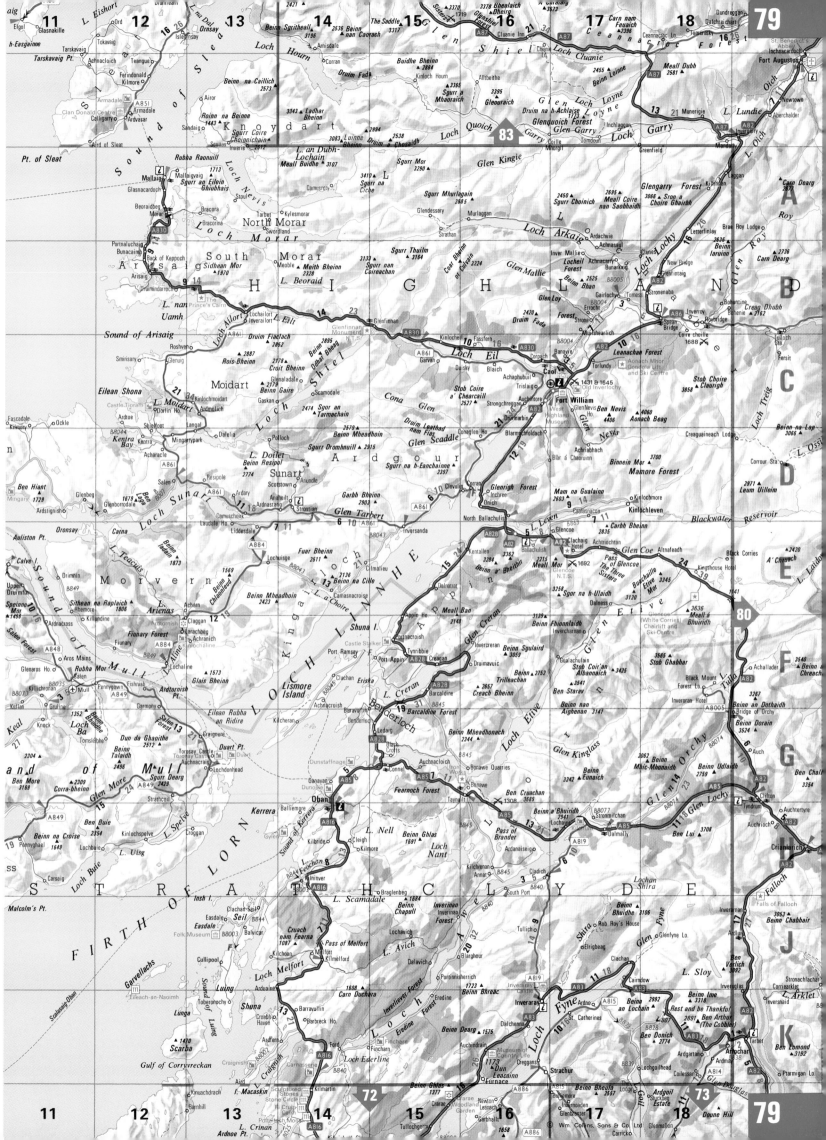

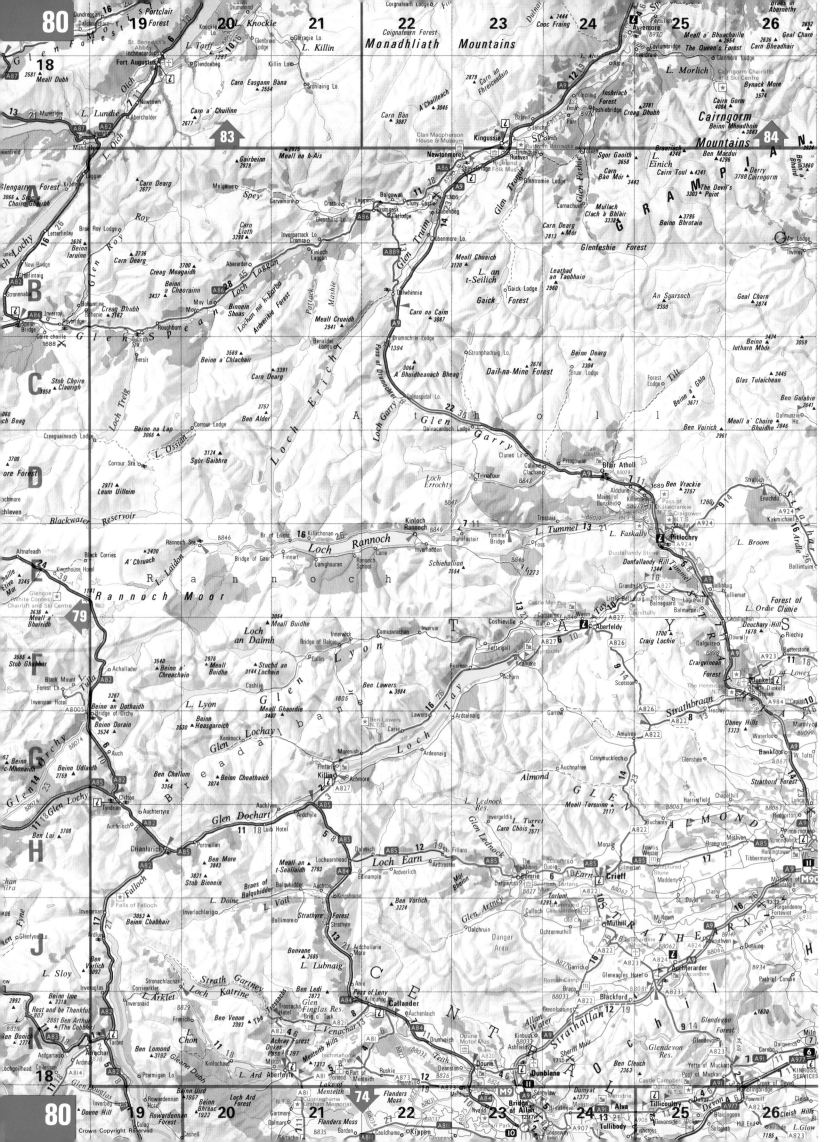

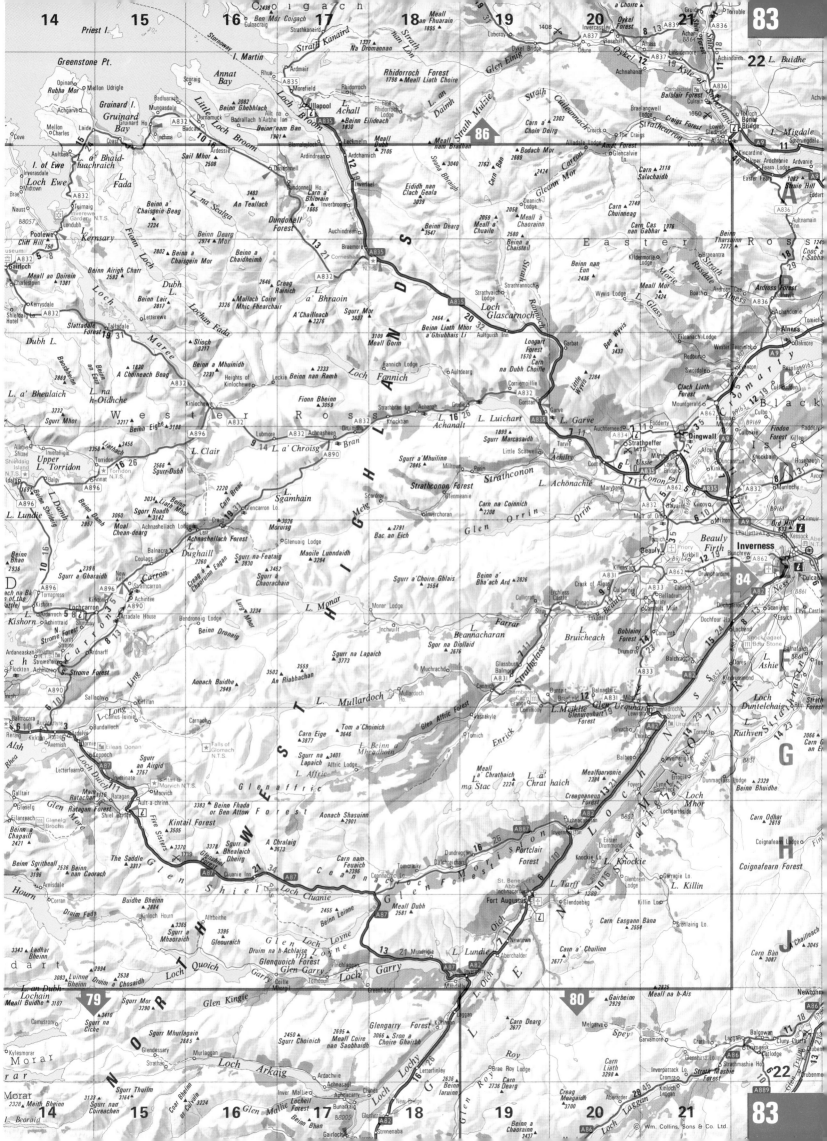

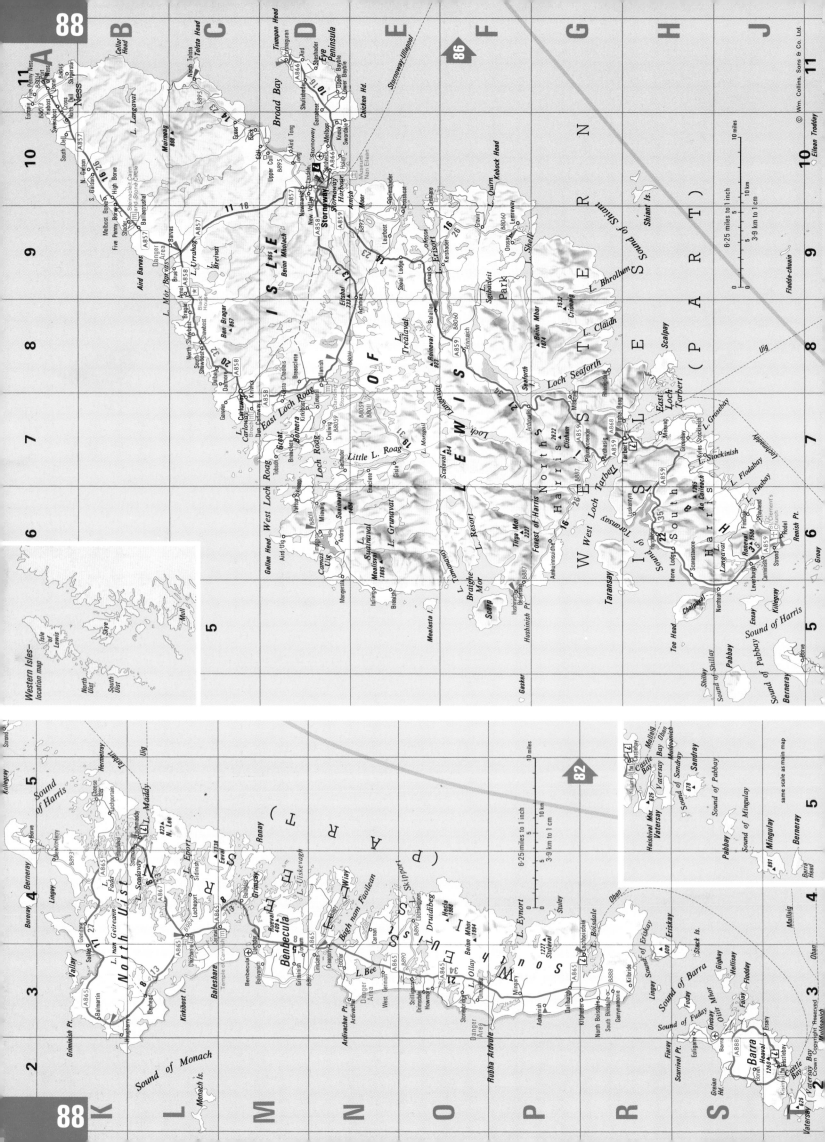

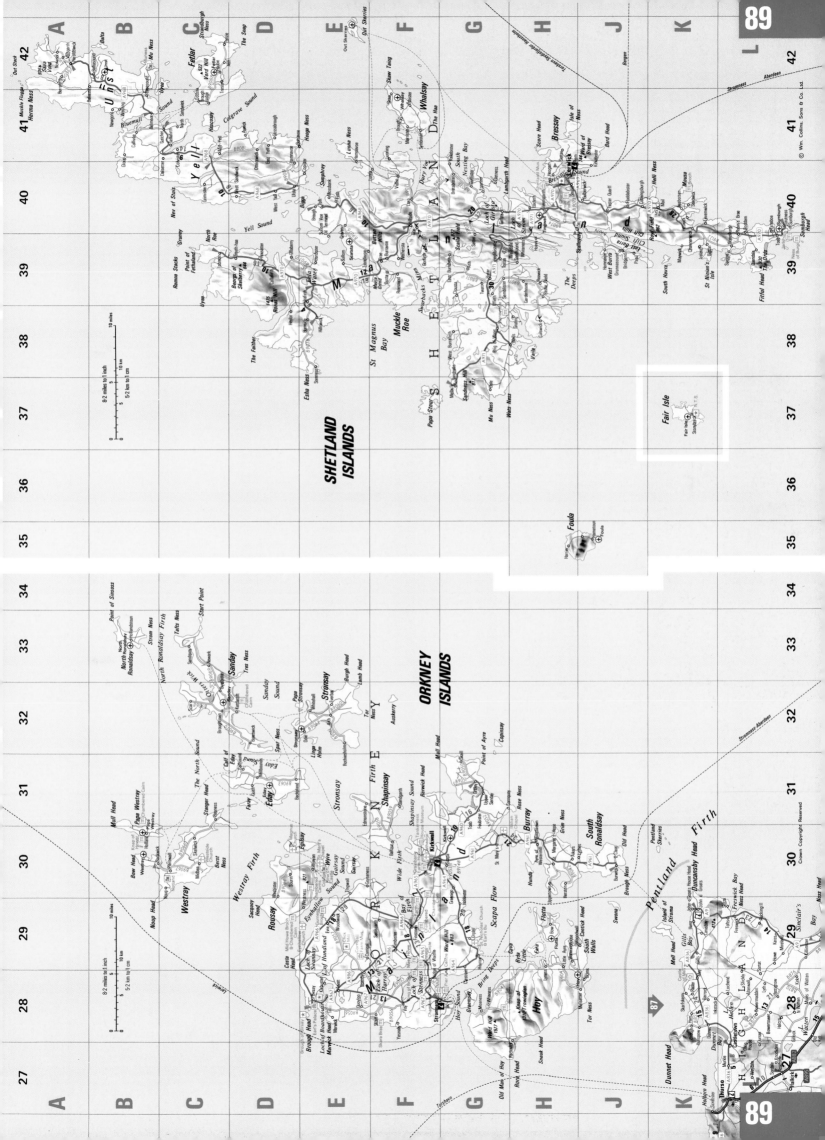

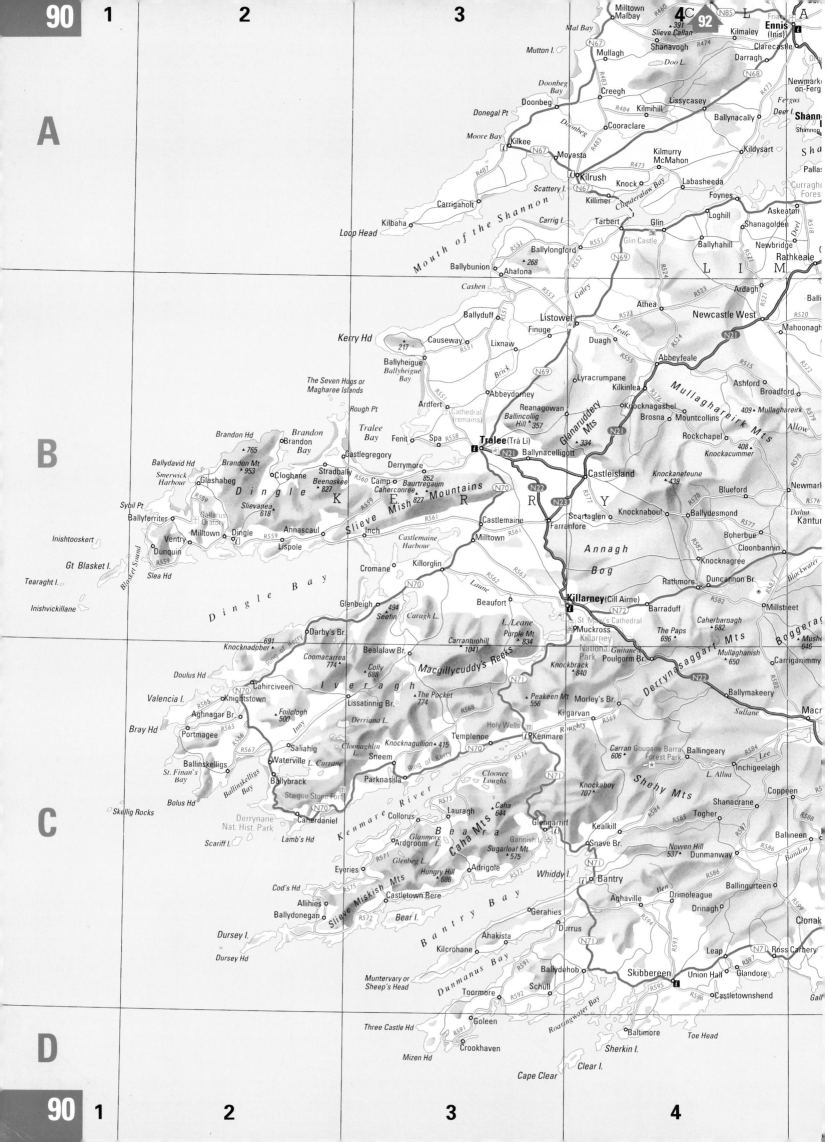

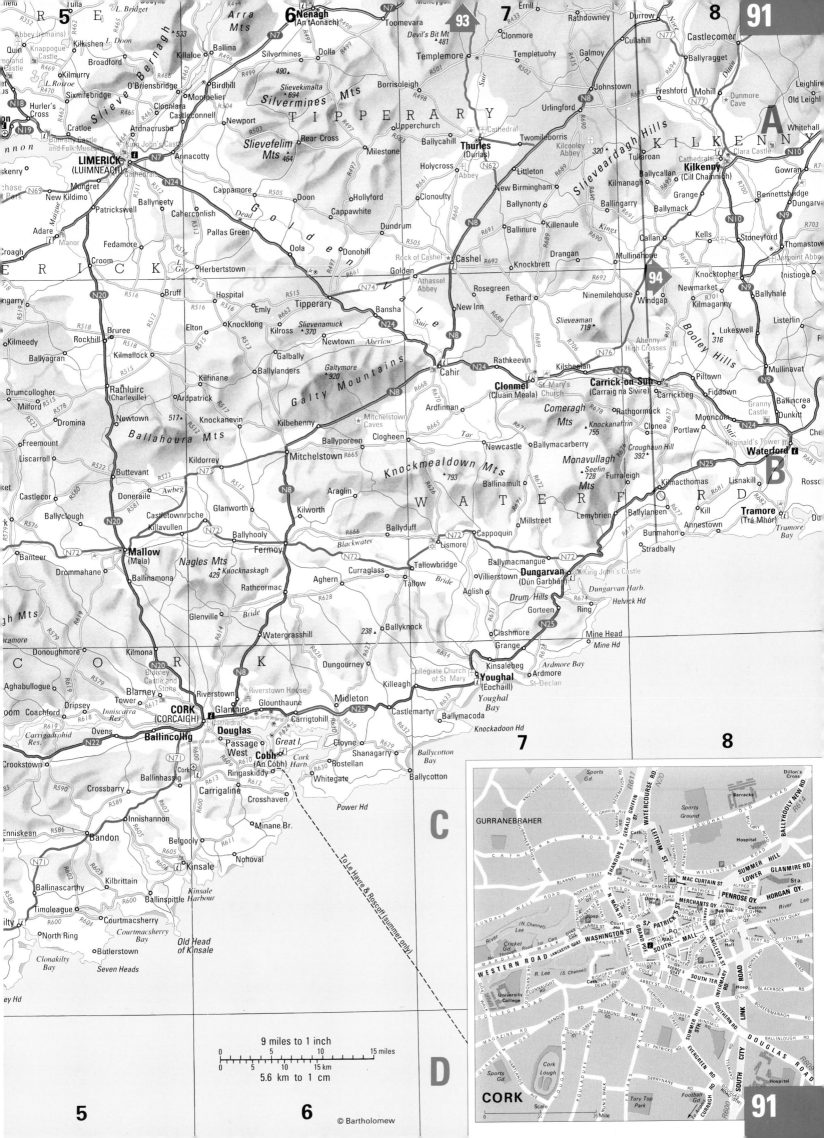

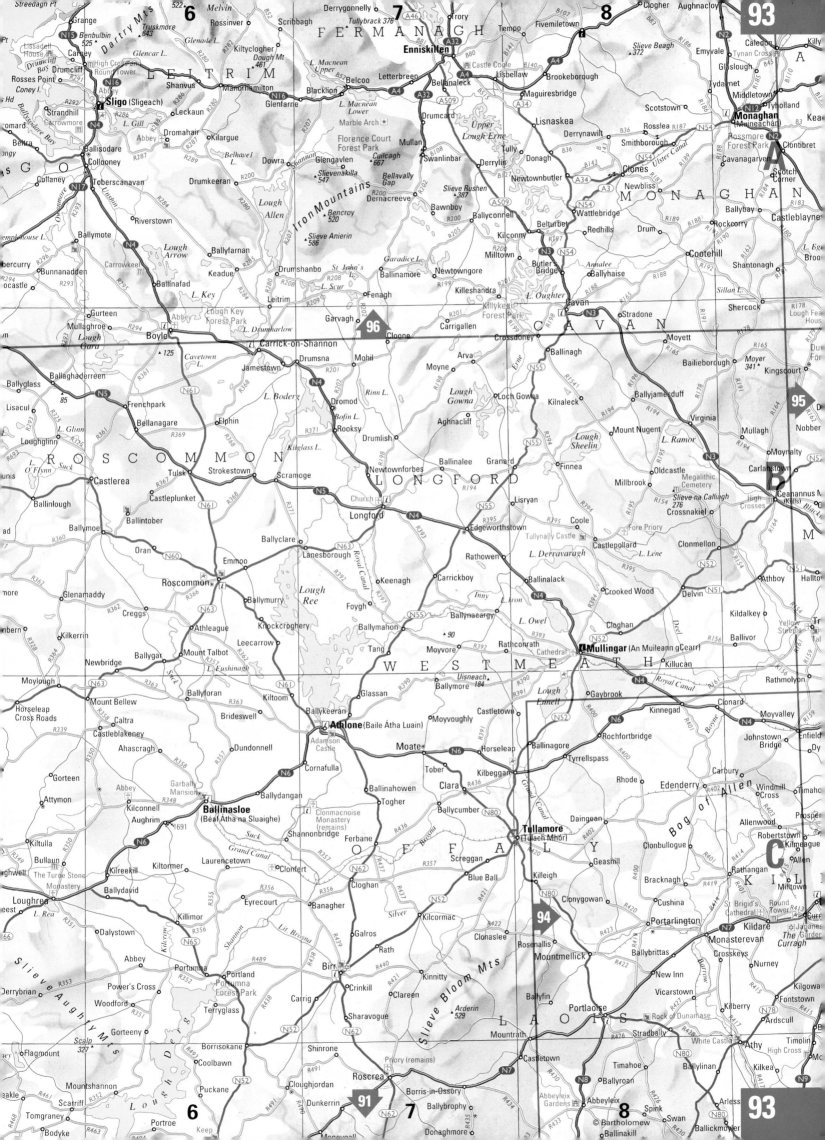

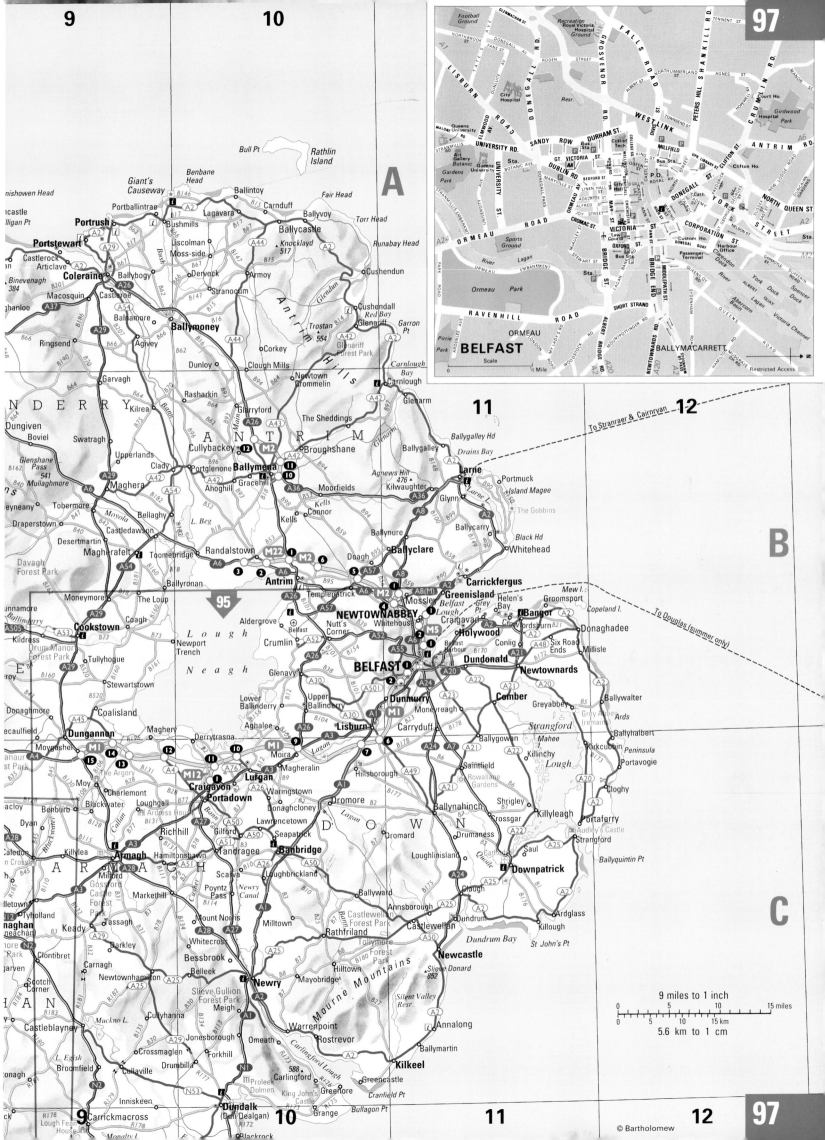

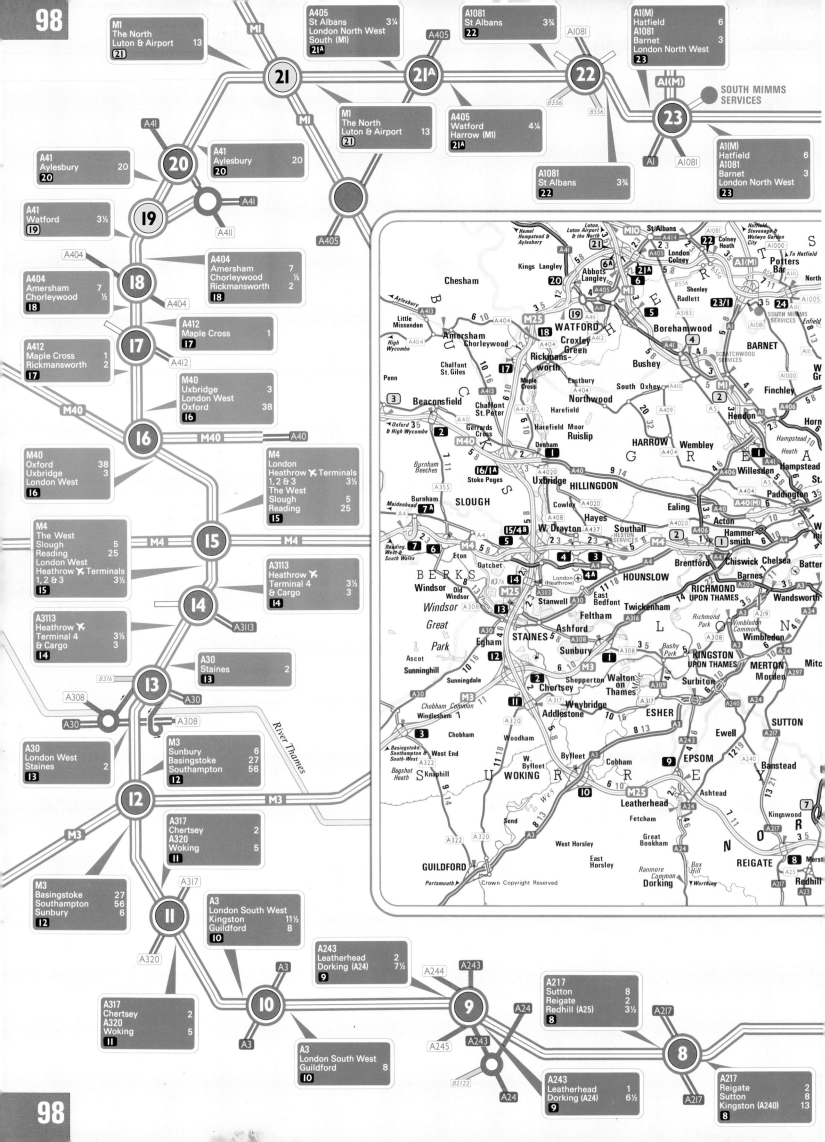

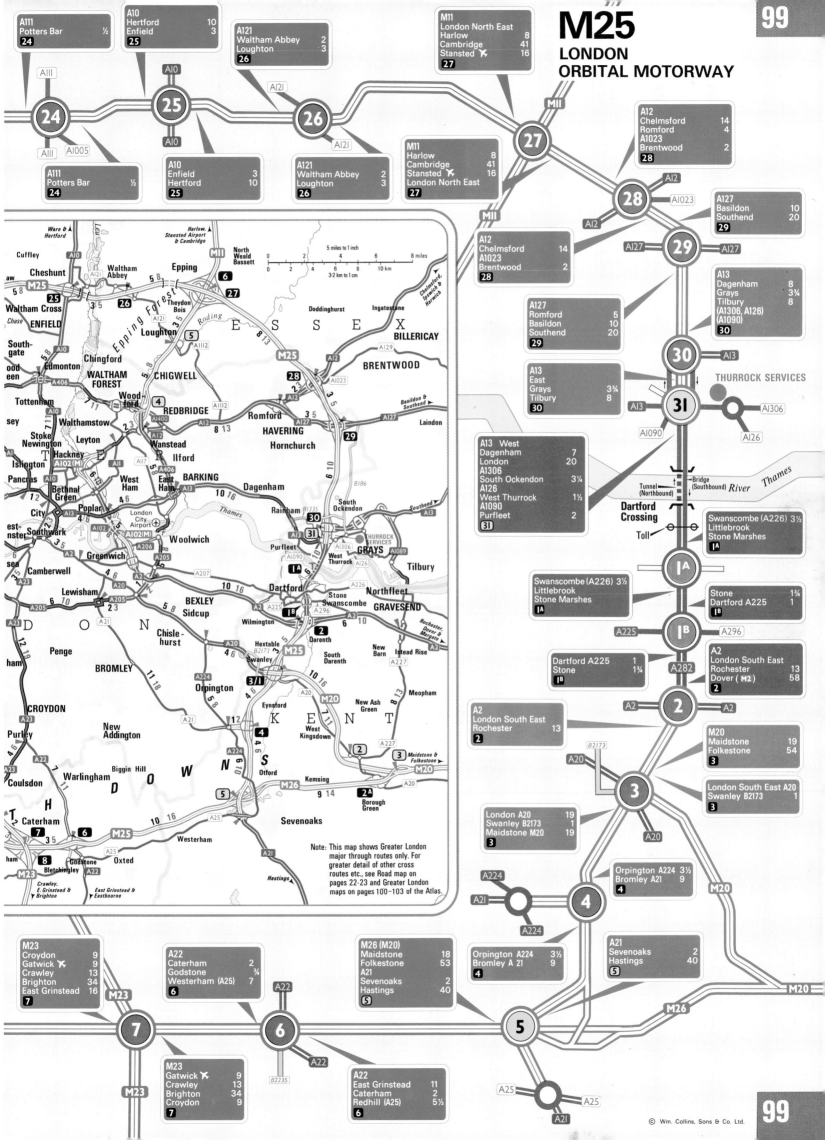

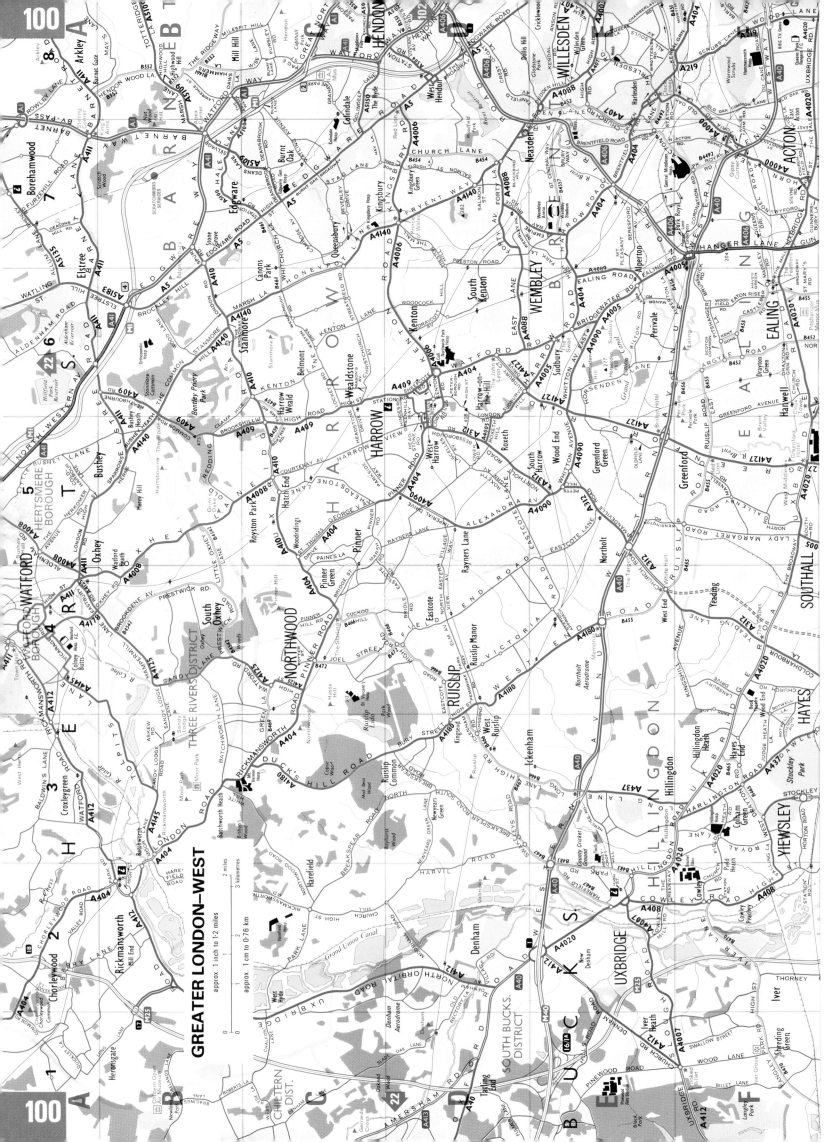

GREATER LONDON—WEST

CENTRAL LONDON

4 inches to 1 mile

| 0 | 1/4 | 1/2 mile |
| 0 | 400 | 800 metres |

OXFORD STREET
Oxford Street is closed to through traffic (except buses and taxis) between 7 a.m. and 7 p.m. Monday-Saturday.

REGENT'S PARK

HYDE PARK

The Serpentine
The Lido

GREEN PARK

BUCKINGHAM PALACE GARDENS

ST. JAMES'S PARK

Constitution Hill

Buckingham Palace

VICTORIA

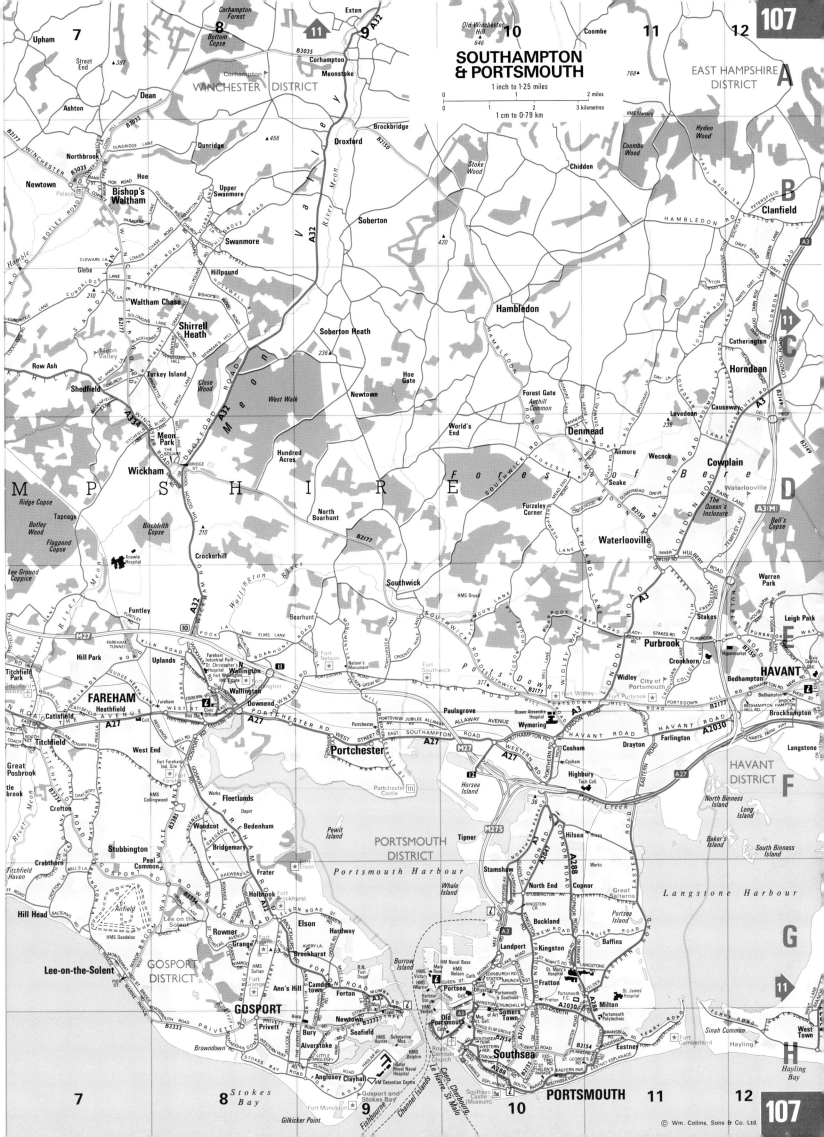

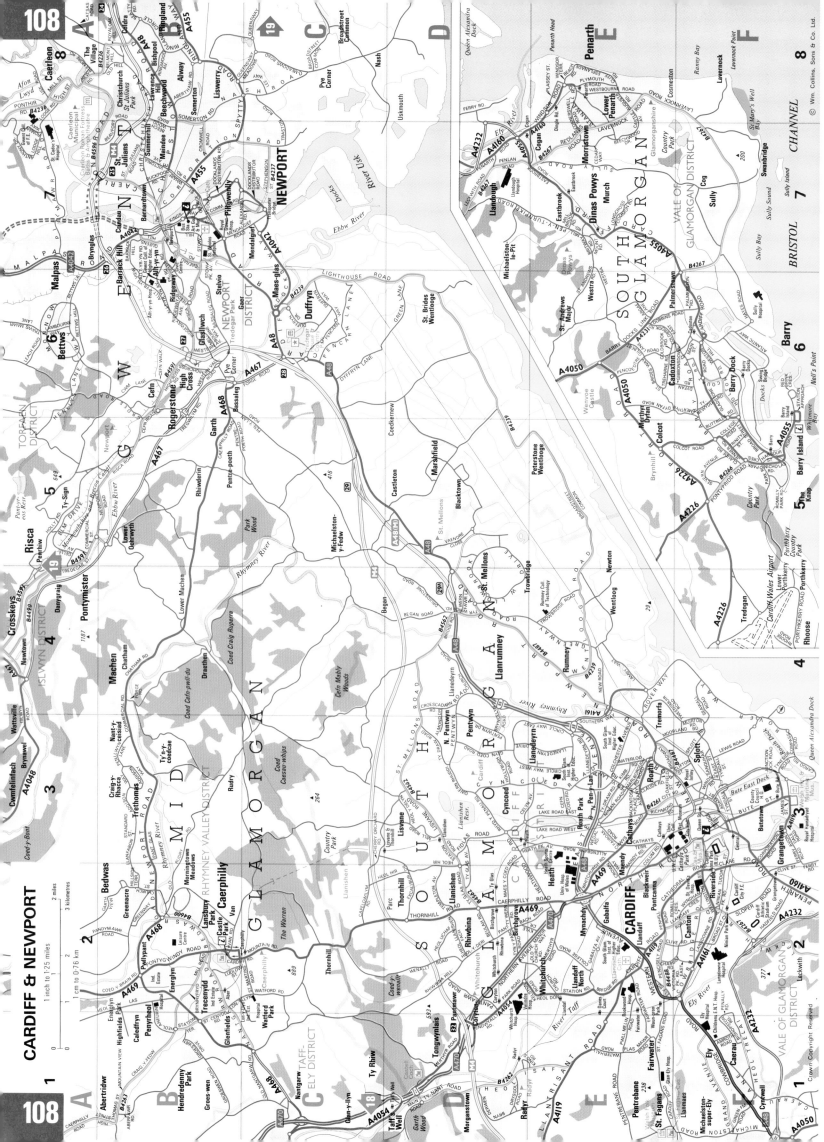

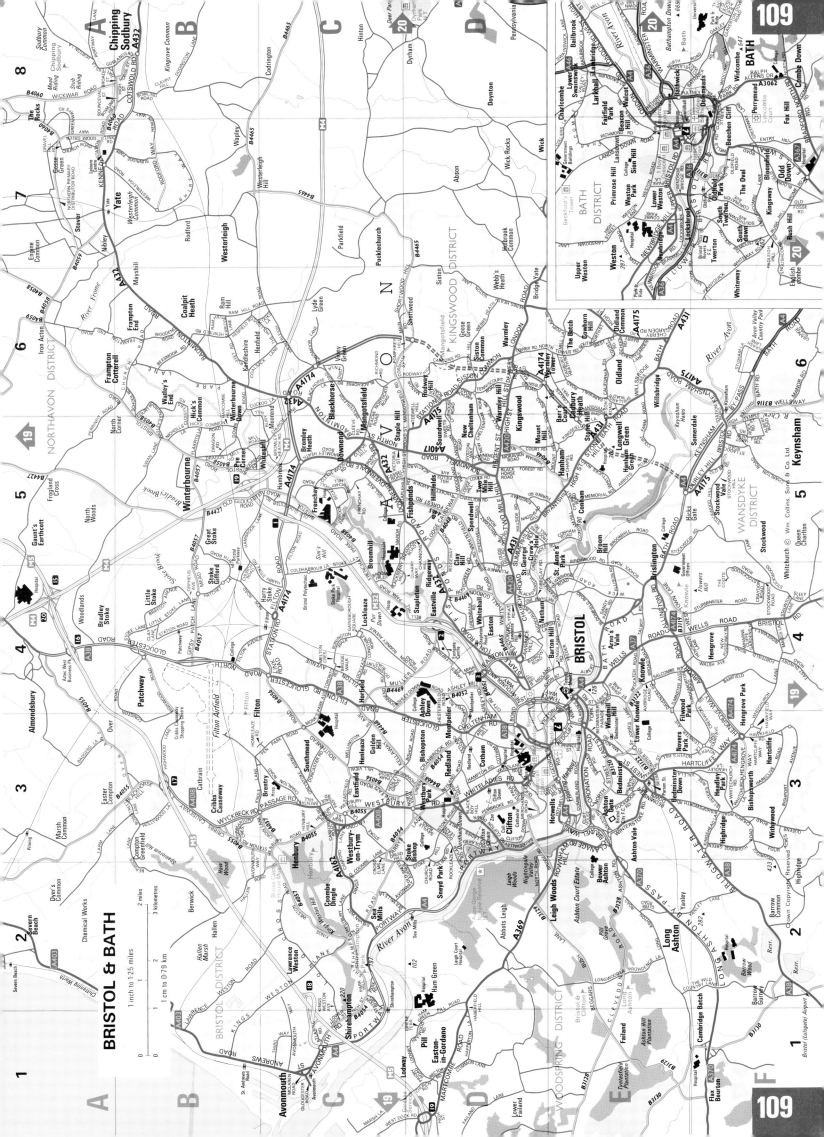

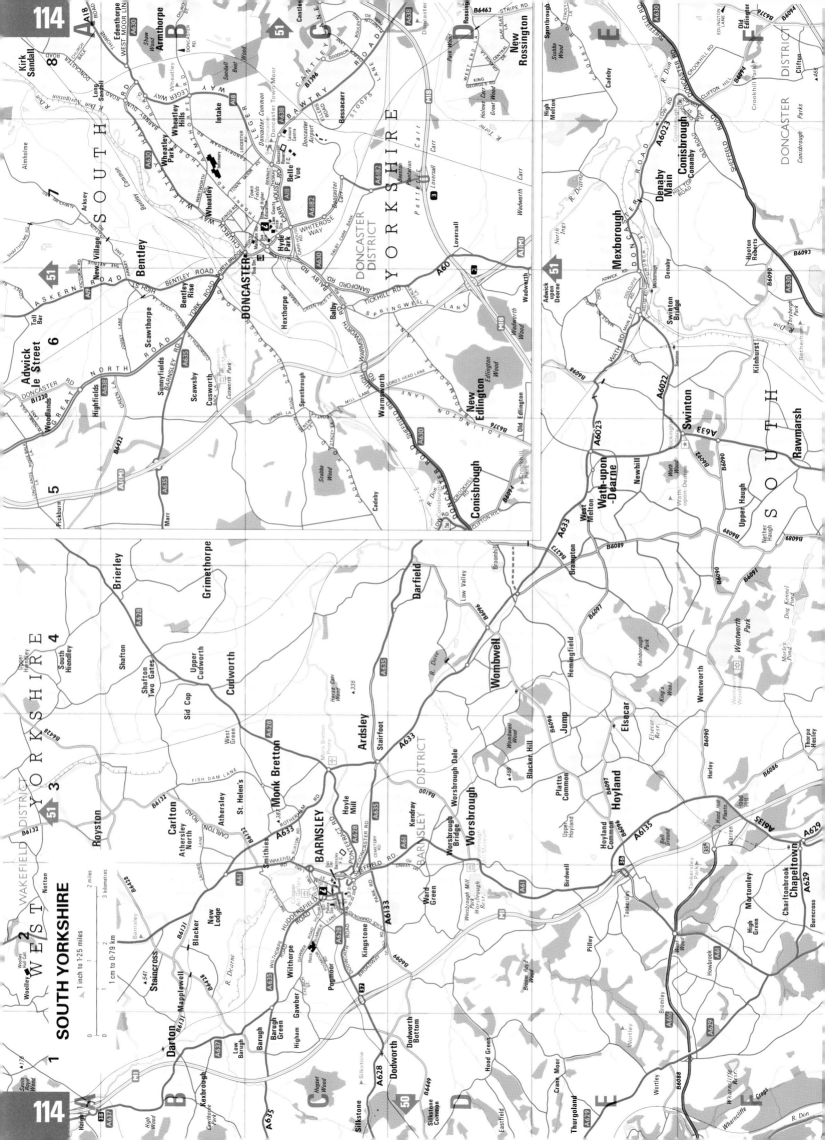

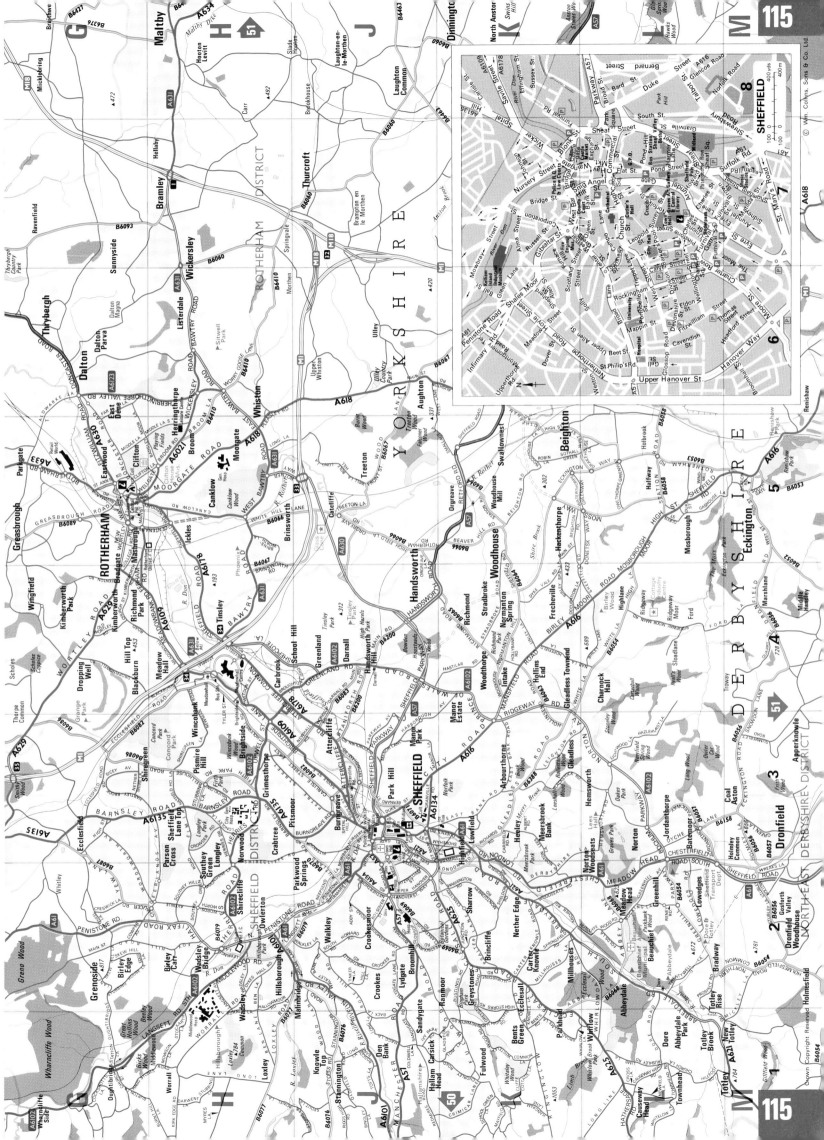

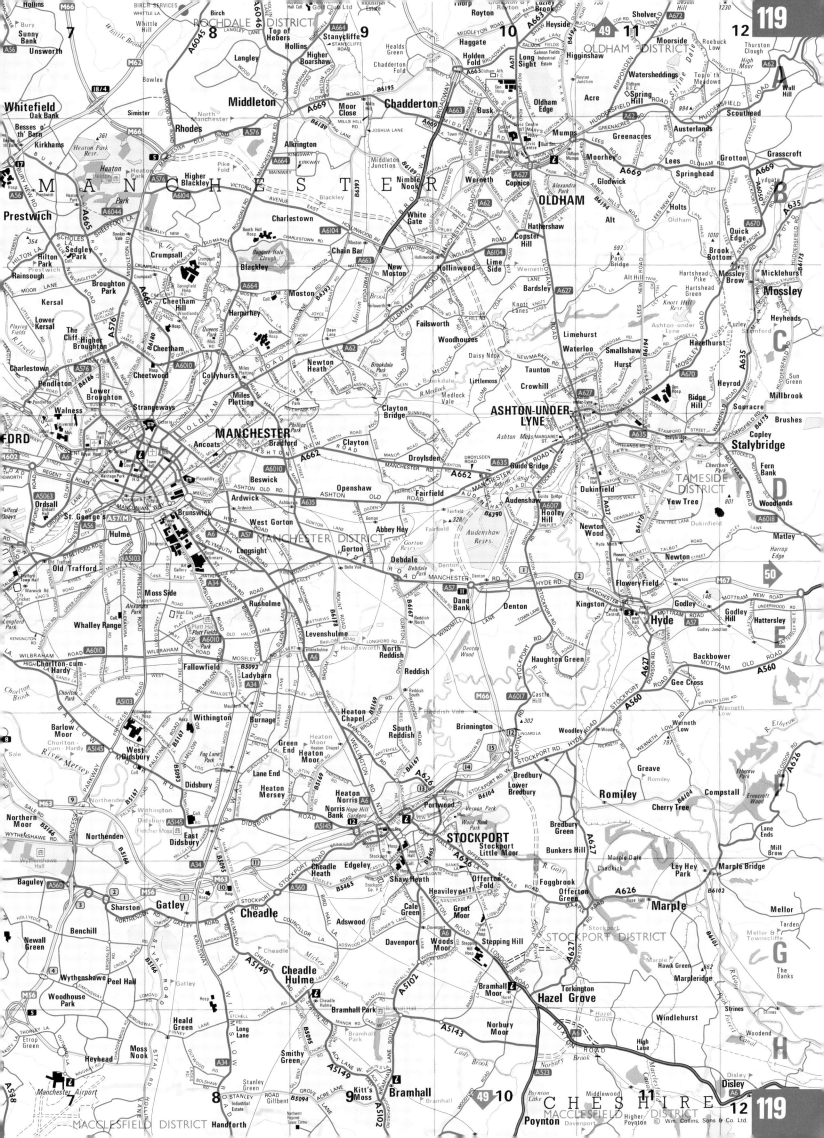

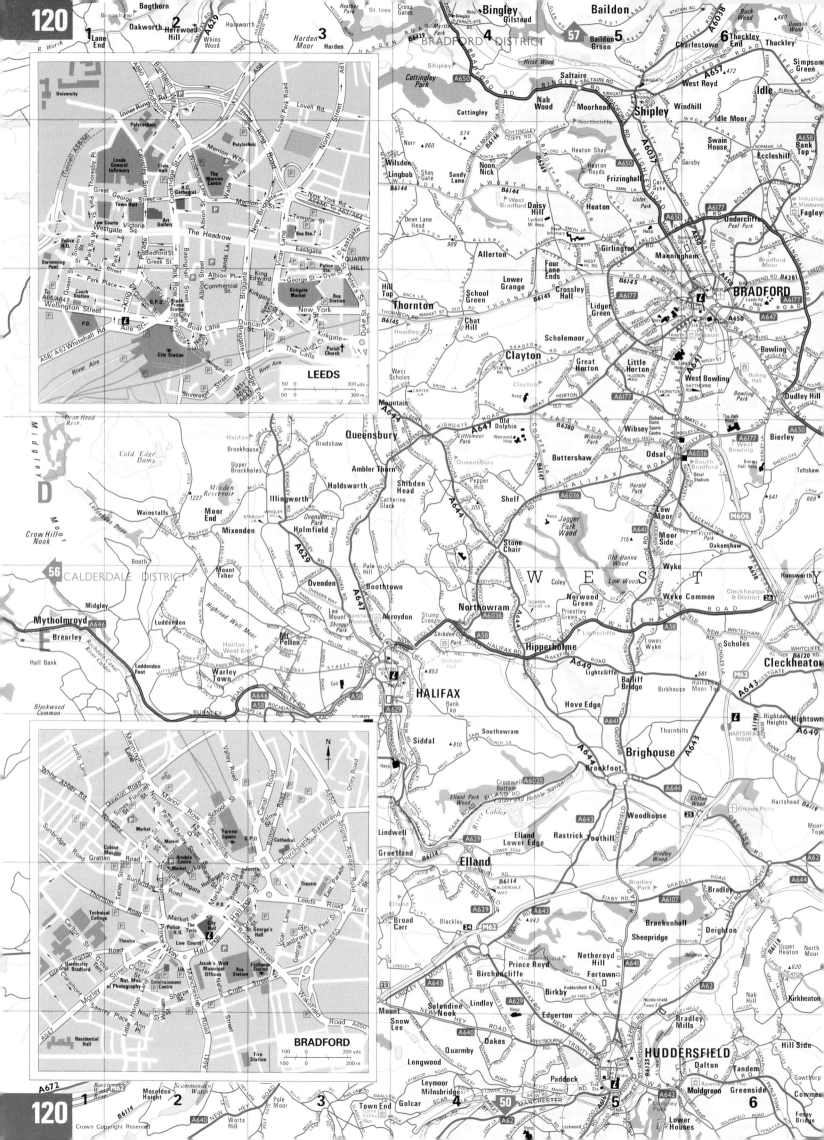

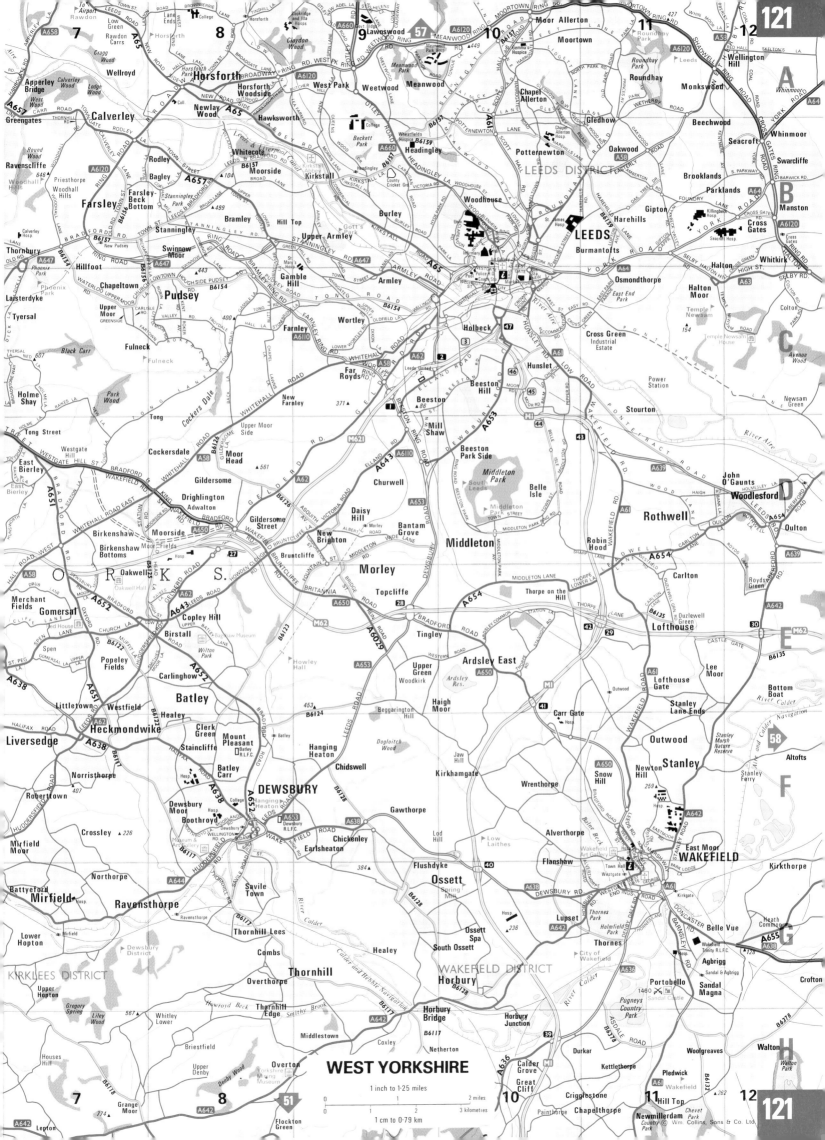

WEST YORKSHIRE

1 inch to 1·25 miles

1 cm to 0·79 km

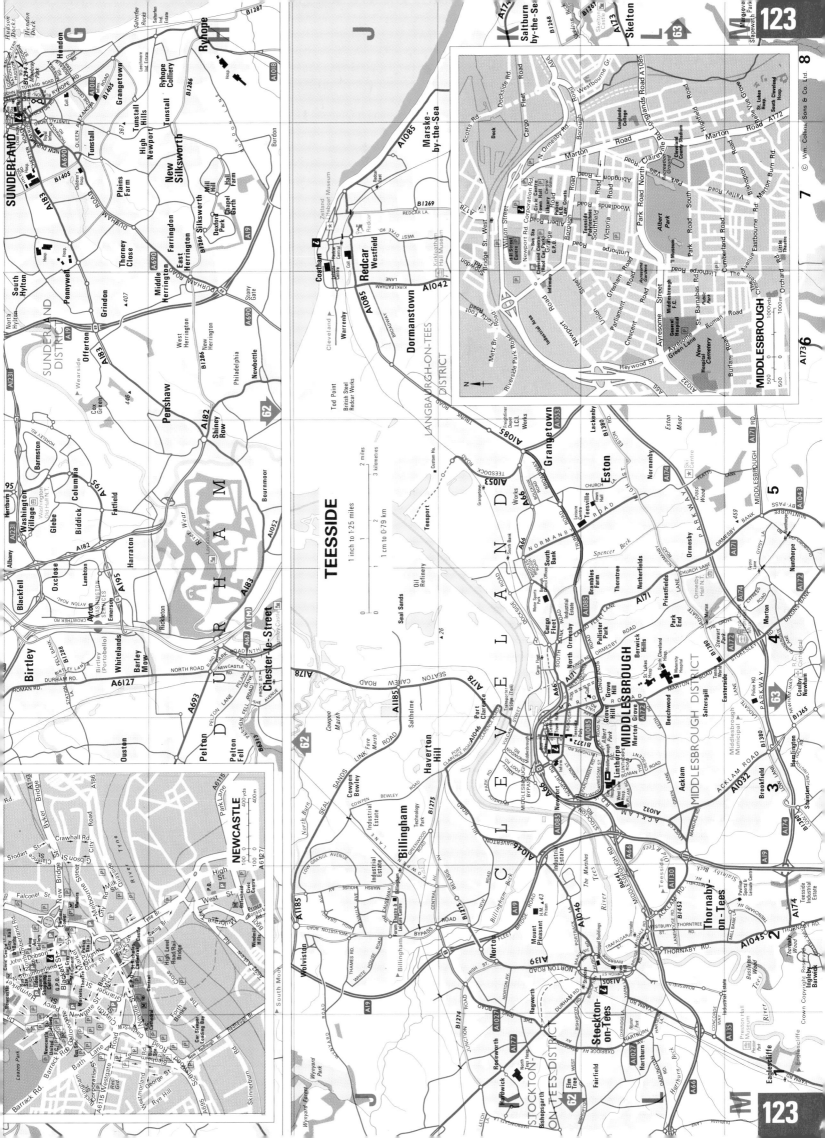

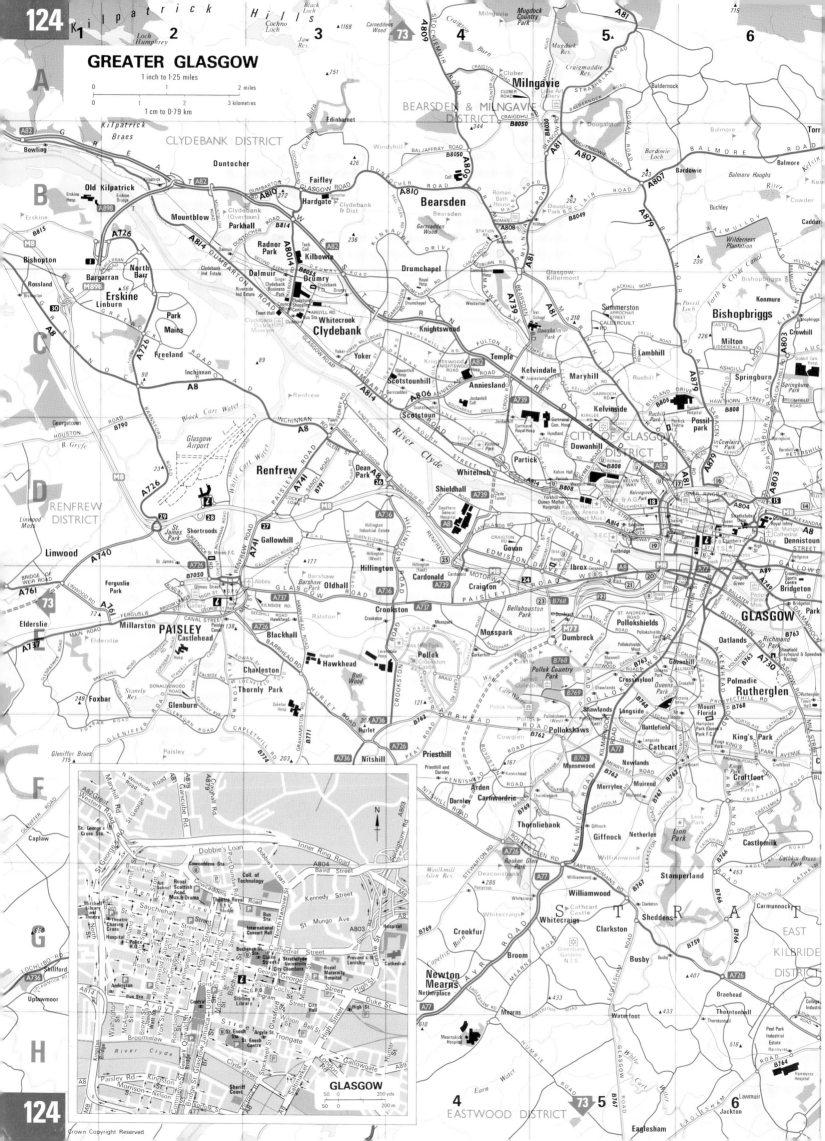

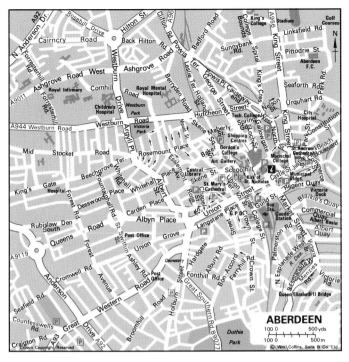

ABERDEEN

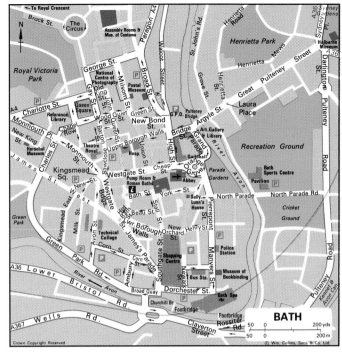

BATH

BLACKPOOL

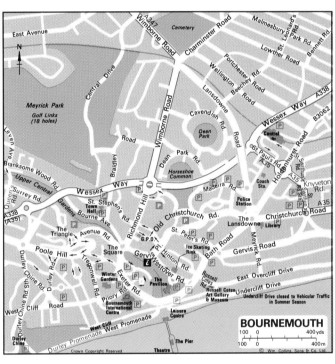

BOURNEMOUTH

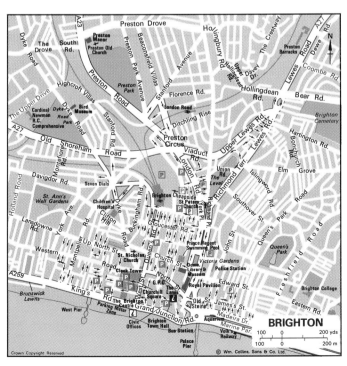

BRIGHTON

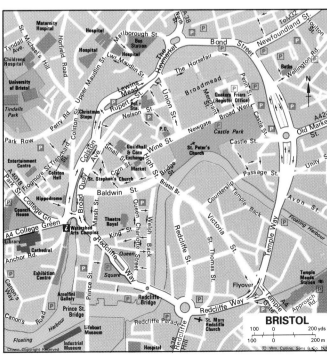

BRISTOL

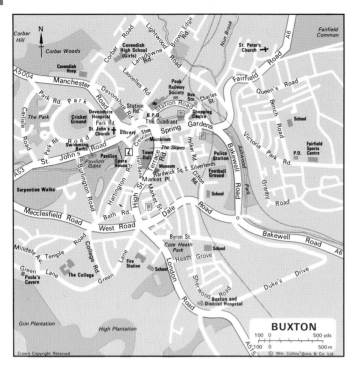

BUXTON

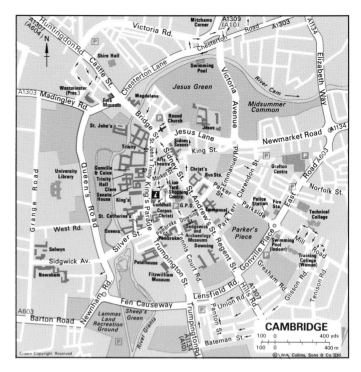

CAMBRIDGE

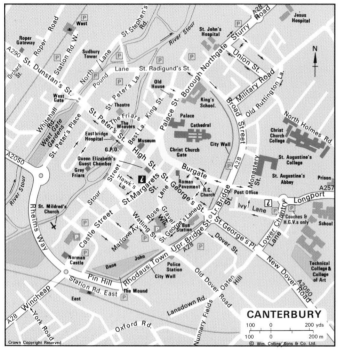

CANTERBURY

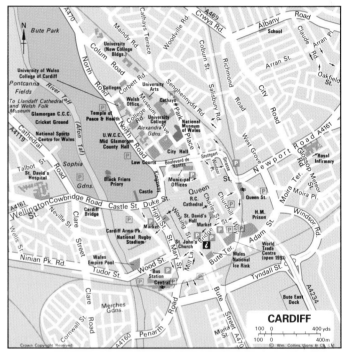

CARDIFF

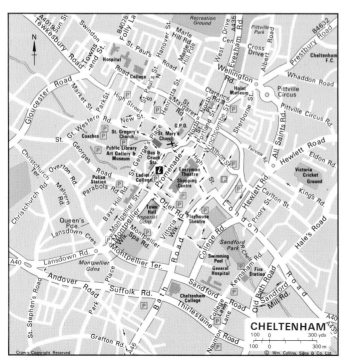

CHELTENHAM

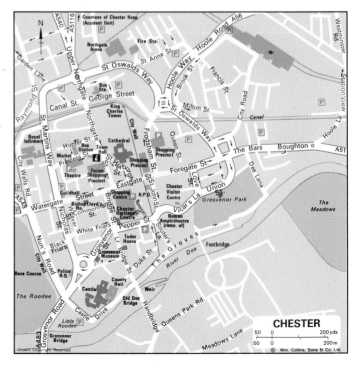

CHESTER

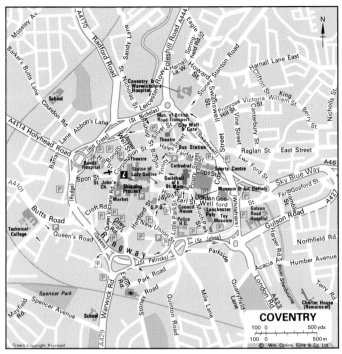

COVENTRY

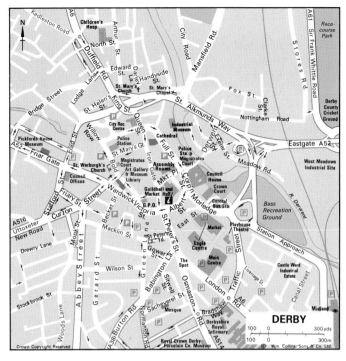

DERBY

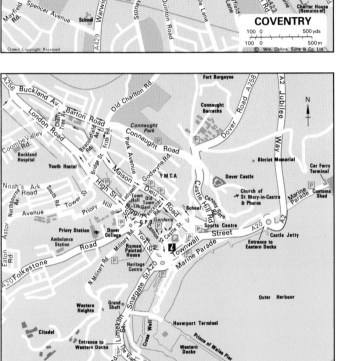

DOVER

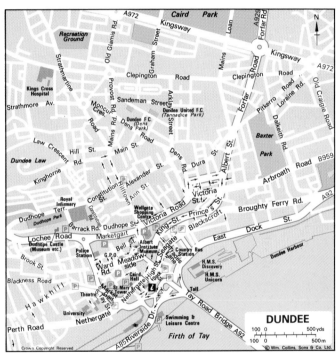

DUNDEE

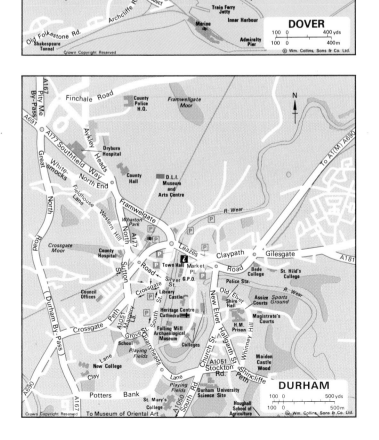

DURHAM

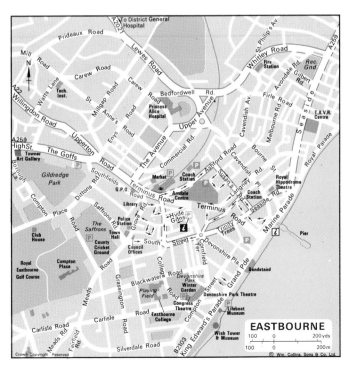

EASTBOURNE

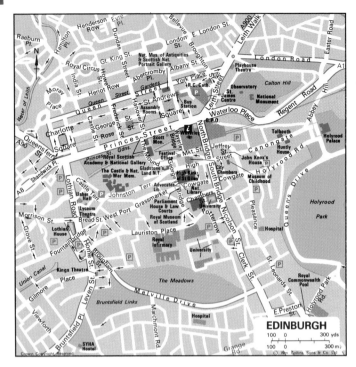

EDINBURGH

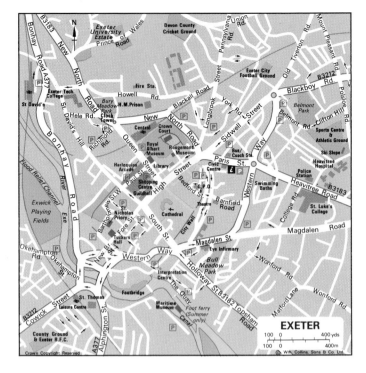

EXETER

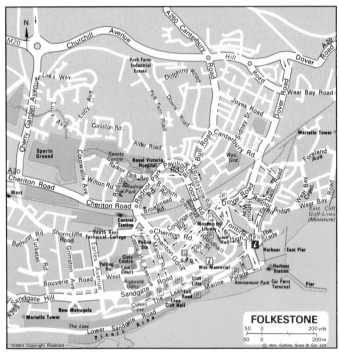

FOLKESTONE

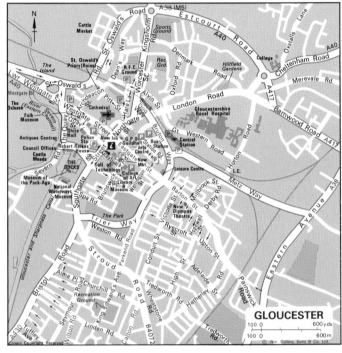

GLOUCESTER

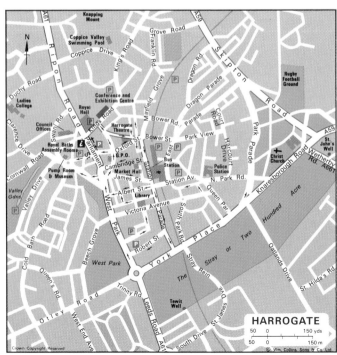

HARROGATE

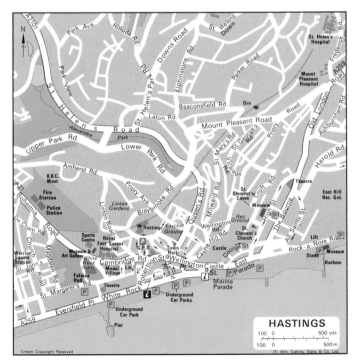

HASTINGS

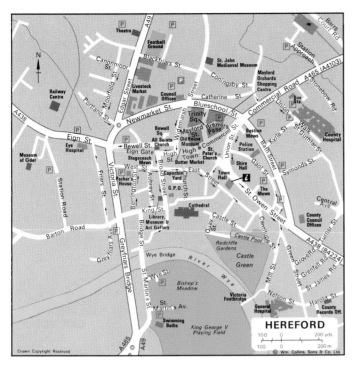

HEREFORD

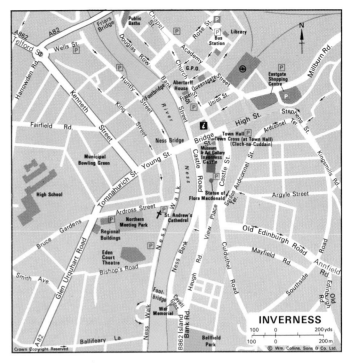

INVERNESS

KINGSTON-UPON-HULL

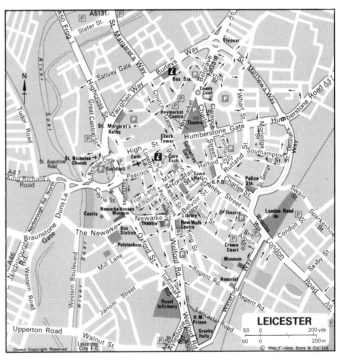

LEICESTER

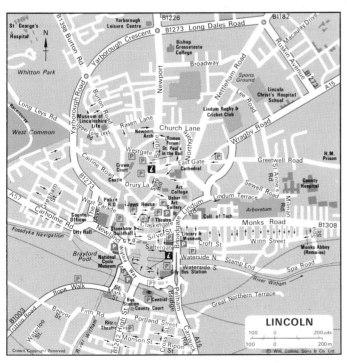

LINCOLN

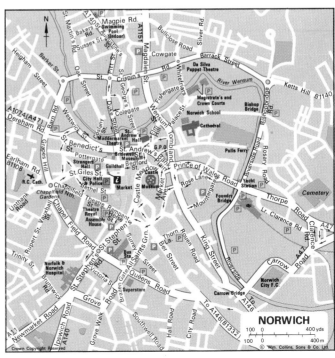

NORWICH

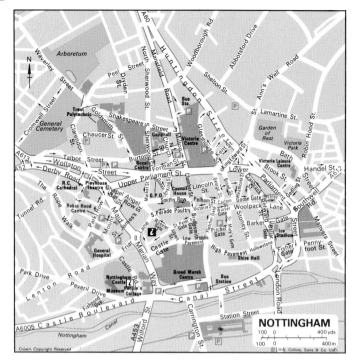

NOTTINGHAM

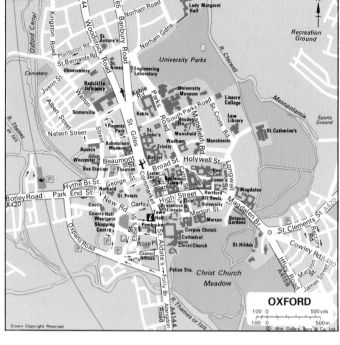

OXFORD

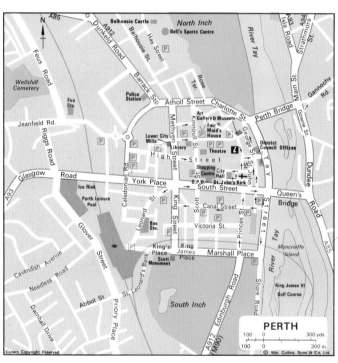

PERTH

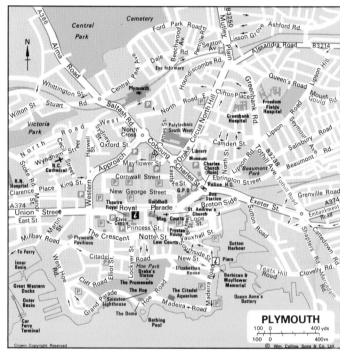

PLYMOUTH

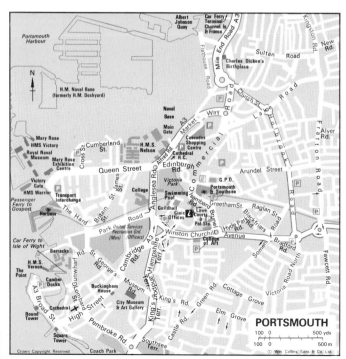

PORTSMOUTH

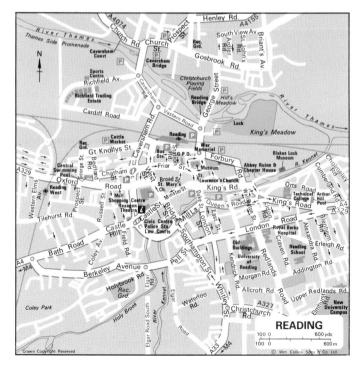

READING

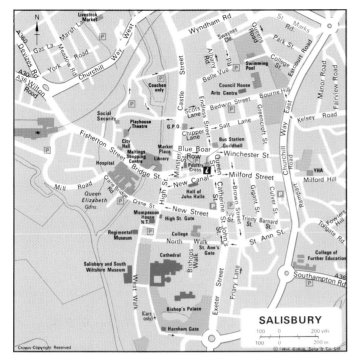

SALISBURY

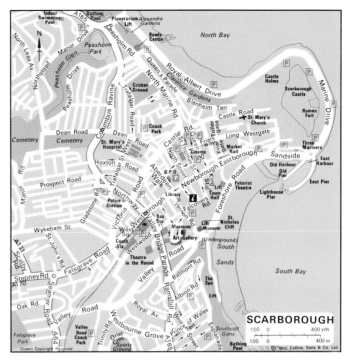

SCARBOROUGH

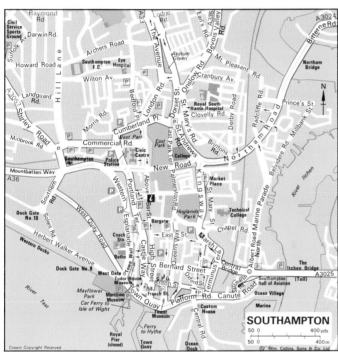

SOUTHAMPTON

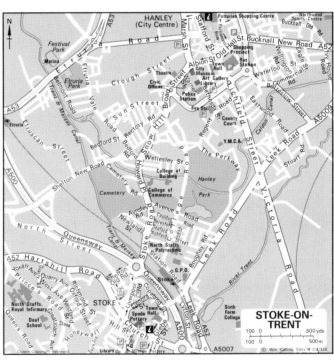

STOKE-ON-TRENT

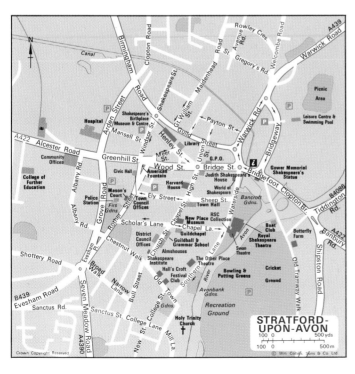

STRATFORD-UPON-AVON

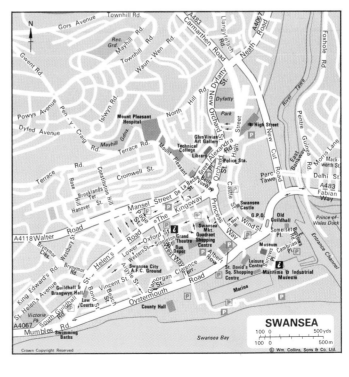

SWANSEA

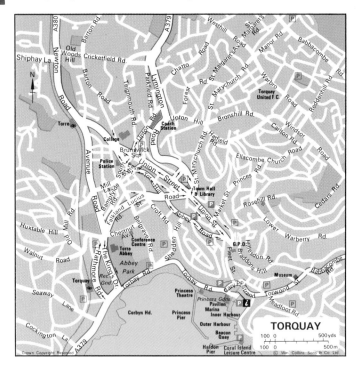

TORQUAY

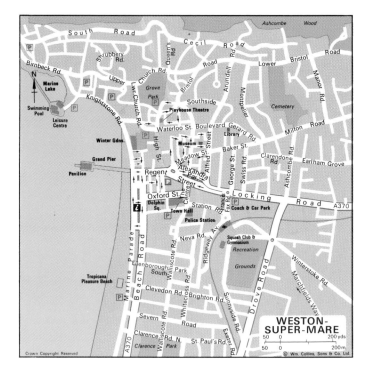

WESTON-SUPER-MARE

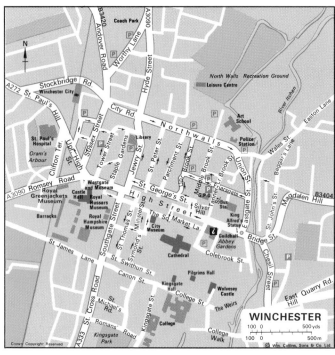

WINCHESTER

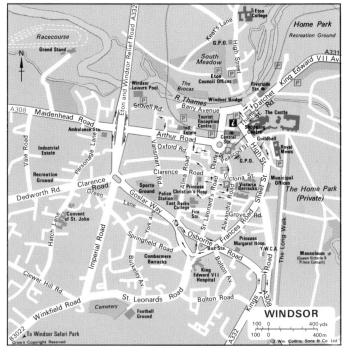

WINDSOR

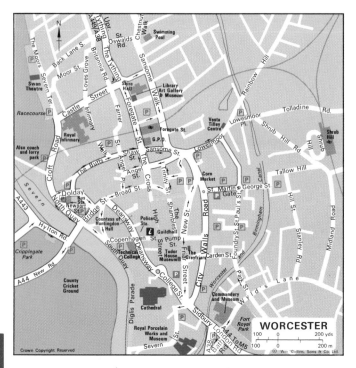

WORCESTER

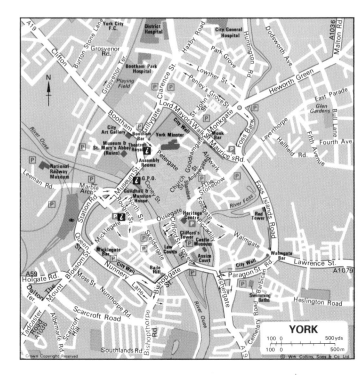

YORK

Ardmolich

INDEX TO PLACE NAMES IN BRITAIN

Abbreviations

Bfd.	Bedfordshire
Bkh.	Buckinghamshire
Bor.	Borders
Brk.	Berkshire
Cbs.	Cambridgeshire
Cen.	Central
Che.	Cheshire
Cle.	Cleveland
Clw.	Clwyd
Cnw.	Cornwall
Cum.	Cumbria
Dby.	Derbyshire
Dev.	Devonshire
D.&G.	Dumfries & Galloway
Dor.	Dorset
Drm.	Durham
Dyf.	Dyfed
E.S.	East Sussex
Esx.	Essex
G.L.	Greater London
Glo.	Gloucestershire
G.M.	Greater Manchester
Gny.	Guernsey
Grm.	Grampian
Gwe.	Gwent
Gwy.	Gwynedd
Ham.	Hampshire
Hfs.	Hertfordshire
Hgh.	Highland
Hum.	Humberside
H.&W.	Hereford & Worcester
I.o.M.	Isle of Man
I.o.W.	Isle of Wight
Jer.	Jersey
Lan.	Lancashire
Lcn.	Lincolnshire
Lei.	Leicestershire
Ltn.	Lothian
Mer.	Merseyside
M.G.	Mid Glamorgan
Nfk.	Norfolk
Nmp.	Northamptonshire
Nor.	Northumberland
Not.	Nottinghamshire
N.Y.	North Yorkshire
Ork.	Orkney Islands
Oxf.	Oxfordshire
Pow.	Powys
Sfk.	Suffolk
S.G.	South Glamorgan
She.	Shetland Islands
Shr.	Shropshire
Som.	Somerset
Sry.	Surrey
Stf.	Staffordshire
Str.	Strathclyde
S.Y.	South Yorkshire
Tay.	Tayside
T.&W.	Tyne & Wear
War.	Warwickshire
W.G.	West Glamorgan
W.I.	Western Isles
W.M.	West Midlands
W.S.	West Sussex
Wts.	Wiltshire
W.Y.	West Yorkshire

A

Abbas Combe **9** B33
Abberley **29** B33
Abberton *Esx.* **34** G56
Abberton *H.& W.* **29** C35
Abberwick **71** B37
Abbess Roding **33** G51
Abbeycwmhir **27** A26
Abbey Dore **28** E29
Abbey St. Bathans **76** D33
Abbeystead **55** D31
Abbeytown **60** A27
Abbey Village **56** G32
Abbotrule **70** B32
Abbots Bickington **6** D19
Abbots' Bromley **40** C36
Abbotsbury **8** F31
Abbotsham **6** C20
Abbotskerswell **5** D24
Abbots Langley **22** A46
Abbots Leigh **19** D31
Abbots Lench **30** C36
Abbotsley **33** C48
Abbots Morton **30** C36
Abbots Ripton **33** A48
Abbots Worthy **11** A41
Abbotts Ann **21** G39
Abdon **38** G31
Aber **46** E22
Aberaeron **26** B20
Aberaman **18** A26
Aberangell **37** D24
Aberarder **80** B20
Aberargie **81** J27
Aberarth **26** B20
Aberavon **18** B23
Aber-banc **26** D19
Aberbargoed **18** B27
Aberbeeg **19** A28
Aber Bowlan **17** A22
Aber-Bran **27** E25
Abercanaid **18** A26
Abercarn **19** B28
Aberchalder **83** J19
Aberchirder **85** D32
Abercoed **27** C22
Abercorn **75** C26
Abercraf **27** G24
Abercregan **18** B24
Abercych **26** D18
Abercynafon **27** G26
Abercynon **18** B26
Aberdare **18** A25
Aberdaron **36** C17
Aberdeen **85** J35
Aberdeen Airport **85** H34
Aberdesach **46** G20
Aberdour **75** B27
Aberdulais **18** B23
Aberdyfi **37** F22
Aberedw **27** D26
Abereiddy **16** A14
Abererch **36** B19
Aberfan **18** A26
Aberfeldy **80** F24
Aberffraw **46** F19
Aberffrwd **27** A22
Aberford **57** F40
Aberfoyle **80** K21
Abergavenny **28** G29
Abergele **47** E25
Abergiar **26** D21
Abergorlech **17** A21
Abergwesyn **27** C24
Abergwili **17** B20
Abergwydol **37** E23
Abergwynant **37** D22
Abergwynfi **18** B24
Abergynolwyn **37** E22
Aberhafesp **37** F26
Aberhosan **37** F24
Aberkenfig **18** C24
Aberlady **76** C30
Aberlemno **81** E31
Aberllefenni **37** D23
Abermorddu **48** G29
Abermule **38** F27
Abernant *Dyf.* **17** B19
Aber-nant *M.G.* **18** A26
Abernethy **81** J27
Abernyte **81** G28
Aberporth **26** C18
Abersoch **36** C19
Abersychan **19** A28
Aberthin **18** D26
Abertillery **19** A28
Abertridwr *M.G.* **18** C27
Abertridwr *Pow.* **37** D26
Abertysswg **18** A27
Aberuthven **80** J25
Aberyscir **27** E26
Aberystwyth **36** G21
Abingdon **21** B41
Abinger Common **22** G47
Abinger Hammer **22** G46
Abington *Str.* **68** A25
Abington Pigotts **33** D49
Abingworth **12** C47
Ab Kettleby **42** C43
Ablington **20** A37
Aboyne **81** A31
Abram **49** B32
Abridge **23** B50
Abson **20** D33
Abthorpe **31** D42
Aby **53** E50
Acaster Malbis **58** E41
Acaster Selby **58** E41
Accrington **56** G33
Acha **78** E7
Achachork **82** E10
Achadhchaorunn **72** E13
Achaetagan **72** B16
Achahoish **72** C13
Achallader **80** F19
Achanalt **83** C18
Achanamara **72** B13
Achandunie **84** B22
Achany **86** H21
Achaphubuil **79** C16
Acharacle **79** D12
Acharn *Hgh.* **79** E12
Acharn *Tay.* **80** F23
Acharole **87** C28
Acharosson **72** C15
Achavanich **87** D27
Achdacherranmore **72** B16
Achentoul **87** E24
Achfary **86** E18
Achgarve **86** J14
Achiemore *Hgh.* **87** C24
Achiemore *Hgh.* **86** B19
A'Chill *Hgh.* **82** J8
Achiltibuie **86** H16
Achinduich **86** J21
Achintee **83** E15
Achintraid **83** F14
Achleck **78** F10
Achlyness **86** C18
Achmelvich **86** F16
Achmore *Cen.* **80** G21
Achmore *Hgh.* **83** F14
Achmore *W.I.* **88** E9
Achnaba **72** B15
Achnacarnin **86** E16
Achnacarry **79** B17
Achnacloich **82** J11
Achnaconeran **83** H20
Achnacroish **79** F14
Achnaha **78** D10
Achnahanat **86** J21
Achnaluachrach **87** H22
Achnasaul **79** B17
Achnasheen **83** D17
Achnashellach Lodge **83** E16
Achnashelloch **72** A14
Achosnich **78** D10
Achranich **79** F13
Achriabhach **79** D17
Achriesgill **86** C18
Achtriochtan **79** E17
Achurch **42** G46
Achuvoldrach **86** C21
Achvaich **87** J23
Ackergill **87** C29
Acklam *Cle.* **62** E40
Acklam *N.Y.* **58** C43
Ackleton **39** F33
Acklington **71** C38
Ackton **57** G40
Ackworth Moor Top **51** A40
Acle **45** D60
Acock's Green **40** G37
Acol **25** E59
Acomb **70** G35
Aconbury **28** E31
Acrefair **38** A28
Acton *Che.* **49** G32
Acton *Sfk.* **34** D54
Acton *Shr.* **38** G29
Acton *Stf.* **40** A34
Acton Bridge **48** E31
Acton Burnell **38** E31
Acton Green **29** C32
Acton Round **39** F32
Acton Scott **38** G30
Acton Trussel **40** D35
Acton Turville **20** C34
Adbaston **39** C33
Adderbury **31** E40
Adderley **39** A32
Adderstone **77** G37
Addiewell **75** D25
Addingham **57** E36
Addington *Bkh.* **31** F43
Addington *G.L.* **23** E49
Addington *Kent* **23** F52
Addlestone **22** E46
Adforton **28** A30
Adisham **15** B58
Adlestrop **30** F38
Adlingfleet **58** G44
Adlington *Che.* **49** D35
Adlington *Lan.* **48** A31
Admaston *Shr.* **39** D32
Admaston *Stf.* **40** C36
Admington **30** D38
Adsborough **8** B28
Adstock **31** E43
Adstone **31** C41
Adversane **12** B46
Advie **84** F27
Adwalton **57** G38
Adwick le Street **51** B41
Adwick upon Dearne **51** B40
Adziel **85** D35
Ae Bridgend **69** E26
Ae Village **68** E25
Affpuddle **9** E34
Affric Lodge **83** G17
Afon-wen **47** E27
Afton Bridgend **68** B22
Agglethorpe **57** A36
Agneash **54** E26
Aigburth **48** D29
Aike **59** E46
Aikers **89** H30
Aiketgate **61** B30
Aikton **60** A28
Ailsworth **42** F47
Ainderby Quernhow **57** A39
Ainderby Steeple **62** G39
Ainsdale **48** A29
Ainsdale on Sea **48** A28
Ainstable **61** B31
Ainsworth **49** A33
Ainthorpe **63** F43
Aintree **48** C29
Aird *Str.* **79** K13
Aird *W.I.* **88** D11
Aird Of Sleat **82** J11
Airdrie **74** D23
Aird Tong **88** D10
Aird Uig **88** D6
Airies **66** G15
Airmyn **58** G43
Airntully **80** G26
Airor **82** J13
Airth **74** B24
Airton **56** D34
Aisby *Lcn.* **42** B46
Aisby *Lcn.* **52** C44
Aisgill **61** G33
Aiskew **57** A38
Aislaby *N.Y.* **58** A43
Aislaby *N.Y.* **63** F44
Aisthorpe **52** D45
Aith *Ork.* **89** E32
Aith *She.* **89** C42
Aith *She.* **89** G39
Aitnoch **84** F25
Akeld **70** A35
Akeley **31** E43
Akenham **35** D57
Albaston **4** C20
Alberbury **38** D29
Albourne **13** C48
Albourne Green **13** C48
Albrighton *Shr.* **40** E34
Albrighton *Shr.* **38** D30
Alburgh **45** G58
Albury *Hfs.* **33** F50
Albury *Sry.* **22** G46
Alcaig **83** D21
Alcester **30** C36
Alciston **13** D51
Alcombe **7** A25
Alconbury **32** A47
Alconbury Hill **32** A47
Alconbury Weston **32** A47
Aldborough *Nfk.* **45** B57
Aldborough *N.Y.* **57** C40
Aldbourne **21** D38
Aldbrough *Hum.* **59** F48
Aldbrough *N.Y.* **62** E38
Aldbury **32** G45
Aldcliffe **55** C30
Aldclune **80** D24
Aldeburgh **35** C60
Aldeby **45** F60
Aldenham **22** B47
Alderbury **10** B37
Alderford **45** D57
Alderholt **10** C37
Alderley **20** B33
Alderley Edge **49** E34
Aldermaston **21** E41
Aldermaston Wharf **21** E42
Alderminster **30** D38
Alderney Airport **3** D17
Aldershot **22** F44
Alderton *Glo.* **30** E36
Alderton *Nmp.* **31** D43
Alderton *Sfk.* **35** D59
Alderton *Shr.* **38** C30
Alderton *Wts.* **20** C34
Alderwasley **51** G39
Aldfield **57** C38
Aldford **48** G30
Aldham **34** F55
Aldingbourne **12** D45
Aldingham **54** B28
Aldington *H.& W.* **30** D36
Aldington *Kent* **15** D56
Aldington Corner **15** D56
Aldochlay **73** A19
Aldreth **33** A50
Aldridge **40** E36
Aldringham **35** B60
Aldrington **13** D48
Aldsworth **30** G37
Aldunie **84** G29
Aldwark *Dby.* **50** G38
Aldwark *N.Y.* **57** C40
Aldwick **12** E45
Aldwincle **42** G46
Aldworth **21** D41
Alexandria **73** C19
Alfington **7** F27
Alfold **12** A46
Alfold Crossways **12** A46
Alford *Grm.* **85** H31
Alford *Lcn.* **53** E50
Alford *Som.* **9** A32
Alfreton **51** G39
Alfrick **29** C33
Alfriston **13** D51
Algarkirk **43** B48
Alhampton **9** A32
Alkborough **58** G44
Alkerton **30** D39
Alkham **15** C58
Alkmonton **40** B37
Alladale Lodge **83** A20
Allanton *Bor.* **77** E34
Allanton *Str.* **74** E24
Allanton *Str.* **74** E23
Allanton Plains **74** G22
Allbrook **11** B40
All Cannings **20** E36
Allendale Town **61** A34
Allenheads **61** B34
Allensford **62** A36
Allensmore **28** E30
Aller **8** B29
Allerby **60** C26
Allerford **7** A25
Allerston **58** A44
Allerthorpe **58** E43
Allerton *Mer.* **48** D29
Allerton *W.Y.* **57** F37
Allerton Bywater **57** G40
Allerton Mauleverer **57** D40
Allerwash **70** G34
Allesley **41** G39
Allestree **41** B39
Allexton **42** E44
Allgreave **49** F35
Allhallows **24** D54
Alligin Shuas **83** D14
Allington *Dor.* **8** E30
Allington *Lcn.* **42** A44
Allington *Wts.* **10** A38
Allington *Wts.* **20** E36
Allithwaite **55** B29
Allnabad **86** D20
Alloa **74** A24
Allonby **60** B26
Allostock **49** E33
Alloway **67** B19
All Stretton **38** F30
Allt **17** D21
Alltami **48** F28
Alltbeithe **83** J16
Alltgobhlach **72** F14
Alltmawr **27** D26
Alltnacaillich **86** D20
Allt na h'Airbhe Inn **86** J17
Alltwalis **17** A20
Alltwen **18** A23
Alltyblacca **26** D21
Allweston **9** C32
Almeley **28** C29
Almer **9** E35
Almington **39** B33
Alminstone Cross **6** C19
Almondbank **80** H26
Almondbury **50** A37
Almondsbury **19** C32
Almont **67** E17
Alne **57** C40
Alness **84** C22
Alnham **70** B35
Alnmouth **71** B38
Alnwick **71** B37
Alphamstone **34** E54
Alpheton **34** C54
Alphington **7** G25
Alport **50** F38
Alpraham **48** G31
Alresford **34** F56
Alrewas **40** D37
Alsager **49** G33
Alsagers Bank **40** A34
Alsop en le Dale **50** G37
Alston *Cum.* **61** B33
Alston *Dev.* **8** D29
Alstone **29** E35
Alstonfield **50** G37
Alswear **7** C23
Altandhu **86** G15
Altanduin **87** F24
Altarnun **4** B18
Altass **86** H21
Alterwall **87** B28
Altgaltraig **72** C16
Altham **56** F33
Althorne **25** B55
Althorpe **52** B44
Alticry **64** D18
Altimeg **66** F16
Altnabea **87** F26
Altnabreac Station **87** D26
Altnacealgach Hotel **86** G18
Altnafeadh **79** E18
Altnaharra **86** E21
Altofts **57** G39
Alton *Dby.* **51** F39
Alton *Ham.* **11** A43
Alton *Stf.* **40** A36
Alton Barnes **20** E37
Alton Pancras **9** D32
Alton Priors **20** E37
Altrincham **49** D33
Alva **74** A24
Alvanley **48** E30
Alvaston **41** B39
Alvechurch **30** A36
Alvediston **9** B35
Alveley **39** G33
Alverdiscott **6** C21
Alverstoke **11** E42
Alverstone **11** F41
Alverton **42** A43
Alvescot **21** A38
Alveston *Avon* **19** C32
Alveston *War.* **30** C38
Alvie **84** J24
Alvingham **53** C49
Alvington **19** A32
Alwalton **42** F47
Alwinton **70** C35
Alwoodley **57** E38
Alyth **81** F28
Ambergate **51** G39
Amberley *Glo.* **20** A34
Amberley *W.S.* **12** C46
Amble **71** C38
Amblecote **40** G34
Ambleside **60** F29
Ambleston **16** B16
Ambrismore **72** E16
Ambrosden **31** G42
Amcotts **52** A44
Amersham **22** B45
Amesbury **20** G37
Amhuinnsuidhe **88** G6
Amington **40** E38
Amisfield Town **68** E25
Amlwch **46** C20
Amlwch Port **46** C20
Ammanford **17** C22
Amotherby **58** B43
Ampfield **10** B39
Ampleforth **58** B41
Ampney Crucis **20** A36
Ampney St. Mary **20** A36
Ampney St. Peter **20** A36
Amport **21** G39
Ampthill **32** E46
Ampton **34** A54
Amroth **16** D17
Amulree **80** G24
Anaheilt **79** D14
Ancaster **42** A45
Anchor **38** G27
Ancroft **77** F35
Ancrum **70** A32
Anderby **53** E51
Anderson **9** E34
Anderton **49** E32
Anderton Services **49** A32
Andover **21** G39
Andoversford **30** G36
Andreas **54** D26
Anelog **36** C17
Angarrack **2** E11
Angersleigh **7** D27
Angerton **60** A28
Angle **16** D14
Angmering **12** D46
Angmering-by-Sea **12** D46
Angram *N.Y.* **58** E41
Angram *N.Y.* **61** G34
Anie **80** J21
Ankerville **84** B24
Anlaby **59** G46
Anmer **44** C53
Annan **69** G27
Annat *Hgh.* **83** D14
Annat *Str.* **79** H16
Anna Valley **21** G39
Annbank **67** A20
Annesley **51** G41
Annesley Woodhouse **51** G40
Annfield Plain **62** A37
Annitsford **71** F38
Ansford **9** A32
Ansley **40** F38
Anslow **40** C38
Anstey *Hfs.* **33** E50
Anstey *Lei.* **41** E41
Anstruther **81** K31
Ansty *War.* **41** G39
Ansty *W.S.* **13** B48
Ansty *Wts.* **9** B35
Ansty Cross **9** D33
Anthorn **60** A27
Antingham **45** B58
Antony **4** E19
Anvil Corner **6** E19
Anwick **52** G47
Anwoth **65** C21
Apethorpe **42** F46
Apley **52** E47
Apperley **29** F34
Apperley Dene **62** A36
Appersett **61** G34
Appin House **79** E15
Appleby **52** A45
Appleby in Westmorland **61** E32
Appleby Magna **41** D39
Appleby Parva **41** E39
Applecross **82** E13
Appledore *Dev.* **6** B20
Appledore *Dev.* **7** D26
Appledore *Kent* **14** E55
Appledore Heath **14** D55
Appleford **21** B41
Applegarth Town **69** E27
Appleshaw **21** G39
Applethwaite **60** D28
Appleton **21** A40
Appleton-le-Moors **58** A43
Appleton-le-Street **58** B43
Appleton Roebuck **58** E41
Appleton Thorn **49** D32
Appleton Wiske **62** F39
Appletreehall **70** B31
Appletreewick **57** C36
Appley Bridge **48** B31
Apse Heath **11** F41
Apsley End **32** E47
Apuldram **12** D44
Arbigland **65** C25
Arbirlot **81** F31
Arboll **84** A24
Arborfield **22** E43
Arborfield Cross **22** E43
Arbroath **81** F32
Arbuthnott **81** C33
Archiestown **84** E28
Arclid Green **49** F33
Ard a' Chapuill **72** C16
Ardachearanbeg **72** B16
Ardachvie **79** A17
Ardalanish **78** J9
Ardanaiseig **79** H16
Ardaneaskan **83** F14
Ardarroch **83** F14
Ardary **79** D13
Ardbeg *Str.* **72** D16
Ardbeg *Str.* **73** B17
Ardbeg *Str.* **78** K5
Ardcharnich **83** A17
Ardchiavaig **78** J9
Ardchullarie More **80** J21
Ardchyle **80** H21
Arddarroch **73** A18
Arddleen **38** D28
Ardeer **73** F18
Ardeley **33** F49
Ardelve **83** G14
Arden **73** B19
Ardendee **65** C22
Ardentinny **73** B17
Ardentraive **72** C16
Ardeonaig **80** G22
Ardersier **84** D23
Ardessie **83** A16
Ardfern **79** K14
Ardgartan **79** K18
Ardgay **86** J21
Ardgowan **73** C18
Ardhasig **88** G7
Ardindrean **83** A17
Ardingly **13** B49
Ardington **21** C40
Ardivachar **88** N3
Ardlair **85** G31
Ardleigh **34** F56
Ardler **81** F28
Ardley **31** F41
Ardlui **80** J19
Ardlussa **72** B12
Ardmair **86** J17
Ardmaleish **72** D16
Ardmay **79** K18
Ardminish **72** F12
Ardmolich **79** C13

Ardmore

Ardmore Str. 73 C19
Ardnackaig 72 A13
Ardnacross 79 F11
Ardnadam 73 B17
Ardnarff 83 F14
Ardnastang 79 D14
Ardnave 78 H4
Ardno 79 K17
Ardochu 87 H22
Ardock 68 C24
Ardpeaton 73 B18
Ardrishaig 72 B14
Ardroil 88 D6
Ardrossan 73 F18
Ardross Castle 84 B22
Ardscalpsie 72 E16
Ardsley 51 B39
Ardsley East 57 G39
Ardslignish 79 D11
Ardtalla 78 J6
Ardtalnaig 80 G23
Ardtarig 72 B16
Ardtoe 79 C12
Ardtrostan 80 H22
Arduaine 79 J13
Ardvanie 84 A22
Ardvasar 82 J12
Ardvorlich 80 H22
Ardvourlie 88 F7
Ardwell D.& G. 64 D17
Ardwell Str. 67 D17
Areley Kings 29 A34
Arford 12 A44
Argoed 18 B27
Argoed Mill 27 B25
Arinacrinachd 82 D13
Arinagour 78 E8
Arisaig 79 B12
Ariundle 79 D14
Arivruaich 88 F8
Arkendale 57 C39
Arkesden 33 E50
Arkholme 55 B31
Arkland 68 D24
Arkleby 60 C27
Arkleton 69 D29
Arkle Town 62 F36
Arkley 23 B48
Arksey 51 B41
Arkwright Town 51 E40
Arlecdon 60 E26
Arlesey 32 E47
Arley Che. 49 D32
Arley War. 40 F38
Arlingham 29 G33
Arlington Dev. 6 A22
Arlington E.S. 13 D51
Arlington Glo. 20 A37
Arlington Beccott 6 A22
Armadale Hgh. 87 B23
Armadale Hgh. 82 J12
Armadale Ltn. 75 D25
Armathwaite 61 B31
Arminghall 45 E58
Armitage 40 D36
Armley 57 F38
Armscote 30 D38
Armthorpe 51 B42
Arnburn 73 B19
Arncliffe 56 B35
Arncroach 81 K31
Arne 9 F35
Arnesby 41 F42
Arnicle 72 G13
Arnisdale 83 H14
Arnish 82 E11
Arniston 75 D29
Arnol 88 C9
Arnold Hum. 59 E47
Arnold Not. 41 A41
Arnprior 74 A22
Arnside 55 B30
Aros Mains 79 F11
Arrad Foot 55 A29
Arram 59 E46
Arrathorne 62 G37
Arreton 11 F41
Arrington 33 C49
Arrochar 79 K18
Arrow 30 C36
Arscaig 86 G21
Arthington 57 E38
Arthingworth 42 G43
Arthog 37 D22
Arthrath 85 F35
Artnoch 67 E18
Arundel 12 D46
Ascog 73 D17
Ascot 22 E45
Ascott under Wychwood 30 G39
Asenby 57 B39
Asfordby 42 D43
Asgarby Lcn. 53 F49
Asgarby Lcn. 42 A47
Ash Dev. 5 E24
Ash Kent 15 B58
Ash Kent 24 E52
Ash Som. 8 B30
Ash Sry. 22 F44
Ashampstead 21 D41
Ashbocking 35 C57
Ashbourne Dby. 40 A37
Ashbrittle 7 C26
Ashburton 5 C23
Ashbury Dev. 6 F21
Ashbury Oxf. 21 C38
Ashby 52 B45
Ashby by Partney 53 F50
Ashby cum Fenby 53 B48
Ashby de la Launde 52 G46
Ashby de la Zouch 41 D39
Ashby Dell 45 F60
Ashby Folville 42 D43
Ashby Magna 41 F41
Ashby Parva 41 G41
Ashby Puerorum 53 E49
Ashby St. Ledgers 31 B41
Ashby St. Mary 45 E59
Ashchurch 29 E35
Ashcombe 5 C25
Ashcott 8 A30
Ashdon 33 D51
Ashe 21 F41
Asheldham 25 A55
Ashen 34 D53
Ashendon 31 G43
Ashfield Cen. 80 K23
Ashfield H.& W. 28 F31
Ashfield Sfk. 35 B58
Ashfield Str. 74 B20
Ashfield Green 35 A58
Ashford Dby. 50 F37
Ashford Dev. 5 F22
Ashford Dev. 6 B21
Ashford Kent 15 C56
Ashford Sry. 22 D46
Ashford Bowdler 28 A31
Ashford Carbonel 28 A31
Ashford Hill 21 E41
Ashgill 74 F23
Ashgill Head 61 C34
Ashgillside 61 B33
Ashieburn 70 A32
Ashill Dev. 7 D26
Ashill Nfk. 44 E54
Ashill Som. 8 C29
Ashingdon 24 B54
Ashington Nor. 71 E38
Ashington W.S. 12 C47
Ashkirk 69 A30
Ashleworth 29 F34
Ashley Cbs. 33 B52
Ashley Che. 49 D33
Ashley Dor. 10 D37
Ashley Glo. 20 B35
Ashley Ham. 10 A39
Ashley Ham. 10 E38
Ashley Kent 15 C59
Ashley Nmp. 42 F43
Ashley Stf. 39 B33
Ashley Green 22 A45
Ash Magna 38 B31
Ashmansworth 21 F40
Ashmansworthy 6 D19
Ash Mill 7 C23
Ashmore 9 C35
Ashover 51 F39
Ashow 30 A39
Ashperton 29 D32
Ashprington 5 E24
Ash Priors 7 C27
Ashreigney 6 D22
Ashtead 22 F47
Ash Thomas 7 D26
Ashton Cnw. 2 F12
Ashton Cnw. 4 D19
Ashton G.M. 48 F31
Ashton H.& W. 28 B31
Ashton Nmp. 31 C43
Ashton Nmp. 42 G46
Ashton in Makerfield 48 C31
Ashton Keynes 20 B36
Ashton under Hill 29 E35
Ashton-under-Lyne 49 B35
Ashton upon Mersey 49 C33
Ashurst Ham. 10 C39
Ashurst Kent 13 A51
Ashurst W.S. 12 C47
Ashurstwood 13 A50
Ash Vale 22 F44
Ashwater 6 F19
Ashwell Hfs. 33 E48
Ashwell Lei. 42 D44
Ashwellthorpe 45 F57
Ashwick 19 G32
Ashwicken 44 D53
Ashybank 70 B31
Askam in Furness 54 B28
Askern 51 A41
Askernish 88 P3
Askerswell 8 E31
Askham Cum. 61 D31
Askham Not. 51 E43
Askham Bryan 58 E41
Askham Richard 58 E41
Asknish 72 A15
Askrigg 61 G35
Askwith 57 E37
Aslackby 42 B46
Aslacton 45 F57
Aslockton 42 A43
Aspatria 60 B27
Aspenden 33 F49
Aspley Guise 32 E45
Aspull 49 B32
Asselby 58 G43
Assington 34 E55
Astbury 49 F34
Astcote 31 C42
Asterley 38 E29
Asthall 30 G38
Astley G.M. 49 B33
Astley H.& W. 29 B33
Astley Shr. 38 D31
Astley War. 41 G39
Astley Abbotts 39 F33
Astley Bridge 49 A32
Astley Cross 29 B34
Astley Green 49 C33
Aston Che. 39 A32
Aston Che. 48 E31
Aston Clw. 48 F29
Aston Dby. 50 D37
Aston Hfs. 33 F48
Aston H.& W. 28 A30
Aston Oxf. 21 A39
Aston Shr. 40 F34
Aston Stf. 40 B35
Aston Stf. 39 A33
Aston S.Y. 51 D40
Aston W.M. 40 G36
Aston Abbots 32 F44
Aston Blank 30 G37
Aston Botterell 39 G32
Aston Cantlow 30 C37
Aston Clinton 32 G44
Aston Cross 29 E35
Aston Eyre 39 F32
Aston Fields 29 B35
Aston Flamville 41 F40
Aston Ingham 29 F32
Aston juxta Mondrum 49 G32
Aston le Walls 31 C40
Aston Magna 30 E37
Aston on Clun 38 G29
Aston Rowant 22 B43
Aston Sandford 22 A43
Aston Somerville 30 E36
Aston Subedge 30 D37
Aston Tirrold 21 C41
Aston upon Trent 41 C40
Aston Upthorpe 21 C41
Astwick 33 E48
Astwood 32 D45
Astwood Bank 30 B36
Aswarby 42 A46
Aswardby 53 E49
Atcham 38 E31
Athelhampton 9 E33
Athelington 35 A58
Athelstaneford 76 C31
Atherington 6 C21
Atherstone 41 F39
Atherstone on Stour 30 C38
Atherton 49 B32
Atley Hill 62 F38
Atlow 40 A38
Attadale House 83 F15
Atterby 52 C45
Attleborough Nfk. 44 F56
Attleborough War. 41 F39
Attlebridge 45 D57
Attonburn 70 A34
Atwick 59 D47
Atworth 20 E34
Aubourn 52 F45
Auch 80 G19
Auchallater 81 B27
Auchameanach 72 E14
Aucharnie 85 E32
Auchavan 81 D27
Auchbraad 72 B14
Auchenblae 81 C33
Auchenbrack 68 D23
Auchenbreck 72 B16
Auchencairn D.& G. 65 C23
Auchencairn D.& G. 68 E25
Auchencastle 69 C26
Auchencorvie 66 B12
Auchencrosh 66 F16
Auchencrow 77 D34
Auchendinny 75 D28
Auchenfoyle 73 C19
Auchengarth 73 D17
Auchengray 75 E25
Auchengruith 68 C24
Auchenheath 74 F24
Auchenhessnane 68 D24
Auchenlaich 80 K22
Auchenlaich 80 K22
Auchenlochan 72 C15
Auchenmade 73 F19
Auchenmalg Bridge 64 C18
Auchentiber 73 F19
Auchenvennel 73 B18
Auchgourish 84 H25
Auchinadrian 72 E13
Auchincruive 67 A19
Auchindrain 79 K16
Auchindrean 83 A17
Auchinleck 67 A21
Auchinloch 74 C22
Auchintore 79 C16
Auchleand 64 C20
Auchleven 85 G32
Auchlochan 74 G24
Auchlossan 85 J31
Auchlyne 80 H21
Auchmacoy 85 F35
Auchmantle 67 G17
Auchmithie 81 F32
Auchmull 81 C31
Auchnacloich 79 G15
Auchnacraig 79 G13
Auchnacree 81 D30
Auchnafree 80 G24
Auchnagallin 84 F26
Auchnagarran 72 B16
Auchnagatt 85 E35
Aucholzie 81 A29
Auchreddie 85 E34
Auchrioch 80 H19
Auchronie 81 B30
Auchterarder 80 J25
Auchterderran 75 A28
Auchtermuchty 81 J28
Auchterneed 83 D20
Auchtertool 75 A28
Auchtertyre Cen. 80 H19
Auchtertyre Hgh. 83 G14
Auchtoo 80 H21
Auckingill 87 B29
Auckley 51 B42
Audenshaw 49 C35
Audlem 39 A32
Audley 49 G33
Aughton Hum. 58 F43
Aughton Lan. 48 B29
Aughton Lan. 55 C31
Aughton S.Y. 51 D40
Auldearn 84 D25
Auldgirth 68 E25
Auldhame 76 B31
Auldhouse 74 E22
Ault-a-chrinn 83 G15
Aultanrynie 86 E19
Aultbea 83 A14
Aultdearg 83 C18
Aultgrishan 82 A13
Aultguish Inn 83 B19
Aultmore 84 D29
Aultnamain Inn 84 A22
Aundorach 84 H25
Aunsby 42 B46
Aust 19 C31
Austerfield 51 C42
Austonley 50 B37
Austrey 40 E38
Aust Services 19 C31
Austwick 56 C33
Authorpe 53 D50
Avebury 20 D36
Aveley 23 C51
Avening 20 B34
Avenuehead 74 B24
Averham 51 G43
Avernish 83 G14
Aveton Gifford 5 F22
Avielochan 84 H25
Aviemore 84 H24
Avinagillan 72 D14
Avoch 84 D23
Avon 10 E37
Avonbridge 75 C25
Avon Dassett 31 D40
Avonmouth 19 D31
Avonwick 5 E23
Awbridge 10 B39
Awhirk 64 C16
Awliscombe 7 E27
Awre 20 A33
Awsworth 41 A40
Axbridge 19 F30
Axford Ham. 21 G42
Axford Wts. 21 D38
Axminster 8 E28
Axmouth 8 E28
Aycliffe 62 D38
Aydon 71 G36
Aylburton 19 A32
Ayle 61 B33
Aylesbeare 7 F26
Aylesbury 32 G44
Aylesby 53 B48
Aylesford 14 B53
Aylesham 15 B58
Aylestone 41 E41
Aylmerton 45 B57
Aylsham 45 C57
Aylton 29 E32
Aymestrey 28 B30
Aynho 31 E41
Ayot St. Lawrence 32 G47
Ayr 67 A19
Ayre of Westermill 89 H30
Aysgarth 56 A35
Ayside 55 A29
Ayston 42 E44
Ayton 77 D35
Aywick 89 D41
Azerley 57 B38

B

Babbacombe 5 D25
Babcary 8 B31
Babel 27 E24
Babell 47 E27
Babraham 33 C51
Babworth 51 D42
Back 88 C10
Backaland 89 D31
Backbarrow 55 A29
Backfolds 85 D36
Backford 48 E29
Backford Cross 48 E29
Backhill 85 F36
Backies 87 H24
Backmuir of New Gilston 81 K30
Back of Keppoch 79 B12
Backwell 19 E30
Backworth 71 F39
Baconsthorpe 45 B57
Bacton H.& W. 28 E29
Bacton Nfk. 45 B59
Bacton Sfk. 34 B56
Bacup 56 G34
Badachro 82 B13
Badanloch Lodge 87 E23
Badbury 20 C37
Badby 31 C41
Badcall Hgh. 86 C18
Badcall Hgh. 86 D17
Badcaul 86 J16
Baddeley Green 49 G35
Badden 72 B14
Baddesley Ensor 40 F38
Badenscoth 85 F32
Badenyon 84 H29
Badger 39 F33
Badger's Mount 23 E50
Badgeworth 29 G35
Badgworth 19 F29
Badingham 35 B59
Badintagairt 86 G20
Badlesmere 15 B56
Badlipster 87 D28
Badlieu 69 B26
Badluarach 86 J15
Badnabay 86 D18
Badninish 87 J23
Badrallach 86 J16
Badsey 30 D36
Badshot Lea 22 G44
Badsworth 51 A40
Badwell Ash 34 B55
Bagby 57 A40
Bag Enderby 53 E49
Bagendon 20 A36
Bagillt 48 E28
Baginton 30 A39
Baglan 18 B23
Bagley 38 C30
Bagnall 49 G35
Bagnor 21 E40
Bagshot 22 E45
Bagstone 19 C32
Bagthorpe Nfk. 44 B53
Bagthorpe Not. 51 G40
Baguley 49 D33
Bagworth 41 E40
Bagwy Llydiart 28 F30
Baildon 57 F37
Baile Boidheach 72 C13
Baile Mor 78 H8
Baileyhead 70 F31
Bailiehill 69 D28
Bailiff Bridge 57 G37
Bailliemore 79 H14
Baillieston 74 D22
Bainbridge 61 G35
Bainsford 74 B24
Bainton Cbs. 42 E46
Bainton Hum. 59 D45
Bairnkine 70 B32
Baker Street 24 C52
Bakewell 50 F38
Bala 37 B25
Balafark 74 A22
Balaglas 88 M4
Balallan 88 E8
Balavil 84 J23
Balbeg 83 G20
Balbeggie 81 H27
Balblair 84 C23
Balby 51 B41
Balcary 65 D24
Balchladich 86 E16
Balchraggan 83 F21
Balchreick 86 C17
Balcombe 13 A49
Baldersby 52 B39
Baldersby St. James 57 B39
Balderton 52 G44
Baldock 33 E48
Baldrine 54 F26
Baldslow 14 F54
Baldwin 54 F26
Baldwinholme 60 A29
Bale 44 B56
Balemartine 78 F5
Balephuil 78 F5
Balerno 75 D27
Balfield 81 D31
Balfour 89 F30
Balfron 74 B21
Balgedie 81 K27
Balgerran 68 G23
Balgonar 75 A26
Balgowan 80 A22
Balgown 82 C9
Balgray 81 G30
Balgrochan 74 C22
Balgy 83 D14
Balhalgardy 85 G33
Baliasta 89 B42
Baligill 87 B24
Balintore Hgh. 84 B24
Balintore Tay. 81 E28
Balivanich 88 M3
Balkholme 58 G43
Balkissock 67 E17
Ballabeg 54 G25
Ballachulish 79 E16
Ballacraine 54 E25
Ballakilpheric 54 G24
Ballamodha 54 F25
Ballantrae 66 E16
Ballantrushal 88 B9
Ballards Gore 25 B55
Ballasalla 54 G25
Ballater 81 A29
Ballaugh 54 D26
Ballcorach 84 G27
Ballencrieff 76 C30
Ballevullin 78 F5
Ball Green 49 G34
Ball Hill 21 E40
Ballidon 50 G38
Balliekine 72 G14
Balliemore 73 A17
Ballig 54 E25
Balligmorrie 67 D18
Ballikinrain Castle 74 B21
Ballimore Cen. 80 J21
Ballimore Str. 72 B15
Ballimore Str. 72 B14
Ballinaby 78 H3
Ballindalloch 84 F27
Ballingdon 34 D54
Ballinger Common 22 A45
Ballingham 28 E31
Ballingry 75 A27
Ballinluig 80 E25
Ballintuim 80 E26
Balloch Hgh. 84 E23
Balloch Str. 73 B19
Ballochan 81 A31
Ballochdoan 66 F16
Ballochmartin 73 E17
Ballochmorrie 67 E18
Ballochmyle 67 A21
Ballochroy 72 E13
Ballochyle 73 B17
Ballyaurgan 72 C13
Ballycaul 72 D16
Ballygrant 78 H5
Ballymenoch 73 B19
Ballymichael 72 G15
Balmacara 83 G14
Balmaclellan 68 F22
Balmacneil 80 E25
Balmaha 74 A20
Balmangan 65 D22
Balmartin 88 K3
Balmedie 85 H35
Balmerino 81 H29
Balminnoch 67 G18
Balmore Hgh. 83 F19
Balmore Str. 74 C22
Balmule 75 B28
Balmullo 81 H30
Balnaboth 81 D29
Balnacoil Lodge 87 G24
Balnacra 83 E15
Balnafoich 84 F22
Balnageith 84 D26
Balnaglaic 83 F20
Balnaguard 80 E25
Balnaha 84 A24
Balnahard 78 G10
Balnakiel 86 B19
Balnaknock 82 C10
Balnapaling 84 C23
Balquhidder 80 H21
Balsall 30 A38
Balsall Common 30 A38
Balsall Heath 40 G36
Balscott 30 D39
Balsham 33 C51
Baltasound 89 B42
Balterley 49 G33
Balterley Heath 49 G33
Baltersan 67 G20
Baltonsborough 8 A31
Balvaird 83 D21
Balvicar 79 J13
Balwearie 75 A28
Balwyllo 81 E32
Bamber Bridge 55 G31
Bamburgh 77 G37
Bamff 81 E28
Bamford 50 D38
Bampton Cum. 61 E31
Bampton Dev. 7 C25
Bampton Oxf. 21 A39
Bampton Grange 61 E31
Banavie 79 C17
Banbury 31 D40
Bancffosfelen 17 C20
Banchory 81 A32
Banchory-Devenick 85 J35
Bancyfelin 17 C19
Bancymansel 17 C21
Banff 85 C32
Bangor Gwy. 46 E21
Bangor-on-Dee 38 A29
Banham 44 G56
Bank 10 D38
Bankend D.& G. 69 G26
Bankend Str. 74 G23
Bankfoot Str. 73 C18
Bankfoot Tay. 80 G26
Bankglen 67 B21
Bankhead Cen. 74 B24
Bankhead D.& G. 65 D23
Bankhead Grm. 85 H34
Bankhouse 76 F30
Bank Newton 56 D35
Banknock 74 C23
Banks Cum. 70 G31
Banks Lan. 55 G29
Bankshill 69 E27
Bank Street 29 B32
Banningham 45 B58
Bannister Green 33 F52
Bannockburn 74 A24
Banstead 23 F48
Bantham 5 F22
Banton 74 C23
Banwell 19 F29
Bapchild 25 E55
Baptiston 74 B21
Barassie 73 G19
Baravullin 79 F14
Barbaraville 84 B23
Barber Booth 50 D37
Barbieston 67 B20
Barbon 56 A32
Barbreck House 79 K14
Barbrook 7 A23
Barburgh Mill 68 E25
Barby 31 A41
Barcaldine 79 F15
Barcaple 65 C22
Barcheston 30 E38
Barclose 69 G30
Barcombe 13 C50
Barcombe Cross 13 C50
Barden 62 G37
Bardennoch 67 D21
Barden Scale 57 D36
Bardister 89 E39
Bardnabeinne 87 J23
Bardney 52 F47
Bardon 41 D40
Bardon Mill 70 G33
Bardowie 74 C21
Bardsea 54 B28
Bardsey 57 E39
Bardsley 49 B35
Bardwell 34 A55
Bare 55 C30
Barend 65 C24
Barfad 72 D14
Barford Nfk. 45 E57
Barford War. 30 B38
Barford St. Martin 10 A36
Barford St. Michael 31 E40
Barfreston 15 B58
Bargaly 67 G20
Bargany 67 C18

Bishopstoke

Bargoed 18 A27
Bargower 74 G20
Bargrennan 67 F19
Barham Cbs. 32 A47
Barham Kent 15 B58
Barharrow 65 C22
Barhaugh 61 A32
Bar Hill 33 B49
Barholm 42 D46
Barkby 41 D42
Barkestone 42 B43
Barkham 22 E43
Barking G.L. 23 C50
Barking Sfk. 34 C56
Barkisland 50 A36
Barkston Lcn. 42 A45
Barkston N.Y. 57 F40
Barkway 33 E49
Barlae 67 G18
Barlaston 40 B34
Barlavington 12 C45
Barlborough 51 E40
Barlby 58 E42
Barlestone 41 E40
Barley Hfs. 33 E50
Barley Lan. 56 E34
Barleyhill 62 A36
Barley Mow Oxf. 31 E41
Barley Mow T.& W. 62 A38
Barleythorpe 42 E44
Barling 25 C55
Barlings 52 E46
Barlow Dby. 51 E39
Barlow N.Y. 58 G42
Barlow T.& W. 71 G37
Barmby Moor 58 E43
Barmby on the Marsh 58 G42
Barmer 44 B54
Barming Heath 14 B53
Barmollack 72 F14
Barmoor Lane End 77 G36
Barmouth 37 D22
Barmston 59 D47
Barmurrie 68 F22
Barnacabber 73 B17
Barnacarry 72 A16
Barnack 42 E46
Barnard Castle 62 E36
Barnardiston 34 D53
Barnbarroch 65 C24
Barnburgh 51 B40
Barnby 45 F60
Barnby Dun 51 B42
Barnby-in-the-Willows 52 G44
Barnby Moor 51 D42
Barncaughlaw 67 G20
Barncorkie 64 E16
Barndennoch 68 E24
Barnes Street 23 G52
Barnet 23 B48
Barnetby le Wold 52 B46
Barney 44 B55
Barnglieshead 69 F29
Barnham Sfk. 34 A54
Barnham W.S. 12 D45
Barnham Broom 44 E56
Barnhill Grm. 84 D27
Barnhill Str. 72 A13
Barningham Drm. 62 E36
Barningham Sfk. 34 A55
Barnoldby le Beck 53 B48
Barnoldswick 56 E34
Barns 70 C31
Barnsallie 64 C18
Barnsdale Bar 51 A41
Barns Green 12 B47
Barnsley Glo. 20 A36
Barnsley S.Y. 51 B39
Barnsoul 68 F24
Barnstaple 6 B21
Barnston Esx. 33 G52
Barnston Mer. 48 D28
Barnstone 42 B43
Barnt Green 30 A36
Barnton 49 E32
Barnwell All Saints 42 G46
Barnwell St. Andrew 42 G46
Barnwood 29 G34
Baronwood 61 B31
Barr 67 D18
Barra Airport 88 S2
Barrachan 64 D19
Barraford Park 70 F35
Barrahormid 72 B13
Barrapoll 78 F5
Barrasford 70 F35
Barravullin 79 K14
Barregarrow 54 E25
Barrhead 74 E20
Barrhill 67 E18
Barrington Cbs. 33 D49
Barrington Som. 8 C29
Barripper 2 E12
Barrmill 73 E19
Barrock 89 K28
Barrow Lan. 56 F33
Barrow Lei. 42 D44
Barrow Sfk. 34 B53
Barrow Shr. 39 E32
Barroway Drove 43 E51
Barrowburn 70 B34
Barrowby 42 B44
Barrowden 42 E45
Barrowford 56 F34
Barrow Gurney 19 E31
Barrow Haven 59 G46
Barrow Hill 51 E40
Barrow in Furness 54 B27
Barrows Green 49 G32
Barrow upon Humber 59 G46
Barrow upon Soar 41 D41
Barrow upon Trent 41 C39
Barrow (Walney Island) Airport 54 B27
Barry S.G. 18 E27
Barry Tay. 81 G31
Barry Island 18 E27
Barsby 41 D42
Barsham 45 G59
Barskimming 67 A20
Barstibly 65 C23
Barston 30 A38
Bartestree 28 D31
Barthol Chapel 85 F34
Barthomley 49 G33
Bartley 10 C39
Bartlow 33 D51
Barton Cbs. 33 C50
Barton Che. 48 G30
Barton Dev. 6 C21
Barton Glo. 30 F37
Barton H.& W. 28 C28
Barton Lan. 55 F31
Barton N.Y. 62 F38
Barton Oxf. 21 A41
Barton Bendish 44 E53
Barton Common 45 C59
Barton End 20 B34
Barton Hartshorn 31 E42
Barton Hill 58 C43
Barton in Fabis 41 B41
Barton-in-the-Clay 32 E46
Barton-le-Street 58 B43
Barton le Willows 58 C43
Barton Mills 34 A53
Barton on Sea 10 E38
Barton-on-the-Heath 30 E38
Barton St. David 8 A31
Barton Seagrave 32 A44
Barton Stacey 21 G40
Barton under Needwood 40 D37
Barton upon Humber 59 G46
Barton upon Irwell 49 C33
Barvas 88 C9
Barwell 41 F40
Barwick 8 C31
Barwick in Elmet 57 F39
Baschurch 38 C30
Bashall Eaves 56 E32
Bashley 10 E38
Basildon Brk. 21 D42
Basildon Esx. 24 C53
Basing 21 F42
Basingstoke 21 F42
Baslow 50 E38
Bason Bridge 19 G29
Bassendean 76 F32
Bassenfell 60 C28
Bassenthwaite 60 C28
Bassett 11 C40
Bassingbourn 33 D49
Bassingham 52 G45
Baston 42 D47
Bastwick 45 D60
Batcombe Dor. 9 D32
Batcombe Som. 9 A32
Bate Heath 49 E32
Bath 20 E33
Bathampton 20 E33
Bathealton 7 C26
Batheaston 20 E33
Bathford 20 E33
Bathgate 75 D25
Bathley 51 G43
Bathpool 4 C18
Batley 57 G38
Batsford 30 E37
Batson 5 F23
Battersby 63 F41
Battisford Tye 34 C56
Battle E.S. 14 F53
Battle Pow. 27 E26
Battlefield 38 D31
Battlesbridge 24 B53
Batt's Corner 22 G44
Baugh 78 F6
Baughton 29 D34
Baughurst 21 E41
Baulking 21 B39
Baumber 53 E48
Baverstock 10 A36
Bawburgh 45 E57
Bawdeswell 44 C56
Bawdrip 8 A29
Bawdsey 35 D59
Bawtry 51 C42
Baxenden 56 G33
Baxterley 40 F38
Baybridge 62 B35
Baycliff 54 B28
Baydon 21 D38
Bayford Hfs. 23 A49
Bayford Som. 9 B33
Bayhead 88 L3
Bayhead 88 J6
Bayles 61 B33
Baylham 35 C57
Baynard's Green 31 F41
Bayston Hill 38 E30
Baythorn End 34 D53
Bayton 29 A32
Beachampton 31 E43
Beachley 19 B31
Beacon End 34 F55
Beacon Hill 12 A44
Beacon's Bottom 22 B43
Beaconsfield 22 B45
Beadlam 58 A42
Beadnell 71 A38
Beaford 6 D21
Beal Nor. 77 F36
Beal N.Y. 58 G41
Beaminster 8 D30
Beamish 62 A38
Beamsley 57 D36
Bean 23 D51
Beanacre 20 E35
Beanley 71 B36
Beardon 6 G21
Beare Green 22 G47
Bearl 71 G36
Bearley 30 B37
Bearley Cross 30 B37
Bearpark 62 B38
Bearsbridge 61 A33
Bearsden 74 C21
Bearsted 14 B53
Beattock 69 C26
Beauchamp Roding 23 A51
Beaufort Gwe. 28 G27
Beaulieu 10 D39
Beauly 83 E21
Beaumaris 46 E22
Beaumont Cum. 60 A29
Beaumont Esx. 35 F57
Beausale 30 A38
Beauworth 11 B41
Beaworthy 6 F20
Beazley End 34 F53
Bebington 48 D29
Bebside 71 E38
Beccles 45 F60
Becconsall 55 G30
Beckbury 39 E33
Beckermet 60 F26
Beck Foot 61 G32
Beckfoot Cum. 60 B26
Beckfoot Cum. 60 F27
Beckford 29 E35
Beckhampton 20 E36
Beck Hole 63 F44
Beckingham Lcn. 52 G44
Beckingham Not. 51 C43
Beckington 20 F34
Beckley E.S. 14 E54
Beckley Oxf. 31 G41
Beck Row 33 A52
Beck Side 54 A28
Beckwithshaw 57 D38
Becontree 23 C50
Bedale 57 A38
Bedburn 62 C36
Bedchester 9 C34
Beddau 18 C26
Beddgelert 36 A21
Beddingham 13 D50
Beddington 23 E48
Bedersaig 88 F5
Bedfield 35 B58
Bedford Bfd. 32 D46
Bedford G.M. 49 C32
Bedhampton 11 D43
Bedingfield 35 B57
Bedlam 57 C38
Bedlington 71 E38
Bedlington Station 71 E38
Bedlinog 18 A26
Bedmond 22 A46
Bednall 40 D35
Bedrule 70 B32
Bedstone 28 A29
Bedwas 18 C27
Bedwellty 18 A27
Bedworth 41 G39
Bedworth Heath 41 G39
Beeby 41 E42
Beech 11 A42
Beechamwell 44 E53
Beech Hill Brk. 21 E42
Beech Hill Cum. 61 F30
Beechingstoke 20 F36
Beechpike 29 G35
Beedon 21 D40
Beedon Hill 21 D40
Beeford 59 D47
Beeley 50 F38
Beelsby 53 B48
Beenham 21 E41
Beer 8 F28
Beercrocombe 8 B29
Beesby 53 D50
Beeston Bfd. 32 D47
Beeston Che. 48 G31
Beeston Nfk. 44 D55
Beeston Not. 41 B41
Beeston Regis 45 A57
Beeswing 68 G24
Beetham 55 B30
Beetley 44 D55
Began 19 C28
Begbroke 31 G40
Begelly 16 D17
Beggar's Bush 28 B28
Beguildy 28 A27
Beighton Dby. 51 D40
Beighton Nfk. 45 E59
Beighton Hill 50 G38
Beith 73 E19
Bekesbourne 15 B58
Belaugh 45 D58
Belbroughton 29 A35
Belchamp Otten 34 D54
Belchamp St. Paul 34 D53
Belchamp Walter 34 D54
Belchford 53 E48
Belford 77 G37
Belford Mains 77 G36
Belhaven 76 C32
Belhelvie 85 H35
Bellabeg 84 H29
Bellacarnane Beg 54 E25
Belladrum 83 E21
Bellanoch 72 A14
Bellaty 81 E28
Bell Bar 23 A48
Bell Busk 56 D35
Belleau 53 E50
Bellehiglash 84 F27
Bellerby 62 G37
Belle Vue Cum. 60 A29
Belle Vue W.Y. 51 A39
Bellfield 74 G24
Bellingdon 22 A45
Bellingham 70 E34
Belloch 72 G12
Bellochantuy 72 G12
Bellsbank 67 C20
Bellshill Nor. 77 G37
Bellshill Str. 74 E23
Bellside 74 E24
Bellspool 75 G27
Bellsquarry 75 D26
Bell's Yew Green 13 A52
Bellymack 68 G22
Belmesthorpe 42 D46
Belmont Lan. 49 A32
Belmont She. 89 B41
Belnacraig 84 H29
Belper 41 A39
Belsay 71 F37
Belstead 35 D57
Belston 67 A19
Belstone 6 F22
Belstone Corner 6 F22
Belthorn 56 G33
Beltinge 25 E57
Beltoft 52 B44
Belton Hum. 51 B43
Belton Lcn. 42 B45
Belton Lei. 41 C40
Belton Nfk. 45 E60
Belton in Rutland 42 E44
Beltring 23 G52
Belvedere 23 D51
Belvoir 42 B44
Bembridge 11 F42
Bemersyde 76 G31
Bempton 59 B47
Benalder Lodge 80 C21
Ben Armine Lodge 87 G23
Benbecula Airport 88 M3
Benbuie 68 D23
Benderloch 79 G15
Bendronaig Lodge 83 F16
Benenden 14 D54
Benfield 67 G19
Benfieldside 62 A37
Bengeworth 30 D36
Benhall Green 35 B59
Benholm 81 D34
Beningbrough 58 D41
Benington Hfs. 33 F48
Benington Lcn. 43 A49
Benllech 46 D21
Benmore 73 B17
Benmore Lodge Hotel 86 G19
Bennan 66 A15
Bennecarrigan 66 A15
Benniworth 53 D48
Benover 14 C53
Ben Rhydding 57 E37
Benson 21 B42
Benthall Nor. 71 A38
Benthall Shr. 39 E32
Bentley Ham. 22 G43
Bentley Hum. 59 F46
Bentley S.Y. 51 B41
Bentley War. 40 F38
Bentley Heath 30 A37
Bentpath 69 E29
Bentworth 21 G42
Benwick 43 F49
Beoch 66 G16
Beoraidbeg 79 A12
Bepton 12 C44
Berden 33 E50
Bere Alston 4 D20
Bere Ferrers 4 D20
Berepper 2 F12
Bere Regis 9 E34
Bergh Apton 45 E59
Berinsfield 21 B41
Berkeley 19 B32
Berkeley Road 20 A33
Berkhamsted 22 A45
Berkley 20 G34
Berkswell 30 A38
Berney Arms Sta. 45 E60
Bernice 73 A17
Bernisdale 82 D10
Berrick Salome 21 B42
Berriedale 87 F27
Berrier 60 D29
Berriew 38 E27
Berrington Nor. 77 F36
Berrington Shr. 38 E31
Berrow 19 F28
Berrow Green 29 C33
Berry Brow 50 A37
Berry Down Cross 6 A21
Berry Hill 28 G31
Berryhillock 85 C31
Berrynarbor 6 A21
Berry Pomeroy 5 D24
Berryscaur 69 D27
Bersham 38 A29
Berwick 13 D51
Berwick Bassett 20 D36
Berwick Hill 71 F37
Berwick St. James 10 A36
Berwick St. John 9 B35
Berwick St. Leonard 9 A35
Berwick upon Tweed 77 E36
Bescar 48 A29
Besford 29 D35
Bessacarr 51 B41
Bessels Leigh 21 A40
Bessingby 59 C47
Bessingham 45 B57
Bestbeech Hill 13 A52
Besthorpe Nfk. 44 F56
Besthorpe Not. 52 F44
Beswick 59 E46
Betchworth 23 G48
Bethania Dyf. 26 B21
Bethania Gwy. 37 A23
Bethel Gwy. 46 F21
Bethel Gwy. 37 A25
Bethel Gwy. 46 E19
Bethersden 14 C55
Bethesda Dyf. 16 C16
Bethesda Gwy. 46 F22
Bethlehem 17 B22
Betley 39 A33
Betsham 24 D52
Betteshanger 15 B59
Bettiscombe 8 D29
Bettisfield 38 B30
Betton Shr. 39 B32
Betton Shr. 38 E29
Bettws Gwe. 19 B28
Bettws Bledrws 26 C21
Bettws Cedewain 38 F27
Bettws-Evan 26 D19
Bettws Gwerfil Goch 37 A26
Bettws Newydd 19 A29
Bettyhill 87 B23
Betws Dyf. 17 C22
Betws M.G. 18 C24
Betws-Garmon 46 G21
Betws-y-Coed 47 G23
Betws-yn-Rhos 47 E25
Beuklay 70 F35
Beulah Dyf. 26 D18
Beulah Pow. 27 C25
Bevercotes 51 E42
Beverley 59 F46
Beverstone 20 B34
Bevington 19 B32
Bewaldeth 60 C28
Bewcastle 70 F31
Bewdley 29 A33
Bewerley 57 C37
Bewholme 59 E47
Bexhill 14 G53
Bexley 23 D50
Bexley Heath 23 D50
Bexwell 44 E52
Beyton 34 B55
Beyton Green 34 B55
Bibbington 50 E36
Bibury 20 A37
Bicester 31 F42
Bickenhall 8 C28
Bickenhill 40 G37
Bicker 43 B48
Bickerstaffe 48 B30
Bickerton Che. 48 G31
Bickerton N.Y. 57 D40
Bickington Dev. 6 B21
Bickington Dev. 5 C23
Bickleigh Dev. 5 D21
Bickleigh Dev. 7 E25
Bickley 23 E50
Bickley Moss 38 A31
Bicknacre 24 A53
Bicknoller 7 B27
Bicknor 14 B54
Bickton 10 C37
Bicton Shr. 38 D30
Bicton Shr. 38 G28
Bidborough 23 G51
Biddenden 14 D54
Biddenden Green 14 C54
Biddenham 32 C46
Biddestone 20 D34
Biddisham 19 F29
Biddlesden 31 D42
Biddulph 49 G34
Biddulph Moor 49 G35
Bideford 6 C20
Bidford-on-Avon 30 C36
Bidston 48 C28
Biel 76 C32
Bielby 58 E43
Bieldside 85 J34
Bierton 32 G44
Big Balcraig 64 D19
Bigbury 5 F22
Bigbury-on-Sea 5 F22
Bigby 52 B46
Big Corlae 68 D22
Biggar Cum. 54 C27
Biggar Str. 75 G26
Biggin Dby. 50 G37
Biggin Dby. 40 A38
Biggin Hfs. 33 E49
Biggin N.Y. 58 F41
Biggin Hill 23 F50
Biggleswade 32 D47
Bigholm 69 E29
Bighouse 87 B24
Bighton 11 A42
Biglands 60 A28
Bignor 12 C45
Big Sand 82 B13
Bigton 89 K39
Bilberry 4 D16
Bilborough 41 A41
Bilbrook 7 A26
Bilbrough 58 E41
Bilbster 87 C28
Bildershaw 62 D37
Bildeston 34 D55
Billericay 24 B52
Billesdon 42 E43
Billholm 69 D28
Billie Mains 77 E34
Billingborough 42 B47
Billinge 48 B31
Billingford Nfk. 35 A57
Billingford Nfk. 44 C56
Billingham 62 D40
Billinghay 52 G47
Billingley 51 B40
Billingshurst 12 B46
Billingsley 39 G33
Billington Bfd. 32 F45
Billington Lan. 56 F33
Billockby 45 D60
Billy Row 62 C37
Bilsborrow 55 F31
Bilsby 53 E50
Bilsdean 76 C33
Bilsington 15 D56
Bilsthorpe 51 F42
Bilston Ltn. 75 D28
Bilston W.M. 40 F35
Bilstone 41 E39
Bilting 15 C56
Bilton Hum. 59 F47
Bilton Nor. 71 B38
Bilton N.Y. 57 D40
Bilton Banks 71 C38
Bimbister 89 F29
Binbrook 53 C48
Binegar 19 G32
Bines Green 12 C47
Binfield 22 D44
Binfield Heath 22 D43
Bingfield 70 F35
Bingham 42 A43
Bingham's Melcombe 9 D33
Bingley 57 F37
Bings 38 D31
Binham 44 B55
Binley Ham. 21 F40
Binley War. 30 A39
Binniehill 74 C24
Binnington 59 B45
Binsoe 57 A38
Binstead 11 E41
Binsted 22 G43
Binton 30 C37
Bintree 44 C56
Birch Esx. 34 F55
Birch G.M. 49 B34
Bircham Newton 44 B53
Bircham Tofts 44 B53
Birchanger 33 F51
Bircher 28 B30
Birch Green 34 G55
Birchgrove S.G. 18 D27
Birchgrove W.G. 18 B23
Birchington 25 E58
Birchington Bay 25 E58
Birchover 50 F38
Birch Services 49 B34
Birch Vale 50 D36
Birchwood 49 C32
Bircotes 51 C42
Birdbrook 34 D53
Birdfield 72 A15
Birdforth 57 B40
Birdham 12 D44
Birdingbury 31 B40
Birdlip 29 G35
Birdsall 58 C44
Birds Edge 50 B38
Birdsmoor Gate 8 D29
Birdston 74 C22
Birdwell 51 B39
Birgham 76 G33
Birkbush 68 E24
Birkby Cum. 60 C26
Birkby N.Y. 62 F39
Birkdale 48 A29
Birkenhead 48 D29
Birkenhills 85 E33
Birkenshaw Str. 74 D22
Birkenshaw W.Y. 57 G38
Birkenside 76 F31
Birkhill D.& G. 69 B28
Birkhill Nor. 70 D34
Birkhill Feus 81 G29
Birkin 58 G41
Birley 28 C30
Birling Kent 24 E52
Birling Nor. 71 C38
Birlingham 29 D35
Birlsmorton 29 E34
Birmingham 40 G36
Birmingham Airport 40 G37
Birnam 80 F26
Birsay 89 E28
Birse 81 A31
Birsemore 81 A31
Birstall Lei. 41 E41
Birstall W.Y. 57 G38
Birstwith 57 D38
Birtley Drm. 62 A38
Birtley H.& W. 28 B29
Birtley Nor. 70 F34
Bisbrooke 42 F44
Bisham 22 C44
Bishampton 29 C35
Bish Mill 7 C23
Bishop Auckland 62 D37
Bishopbridge 52 C46
Bishopbriggs 74 C22
Bishop Burton 59 F45
Bishop Middleham 62 C39
Bishop Monkton 57 C39
Bishop Norton 52 C45
Bishopsbourne 15 B57
Bishop's Cannings 20 E36
Bishop's Castle 38 G29
Bishop's Caundle 9 C32
Bishop's Cleeve 29 F35
Bishop's Fonthill 9 A35
Bishops Frome 29 D32
Bishop's Green 33 G52
Bishop's Hull 8 B28
Bishop's Itchington 30 C39
Bishop's Lydeard 7 C27
Bishopsmoat 38 G28
Bishop's Nympton 7 C23
Bishop's Offley 39 B33
Bishop's Stortford 33 F50
Bishops Sutton 11 A42
Bishop's Tachbrook 30 B39
Bishop's Tawton 6 B21
Bishopsteignton 5 C25
Bishopstoke 11 C40

Bishopston

Bishopston 17 F21
Bishopstone *Bkh.* 32 G44
Bishopstone E.S. 13 D50
Bishopstone *H.& W.* 28 D30
Bishopstone *Wts.* 10 B36
Bishopstone *Wts.* 21 C38
Bishopstrow 20 G34
Bishop Sutton 19 F31
Bishop's Waltham 11 C41
Bishopswood *Som.* 8 C28
Bishop's Wood *Stf.* 40 E34
Bishopsworth 19 E31
Bishopton 19 E31
Bishop Thornton 57 C38
Bishopthorpe 58 E41
Bishopton *D.& G.* 64 D20
Bishopton *Drm.* 62 D39
Bishopton *N.Y.* 57 B38
Bishopton *Str.* 74 C20
Bishop Wilton 58 D43
Bishton 19 C29
Bisley *Glo.* 20 A35
Bisley *Sry.* 22 F45
Bisley Camp 22 F45
Bispham 55 E29
Bisterne 10 D37
Bitchfield 42 C45
Bittadon 6 A21
Bittaford 5 E22
Bitterley 28 A31
Bitterne 11 C40
Bitteswell 41 G41
Bitton 19 E32
Bix 22 C43
Bixter 89 G39
Blaby 41 F41
Blackacre 69 D26
Blackawton 5 E24
Blackborough End 44 D52
Black Bourton 21 A38
Blackboys 13 B51
Black Bridge 46 D18
Blackbrook *Mer.* 48 C31
Blackbrook *Stf.* 39 B33
Blackburn *Bor.* 77 E34
Blackburn *Grm.* 85 H34
Blackburn *Lan.* 56 G32
Blackburn *Ltn.* 75 D25
Blackburn *Str.* 68 A24
Black Corries 79 E18
Blackcraig *Str.* 68 C22
Blackcraig *Tay.* 81 E27
Black Crofts 79 G15
Blackditch Cross 7 E23
Black Dog 7 E24
Blackdown 8 D29
Blackdown Hill 10 B39
Blackdyke 60 A27
Blackfield 11 D40
Blackford *Cum.* 69 G29
Blackford *Som.* 8 B32
Blackford *Som.* 19 G30
Blackford *Tay.* 80 K24
Blackford Bridge 49 B33
Blackfordby 41 D39
Blackgang 11 G40
Blackhall Colliery 62 C40
Blackham 13 A51
Blackhaugh 76 G30
Blackheath *Esx.* 34 F55
Blackheath *Sfk.* 35 A60
Blackheath *W.M.* 40 G35
Blackhedobon Hall 71 F36
Blackhill *Drm.* 62 A36
Blackhill *Grm.* 85 D36
Blackhill *Grm.* 85 E36
Blackhill *Hgh.* 82 D9
Blackhills *Grm.* 85 C35
Blackhills *Grm.* 84 D28
Blackhorse 19 D32
Blacklaw 69 C26
Blackley 49 B34
Blacklunans 81 D27
Blackmill 18 C25
Blackmoor *G.M.* 49 B32
Blackmoor *Ham.* 11 A43
Blackmoor Gate 6 A22
Blackmore 24 A52
Blackmore End 34 E53
Black Mount 79 F18
Blackness 75 C26
Blacknest 13 A51
Black Notley 34 F53
Blacko 56 E34
Blackpark 68 E25
Black Pill 17 E22
Blackpool 54 F28
Blackpool Airport 55 F29
Blackridge 74 D24
Blackrock *Gwe.* 28 G28
Blackrock *Str.* 78 J4
Blackrod 49 A32
Blackshaw 69 G26
Blackshaw Head 56 G35
Blacksnape 56 G33
Blackthorn 31 G42
Blacktoft 58 G44
Black Torrington 6 E20
Blackwater *Cnw.* 2 D13
Blackwater *Ham.* 22 E44
Blackwater *I.o.W.* 11 F41
Blackwater *Sfk.* 35 A61
Blackwaterfoot 66 A14
Blackwater Lodge 84 G29
Blackwell *Cum.* 61 A30
Blackwell *Dby.* 51 G40
Blackwell *Dby.* 50 E37
Blackwell *Drm.* 62 E38
Blackwell *War.* 30 D38
Blackwood *D.& G.* 68 E25
Blackwood *Gwe.* 18 B27
Blackwood *Str.* 74 F23
Bladnoch 64 C20

Bladon 31 G40
Blaenannerch 26 D18
Blaenau Dolwyddelan 47 G23
Blaenau-Ffestiniog 37 A23
Blaenau Uchaf 38 A28
Blaenavon 19 A28
Blaen Clydach 18 B25
Blaencwm 18 B25
Blaenffos 16 A17
Blaengarw 18 B25
Blaengwrach 18 A24
Blaengwynfi 18 B24
Blaenpennal 27 B22
Blaenplwyf 26 A21
Blaenporth 26 D18
Blaenrhondda 18 B25
Blaenwaun 17 B18
Blagdon *Avon* 19 F30
Blagdon *Dev.* 5 D24
Blagdon Hill 8 C28
Blagill 61 B33
Blaich 79 C16
Blaina 19 A28
Blairadam 75 A27
Blair Atholl 80 D24
Blair Drummond 74 A23
Blairgorts 74 A21
Blairgowrie 81 F27
Blairhall 75 B26
Blairkip 67 A21
Blairlogie 74 A24
Blairmore *Hgh.* 86 C17
Blairmore *Str.* 73 B17
Blairnairn 73 B18
Blairpark 73 E18
Blairquhan 67 C19
Blairquhosh 74 B21
Blair's Ferry 72 D15
Blairvadach 73 B18
Blaisdon 29 G33
Blakebrook 29 A34
Blakedown 29 A34
Blake End 34 F53
Blakelaw 76 G33
Blakemere 28 D29
Blakeney *Glo.* 19 B62
Blakeney *Nfk.* 44 A56
Blakenhall *Che.* 39 A33
Blakenhall *Stf.* 40 F35
Blakesley 31 C42
Blanchland 62 A35
Blandford Forum 9 D34
Blandford St. Mary 9 D34
Bland Hill 57 D38
Blanefield 74 C21
Blankney 52 F46
Blantyre 74 E22
Blàr a'Chaoruinn 79 D17
Blarghour 79 J15
Blarglas 73 B19
Blarmachfoldach 79 D16
Blarnaleyloch 86 J17
Blashaval 88 L4
Blashford 10 D37
Blaston 42 F44
Blatherwycke 42 F45
Blawith 54 A28
Blawquhairn 68 E22
Blaxhall 35 C59
Blaxton 51 B42
Blaydon 71 G37
Bleadney 19 G30
Bleadon 19 F29
Blean 25 E57
Bleasby 42 A43
Bleasby Moor 52 D47
Bleddfa 28 B28
Bledington 30 F38
Bledlow 22 A43
Bledlow Ridge 22 B43
Blencarn 61 C32
Blencogo 60 B27
Blendworth 11 C43
Blennerhasset 60 B27
Bletchingdon 31 G41
Bletchingley 23 F49
Bletchley *Bkh.* 32 E44
Bletchley *Shr.* 39 B32
Bletherston 16 B16
Bletsoe 32 C46
Blewbury 21 C41
Blickling 45 C57
Blidworth 51 G41
Blindcrake 60 C27
Blindley Heath 23 G49
Blisland 4 C16
Blisworth 31 C43
Blithbury 40 C36
Blitterlees 60 A27
Blockley 30 E37
Blofield 45 E59
Blo'Norton 34 A56
Bloomfield 68 F25
Blore 40 A37
Blount's Green 40 B36
Blowick 48 A29
Bloxham 31 E40
Bloxholm 52 G46
Bloxwich 40 E35
Bloxworth 9 E34
Blubberhouses 57 D37
Blue Anchor 7 A26
Bluebell Hill 24 E53
Blue Harbour Inn 42 B45
Blundellsands 48 B28
Blundeston 45 F61
Blunham 32 C47
Blunsdon St. Andrew 20 B37
Bluntisham 33 A49
Blyford 35 A60
Blymhill 40 D34
Blyth *Nor.* 71 E39

Blyth *Not.* 51 D42
Blyth Bridge 75 F27
Blythburgh 35 A60
Blythe Bridge 40 A35
Blythe Marsh 40 A35
Blyton 52 C44
Boarhills 81 J31
Boarhunt 11 D42
Boarshead 13 A51
Boarstall 31 G42
Boasley Cross 6 F20
Boath 83 B21
Bobbing 24 E54
Bobbington 40 F34
Bobbingworth 23 A51
Bocking Churchstreet 34 F53
Boconnoc 4 D17
Boddam *Grm.* 85 E37
Boddam *She.* 89 L39
Boddington 29 F34
Bodedern 46 D19
Bodelwyddan 47 E26
Bodenham *H.& W.* 28 C31
Bodenham *Wts.* 10 B37
Bodesbeck 69 C27
Bodewryd 46 C20
Bodfari 47 E26
Bodffordd 46 E20
Bodfuan 36 B19
Bodham Street 45 A57
Bodiam 14 E53
Bodicote 31 E40
Bodieve 3 A15
Bodinnick 4 E17
Bodmin 4 D16
Bodney 44 F54
Bogbrae 85 F36
Bogend *Bor.* 76 F33
Bogend *Str.* 73 G19
Boghall *Ltn.* 75 D28
Boghall *Str.* 67 B19
Boghead *Str.* 74 F23
Boghead *Str.* 68 A22
Bogmoor 84 C29
Bogniebrae 85 E31
Bognor Regis 12 E45
Bogside *Fife* 75 A25
Bogside *Str.* 74 E24
Bogton 85 D32
Bogue 68 E22
Bohenie 79 B18
Bohuntine 79 B18
Bolam 62 D37
Bolberry 5 G22
Bold Heath 48 D31
Boldon 71 G39
Boldon Colliery 71 G39
Boldre 10 E39
Boldron 62 E36
Bole 51 D43
Bolehill 50 G38
Boleside 76 G30
Bolham 7 D25
Bolingey 2 C13
Bollington *Che.* 49 E35
Bollington *Che.* 49 D33
Bollington Cross 49 E35
Bolney 13 B48
Bolnhurst 32 C46
Bolsover 51 E40
Bolsterstone 50 C38
Bolstone 28 E31
Boltby 57 A40
Bolter End 22 B43
Bolton *Cum.* 61 D32
Bolton *G.M.* 49 B32
Bolton *Hum.* 58 D43
Bolton *Ltn.* 76 D31
Bolton *Nor.* 71 B37
Bolton Abbey 57 D36
Bolton Bridge 57 D36
Bolton-by-Bowland 56 E33
Boltonfellend 69 G30
Boltongate 60 B28
Bolton-le-Sands 55 C30
Bolton Low Houses 60 B28
Bolton-on-Swale 62 G38
Bolton Percy 58 E41
Bolton Town End 55 C30
Bolton upon Dearne 51 B40
Bolventor 4 C17
Bombie 65 D23
Bomere Heath 38 C30
Bonar Bridge 87 J22
Bonawe 79 G16
Bonawe Quarries 79 G16
Bonby 52 A46
Boncath 17 A18
Bonchester Bridge 70 B31
Bonchurch 11 G41
Bondleigh 6 E22
Bonds 55 E30
Bo'ness 75 B25
Bonhill 73 C19
Boningale 40 E34
Bonjedward 70 A32
Bonkle 74 E24
Bonnington 15 D56
Bonnybridge 74 B24
Bonnykelly 85 D34
Bonnyrigg 75 D29
Bonsall 50 G38
Bontddu 37 D22
Bont-dolgadfan 37 E24
Bontgoch 37 G22
Bont Newydd *Gwy.* 37 A23
Bont Newydd *Gwy.* 37 C23
Bontnewydd *Gwy.* 46 F20
Bontrhygaled 37 G23
Bontuchel 47 G26

Bonvilston 18 D26
Bon-y-maen 17 E22
Boohay 52 F24
Boosbeck 63 E42
Boot *Cnw.* 4 A18
Boot *Cum.* 60 F27
Booth 58 G43
Boothby Graffoe 52 G45
Boothby Pagnell 42 B45
Boothstown 49 B33
Bootle *Cum.* 54 A27
Bootle *Mer.* 48 C29
Boquhan 74 B21
Boraston 29 A32
Borden 24 E54
Bordley 56 C35
Bordon Camp 11 A43
Boreham *Esx.* 24 A53
Boreham *Wts.* 20 G34
Boreham Street 13 C52
Borehamwood 22 B47
Boreland *D.& G.* 67 G19
Boreland *D.& G.* 65 C21
Boreland *D.& G.* 69 D27
Boreraig 82 D7
Borgue *D.& G.* 65 D22
Borgue *Hgh.* 87 F27
Borness 65 D22
Boroughbridge 57 C39
Borough Green 23 F52
Borrobol Lodge 87 F24
Borrowash 41 B40
Borrowby 57 A40
Borrowdale 60 E28
Borth 37 G22
Borthwick 75 E29
Borthwickbrae 69 B30
Borthwick Hall 75 E29
Borthwickshiels 69 B30
Borth-y-Gêst 36 B21
Borve *Hgh.* 82 E10
Borve *W.I.* 88 S2
Borve *W.I.* 88 J5
Borve Lodge 88 H6
Borwick 55 B31
Bosbury 29 D32
Boscastle 4 A16
Boscombe *Dor.* 10 E37
Boscombe *Wts.* 10 A38
Bosham 12 D44
Bosherston 16 E15
Bosley 49 F35
Bossall 58 C43
Bossiney 4 B16
Bossingham 15 C57
Bossington 7 A24
Bostock Green 49 F32
Boston 43 A49
Boston Spa 57 E40
Boswinger 3 D15
Botallack 2 E9
Botany Bay 23 B48
Botcherby 61 A30
Botesdale 34 A56
Bothal 71 E38
Bothamsall 51 E42
Bothel 60 C27
Bothenhampton 8 E30
Bothwell 74 E22
Bothwell Services 74 E23
Botley *Bkh.* 22 A45
Botley *Ham.* 11 C41
Botley *Oxf.* 21 A40
Botleys 22 E46
Botolphs 12 D47
Bottesford *Hum.* 52 B45
Bottesford *Lei.* 42 B44
Bottisham 33 B51
Bottom House 50 G36
Bottom o' th' Moor 49 A32
Botusfleming 4 D20
Bough Beech 23 G50
Boughrood 28 E27
Boughspring 19 B48
Boughton *Nfk.* 44 E53
Boughton *Nmp.* 31 B43
Boughton *Not.* 51 F42
Boughton Green 14 B53
Boughton Lees 15 C56
Boughton Street 15 B56
Boulby 63 E43
Boulmer 71 B38
Boultenstone 85 H30
Boultham 52 E45
Bourn 33 C49
Bourne 42 C46
Bournebridge 23 B51
Bourne End *Bkh.* 22 C44
Bourne End *Hfs.* 22 A46
Bournemouth 10 E36
Bournemouth Airport 10 E37
Bournes Green 25 C55
Bournheath 29 A35
Bournmoor 62 A39
Bourton *Dor.* 9 A33
Bourton *Oxf.* 21 C38
Bourton *Shr.* 38 F31
Bourton on Dunsmore 31 A40
Bourton-on-the-Hill 30 E37
Bourton on the Water 30 F37
Boustead Hill 60 A28
Bouth 55 A29
Bouthwaite 57 B37
Boverton 18 E25
Bovey Tracey 5 C24
Bovingdon 22 A46
Bovington Camp 9 F34
Bow *Bor.* 76 F30
Bow *Dev.* 7 E23
Bow *Ork.* 89 H29
Bowbank 61 D35
Bow Brickhill 32 E45
Bowbridge 20 A34
Bowburn 62 C39

Bowcombe 11 F40
Bowden *Bor.* 76 G31
Bowden *Dev.* 5 F24
Bowdon 49 D33
Bower 70 E33
Bowerchalke 10 B36
Bower Hinton 8 C30
Bowermadden 87 B28
Bowershall 75 A26
Bowertower 87 B28
Bowes 62 E35
Bowgreave 55 E30
Bowhill 69 A30
Bowland 76 F30
Bowland Bridge 55 A30
Bowling 74 C20
Bowling Bank 38 A29
Bowling Green 29 C34
Bowmanstead 60 G28
Bowmore 78 J4
Bowness-on-Solway 69 G28
Bowness-on-Windermere 61 G30
Bowsden 77 F35
Bowside Lodge 87 B24
Bow Street 37 G22
Box *Glo.* 20 A34
Box *Wts.* 20 E34
Boxford *Brk.* 21 D40
Boxford *Sfk.* 34 D55
Boxgrove 12 D45
Boxley 14 B53
Boxmoor 22 A46
Box's Shop 6 E18
Boxted *Esx.* 34 E56
Boxted *Sfk.* 34 C54
Boxted Cross 34 E56
Boxwell 20 B34
Boxworth 33 B49
Boyden Gate 25 E58
Boylestone 40 B37
Boyndie 85 C32
Boyndlie 85 C35
Boynton 59 C47
Boyton *Cnw.* 6 F19
Boyton *Sfk.* 35 D59
Boyton *Wts.* 9 A35
Boyton Cross 24 A52
Bozeat 32 C45
Braaid 54 F25
Braal Castle 87 B27
Brabourne 15 C57
Brabourne Lees 15 C56
Bracadale 82 F9
Braceborough 42 D46
Bracebridge Heath 52 F45
Braceby 42 B46
Bracewell 56 E34
Brackenber 61 E33
Brackenbottom 56 B34
Brackenfield 51 G39
Bracklesham 12 E44
Brackley 31 E41
Bracknell 22 E44
Braco 80 J24
Bracon Ash 45 F57
Bracora 79 A13
Bracorina 79 A13
Bradbourne 50 G38
Bradbury 62 D39
Bradda West 54 G24
Bradden 31 D42
Bradenham 22 B44
Bradenstoke cum Clack 20 D35
Bradfield *Brk.* 21 D42
Bradfield *Dev.* 7 E26
Bradfield *Esx.* 35 E57
Bradfield *S.Y.* 50 C38
Bradfield Combust 34 C54
Bradfield Green 49 G32
Bradfield Heath 35 F57
Bradfield St. Clare 34 C55
Bradfield St. George 34 B55
Bradford *Dby.* 50 F38
Bradford *Dev.* 6 E20
Bradford *Nor.* 77 G37
Bradford *W.Y.* 57 F37
Bradford Abbas 8 C31
Bradford on Avon 20 E34
Bradford-on-Tone 7 C27
Bradford Peverell 9 E32
Brading 11 F42
Bradley *Dby.* 40 A38
Bradley *Ham.* 21 G42
Bradley *Hum.* 53 B48
Bradley *H.& W.* 29 B35
Bradley *N.Y.* 57 B36
Bradley *Shr.* 29 A33
Bradley *Stf.* 40 D34
Bradley *W.Y.* 57 G37
Bradley Green *Che.* 38 A31
Bradley Green *H.& W.* 29 B35
Bradmore 41 B41
Bradninch 7 E25
Bradnop 50 G36
Bradpole 8 E30
Bradshaw 49 A33
Bradstone 6 G19
Bradwell *Bkh.* 32 D44
Bradwell *Dby.* 50 D37
Bradwell *Esx.* 34 F54
Bradwell *Nfk.* 45 E61
Bradwell-on-Sea 25 A56
Bradwell Waterside 25 A55
Bradworthy 6 D19
Brae *D.& G.* 68 F24
Brae *Hgh.* 86 H20
Brae *Hgh.* 83 A14
Brae *She.* 89 F39
Braeantra 83 B21
Braedownie 81 C28
Braefield 83 F20
Braegrum 80 H26
Braehead *D.& G.* 64 C20

Braehead *Str.* 75 E25
Braehead *Tay.* 81 E32
Braelangwell Lodge 86 J21
Braemar 81 A27
Braemore *Hgh.* 87 F26
Braemore *Hgh.* 83 B17
Brae of Achnahaird 86 G16
Brae Roy Lodge 80 A19
Braeside 73 C18
Braeswick 89 D32
Braetongue 86 C21
Brafferton *Drm.* 62 D38
Brafferton *N.Y.* 57 B40
Brafield-on-the-Green 32 C44
Bragar 88 C8
Bragbury End 33 F48
Braglenbeg 79 H15
Braides 55 D30
Braidwood 74 F24
Braigo 78 H3
Brailsford 40 A38
Braintree 34 F53
Braishfield 10 B39
Braithwaite *Cum.* 60 D28
Braithwaite *S.Y.* 51 A42
Braithwell 51 C41
Brakenthwaite 60 D27
Bramber 12 C47
Bramcote 41 B41
Bramdean 11 B42
Bramerton 45 E58
Bramfield *Hfs.* 33 G48
Bramfield *Sfk.* 35 A60
Bramford 35 D57
Bramhall 49 D35
Bramham 57 E40
Bramhope 57 E38
Bramley *Ham.* 21 F42
Bramley *Sry.* 22 G46
Bramley *S.Y.* 51 C40
Bramley *W.Y.* 57 F38
Bramling 15 B58
Brampford Speke 7 F25
Brampton *Cbs.* 33 A48
Brampton *Cum.* 70 G31
Brampton *Cum.* 61 D32
Brampton *Lcn.* 52 E44
Brampton *Nfk.* 45 C58
Brampton *Sfk.* 45 G60
Brampton *S.Y.* 51 B40
Brampton Abbots 29 F32
Brampton Ash 42 G43
Brampton Bryan 28 A29
Bramshall 40 B36
Bramshaw 10 C38
Bramshill 22 E43
Bramshott 12 A44
Bramstead Heath 39 D33
Brancaster 44 A53
Brancaster Staithe 44 A53
Brancepeth 62 C38
Branch End 71 G36
Branchill 84 D26
Branderburgh 84 B28
Brandesburton 59 E47
Brandeston 35 B58
Brandis Corner 6 E20
Brandish Street 7 A25
Brandiston 45 C57
Brandon *Drm.* 62 B38
Brandon *Lcn.* 42 A45
Brandon *Nor.* 71 B36
Brandon *Sfk.* 44 G53
Brandon *War.* 31 A40
Brandon Creek 44 F52
Brandsby 58 B41
Brandy Wharf 52 C46
Bran End 33 F52
Branksome 10 E36
Branscombe 7 G27
Bransford 29 C33
Bransgore 10 E37
Branson's Cross 30 A36
Branston *Lcn.* 52 F46
Branston *Lei.* 42 B44
Branston *Stf.* 40 C38
Branston Booths 52 F46
Brant Broughton 52 G45
Brantham 35 E57
Branthwaite *Cum.* 60 D26
Branthwaite *Cum.* 60 C28
Brantingham 59 G45
Branton *Nor.* 71 B36
Branton *S.Y.* 51 B42
Branxholme 69 B30
Branxholme Park 69 B30
Branxton 77 G35
Brassington 50 G38
Brasted 23 F50
Bratoft 53 F50
Brattleby 52 D45
Bratton *Shr.* 39 D32
Bratton *Wts.* 20 F35
Bratton Clovelly 6 F20
Bratton Fleming 6 B22
Bratton Seymour 9 B32
Braughing 33 F49
Braunston *Lei.* 42 E44
Braunston *Nmp.* 31 B41
Braunstone 41 E41
Braunton 6 B20
Brawby 58 B43
Brawl 87 B24
Brawlbin 87 C26
Bray *Brk.* 22 D45
Braye 3 D17
Brayford 6 B22
Bray Shop 4 C19
Braystones 60 F26
Brayton 58 F41
Braytown 9 F34
Bray Wick 22 D44
Breach 15 C58

Breachwood Green 32 F47
Breaclete 88 D7
Breadsall 41 B39
Breadstone 20 A33
Breage 2 F12
Breakish 82 G12
Breamore 10 C37
Brean 19 F28
Brearton 57 F39
Breasclete 88 D8
Breaston 41 B40
Brechfa 17 A21
Brechin 81 D31
Breckonside 68 C24
Brecon 27 F26
Breconside 69 C27
Bredbury 49 C35
Brede 14 F54
Bredenbury 29 C32
Bredfield 35 C58
Bredgar 24 E54
Bredhurst 24 E53
Bredicot 29 C35
Bredon 29 E35
Bredon's Norton 29 E35
Bredwardine 28 D29
Breedon on the Hill 41 C40
Breich 75 D25
Breighton 58 F43
Breinton 28 E30
Bremhill 20 D35
Brenchley 23 G52
Brendon 7 A23
Brenfield 72 B14
Brenish 88 E5
Brent Eleigh 34 D55
Brent Knoll 19 F29
Brent Pelham 33 E50
Brentwood 24 B52
Brenzett 15 E56
Brereton 40 D36
Brereton Green 49 F33
Brereton Heath 49 F34
Bressingham 44 G56
Bretabister 89 G40
Bretby 40 C38
Bretford 31 A40
Bretforton 30 D36
Bretherton 55 G30
Brettenham 34 C55
Bretton 48 F29
Brewood 40 E34
Bricket Wood 22 A47
Bricklehampton 29 D35
Bride 54 D27
Bridekirk 60 C27
Bridell 26 D17
Bridestowe 6 G21
Brideswell Grm. 85 F31
Bridford 7 G24
Bridge Cnw. 2 D12
Bridge Kent 15 B57
Bridge End Bfd. 32 C46
Bridge End Cum. 60 G27
Bridge End Lcn. 42 B47
Bridge End Pow. 28 B28
Bridgefoot 60 D26
Bridge Hewick 57 B39
Bridgemary 11 D41
Bridgend 89 J39
Bridgend Cnw. 4 E17
Bridgend Cum. 60 E29
Bridgend D.& G. 69 C26
Bridgend Grm. 84 F29
Bridgend Grm. 85 G35
Bridgend Ltn. 75 C26
Bridgend M.G. 18 C25
Bridgend Str. 78 J4
Bridgend Str. 72 A14
Bridgend Tay. 81 D31
Bridgend of Lintrathen 81 E28
Bridge of Alford 85 H31
Bridge of Allan 74 A23
Bridge of Aln Hotel 71 B36
Bridge of Avon 84 G27
Bridge of Balgie 80 F21
Bridge of Balgie 80 F21
Bridge of Brewlands 81 D27
Bridge of Brown 84 G27
Bridge of Buchat 84 H29
Bridge of Cally 81 E27
Bridge of Canny 81 A32
Bridge of Craigisla 81 E28
Bridge of Dee 65 G23
Bridge of Don 85 J35
Bridge of Dye 81 B32
Bridge of Earn 81 J27
Bridge of Ericht 80 E21
Bridge of Forss 87 B26
Bridge of Gaur 80 E21
Bridge of Orchy 80 G19
Bridge of Waithe 89 F28
Bridge of Weir 73 D19
Bridge Reeve 6 D22
Bridgerule 6 E18
Bridges 38 F29
Bridge Sollers 28 D30
Bridge Street 34 D54
Bridge Trafford 48 E30
Bridgham 44 G55
Bridgnorth 39 F33
Bridgtown 40 E35
Bridgwater 8 A28
Bridlington 59 C47
Bridport 8 E30
Brierfield 56 F34
Brierley H.& W. 28 C30
Brierley S.Y. 51 A40
Brierley Hill 40 G35
Brierton 62 D40
Brieryside 67 A19
Brigg 52 B46

Briggswath 63 F44
Brigham Cum. 60 C26
Brigham Hum. 59 D46
Brighouse 57 G37
Brighstone 11 F40
Brighthampton 21 A39
Brightling 13 B52
Brightlingsea 34 G56
Brighton Cnw. 3 C15
Brighton E.S. 13 D49
Brightons 75 C25
Brightwalton 21 D40
Brightwell 35 D58
Brightwell Baldwin 21 B42
Brightwell-cum-Sotwell 21 B41
Brignall 62 E36
Brig of Waas 89 G38
Brig O'Turk 80 K21
Brigsley 53 B48
Brigsteer 55 A30
Brigstock 42 G45
Brill 31 G42
Brilley 28 D28
Brimfield 28 B31
Brimington 51 E40
Brimpsfield 29 G35
Brimpton 21 E41
Brims 89 J28
Brimscombe 20 A34
Brimstage 48 D29
Brin 84 G22
Brindle 55 G31
Brindley Ford 49 G34
Brindley Lea 48 G31
Brineton 40 D34
Brington 32 A46
Briningham 44 B56
Brinkhill 53 E49
Brinkley 33 C52
Brinklow 41 G40
Brinkworth 20 C36
Brinscall 56 G32
Brinsley 41 A40
Brinsop 28 D30
Brinton 44 B56
Brinyan 89 E30
Brisco 61 A30
Brisley 44 C55
Brislington 19 D32
Bristol 19 D32
Bristol Airport 19 E31
Briston 44 B56
Britannia 56 G34
Britford 10 B37
Brithdir D23
Brithem Bottom 7 D26
British Legion Village 14 B53
Briton Ferry 18 B23
Britwell Salome 21 B42
Brixham 5 E25
Brixton 5 E21
Brixton Deverill 9 A34
Brixworth 31 A43
Brize Norton 21 A39
Broad Blunsdon 20 B37
Broadbottom 49 C35
Broadbridge 12 D44
Broadbridge Heath 12 A47
Broad Campden 30 E37
Broad Chalke 10 B36
Broad Clyst 7 F25
Broadford Hgh. 82 G12
Broadford Bridge 12 B46
Broadgate 54 A27
Broad Green 32 D45
Broadhaugh 69 C30
Broad Haven Dyf. 16 C14
Broadhaven Hgh. 87 C29
Broadheath G.M. 49 D33
Broad Heath H.& W. 29 B32
Broadhembury 7 E27
Broadhempston 5 D24
Broad Hinton 20 D37
Broadland Row 14 F54
Broadlay 17 D19
Broad Laying 21 E40
Broadley 84 C29
Broadmayne 9 F33
Broadmeadows 76 G30
Broadmoor 16 D16
Broad Oak Dyf. 17 B21
Broad Oak E.S. 14 E54
Broadoak E.S. 13 B52
Broad Oak H.& W. 28 F30
Broadoak Kent 25 E57
Broadstairs 25 E60
Broadstone 10 E36
Broad Street 14 B54
Broad Street Green 34 G54
Broad Town 20 D36
Broadtown Lane 20 D36
Broadwas 29 C33
Broadwater 33 F48
Broadway H.& W. 30 E36
Broadway Som. 8 C29
Broadwell Glo. 30 F38
Broadwell Oxf. 21 A38
Broadwell War. 31 B40
Broadwey 9 F32
Broadwindsor 8 D30
Broadwood-Kelly 6 E22
Broadwoodwidger 6 G20
Broats 69 G28
Brochel 82 E11
Brochloch 67 D21
Brockdish 35 A58
Brockenhurst 10 D38
Brocketsbrae 74 G24
Brockhall 31 B42
Brockham 22 G47
Brockhampton Glo. 30 F36
Brockhampton H.& W. 28 E31
Brockhill 69 A29
Brockholes 50 A37

Brockhurst 11 D42
Brocklebank 60 B29
Brocklesby 52 A47
Brockley 19 E30
Brockley Green 34 C54
Brockton Shr. 38 E29
Brockton Shr. 39 E33
Brockton Shr. 38 G29
Brockton Shr. 38 F31
Brockweir 19 A31
Brockworth 29 G34
Brocton 40 D35
Brodick 72 G16
Brodsworth 51 B40
Brokenborough 20 C35
Broken Cross 49 E34
Bromborough 48 D29
Brome 35 A57
Bromfield Cum. 60 B27
Bromfield Shr. 28 A30
Bromham Bfd. 32 C46
Bromham Wts. 20 E35
Bromley 23 E50
Bromley Cross 49 A33
Bromley Green 14 D55
Bromleysmill 38 F29
Brompton N.Y. 62 G39
Brompton N.Y. 59 A45
Brompton-on-Swale 62 G38
Brompton Ralph 7 B26
Brompton Regis 7 B25
Bromsash 29 F32
Bromsberrow 29 E33
Bromsberrow Heath 29 E33
Bromsgrove 29 A35
Bromyard 29 C32
Bromyard Downs 29 C32
Bronaber 37 B23
Brongest 26 D19
Bronington 38 B30
Bronllys 28 E27
Bronnant 27 B22
Bron-y-garth 38 B28
Brook Ham. 10 C38
Brook I.o.W. 10 F39
Brook Kent 15 C56
Brook Sry. 12 A45
Brooke Lei. 42 E44
Brooke Nfk. 45 F58
Brookend 19 B31
Brookfield 74 D20
Brookhouse Che. 49 E35
Brookhouse Lan. 55 C31
Brookhouse Green 49 F34
Brookland 14 E55
Brookmans Park 23 A48
Brook Street Kent 14 D55
Brook Street W.S. 13 B49
Brookthorpe 29 G34
Brookwood 22 F45
Broom Bfd. 32 D47
Broom War. 30 C36
Broome H.& W. 29 A35
Broome Nfk. 45 F59
Broome Shr. 38 G30
Broomedge 49 D33
Broome Park 71 B37
Broomfield Esx. 34 G53
Broomfield Kent 14 B54
Broomfield Kent 25 E58
Broomfield Som. 8 A28
Broomfleet 58 G44
Broom Green 44 C55
Broomhaugh 71 G36
Broomhill E.S. 14 F55
Broomhill Hgh. 84 G25
Broomhill Nor. 71 C38
Broomholm 45 B59
Broomielaw 62 E36
Broomley 62 A36
Broompark 62 B38
Brora 87 H25
Broseley 39 E32
Brotherlee 61 C35
Brothertoft 43 A48
Brotherton 57 G40
Brotton 63 E42
Brough Cum. 61 E33
Brough Hgh. 89 K28
Brough Hum. 59 G45
Brough She. 89 F41
Brough She. 89 F40
Brough Lodge 89 C41
Brough Sowerby 61 E33
Broughton Bkh. 32 E44
Broughton Bor. 75 G27
Broughton Cbs. 33 A48
Broughton Clw. 48 F29
Broughton G.M. 49 B34
Broughton Ham. 10 A39
Broughton Lan. 55 F31
Broughton Lcn. 52 B45
Broughton M.G. 18 D25
Broughton Nmp. 32 A44
Broughton N.Y. 58 B43
Broughton N.Y. 63 F41
Broughton N.Y. 56 F35
Broughton Oxf. 31 E40
Broughton Astley 41 F41
Broughton Beck 54 A28
Broughton Gifford 20 E34
Broughton Hackett 29 C35
Broughton in Furness 54 A28
Broughton Mills 54 A28
Broughton Moor 60 C26
Broughton Poggs 21 A38
Broughtown 89 C32
Broughty Ferry 81 G30
Brown Candover 11 A41
Brownedge Lan. 55 G31
Brown Edge Stf. 49 G35
Brownhill Lan. 56 F32
Brownhill Shr. 38 C30
Brownhills 40 E36

Brownridge 77 G36
Brownsover 31 A41
Brownston 5 E22
Brownyside 71 A37
Brox 22 E46
Broxa 63 G45
Broxbourne 23 A49
Broxburn Ltn. 76 C32
Broxburn Ltn. 75 C26
Broxted 33 F51
Broxton 48 G30
Broxwood 28 C29
Bruar Lodge 80 C24
Brue 88 C9
Bruera 48 F30
Bruichladdich 78 J4
Bruisyard 35 B59
Bruisyard Street 35 B59
Brumby 52 B45
Brundall 45 E59
Brundish 35 B58
Brunstock 61 A30
Brunswick 71 F38
Bruntcliffe 57 G38
Bruntingthorpe 41 F42
Brunton Fife 81 H29
Brunton Nor. 71 A38
Brushford 7 C25
Bruton 9 A32
Brydekirk 69 F27
Brymbo 48 G28
Brympton 8 C31
Bryn Dyf. 27 A23
Bryn G.M. 48 B31
Bryn W.G. 18 B24
Brynaman 27 G23
Brynawel 28 F28
Brynberian 16 A17
Bryncethin 18 C25
Bryncir 36 A20
Bryn-côch 18 B23
Bryncroes 36 B18
Bryncrug 37 E22
Bryneglwys 38 A27
Brynford 47 E27
Bryngwran 46 E19
Bryngwyn Gwe. 19 A29
Bryngwyn Pow. 28 D27
Bryn-henllan 16 A16
Brynhoffnant Inn 26 C19
Bryn-lfan 37 B24
Brynmawr 28 G27
Brynmenyn 18 C25
Brynmill 17 E22
Brynna 18 C25
Brynrefail Gwy. 46 F21
Brynrefail Gwy. 46 D20
Brynsadler 18 C26
Brynsiencyn 46 F20
Bryn-y-Cae 18 C25
Bubbenhall 31 A40
Bubwith 58 F43
Buccleuch 69 B29
Buchanan Castle 74 B20
Buchanhaven 85 E37
Buchanty 80 H25
Buchlyvie 74 A21
Buchtrig 70 B33
Buckabank 60 B29
Buckby Folly 31 B42
Buckden N.Y. 56 B35
Buckerell 7 E27
Buckfast 5 D23
Buckfastleigh 5 D23
Buckhaven 75 A29
Buckholm 76 G30
Buckhorn Weston 9 B33
Buckie 85 C30
Buckingham 31 E42
Buckland Bkh. 32 G44
Buckland Dev. 5 F22
Buckland Glo. 30 E36
Buckland Hfs. 33 E49
Buckland Kent 15 C58
Buckland Oxf. 21 B39
Buckland Sry. 23 F48
Buckland Brewer 6 C20
Buckland Common 22 A45
Buckland Dinham 20 F33
Buckland Filleigh 6 E20
Buckland in the Moor 5 C23
Buckland Monachorum 4 D20
Buckland Newton 9 D32
Buckland St. Mary 8 C28
Bucklebury 21 D41
Bucklers Hard 11 E40
Bucklesham 35 D58
Buckley 48 F28
Buckminster 42 C44
Bucknall Lcn. 52 F47
Bucknall Stf. 40 A35
Bucknell Oxf. 31 F41
Bucknell Shr. 28 A29
Bucksburn 85 J34
Buck's Cross 6 C19
Bucks Green 12 A46
Bucks Horn Oak 22 G44
Buck's Mills 6 C19
Buckton Hum. 59 B47
Buckton H.& W. 28 A29
Buckton Nor. 77 G36
Buckworth 32 A47
Budbrooke 30 B38
Budby 51 E42
Bude 6 E18
Budle 77 G37
Budleigh Salterton 7 G26
Budock Water 2 E13
Buerton 39 A32
Bugbrooke 31 C42
Buglawton 49 F34
Bugle 4 E16

Bugthorpe 58 D43
Buildwas 39 E32
Builth Road 27 C26
Builth Wells 27 C26
Buittle 65 C24
Bulcote 41 A42
Buldoo 87 B25
Bulford 20 G37
Bulford Camp 20 G37
Bulkeley 48 G31
Bulkington War. 41 G39
Bulkington Wts. 20 F35
Bulkworthy 6 D19
Bull Bay 46 C20
Bullbrook 22 E44
Bulley 29 G33
Bullgill 60 C26
Bullington Ham. 21 G40
Bullington Lcn. 52 E46
Bullwood 73 C17
Bulmer Esx. 34 D54
Bulmer N.Y. 58 C42
Bulmer Tye 34 E54
Bulphan 24 C52
Bulverton 7 G27
Bulwell 41 A41
Bulwick 42 F45
Bumbles Green 23 A50
Bunacaimb 79 B12
Bunarkaig 79 B17
Bunavoneader 88 G7
Bunbury 48 G31
Bunbury Heath 48 G31
Bunchrew 84 E22
Bundalloch 83 G14
Bunessan 78 H9
Bungalow Hotel 54 E26
Bungay 45 F59
Bunlarie 72 G13
Bunnahabhainn 78 H5
Bunny 41 C41
Buntait 83 F19
Buntingford 33 F49
Bunwell 45 F57
Bunwell Street 45 F57
Burbage Dby. 50 E36
Burbage Lei. 41 F40
Burbage Wts. 21 E38
Burchett's Green 22 C44
Burcombe 10 A36
Burcot H.& W. 29 A35
Burcot Oxf. 21 B41
Burdale 58 C44
Bures 34 E55
Burford H.& W. 28 B31
Burford Oxf. 30 G38
Burgate 10 C37
Burgess Hill 13 C49
Burgh 35 C58
Burgh by Sands 60 A29
Burgh Castle 45 E60
Burghclere 21 E40
Burghead 84 C27
Burghfield 21 E42
Burghfield Common 21 E42
Burgh Heath 23 F48
Burghill 28 D30
Burgh le Marsh 53 F51
Burgh next Aylsham 45 C58
Burgh on Bain 53 D48
Burgh St. Margaret 45 D60
Burgh St. Peter 45 F60
Burghwallis 51 A41
Burham 24 E53
Buriton 11 B43
Burland 49 G32
Burlawn 3 A15
Burleigh 22 E45
Burlescombe 7 D26
Burleston 9 E33
Burley Ham. 10 D38
Burley Lei. 42 D44
Burleydam 39 A32
Burley Gate 28 D31
Burley in Wharfedale 57 E37
Burley Street 10 D38
Burlingjobb 28 C28
Burlow 13 C51
Burlton 38 C30
Burmarsh 15 D57
Burmington 30 E38
Burn 58 G41
Burnaston 40 B38
Burnbank 74 E22
Burnby 58 E44
Burncross 51 C39
Burndell 12 D45
Burnedge 49 A35
Burneside 61 G31
Burneston 57 A39
Burnett 19 E32
Burnfoot Bor. 69 B30
Burnfoot D.& G. 69 E29
Burnfoot D.& G. 69 F28
Burnfoot D.& G. 69 D29
Burnfoot Str. 67 E17
Burnham 22 C45
Burnham Deepdale 44 A54
Burnham Green 33 G48
Burnham Market 44 A54
Burnham Norton 44 A54
Burnham-on-Crouch 25 B55
Burnham on Sea 19 G28
Burnham Overy 44 A54
Burnham Thorpe 44 A54
Burnhaven 85 E37
Burnhead 68 D24
Burnhervie 85 H33
Burnhill Green 39 E33
Burnhope 62 B37
Burnhouse 73 F19
Burnhouses 76 E33
Burniston 63 G46
Burnley 56 F34

Burnmouth 77 D35
Burn Naze 55 E29
Burnopfield 62 A37
Burnsall 57 C36
Burnside Ltn. 75 C26
Burnside Ltn. 75 C26
Burnside She. 89 E38
Burnside Str. 67 B21
Burnt Houses 62 D37
Burntisland 75 B28
Burnton 67 C20
Burntwood 40 E36
Burnt Yates 57 C38
Burpham 12 D46
Burradon 70 C35
Burrafirth 89 A42
Burras 2 E12
Burravoe She. 89 E41
Burravoe She. 89 F39
Burrells 61 E32
Burrelton 81 G27
Burrill 57 A38
Burringham 52 B44
Burrington Dev. 6 D22
Burrington H.& W. 28 A30
Burrington Som. 19 F30
Burrough Green 33 C52
Burrough on the Hill 42 D43
Burrow Bridge 8 A29
Burrowhill 22 E45
Burry Port 17 D20
Burscough 48 A30
Burscough Bridge 48 A30
Bursea 58 F44
Burshill 59 E46
Bursledon 11 D40
Burslem 49 G34
Burstall 35 D57
Burstock 8 D30
Burston Nfk. 45 G57
Burston Stf. 40 B35
Burstow 23 G49
Burstwick 59 G48
Burtersett 56 A34
Burton Che. 48 F31
Burton Che. 48 E29
Burton Dor. 10 E37
Burton Dyf. 16 D15
Burton Lcn. 52 E45
Burton Som. 7 A27
Burton Wts. 20 D34
Burton Agnes 59 C47
Burton Bradstock 8 F30
Burton Coggles 42 C45
Burton Constable 59 F47
Burton Hastings 41 F40
Burton-in-Kendal 55 B31
Burton in Lonsdale 56 B32
Burton Joyce 41 A42
Burton Latimer 32 A45
Burton Lazars 42 D43
Burton Leonard 57 C39
Burton on the Wolds 41 C41
Burton Overy 41 F42
Burton Pedwardine 42 A47
Burton Pidsea 59 F48
Burton Salmon 57 G40
Burton upon Stather 52 A44
Burton upon Trent 40 C38
Burtonwood 48 C31
Burtonwood Services 48 C31
Burtree Ford 61 B34
Burwardsley 48 G31
Burwarton 39 G32
Burwash 13 B52
Burwash Common 13 B51
Burwash Weald 13 B52
Burwell Cbs. 33 B51
Burwell Lcn. 53 E49
Burwen 46 C20
Burwick 89 J30
Bury Cbs. 43 G48
Bury G.M. 49 A33
Bury Som. 7 C25
Bury W.S. 12 C46
Buryas Bridge 2 F10
Bury St. Edmunds 34 B54
Burythorpe 58 C43
Busby 74 E21
Buscot 21 B38
Bush Bank 28 C30
Bushbury 40 E35
Bushey 22 B47
Bush Hill Park 23 B49
Bush Lawsie 81 A28
Bushley 29 E34
Bushton 20 D36
Buslingthorpe 52 D46
Busta 89 F39
Butcher's Cross 13 B51
Butcher's Pasture 33 F52
Butcombe 19 E31
Butleigh 8 A31
Butler's Cross 22 A44
Butlers Marston 30 D39
Butley 35 C59
Butterburn 70 F32
Buttercrambe 58 D43
Butterdean 76 D33
Butterknowle 62 D37
Butterleigh 7 E25
Buttermere 60 E27
Butterstone 80 F26
Butterton 50 G36
Butterwick Cum. 61 E31
Butterwick Drm. 62 D39
Butterwick Lcn. 43 A49
Butterwick N.Y. 58 B43
Butterwick N.Y. 59 B45
Buttington 38 E28
Butt Lane 49 G34
Buttonbridge 29 A33
Buttonoak 29 A33

Buxhall 34 C56
Buxted 13 B51
Buxton Dby. 50 E36
Buxton Nfk. 45 C58
Buxton Heath 45 C57
Bwlch 28 F27
Bwlchgwyn 48 G28
Bwlchllan 26 C21
Bwlchnewydd 17 B19
Bwlch-y-cibau 38 D27
Bwlchyddar 38 C27
Bwlchyfadfa 26 D20
Bwlch-y-ffridd 37 F26
Bwlch-y-groes 17 A18
Bwlch-y-tocyn 36 C19
Byers Green 62 C38
Byfield 31 C41
Byfleet 22 E46
Byford 28 D29
Bygrave 33 E48
Byland Abbey 58 B41
Bylbster 87 C28
Bylchau 47 F25
Byley 49 F33
Bynea 17 E21
Byreburnfoot 69 F29
Byrness 70 C33
Bythorn 32 A46
Byton 28 B29
Bywell 71 G36
Byworth 12 B45

C

Caarnduncan 78 H3
Cabourne 52 B47
Cabrach Grm. 84 G29
Cabrach Str. 78 H6
Cabrich 83 E21
Cackle Street 14 F54
Cacrabank 69 B29
Cadbury 7 E25
Cadbury Heath 19 D32
Cadder 74 C22
Caddington 32 F46
Cadeby Lei. 41 E40
Cadeby S.Y. 51 B41
Cadeleigh 7 E25
Cadgwith 2 G13
Cadishead 49 C33
Cadley 21 E38
Cadmore End 22 B43
Cadnam 10 C38
Cadney 52 B46
Cadole 48 F28
Cadoxton 18 E27
Cadshaw 49 A33
Caeathro 46 F21
Cae Dafydd 37 A22
Caehopkin 27 G24
Caenby 52 D46
Caenby Corner 52 D45
Caeo 27 D22
Caerau 18 B24
Caerdeon 37 D22
Caer Farchell 16 B13
Caergeiliog 46 E19
Caergwrle 48 G29
Caerlanrig 69 C29
Caerleon 19 B29
Caernarfon 46 F20
Caerphilly 18 C27
Caersws 37 F26
Cae'r-tyddyn 37 D23
Caerwent 19 B30
Caerwys 47 E27
Caethle 37 F22
Caggan 84 H24
Cairnbaan 72 A14
Cairnborrow 85 E30
Cairncross 77 D34
Cairncurran 73 D19
Cairndow 79 J17
Cairness 85 C36
Cairneyhill 75 B26
Cairnhouses 74 G24
Cairnie 85 E30
Cairnorrie 85 E34
Cairnpark 68 D24
Cairnpat 64 C16
Cairnryan 66 G16
Cairnsmore 67 G20
Cairntable 67 B20
Cairnwhin 67 D18
Caister-on-Sea 45 D61
Caistor 52 B47
Caistor St. Edmund 45 E58
Calbourne 11 F40
Calceby 53 E49
Calcot 38 F28
Calcot Farm 20 B34
Calcot Row 21 D42
Calcott 25 E57
Caldbeck 60 C29
Caldbergh 57 A36
Caldecot 15 E56
Caldecote Cbs. 42 G47
Caldecote Cbs. 33 C49
Caldecote Nmp. 31 C42
Caldecote War. 41 F39
Caldecott Lei. 42 F44
Caldecott Nmp. 32 B45
Calder 60 F26
Calderbank 74 D23
Calder Bridge 60 F26
Calderbrook 49 A35
Calder Mains 87 C26
Caldermill 74 F22
Calder Vale 55 E31

Caldicot 19 C30
Caldwell Dby. 40 D38
Caldwell N.Y. 62 E37
Caldy 48 D28
Caledfwlch 17 B22
Calfsound 89 D31
Calgary 78 E9
Calgow 67 G20
California Cen. 75 C25
California Nfk. 45 D61
California Sfk. 35 D57
California Cross 5 E23
Callaly 71 C36
Callander 80 K22
Callands House 75 F27
Callestick 2 C13
Calligarry 82 J12
Callington 6 C27
Callow H.&W. 28 E30
Callow Hill H.&W. 29 A33
Callow Hill Wts. 20 C36
Calmore 10 C39
Calne 20 D35
Calow 51 E40
Calshot 11 D40
Calstock 4 D20
Calstone Wellington 20 E36
Calthorpe 45 B57
Calthwaite 61 C30
Calton N.Y. 56 D35
Calton Stf. 50 G37
Calveley 48 G31
Calver 50 E38
Calverhall 39 B32
Calverleigh 7 D25
Calverley 57 F38
Calverton Bkh. 31 E43
Calverton Not. 41 A42
Calvine 80 D24
Calvo 60 A27
Calzeat 75 G27
Cam 20 B33
Camasnacroise 79 E14
Camasterach 82 E13
Camastianavaig 82 F11
Camault Muir 83 E21
Camber 14 F55
Camberley 22 E44
Camblesforth 58 G42
Cambo 71 E36
Cambois 71 E39
Camborne 2 E12
Cambridge Cbs. 33 C50
Cambridge Glo. 20 A33
Cambus 74 A24
Cambusavie 87 J23
Cambusbarron 74 A23
Cambuslang 74 D23
Cambuswallace 75 G26
Cameley 19 F32
Camelford 4 B17
Camelon 74 B24
Camer 24 E52
Camer-fawr 27 B22
Camerton Cum. 60 C26
Camerton Som. 19 F32
Camghouran 80 D21
Cammachmore 81 A35
Cammeringham 52 D45
Campbelltown 84 D23
Campbeltown 66 A13
Campbeltown Airport 66 A12
Cample 68 D24
Campmuir 81 G28
Campsall 51 A41
Camps End 33 D52
Campsey Ash 35 C59
Campton 32 E47
Camptown 70 B32
Camrose 16 B15
Camserney 80 F24
Camuschoirk 79 D13
Camus-luinie 83 G15
Camusrory 79 A14
Camusteel 82 E13
Camusvrachan 80 F22
Canada 10 C38
Candlesby 53 F50
Candy Mill 75 F26
Canewdon 25 B55
Canfield End 33 F51
Canford Bottom 10 D36
Canford Magna 10 E36
Canisbay 89 K29
Cann 9 B34
Cannard's Grave 19 G32
Cannich 83 F19
Cannington 8 A28
Cannock 40 D35
Cannock Wood 40 D36
Cannop 29 G32
Canon Frome 29 D32
Canon Pyon 28 D30
Canons Ashby 31 C41
Canonstown 2 E11
Canterbury 15 B57
Cantley Nfk. 45 E59
Cantley S.Y. 51 B42
Canton 18 D27
Cantraybruich 84 E23
Cantsfield 56 B32
Canvey 24 C54
Canwick 52 F45
Canworthy Water 4 A18
Caol 79 C17
Caolasnacon 79 D17
Caoles 78 F6
Capel 22 G47
Capel Bangor 37 G22
Capel-Betws-Lleucu 27 C22
Capelcoch 46 D20
Capel Curig 47 G23

Capel Cynon 26 C19
Capel Dewi Dyf. 37 G22
Capel Dewi Dyf. 26 D20
Capel Garmon 47 G24
Capel Gwynfe 27 F23
Capel Hendre 17 C21
Capel Isaac 17 B21
Capel Iwan 17 A18
Capel le Ferne 15 D58
Capel Parc 46 D20
Capel St. Mary 35 E57
Capeluchaf 36 A20
Capel y ffin 28 E28
Capel-y-graig 46 F21
Capenhurst 48 E29
Caplaw 74 E20
Cappercleuch 69 A28
Capplegill 69 C27
Caputh 80 F26
Carbis Bay 2 E11
Carbost Hgh. 82 F9
Carbost Hgh. 82 E10
Carbrooke 44 E55
Carburton 51 E42
Carcluie 67 B19
Carco 68 B23
Car Colston 42 A43
Carcroft 51 B41
Cardenden 75 B28
Cardeston 38 D29
Cardiff 19 D28
Cardigan 26 D17
Cardington Bfd. 32 D46
Cardington Shr. 38 F31
Cardinham 4 D17
Cardow 84 E27
Cardrona 75 G29
Cardrona Mains 75 G29
Cardross 73 C19
Cardurnock 60 A27
Careby 42 D46
Careston 81 D31
Carew 16 D16
Carew Newton 16 D16
Carfin 74 E23
Carfrae 76 D31
Carfraemill Hotel 76 E31
Cargen 68 F25
Cargenbridge 68 F25
Cargill 81 G27
Cargo 60 A29
Cargreen 4 D20
Carham 76 G33
Carhampton 7 A26
Carharrack 2 D13
Carie Tay. 80 E22
Carie Tay. 80 G22
Carinish 88 M4
Carisbrooke 11 F40
Cark 55 B29
Carkeel 4 D20
Carland Cross 3 C14
Carlby 42 D46
Carlecotes 50 B38
Carleton Cum. 61 D31
Carleton Cum. 61 A30
Carleton Lan. 55 F29
Carleton N.Y. 56 E35
Carleton W.Y. 57 G40
Carleton Forehoe 44 E56
Carleton Rode 45 F57
Carlingcott 19 F32
Carlin How 63 E43
Carlisle 60 A29
Carlops 75 E27
Carloway 88 C8
Carlton Bfd. 32 C45
Carlton Cbs. 33 C52
Carlton Drm. 62 D39
Carlton Lei. 41 E39
Carlton Not. 41 A41
Carlton N.Y. 63 F41
Carlton N.Y. 58 A42
Carlton N.Y. 58 G42
Carlton N.Y. 57 A36
Carlton Sfk. 35 B59
Carlton S.Y. 51 B39
Carlton W.Y. 57 G39
Carlton Colville 45 F61
Carlton Curlieu 41 F42
Carlton Husthwaite 57 B40
Carlton in Lindrick 51 D41
Carlton le Moorland 52 G45
Carlton Miniott 57 A39
Carlton Scroop 42 A45
Carlton-on-Trent 52 F44
Carluke 74 E24
Carmacoup 68 A23
Carmarthen 17 B19
Carmel Clw. 47 E27
Carmel Dyf. 17 C21
Carmel Gwy. 46 G20
Carmel Gwy. 46 D19
Carminish 88 J6
Carmunnock 74 E21
Carmyle 74 D22
Carnaby 59 C47
Carnach Grm. 84 E26
Carnach Hgh. 83 G16
Carnachuin 80 A24
Carnachy 87 C23
Carnan 88 N4
Carnbee 81 K31
Carnbo 80 K26
Carnell 74 G20
Carnforth 55 B30
Carnhell Green 2 E12
Carno 37 F25
Carnoch 84 F24
Carnock 75 B26
Carnon Downs 2 D13
Carnousie 85 C59
Catforth 55 F30
Cathcart 74 D21
Cathedine 28 F27
Catherington 11 C42

Carperby 57 A36
Carradale 72 G14
Carrbridge 84 G25
Carr Cross 48 A29
Carrefour Selous 3 G17
Carreglefn 46 D19
Carrick Fife 81 H30
Carrick Str. 72 B15
Carrick Str. 73 A17
Carriden 59 B26
Carrifran 69 B27
Carrington G.M. 49 C33
Carrington Lcn. 53 G49
Carrington Ltn. 75 D29
Carrog 38 A27
Carron Cen. 74 B24
Carron Grm. 84 E28
Carron Bridge Cen. 74 B23
Carronbridge D.& G. 68 D24
Carronshore 74 B24
Carr Shield 61 B34
Carrutherstown 69 F26
Carruthmuir 73 D19
Carrutchan 65 C25
Carsaig Str. 79 H11
Carsaig Str. 72 B13
Carscreugh 67 G18
Carse 72 D13
Carsegown 64 C20
Carseriggan 67 G19
Carsethorn 65 C25
Carshalton 23 E48
Carsington 50 G38
Carskiey 66 C12
Carsluith 64 C20
Carson 69 F30
Carstairs 75 F25
Carstairs Junction 75 F25
Carter Bar 70 C32
Carterton 21 A38
Carterway Heads 62 A36
Carthew 4 E16
Carthorpe 57 A39
Cartington 71 C36
Cartland 74 E23
Cartmel 55 B29
Cartmel Fell 55 A30
Cartworth 50 B37
Carwinley 69 F30
Carwood 75 G26
Cashell 74 A20
Cashlie 80 F20
Cashmoor 9 C35
Cassencarrie 64 C20
Cassington 31 G40
Cassop 62 C39
Casterton 56 B32
Castle Acre 44 D54
Castle Ashby 32 C44
Castlebay 81 T2
Castle Bolton 62 G36
Castle Bromwich 40 G37
Castle Bytham 42 D45
Castlebythe 16 B16
Castle Caereinion 38 E27
Castle Camps 33 D52
Castle Carrock 61 A31
Castle Cary 9 A32
Castlecary 74 C23
Castle Combe 20 D34
Castlecraig Bor. 75 F27
Castlecraig Hgh. 84 C24
Castle Donington 41 C40
Castle Douglas 68 E23
Castle Eaton 20 B37
Castle Eden 62 C40
Castlefield 57 G40
Castlefairn 68 E23
Castleford 57 G40
Castle Frome 29 D32
Castle Gresley 40 D38
Castle Hedingham 34 E53
Castlehill Bor. 75 G28
Castle Hill D.& G. 68 F25
Castle Hill Gwe. 19 C28
Castle Kennedy 64 C17
Castlemartin 16 E15
Castlemilk 69 F27
Castlemorris 16 A15
Castlemorton 29 E33
Castle Nook 61 B32
Castle O'er 69 D28
Castle Rising 44 C52
Castleside Bor. 69 A30
Castleside Drm. 62 B36
Castlesteads 70 G31
Castlethorpe 31 D43
Castlethwaite 61 F33
Castleton Cum. 70 E31
Castleton Dby. 50 D39
Castleton Gwe. 19 C28
Castleton Lan. 49 A34
Castleton N.Y. 63 F42
Castleton Str. 72 B14
Castletown Drm. 62 A39
Castletown Hgh. 87 B27
Castletown I.o.M. 54 G25
Castleweary 69 C30
Castley 57 F38
Caston 44 F55
Castor 42 F47
Castramont 67 G21
Catacol 72 F15
Catchall 2 F10
Catchems Corner 30 A38
Catchgate 62 A37
Catcleugh 70 C33
Catcliffe 51 D40
Catcott 8 A29
Catfield 45 C59
Carnoustie 81 G31
Carnwath 75 F25

Catherston Leweston 8 E29
Catlodge 80 A22
Catlowdy 69 F30
Catmore 21 C40
Caton 55 C31
Catrine 67 A21
Catsfield 14 F53
Catshill 29 A35
Cattal 57 D40
Cattawade 35 E57
Catterall 55 E30
Catterick 62 G38
Catterick Bridge 62 G38
Catterick Camp 62 G37
Catterlen 61 C30
Catterline 81 C34
Catterton 58 E41
Catthorpe 31 A41
Cattistock 8 E31
Catton Nfk. 45 D58
Catton Nor. 61 A34
Catton N.Y. 57 B39
Catwick 59 E47
Catworth 32 A46
Caudle Green 29 G35
Cauldcots 81 F41
Cauldhame 74 A22
Cauldmill 70 B31
Cauldon 40 A36
Cauldonlow 40 A36
Cauldside 69 F30
Caulkerbush 65 C25
Caunsall 40 G34
Caunton 51 F43
Causeway End D.& G. 64 C20
Causeway End Lan. 48 A30
Causewayhead Cen. 74 A24
Causewayhead Cum. 60 A27
Causey Park Bridge 71 D37
Cautley 61 G32
Cavendish 34 D54
Cavenham 34 A53
Caversfield 31 F41
Caversham 22 D43
Caverswall 40 A35
Cavil 58 F43
Cawdor 84 E24
Cawkwell 53 D48
Cawood 58 F41
Cawsand 4 E20
Cawston 45 C57
Cawthorn 58 A43
Cawthorne 50 B38
Cawton 58 B42
Caxton 33 C49
Caxton Gibbet 33 B48
Caynham 28 A31
Caythorpe Lcn. 42 A45
Caythorpe Not. 41 A42
Cayton 59 A46
Ceannacroc Lo. 83 H18
Cefn brîth 47 G25
Cefn-Bychan 38 A28
Cefn Coed-y-Cymmer 18 A26
Cefn Cribwr 18 C24
Cefn-ddwysarn 37 B25
Cefn Einion 38 G28
Cefneithin 17 C21
Cefngorwydd 27 D25
Cefn-Mawr 38 A28
Cefn-y-bedd 48 G29
Cefn-y-coed 38 F27
Cefn-y-pant 16 B17
Cellan 27 D22
Cellarhead 40 A35
Cemaes 46 C19
Cemmaes 37 E24
Cemmaes Road 37 E24
Cenarth 26 D18
Ceres 81 J29
Cerist 37 G25
Cerne Abbas 9 D32
Cerney Wick 20 B36
Cerrigceinwen 46 E20
Cerrigydrudion 37 A25
Cessford 70 A33
Chaceley 29 E34
Chacewater 2 D13
Chackmore 31 E42
Chacombe 31 D40
Chadderton 49 B35
Chaddesden 41 B39
Chaddesley Corbett 29 A34
Chaddleworth 21 D40
Chadlington 30 F39
Chadshunt 30 C39
Chadwell Heath 23 C50
Chadwell St. Mary 24 D52
Chadwick End 30 A38
Chaffcombe 8 C29
Chagford 6 G22
Chailey 13 C49
Chainbridge 43 E50
Chainhurst 14 C53
Chalbury Common 10 D36
Chaldon 23 F49
Chaldon Herring 9 F33
Chale 11 G40
Chale Green 11 G40
Chalfont St. Giles 22 B45
Chalfont St. Peter 22 B46
Chalford 20 A34
Chalgrave 32 F46
Chalgrove 31 B42
Chalk 24 D52
Challacombe 6 A22
Challoch 67 G19
Challochmunn 64 C18
Challock 15 B56
Chalmington 8 D31
Chalton Bfd. 32 F46
Chalton Ham. 11 C43

Chalvington 13 D51
Champany 75 C26
Chancery 26 A21
Chandler's Ford 11 B40
Changue 64 D18
Channerwick 89 K40
Chantry Fife 35 D57
Chantry Som. 20 G33
Chapel 65 C22
Chapel Allerton 19 F30
Chapel Amble 3 A15
Chapel Brampton 31 B43
Chapel Chorlton 40 B34
Chapeldonan 67 C17
Chapelend Way 34 E53
Chapel en le Frith 50 D36
Chapel Green 40 G38
Chapel Haddlesey 58 G41
Chapelhall 74 D23
Chapel Hill Grm. 85 F36
Chapel Hill Gwe. 19 B31
Chapel Hill Lcn. 53 G48
Chapelhill Tay. 80 G26
Chapelhill Tay. 81 H28
Chapelknowe 69 F29
Chapel Lawn 28 A29
Chapel le Dale 56 B33
Chapel of Garioch 85 G33
Chapel Rossan 64 D17
Chapel Row 21 E41
Chapels 54 A28
Chapel St. Leonards 53 E51
Chapel Stile 60 F29
Chapelton Dev. 6 C21
Chapelton Hgh. 84 H25
Chapelton Str. 74 F22
Chapelton Tay. 81 F32
Chapeltown Grm. 84 G28
Chapeltown Lan. 49 A33
Chapeltown S.Y. 51 C39
Chapmanslade 20 G34
Chapmans Well 6 F19
Chappel 34 F54
Chard 8 D29
Chardstock 8 D29
Charfield 20 B33
Charing 14 C55
Charing Heath 14 C55
Charingworth 30 E38
Charlbury 30 G39
Charlcombe 20 E33
Charlcote 30 C38
Charles 6 B22
Charleshill 22 G44
Charleston 81 F29
Charlestown Cnw. 4 E16
Charlestown Fife 75 B26
Charlestown Grm. 85 J35
Charlestown Hgh. 84 E22
Charlestown Hgh. 83 B14
Charlestown W.Y. 56 G35
Charlestown of Aberlour 84 E28
Charlesworth 50 C36
Charlinch 8 A28
Charlton 63 E42
Charlton Ham. 21 G39
Charlton H.& W. 30 D36
Charlton Nmp. 31 E41
Charlton Nor. 70 E34
Charlton Oxf. 21 C40
Charlton W.S. 12 C44
Charlton Wts. 9 B35
Charlton Wts. 20 C35
Charlton Wts. 10 B37
Charlton Wts. 20 F37
Charlton Adam 8 B31
Charlton Horethorne 9 B32
Charlton Kings 29 F35
Charlton Mackrell 8 B31
Charlton Marshall 9 D35
Charlton Mires 71 A37
Charlton Musgrove 9 A33
Charlton on Otmoor 31 G41
Charlwood 23 G48
Charminster 9 E32
Charmouth 8 E29
Charndon 31 F42
Charney Bassett 21 B39
Charnock Richard 48 A31
Charnock Richard Services 48 A31
Charsfield 35 C58
Chart Corner 14 B53
Charterhall 76 F33
Charterhouse 19 F30
Chartershall 74 A23
Chartham 15 B57
Chartridge 22 A45
Chart Sutton 14 C54
Charwelton 31 C41
Chase Terrace 40 E36
Chasetown 40 E36
Chastleton 30 F38
Chatburn 56 E33
Chatham 24 E53
Chathill 71 A37
Chattenden 24 D53
Chatteris 43 G49
Chattisham 34 D56
Chatto 70 B33
Chatton 71 A36
Chavel 38 D30
Chawleigh 7 D23
Chawton 11 A43
Cheadle G.M. 49 D34
Cheadle Stf. 40 A36
Cheadle Hulme 49 D34
Chealamy 87 C23
Cheam 23 E48
Cheapside 22 E45
Chearsley 31 G43
Chebsey 40 C34

Checkendon 21 C42
Checkley Che. 39 A33
Checkley Stf. 40 B36
Chedburgh 34 C53
Cheddar 19 F30
Cheddington 32 G45
Cheddleton 49 G35
Cheddleton Heath 49 G35
Chedglow 20 B35
Chedgrave 45 F59
Chedington 8 D30
Chediston 35 A59
Chedworth 30 G36
Chedzoy 8 A29
Cheeklaw 76 E33
Cheese Bay 88 K5
Cheldon Barton 7 D23
Chelford 49 E34
Chellaston 41 B39
Chellington 32 C45
Chelmarsh 39 G33
Chelmondiston 35 E58
Chelmorton 50 E37
Chelmsford 24 A53
Chelmsley Wood 40 G37
Chelsea 23 E48
Chelsfield 23 E50
Chelsworth 34 D55
Cheltenham 29 F35
Chelveston 32 B45
Chelvey 19 E30
Chelwood 19 E32
Chelwood Gate 13 A50
Cheney Longville 38 G30
Chenies 22 B46
Chepstow 19 B31
Cherhill 20 D36
Cherington Glo. 20 B35
Cherington War. 30 E38
Cheriton Dyf. 16 E15
Cheriton Ham. 11 B41
Cheriton Kent 15 D58
Cheriton W.G. 17 E20
Cheriton Bishop 7 F23
Cheriton Cross 7 F23
Cheriton Fitzpaine 7 E24
Cherrington 39 D32
Cherry Burton 59 E45
Cherry Hinton 33 C50
Cherry Orchard 29 C34
Cherry Willingham 52 E46
Chertsey 22 E46
Cheselbourne 9 D33
Chesham 22 A45
Chesham Bois 22 A45
Cheshunt 23 A49
Cheslyn Hay 40 E35
Chessington 22 E47
Chester 48 F29
Chesterblade 19 G32
Chesterfield 51 E39
Chesterfield Village 25 E57
Chesterholm 70 G33
Chester le Street 62 A38
Chester Moor 62 B38
Chesters Bor. 70 A32
Chesters Bor. 70 B32
Chesterton Cbs. 42 F47
Chesterton Oxf. 31 F41
Chesterton Shr. 39 F33
Chesterton Stf. 40 A34
Chesterwood 70 G34
Cheswardine 39 B33
Cheswick 77 F36
Cheswick Green 30 A37
Chetnole 8 D31
Chettisham 43 G51
Chettle 9 C35
Chetton 39 F32
Chetwynd 39 C33
Chetwynd Aston 39 D33
Cheveley 33 B52
Chevington 34 B53
Chevington Drift 71 D38
Chevithorne 7 D25
Chew Magna 19 E31
Chew Stoke 19 E31
Chewton Keynsham 19 E32
Chewton Mendip 19 F31
Chicheley 32 D45
Chicherell 9 F32
Chichester 12 D44
Chickering 35 A58
Chicklade 9 A35
Chiddingfold 12 A45
Chiddingly 13 C51
Chiddingstone 23 G51
Chiddingstone Causeway 23 G51
Chideock 8 E30
Chidham 11 D43
Chieveley 21 D40
Chignall St. James 33 G52
Chigwell 23 B50
Chigwell Row 23 B50
Chilbolton 21 G39
Chilcomb 11 B41
Chilcombe 8 E31
Chilcompton 19 F32
Chilcote 40 D38
Childer Thornton 48 E29
Child Okeford 9 C34
Childrey 21 C39
Child's Ercall 39 C32
Childswickham 30 E36
Childwall 48 D30
Childwick Green 32 G47
Chilgrove 12 C44
Chilham 15 B56
Chillaton 6 G20
Chillenden 15 B58
Chillerton 11 F40
Chillesford 35 C59
Chillingham 71 A36
Chillington Dev. 5 F23

Chillington Som. 8 C29
Chilmark 9 A35
Chilsworthy 6 E19
Chilthorne Domer 8 C31
Chilton Bkh. 31 G42
Chilton Drm 62 D38
Chilton Oxf. 21 C40
Chilton Candover 21 G41
Chilton Cantelo 8 B31
Chilton Foliat 21 D39
Chilton Lane 62 C39
Chilton Polden 19 G29
Chilton Street 34 D53
Chilton Trinity 8 A28
Chilvers Coton 41 F39
Chilwell 41 B41
Chilworth Ham. 11 C40
Chilworth Sry. 22 G46
Chineham 21 F42
Chingford 23 B49
Chinley 50 D36
Chinley Head 50 D36
Chinnor 22 A43
Chipchase Castle 70 F34
Chipnall 39 B33
Chippenham Cbs. 33 A52
Chippenham Wts. 20 D35
Chipperfield 22 A46
Chipping Hfs. 33 E49
Chipping Lan. 56 E32
Chipping Campden 30 E37
Chipping Ongar 23 A51
Chippinghill 34 G54
Chipping Norton 30 F39
Chipping Sodbury 20 C33
Chipping Warden 31 D41
Chipstable 7 C26
Chipstead Kent 23 F51
Chipstead Sry. 23 F48
Chirbury 38 F28
Chirk 38 B28
Chirk Green 38 B28
Chirmorie 67 F18
Chirnside 77 E34
Chirnsidebridge 77 E34
Chirton Wts. 20 F36
Chisbury 21 E38
Chiselborough 8 C30
Chiseldon 20 D37
Chiseldon Camp 20 D37
Chisholme 69 B30
Chislehampton 21 B41
Chislehurst 23 D50
Chislet 25 E58
Chiswellgreen 22 A47
Chisworth 49 C35
Chithurst 12 B44
Chittering 33 A50
Chitterne 20 G35
Chittlehamholt 6 C22
Chittlehampton 6 C22
Chittoe 20 E35
Chivelstone 5 G23
Chobham 22 E45
Choicelee 76 E33
Cholderton 21 G38
Cholesbury 22 A45
Chollerford 70 F35
Chollerton 70 F35
Cholsey 21 C41
Cholstrey 28 C30
Chop Gate 63 G41
Choppington 71 E38
Chopwell 62 A37
Chorley Che. 48 G31
Chorley Lan. 48 A31
Chorley Stf. 40 D36
Chorleywood 22 B46
Chorlton 49 G33
Choseley Farm 44 A53
Chrishall 33 E50
Chrisswell 73 C18
Christchurch Cbs. 43 F50
Christchurch Dor. 10 E37
Christian Malford 20 D35
Christleton 48 F30
Christmas Common 22 B43
Christon 19 F29
Christon Bank 71 A38
Christow 7 G24
Chudleigh 5 C24
Chudleigh Knighton 5 C24
Chulmleigh 6 D22
Chunal 50 C36
Church 56 G33
Churcham 29 G33
Church Aston 39 D33
Church Brampton 31 B43
Church Broughton 40 B38
Church Crookham 22 F43
Churchdown 29 G34
Church Eaton 40 D34
Churchend Avon 20 B33
Church End Bfd. 32 E47
Church End Cbs. 43 E49
Church End Cbs. 33 A49
Church End Esx. 33 D51
Church End Esx. 34 F53
Churchend Esx. 25 B56
Churchend Esx. 33 F52
Church End Hfs. 32 G47
Church End Lcn. 53 C50
Church End War. 40 F38
Church End War. 40 F38
Church End Wts. 20 D36
Church Enstone 30 F39
Church Fenton 58 F41
Church Green 7 F27
Church Gresley 40 D38
Church Houses 63 G42
Churchill Avon 19 F30
Churchill H.& W. 29 A35
Churchill H.& W. 29 A34

Churchill Oxf. 30 F38
Churchingford 8 C28
Church Knowle 9 F35
Church Langton 42 F43
Church Lawford 31 A40
Church Lawton 49 G34
Church Leigh 40 B36
Church Lench 30 C36
Church Norton 12 E44
Church Preen 38 F31
Church Pulverbatch 38 E30
Church Stoke 38 F28
Churchstanton 7 D27
Church Stowe 31 C42
Church Street 45 G60
Church Street 24 D53
Church Stretton 38 F30
Church Town Cum. 61 G30
Churchtown I.o.M. 54 D26
Churchtown Lan. 55 E30
Churchtown Mer. 48 A29
Church Village 18 C26
Church Warsop 51 F41
Churston Ferrers 5 E24
Churt 12 A44
Churton 48 G30
Churwell 57 F38
Chwilog 36 B20
Cilcain 47 F27
Cilcennin 26 B21
Cilfrew 18 A23
Cilfynydd 18 B26
Cilgerran 26 D17
Cilgwyn 27 E23
Ciliau-Aeron 26 C21
Cilmaengwyn 18 A23
Cilmalieu 79 E14
Cilmery 27 C26
Cilybebyll 18 A23
Cilycwm 27 D23
Cimla 18 B23
Cinderford 29 G32
Cinderhill 41 A41
Cippyn 26 D17
Cirencester 20 A36
Citadilla 62 G38
City Dulas 46 D20
Clabhach 78 E7
Clachaig 73 B17
Clachaig Hotel 79 E17
Clachan Hgh. 82 F11
Clachan Str. 72 E13
Clachan Str. 79 F14
Clachan Str. 79 J17
Clachan Tay. 80 D24
Clachan-a-Luib 88 L4
Clachaneasy 67 F19
Clachan of Campsie 74 C22
Clachan of Glendaruel 72 B15
Clachan-Seil 79 J13
Clachbreck 72 C13
Clachnabrain 81 D29
Clachtoll 86 F16
Clackmannan 75 A25
Clacton-on-Sea 35 G57
Cladich 79 H16
Claggan 79 F12
Claigan 82 D8
Clandown 19 F32
Clanfield Ham. 11 C42
Clanfield Oxf. 21 A38
Clannaborough 7 E23
Clanville 21 G39
Claonaig 72 E14
Clapham Bfd. 32 C46
Clapham N.Y. 56 C33
Clapham W.S. 12 D46
Clapham Hill 25 E57
Clappers 77 E35
Clappersgate 60 F29
Clapton 8 D30
Clapton-in-Gordano 19 D30
Clapton-on-the-Hill 30 G37
Clapworthy 6 C22
Clarach 36 G21
Clarbeston 16 B16
Clarbeston Road 16 B16
Clarborough 51 D43
Clare Sfk. 34 D53
Clarebrand 68 G23
Clarencefield 69 G26
Clarewood 71 G36
Clarilaw 70 B31
Clarkston 74 E21
Clashmore Hgh. 84 A23
Clashnessie 86 E16
Clathy 80 H25
Clatt 85 G31
Clatter 37 F26
Clatterford End 23 A51
Clattering Bridge 81 C32
Clatteringshaws 67 F21
Clatworthy 7 B26
Claughton Lan. 55 C31
Claughton Lan. 55 F31
Claughton Lan. 48 D29
Claverdon 30 B37
Claverham 19 E30
Clavering 33 E50
Claverley 39 F33
Claverton 20 E33
Claw Cross 6 D19
Clawdd-newydd 47 F27
Clawton 6 F19
Claxby 52 C47
Claxton Nfk. 45 E59
Claxton N.Y. 58 D42
Claybrooke Magna 41 G40
Claybrooke Parva 41 G40
Claycoton 31 A41
Clay Cross 51 F39

Claydon Oxf. 31 C40
Claydon Sfk. 35 C57
Claygate D.& G. 69 F29
Claygate Kent 14 C53
Claygate Sry. 22 E47
Clayhanger Dev. 7 C26
Clayhanger W.M. 40 E36
Claypole 42 A44
Clayton Stf. 40 A34
Clayton W.S. 13 C49
Clayton W.Y. 57 F37
Clayton-le-Moors 56 F33
Clayton-le-Woods 55 G31
Clayton West 50 A38
Clayworth 51 D43
Cleadale 78 B10
Cleadon 71 G39
Clearbrook 5 D21
Clearwell 19 A31
Cleasby 62 E38
Cleat 89 J30
Cleatlam 62 E37
Cleator 60 E26
Cleator Moor 60 E26
Cleckheaton 57 G37
Cleedownton 38 G31
Cleehill 28 A31
Clee St. Margaret 38 G31
Cleethorpes 53 B49
Cleeton St. Mary 29 A32
Cleeve Avon 19 E30
Cleeve Oxf. 21 C42
Cleeve Hill 29 F35
Cleeve Prior 30 D36
Cleghorn 74 F24
Clehonger 28 E30
Cleigh 79 H14
Cleish 75 A26
Cleland 74 E23
Clenchwarton 43 C51
Clent 29 A35
Cleobury Mortimer 29 A32
Cleobury North 39 G32
Cleongart 72 G12
Clerkhill 69 D28
Clerklands 70 A31
Clestrain 89 G29
Cleuchbrae 69 F26
Cleuch Head 70 C31
Cleuchside 69 F27
Clevancy 20 D36
Clevedon 19 D29
Cleveland Tontine Inn 62 G40
Cleveleys 55 E29
Cleverton 20 C35
Clewer 19 F30
Cley next the Sea 44 A56
Cliburn 61 D31
Cliddesden 21 G42
Cliffe Kent 24 D53
Cliffe N.Y. 62 E38
Cliffe N.Y. 58 F42
Cliff End 14 F54
Clifford H.& W. 28 D28
Clifford W.Y. 57 E40
Clifford Chambers 30 C37
Clifford's Mesne 29 F33
Cliffsend 25 E59
Clifton Avon 19 D31
Clifton Bfd. 32 E47
Clifton Cen. 80 G19
Clifton Cum. 61 D31
Clifton Dby. 40 A37
Clifton H.& W. 29 D34
Clifton Lan. 55 F30
Clifton Nor. 71 E38
Clifton Not. 41 B41
Clifton N.Y. 57 E37
Clifton Oxf. 31 E40
Clifton S.Y. 51 C41
Clifton Campville 40 D38
Clifton Hampden 21 B41
Clifton Reynes 32 C45
Clifton upon Dunsmore 31 A41
Clifton upon Teme 29 B33
Cliftonville 25 D59
Climping 12 D46
Climpy 75 E25
Clint 57 D38
Clintmains 76 G32
Clipiau 37 D24
Clippesby 45 D60
Clipsham 42 D45
Clipston Nmp. 42 G46
Clipston Not. 41 B42
Clitheroe 56 E33
Clive 38 C31
Clixby 52 B47
Clocaenog 47 G26
Clochan 85 C30
Clodock 28 F29
Cloford 20 G33
Clola 85 E35
Clophill 32 E46
Clopton Nmp. 42 G46
Clopton Sfk. 35 C58
Closeburn 68 D24
Closeburnmill 68 D25
Closworth 8 C31
Clothall 33 E48
Clotton 48 F31
Clough G.M. 49 B35
Clough Foot 56 G35
Cloughton 63 G46
Cloughton Newlands 63 G46
Clousta 89 G39
Clova Grm. 85 G30
Clova Tay. 81 C29
Clovelly 6 C19
Clovenfords 76 G30
Clovulin 79 D16
Clowne 51 E40
Clows Top 29 A33
Cloy 38 A29

Cloyntie 67 C19
Cluanach 78 J5
Cluanie Inn 83 H16
Cluanie Lo. 83 H16
Clugston 64 C19
Clun 38 G28
Clunbury 38 G29
Clune 84 G23
Clunes 79 B18
Clunes Lodge 80 D23
Clungunford 28 A29
Clunton 38 G29
Cluny Castle 80 A22
Clutton Avon 19 F32
Clutton Che. 48 G30
Clydach Gwe. 28 G28
Clydach W.G. 17 D22
Clydach Vale 18 B25
Clydebank 74 D20
Clyffe Pypard 20 D36
Clynder 73 B18
Clynnogfawr 46 G20
Clyro 28 D28
Clyst Honiton 7 F25
Clyst Hydon 7 E26
Clyst St. George 7 G25
Clyst St. Lawrence 7 E26
Clyst St. Mary 7 F25
Coad's Green 4 C18
Coal Aston 51 E39
Coalbrookdale 39 E32
Coalbrookvale 18 A27
Coalburn 74 G24
Coalcleugh 61 B34
Coaley 20 A33
Coalfell 61 A31
Coalhall 67 B20
Coalpit Heath 19 C32
Coalpit Hill 49 G34
Coal Pool 40 E36
Coalport 39 E32
Coalsnaughton 75 A25
Coaltown of Balgonie 75 A29
Coaltown of Wemyss 75 A29
Coalville 41 D40
Coast 86 J15
Coastley 70 G34
Coatbridge 74 D23
Coatdyke 74 D23
Coate Wts. 20 C37
Coate Wts. 20 D36
Coates Cbs. 43 F49
Coates Glo. 20 A35
Coates Lcn. 52 D45
Coatham 63 D41
Coatham Mundeville 62 E38
Cobbaton 6 C22
Coberley 29 G35
Cobham Kent 24 E52
Cobham Sry. 22 F47
Cobleland 74 A21
Cockayne 63 G42
Cockayne Hatley 33 D48
Cock Bridge 84 J28
Cockburnspath 76 C33
Cock Clarks 24 A54
Cockenzie 75 C29
Cockerham 55 D30
Cockermouth 60 C27
Cockfield Drm. 62 D37
Cockfield Sfk. 34 C55
Cockfosters 23 B48
Cocking 12 C44
Cockington 5 D24
Cocklake 19 G30
Cocklaw 70 F35
Cocklawfoot 70 B34
Cockley Cley 44 E53
Cockshutt 38 C30
Cockwood 7 G25
Coddenham 35 C57
Coddington 29 D33
Coddington Che. 48 G30
Coddington Not. 52 G44
Codford St. Mary 9 A35
Codford St. Peter 20 G35
Codicote 33 G48
Codmore Hill 12 B46
Codnor 41 A40
Codrington 20 D33
Codsall 40 E34
Codsall Wood 40 E34
Coedana 46 D20
Coed-ddôl 37 E23
Coedkernew 19 C28
Coedmawr 27 C26
Coed Morgan 28 G29
Coedpoeth 48 G28
Coedway 38 D29
Coed-y-paen 19 B29
Coed-yr-ynys 28 F27
Coed Ystrum-gwern 36 C21
Coelbren 27 G24
Coffinswell 5 D24
Cofton Hackett 30 A36
Cogan 18 D27
Cogenhoe 32 B44
Coggeshall 34 F54
Coggeshall Hamlet 34 F54
Coignafearn Lodge 84 H22
Coignafeuinternich 84 H23
Coilessan 81 J28
Coille Mhorgil 83 J16
Coillore 82 F9
Coity 18 C25
Colaboll 86 G21
Colan 3 B14
Colaton Raleigh 7 G26
Colbost 82 E8
Colburn 62 G37
Colbury 10 C39
Colby Cum. 61 D32

Colby I.o.M. 54 G24
Colby Nfk. 45 B58
Colchester 34 F56
Colcot 18 E27
Cold Ash 21 E41
Cold Ashby 31 A42
Cold Ashton 20 D33
Coldbackie 87 C22
Cold Brayfield 32 C45
Coldeast 5 C24
Colden Common 11 B40
Coldfair Green 35 B60
Coldham 43 E50
Cold Hanworth 52 D46
Coldharbour 22 G47
Cold Hatton 39 C32
Cold Hatton Heath 39 C32
Cold Hesledon 62 B40
Cold Higham 31 C42
Coldingham 77 D35
Cold Kirby 58 A41
Cold Norton 24 A54
Cold Overton 42 D44
Coldrain 75 A26
Coldred 15 C58
Coldridge 6 E22
Coldstream 77 G34
Coldwaltham 12 C46
Coldwells 85 F37
Cole 9 A32
Colebatch 38 G29
Colebrook 5 E21
Colebrooke 7 E23
Coleby Hum. 52 A44
Coleby Lcn. 52 F45
Coleford Dev. 7 E23
Coleford Glo. 28 G31
Coleford Som. 19 G32
Cole Green 33 G48
Cole Henley 21 F40
Colehill 10 D36
Coleman's Hatch 13 A50
Coleorton 41 D40
Colerne 20 D34
Colesbourne 30 G36
Coleshill Bkh. 22 B45
Coleshill Oxf. 21 B38
Coleshill War. 40 G38
Colgate 13 A48
Colgrain 73 B19
Colinsburgh 81 K30
Colinton 75 D28
Colintraive 72 C16
Colkirk 44 C55
Collacriech 81 A29
Collafirth 89 D39
Collaton St. Mary 5 D24
Collessie 81 J28
Colleton Mills 6 D22
Collier Row 23 B51
Collier's End 33 F49
Collier Street 14 C53
Collieston 85 G36
Collin 69 F26
Collingbourne Ducis 21 F38
Collingbourne Kingston 21 F38
Collingham Not. 52 F44
Collingham S.Y. 57 E39
Collington 29 B32
Collingtree 31 C43
Colliston 81 F32
Colliton 7 E26
Collyweston 42 E45
Colmonell 67 E17
Colmworth 32 C47
Colnabaichin 84 J28
Colnbrook 22 D46
Colne Cbs. 33 A49
Colne Lan. 56 E34
Colne Engaine 34 E54
Colney 45 E57
Colney Heath 23 A48
Colney Street 22 A47
Coln Rogers 20 A36
Coln St. Aldwyn 20 A37
Coln St. Dennis 30 G36
Colpy 85 F32
Colquhar 75 F29
Colsterdale 57 A37
Colsterworth 42 C45
Colston Bassett 42 B43
Coltishall 45 C58
Colton Cum. 55 A29
Colton Nfk. 45 D57
Colton N.Y. 58 E41
Colton Stf. 40 C36
Colvend 65 C24
Colvister 89 C41
Colwall 29 D33
Colwall Green 29 D33
Colwall Stone 29 D33
Colwell 70 F35
Colwich 40 C36
Colwick 41 A42
Colwinston 18 D25
Colworth 12 D45
Colwyn Bay 47 E24
Colyford 8 E28
Colyton 8 E28
Combe Brk. 21 E39
Combe Cnw. 6 D18
Combe H.& W. 28 B29
Combe Oxf. 31 G40
Combe Down 20 E33
Combe Florey 7 B27
Combe Hay 20 F33
Combeinteignhead 5 C25
Combe Martin 6 A21
Combe Moor 28 B29
Combe Raleigh 7 E27
Comberbach 49 E32
Comberton 33 C49

Combe St Nicholas

Combe St. Nicholas 8 C29
Combrook 30 C39
Combs Ford 34 C56
Combwich 19 G28
Comers 85 J32
Commins 38 C27
Commins Coch 37 E24
Commondale 63 E42
Commonmoor 4 D18
Commonside Bor. 69 C30
Commonside Dby. 40 A38
Compstall 49 C35
Compstonend 65 C22
Compton Brk. 21 C41
Compton Dev. 5 D24
Compton Ham. 11 B40
Compton Ham. 10 B39
Compton Sry. 22 G45
Compton W.S. 11 C43
Compton Abbas 9 C34
Compton Abdale 30 G36
Compton Bassett 20 D36
Compton Beauchamp 21 C38
Compton Bishop 19 E29
Compton Chamberlayne 10 B36
Compton Dando 19 E32
Compton Dundon 8 A30
Compton Martin 19 F31
Compton Pauncefoot 9 B32
Compton Valence 8 E31
Compton Verney 30 C39
Comrie Fife 75 B26
Comrie Tay. 80 H23
Conaglen House 79 D16
Conchra 72 B16
Conder Green 55 D30
Conderton 29 E35
Condicote 30 F37
Condorrat 74 C23
Condover 38 E30
Coneyhurst Common 12 B47
Coneysthorpe 58 B43
Coney Weston 34 A55
Congalton Mains 76 B31
Congash 84 G26
Congdons Shop 4 C18
Congerstone 41 E39
Congleton 49 F34
Congresbury 19 E30
Conicavel 84 D25
Coningsby 53 G48
Conington Cbs. 42 G47
Conington Cbs. 33 B49
Conisbrough 51 C41
Conisholme 53 C50
Coniston Cum. 60 G29
Coniston Hum. 59 F47
Coniston Cold 56 D35
Conistone 56 C35
Connah's Quay 48 F28
Connel 79 G15
Connel Park 68 B22
Connor Downs 2 E11
Conon Bridge 83 D21
Cononley 56 E35
Consall 40 A35
Consett 62 A37
Constable Burton 62 G37
Constantine 2 F13
Constantine Bay 3 A14
Contin 83 D20
Convinth 83 F21
Conwy 47 E23
Conyer 25 E55
Cooden 14 G53
Coodham 73 G19
Cookbury 6 E20
Cookham 22 C44
Cookham Dean 22 C44
Cookham Rise 22 C44
Cook Hill 30 C36
Cookley H.& W. 40 G34
Cookley Sfk. 35 A59
Cookley Green 21 B42
Cookridge 57 F38
Cooksbridge 13 C50
Coolham 12 B47
Cooling 24 D53
Cooling Street 24 D53
Coombe 3 C15
Coombe Bissett 10 B37
Coombe Hill 29 F34
Coombe Keynes 9 F34
Coombes 12 D47
Coopersale Common 23 A50
Cooper's Corner 23 G50
Cooper's Green 13 B50
Cootham 12 C46
Copdock 35 D57
Copford Green 34 F55
Copgrove 57 C39
Copister 89 E40
Cople 32 D47
Copley Drm. 62 D36
Copley G.M. 49 C35
Copmanthorpe 58 E41
Copp 55 F30
Coppathorne 6 E18
Coppenhall 40 D35
Copperhouse 2 E11
Copplestone 7 E23
Coppull 48 A31
Coppull Moor 48 A31
Copsale 12 B47
Copster Green 56 E33
Copston Magna 41 F41
Copt Heath 30 A37
Copt Hewick 57 B39
Copthorne 13 A49
Copt Oak 41 D40
Copythorne 10 C39
Corbridge 70 G35
Corby 42 G44

Corby Glen 42 C45
Cordach 81 A32
Cordorcan 67 F19
Coreley 29 A32
Corfe 8 C28
Corfe Castle 9 F35
Corfe Mullen 9 E35
Corgarff 84 J28
Corhampton 11 B42
Corley 41 G39
Corley Ash 40 G38
Corley Services 41 G39
Cornabus 78 K4
Cornforth 62 C39
Cornhill 85 D31
Cornhill-on-Tweed 77 G34
Cornhills 70 E35
Cornholme 56 G35
Cornish Hall End 33 E52
Cornquoy 89 G31
Cornriggs 62 B37
Cornsay 62 B37
Cornsay Colliery 62 B37
Cornwell 30 F38
Cornwood 5 E22
Cornworthy 5 E24
Corpach 79 C16
Corpusty 45 B57
Corra 72 D15
Corran Hgh. 83 J14
Corran Hgh. 79 D16
Corranbuie 72 D14
Corrany 54 E27
Corrie 72 F16
Corrie 72 F16
Corriearklet 80 J19
Corrie Common 69 E28
Corriecravie 66 A15
Corriedoo 68 E22
Corriemoillie 83 C19
Corrievorrie 84 G23
Corrimony 83 F19
Corringham Esx. 24 C53
Corringham Lcn. 52 C44
Corris 37 E23
Corris Uchaf 37 E23
Corrour Lodge 80 C20
Corrour Station 80 D19
Corry 82 G12
Corrygills 72 G16
Corrylach 72 G13
Corrymuckloch 80 G24
Corscombe 8 D31
Corsebank 68 B24
Corseclays 66 E16
Corsham 20 D34
Corsley 20 G34
Corsley Heath 20 G34
Corsliehill 74 D20
Corsock 68 F23
Corston Avon 19 E32
Corston Wts. 20 C35
Corstorphine 75 C27
Cortachy 81 E29
Corton Sfk. 45 F61
Corton Wts. 20 G35
Corton Denham 9 B32
Corwen 37 A26
Coryton Dev. 6 G20
Coryton Esx. 24 C53
Cosby 41 F41
Coseley 40 F35
Cosgrove 31 D43
Cosham 11 D42
Cosheston 16 D16
Coshieville 80 F23
Cossall 41 A40
Cossington Lei. 41 D42
Cossington Som. 19 G29
Costessey 45 D57
Costock 41 C41
Coston 42 C44
Cote 21 A39
Cote Brook 48 F31
Cotehill 61 A30
Cotes 41 C41
Cotesbach 41 G41
Cotgrave 41 B42
Cothall 85 H34
Cothelstone 7 B27
Cotheridge 29 C33
Cotherstone 62 E36
Cotleigh 8 D28
Coton Cbs. 33 C50
Coton Stf. 40 C34
Coton Stf. 40 B35
Coton in the Elms 40 D38
Cott 5 D23
Cottam Lan. 55 F30
Cottam Not. 52 E44
Cottartown 84 F26
Cottenham 33 B50
Cotterdale 61 G34
Cottered 33 F49
Cotterstock 42 F46
Cottesbrooke 31 A43
Cottesmore 42 D45
Cotteylands 7 D25
Cottingham Hum. 59 F46
Cottingham Nmp. 42 F44
Cottingley 57 F37
Cottisford 31 E41
Cotton 34 B56
Cotton End 32 D46
Cot-town 85 E34
Cotwall 39 D32
Couch's Mill 4 E17
Coughton H.& W. 28 F31
Coughton War. 30 B36
Coulaghailtro 72 D13
Coulags 83 E15
Coulderton 60 F25
Coull 85 J31
Coulport 73 B18

Coulsdon 23 F48
Coulston 20 F35
Coulter 75 G26
Coultershaw Bridge 12 C45
Coulton 58 B42
Cound 38 E31
Coundon Drm. 62 D38
Coundon W.M. 41 G39
Coundon Grange 62 D38
Countersett 56 A35
Countesthorpe 41 F41
Countisbury 7 A23
Coupar Angus 81 F28
Coupland Cum. 61 D33
Coupland Nor. 77 G35
Cour 72 F14
Courance 69 E26
Court-at-Street 15 D56
Courteenhall 31 C43
Courthill 81 E32
Courtsend 25 B56
Cousland 75 D29
Couslewood 13 A52
Coustonn 72 C16
Cove Dev. 7 D25
Cove Ham. 22 F44
Cove Hgh. 86 J14
Cove Ltn. 76 C33
Cove Str. 73 B18
Cove Bay 85 J35
Covehithe 45 G61
Coven 40 E35
Coveney 43 G50
Covenham St. Bartholomew 53 C49
Covenham St. Mary 53 C49
Coventry 30 A39
Coverack 2 G13
Coverham 57 A36
Covington Cbs. 32 A46
Covington Str. 75 G25
Cowan Bridge 56 B32
Cowbeech 13 C52
Cowbit 43 D48
Cowbridge Lcn. 43 A49
Cowbridge S.G. 18 D25
Cowden 23 G50
Cowdenbeath 75 A27
Cowdenburn 75 E28
Cowerslane 41 A39
Cowes 11 E40
Cowesby 57 A40
Cowfold 13 B48
Cowie Cen. 74 B24
Cowie Grm. 81 B34
Cowley Dev. 7 F25
Cowley G.L. 22 C46
Cowley Glo. 29 G35
Cowley Oxf. 21 A41
Cowling N.Y. 56 E35
Cowling N.Y. 57 A38
Cowlinge 34 C53
Cowpen 71 E38
Cowpen Bewley 62 D40
Cowplain 11 C43
Cowshill 61 B34
Cowstrandburn 75 A26
Cowthorpe 57 D40
Coxbank 39 A32
Coxford 44 C54
Coxhoe 62 C39
Coxley 19 G31
Coxwold 58 B41
Coychurch 18 D25
Coylton 67 B20
Coylumbridge 84 H25
Coytrahen 18 C24
Crabbs Cross 30 B36
Crabtree 13 B48
Crabtree Green 38 A29
Crackenthorpe 61 D32
Crackley 30 A38
Crackleybank 39 D33
Crackpot 62 G35
Cracoe 56 D35
Craddock 7 D26
Cradley H.& W. 29 D33
Cradley W.M. 40 G35
Crafthole 4 E19
Cragg 57 G36
Craggan Hgh. 84 G26
Craggan Str. 73 A18
Craggie 87 G24
Craghead 62 A38
Craibstone 85 H34
Craichie 81 F31
Craig Hgh. 83 E16
Craig Hgh. 82 C13
Craig Str. 72 C16
Craig Str. 77 B21
Craigandaive 72 B16
Craigbrack 73 A17
Craigcaffie 66 G16
Craig Castle 85 G30
Craigcefnparc 17 D22
Craigcleugh 69 E29
Craigdarroch D.& G. 68 D23
Craigdarroch Str. 68 C22
Craigdews 67 F21
Craig Douglas 69 A28
Craigearn 85 H33
Craigellachie 84 E28
Craigencross 66 G16
Craigendarroch 81 A29
Craigendoran 73 B19
Craigengillan 67 C20
Craigenrae 67 E18
Craigens Dyf. 16 D16
Craigens Str. 77 B21
Craigens Str. 78 H4
Craiggiecat 81 A34
Craighat 74 B20
Craighead 67 C18

Craighouse 78 H6
Craigie Str. 74 G20
Craigie Tay. 81 F27
Craigieburn 69 C27
Craigielaw 76 C30
Craiglemine 64 E20
Craigmaud 85 D34
Craigmill 74 A24
Craigmillar 75 C28
Craigmore 73 D17
Craignafeich 72 C15
Craignant 38 B28
Craigneil 67 E17
Craigneuk 74 E23
Craignure 79 G13
Craigo 81 D32
Craigoch 67 C18
Craigrothie 81 J29
Craigs D.& G. 69 F28
Craigs Str. 66 A12
Craigton Tay. 81 G31
Craigton Tay. 81 E29
Craigtown 87 C24
Craig-y-nos 27 G24
Craik 69 C29
Crail 81 K32
Crailing 70 A32
Crailinghall 70 A33
Craiselound 51 C43
Crambe 58 C43
Cramlington 71 F38
Cramond 75 C27
Cramond Bridge 75 C27
Cranage 49 F33
Cranberry 40 B34
Cranborne 10 C36
Cranbourne 22 D45
Cranbrook 14 D53
Crane Moor 51 B39
Cranfield 32 D45
Cranford St. Andrew 32 A45
Cranford St. John 32 A45
Cranham Esx. 23 C51
Cranham Glo. 29 G34
Crank 34 C31
Cranleigh 12 A46
Cranmore 19 G31
Cranna 85 D34
Cranoe 42 F43
Cransford 35 B59
Cranshaws 76 D32
Cranstal 54 C27
Cranstoun Riddel 75 D29
Crantock 2 B13
Cranwell 52 G46
Cranwich 44 F53
Cranworth 44 E55
Crapstone 5 D21
Crarae 72 A15
Crask Inn 86 F21
Crask of Aigas 83 E20
Craster 71 B38
Craswall 28 E28
Cratfield 35 A59
Crathes 81 A33
Crathie Grm. 81 A28
Crathie Hgh. 80 A21
Crathorne 62 F40
Craven Arms 38 G30
Craw 72 F14
Crawcrook 71 G37
Crawford Lan. 48 B30
Crawford Str. 68 A25
Crawfordjohn 68 A24
Crawick 68 B23
Crawley Ham. 11 A40
Crawley Oxf. 30 G39
Crawley W.S. 13 A48
Crawley Down 13 A49
Crawleyside 62 B35
Crawshawbooth 56 G34
Crawton 81 C34
Cray N.Y. 56 B35
Cray Pow. 27 F24
Cray Tay. 81 D27
Crayford 23 D51
Crayke 58 B41
Crays Hill 24 B53
Cray's Pond 21 C42
Creacombe 7 D24
Creagan 79 F15
Creaguaineach Lodge 80 D19
Creaton 31 A43
Creca 69 F28
Credenhill 28 D30
Crediton 7 E24
Creebank 67 F19
Creebridge 67 G20
Creech St. Michael 8 B28
Creed 3 D15
Creekmouth 23 C50
Creeside 67 E18
Creeting St. Mary 35 C57
Creeton 42 C46
Creetown 64 C20
Creggan Str. 72 E14
Creggans 79 K16
Cregneish 54 G24
Creg-ny-Baa 54 E26
Cregrina 28 C27
Creich 81 H29
Creigiau 18 D25
Cremyll 4 E20
Cressage 38 E31
Cresselly 16 D16
Cressing 34 F53
Cresswell Dyf. 16 D16
Cresswell Nor. 71 D38
Creswell Stf. 40 B35
Creswell 51 E41
Cretingham 35 B58
Cretshengan 72 D13
Crewe Che. 49 G32
Crewe Che. 48 G30
Crew Green 38 D29

Crewkerne 8 D30
Crianlarich 80 H19
Cribarth 27 C25
Cribyn 26 C21
Criccieth 36 B20
Crich 51 G39
Crichton 75 D29
Crichton Dean 76 D30
Crick Gwe. 19 B30
Crick Nmp. 31 A41
Crickadarn 27 D26
Cricket St. Thomas 8 D29
Crickheath 38 C28
Crickhowell 28 G28
Cricklade 20 B36
Cricklewood 23 C48
Cridling Stubbs 58 G41
Crieff 80 H24
Criggion 38 D28
Crigglestone 51 A39
Crimond 85 D36
Crimonmogate 85 D36
Crimplesham 44 E52
Crinaglack 83 E20
Crinan 72 A13
Crinan Ferry 72 A13
Crindledyke 74 E24
Cringleford 45 E57
Cripp's Corner 14 E53
Croabh Haven 79 K13
Crockenhill 23 E51
Crockernwell 7 F23
Crockerton 20 G34
Crocketford 68 F24
Crockey Hill 58 E42
Crockham Hill 23 F50
Crockhurst Street 23 G52
Crockleford Hill 34 F56
Croeserw 18 B24
Croesgoch 16 A14
Croes-gwyn 26 C20
Croes-lan 26 D19
Croesor 37 A22
Croesyceiliog 19 B29
Croes-y-mwyalch 19 B29
Croft Che. 49 C32
Croft Lcn. 53 F51
Croft Lei. 41 F41
Croftamie 74 B20
Crofthead 69 F29
Crofton 51 A39
Croft-on-Tees 62 F38
Crofts 68 F23
Crofts of Savoch 85 D36
Crogga 54 E25
Croggan 79 H13
Croglin 61 B31
Crogo 68 F23
Croick 86 J20
Croig 78 E9
Cromarty 84 C23
Crombie 75 B26
Cromdale 84 G26
Cromer Hfs. 33 F48
Cromer Nfk. 45 A58
Cromford 50 G38
Cromhall 19 B32
Cromore 88 E9
Cromra 80 A21
Cromwell 51 F43
Cronberry 68 A22
Crondall 22 G43
Cronton 48 D30
Crook Cum. 70 F31
Crook Cum. 61 G30
Crook Drm. 62 C37
Crooke 48 B31
Crookedholm 74 G20
Crookham 77 G35
Crookham Village 22 F43
Crookhaugh 69 A27
Crook Inn 69 A27
Crooklands 55 A31
Crook of Alves 84 C27
Crook of Devon 75 A26
Crookston 74 D21
Crookston Ho. 76 E30
Crookston North Mains 76 E30
Cropredy 31 D40
Cropston 41 D41
Cropthorne 29 D35
Cropton 58 A43
Cropwell Bishop 41 B42
Cropwell Butler 41 B42
Crosbie 73 E18
Crosby Cum. 60 C26
Crosby Hum. 52 A44
Crosby I.o.M. 54 F25
Crosby Mer. 48 C28
Crosby Garrett 61 F33
Crosby Ravensworth 61 E32
Crosby Villa 60 C26
Croscombe 19 G31
Crosemere 38 C30
Cross W.I. 88 A10
Crossaig 72 E14
Crossapoll 78 F5
Cross Ash 28 G30
Cross-at-Hand 14 C53
Crossbost 88 E9
Crosscanonby 60 C26
Crossdale Street 45 B58
Crossford D.& G. 68 E24
Crossford Fife 75 B26
Crossford Str. 74 F24
Cross Foxes Inn 37 D23
Crossgatehall 75 D29
Crossgates Fife 75 B27
Crossgates Pow. 27 B26
Crossgill 55 C31
Cross Green Sfk. 34 C54
Cross Green Sfk. 34 C55
Crossgreen Shr. 38 D30
Cross Hands Dyf. 17 C21
Cross Hands Dyf. 16 C16
Crosshands Str. 74 G20

Crosshill Fife 75 A27
Crosshill Str. 67 C19
Crosshills 57 E36
Crosshouse 73 G19
Cross Houses 38 E31
Crossings 70 F31
Cross in Hand 13 B51
Cross Inn Dyf. 26 B21
Cross Inn Dyf. 26 C19
Cross Inn M.G. 18 C26
Crosskeys Gwe. 19 B28
Cross Keys Nfk. 43 C51
Cross Keys Wts. 20 D34
Crosskirk 87 A26
Cross Lane 38 E27
Crosslanes Clw. 38 A29
Cross Lanes Cnw. 2 F12
Cross Lanes N.Y. 58 C41
Crosslee Bor. 69 B29
Crosslee Str. 74 D20
Crossmichael 68 G23
Crossmoor 55 F30
Cross o' th' hands 40 A38
Crossroads Grm. 85 J31
Crossroads Str. 74 G20
Cross Street 35 A57
Crossway H.& W. 29 E32
Crossway Pow. 27 C26
Crossway Green 29 B34
Crossways 9 F33
Crossways 28 G31
Crosswell 16 A17
Crosswoodhill 75 E26
Crosthwaite Green 61 G30
Croston 48 A30
Crostwick 45 D58
Crouch 23 F52
Croughton 31 E41
Crovie 85 C34
Crow 10 D37
Crowan 2 E12
Crowborough 13 A51
Crowcombe 7 B27
Crowden 50 C36
Crowdhill 11 C40
Crowdicote 50 F37
Crow Edge 50 B37
Crowell 22 A43
Crow Hill 29 F32
Crowfield 35 C57
Crowhurst E.S. 14 F53
Crowhurst Sry. 23 G49
Crowhurst Lane End 23 G49
Crowland 43 D48
Crowlas 2 E11
Crowle Hum. 51 A43
Crowle H.& W. 29 C35
Crowmarsh Gifford 21 C42
Crownhill 4 E21
Crownpits 22 G45
Crownthorpe 44 E56
Crowntown 2 E12
Crows 64 C19
Crowthorne 22 E44
Crowton 48 E31
Croxall 40 D37
Croxby 52 C47
Croxdale 62 C38
Croxden 40 B36
Croxley Green 22 B46
Croxton Cbs. 33 B48
Croxton Hum. 52 A46
Croxton Nfk. 44 G54
Croxton Stf. 39 B33
Croxton Kerrial 42 C44
Croy Hgh. 84 E23
Croy Str. 74 C23
Croy Cunningham 74 B21
Croyde 6 B22
Croydon Cbs. 33 D49
Croydon Sry. 23 E49
Crubenbeg 80 A22
Crubenmore Lodge 80 A22
Cruckmeole 38 E30
Cruckton 38 D30
Cruden Bay 85 F36
Crudgington 39 D32
Crudwell 20 B35
Crug 28 A27
Crugybar 17 A22
Crulivig 88 D7
Crumlin Gwe. 19 B28
Crundale Dyf. 16 C15
Crundale Kent 15 C56
Crux Easton 21 F40
Crwbin 17 C20
Cryers Hill 22 B44
Crymych 16 A17
Crynant 18 A23
Crynfryn 26 B21
Cuaig 82 D13
Cubbington 30 B39
Cubert 2 C13
Cublington 32 F44
Cuckfield 13 B49
Cucklington 9 B33
Cuckney 51 E41
Cuddesdon 21 A42
Cuddington Bkh. 31 G43
Cuddington Che. 49 E32
Cuddington Heath 38 A30
Cuddy Hill 55 F30
Cudham 23 F50
Cudworth Som. 8 C29
Cudworth S.Y. 51 B39
Cuerdley Cross 48 D31
Cuffley 23 A49
Cuil 67 G20
Culag 73 A19
Culbo 84 C22
Culbokie 84 D22
Culburnie 83 E20
Culcabock 84 E22
Culcharry 84 E24
Culcheth 49 C32
Culcronchie 67 G21

Culdrain 85 F31
Culford 34 A54
Culgaith 61 D32
Culham 21 B41
Culindrach 72 E15
Culkein 86 E16
Culkerton 20 B35
Cullen *Grm.* 85 C31
Cullercoats 71 F39
Cullerlie 85 J33
Cullicudden 84 C22
Culligran 83 E19
Cullingworth 57 F36
Cullivoe 89 B41
Culloch 80 J23
Cullompton 7 E26
Culmaily 87 J24
Culmalzie 64 C19
Culmington 38 G30
Culmstock 7 D27
Culnacraig 86 H16
Culnaknock 82 C11
Culquhirk 64 C20
Culrain 86 J21
Culross 75 B25
Culroy 67 B19
Culscadden 64 D20
Culshabbin 64 C20
Culswick 89 H38
Cults *D.& G.* 64 D20
Cults *Grm.* 85 J34
Culverthorpe 42 A46
Culworth 31 D41
Cumberhead 74 G23
Cumbernauld 74 C23
Cumber's Bank 38 B30
Cumberworth 53 E51
Cuminestown 85 E34
Cumledge 76 E33
Cummersdale 60 A29
Cummertrees 69 G27
Cummingstown 84 C27
Cumnock 67 B21
Cumnor 21 A40
Cumrew 61 A31
Cumwhinton 61 A30
Cumwhitton 61 A31
Cundall 57 B40
Cunninghamhead 73 F19
Cunningsburgh 89 J40
Cupar 81 J29
Curbar 50 E38
Curborough 40 D37
Curbridge *Ham.* 11 C41
Curbridge *Oxf.* 21 A39
Curdridge 11 C41
Curdworth 40 F37
Curland 8 C28
Curload 8 B29
Curridge 21 D40
Currie 75 D27
Curry Mallet 8 B29
Curry Rivel 8 B29
Curtisden Green 14 C53
Cury 2 F12
Cusop 28 D28
Cutcloy 64 E20
Cutcombe 7 B25
Cuthill 75 C29
Cutiau 37 D22
Cutnall Green 29 B34
Cutsdean 30 E36
Cutsyke 57 G40
Cutthorpe 51 E39
Cuxham 21 B42
Cuxton 24 E53
Cuxwold 52 B47
Cwm *Clw.* 47 E26
Cwm *Gwe.* 18 A27
Cwmafan 18 B23
Cwmaman 18 B26
Cwmann 26 D21
Cwmbach *Dyf.* 17 B18
Cwmbâch *M.G.* 18 A26
Cwmbelan 37 G25
Cwmbrân 19 B28
Cwmcarn 19 B28
Cwmcarvan 19 A30
Cwm Cewydd 37 D24
Cwmcoy 26 D18
Cwm Crawnon 28 G27
Cwmdare 18 A25
Cwmdu *Dyf.* 17 A22
Cwmdu *Pow.* 28 F27
Cwmdu *W.G.* 17 E22
Cwmduad 17 A19
Cwmdwr 27 E23
Cwmfelin 18 A26
Cwmfelin Boeth 16 C17
Cwmfelinfach 18 B27
Cwmfelin Mynach 17 B18
Cwmffrwd 17 C20
Cwmgors 27 G23
Cwmllynfell 27 G23
Cwmorgan 17 A18
Cwm Owen Inn 27 D26
Cwmparc 18 B25
Cwmpengraig 17 A19
Cwm Penmachno 37 A23
Cwmrhos 28 F27
Cwmsychpant 26 D20
Cwmtillery 19 A28
Cwmtwrch-isaf 27 G23
Cwmtwrch-uchaf 27 G23
Cwm-y-glo 46 F21
Cwmyoy 28 F29
Cwmystwyth 27 A23
Cwrt 37 E22
Cwrt-newydd 26 D20
Cyffylliog 47 G26
Cymer 18 B24
Cymmer 18 B26
Cynghordy 27 E24
Cynheidre 17 D20

Cynwyd 37 A26
Cynwyl Elfed 17 B19

D

Daccombe 5 D25
Dacre *Cum.* 61 D30
Dacre *N.Y.* 57 C37
Dacre Banks 57 C37
Daddry Shield 61 C34
Dadford 31 E42
Dadlington 41 F40
Dafen 17 D21
Dagenham 23 C51
Daggons 10 C37
Daglingworth 20 A35
Dagnall 32 G45
Dailly 67 C18
Dairsie 81 J30
Daisy Hill 49 B33
Dalavich 79 J15
Dalbeattie 68 G24
Dalbeg 88 C8
Dalblair 81 C31
Dalbog 81 C31
Dalbreck 87 G23
Dalby *I.o.M.* 54 F24
Dalby *Lcn.* 53 E50
Dalchenna 79 K16
Dalchork 86 G21
Dalchreichart 83 H18
Dalchruin 80 J23
Dalderby 53 F48
Dale *Dyf.* 16 D14
Dale *She.* 89 G37
Dale Abbey 41 B40
Dalehouse 63 E43
Dalelia 79 D13
Dalfibble 69 E26
Dalgarven 73 F18
Dalgety Bay 75 B27
Dalgig 67 B21
Dalginross 80 H23
Dalguise 80 F25
Dalhalvaig 87 C24
Dalham 34 B53
Daligan 73 B19
Dalinlongart 73 B17
Daljarrock 67 E17
Dalkeith 75 D29
Dallas 84 D27
Dalleagles 67 B21
Dallinghoo 35 C58
Dallington *E.S.* 13 C52
Dallington *Nmp.* 31 B43
Dally 66 G15
Dalmahoy 75 D27
Dalmally 79 H17
Dalmary 74 A21
Dalmellington 67 C20
Dalmeny 75 C27
Dalmigavie 84 H23
Dalmigavie Lodge 84 G23
Dalmore *Hgh.* 84 C22
Dalmore *W.I.* 88 C8
Dalmuir 74 C20
Dalmunzie House 80 C26
Dalnacardoch Lodge 80 C23
Dalnahaitnach 84 H24
Dalnaspidal Lodge 80 C22
Dalnatrat 79 E15
Dalnavie 84 B22
Dalnawillan Lodge 87 D26
Dalness 79 E17
Dalnessie 87 G22
Dalpeddar 68 C24
Dalqueich 80 K26
Dalquhairn 67 D19
Dalreavoch 87 H23
Dalry 73 F18
Dalrymple 67 B19
Dalserf 74 E23
Dalsetter 89 C41
Dalshangan 67 E21
Dalston 60 B29
Dalswinton 68 E25
Dalton *D.& G.* 69 F27
Dalton *Lan.* 48 B30
Dalton *Nor.* 61 A35
Dalton *Nor.* 71 F37
Dalton *N.Y.* 57 B40
Dalton *N.Y.* 62 F37
Dalton *S.Y.* 51 C40
Dalton in Furness 54 C28
Dalton le Dale 62 B40
Dalton-on-Tees 62 F38
Dalton Piercy 62 C40
Daltot 72 B13
Dalvadie 64 C16
Dalveich 80 H22
Dalvennan 67 B19
Dalvina Lodge 87 D22
Dalwhat 68 D23
Dalwhinnie 80 B22
Dalwood 8 D28
Damerham 10 C37
Damgate 45 E60
Damnaglaur 64 E17
Damside 75 F27
Danbury 24 A53
Danby 63 F43
Danby Wiske 62 G39
Dandaleith 84 E28
Danderhall 75 D29
Danebridge 49 F35
Danehill 13 B50
Danskine 76 D31
Darby's Corner 10 E36
Daren-felen 28 G28
Darenth 23 D51

Daresbury 48 D31
Darfield 51 B40
Dargate 25 E56
Darite 4 D18
Darlaston 40 F35
Darley 57 D38
Darley Bridge 50 F38
Darley Head 57 D37
Darlingscott 30 D38
Darlington 62 E38
Darliston 38 B31
Darlton 51 E43
Darnall 51 D39
Darnconner 67 A21
Darngarroch 68 G22
Darnick 76 G31
Darowen 37 E24
Darra 85 E33
Darras Hall 71 F37
Darrington 57 G40
Darsham 35 A60
Dartford 23 D51
Dartington 5 D23
Dartmeet 5 C22
Dartmouth 5 E24
Darton 51 B39
Darvel 74 G21
Darwen 56 G33
Datchet 22 D45
Datchworth 33 G48
Datchworth Green 33 G48
Daubhill 49 B33
Dauntsey 20 C35
Dauntsey Green 20 C35
Dava 84 F26
Davenham 49 E32
Davenport Green 49 D34
Daventry 31 B41
Davidson's Mains 75 C28
Davidstow 4 B17
Davington 69 C28
Daviot *Grm.* 85 G33
Daviot *Hgh.* 84 H23
Davoch of Grange 85 D30
Davyhulme 49 C33
Daw Cross 57 D38
Dawley 39 E32
Dawlish 5 C25
Dawlish Warren 5 C25
Dawn 47 E24
Daws Heath 24 C54
Daylesford 30 F38
Deadwater 70 D32
Deadwaters 74 F23
Deal 15 B59
Dean *Cum.* 60 D26
Dean *Dev.* 5 D23
Dean *Dor.* 9 C35
Deanburnhaugh 69 B29
Deane *G.M.* 49 B32
Deane *Ham.* 21 F41
Dean Hill 49 G33
Deanich Lodge 83 A19
Dean Prior 5 D23
Deanscales 60 D26
Deanshanger 31 E43
Deanston 80 K23
Dean Street 14 B53
Dearham 60 C26
Debate 69 E28
Debden 33 E51
Debenham 35 B57
Dechmont 75 C26
Deddington 31 E40
Dedham 34 E56
Deene 42 F45
Deenethorpe 42 F45
Deepcar 50 C38
Deepdale *Cum.* 56 A33
Deepdale *N.Y.* 56 B34
Deephole 69 B28
Deeping Gate 42 E47
Deeping St. James 42 E47
Deeping St. Nicholas 43 D48
Deerhurst 29 F34
Defford 29 D35
Defynnog 27 F25
Deganwy 47 E23
Deighton *N.Y.* 62 F39
Deighton *N.Y.* 58 E42
Deiniolen 46 F21
Delabole 4 B16
Delamere 48 F31
Delliefure 84 F26
Dell Lodge 84 H26
Delnadamph Lodge 84 J28
Delph 49 B35
Dembleby 42 B46
Denaby 51 C40
Denaby Main 51 C40
Denbie Mains 69 F27
Denbigh 47 F26
Denbury 5 D24
Denby 41 A39
Denby Dale 50 B38
Denchworth 21 B39
Denford 32 A45
Dengie 25 A55
Denham *Bkh.* 22 C46
Denham *Sfk.* 34 B53
Denham *Sfk.* 35 A57
Denhead 85 D35
Denholm 70 B31
Denholme 57 F36
Denholme Gate 57 F36
Denio 36 B19
Denmead 11 C42
Den Moss 87 E27
Dennington 35 B58
Denny 74 B24
Dennyloanhead 74 C24
Denshaw 49 A35
Denside 81 A34
Densole 15 C58

Denston 34 C53
Denstone 40 A37
Dent 56 A33
Denton *Cbs.* 42 G47
Denton *Drm.* 62 E38
Denton *E.S.* 13 D50
Denton *G.M.* 49 C35
Denton *Kent* 15 C58
Denton *Lcn.* 42 B44
Denton *Nfk.* 45 G58
Denton *Nmp.* 32 C44
Denton *N.Y.* 57 E37
Denton *Oxf.* 21 A41
Denver 44 E52
Denwick 71 B38
Deopham 44 E56
Deopham Green 44 F56
Deptford 10 A36
Derby 41 B39
Derbyhaven 54 G25
Dergoals 64 C18
Deri 18 A27
Derringstone 15 C58
Derry Hill 20 D35
Derrythorpe 52 B44
Dersingham 44 B52
Dervaig 78 E10
Derwen 47 G26
Derwenlas 37 F23
Desborough 42 G43
Desford 41 E40
Detchant 77 G36
Detling 14 B53
Deuxhill 39 G32
Devauden 19 B30
Devil's Bridge 27 A23
Deviock 4 E19
Devizes 20 E36
Devonport 4 E20
Devonside 75 A25
Devoran 2 E13
Dewartown 75 D29
Dewlish 9 E33
Dewsbury 57 G38
Dhoon 54 E27
Diabaig 82 C13
Dial Post 12 C47
Dibden 11 D40
Dibden Purlieu 11 D40
Dickleburgh 45 G57
Dickstree 69 G29
Didbrook 30 E36
Didcot 21 B41
Diddington 32 B47
Diddlebury 38 G31
Didley 28 E30
Didling 12 C44
Didmarton 20 C34
Didworthy 5 D22
Digby 52 G46
Digg 82 C10
Diggle 50 B36
Digswell 33 G48
Dihewyd 26 C20
Dilham 45 C59
Dilhorne 40 A35
Dilston 70 G35
Dilton Marsh 20 G34
Dilwyn 28 C30
Dinas *Dyf.* 16 A16
Dinas *Dyf.* 17 A18
Dinas *Gwy.* 46 G20
Dinas *Gwy.* 36 B18
Dinas Powys 18 D27
Dinder 19 G31
Dinedor 28 E31
Dingestow 28 G30
Dingle *Mer.* 48 D29
Dingleton 76 G31
Dingley 42 G43
Dingwall 83 D21
Dinlabyre 70 D31
Dinley 69 D30
Dinnans 64 D20
Dinnet 81 A30
Dinnington *Som.* 8 C30
Dinnington *S.Y.* 51 D41
Dinnington *T.& W.* 71 F38
Dinorwic 46 F21
Dinsdale 62 E39
Dinton *Bkh.* 31 G43
Dinton *Wts.* 10 A36
Dinvin 64 C16
Dinwoodiegreen 69 E27
Dippen 72 G13
Dippin 66 A16
Dipple 67 C17
Diptford 5 C40
Dipton 62 A37
Dirleton 76 B31
Dirt Pot 61 B34
Discoed 28 B28
Diseworth 41 C40
Dishforth 57 B39
Disley 49 D35
Diss 45 G57
Distington 60 D26
Ditcheat 9 A32
Ditchingham 45 F59
Ditchling 13 C49
Ditherington 38 D31
Dittisham 5 E24
Ditton *Che.* 48 D30
Ditton *Kent* 14 B53
Ditton Priors 39 G32
Divach 83 G20
Dixton 28 G31
Dobcross 49 B35
Dobwalls 4 D18
Doccombe 7 G23
Dochfour House 84 F22
Dochgarroch 84 E22
Docking 44 B53

Docklow 28 C31
Dockray 60 D29
Dodburn 69 C30
Doddenham 29 C33
Doddinghurst 23 B51
Doddington *Cbs.* 43 F49
Doddington *Kent* 14 B53
Doddington *Lcn.* 52 E45
Doddington *Nor.* 77 G35
Doddington *Shr.* 29 A32
Doddiscombsleigh 7 G24
Dodford 31 B42
Dodington 20 C33
Dodington Ash 20 D33
Dodleston 48 F29
Dodside 74 E20
Dodworth 51 B39
Doe Lea 51 F40
Dogdyke 53 G48
Dogmersfield 22 F43
Dog Village 7 F25
Dolanog 37 D26
Dolau *Pow.* 27 B26
Dolau *Pow.* 28 B27
Dolaucothi 27 D22
Dolbenmaen 36 A21
Dolfach 27 A25
Dolfor 38 G27
Dolgarrog 47 F23
Dolgellau 37 D23
Dolgoch 37 E22
Dol-gran 17 A20
Dolhelfa 27 A25
Dollar 75 A25
Dollarbeg 75 A25
Dollwen 37 G22
Dolphin 47 E27
Dolphinholme 55 D31
Dolphinton 75 F27
Dolton 6 D21
Dol-wen 47 E24
Dolwyd 47 E24
Dolwyddelan 47 G23
Dol-y-bont 37 G22
Dol-y-gaer 27 G26
Dolygarn 27 A26
Doncaster 51 B41
Donhead St. Andrew 9 B35
Donhead St. Mary 9 B35
Donibristle 75 B27
Doniford 7 A26
Donington *Lcn.* 43 B48
Donington *Shr.* 40 E34
Donington on Bain 53 D48
Donington South Ing 43 B48
Donisthorpe 41 D39
Donklewyood 70 E33
Donnington *Brk.* 21 E40
Donnington *Glo.* 30 F37
Donnington *Shr.* 39 D33
Donnington *W.S.* 12 D44
Donyatt 8 C29
Doonfoot 67 B19
Dorback 84 E37
Dorchester *Dor.* 9 E32
Dorchester *Oxf.* 21 B41
Dordon 40 E38
Dore 51 D39
Dores 84 F22
Dorking 22 F47
Dorlin House 79 C12
Dormans Land 23 G50
Dormanstown 63 D41
Dormington 28 D31
Dornal 67 F18
Dorney 22 D45
Dornie 83 G14
Dornoch 84 A24
Dornock 69 G28
Dorrery 87 C26
Dorridge 30 A37
Dorrington *Lcn.* 52 G46
Dorrington *Shr.* 38 E30
Dorsington 30 D37
Dorstone 28 D29
Dorton 31 G42
Dosthill 40 E38
Dottery 8 E30
Doublebois 4 D17
Dougarie 72 G14
Doughton 20 B34
Douglas *I.o.M.* 54 F26
Douglas *Str.* 74 G24
Douglastown 81 F30
Douglas Water 74 G24
Doulang 67 D18
Doulting 19 G32
Dounby 89 E28
Doune *Cen.* 80 K23
Doune *Hgh.* 86 H20
Dounepark 67 D17
Dounie 86 J21
Dounreay 87 B25
Dousland 5 D21
Dove Holes 50 E36
Dovenby 60 C26
Dover 15 C59
Dovercourt 35 E58
Doverdale 29 B34
Doveridge 40 B37
Doversgreen 23 G48
Dowally 80 F26
Dowbridge 55 F30
Dowdeswell 30 G36
Dowhill 67 C18
Dowlais 18 A26
Dowland 6 D21
Dowles 29 A33
Dowlish Wake 8 C29
Down Ampney 20 B36
Downcraig Ferry 73 E17
Downderry 4 E19
Downe 23 F50
Downend *Avon* 19 D32
Downend *I.o.W.* 11 F41

Downfield *Cbs.* 33 A52
Downfield *Tay.* 81 G29
Downgate 4 C19
Downham *Esx.* 24 B53
Downham *Lan.* 56 E33
Downham *Nor.* 77 G34
Downham Market 44 E52
Down Hatherley 29 F34
Downhead 19 G32
Downholland Cross 48 B29
Downholme 62 G37
Downies 81 A35
Down St. Mary 7 E23
Downside 22 F47
Down Thomas 5 E21
Downton *Ham.* 10 E38
Downton *Wts.* 10 B37
Dowsby 42 C47
Doynton 20 D33
Draffan 74 F23
Dragley Beck 54 C28
Drakemyre 73 E18
Drake's Boughton 29 D35
Drannandow 67 F19
Draughton *Nmp.* 31 A43
Draughton *N.Y.* 57 D36
Drax 58 G42
Draycott *Dby.* 41 B40
Draycott *Glo.* 30 E37
Draycott *Som.* 19 F30
Draycott in the Clay 40 C37
Draycott in the Moors 40 A35
Drayford 7 D23
Drayton *Lcn.* 43 B48
Drayton *Lei.* 42 F44
Drayton *Nfk.* 45 D57
Drayton *Oxf.* 31 D40
Drayton *Oxf.* 21 B40
Drayton *Som.* 8 B30
Drayton Bassett 40 E37
Drayton Beauchamp 32 G45
Drayton Parslow 32 F44
Drayton St. Leonard 21 B42
Drebley 57 D36
Dreemskerry 54 E27
Drefach *Dyf.* 17 C21
Drefach *Dyf.* 17 A19
Drefach *Dyf.* 26 D21
Dreghorn 73 G19
Drellingore 15 C58
Drem 76 C31
Drewsteignton 7 F23
Driby 53 E49
Driffield 20 B36
Drigg 60 G26
Drighlington 57 G38
Drimnin 79 E11
Drimpton 8 D30
Drimsdale 88 O3
Drimvore 72 A14
Drinkstone 34 B55
Drinkstone Green 34 B55
Drochil 75 F27
Drointon 40 C36
Droitwich 29 B34
Dron 81 J27
Dronfield 51 E39
Dronfield Woodhouse 51 E39
Drongan 67 B20
Drovers' Arms 27 D25
Droxford 11 C42
Droylsden 49 C35
Druid 37 A26
Druimarbin 79 C16
Druimavuic 79 F16
Druimdhu 83 D17
Druimdrishaig 72 C13
Druimavuic 79 B12
Druimindarroch 79 B12
Drum *Str.* 72 C15
Drumachloy 72 D16
Drumbeg 86 E17
Drumblade 85 E31
Drumbuie 82 F13
Drumburgh 60 A28
Drumburn 68 G25
Drumchapel 74 C21
Drumchardine 83 E21
Drumclog 74 G22
Drumcoltran 68 G24
Drumcroy 83 F20
Drumelzier 75 G27
Drumfearn 82 H12
Drumgask 80 A22
Drumguish 80 A23
Drumhead 81 A32
Drumjohn 67 D21
Drum Kilavie 66 B13
Drumlanrig Castle 68 D24
Drumlasie 85 J32
Drumlemble 66 B12
Drumlithie 81 B33
Drummore *D.& G.* 68 F24
Drummore *D.& G.* 64 E17
Drummore *D.& G.* 65 D22
Drummuckloch 65 C21
Drummuir Castle 84 E29
Drumnadrochit 83 G21
Drumnagorrach 85 D31
Drumochter Lodge 80 C22
Drumore 66 A13
Drumpail 67 G18
Drumpark 68 F24
Drumrash 68 F22
Drumrunie 86 H17
Drums 85 G35
Drumshang 67 B18
Drumshinnoch 68 D24
Drumstinchall 65 C24
Drumtochty Castle 81 B32
Drumuie 82 E10
Drumuillie 84 H25
Drumvaich 80 K22
Drumwalt 64 C19
Drumwhirn 68 E23

Drybeck 61 E32
Drybridge *Grm.* 85 C30
Drybridge *Str.* 73 G19
Drybrook 29 G32
Dryburgh 76 G31
Dryden 69 A30
Dry Doddington 42 A44
Dry Drayton 33 B49
Dryfesdale Gate 69 E27
Dryhope 69 A28
Drymen 74 B20
Drymuir 85 E35
Drynoch 82 F10
Duartmore Bridge 86 E17
Dubford 85 C33
Dubhchladach 72 D14
Duchally 86 G19
Duck Bay 73 B19
Duck End 33 F52
Duckington 48 G30
Ducklington 21 A39
Dudbridge 20 A34
Duddingston 75 C28
Duddington 42 E45
Duddleswell 13 B50
Duddo 77 F35
Duddon 48 F31
Dudleston 38 B29
Dudleston Heath 38 B29
Dudley *T.& W.* 71 F38
Dudley *W.M.* 40 G35
Dudley Hill 57 F37
Duffield 41 A39
Dufftown 84 F29
Dufton 61 D32
Duggleby 58 C44
Duiar 84 F27
Duirinish 82 F13
Duisky 79 C16
Dukestown 28 G27
Dukinfield 49 C35
Dulcote 19 G31
Dulford 7 E26
Dull 80 F24
Dullatur 74 C23
Dullingham 33 C52
Dulnain Bridge 84 G25
Duloe 4 E18
Dulsie 84 E25
Dulverton 7 C25
Dumbarton 74 C20
Dumbleton 30 E36
Dumcrieff 69 C26
Dumfin 73 B19
Dumfries 68 F25
Dumgoyne 74 B21
Dummer 21 G41
Dun 81 D32
Dunalastair 80 E23
Dunan *Hgh.* 82 G11
Dunan *Str.* 73 C17
Dunans 72 A16
Dunball 19 G29
Dunbar 76 C32
Dunbeath 87 F27
Dunblane 80 K23
Dunbog 81 J28
Duncanston *Grm.* 85 G31
Duncanston *Hgh.* 83 D21
Dun Carloway 88 C7
Dunchurch 31 A40
Duncote 31 C42
Duncow 68 E25
Duncton 12 C45
Dundas 75 C27
Dundee 81 G30
Dundee Airport 81 H29
Dundon 8 A30
Dundonald *Str.* 73 G19
Dundonnell *Hgh.* 83 A16
Dundonnell House 83 A17
Dundraw 60 B28
Dundreggan 83 H19
Dundrennan 65 D23
Dundry 19 E31
Dunduff *Fife* 75 A26
Dunduff *Str.* 67 B18
Dunearn 75 B28
Dunecht 85 J33
Dunfermline 75 B26
Dunford Bridge 50 B37
Dungavel 74 G22
Dunglass 76 C33
Dungworth 50 D38
Dunham on the Hill 48 E30
Dunham-on-Trent 52 E44
Dunham Town 49 D33
Dunham Woodhouses 49 D33
Dunholme 52 E46
Dunino 81 J31
Dunipace 74 B24
Dunkeld 80 F26
Dunkerton 20 F33
Dunkeswell 7 E27
Dunkeswick 57 E39
Dunkirk 15 B56
Dunlappie 81 D31
Dunley 29 B33
Dunlop 74 F20
Dunmaglass Lodge 83 G21
Dunmere 4 D16
Dunmore *Cen.* 74 B24
Dunmore *Str.* 72 D13
Dunnet 89 K28
Dunnichen 81 F31
Dunning 80 J26
Dunnington *Hum.* 59 D47
Dunnington *N.Y.* 58 D42
Dunnington *War.* 30 C36
Dunnockshaw 56 G34
Dunoon 73 C17
Dunragit 64 C17

Dunrostan 72 B13
Duns 76 E33
Dunsby 42 C47
Dunscore 68 E24
Dunscroft 51 B42
Dunsdale 63 E42
Dunsfold 12 A46
Dunsford 7 G24
Dunshelt 81 J28
Dunsley 63 E44
Dunsmore 22 A44
Dunsop Bridge 56 D32
Dunstable 32 F45
Dunstall 40 C37
Dunstan 71 B38
Dunster 7 A25
Duns Tew 31 F40
Dunston *Lcn.* 52 F46
Dunston *Nfk.* 45 D58
Dunston *Stf.* 40 D35
Dunston *T.& W.* 71 G38
Dunstone 5 C23
Dunsville 51 B42
Dunswell 59 F46
Dunsyre 75 F26
Dunterley 70 E34
Dunterton 4 C19
Duntisbourne Abbots 20 A35
Duntish 9 D32
Duntocher 74 C20
Dunton *Bfd.* 33 D48
Dunton *Bkh.* 32 F44
Dunton *Nfk.* 44 B54
Dunton Bassett 41 F41
Dunton Green 23 F51
Dunure 67 B18
Dunvant 17 E21
Dunvegan 82 E8
Dunwich 35 A60
Dupin 66 F16
Durdar 61 A30
Durham 62 B38
Durisdeer 68 C24
Durisdeermill 68 C24
Durleigh 8 A28
Durley *Ham.* 11 C41
Durley *Wts.* 21 E38
Durnamuck 86 J16
Durness 86 B20
Durno 85 G33
Durran 87 B27
Durrington *W.S.* 12 D47
Durrington *Wts.* 20 G37
Dursley 20 B33
Durston 8 B28
Durweston 9 D34
Duston 31 B43
Duthill 84 G25
Duthlas 28 A28
Dutton 48 E31
Duxford 33 D50
Dwygyfylchi 47 E23
Dwyran 46 F20
Dyce 85 H34
Dye House 61 A35
Dyfatty 17 D20
Dyffryn 18 B24
Dyffryn Ardudwy 36 C21
Dyffryn-Castell 37 G23
Dyffryn Cellwen 27 G24
Dyke *Grm.* 84 D25
Dyke *Lcn.* 42 C47
Dykehead *Bor.* 69 A26
Dykehead *Cen.* 74 A21
Dykehead *Str.* 74 E24
Dykehead *Str.* 74 G22
Dykehead *Tay.* 81 D29
Dykends 81 E28
Dylife 37 F24
Dymchurch 15 E57
Dymock 29 E33
Dyrham 20 D33
Dysart *Fife* 75 A29
Dyserth 47 E26

E

Eagland Hill 55 E30
Eagle 52 F44
Eaglescliffe 62 E40
Eaglesfield *Cum.* 60 D26
Eaglesfield *D.& G.* 69 F28
Eaglesham 74 E21
Eaglethorpe 42 F46
Eagley 49 A33
Ealand 51 A43
Eals 61 A32
Eamont Bridge 61 D31
Earby 56 E35
Earcroft 56 G32
Eardington 39 F33
Eardisland 28 C30
Eardisley 28 D29
Earith 33 A49
Earle 70 A35
Earley 22 D43
Earlish 82 C9
Earls Barton 32 B44
Earls Colne 34 F54
Earls Croome 29 D34
Earlsdon 30 A39
Earlsferry 76 A30
Earlsford 85 F34
Earl Shilton 41 F40
Earl Soham 35 B58
Earl Sterndale 50 F36
Earlston 76 G31
Earl Stonham 35 C57
Earlswood *Sry.* 23 G48

Earlswood *War.* 30 A37
Earlswood Common 19 B30
Earnley 12 E44
Earsdon 71 F39
Earsham 45 G59
Earswick 58 D42
Eartham 12 D45
Earthcott Green 19 C32
Easby *N.Y.* 62 F37
Easby *N.Y.* 63 F41
Eascairt 72 E14
Easdale 79 J13
Easebourne 12 B44
Easenhall 31 A40
Eashing 22 G45
Easington *Cle.* 63 E43
Easington *Drm.* 62 B40
Easington *Hum.* 53 A50
Easington *Nor.* 77 G37
Easington Colliery 62 B40
Easington Lane 62 B39
Easingwold 58 C41
Easole Street 15 B58
Eassie and Nevay 81 F29
East Aberthaw 18 E26
East Allington 5 F23
East Anstey 7 C24
East Appleton 62 G38
East Ashling 12 D44
East Ayton 59 A45
East Barkwith 52 D47
East Barming 14 B53
East Barnby 63 E44
East Barnet 23 B48
East Barns 76 C33
East Barsham 44 B55
East Beckham 45 A57
East Bedfont 22 D46
East Bergholt 34 E56
East Bierley 57 G37
East Bilney 44 D55
East Blatchington 13 D50
East Boldon 71 G39
East Boldre 10 D39
East Bolton 71 B37
Eastbourne 13 E52
East Bradenham 44 E55
East Brent 19 F29
East Bridgford 41 A42
East Buckland 6 B22
East Budleigh 7 G26
Eastburn *Hum.* 59 D45
Eastburn *W.Y.* 57 E36
East Burrafirth 89 G39
Eastbury *Brk.* 21 D39
Eastbury *G.L.* 22 B46
East Butterwick 52 B44
Eastby 57 D36
East Calder 75 D26
East Carleton 45 E57
East Carlton *Hum.* 59 F48
East Carlton *Nmp.* 42 G44
East Chaldon 9 F33
East Challow 21 C39
East Charleton 5 F23
East Chelborough 8 D31
East Chiltington 13 C49
East Chinnock 8 C30
East Chisenbury 20 F37
Eastchurch 25 D55
East Clandon 22 F46
East Claydon 31 F43
East Clyne 87 H24
East Coker 8 C31
Eastcombe 20 A34
East Cote *Cum.* 60 A27
Eastcote *G.L.* 22 C47
Eastcote *W.M.* 30 A37
Eastcott *Cnw.* 6 D18
Eastcott *Wts.* 20 F36
East Cottingwith 58 E43
Eastcourt 20 B35
East Cowes 11 E41
East Cowick 58 G42
East Cowton 62 F39
East Cranmore 19 G32
East Darlochan 66 A12
Eastdean *E.S.* 13 E51
East Dean *Ham.* 10 B38
East Dean *W.S.* 12 C45
East Dereham 44 D55
East Down 6 A21
East Drayton 51 E43
Eastend *Esx.* 25 B55
East End *Ham.* 21 E40
East End *Ham.* 10 E39
Eastend *Str.* 75 G25
Easter Balmoral 81 A28
Easter Buckieburn 74 B23
Easter Calcots 84 C28
Easter Compton 19 C31
Easter Grey 20 C34
Easter Fearn 84 A22
Eastergate 12 D45
Easter Hatton Mains 75 D27
Easterhouse 74 D22
Easter Howgate 75 D28
Easter Lednathie 81 C28
Easter Pencaitland 76 D30
Easter Quarff 89 J40
Easter Skeld 89 H39
Easterton 20 F36
Easterton 68 A24
East Farleigh 14 B53
East Farndon 42 G43
East Ferry 52 C44
Eastfield *N.Y.* 59 A46
Eastfield *Str.* 74 E24
Eastfield *Str.* 75 G26
East Flatt 74 E22
East Galdenoch 64 C17
East Garston 21 D39
Eastgate *Drm.* 62 C35
Eastgate *Lcn.* 42 C47

Eastgate *Nfk.* 45 C57
East Goscote 41 D42
East Grafton 21 E38
East Grimstead 10 B38
East Grinstead 13 A50
East Guldeford 14 E55
East Haddon 31 B42
East Hagbourne 21 C41
East Halton 52 A47
Eastham 48 D29
Eastham Ferry 48 D29
East Hanney 21 B40
East Hanningfield 24 A53
East Hardwick 51 A40
East Harling 44 G55
East Harlsey 62 G40
East Harptree 19 F31
East Harting 11 C43
East Hatley 33 C48
East Hauxwell 62 G37
East Haven 81 G31
Eastheath 22 E44
East Heckington 42 A47
East Hedleyhope 62 B37
East Hendred 21 C40
East Heslerton 59 B45
East Hoathly 13 C51
East Holme 9 F34
Easthope 38 F31
East Horndon 24 C52
East Horrington 19 G31
East Horsley 22 F46
East Horton 77 G36
East Hyde 32 G47
East Ilsley 21 C40
Eastington *Glo.* 30 G37
Eastington *Glo.* 20 A33
East Keal 53 F49
East Kennett 20 E37
East Keswick 57 E39
East Kilbride 74 E22
East Kirkby 53 F49
East Knighton 9 F34
East Knowstone 7 C24
East Knoyle 9 A34
East Lambrook 8 C30
Eastlands 68 F24
East Langdon 15 C59
East Langton 42 F43
East Langwell 87 H23
East Lavant 12 D45
East Lavington 12 C45
East Layton 62 F37
Eastleach Martin 21 A38
Eastleach Turville 20 A37
East Leake 41 C41
East Learmouth 77 G34
Eastleigh *Dev.* 6 C20
Eastleigh *Ham.* 11 C40
East Lexham 44 D54
Eastling 14 B55
East Linton 76 C31
East Liss 11 B43
East Looe 4 E18
East Lound 51 C43
East Lulworth 9 F34
East Lutton 59 C45
East Malling 14 B53
East Marden 12 C44
East Markham 51 E43
East Marton 56 D35
East Meon 11 B42
East Mere 7 D25
East Mersea 34 G56
East Midlands Airport 41 C40
East Morden 9 E35
East Morriston 76 F32
East Morton 57 E36
Eastnor 29 E33
East Norton 42 E43
East Oakley 21 F41
Eastoft 52 A44
East Ogwell 5 C24
Eastoke 11 E43
Easton *Cbs.* 32 A47
Easton *Cum.* 69 F30
Easton *Cum.* 60 A28
Easton *Dev.* 7 G23
Easton *Dor.* 8 G31
Easton *Ham.* 11 A41
Easton *I.o.W.* 10 F39
Easton *Lcn.* 42 C45
Easton *Nfk.* 45 D57
Easton *Sfk.* 35 C58
Easton *Som.* 19 G31
Easton Grey 20 C34
Easton-in-Gordano 19 D31
Easton Maudit 32 C44
Easton on the Hill 42 E46
Easton Royal 21 E38
East Orchard 9 C34
East Ord 77 E35
East Peckham 23 G52
East Pennar 16 D15
East Pennard 8 A31
East Plean 74 B24
East Portlemouth 5 G23
East Prawle 5 G23
East Preston 12 D46
East Putford 6 D19
East Quantoxhead 7 A27
East Rainham 24 E54
East Rainton 62 B39
East Ravendale 53 C48
East Raynham 44 C54
Eastrea 43 F48
East Retford 51 D43
East Rhidorroch Lodge 86 J18

Eastriggs 69 G28
East Rigton 57 E39
Eastrington 58 G43
East Rounton 62 F40
East Row 63 E44
East Rudham 44 C54
East Runton 45 A57
East Ruston 45 C59
Eastry 15 B59
East Saltoun 76 D30
East Scrafton 57 A36
East Shefford 21 D39
East Sleekburn 71 E38
East Somerton 45 C60
East Stockwith 51 C43
East Stoke *Dor.* 9 F34
East Stoke *Not.* 42 A43
East Stour 9 B33
East Stourmouth 25 E58
East Stratton 21 G41
East Studdal 15 C59
East Suisnish 82 F11
East Taphouse 4 D17
East-the-Water 6 C20
East Thirston 71 D37
East Tilbury 24 D52
East Tisted 11 A43
East Trewick 71 F37
East Tuddenham 44 D56
East Tytherley 10 B38
East Tytherton 20 D35
Eastville 53 G50
East Walton 44 D53
East Wellow 10 B39
East Wemyss 75 A29
East Whitburn 75 D25
Eastwick 33 G50
East Williamston 16 D17
East Winch 44 D52
East Wittering 11 E43
East Witton 57 A37
Eastwood *Esx.* 24 C54
Eastwood *Not.* 41 A40
East Woodburn 70 E35
East Woodhay 21 E40
East Worldham 11 A43
East Worlington 7 D23
East Wretham 44 F55
East Yell 89 D41
Eathorpe 30 B39
Eaton *Che.* 49 F34
Eaton *Che.* 48 F31
Eaton *Lei.* 42 C43
Eaton *Nfk.* 45 E58
Eaton *Not.* 51 E43
Eaton *Shr.* 38 G29
Eaton Bishop 28 E30
Eaton Bray 32 F45
Eaton Constantine 38 E31
Eaton Hastings 21 B38
Eaton Socon 32 C47
Eaton upon Tern 39 C32
Ebberston 58 A44
Ebbesborne Wake 9 B35
Ebbw Vale 18 A27
Ebchester 62 A36
Ebford 7 G25
Ebley 20 A34
Ebrington 30 E37
Ecchinswell 21 E41
Ecclaw 76 D33
Ecclefechan 69 F27
Eccles *Bor.* 76 F33
Eccles *G.M.* 49 C33
Eccles *Kent* 24 E53
Ecclesfield 51 C39
Eccleshall *Stf.* 40 C34
Eccleshall *S.Y.* 51 C39
Eccleshill 57 F37
Ecclesmachan 75 C26
Eccles Road 44 F56
Eccleston *Che.* 48 F30
Eccleston *Lan.* 48 A31
Eccleston *Mer.* 48 C30
Eccleston Green 48 A31
Eccup 57 E38
Echt 85 J33
Eckford 70 A33
Eckington *Dby.* 51 E40
Eckington *H.& W.* 29 D35
Ecton 32 B44
Edale 50 D37
Eday Airport 89 D31
Edderside 60 B27
Edderton 84 A23
Eddington *Brk.* 21 E39
Eddington *Kent* 25 E57
Eddleston 75 F28
Edenbridge 23 G50
Edenfield 49 A34
Edenhall 61 C31
Edenham 42 C46
Edensor 50 F38
Edentaggart 73 A19
Edenthorpe 51 B42
Edern 36 B18
Edgarley 8 A31
Edgbaston 40 G36
Edgcott 31 F42
Edgcumbe 2 E13
Edge *Glo.* 20 A34
Edge *Shr.* 38 E30
Edgefield 44 B56
Edgefield Green 45 B57
Edge Green 48 G30
Edge Hill 48 C29
Edgerston 70 B32
Edgeside 56 G34
Edginswell 5 D24
Edgmond 39 D33
Edgton 38 G29
Edgware 22 B47
Edgworth 49 A33

Edinample 80 H21
Edinbane 82 D9
Edinburgh 75 C28
Edinburgh Airport 75 C27
Edingale 40 D38
Edingham 68 G24
Edingley 51 G42
Edingthorpe 45 B59
Edington *Bor.* 77 E34
Edington *Som.* 19 G30
Edington *Wts.* 20 F35
Edington Burtle 19 G29
Edith Weston 42 E45
Edlesborough 32 G45
Edlingham 71 C37
Edlington 53 E48
Edmondbyers 62 B36
Edmondsham 10 C36
Edmondsley 62 B38
Edmondthorpe 42 D44
Edmonstone 89 E31
Edmonton 23 B48
Ednam 76 G33
Ednaston 40 A37
Edney Common 24 A53
Edradynate 80 E24
Edrom 77 E34
Edstaston 38 B31
Edvin Ralph 29 C32
Edwalton 41 B42
Edwardstone 34 D55
Edwinsford 17 A22
Edwinstowe 51 F42
Edworth 33 D48
Edwyn Ralph 29 C32
Edzell 81 D31
Efail Isaf 18 C26
Efailnewydd 36 B19
Efail-rhyd 38 C27
Efailwen 16 B17
Efenechtyd 47 G27
Effingham 22 F47
Effirth 89 G39
Egdean 12 B46
Egerton *G.M.* 49 A33
Egerton *Kent* 14 C55
Eggbuckland 5 E21
Eggesford 6 D22
Eggington 32 F45
Egginton 40 C38
Egglescliffe 62 E40
Eggleston 62 D35
Egham 22 D46
Egleton *H.& W.* 29 D32
Egleton *Lei.* 42 E44
Eglingham 71 B37
Egloshayle 3 A15
Egloskerry 4 B18
Eglwysbach 47 E24
Eglwys Cross 38 A30
Eglwysfach 37 F22
Eglwyswrw 16 A17
Egmanton 51 F43
Egremont *Cum.* 60 E26
Egremont *Mer.* 48 C29
Egton 63 F44
Egton Bridge 63 F44
Eight Ash Green 34 F55
Eilanreach 83 H14
Eileanach Lodge 83 C21
Eisingrug 37 B22
Eisteddfa-Gurig 37 G24
Elan Village 27 B25
Elberton 19 C31
Elburton 5 E21
Eldernell 43 F49
Eldersfield 29 E34
Elderslie 74 D20
Eldon 62 D38
Eldrick 67 E18
Eldroth 56 C33
Eldwick 57 E37
Elford *Nor.* 77 G37
Elford *Stf.* 40 D37
Elgin 84 C28
Elgol 82 H11
Elham 15 C57
Elibank 75 G29
Elie 76 A30
Elilaw 70 C35
Elim 46 E19
Eling 10 C39
Eliock 68 C23
Elishader 82 C11
Elishaw 70 D34
Elkesley 51 E42
Elkstone 29 G35
Elland 57 G36
Ellary 72 C13
Ellastone 40 A37
Ellel 55 D30
Ellemford 76 D33
Ellemford Bridge 76 E33
Ellenborough 60 C26
Ellenhall 40 C34
Ellen's Green 12 A47
Ellerbeck 62 G40
Eller Beck Bridge 63 G44
Ellerby *Hum.* 59 F47
Ellerby *N.Y.* 63 E43
Ellerdine Heath 39 C32
Ellerker 59 G45
Ellerton 58 F43
Ellesborough 22 A44
Ellesmere 38 B30
Ellesmere Port 48 E30
Ellingham *Ham.* 10 D37
Ellingham *Nfk.* 45 F59
Ellingham *Nor.* 71 A37
Ellingstring 57 A37
Ellington *Cbs.* 32 A47
Ellington *Nor.* 71 D38
Ellisfield 21 G42
Ellister 78 K3
Ellistown 41 D40
Ellon 85 F35
Ellonby 61 C30
Elloughton 59 G45
Elm 43 E50
Elmbridge 29 B34

Fornham St Martin

Elmdon Esx. 33 E50
Elmdon W.M. 40 G37
Elmers End 23 E49
Elmesthorpe 41 F40
Elmfield 11 E42
Elmley Castle 29 D35
Elmley Lovett 29 B34
Elmore 29 G33
Elmscott 6 C18
Elmsett 34 D56
Elmstead Market 34 F56
Elmstone 25 E58
Elmstone Hardwicke 29 F35
Elmswell Hum. 59 D45
Elmswell Sfk. 34 B55
Elmton 51 E41
Elphin Hgh. 86 G18
Elphinstone 75 D29
Elrick 85 J34
Elrig 64 D19
Elrigbeag 79 J17
Elrington 70 G34
Elsdon 70 D35
Elsecar 51 C39
Elsenham 33 F51
Elsfield 31 G41
Elsham 52 A46
Elsing 44 D56
Elslack 56 E35
Elson 38 B29
Elsrickle 75 F26
Elstead 22 G45
Elsted 12 C44
Elston 42 A43
Elstone 6 D22
Elstow 32 D46
Elstree 22 B47
Elstronwick 59 F48
Elswick 55 F30
Elsworth 33 B49
Elterwater 60 F29
Eltisley 33 B48
Elton Cbs. 42 F46
Elton Che. 48 E30
Elton Cle. 62 E40
Elton Dby. 50 F38
Elton H.& W. 28 A30
Elton Not. 42 B43
Elvanfoot 68 B25
Elvaston 41 B40
Elveden 44 G54
Elvington Kent 15 B58
Elvington N.Y. 58 E42
Elwick Cle. 62 C40
Elwick Nor. 77 G37
Elworth 49 F33
Elworthy 7 B26
Ely Cbs. 43 G51
Ely S.G. 18 D27
Emberton 32 D44
Embleton Cum. 60 C27
Embleton Nor. 71 A38
Embo 87 J24
Emborough 19 F32
Embo Street 87 J24
Embsay 57 D36
Emery Down 10 D38
Emley 50 A38
Emneth 43 E50
Empingham 42 E45
Empshott 11 A43
Emsworth 11 D43
Enaclete 88 E7
Enborne 21 E40
Enderby 41 F41
Endmoor 55 A31
Endon 49 G35
Endon Bank 49 G35
Enfield G.L. 23 B49
Enford 20 F37
Engine Common 19 C32
England's Gate 28 C31
Englefield 21 D42
Englefield Green 22 D45
English Bicknor 28 G31
Englishcombe 20 E33
Enham Alamein 21 G39
Enmore 8 A28
Ennerdale Bridge 60 E26
Enoch 68 C24
Enochdu 80 D26
Ensdon 38 D30
Enson 40 C35
Enstone 30 F39
Enterkinfoot 68 C24
Enville 40 G34
Eochar 88 N3
Eoligarry 88 S3
Eoropie 88 A11
Epney 29 G33
Epperstone 41 A42
Epping 23 A50
Epping Green 23 A50
Epping Upland 23 A50
Eppleby 62 E37
Epsom 22 E47
Epwell 30 D39
Epworth 51 B43
Erbistock 38 A29
Erbusaig 82 G13
Erchless Castle 83 E20
Erdington 40 F37
Eredine 79 K15
Eriboll 86 C20
Ericstane 69 B26
Eridge Green 13 A51
Eriff 67 C21
Erines 72 C14
Eriswell 34 A53
Erith 23 D51
Erlestoke 20 F35
Ermington 5 E22
Erminzie 68 G23
Erpingham 45 B57
Errocht 79 B17
Errogie 83 G21
Errol 81 H28
Erryrys 48 G28
Ersary 88 T3
Erskine 74 C20
Ervie 66 G15
Erwarton 35 E58
Eryholme 62 F39
Escart 72 D14
Escomb 62 C37
Escrick 58 E42
Esgair 26 B21
Esgairgeiliog 37 E23
Esgyryn 47 E24
Esh 62 B37
Esher 22 E47
Esholt 57 E37
Eshott 71 D38
Eshton 56 D35
Esh Winning 62 B37
Eskadale 83 F20
Eskbank 75 D29
Eskdale Green 60 F27
Eskdalemuir 69 D28
Eske 59 E46
Eskham 53 C49
Esknish 78 H5
Espershields 62 A35
Esprick 55 F30
Essendine 42 D46
Essendon 23 A48
Essich 84 F22
Essington 40 E35
Eston 63 E41
Etal 77 G35
Etchilhampton 20 E36
Etchingham 14 E53
Etchinghill Kent 15 D57
Etchinghill Stf. 40 D36
Etling Green 44 D56
Eton 22 D45
Eton Wick 22 D45
Ettersgill 61 D34
Ettington 30 D38
Etton Cbs. 42 E47
Etton Hum. 59 E45
Ettrick 69 B28
Ettrickbridge 69 A29
Ettrickhill 69 B28
Etwall 40 B38
Euston 34 A54
Euxton 48 A31
Evanton 84 C22
Evedon 42 A46
Evelaw 76 E32
Evelix 87 J23
Evenjobb 28 B28
Evenley 31 E41
Evenlode 30 F38
Evenwood 62 D37
Evenwood Gate 62 D37
Everbay 89 E32
Evercreech 9 A32
Everdon 31 C41
Everingham 58 E44
Everleigh 21 F38
Everley 59 A45
Eversholt 32 E45
Evershot 8 D31
Eversley 22 E43
Eversley Cross 22 E43
Everton Bfd. 33 C48
Everton Ham. 10 E38
Everton Mer. 48 C29
Everton Not. 51 C42
Evertown 69 F29
Evesham 30 D36
Evie 89 E29
Evington 41 E42
Ewden Village 50 C38
Ewell 23 E48
Ewelme 21 B42
Ewen 20 B36
Ewenny 18 D25
Ewerby 42 A47
Ewesley 71 D36
Ewhurst E.S. 14 E53
Ewhurst Sry. 22 G46
Ewhurst Green 12 A46
Ewloe 48 F28
Ewshot 22 G44
Ewyas Harold 28 F29
Exbourne 6 E21
Exbury 11 D40
Exebridge 7 C25
Exelby 57 A38
Exeter 7 F25
Exeter Airport 7 F26
Exeter Services 7 F25
Exford 7 B24
Exhall War. 41 G39
Exhall War. 30 C37
Exminster 7 G25
Exmouth 7 G26
Exnaboe 89 L40
Exning 33 B52
Exton Dev. 7 G25
Exton Ham. 11 B42
Exton Lei. 42 D45
Exton Som. 7 B25
Eyam 50 E38
Eydon 31 C41
Eye Cbs. 43 E48
Eye Sfk. 35 A57
Eye Green 43 E48
Eyemouth 77 D35
Eyeworth 33 D48
Eyhorne Street 14 B54
Eyke 35 C59
Eynesbury 32 C47
Eynort 82 G9
Eynsford 23 E51
Eynsham 21 A40
Eype 8 E30
Eyre Hgh. 82 D10
Eyre Hgh. 82 F11
Eythorne 15 C58
Eyton Clw. 38 A29
Eyton H.& W. 28 B30
Eyton upon the Weald Moors 39 D32

F

Faccombe 21 F39
Faceby 62 F40
Fachwen 46 F21
Facit 49 A34
Faddiley 48 G31
Fadmoor 58 A42
Fail 67 A20
Failand 19 D31
Failford 67 A20
Failsworth 49 B35
Fairbourne 37 D22
Fairburn 57 G40
Fairfield Dby. 50 E36
Fairfield H.& W. 29 A35
Fairfield H.& W. 30 D36
Fairfield Mer. 48 C29
Fairford 20 A37
Fair Isle Airport 89 C37
Fairlie 73 E18
Fairlight 14 F54
Fairlight Cove 14 F54
Fairmile 7 F26
Fair Oak Ham. 11 C40
Fair Oak Ham. 21 E41
Fairseat 24 E52
Fairstead 45 C58
Fair Thorn 23 G52
Fairwarp 13 B50
Fairy Cross 6 C20
Fairyhill 17 E20
Fakenham 44 C55
Fala 76 D30
Falahill 75 E29
Falcon 29 E32
Falcon Inn 63 G45
Faldingworth 52 D46
Faldonside 76 G31
Falfield 19 B32
Falkenham 35 E58
Falkirk 74 B24
Falkland 81 K28
Falla 70 B33
Fallford 69 E28
Fallgate 51 F39
Fallin 74 A24
Fallowfield 70 G35
Falmer 13 D49
Falmouth 3 E13
Falnash 69 C29
Falsgrave 59 A46
Falstone 70 E33
Fanagmore 86 D17
Fangdale Beck 63 G41
Fangfoss 58 D43
Fanmore 78 F10
Fannich Lodge 83 C18
Fans 76 F32
Farcet 43 F48
Far Cotton 31 C43
Far Duckmanton 51 E40
Fareham 11 D41
Farewell 40 D36
Far Forest 29 A33
Faringdon 21 B38
Farington 55 G31
Farlam 61 A31
Farleigh 20 F34
Farleigh Avon 19 E30
Farleigh Sry. 23 E49
Farleigh Wallop 21 G42
Farleton 55 A31
Farley Stf. 40 A36
Farley Wts. 10 B38
Farlington 58 C42
Farlow 39 G32
Farmborough 19 E32
Farmers 27 D22
Farmington 30 G37
Far Moor G.M. 48 B31
Farmoor Oxf. 21 A40
Farmtown 85 D31
Farnborough Brk. 21 C40
Farnborough Ham. 22 F44
Farnborough War. 31 D40
Farnborough Green 22 F44
Farncombe 22 G45
Farndon Che. 48 G30
Farndon Not. 51 G43
Farnell 81 E32
Farnham Dor. 9 C35
Farnham Esx. 33 F50
Farnham N.Y. 57 C39
Farnham Sfk. 35 B59
Farnham Sry. 22 G44
Farnham Common 22 C45
Farnham Royal 22 C45
Farnhill 57 E36
Farningham 23 E51
Farnley 57 E38
Farnley Tyas 50 A37
Farnsfield 51 G42
Farnworth Che. 48 D31
Farnworth G.M. 49 B33
Farr Hgh. 84 F22
Farr Hgh. 84 J24
Farr Hgh. 87 B23
Farringdon Dev. 7 F26
Farringdon Ham. 11 A43
Farrington Gurney 19 F32
Far Sawrey 60 G29
Farsley 57 F38
Farthing Corner Services 24 E54
Farthinghoe 31 E41
Farthingloe 15 C58
Farthingstone 31 C42
Farway 7 F27
Fascadale Hgh. 79 C11
Fascadale Str. 72 B14
Faslane 73 B18
Fasnakyle 83 G19
Fasque 81 C32
Fassfern 79 C16
Fatfield 62 A39
Faugh 61 A31
Fauldhouse 75 D25
Faulkbourne 34 G53
Faulkland 20 F33
Faversham 25 E56
Fawfieldhead 50 F36
Fawkham Green 23 E51
Fawler 30 G39
Fawley Bkh. 22 C43
Fawley Brk. 21 C39
Fawley Ham. 11 D40
Faxfleet 58 G44
Faygate 13 A48
Fazakerley 48 C29
Fazeley 40 E38
Fearby 57 A37
Fearnan 80 F23
Fearnbeg 82 D13
Fearnhead 49 C32
Fearn Lodge 84 A22
Fearnmore 82 C13
Featherstone Stf. 40 E35
Featherstone W.Y. 57 G40
Fechan 73 E18
Feckenham 30 B36
Feering 34 F54
Feetham 62 G35
Feizor 56 C33
Felbridge 13 A49
Felbrigg 45 B58
Felcourt 23 G49
Felindre Dyf. 26 C21
Felindre Pow. 38 G27
Felindre W.G. 17 D22
Felin-fach 27 E26
Felin-foel 17 D21
Felingwm Uchaf 17 B21
Felixkirk 57 A40
Felixstowe 35 E59
Felixstoweferry 35 E59
Felkington 77 F35
Fell End 70 E34
Felling 71 G38
Fell Side 60 C29
Felmersham 32 C45
Felmingham 45 C58
Felpham 12 E45
Felsham 34 C55
Felsted 33 F52
Feltham 22 D46
Felthorpe 45 D57
Felton Avon 19 E31
Felton H.& W. 28 D31
Felton Nor. 71 C37
Feltwell 44 F53
Feltwell Anchor 44 G52
Fenay Bridge 50 A37
Fence 56 F34
Fence Houses 62 A39
Fen Ditton 33 B50
Fen Drayton 33 B49
Feniscowles 56 G32
Feniton 7 F27
Fenny Bentley 50 G37
Fenny Compton 31 C40
Fenny Drayton 41 F39
Fenny Stratford 32 E44
Fenrother 71 D37
Fenstanton 33 B49
Fenton Lcn. 52 E44
Fenton Lcn. 52 G44
Fenton Stf. 40 A35
Fenton Barns 76 B31
Fenton Town 77 G35
Fenwick Nor. 77 G36
Fenwick Nor. 71 F36
Fenwick Str. 74 F20
Fenwick S.Y. 51 A41
Feochaig 66 B13
Feock 3 E14
Feolin Ferry 78 H5
Ferindonald 82 J12
Feriniquarrie 82 D7
Fern 81 D30
Ferndale 18 B26
Ferndown 10 D36
Ferness 84 E25
Fernham 21 B38
Fernhill Heath 29 C34
Fernhurst 12 B45
Ferniegair 74 E23
Fernilee 50 E36
Ferrensby 57 C39
Ferring 12 D47
Ferrybridge 57 G40
Ferryden 81 E33
Ferryhill 62 C38
Ferryside 17 C19
Fersfield 44 G56
Fersit 80 C19
Feshiebridge 84 J24
Fetcham 22 F47
Fetlar Airport 89 C42
Fetterangus 85 D35
Fettercairn 81 C32
Feus of Caldhame 81 D32
Fewston 57 D37
Ffairfach 17 B22
Ffair-rhos 27 B23
Ffald-y-Brenin 27 D22
Ffestiniog 37 A23
Fforddlas 47 E24
Fforest 17 D21
Fforest-fâch 17 E22
Ffostrasol 26 D19
Ffos-y-ffin 26 B20
Ffynnongroyw 47 D27
Ffynnon-oer 26 C21
Fiddes 81 B34
Fiddington Glo. 29 E35
Fiddington Som. 19 G28
Fiddleford 9 C34
Field 40 B36
Field Broughton 55 A29
Field Dalling 44 B56
Field Head 41 E40
Fifehead Magdalen 9 B33
Fifehead Neville 9 C33
Fifield Brk. 22 D45
Fifield Oxf. 30 G38
Fifield Bavant 10 B36
Figheldean 20 G37
Fighting Cocks 62 E39
Filby 45 D60
Filey 59 A47
Filkins 21 A38
Filleigh 6 C22
Fillingham 52 D45
Fillongley 40 G38
Filton 19 D32
Fimber 58 C44
Finavon 81 E30
Fincham 44 E52
Finchampstead 22 E43
Fincharn 79 K14
Finchdean 11 C43
Finchingfield 33 E52
Findern 41 B39
Findhorn 84 C26
Findochty 85 C30
Findon Grm. 81 A35
Findon W.S. 12 D47
Findon Mains 84 C22
Finedon 32 A45
Fingerpost 29 A33
Fingest 22 B43
Finghall 57 A37
Fingland Cum. 60 A28
Fingland D.& G. 68 B23
Fingringhoe 34 F56
Finlarig 80 G21
Finmere 31 E42
Finnart Str. 73 A18
Finnart Tay. 80 E21
Finningham 34 B56
Finningley 51 C42
Finnygaud 85 D31
Finsbay 88 J6
Finstall 29 A35
Finsthwaite 55 A29
Finstock 30 G39
Finstown 89 F29
Fintry Cen. 74 B22
Fintry Grm. 85 D33
Fintry Tay. 81 G30
Fionnphort 78 H9
Firbank 61 G32
Firbeck 51 D41
Firby 57 A38
Firsby 53 F50
Firth 89 E40
Fir Tree 62 C37
Fishbourne I.o.W. 11 E41
Fishbourne W.S. 12 D44
Fishburn 62 C39
Fishcross 75 A25
Fisherford 85 F32
Fisherrow 75 C29
Fisher's Pond 11 B40
Fisher's Row 55 E30
Fisherstreet W.S. 12 A45
Fisherton Hgh. 84 D23
Fisherton Str. 67 B18
Fisherton de la Mere 10 A36
Fishguard 16 A15
Fishlake 51 A42
Fishnish 79 F12
Fish-ponds 19 D32
Fish Pools 28 B27
Fishtoft 43 A49
Fishtown of Usan 81 E33
Fishwick 77 E35
Fiskavaig 82 F9
Fiskerton Lcn. 52 E46
Fiskerton Not. 51 G43
Fitling 59 F48
Fittleton 20 G37
Fittleworth 12 C46
Fitzhead 7 C27
Fitzwilliam 51 A40
Fiunary 79 F12
Five Ashes 13 B51
Five Bridges 29 D32
Fivecrosses 48 E31
Fivehead 8 B29
Five Oak Green 23 G52
Five Oaks 12 B46
Five Penny Borve 88 B10
Five Penny Ness 88 A11
Five Roads 17 D20
Five Turnings 28 A28
Five Ways 30 A38
Five Wents 14 B54
Flackwell Heath 22 C44
Fladbury 29 D35
Fladdabister 89 J40
Flagg 50 F37
Flamborough 59 B48
Flamstead 32 G46
Flash 50 F36
Flashader 82 D9
Flask Inn 63 F45
Flaunden 22 A46
Flawborough 42 A43
Flawith 57 C40
Flax Bourton 19 E31
Flaxby 57 D39
Flaxley 29 G32
Flaxton 58 C42
Fleckney 41 F42
Flecknoe 31 B41
Fledborough 52 E44
Fleet Dor. 9 F32
Fleet Ham. 22 F44
Fleet Lcn. 43 C49
Fleetham 71 A37
Fleet Hargate 43 C49
Fleet Services 22 F44
Fleetwood 55 E29
Flemingston 18 D26
Flempton 34 A54
Fletchertown 60 B28
Fletching 13 B50
Flexbury 6 E18
Flexford 22 F45
Flimby 60 C26
Flimwell 14 D53
Flint 48 E28
Flint Cross 33 D50
Flintham 42 A43
Flinton 59 F48
Flishinghurst 14 D53
Flitcham 44 C53
Flitton 32 E46
Flitwick 32 E46
Flixborough 52 A44
Flixton G.M. 49 C33
Flixton N.Y. 59 B46
Flockton 50 A38
Flockton Green 50 A38
Flodden 77 G35
Flodigarry 82 B10
Flookburgh 55 B29
Flordon 45 F57
Flore 31 B42
Flosh 69 G27
Flotta Airport 89 H29
Flotterstone 75 D28
Flotterton 70 C35
Flouch Inn 50 B37
Flushing 3 E14
Flyford Flavell 29 C35
Fobbing 24 C53
Fochabers 84 D29
Fochriw 18 A27
Fockerby 52 A44
Fodderletter 84 G27
Fodderty 83 D21
Foel Gwy. 46 F20
Foel Pow. 37 D25
Foggathorpe 58 F43
Fogo 76 F33
Fogorig 76 F33
Foindle 86 D17
Folda 81 D27
Fole 40 B36
Foleshill 41 G39
Folke 9 C32
Folkestone 15 D58
Folkingham 42 B46
Folkington 13 D51
Folksworth 42 F47
Folkton 59 B46
Folla Rule 85 F33
Follifoot 57 D39
Folly Gate 6 F21
Folly Hill 22 G44
Fonthill Gifford 9 A35
Fontmell Magna 9 C34
Foolow 50 E37
Ford Bkh. 22 A43
Ford Dev. 5 F23
Ford Dev. 6 C20
Ford Glo. 30 F36
Ford Kent 25 E58
Ford Ltn. 75 D29
Ford Nor. 77 G35
Ford Shr. 38 D30
Ford Str. 79 K14
Ford W.S. 12 D46
Ford Wts. 20 D34
Fordcombe 23 G51
Fordell 75 B27
Forden 38 E28
Ford End 33 G52
Fordham Cbs. 33 A52
Fordham Esx. 34 F55
Fordham Nfk. 44 F52
Fordingbridge 10 C37
Fordon 59 B46
Fordoun 81 C33
Fordstreet 34 F55
Fordwich 15 B57
Fordyce 85 C31
Forebridge 40 C35
Foreland House 78 H4
Foremark 41 C39
Forest 3 F17
Forestburn Gate 71 D36
Forest Green 22 G47
Forest Hall 71 G38
Forest Head 61 A31
Forest Hill 21 A41
Forest-in-Teesdale 61 D34
Forest Lodge Bor. 70 A32
Forest Lodge Hgh. 84 H26
Forest Lodge Str. 79 F18
Forest Lodge Tay. 80 C25
Forest Mill 75 A25
Forest Row 13 A50
Forestside 11 C43
Forest Town 51 F41
Forfar 81 E30
Forgandenny 80 J26
Forgie 84 D29
Formby 48 B28
Forncett End 45 F57
Forncett St. Mary 45 F57
Fornham All Saints 34 B54
Fornham St. Martin 34 B54

Fornside

Fornside 60 D29
Forres 84 D26
Forrestfield 74 D24
Forsbrook 40 A35
Forsinain 87 D25
Forsinard 87 D24
Fort Argyll 66 A13
Fort Augustus 83 J19
Forter 81 D27
Forteviot 80 J26
Fort George 84 D23
Forth 75 E25
Forthampton 29 E34
Fortingall 80 F23
Forton Ham. 21 G40
Forton Lan. 55 D30
Forton Som. 8 D29
Forton Stf. 39 C33
Forton Services 55 D31
Fortrie 85 E32
Fortrose 84 D23
Fortuneswell 9 G32
Fort William 79 C17
Forward Green 34 C56
Fosdyke 43 B49
Foss 80 E23
Foss Cross 20 A36
Fossebridge 30 G36
Foster Street 23 A50
Foston Dby. 40 B37
Foston Lcn. 42 A44
Foston on the Wolds 59 D46
Fotherby 53 C49
Fothergill 60 C26
Fotheringhay 42 F46
Foubister 89 G31
Foulbog 69 C28
Foulden Bor. 77 E35
Foulden Nfk. 44 F53
Foul Mile 13 C52
Foulridge 56 E34
Foulsham 44 C56
Foulshiels 69 A30
Fountainhall 76 F30
Four Ashes Sfk. 34 A56
Four Ashes Stf. 40 G34
Four Ashes Stf. 40 E35
Four Crosses Pow. 37 E26
Four Crosses Pow. 38 D28
Four Crosses Stf. 40 E35
Four Cross Way 6 B22
Four Elms 23 G50
Four Forks 8 A28
Four Gates 49 B32
Four Gotes 43 D50
Four Lane Ends Che. 48 F31
Fourlane Ends Dby. 51 G39
Four Lane Ends N.Y. 58 D42
Four Lane Ends N.Y. 57 D38
Four Lanes 2 E12
Fourlanes End 49 G34
Four Marks 11 A42
Four Mile Bridge 46 E18
Four Mile Elm 29 G33
Four Oaks E.S. 14 E54
Four Oaks Glo. 29 F32
Four Oaks W.M. 40 F37
Four Roads I.o.M. 54 G24
Fourstones 70 G34
Fovant 9 B35
Foveran 85 G35
Fowberry Tower 71 A36
Fowey 4 E17
Fowlis 81 G29
Fowlis Wester 80 H25
Fowlmere 33 D50
Fownhope 28 E31
Foxdale 54 F25
Foxearth 34 D54
Foxendale 53 E48
Foxfield 54 A28
Foxham 20 D35
Foxhole 3 C15
Foxholes 59 B46
Foxhunt Green 13 C51
Fox Lane 22 F44
Foxley Nfk. 44 C56
Foxley Wts. 20 C34
Foxley Bridge 49 G34
Fox Street 34 F56
Foxton Cbs. 33 D50
Foxton Lei. 42 F43
Foxton N.Y. 62 G40
Foxup 56 B34
Foxwood 29 A32
Foy 28 F31
Foyers 83 G20
Fraddam 2 E11
Fraddon 3 C15
Fradley 40 D37
Fradswell 40 B35
Fraisthorpe 59 C47
Framfield 13 B51
Framilode 29 G33
Framingham Earl 45 E58
Framingham Pigot 45 E58
Framlingham 35 B58
Frampton Dor. 9 E32
Frampton Lcn. 43 B49
Frampton Cotterell 19 C32
Frampton Mansell 20 A35
Frampton on Severn 20 A33
Framsden 35 C58
Framwellgate Moor 62 B38
Franche 29 A34
Frandley 49 E32
Frankby 48 D28
Frankley 40 G35
Frankley Services 40 G35
Frank's Bridge 28 C27
Frankton 31 A40
Frankwell Pow. 37 F25
Frankwell Shr. 38 D30
Frant 13 A51

Fraserburgh 85 C35
Frating Green 34 F56
Fratton 11 D42
Freckenham 33 A52
Freckleton 55 G30
Freeby 42 C44
Freefolk Priors 21 G40
Freeland 31 G40
Freester 89 G40
Freethorpe 45 E60
Freiston 43 A49
Fremington 6 B21
Frenchay 19 D32
Frenich 80 K20
Frensham 22 G44
Freshfield 48 B28
Freshford Avon 20 E33
Freshwater 10 F39
Freshwater East 16 E16
Fressingfield 35 A58
Freswick 87 B29
Fretherne 20 A33
Frettenham 45 D58
Freuchie 81 K28
Freystrop Cross 16 C15
Friars Gate 13 A50
Friday Bridge 43 E50
Friday Street E.S. 13 D52
Friday Street Sry. 22 G47
Fridaythorpe 58 D44
Friesthorpe 52 D46
Frieston 42 A45
Frieth 22 B43
Frilford 21 B40
Frilsham 21 D41
Frimley 22 F44
Frimley Green 22 F44
Fring 44 B53
Fringford 31 F42
Frinsted 14 B54
Frinton 35 G58
Friockheim 81 F31
Friog 37 D22
Frisby on the Wreake 41 D42
Friskney 53 G50
Friston E.S. 13 E51
Friston Sfk. 35 B60
Fritham 10 C38
Frith Bank 43 A49
Frithelstock 6 D20
Frithelstock Stone 6 D20
Frithville 53 G49
Frittenden 14 C54
Fritton Nfk. 45 F58
Fritton Nfk. 45 E60
Fritwell 31 F41
Frizington 60 E26
Frocester 20 A33
Frochas 38 E28
Frodesley 38 E31
Frodingham 52 A45
Frodsham 48 E31
Frogden 70 A33
Froggatt 50 E38
Froghall 40 A36
Frogmore 5 F23
Frolesworth 41 F41
Frome 20 G33
Frome St. Quintin 8 D31
Fromes Hill 29 D32
Fron 27 B26
Froncysyllte 38 A28
Frongoch 37 B25
Fronsaf 38 A28
Frosterley 62 C36
Froxfield 21 E38
Froxfield Green 11 B43
Froyle 22 G43
Fryerning 24 A52
Fryton 58 B42
Fualt 28 C27
Fulbeck 52 G45
Fulbourn 33 C51
Fulbrook 30 G38
Fulford N.Y. 58 E42
Fulford Stf. 40 B35
Fulfordlees 76 D33
Fulking 13 C48
Fullarton 73 G19
Fuller Street 34 G53
Fullerton 10 A39
Fulletby 53 E48
Full Sutton 58 D43
Fullwood 74 E20
Fulmer 22 C45
Fulmodeston 44 B55
Fulnetby 52 E46
Fulney 43 C48
Fulstow 53 C49
Fulwell 62 A39
Fulwood 55 F31
Fundenhall 45 F57
Funtington 11 D43
Funzie 89 C42
Furnace Dyf. 17 D21
Furnace Str. 72 A16
Furness Vale 50 D36
Furneux Pelham 33 F50
Furze Platt 22 C44
Fyfield Esx. 23 A51
Fyfield Ham. 21 G38
Fyfield Oxf. 21 B40
Fyfield Wts. 20 E37
Fyling Thorpe 63 F45
Fyvie 85 F33

G

Gabroc Hill 74 E20
Gaddesby 41 D42
Gadgirth 67 A20
Gaer 28 F27
Gaerwen 46 E20
Gaick Lodge 80 B23
Gailey 40 D35
Gainford 62 E37
Gainsborough 52 C44
Gairloch 83 B14
Gairlochy 79 B17
Gairnshiel Lodge 84 J28
Gaisgill 61 F32
Gaitsgill 60 B29
Galashiels 76 G30
Galgate 55 D30
Galhampton 9 B32
Gallantry Bank 48 G31
Gallatown 75 A28
Gallchoille 72 A13
Galleyend 24 A53
Galleywood 24 A53
Gallin 80 F21
Gallowfauld 81 F30
Gallows Green 40 A36
Galltair 83 G14
Galmisdale 78 B10
Galmpton Dev. 5 F22
Galmpton Dev. 5 E24
Galphay 57 B38
Galston 74 G21
Galtrigill 82 D7
Galtway 65 D23
Gamblesby 61 C32
Gamlingay 33 C48
Gammersgill 57 A36
Gamston Not. 51 E43
Gamston Not. 41 B42
Ganavan 79 G14
Ganllwyd 37 C23
Gannachy 81 C31
Gannow Hill 38 B29
Ganstead 59 F47
Ganthorpe 58 B42
Ganton 59 B45
Gara Bridge 5 E23
Garbat 83 C20
Garbhallt 72 A16
Garboldisham 44 G56
Garden 74 A21
Garden City 48 F29
Gardenholm 69 C26
Gardenstown 85 C33
Garden Village 57 F40
Garderhouse 89 H39
Gardner Street 13 C52
Garelochhead 73 A18
Garenin 88 C7
Garford 21 B40
Garforth 57 F40
Garforth Bridge 57 F39
Gargrave 56 D35
Gargunnock 74 A23
Garizim 46 E22
Garlieston 64 D20
Garlinge 25 E59
Garlinge Green 15 C56
Garlogie 85 J33
Garmond 85 D34
Garmony 79 F12
Garmouth 84 C29
Garnant 17 C22
Garn Dolbenmaen 36 A20
Garnett Bridge 61 G31
Garnkirk 74 D22
Garnswllt 17 D22
Garrabost 88 D11
Garragie Lodge 83 H21
Garras 2 F12
Garrauld 74 A21
Garreg 37 A22
Garrick 80 J24
Garrigill 61 B33
Garrow 80 F24
Garrynamonie 88 R3
Garsdale Head 61 G33
Garsdon 20 C35
Garsington 21 A41
Garstang 55 E30
Garston Hfs. 22 A47
Garston Mer. 48 D29
Garswood 48 C31
Gartachoil 74 A21
Gartcosh 74 D22
Garth Clw. 38 A28
Garth Pow. 28 A28
Garth Pow. 27 D25
Garthbrengy 27 E26
Gartheli 26 C21
Garthmyl 38 F27
Garthorpe Hum. 52 A44
Garthorpe Lei. 42 C44
Garth Penrhyncoch 37 G22
Gartley Station 85 F31
Gartmore 74 A21
Gartnagrenach 72 E13
Gartness 74 B20
Gartocharn 74 B20
Garton 59 F48
Garton on the Wolds 59 D45
Gartsherrie 74 D23
Gartwhinzean Feus 75 A26
Gartymore 87 G26
Garvald Bor. 75 E29
Garvald Ltn. 76 C31
Garvamore 80 A21
Garvan 79 C15
Garvard 78 K9
Garve 83 C19
Garvestone 44 E56
Garvie 72 A16

Garvock 73 C18
Garwald 69 C28
Garway 28 F30
Gaskan 79 C13
Gass 67 C20
Gasstown 68 F25
Gastard 20 E34
Gateacre 48 D30
Gatebeck 55 A31
Gateforth 58 G41
Gatehead 73 G19
Gate Helmsley 58 D42
Gatehouse 70 E33
Gatehouse of Fleet 65 C21
Gatelawbridge 68 D25
Gateley 44 C55
Gatenby 57 A39
Gatesgarth 60 E27
Gateshaw 70 A33
Gateshead 62 A38
Gateside Fife 81 K27
Gateside Str. 73 E19
Gateside Str. 74 E20
Gateside Tay. 81 F30
Gateslack 68 C24
Gathurst 48 B31
Gatley 49 D34
Gattonside 76 G31
Gatwick Airport 23 G48
Gaulby 41 E42
Gauldry 81 H29
Gaultree 43 E50
Gavinton 76 E33
Gawcott 31 E42
Gawsworth 49 F34
Gawthrop 56 A32
Gawthwaite 54 A28
Gaydon 30 C39
Gayhurst 32 D44
Gayle 56 A34
Gayles 62 F37
Gayton Mer. 48 D28
Gayton Nfk. 44 D53
Gayton Nmp. 31 C43
Gayton Stf. 40 C35
Gayton le Marsh 53 D50
Gayton Thorpe 44 D53
Gaywood 44 C52
Gazeley 34 B53
Gearnsary 87 E23
Geary 82 C8
Gedding 34 C55
Geddington 42 G44
Gedintailor 82 F11
Gedney 43 C50
Gedney Broadgate 43 C50
Gedney Drove End 43 C50
Gedney Dyke 43 C50
Gedney Hill 43 D49
Gee Cross 49 C35
Geilston 73 C19
Geise 87 B27
Geldeston 45 F59
Gell 47 F24
Gelli 18 B25
Gellideg 18 A26
Gellifor 47 F27
Gelligaer 18 B27
Gelly 16 C16
Gellywen 17 B18
Gelston 65 C23
Gembling 59 D47
Gentleshaw 40 D36
Georgefield 69 D28
George Green 22 C46
Georgeham 6 A20
George Nympton 6 C22
Georgetown D.& G. 68 F25
Georgetown Gwe. 18 A27
Georgetown Str. 74 D20
Gerlan 47 F21
Germansweek 6 F20
Germoe 2 F11
Gerrans 3 E14
Gerranton 68 G23
Gerrards Cross 22 C45
Geshader 88 D7
Gestingthorpe 34 E54
Geufford 38 D28
Gibbshill 68 F23
Gibraltar 53 G51
Gidleigh 6 G22
Giffnock 74 E21
Gifford 76 D31
Giffordland 73 F19
Giffordtown 81 K28
Giggleswick 56 C34
Gilberdyke 58 G44
Gilcrux 60 C27
Gildersome 57 G38
Gildingwells 51 D41
Gileston 18 E26
Gilfach M.G. 18 B27
Gilfach M.G. 18 C25
Gilfach Goch 18 C25
Gilfachrheda 26 C20
Gillamoor 58 A42
Gillenbie 69 E27
Gillesbie 69 D27
Gillfoot 68 F25
Gill Head 60 G29
Gilling East 58 B42
Gillingham Dor. 9 B34
Gillingham Kent 24 E53
Gillingham Nfk. 45 F60
Gilling West 62 F37
Gillock 87 C28
Gillow Heath 49 G34
Gillroanie 65 D22
Gills 89 K29
Gill's Green 14 D53
Gillside 69 E30
Gilmanscleuch 69 A29
Gilmerton Ltn. 75 D28

Gilmerton Tay. 80 H24
Gilmonby 62 E35
Gilmorton 41 G41
Gilsland 70 G32
Gilston 76 E30
Gilwern 28 G28
Gimingham 45 B58
Ginclough 49 E35
Gipping 34 B56
Gipsey Bridge 43 A48
Girdle Toll 73 G19
Girlsta 89 G40
Girthon 65 C22
Girton Cbs. 33 B50
Girton Not. 52 F44
Girvan 67 D17
Gisburn 56 E34
Gisla 88 E7
Gislingham 34 A56
Gissing 45 G57
Gittisham 7 F27
Gladdish 14 C54
Gladestry 28 C28
Gladsmuir 76 C30
Glais 18 A23
Glaisdale 63 F43
Glame 82 E11
Glamis 81 F29
Glanaber 46 G22
Glanaman 17 C22
Glandford 44 A56
Glandwr Dyf. 16 B17
Glandwr Gwe. 19 A28
Glan Dwyfach 36 A20
Glandyfi 37 F22
Glangrwyne 28 G28
Glanmule 38 F27
Glanrhyd 26 D17
Glanton 71 B36
Glanton Pike 71 B36
Glanvilles Wootton 9 D32
Glan-y-don 47 E27
Glan-yr-afon Gwy. 37 A26
Glan-yr-afon Gwy. 37 A25
Glapthorn 42 F46
Glapwell 51 F40
Glasbury 28 E27
Glascoed Clw. 47 E25
Glascoed Pow. 38 D27
Glascote 40 E38
Glascwm 28 C27
Glasfryn 47 G25
Glasgow 74 D21
Glasgow (Abbotsinch) Airport 74 D20
Glasinfryn 46 F21
Glasnacardoch 79 A12
Glasnakille 82 H11
Glassburn 83 F19
Glassel 81 A32
Glassenbury 14 D53
Glasserton 64 E20
Glassford 74 F23
Glass Houghton 57 G40
Glasshouse 29 F33
Glasshouses 57 C37
Glassoch 67 G19
Glasson Cum. 69 G28
Glasson Lan. 55 D30
Glassonby 61 C31
Glaston 42 E44
Glastonbury 8 A30
Glatton 42 G47
Glazebrook 49 C32
Glazebury 49 C32
Glazeley 39 G33
Gleadless 51 D39
Gleaston 54 B28
Glecknabae 72 D16
Glemanuilt 66 C12
Glemsford 34 D54
Glen D.& G. 65 C21
Glenaladale 79 C14
Glenalmond 80 H24
Glenancross 79 F11
Glen Auldyn 54 D26
Glenbarr 72 G12
Glen Barry 85 D31
Glenbeg 79 D11
Glenbervie 81 B33
Glenboig 74 D23
Glenborrodale 79 D12
Glenbranter 73 A17
Glenbreck 69 A26
Glenbrein Lodge 83 H20
Glenbrittle Ho. 82 G10
Glenbuck 68 A23
Glencaird 67 F19
Glencally 81 D29
Glencalvie Lodge 83 A20
Glencanisp Lodge 86 F17
Glencaple 68 G25
Glencarron Lodge 83 D16
Glencarse 81 H27
Glencartholm 69 F29
Glencassley Castle 86 H20
Glen Clunie Lodge 81 B27
Glencoe 79 E17
Glencoyne 60 E29
Glencraig 75 A27
Glencrosh 68 E23
Glendearg Bor. 76 G31
Glendearg D.& G. 69 C28
Glendessary 79 A15
Glendevon 80 K25
Glendissaig 67 D17
Glendye Lodge 81 B32
Gleneagles Hotel 80 J25
Glenegedale 78 K4
Glenelg 83 H14

Glenernie 84 E26
Glenfarg 81 J27
Glenferness House 84 E25
Glenfield 41 E41
Glenfinnan 79 B15
Glenfintaig 79 B18
Glenfyne Lodge 79 J18
Glengap 65 C22
Glengarnock 73 E19
Glengarrisdale 72 A12
Glengrasco 82 E10
Glenhapple 67 F19
Glenhoul 68 E22
Glen House 75 G28
Glenkerry 69 B28
Glenkindie 85 H30
Glenlean 72 B16
Glenlee 68 F22
Glenlochar 68 G23
Glenloig 72 G15
Glenluce 64 C17
Glenlude 69 A29
Glenmallan 73 A18
Glenmanna 68 C23
Glenmark 81 B30
Glenmavis 74 D23
Glenmaye 54 F24
Glenmeanie 83 D18
Glen Mona 54 E27
Glenmore Lodge 84 J25
Glenmoy 81 D29
Glenmuck 67 C21
Glen Nevis Ho. 79 C17
Glenochar 68 B25
Glen Parva 41 F41
Glenprosen Village 81 D29
Glenree 66 A15
Glenridding 60 E29
Glenrisdell 72 E14
Glenrothes 81 K28
Glenshee 80 G25
Glenshirra Lodge 80 A21
Glenside 68 G16
Glensluain 72 A16
Glenstriven 72 C16
Glentaggart 68 A24
Glen Tanar House 81 A30
Glentham 52 C46
Glentress 75 G28
Glentromie Lodge 80 A23
Glen Trool Lodge 67 E20
Glentrool Village 67 F19
Glentworth 52 D45
Glenuaig Lodge 83 E17
Glenuig 79 C12
Glenvarragill 82 E10
Glenveg 69 A27
Glen Village 74 C24
Glen Vine 54 F25
Glenwhilly 67 F17
Glespin 68 A24
Gletness 89 G40
Glewstone 28 F31
Glinton 42 E47
Glooston 42 F43
Glororum 77 G37
Glossop 50 C36
Gloucester 29 G34
Gloucester Airport 29 F34
Gloup 89 B41
Gloweth 2 D13
Glusburn 56 E35
Glutt Lodge 87 E25
Glympton 31 F40
Glyn 47 G23
Glynarthen 26 D19
Glyn Ceiriog 38 B28
Glyncoch 18 B26
Glyncorrwg 18 B24
Glyn Cywarch 37 B22
Glynde 13 D50
Glyndebourne 13 C50
Glyndyfrdwy 38 A27
Glynneath 18 A24
Glyntaff 18 C26
Gnosall 40 C34
Gnosall Heath 40 C34
Goadby 42 F43
Goadby Marwood 42 C43
Goatacre 20 D36
Goathland 63 F44
Goathurst 8 A28
Goat Lees 15 C56
Gobernuisgach Lodge 86 D20
Gobowen 38 B29
Godalming 22 G45
Godford Cross 7 E27
Godmanchester 33 A48
Godmanstone 9 E32
Godmersham 15 B56
Godolphin Cross 2 E12
Godshill Ham. 10 C37
Godshill I.o.W. 11 F41
Godstone 23 F49
Goetre 18 C23
Goff's Oak 23 A49
Gogar 75 C27
Goginan 37 G22
Golan 36 A21
Golant 4 E17
Golberdon 4 C19
Golborne 49 C32
Golcar 50 A36
Goldcliff 19 C29
Golden Cross 13 C51
Golden Fleece 61 A30
Golden Green 23 G52
Goldenhill 49 G34
Golden Pot 22 G43
Goldhanger 25 A55
Gold Hill 43 F51

Goldington 32 C46
Goldsborough *N.Y.* 63 E44
Goldsborough *N.Y.* 57 D39
Goldsithney 2 E11
Goldthorpe 51 B40
Goldworthy 6 C19
Golspie 87 H24
Golval 87 B24
Gomeldon 10 A37
Gomersal 57 G38
Gomshall 22 G46
Gonachan 74 C22
Gonalston 41 A42
Gonfirth 89 F39
Good Easter 33 G52
Gooderstone 44 E53
Goodhope 69 D26
Goodleigh 6 B21
Goodmanham 58 E44
Goodnestone *Kent* 15 B58
Goodnestone *Kent* 25 E56
Goodrich 28 G31
Goodrington 5 E25
Goodshaw 56 G34
Goodwick 16 A15
Goodworth Clatford 21 G39
Goole 58 G43
Goonbell 2 D13
Goonhavern 2 C13
Goosecruives 81 B33
Goose Green 23 F52
Gooseham 6 D18
Goosewell 5 E21
Goosey 21 B39
Goosnargh 55 F31
Goostrey 49 F33
Gorcott Hill 30 B36
Gordano Services 19 D31
Gorddinog 46 E22
Gordon 76 F32
Gordonbush 87 H24
Gordonstown 85 F33
Gordonstown 85 D31
Gore 28 C28
Gorebridge 75 D29
Gorefield 43 D50
Gorey *Jer.* 3 G18
Goring 21 C42
Goring-by-Sea 12 D47
Goring Heath 21 D42
Gorleston on Sea 45 E61
Gornalwood 40 F35
Gorran Churchtown 3 D15
Gorran Haven 4 F16
Gorrenberry 69 D30
Gorsedd 47 E27
Gorseinon 17 E21
Gorseness 89 E30
Gorseybank *Dby.* 50 G38
Gorsey Bank *Shr.* 39 D33
Gorslas 17 C21
Gorsley 29 F32
Gorstan 83 C19
Gorsty Common 28 E30
Gortantaoid 78 H4
Gorton 49 C34
Gortonallister 66 A16
Gosbeck 35 C57
Gosberton 43 B48
Gosfield 34 F53
Gosford House 76 C30
Gosforth *Cum.* 60 F26
Gosforth *T.& W.* 71 G38
Gospel End 40 F35
Gosport 11 E42
Gossabrough 89 D41
Gossops Green 13 A48
Gotham 41 B41
Gotherington 29 F35
Goudhurst 14 D53
Goulceby 53 E48
Gourdon 81 C34
Gourock 73 C18
Govan 74 D21
Govilon 28 G28
Gowdall 58 G42
Gowerton 17 E21
Gowkhall 75 B26
Goxhill *Hum.* 59 E47
Goxhill *Hum.* 59 G46
Graffham 12 C45
Grafham *Cbs.* 32 B47
Grafham *Sry.* 22 G46
Grafton *N.Y.* 57 C40
Grafton *Oxf.* 21 A38
Grafton Regis 31 D43
Grafton Underwood 42 G45
Grafty Green 14 C54
Graianrhyd 48 G28
Graig Penllyn 18 D25
Grain 24 D54
Grains Bar 49 B35
Grainsby 53 C48
Grains o' th' Beck Bridge 61 D34
Grainthorpe 53 C49
Grampound 3 D15
Grampound Road 3 C15
Granborough 31 F43
Granby 42 B43
Grandborough 31 B40
Grandtully 80 E25
Grange *Cum.* 60 E28
Grange *Hgh.* 83 F19
Grange *Mer.* 48 D28
Grange *N.Y.* 63 E44
Grangemill 50 G38
Grange Moor 50 A38
Grangemouth 75 B25
Grange-over-Sands 55 B30
Grangepans 75 B26
Grangestone 67 D18
Grangetown *Cle.* 63 D41
Grangetown *S.G.* 18 D27

Gransmoor 59 D47
Granston 16 A14
Grantchester 33 C50
Grantham 42 B45
Granton *D.& G.* 69 C26
Granton *Ltn.* 75 C28
Grantown-on-Spey 84 G26
Grantshouse 77 D34
Grappenhall 49 D32
Grasby 52 B46
Grasmere 60 F29
Grasscroft 49 B35
Grassendale 48 D29
Grassholme 61 D35
Grassington 57 C36
Grassmoor 51 F40
Grassthorpe 51 F43
Grateley 21 G38
Gravel 28 A27
Graveley *Cbs.* 33 B48
Graveley *Hfs.* 33 F48
Gravelly Hill 40 F37
Graven 89 E40
Graveney 25 E56
Gravesend 24 D52
Gravir 89 F8
Grawen 27 G26
Grayingham 52 C45
Grayrigg 61 G31
Grays 24 D52
Grayshott 12 A44
Grayswood 12 A45
Greasbrough 51 C40
Greasby 48 D28
Greasley 41 A40
Great Abington 33 D51
Great Addington 32 A45
Great Alne 30 C37
Great Altcar 48 B29
Great Amwell 33 G49
Great Asby 61 E32
Great Ashfield 34 B56
Great Ayton 63 E41
Great Baddow 24 A53
Great Badminton 20 C34
Great Bardfield 33 E52
Great Barford 32 C47
Great Barr 40 F36
Great Barrington 30 G38
Great Barrow 48 F30
Great Barton 34 B54
Great Barugh 58 A42
Great Bavington 70 E35
Great Bealings 35 D58
Great Bedwyn 21 E38
Great Bentley 35 F57
Great Billing 32 B44
Great Bircham 44 B53
Great Blakenham 35 C57
Great Blencow 61 C30
Great Bolas 39 C32
Great Bookham 22 F47
Great Bourton 31 D40
Great Bowden 42 G43
Great Bradley 33 C52
Great Braxted 34 G54
Great Bricett 34 C56
Great Brickhill 32 E45
Great Bridgeford 40 C34
Great Brington 31 B42
Great Bromley 34 F56
Great Broughton 60 C26
Great Budworth 49 E32
Great Burstead 24 B52
Great Busby 63 F41
Great Carlton 53 D50
Great Casterton 42 E46
Great Chart 14 C55
Great Chatwell 39 D33
Great Chesterford 33 D51
Great Cheverell 20 F35
Great Chishill 33 E50
Great Clacton 35 G57
Great Clifton 60 D26
Great Coates 53 A48
Great Comberton 29 D35
Great Corby 61 A30
Great Cornard 34 D54
Great Coxwell 21 B38
Great Crakehall 57 A38
Great Cransley 32 A44
Great Cressingham 44 E54
Great Crosby 48 C29
Great Cubley 40 B37
Great Dalby 42 D43
Great Doddington 32 B44
Great Driffield 59 D46
Great Dunham 44 D54
Great Dunmow 33 F52
Great Durnford 10 A37
Great Easton *Esx.* 33 F52
Great Easton *Lei.* 42 F44
Great Eccleston 55 E30
Great Edstone 58 A43
Great Ellingham 44 F56
Great Elm 20 G33
Great Eversden 33 C49
Great Fencote 62 G38
Great Finborough 34 C56
Greatford 42 D46
Great Fransham 44 D54
Great Gaddesden 32 G46
Great Gidding 42 G47
Great Givendale 58 D44
Great Glemham 35 B59
Great Glen 41 F42
Great Gonerby 42 B44
Great Gransden 33 C48
Greatham *Brk.* 21 E40
Greatham *Ham.* 58 B43
Great Hale 42 A47
Great Hallingbury 33 G51
Greatham *Cle.* 62 D40
Greatham *Ham.* 11 A43

Great Hanwood 38 D30
Great Harrowden 32 A44
Great Harwood 56 F33
Great Haseley 21 A42
Great Hatfield 59 E47
Great Haywood 40 C35
Great Heck 58 G41
Great Hinton 20 F35
Great Hockham 44 F55
Great Holland 35 G58
Great Horkesley 34 E55
Great Hormead 33 E50
Great Horton 57 F37
Great Horwood 31 E43
Great Houghton *Nmp.* 31 C43
Great Houghton *S.Y.* 51 B40
Great Hucklow 50 E37
Great Kelk 59 D47
Great Kendale 59 D46
Great Kimble 22 A44
Great Kingshill 22 B44
Great Langton 62 G38
Great Leighs 34 G53
Great Limber 52 B47
Great Linford 32 D44
Great Livermere 34 A54
Great Longstone 50 E37
Great Lumley 62 B38
Great Malvern 29 D34
Great Maplestead 34 E54
Great Marton 55 F29
Great Massingham 44 C53
Great Milton 21 A42
Great Missenden 22 A44
Great Mitton 56 F33
Great Mongeham 15 B59
Great Moss 48 B31
Great Musgrave 61 E32
Great Ness 38 D29
Great Oakley *Esx.* 35 F57
Great Oakley *Nmp.* 42 G44
Great Offley 32 F47
Great Ormside 61 E33
Great Orton 60 A29
Great Ouseburn 57 C40
Great Oxendon 42 G43
Great Oxney Green 24 A52
Great Parndon 23 A50
Great Paxton 33 B48
Great Plumpton 55 F29
Great Plumstead 45 D59
Great Ponton 42 B45
Great Preston 57 G40
Great Raveley 43 G48
Great Rissington 30 G38
Great Rollright 30 E39
Great Ryburgh 44 C55
Great Ryle 71 B36
Great Saling 34 F53
Great Salkeld 61 C31
Great Sampford 33 E52
Great Sankey 48 D31
Great Shefford 21 D39
Great Shelford 33 C50
Great Smeaton 62 F39
Great Snoring 44 B55
Great Somerford 20 C35
Great Soudley 39 C33
Great Stainton 62 D39
Great Stambridge 25 B55
Great Staughton 32 B47
Great Steeping 53 F50
Great Stonar 15 B59
Greatstone-on-Sea 15 E56
Great Strickland 61 D31
Great Stukeley 33 A48
Great Sutton 48 E29
Great Swinburne 70 F35
Great Tew 30 F39
Great Tey 34 F54
Great Thurlow 33 C52
Great Torrington 6 D20
Great Tosson 71 C36
Great Totham *Esx.* 34 G54
Great Totham *Esx.* 34 G54
Great Urswick 54 B28
Great Wakering 25 C55
Great Waldingfield 34 D55
Great Walsingham 44 B55
Great Waltham 33 G52
Great Warley 23 B51
Great Washbourne 29 E35
Great Wenham 34 E56
Great Whittington 71 F36
Great Wigborough 34 G55
Great Wilbraham 33 C51
Great Wishford 10 A36
Great Witcombe 29 G35
Great Witley 29 B33
Great Wolford 30 E38
Greatworth 31 D41
Great Wratting 33 D52
Great Wymondley 33 F48
Great Wyrley 40 E35
Great Wytheford 38 D31
Great Yarmouth 45 E61
Great Yeldham 34 E53
Greeba 54 F25
Greendale 60 F27
Greendikes 71 A36
Greenfield *Bfd.* 32 E46
Greenfield *Clw.* 47 E27
Greenfield *G.M.* 49 B35
Greenfield *Hgh.* 83 J17
Greenford 22 C47
Greengairs 74 C23
Greengates 57 F38
Greenham *Brk.* 21 E40
Greenham *Som.* 7 C26
Green Hammerton 57 D40
Greenhaugh 70 E33
Greenhead *Fife* 75 A28
Greenhead *Nor.* 70 G32
Greenhill *Bor.* 70 B33

Greenhill *Cen.* 74 C24
Greenhill *Str.* 75 G25
Greenhithe 23 D51
Greenholm 74 G21
Greenhow Hill 57 C37
Greenigo 89 G30
Greenknowe 76 F32
Greenlands 22 C43
Green Lane 38 F27
Greenlaw 76 F33
Greenloaning 80 K24
Greenmount 49 A33
Greenock 73 C18
Greenodd 55 A29
Green Ore *Som.* 19 F31
Greenridge 70 G34
Greenrigg 75 D25
Greensfield Moorhouse 71 B37
Greenside 71 G37
Greensidehill 70 B35
Greens Norton 31 D42
Greenstead Green 34 F54
Green Street 29 D34
Green Street Green *G.L.* 23 E50
Green Street Green *Kent* 23 D51
Greenway *Dyf.* 16 A16
Greenway *H.& W.* 29 E33
Greenway *Som.* 8 B29
Greete 28 A31
Greetham *Lcn.* 53 E49
Greetham *Lei.* 42 D45
Greetland 57 G36
Greinton 8 A30
Grendon *Nmp.* 32 B44
Grendon *War.* 40 F38
Grendon Green 28 C31
Grendon Underwood 31 F42
Grenitote 88 K4
Grennan 68 F22
Grenoside 51 C39
Gresford 48 G29
Gresham 45 B57
Greshornish 82 D9
Gress 88 C10
Gressenhall 44 D55
Gressingham 55 C31
Greta Bridge 62 E36
Gretna 69 G29
Gretna Green 69 G29
Gretton *Glo.* 30 E36
Gretton *Nmp.* 42 F45
Gretton *Shr.* 38 F31
Grewelthorpe 57 B38
Greygarth 57 B37
Greynor 17 C21
Greyrigg 69 E26
Greysouthen 60 D26
Greystoke 61 C31
Greystone 56 E34
Greywell 22 F43
Gridley Corner 6 F19
Griffithstown 19 B28
Grigghall 61 G30
Grimethorpe 51 B40
Griminish 88 M3
Grimister 89 C40
Grimley 29 B34
Grimmet 67 B19
Grimoldby 53 D49
Grimsargh 55 F31
Grimsby 53 A48
Grimscote 31 C42
Grimscott 6 E18
Grimshader 88 E10
Grimsthorpe 42 C46
Grimston *Lei.* 41 C42
Grimston *Nfk.* 44 C53
Grimstone 9 E32
Grindale 59 B47
Grindleford Bridge 50 E38
Grindleton 56 E33
Grindley brook 38 A31
Grindlow 50 E37
Grindon *Cle.* 62 D39
Grindon *Nor.* 77 F35
Grindon *Stf.* 50 G36
Grindon Hill 70 G34
Gringley on the Hill 51 C43
Grinsdale 60 A29
Grinshill 38 C31
Grinton 62 G36
Gristhorpe 59 A46
Griston 44 F55
Gritley 89 G31
Grittenham 20 C36
Grittleton 20 C34
Grizebeck 54 A28
Groby 41 E41
Groes 47 F26
Groesllwyd 38 D28
Groeslon 46 G20
Grogport 72 F14
Gronant 42 D50
Groombridge 13 A51
Grosebay 88 H7
Grosmont *Gwe.* 28 F30
Grosmont *N.Y.* 63 F44
Groton 34 D55
Grouville 3 G18
Grove *Dor.* 9 G32
Grove *Not.* 51 E43
Grove Vale 40 F36
Grove *Oxf.* 21 B40
Grovehall *Hum.* 57 F60
Grovesend *Avon* 19 C32
Grovesend *W.G.* 17 D21
Grudie 83 C19
Gruids 85 J7
Gruinard House 86 J15
Gruinart 78 H4
Gruline 79 F11
Grundisburgh 35 C58

Grunnasound 89 J39
Gruting 89 H38
Grutness 89 L40
Gualachulain 79 F17
Gualin House 86 C19
Guard Bridge 81 H30
Guarlford 29 D34
Guay 80 E24
Guernsey Airport 3 F16
Guestling Green 14 F54
Guestwick 44 C56
Guide 56 G33
Guide Post 71 E38
Guilden Morden 33 D48
Guilden Sutton 48 F30
Guildford 22 F45
Guildtown 81 G27
Guilsborough 31 A42
Guisborough 63 E41
Guiseley 57 E37
Guist 44 C55
Guith 89 D31
Guiting Power 30 F36
Gulberwick 89 H39
Gullane 76 B30
Gulval 2 E10
Gulworthy 4 C20
Gumfreston 16 D17
Gumley 41 F42
Gunby 42 C45
Gun Green 14 E40
Gunn 6 B22
Gunnerside 61 G35
Gunnerton 70 F35
Gunness 52 A44
Gunnislake 4 C20
Gunthorpe *Nfk.* 44 B56
Gunthorpe *Not.* 41 A42
Gunwalloe 2 F12
Gurnard 11 E40
Gurney Slade 19 G32
Gurnos 27 G23
Gussage All Saints 9 C35
Gussage St. Michael 9 C35
Guston 15 C59
Gutcher 89 C41
Guthrie 81 E31
Guyance 71 C38
Guyhirn 43 E50
Gwaelod-y-Garth 18 C27
Gwaenysgor 47 D26
Gwalchmai 46 E19
Gwaun-Cae-Gurwen 27 G23
Gwbert 26 D17
Gweek 2 F13
Gwehelog 19 A30
Gwenddwr 27 D26
Gwennap 2 D13
Gwernesney 19 A30
Gwernogle 17 A21
Gwernymynydd 48 F28
Gwersyllt 48 G29
Gwespyr 47 D27
Gwinear 2 E11
Gwithian 2 D11
Gwyddelwern 37 A26
Gwyddgrug 17 A20
Gwyn Arms 27 G24
Gwystre 27 B26
Gwytherin 47 F24
Gyfelia 38 A29
Gyffin 47 E23
Gyrn-gôch 36 A20

H

Habberley 38 E30
Habost 88 A11
Habrough 52 A47
Haceby 42 B46
Hacheston 35 C59
Hackford 44 E56
Hackforth 62 G38
Hackleton 32 C44
Hacklinge 15 B59
Hackness 59 A45
Hackthorn 52 D45
Hackthorpe 61 D31
Hadden 76 G33
Haddenham *Bkh.* 22 A43
Haddenham *Cbs.* 33 A50
Haddington *Lcn.* 52 F45
Haddington *Ltn.* 76 C31
Haddiscoe 45 F60
Haddon 42 F47
Hadfield 50 C36
Hadham Cross 33 G50
Hadham Ford 33 F50
Hadleigh *Esx.* 24 C53
Hadleigh *Sfk.* 34 D56
Hadley *H.& W.* 29 B34
Hadley *Shr.* 39 D32
Hadley Wood 23 B48
Hadlow 23 G52
Hadlow Down 13 B51
Hadnall 38 C31
Hadspen 9 A32
Hadstock 33 D51
Hadzor 29 B35
Hafod-garegog 37 A22
Haggate 56 F34
Haggerston 77 F36
Haggs 74 C23
Hagley 40 G35
Hagnaby 53 F49
Hagworthingham 53 F49
Haigh *G.M.* 49 B32
Haigh *W.Y.* 50 A38
Haile 60 F26
Hailes 30 E36
Hailey 30 D38
Hailsham 13 D51
Hail Weston 32 B47
Hainault 23 B50
Haine 25 E59

Hainford 45 D58
Hainton 52 D47
Hairlaw 74 F20
Haisthorpe 59 C47
Halam 51 G42
Halbeath 75 B27
Halberton 7 D26
Halcro 87 B28
Hale *Che.* 48 D30
Hale *Cum.* 55 B31
Hale *G.M.* 49 D33
Hale *Ham.* 10 C37
Hale *Sry.* 22 G44
Halebarns 49 D33
Halesfield 39 D33
Halesowen 40 G35
Hales Place 15 B57
Hale Street 23 G52
Halesworth 35 A59
Halewood 43 D30
Halford *Shr.* 38 G30
Halford *War.* 30 D38
Halfpenny Green 40 F34
Halfway *Dyf.* 17 A22
Halfway *Dyf.* 27 E24
Halfway *S.Y.* 51 D40
Halfway Hotel 7 F26
Halfway House *D.& G.* 67 G19
Halfway House *Shr.* 38 D29
Halfway House Inn *Cnw.* 4 D17
Halfway Houses 25 D55
Halifax 57 G36
Halistra 82 D8
Halkirk 87 C27
Halkyn 48 E28
Halland 13 C51
Hallaton 42 F43
Hallatrow 19 F32
Hallbankgate 61 A31
Hallcrofts 69 E29
Hall Dunnerdale 60 G28
Hallen 19 C31
Hallfield Gate 51 G39
Hall Green *Lan.* 48 B31
Hall Green *W.M.* 40 G37
Halliburton 76 F32
Hallin 82 D8
Halling 24 E53
Hallington 70 F35
Halliwell 49 B32
Hall of Caldwell 74 E20
Hall of the Forest 38 G28
Halloughton 51 F42
Hallow 29 C34
Hallrule 70 B31
Halls 76 C32
Hallsands 5 G24
Hallsgreen 23 A50
Hallthwaites 54 A27
Halltoft End 43 A49
Hall Waberthwaite 60 G26
Hallworthy 4 B17
Hallydown 77 D35
Hallyne 75 F27
Halmore 19 A32
Halmyre Mains 75 F27
Halnaker 12 D45
Halsall 48 A29
Halse 7 C27
Halsetown 2 E11
Halsfordwood 7 F24
Halsham 59 G48
Halstead *Esx.* 34 E54
Halstead *Kent* 23 E50
Halstead *Lei.* 42 E43
Halstock 8 D31
Haltham 53 F48
Halton *Bkh.* 32 G44
Halton *Che.* 48 D31
Halton *Lan.* 55 C31
Halton *Nor.* 70 G35
Halton *W.Y.* 57 F39
Halton East 57 D36
Halton Gill 56 B34
Halton Holegate 53 F50
Halton Lea Gate 61 A32
Halton Shields 71 G36
Halton West 56 D34
Haltwhistle 70 G33
Halvergate 45 E60
Halwell 5 E23
Halwill 6 F20
Halwill Junction 6 E20
Ham 89 K28
Ham *Dev.* 4 E20
Ham *Glo.* 19 B32
Ham *She.* 89 J35
Ham *She.* 89 J40
Ham *Wts.* 21 E39
Hamble 11 D40
Hambleden 22 C43
Hambledon *Ham.* 11 C42
Hambledon *Sry.* 12 A45
Hambleton *Lan.* 55 E29
Hambleton *N.Y.* 58 F41
Hambridge 8 B29
Hambrook *Avon* 19 D32
Hambrook *W.S.* 11 D43
Hameringham 53 F49
Hamerton 42 G47
Hametoun 89 J35
Hamilton 74 E23
Hamilton Services 74 E23
Hammer 12 A44
Hammerwich 40 E36
Hammond Street 23 A49
Hammoon 9 C34
Hamnavoe *She.* 89 J39
Hamnavoe *She.* 89 D40
Hamnavoe *She.* 89 E40
Hampden Park 13 D52
Hampnett 30 G37

Hampole

Hampole 51 A41
Hampreston 10 E36
Hampstead Norreys 21 D41
Hampsthwaite 57 D38
Hampton G.L. 22 D47
Hampton H.& W. 30 D36
Hampton Shr. 39 G33
Hampton Bishop 28 E31
Hampton Heath 38 A31
Hampton-in-Arden 40 G38
Hampton Loade 39 G33
Hampton Lovett 29 B34
Hampton Lucy 30 C38
Hampton on the Hill 30 B38
Hampton Poyle 31 G41
Hamptworth 10 C38
Hamsey 13 C50
Hamstall Ridware 40 D37
Hamstead 40 F36
Hamstead Marshall 21 E40
Hamsterley Drm. 62 A37
Hamsterley Drm. 62 C37
Hamsterley Mill 62 A37
Ham Street 8 A31
Hamstreet 15 D56
Hanbury H.& W. 29 B35
Hanbury Stf. 40 C37
Hanchurch 40 A34
Handbridge 48 F30
Handcross 13 A48
Handforth 49 D34
Handley 48 G30
Handsacre 40 D36
Handsworth S.Y. 51 D40
Handsworth W.M. 40 F36
Handy Cross 22 B44
Hanford 40 A34
Hanging Langford 10 A36
Hangingshaw Bor. 69 A29
Hangingshaw D.& G. 69 E27
Hanham 19 D32
Hankelow 39 A32
Hankerton 20 B35
Hanley 40 A34
Hanley Castle 29 D34
Hanley Swan 29 D34
Hanley William 29 B32
Hanlith 56 C35
Hannington Ham. 21 F41
Hannington Nmp. 32 A44
Hannington Wts. 20 B37
Hanslope 32 D44
Hanthorpe 42 C46
Hanwell 31 D40
Hanworth G.L. 22 D47
Hanworth Nfk. 45 B57
Happendon 74 G24
Happisburgh 45 B59
Happisburgh Common 45 C59
Hapsford 48 E30
Hapton Lan. 56 F33
Hapton Nfk. 45 F57
Harberton 5 E23
Harbertonford 5 E23
Harbledown 15 B57
Harborne 40 G36
Harborough Magna 31 A40
Harbottle 70 C35
Harbury 30 C39
Harby Lei. 42 B43
Harby Not. 52 E44
Harcombe 7 G24
Harden 57 F36
Hardenhuish 20 D35
Hardgate D.& G. 68 G24
Hardgate Grm. 85 J33
Hardgrove 69 F27
Hardham 12 C46
Hardhorn 55 F29
Hardingham 44 E56
Hardingstone 31 C43
Hardings Wood 49 G34
Hardington Mandeville 8 C31
Hardley 11 D40
Hardrow 61 G34
Hardstoft 51 F40
Hardwick Bkh. 32 G44
Hardwick Cbs. 33 C49
Hardwick H.& W. 28 D28
Hardwick Nfk. 45 F58
Hardwick Nmp. 32 A44
Hardwick W.M. 40 F36
Hardwicke 29 G33
Hare and Hounds Inn 7 F27
Hareby 53 F49
Hareden 56 D32
Harefield 22 B46
Harefield Moor 22 C46
Hare Green 35 F57
Hare Hatch 22 D44
Harehead 76 D32
Harelaw 77 E34
Harelawhole 69 F30
Haresceugh 61 B32
Harescombe 29 G34
Haresfield 29 G34
Hareshaw 74 D24
Hareshaw Head 70 E34
Hare Street 33 F49
Harewood 57 E39
Harewood End 28 F31
Harford 5 E22
Hargate 45 F57
Hargrave Nmp. 32 A46
Hargrave Sfk. 34 B53
Harker 69 G29
Harkstead 35 E57
Harlaston 40 D38
Harlaxton 42 B44
Harlech 36 B21
Harleston Nfk. 45 G58
Harleston Sfk. 34 B56
Harlestone 31 B43
Harle Syke 56 F34
Harley 38 E31
Harleyholm 75 G25
Harlington Bfd. 32 E46
Harlington G.L. 22 D46
Harlington S.Y. 51 B40
Harlosh 82 E8
Harlow 33 G50
Harlow Hill 71 G36
Harlthorpe 58 F43
Harlton 33 C49
Harmby 57 A37
Harmerhill 38 C30
Harmston 52 F45
Harnham 10 B37
Harnham 71 E36
Harold Hill 23 B51
Haroldston West 16 C14
Haroldswick 89 A42
Harold Wood 23 B51
Harome 58 A42
Harpenden 32 G47
Harpford 7 F26
Harpham 59 C46
Harpley 44 C53
Harpole 31 B42
Harpsden 22 C43
Harpswell 52 D45
Harpurhill 50 E36
Harrier 89 H35
Harrietfield 80 G25
Harrietsfield 70 A32
Harrietsham 14 B54
Harrington Cum. 60 D25
Harrington Lcn. 53 E49
Harrington Nmp. 42 G43
Harringworth 42 F45
Harris 78 A9
Harrisea Head 49 G34
Harrogate 57 D39
Harrold 32 C45
Harrow 22 C47
Harrowbarrow 4 C19
Harrowgate Hill 62 E38
Harrow Weald 22 B47
Harston Cbs. 33 C50
Harston Lei. 42 B44
Harswell 58 E44
Hart 62 C40
Hartburn Cle. 71 E36
Hartburn Nor. 62 E40
Hartest 34 C54
Hartfield 13 A50
Hartford Cbs. 33 A48
Hartford Che. 49 E32
Hartfordbeach 49 E32
Hartfordbridge 22 F43
Hartford End 33 G52
Harthill Che. 48 G31
Harthill Ltn. 75 D25
Harthill S.Y. 51 D40
Harthill Services 75 D25
Hartington 50 F37
Hartland 6 C18
Hartland Quay 6 C18
Hartleap 69 A28
Hartlebury 29 A34
Hartlepool 63 C41
Hartley Cum. 61 F33
Hartley Kent 14 D53
Hartley Kent 24 E52
Hartley T.& W. 71 F39
Hartley's Village 48 C29
Hartley Wespall 22 F43
Hartley Wintney 22 F43
Hartlington 57 C36
Hartlip 24 E54
Harton N.Y. 58 C43
Harton Shr. 38 G30
Harton T.& W. 71 G39
Hartpury 29 F33
Hartrigge 70 A32
Hartshead Moor Services 57 G37
Hartshill 41 F39
Hartshorne 41 C39
Hartside 68 A25
Hartsop 61 E30
Hartwell Bkh. 31 G43
Hartwell Nmp. 31 C43
Hartwood 74 E24
Harvel 24 E52
Harvieston 87 E24
Harvington 30 D36
Harwell 21 C40
Harwich 35 E58
Harwood Bor. 69 C30
Harwood Drm. 61 C34
Harwood Nor. 71 E36
Harwood Dale 63 G45
Harworth 51 C42
Hasbury 40 G35
Hascombe 12 A46
Haselbech 31 A43
Haselbury Plucknett 8 C30
Haseley 30 B38
Haselor 30 C37
Hasfield 29 F34
Haskayne 48 B29
Hasketon 35 C58
Hasland 51 F39
Haslemere 12 A45
Haslingden 56 G33
Haslingfield 33 C50
Haslington 49 G33
Hassall 49 G33
Hassendean 70 A31
Hassness 60 E27
Hassocks 13 C49
Hassop 50 E38
Hastigrow 87 B28
Hastingleigh 15 C57
Hastings 14 G54
Hastingwood 23 A50
Haswell 62 B39
Haswell Plough 62 B39
Hatch 21 F42
Hatch Beauchamp 8 B29
Hatchednize 77 F34
Hatch Green 8 C28
Hatcliffe 53 B48
Hatfield Hfs. 23 A48
Hatfield H.& W. 28 C31
Hatfield H.& W. 29 C34
Hatfield S.Y. 51 B42
Hatfield Broad Oak 33 G51
Hatfield Heath 33 G51
Hatfield Peverel 34 G54
Hatfield Woodhouse 51 B42
Hatford 21 B39
Hatherden 21 F39
Hatherleigh 6 E21
Hathern 41 C41
Hatherop 20 A37
Hathersage 50 D38
Hatherton Che. 39 A32
Hatherton Stf. 40 D35
Hatley St. George 33 C48
Hatt 4 D19
Hatton Che. 48 D31
Hatton Dby. 40 C38
Hatton G.L. 22 D46
Hatton Grm. 85 F36
Hatton Lcn. 52 E47
Hatton War. 30 B38
Hatton Heath 48 F30
Hatton of Fintray 85 H34
Haugham 53 D49
Haugh Head Nor. 71 A36
Haughhead Str. 74 C22
Haughley 34 B56
Haughley Green 34 B56
Haugh of Glass 85 F30
Haugh of Urr 68 G24
Haughton Not. 51 E42
Haughton Shr. 38 C29
Haughton Stf. 40 C34
Haughton le Skerne 62 E39
Haunn 78 F9
Haunton 40 D38
Hauxley 71 C38
Hauxton 33 C50
Havant 11 D43
Haven 28 C30
Haven Side 59 G49
Havenstreet 11 E41
Havercroft 51 A39
Haverfordwest 16 C15
Haverhill 33 D52
Haverigg 54 B27
Havering 23 C51
Havering-atte-Bower 23 B51
Haversham 32 D44
Haverthwaite 55 A29
Haverton Hill 62 D40
Hawarden 48 F29
Hawbush Green 34 F53
Hawcoat 54 B27
Hawes 56 A34
Hawick 69 B30
Hawkchurch 8 D29
Hawkedon 34 C54
Hawkeridge 20 F34
Hawkesbury 20 C33
Hawkesbury Upton 20 C33
Hawk Green 49 D35
Hawkhill Nor. 71 B38
Hawkhill Tay. 81 E32
Hawkhurst 14 D53
Hawkinge 15 C58
Hawkley 11 B43
Hawkridge 7 B24
Hawksdale 60 B29
Hawkshead 60 G29
Hawksland 74 G24
Hawkstone 38 B31
Hawkswick 56 B35
Hawksworth Not. 42 A43
Hawksworth W.Y. 57 E37
Hawkwell 24 B54
Hawley Ham. 22 F44
Hawley Kent 23 D51
Hawling 30 F36
Hawnby 58 A41
Haworth 57 F36
Hawstead 34 C54
Hawthorn Drm. 62 B40
Hawthorn Wts. 20 E34
Hawthornside 70 B31
Hawton 51 G43
Haxby 58 D42
Haxey 51 B43
Haxted 23 G50
Haydock 48 C31
Haydon 9 C32
Haydon Bridge 70 G34
Haydon Wick 20 C37
Hayes G.L. 23 E50
Hayes G.L. 22 C46
Hayfield 50 D36
Hayhillock 81 F31
Haylands 11 E41
Hayle 2 E11
Haynes 32 D46
Hay-on-Wye 28 D28
Hayscastle 16 B14
Hayscastle Cross 16 B15
Hay Street 33 F49
Hayton Cum. 61 A31
Hayton Cum. 60 B27
Hayton Hum. 58 E44
Hayton Not. 51 D43
Haytor Vale 5 C23
Haywards Heath 13 B49
Haywood 75 E25
Hazelbank 74 F24
Hazelbury Bryan 9 D33
Hazeley 22 F43
Hazel Grove 49 D35
Hazelside 68 A24
Hazelslade 40 D36
Hazel Wood 23 E50
Hazelwood 41 A39
Hazlemere 22 B44
Hazlerigg 71 F38
Hazleton 30 G36
Heacham 44 B52
Headbourne Worthy 11 A40
Headcorn 14 C54
Headingley 57 F38
Headington 21 A41
Headlam 62 E37
Headless Cross 30 B36
Headley Ham. 21 E41
Headley Ham. 12 A44
Headley Sry. 23 F48
Headley Down 12 A44
Headon 51 E43
Head's Nook 61 A30
Heage 51 G39
Healaugh N.Y. 57 E40
Healaugh N.Y. 62 G36
Heald Green 49 D34
Healey G.M. 49 A34
Healey N.Y. 57 A37
Healeyfield 62 B36
Healing 53 A48
Heamoor 2 E10
Heanor 41 A40
Heanton Punchardon 6 B20
Heap Bridge 49 A34
Heapham 52 D44
Hearthstane 69 A27
Heaste 82 H12
Heath 51 F40
Heath and Reach 32 F45
Heathcote 50 F37
Heath End Ham. 21 E41
Heath End Ham. 22 G44
Heath End W.M. 40 E36
Heather 41 D39
Heathfield Dev. 5 C24
Heathfield D.& G. 69 G28
Heathfield E.S. 13 B51
Heathfield Som. 7 C27
Heathhall 68 F25
Heath Hayes 40 D36
Heath Hill 39 D33
Heathrow Airport 22 D46
Heath Town 40 F35
Heatley 49 D33
Heaton 49 F35
Hebburn 71 G39
Hebden 57 C36
Hebden Bridge 56 G35
Hebron Dyf. 16 B17
Hebron Nor. 71 E37
Heck 69 F26
Heckfield 22 E43
Heckfield Green 35 A57
Heckington 42 A47
Heckmondwike 57 G38
Heddington 20 E35
Heddon on the Wall 71 G37
Hedenham 45 F59
Hedge End 11 C40
Hedgerley 22 C45
Hedley Hill 62 B37
Hedley on the Hill 62 A36
Hednesford 40 D36
Hedon 59 G47
Hedworth 71 G39
Heglibister 89 G39
Heighington Drm. 62 D38
Heighington Lcn. 52 F46
Heights of Kinlochewe 83 C16
Heilam 86 B20
Heiton 76 G33
Hele 7 E25
Helensburgh 73 B18
Helford 2 F13
Helhoughton 44 C54
Helions Bumpstead 33 D52
Helland 4 C16
Hellandbridge 4 C16
Hellesdon 45 D57
Hellidon 31 C41
Hellifield 56 D34
Hellingly 13 C51
Helm 71 D37
Helmdon 31 D41
Helmington Row 62 C37
Helmsdale 87 G26
Helmshore 56 G33
Helmsley 58 A42
Helperby 57 C40
Helperthorpe 59 B45
Helpringham 42 A47
Helpston 42 E47
Helsby 48 E30
Helston 2 F12
Helstone 4 B16
Helton 61 D31
Helwith Bridge 56 C34
Hemel Hempstead 22 A46
Hemheath 40 A34
Hemingbrough 58 F42
Hemingby 53 E48
Hemingford Abbots 33 A48
Hemingford Grey 33 A48
Hemingstone 35 C57
Hemington Lei. 41 C40
Hemington Nmp. 42 G46
Hemington Som. 20 F33
Hemley 35 D58
Hemlington 63 E41
Hempnall 45 F58
Hempstead Esx. 33 E52
Hempstead Nfk. 45 B57
Hempsted 29 G34
Hempton Nfk. 44 C55
Hempton Oxf. 31 E40
Hemsby 45 D60
Hemswell 52 C45
Hemsworth 51 A40
Hemyock 7 D27
Henbury Avon 19 D31
Henbury Che. 49 E34
Hendon 62 A40
Hendre 47 F27
Hendremynach 37 D22
Hendy 17 D21
Heneglwys 46 E20
Henfaes 37 C24
Henfield 13 C48
Henfron 27 D24
Hengoed 18 B27
Hengrave 34 B54
Henham 33 F51
Heniarth 38 E27
Henlade 8 B28
Henley Sfk. 35 C57
Henley Som. 8 A30
Henley W.S. 12 B44
Henley-in-Arden 30 B37
Henley-on-Thames 22 C43
Henllan Clw. 47 F26
Henllan Dyf. 26 D19
Henllys 19 B28
Henlow 32 E47
Hennock 7 G24
Henny Street 34 E54
Henryd 47 E23
Henry's Moat 16 B16
Hensall 58 G41
Henshaw 70 G33
Hensingham 60 E25
Henstead 45 G60
Henstridge 9 C33
Henstridge Ash 9 B33
Henton Oxf. 22 A43
Henton Som. 19 G30
Henwood 4 C18
Heogan 89 H40
Heol Senni 27 F25
Heol-y-Cyw 18 C25
Hepburn 71 A36
Hepple 70 C35
Hepscott 71 E38
Heptonstall 56 G35
Hepworth Sfk. 34 A55
Hepworth W.Y. 50 B37
Herbrandston 16 D14
Hereford 28 E31
Hergest 28 C28
Heriot 75 E29
Hermitage Bor. 70 D31
Hermitage Brk. 21 D41
Hermitage Dor. 9 D32
Hermitage W.S. 11 D43
Hermon Dyf. 17 A18
Hermon Dyf. 17 A19
Hermon Gwy. 46 F19
Herne 25 E57
Herne Bay 25 E57
Herne Common 25 E57
Herner 6 C21
Hernhill 25 E56
Herodsfoot 4 D18
Herongate 24 B52
Heronsford 67 E17
Herriard 21 G42
Herringswell 34 A53
Herstmonceux 13 C52
Herston Dor. 10 G36
Herston Ork. 89 H30
Hertford 33 G49
Hesketh Bank 55 G30
Hesketh Lane 56 E32
Hesket Newmarket 60 C29
Heskin Green 48 A31
Hesleden 62 C40
Hesleyside 70 E34
Heslington 58 D42
Hessay 58 D41
Hessenford 4 E19
Hessett 34 B55
Hessle 59 G46
Hest Bank 55 C30
Heston 22 D47
Heston Services 22 D47
Heswall 48 D28
Hethe 31 F41
Hethersett 45 E57
Hethersgill 69 G30
Hethpool 70 A34
Hett 62 C38
Hetton 56 D35
Hetton Downs 62 B39
Hetton le Hole 62 B39
Heugh Nor. 71 F36
Heugh Nor. 70 E34
Heugh Head Bor. 77 D34
Heugh-head Grm. 84 H29
Heveningham 35 A59
Hever 23 G50
Heversham 55 A30
Hevingham 45 C58
Hewelsfield 19 A31
Hewish Avon 19 E29
Hewish Som. 8 D30
Heworth 71 G38
Hexham 70 G35
Hexpath 76 F32
Hextable 23 D51
Hexthorpe 51 B41
Hexton 32 E47
Hexworthy 5 C22
Hey 56 E34
Heybridge Esx. 24 B52
Heybridge Esx. 24 A54
Heybrook Bay 4 F20
Heydon Cbs. 33 D50
Heydon Nfk. 45 C57
Heydour 42 B46
Hey Houses 55 G29
Heylor 89 D38
Heysham 55 C30
Heyshott 12 C44
Heytesbury 20 G35
Heythrop 30 F39
Heywood G.M. 49 A34
Heywood Wts. 20 F34
Hibaldstow 52 B45
Hickleton 51 B40
Hickling Nfk. 45 C60
Hickling Not. 41 C42
Hickling Green 45 C60
Hickstead 13 B48
Hidcote Bartrim 30 D37
High Ackworth 51 A40
High Airriequhillart 64 C19
Higham 24 D53
Higham Dby. 51 G39
Higham Lan. 56 F34
Higham Sfk. 34 B53
Higham Sfk. 34 E56
Higham S.Y. 51 B39
Higham Dykes 71 F37
Higham Ferrers 32 B45
Higham Gobion 32 E47
Higham on the Hill 41 F39
Highampton 6 E20
High Angerton 71 E36
High Bankhill 61 B31
High Banton 74 B23
High Beach 23 B50
High Bentham 56 C32
High Bickington 6 C21
High Blantyre 74 E22
High Bonnybridge 74 C24
High Borgue 65 C22
High Borve 88 B10
High Bray 6 B22
Highbridge 19 G29
Highbrook 13 A49
High Brooms 23 G51
High Bullen 6 C21
Highburton 50 A37
Highbury 19 G32
High Buston 71 C38
High Catton 58 D43
Highchesters 69 B30
Highclere 21 E40
High Cleughearn 74 F22
Highcliffe 10 E38
High Coniscliffe 62 E38
High Crosby 61 A30
High Cross Ham. 11 B43
High Cross Hfs. 33 G49
High Easter 33 G52
High Ellington 57 A37
High Entercommon 62 F39
Higher Ashton 7 G24
Higher Ballam 55 F29
Higher Boscaswell 2 E9
High Ercall 38 D31
Higher Heysham 55 C30
Higher Kinnerton 48 F29
Higher Porthpean 4 E16
Higher Town Cnw. 2 A11
Highertown Cnw. 3 D14
Higher Walton 55 G31
Higher Wheelton 56 G32
Higher Whitley 49 D32
Higher Wych 38 A31
High Etherley 62 D37
Highfield 73 E19
Highfields 33 C49
High Garrett 34 F53
Highgate 51 A41
High Glenling 64 C19
High Grantley 57 B38
High Green H.& W. 29 D34
High Green S.Y. 51 C39
High Green W.Y. 50 A37
Highgreen Manor 70 D34
High Halden 14 D54
High Halstow 24 D53
High Ham 8 A30
High Harrington 60 D25
High Hartington 71 E36
High Hawsker 63 F45
High Hermitage 62 B36
High Hesket 61 B30
High Hoyland 50 B38
High Hunsley 59 F45
High Hurstwood 13 B50
High Hutton 58 C43
High Ireby 60 C28
High Kilburn 58 B41
Highlane 49 F34
Highlane Dby. 51 D40
High Lane G.M. 49 D35
High Lane H.& W. 29 B32
High Laver 23 A51
Highlaws 60 B27
Highleadon 29 F33
High Legh 49 D33
Highleigh 12 E44
High Leven 62 E40
Highley 39 G33
High Limerigg 74 C24
High Littleton 19 F32
High Lorton 60 D27
High Marishes 58 B44
High Marnham 52 E44
High Melton 51 B41
High Mickley 71 G36
High Moor Cum. 60 B28
High Moor Lan. 55 F29
Highmoor Cross 21 C42
Highnam 29 G33
Highnam Green 29 F33
High Newton 55 A30
High Nibthwaite 54 A28
High Offley 39 C33
High Ongar 23 A51
High Pennyvenie 67 C20
High Roding 33 G52
High Row 60 C29
High Scales 60 B27

High Shaw 61 G34
High Spen 62 A37
Highsted 25 E55
High Street Cnw. 3 C15
Highstreet Kent 14 D53
Highstreet Kent 25 E56
High Street Sfk. 34 D54
High Street Green 34 C56
Hightae 69 F26
Hightown Che. 49 F34
Hightown Mer. 48 B28
High Toynton 53 F48
High Trewhitt 71 C36
High Valleyfield 75 B26
Highweek 5 C24
High Westward 62 A37
High Woolaston 19 B31
Highworth 21 B38
High Wray 60 G29
High Wych 33 G50
High Wycombe 22 B44
Hilborough 44 E54
Hildenborough 23 G51
Hilden Park 23 G51
Hildersham 33 D51
Hilderstone 40 B35
Hilderthorpe 59 C47
Hilgay 44 F52
Hill 19 B32
Hillam 58 G41
Hillbeck 61 E33
Hillberry 54 F26
Hillborough 25 E58
Hill Brow 11 B43
Hill Dale 48 A30
Hill Dyke 43 A49
Hill End Drm. 62 C36
Hill End Fife 75 A26
Hillend Fife 75 B27
Hillend Ltn. 75 D28
Hill End N.Y. 57 D36
Hillend Str. 74 D24
Hillesden 31 F42
Hillfield 9 D32
Hillhead Cnw. 5 E25
Hill Head Ham. 11 D41
Hill Head Nor. 70 G35
Hillingdon 22 C46
Hillmorton 31 A41
Hillockhead 84 J29
Hill of Beath 75 A27
Hill of Fearn 84 B24
Hill Ridware 40 D36
Hillsborough S.Y. 51 D39
Hillside Fife 75 A26
Hillside Grm. 81 A35
Hillside She. 89 F40
Hillside Tay. 81 D33
Hillsley 20 C33
Hillswick 89 E38
Hill Top Drm. 62 A37
Hill Top W.Y. 51 A39
Hill View 9 E35
Hilmarton 20 D36
Hilperton 20 F34
Hilsea 11 D42
Hilston 59 F48
Hilton Cbs. 33 B48
Hilton Cle. 62 E40
Hilton Cum. 61 D33
Hilton Dby. 40 B38
Hilton Dor. 9 D33
Hilton Drm. 62 D37
Hilton Sal. 39 F33
Hilton of Cadboll 84 B24
Hilton Park Services 40 E35
Himbleton 29 C35
Himley 40 F34
Hincaster 55 A31
Hinckley 41 F40
Hinderclay 34 A56
Hinderwell 63 E43
Hindford 38 B29
Hindhead 12 A44
Hindle Fold 56 F33
Hindley G.M. 49 B32
Hindley Nor. 62 A36
Hindlip 29 C34
Hindolveston 44 C56
Hindon 9 A35
Hindringham 44 B55
Hingham 44 E56
Hinstock 39 C32
Hintlesham 34 D56
Hinton Avon 20 D33
Hinton Glo. 19 A32
Hinton Ham. 10 E38
Hinton H.& W. 28 E29
Hinton Shr. 38 E30
Hinton Ampner 11 B42
Hinton Blewett 20 F33
Hinton Charterhouse 20 F33
Hinton Green 30 E36
Hinton in the Hedges 31 E41
Hinton Marsh 11 B41
Hinton Martell 10 D36
Hinton on the Green 30 E36
Hinton Parva Dor. 10 D36
Hinton Parva Wts. 21 C38
Hinton St. George 8 C30
Hinton St. Mary 9 C33
Hinton Waldrist 21 B39
Hints 40 E37
Hinwick 32 B45
Hinxhill 15 C56
Hinxton 33 D50
Hinxworth 33 D48
Hipperholme 57 G37
Hipswell 62 G37
Hiraeth 16 B17
Hirn 81 A33
Hirnant Pow. 37 C26
Hirnant Pow. 27 A24

Hirst 71 E38
Hirst Courtney 58 G42
Hirwaun 18 A25
Histon 33 B50
Hitcham 34 C55
Hitchin 32 E47
Hive 58 F44
Hixon 40 C35
Hoar Cross 40 C37
Hoarwithy 28 F31
Hoath 25 E58
Hobbister 89 G29
Hobkirk 70 B31
Hobson 62 A37
Hoby 41 D42
Hockering 44 D56
Hockerton 51 G43
Hockley Esx. 24 B54
Hockley W.M. 30 A38
Hockley Heath 30 A37
Hockliffe 32 F45
Hockwold cum Wilton 44 G53
Hockworthy 7 D26
Hoddesdon 23 A49
Hoddlesden 56 G33
Hodgeston 16 E16
Hodnet 39 C32
Hodthorpe 51 E41
Hoe 44 D55
Hoff 61 E32
Hoffleet Stow 43 B48
Hoften's Cross 40 A36
Hoggeston 32 F44
Hoghton 56 G32
Hognaston 50 G38
Hogsthorpe 53 E51
Holbeach 43 C49
Holbeach Drove 43 D49
Holbeach Hurn 43 C49
Holbeach St. Johns 43 D49
Holbeach St. Marks 43 B49
Holbeck 51 E41
Holbeton 5 E22
Holborough 24 E53
Holbrook Dby. 41 A39
Holbrook Sfk. 35 E57
Holburn 77 G36
Holbury 11 D40
Holcombe Dev. 5 C25
Holcombe Som. 19 G32
Holcombe Brook 49 A33
Holcombe Rogus 7 D26
Holcot 31 B43
Holden 56 E33
Holdenby 31 B42
Holdenhurst 10 E37
Holdgate 38 F31
Holdingham 42 A46
Holefield 77 G34
Holestane 68 D24
Holford 7 A27
Holker 55 B29
Holkham 44 A54
Hollacombe 6 E19
Holland Ork. 89 B30
Holland Sry. 23 F50
Holland Fen 43 A48
Holland-on-Sea 35 G58
Hollandstoun 89 B33
Hollee 69 G28
Hollesley 35 D59
Hollingbourne 14 B54
Hollington Dby. 40 B38
Hollington E.S. 14 F53
Hollington Stf. 40 B36
Hollingworth 50 C36
Hollin Hall 56 F35
Hollins 49 B34
Hollinsclough 50 F36
Hollins Green 49 C32
Hollins Lane 55 D30
Hollocombe 6 D22
Holloway 51 G39
Hollowell 31 A42
Hollow Meadows 50 D38
Hollows 69 F29
Holly Bush Clw. 38 A30
Hollybush Gwe. 18 A27
Hollybush H.& W. 29 E33
Hollybush Str. 67 B19
Holly End 43 E50
Hollym 59 G49
Hollywood H.& W. 30 A36
Holm 88 D10
Holmbridge 50 B37
Holmbury St. Mary 22 G47
Holme Cbs. 42 G47
Holme Cum. 55 B31
Holme Hum. 52 B45
Holme Not. 52 G44
Holme W.Y. 50 B37
Holmebridge 9 F34
Holme Chapel 56 G34
Holme Hale 44 E54
Holme Lacy 28 E31
Holme Marsh 28 C29
Holmend 69 C26
Holme next the Sea 44 A53
Holme on the Wolds 59 E45
Holme Pierrepont 41 B42
Holmer 28 D31
Holmer Green 22 B45
Holme St. Cuthbert 60 B27
Holmes Chapel 49 F33
Holmeswood 48 A30
Holme upon Spalding Moor 58 F44
Holmewood 51 F40
Holmfirth 50 B37
Holmhead D.& G. 68 E23
Holmhead Str. 67 A21
Holmpton 59 G49
Holmrook 60 G26

Holmside 62 B38
Holne 5 D23
Holnest 9 D32
Holsworthy 6 E19
Holsworthy Beacon 6 E19
Holt Clw. 48 G30
Holt Dor. 10 D36
Holt Nfk. 44 B56
Holt Wts. 20 E34
Holtby 58 D42
Holt End 30 B36
Holt Fleet 29 B34
Holt Heath 29 B34
Holton Lcn. 52 D47
Holton Oxf. 21 A42
Holton Sfk. 35 A60
Holton Som. 9 B32
Holton le Clay 53 B48
Holton le Moor 52 C46
Holton St. Mary 34 E56
Holwell Dor. 9 C32
Holwell Hfs. 32 E47
Holwell Lei. 42 C43
Holwell Oxf. 21 A38
Holwell Som. 20 G33
Holwick 61 D35
Holybourne 22 G43
Holy Cross H.& W. 29 A35
Holyhead 46 D18
Holy Island 77 F37
Holylee 75 G29
Holymoorside 51 F39
Holyport 22 D44
Holystone 70 C35
Holytown 74 D23
Holywell Hfs. 33 A49
Holywell Clw. 47 E27
Holywell Cnw. 2 C13
Holywell Dor. 8 D31
Holywell T.& W. 71 F39
Holywell Green 50 A36
Holywell Row 34 A53
Holywood Avon D.& G. 68 E25
Homersfield 45 G58
Homington 10 B37
Honeyborough 16 D15
Honeybourne 30 D37
Honey Hill 25 E57
Honey Tye 34 E55
Honiley 30 A38
Honing 45 C59
Honingham 45 D57
Honington Lcn. 42 A45
Honington Sfk. 34 A55
Honington War. 30 D38
Honiton 7 E27
Honley 50 A37
Honnington 39 D33
Hoo 24 D53
Hood Green 51 B39
Hooe Dev. 4 E20
Hooe E.S. 13 D52
Hooe Common 13 C52
Hook Dyf. 16 C15
Hook Ham. 22 F43
Hook Hum. 58 G43
Hook Wts. 20 C36
Hooke 8 D31
Hookgate 39 B33
Hook Green 13 A52
Hook Norton 30 E39
Hookwood Common 23 G48
Hooley 23 F48
Hooton Levitt 51 C41
Hooton Pagnell 51 B40
Hooton Roberts 51 C40
Hoove 89 H39
Hope Clw. 48 G30
Hope Dby. 50 D37
Hope Hgh. 86 C20
Hope Pow. 38 E28
Hope Shr. 38 E29
Hope Bagot 28 A31
Hope Bowdler 38 F30
Hopehouse 69 B28
Hope Mansel 29 G32
Hopesay 38 G29
Hope under Dinmore 28 C31
Hopperton 57 D40
Hopsrig 69 E29
Hopton Nfk. 45 E61
Hopton Sal. 38 C31
Hopton Sfk. 34 A55
Hopton Stf. 40 C35
Hopton Cangeford 38 G31
Hopton Castle 28 A29
Hoptonheath 28 A29
Hopton Wafers 29 A32
Hopwas 40 E37
Horam 13 C51
Horbling 42 B47
Horbury 50 A38
Horden 62 B40
Horderley 38 G30
Hordle 10 E38
Hordley 38 B29
Horeb 26 D19
Horgabost 88 H6
Horham 35 A58
Horkesley Heath 34 F55
Horkstow 52 A45
Horley Oxf. 31 D40
Horley W.S. 23 G48
Hornby Lan. 55 C31
Hornby N.Y. 62 G38
Hornby N.Y. 62 F39
Horncastle 53 F48
Horncliffe 77 F35
Horndean Bor. 77 F34
Horndean Ham. 11 C42
Horndon 6 G21
Horndon on the Hill 24 C52

Horning 45 D59
Horninghold 42 F44
Horninglow 40 C38
Horningsea 33 B50
Horningsham 20 G34
Horningtoft 44 C55
Horningtops 4 D18
Hornsby 61 B31
Hornsby Gate 61 A31
Horns Cross Dev. 6 C19
Horns Cross E.S. 14 E54
Hornsea 59 E48
Hornton 30 D39
Horrabridge 5 C21
Horringer 34 B54
Horringford 11 F41
Horsebridge E.S. 13 C51
Horsebridge Ham. 10 A39
Horsehay 39 E32
Horseheath 33 D52
Horsehouse 57 A36
Horsell 22 F45
Horsey 45 C60
Horsford 45 D57
Horsforth 57 F38
Horsham 12 A47
Horsham St. Faith 45 D58
Horsington Lcn. 52 F47
Horsington Som. 9 B32
Horsley Dby. 41 A39
Horsley Glo. 20 B34
Horsley Nor. 71 G36
Horsley Nor. 70 D34
Horsley Cross 35 F57
Horsleycross Street 35 F57
Horsleyhill 70 B31
Horsley Woodhouse 41 A39
Horsmonden 14 C53
Horspath 21 A41
Horstead 45 D58
Horsted Keynes 13 B49
Horton Avon 20 C33
Horton Bkh. 22 D46
Horton Dor. 10 D36
Horton Lan. 56 D34
Horton Nmp. 32 C44
Horton Shr. 38 B30
Horton Som. 8 C29
Horton Stf. 49 G35
Horton W.G. 17 F20
Horton Wts. 20 E36
Horton Cross 8 C29
Horton-cum-Studley 31 G41
Horton Heath 11 C40
Horton Inn 10 D36
Horton in Ribblesdale 56 B34
Horton Kirby 23 E51
Hortonwood 39 D32
Horwich 49 A32
Horwood 6 C21
Hoscote 69 B29
Hose 42 C43
Hoswick 89 K40
Hotham 58 F44
Hothfield 14 C55
Hoton 41 C41
Houbie 89 C42
Houdston 67 D17
Hough Che. 49 G33
Hough Str. 78 F5
Hougham 42 A44
Hougharry 88 K3
Hough on the Hill 42 A45
Houghton Cbs. 33 A48
Houghton Cum. 61 A30
Houghton Dyf. 16 D15
Houghton Ham. 10 A39
Houghton W.S. 12 C46
Houghton Bank 62 D38
Houghton Conquest 32 D46
Houghton Green 49 C32
Houghton Hall 61 B39
Houghton le Spring 62 B39
Houghton on the Hill 41 E42
Houghton Regis 32 F46
Houghton St. Giles 44 B55
Houlsyke 63 F41
Hound 11 D40
Houndslow 76 F32
Houndwood 77 D34
Hounsdown 10 C39
Hounslow 22 D47
Hounslow Green 33 G52
Housetter 89 D39
Houston 74 D20
Houstry 87 E27
Houton 89 G29
Hove 13 D48
Hoveringham 41 A42
Hoveton 45 D59
Hovingham 58 B42
How Caple 29 E32
Howden Bor. 69 A30
Howden Bor. 70 B32
Howden Hum. 58 G43
Howden le Wear 62 C37
Howdens 71 D37
Howe Cum. 55 A30
Howe Hgh. 87 B29
Howe Nfk. 45 E59
Howe Green 24 A53
Howell 42 A47
How End 32 D46
Howe Street 34 G53
Howey 27 C26
Howford 75 G29
Howgate 75 E28
How Head 60 G29
Howick 71 B38
How Man 58 B41
Hownam 70 B33
Hownam Mains 70 B33

Howrigg 60 B29
Howsham Hum. 52 B46
Howsham N.Y. 58 C43
Howtel 77 G34
Howtown 61 E30
Howwell 65 D22
Howwood 73 D19
Hoxne 35 B31
Hoy Airport 89 H28
Hoylake 48 C28
Hoyland 51 B39
Hoyland Swaine 50 B38
Hubberholme 56 B35
Hubbert's Bridge 43 A48
Huby N.Y. 58 C41
Huby N.Y. 57 E38
Hucclecote 29 G34
Hucking 14 B54
Hucknall 41 A41
Huddersfield 50 A37
Huddington 29 C35
Hudscott 6 C22
Hudswell 62 F37
Huggate 58 D44
Hugglescote 41 D40
Hughenden Valley 22 B44
Hughley 38 F31
Hugh Town 2 A11
Huish Dev. 6 D21
Huish Wts. 20 E37
Huish Champflower 7 C26
Huish Episcopi 8 B30
Hulcott 32 G44
Hull, Kingston upon 59 G47
Hulland 40 A38
Hullavington 20 C34
Hullbridge 24 B54
Hulme 49 C34
Hulme End 50 G37
Hulme Walfield 49 F34
Hulverstone 11 F40
Hulver Street 45 G60
Humber Court 52 A46
Humberside Airport 52 A46
Humberston 53 B49
Humberstone 41 E42
Humbie 76 D30
Humbie Ho. 76 D30
Humbleton Hum. 59 F48
Humbleton Nor. 70 A35
Humby 42 B46
Hume 76 F33
Humshaugh 70 F35
Huna 89 K29
Huncoat 56 F33
Huncote 41 F41
Hundalee 70 B32
Hunderthwaite 62 D35
Hundle House 28 C27
Hundleby 53 F49
Hundleton 16 D15
Hundon 34 D53
Hungarton 41 E42
Hungerford Brk. 21 E39
Hungerford Ham. 10 C37
Hungerford Newtown 21 D39
Hunmanby 59 B46
Hunningham 30 B39
Hunsdon 33 G50
Hunsingore 57 D40
Hunsonby 61 C31
Hunspow 89 K28
Hunstanton 44 A52
Hunstanworth 61 B35
Hunston Sfk. 34 B55
Hunston W.S. 12 D44
Hunsworth 57 G37
Huntercombe End 21 C42
Huntershall 76 E30
Hunters Lodge Inn 8 E29
Hunter's Quay 73 C17
Hunterston 73 E17
Huntford 70 C32
Hunthill Lodge 81 C30
Huntingdon 33 A48
Huntingfield 35 A59
Huntington H.& W. 28 C28
Huntington N.Y. 58 D42
Huntington Stf. 40 D35
Huntingtower 80 H26
Huntley 29 G33
Huntly 85 F31
Huntlywood 76 F32
Hunton Ham. 11 A40
Hunton Kent 14 C53
Hunton N.Y. 62 G37
Hunts Cross 48 D30
Huntsham 7 C25
Huntshaw Cross 6 C21
Huntworth 8 A29
Hunwick 62 C37
Hunworth 44 B56
Hurdsfield 50 E34
Hurlet 74 D21
Hurley Brk. 22 C44
Hurley War. 40 F38
Hurley Bottom 22 C44
Hurlford 74 G20
Hurn 10 E37
Hursley 11 B40
Hurst 22 D43
Hurstbourne Priors 21 G40
Hurstbourne Tarrant 21 F39
Hurst Green E.S. 14 E53
Hurst Green Lan. 56 F32
Hurstpierpoint 13 C48
Hurstwood 56 F34
Hurworth-on-Tees 62 E39
Husbands Bosworth 41 G42
Husborne Crawley 32 E45
Hushinish 88 F5
Husthwaite 58 B41
Huthwaite 51 G40
Hutlerburn 69 A30
Huttoft 53 E51
Hutton Avon 19 F29

Hutton Bor. 77 E35
Hutton Cum. 61 D30
Hutton Esx. 24 B52
Hutton Hum. 59 D46
Hutton Lan. 55 G30
Hutton Buscel 59 A45
Hutton Conyers 57 B39
Hutton Cranswick 59 D46
Hutton End 61 C30
Hutton Henry 62 C40
Hutton John 61 D30
Hutton-le-Hole 58 A43
Hutton Magna 62 E37
Hutton Roof Cum. 55 B31
Hutton Roof Cum. 60 C29
Hutton Rudby 62 F40
Hutton Sessay 57 B40
Hutton Village 63 E41
Hutton Wandesley 58 D41
Huxham 7 F25
Huxley 48 F31
Huyton 48 C30
Hycemoor 54 A26
Hyde Glo. 20 A34
Hyde G.M. 49 C35
Hyde Heath 22 A45
Hydestile 22 G45
Hykeham Moor 52 F45
Hyndford-bridge-end 75 F25
Hyndlee 70 C31
Hynish 78 G5
Hyssington 38 F29
Hythe Ham. 11 D40
Hythe Kent 15 D57

I

Ibberton 9 D33
Ible 50 G38
Ibsley 10 D37
Ibstock 41 D40
Ibstone 22 B43
Ibthorpe 21 F39
Iburndale 63 F44
Ibworth 21 F41
Icelton 19 E29
Ickburgh 44 F54
Ickenham 22 C46
Ickford 21 A42
Ickham 15 B58
Ickleford 32 E47
Icklesham 14 F54
Ickleton 33 D50
Icklingham 34 A53
Ickwell Green 32 D47
Icomb 30 F38
Idbury 30 G38
Iddesleigh 6 E21
Ide 7 F24
Ideford 5 C24
Ide Hill 23 F50
Iden 14 E55
Iden Green 14 D54
Idle 57 F37
Idlicote 30 D38
Idmiston 10 A37
Idridgehay 40 A38
Idrigil 82 C9
Idstone 21 C38
Iffley 21 A41
Ifold 12 A44
Iford 13 D50
Ifton 19 C30
Ightfield 38 B31
Ightham 23 F51
Iken 35 C60
Ilam 50 G37
Ilchester 8 B31
Ilderton 71 A36
Ilford 23 C50
Ilfracombe 6 A21
Ilkeston 41 A40
Ilketshall St. Andrew 45 G59
Ilketshall St. Lawrence 45 G59
Ilketshall St. Margaret 45 G59
Ilkley 57 E37
Illingworth 57 G36
Illogan 2 D12
Illston on the Hill 42 F43
Ilmer 22 A43
Ilmington 30 D38
Ilminster 8 C29
Ilsington 5 C23
Ilston 17 E21
Ilton N.Y. 57 B37
Ilton Som. 8 C29
Imachar 72 F14
Immingham 52 A47
Immingham Dock 53 A48
Impington 33 B50
Ince Che. 48 E30
Ince G.M. 48 B31
Ince Blundell 48 B29
Inchbare 81 D32
Inchberry 84 D29
Inchbraoch 81 E33
Inchgrundle 81 C30
Inchina 86 J15
Inchinnan 74 D20
Inchlaggan 83 J17
Inchnacardoch 83 H19
Inchnadamph 86 F18
Inchree 79 D16
Inchture 81 H28
Inchvuilt 83 F18
Indian Queens 3 C15
Indians 74 B21
Inerval 78 L4
Ingatestone 24 B52
Ingbirchworth 50 B38
Ingestre 40 C35
Ingham Lcn. 52 D45

Ingham

Ingham Nfk. 45 C59
Ingham Sfk. 34 A54
Ingleborough 56 C33
Ingleby Dby. 41 C39
Ingleby Lcn. 52 E44
Ingleby Arncliffe 62 F40
Ingleby Barwick 62 E40
Ingleby Cross 62 F40
Ingleby Greenhow 63 F41
Inglesham 21 B38
Ingleton Drm. 62 D37
Ingleton N.Y. 56 B32
Inglewhite 55 E31
Ingoe 71 F36
Ingoldisthorpe 44 B52
Ingoldmells 53 F51
Ingoldsby 42 B46
Ingram 71 B36
Ingrave 24 B52
Ings 61 G30
Ingst 19 C31
Ingworth 45 C57
Injebreck 54 E26
Inkberrow 30 C36
Inkpen 21 E39
Inkstack 89 K28
Innellan 73 C17
Inner Hope 5 F22
Innerleithen 75 G29
Innerleven 75 A29
Innermessan 66 G16
Innerwell Fishery 64 D20
Innerwick Ltn. 76 C33
Innerwick Tay. 80 F21
Insch 85 G32
Insh 84 J24
Inskip 55 F30
Instow 6 B20
Intake 51 D39
Inver Grm. 81 A28
Inver Hgh. 84 A24
Inver Tay. 80 F26
Inverailort 79 B13
Inveralligin 83 D14
Inverallochy 85 C36
Inveraray 79 K16
Inverarish 82 F11
Inverarity 81 F30
Inverarnan 80 J19
Inverasdale 83 A14
Inverbeg Hotel 73 A19
Inverbervie 81 C34
Inverboyndie 85 C32
Inverbroom 83 A17
Invercassley 86 H20
Invercauld House 81 A27
Inverchaolain 72 C16
Invercharnan 79 F17
Inverchoran 83 D18
Inver Cottage 78 H5
Invercreran 79 F16
Inverdruie 84 H25
Inveresk 75 C29
Inverey 80 B26
Inverfarigaig 83 G21
Invergarry 83 J19
Invergeldie 80 H23
Invergordon 84 C23
Invergowrie 81 G29
Inverhadden 80 E22
Inverharroch 84 F29
Inverie 82 J13
Inverinan 79 J15
Inverinate 83 G15
Inverkeilor 81 F32
Inverkeithing 75 B27
Inverkeithny 85 E32
Inverkip 73 C18
Inverkirkaig 86 G16
Inverlael 83 A17
Inverlochlarig 80 J20
Inver Mallie 79 B17
Invermoriston 83 H20
Invernaver 87 B23
Inverness 84 E22
Inverness Airport 84 D23
Invernoaden 73 A17
Inveroran Hotel 79 F18
Inverpattack Lodge 80 A21
Inverpolly Lodge 86 G16
Inverroy 79 B18
Inversanda 79 E15
Inversnaid 80 K19
Inverugie 85 E37
Inveruglas 80 J19
Inverurie 85 G33
Invervar 80 F22
Invervegain 72 C16
Inwardleigh 6 F21
Inworth 34 G54
Iping 12 B44
Ipplepen 5 D24
Ipsden 21 C42
Ipstones 50 G36
Ipswich 35 D57
Irby 48 D28
Irby in the Marsh 53 F50
Irby upon Humber 52 B47
Irchester 32 B45
Ireby Cum. 60 C28
Ireby Lan. 56 B32
Ireland 89 K39
Ireleth 54 B28
Ireshopeburn 61 C34
Irlam 49 C33
Irnham 42 C46
Iron Acton 19 C32
Ironbridge 39 E32
Ironville 51 G40
Irthington 69 G30
Irthlingborough 32 A45
Irton 59 A46
Irvine 73 G19
Isauld 87 B25
Isbister She. 89 F41
Isbister She. 89 C39
Isel 60 C27
Isfield 13 C50
Isham 32 A44
Islay Airport 78 K4
Islay House 78 J4
Isle Abbotts 8 B29
Isle Brewers 8 B29
Isleham 33 A52
Isle of Man Airport 54 G25
Isle of Whithorn 64 E20
Isleornsay 82 H12
Isles of Scilly Airport 2 A11
Islesteps 68 F25
Isleworth 22 D47
Isley Walton 41 C40
Islip Nmp. 32 A45
Islip Oxf. 31 G41
Islivig 88 E5
Istead Rise 24 E52
Itchen 11 C40
Itchen Abbas 11 A41
Itchenfield 12 B47
Itchen Stoke 11 A41
Itchington 19 C32
Itford 13 D50
Itteringham 45 B57
Ivegill 61 B30
Iver 22 C46
Iver Heath 22 C46
Iveston 62 A37
Ivetsey Bank 40 D34
Ivinghoe 32 G45
Ivinghoe Aston 32 G45
Ivington 28 C30
Ivybridge 5 E22
Ivychurch 15 E56
Ivy Hatch 23 F51
Iwade 25 E55
Iwerne Courtney 9 C34
Iwerne Minster 9 C34
Ixworth 34 A55
Ixworth Thorpe 34 A55

J

Jackton 74 E21
Jacobstow 4 A17
Jacobstowe 6 E21
Jameston 16 E16
Jamestown Str. 73 B19
Janefield 84 D23
Janetstown 87 C29
Jarrow 71 G39
Jarvis Brook 13 B51
Jawcraig 74 C24
Jaywick 35 G57
Jaywick Sands 35 G57
Jeater Houses 62 G40
Jedburgh 70 A32
Jeffreston 16 D16
Jemimaville 84 C23
Jersey Airport 3 G17
Jersey Marine 18 B23
Jervaulx 57 A37
Jevington 13 D51
Jodrell Bank 49 E33
Johnby 61 C30
John O'Gaunt 42 D43
John O'Groats 89 K29
John O'Groats House Hotel 89 K29
John's Cross 14 E53
Johnshaven 81 D33
Johnston 16 C15
Johnstone D.& G. 69 D28
Johnstone Str. 74 D20
Johnstonebridge 69 D26
Johnstown Clw. 38 A29
Johnstown Dyf. 17 B19
Joppa Ltn. 75 C29
Joppa Str. 67 B20
Jordans 22 B45
Jump 51 B39
Juniper Green 75 D28
Jurby 54 D26
Justicetown 69 G29

K

Kaber 61 E33
Kailzie 75 G28
Kaimes Ltn. 75 D28
Kaimes Str. 68 A22
Kalemouth 70 A33
Kalnakill 82 D12
Kames 72 C15
Kea 3 D14
Keadby 52 A44
Keal Coates 53 F49
Kearsley G.M. 49 B33
Kearsley Nor. 71 F36
Kearstwick 56 B32
Keasden 56 C33
Keddington 53 D49
Kedington 34 D53
Kedleston 41 A39
Kedslie 76 F31
Keelby 52 A47
Keele 40 A34
Keele Services 40 A34
Keeley Green 32 D46
Keeston 16 C15
Keevil 20 F35
Kegworth 41 C40
Keig 85 H32
Keighley 57 E36
Keilhill 85 D33
Keillmore 72 B12
Keils 78 H6
Keinton Mandeville 8 A31
Keir Mill 68 D24
Keiss 87 B29
Keith 85 D30
Kelbrook 56 E35
Kelby 42 A46
Keld Cum. 61 E31
Keld N.Y. 61 F34
Keld Head 58 A43
Keldholme 58 A43
Kelfield Hum. 52 B44
Kelfield N.Y. 58 F41
Kelham 51 G43
Kelhead 69 G27
Kellan 79 F11
Kellarsbrae 74 A24
Kellas Grm. 84 D27
Kellas Tay. 81 G30
Kellaton 5 G24
Kellaways 20 D35
Kelleth 61 F32
Kelling 44 A56
Kellingley 58 G41
Kellington 58 G41
Kelloe 62 C39
Kelloe Mains 77 E34
Kelloholm 68 B23
Kelly 6 G19
Kelly Bray 4 C19
Kelmarsh 31 A43
Kelmscott 21 B38
Kelsale 35 B59
Kelsall 48 F31
Kelsall Hill 48 F31
Kelshall 33 E49
Kelsick 60 B28
Kelso 76 G33
Kelstedge 51 F39
Kelstern 53 C48
Kelsterton 48 E28
Kelston 19 E32
Kelton 68 F25
Kelton Hill 65 C23
Kelty 75 A27
Kelvedon 34 G54
Kelvedon Hatch 23 B51
Kelynack 2 E9
Kemback 81 J30
Kemberton 39 E33
Kemble 20 B35
Kemerton 29 E35
Kemeys Commander 19 A29
Kemnay 85 H33
Kempley 29 F32
Kempsey 29 D34
Kempsford 20 B37
Kempshott 21 F41
Kempston 32 D46
Kempston Church End 32 D46
Kempton 38 G29
Kemp Town 13 D49
Kemsing 23 F51
Kemsley 25 E55
Kenardington 14 D55
Kenchester 28 D30
Kencott 21 A38
Kendal 61 G31
Kenderchurch 28 F30
Kenfig 18 C24
Kenfig Hill 18 C24
Kenilworth 30 A38
Kenknock 80 G20
Kenley G.L. 23 F49
Kenley Shr. 38 E31
Kenmore Hgh. 82 D13
Kenmore Tay. 80 F23
Kenn Avon 19 E30
Kenn Dev. 7 G25
Kennacraig 72 D14
Kennards House 4 B18
Kennerleigh 7 E24
Kennet 75 A25
Kennethmont 85 G31
Kennett 33 B52
Kennford 7 G25
Kenninghall 44 G56
Kennington Kent 15 C56
Kennington Oxf. 21 A41
Kennoway 81 K29
Kennyhill 33 A52
Kenovay 78 F5
Kensaleyre 82 D10
Kensworth 32 G46
Kensworth Common 32 G46
Kentallen 79 E16
Kentchurch 28 F30
Kentford 34 B53
Kentisbeare 7 E26
Kentisbury 6 A22
Kentisbury Ford 6 A22
Kentmere 61 F30
Kenton Dev. 7 G25
Kenton Sfk. 35 B57
Kenton T.& W. 71 G38
Kenton Bank Foot 71 G38
Kentra 79 D12
Kents Bank 55 B29
Kent's Green 29 F33
Kent's Oak 10 B39
Kent Street 23 F52
Kenwyn 3 D14
Kenyon 49 C32
Keoldale 86 B19
Keose 88 E9
Keppoch 83 G14
Keprigan 66 B12
Kepwick 62 G40
Kerchesters 76 G33
Keresley 41 G39
Kerridge 49 E35
Kerry 38 F27
Kerrycroy 73 D17
Kerrysdale 83 B14
Kersall 51 F43
Kersey 34 D56
Kershader 88 F9
Kershopefoot 69 E30
Kersie Mains 74 A24
Kerswell 7 E26
Kerswell Green 29 D34
Kesgrave 35 D58
Keskadale 60 E28
Kessingland 45 G61
Kessingland Beach 45 G61
Kestle Mill 3 C14
Keston 23 E50
Keswick Cum. 60 D28
Keswick Nfk. 45 B59
Keswick Nfk. 45 E58
Ketley 39 D32
Kettelshiel 76 E33
Kettering 32 A44
Ketteringham 45 E57
Kettins 81 G28
Kettlebaston 34 C55
Kettleburgh 35 B58
Kettleholm 69 F27
Kettleness 63 E44
Kettleshulme 49 E35
Kettlesing Bottom 57 D38
Kettlestone 44 B55
Kettletoft 89 D32
Kettlewell 56 B35
Ketton 42 E45
Kewstoke 19 E29
Kexbrough 51 B39
Kexby Lcn. 52 D44
Kexby N.Y. 58 D43
Key Green 63 F44
Keyham 41 E42
Keyhaven 10 E39
Keyingham 59 G48
Keymer 13 C49
Keynsham 19 E32
Keysoe 32 B46
Keysoe Row 32 B46
Keyston 32 A46
Keyworth 41 B42
Kibblesworth 62 A38
Kibworth Beauchamp 41 F42
Kibworth Harcourt 41 F42
Kiddal Lane End 57 F40
Kidderminster 29 A34
Kiddington 31 F40
Kidlington 31 G40
Kidmore End 22 D43
Kidsdale 64 E20
Kidsgrove 49 G34
Kidstones 56 A35
Kidwelly 17 D20
Kielder 70 D32
Kiells 78 H5
Kilbagie 75 B25
Kilbarchan 73 D19
Kilberry Str. 72 D13
Kilbirnie 73 E19
Kilbride Str. 79 H14
Kilbride W.I. 88 R3
Kilbridemore 72 A16
Kilburn Dby. 41 A39
Kilburn N.Y. 58 B41
Kilby 41 F42
Kilcadzow 74 F24
Kilchamaig 72 D14
Kilchattan Str. 78 K9
Kilchattan Str. 73 E16
Kilchenzie 66 A12
Kilcheran 79 G14
Kilchiaran 78 J3
Kilchoan Hgh. 78 D10
Kilchoan Str. 79 J13
Kilchoman 78 J3
Kilchrenan 79 H16
Kilconquhar 81 K30
Kilcot 29 F32
Kilcoy 83 D21
Kilcreggan 73 B18
Kildale 63 F42
Kildalloig 66 B13
Kildalton Castle 78 K5
Kildary 84 B23
Kildavaig 72 D15
Kildavanan 72 D16
Kildermorie Lodge 83 B21
Kildonan Hgh. 87 F25
Kildonan Str. 66 A16
Kildonnan 78 B10
Kildrochet Ho. 64 C16
Kildrummy 85 H30
Kildwick 57 E36
Kilfinan 72 C15
Kilfinnan 79 A18
Kilford 47 F26
Kilgetty 16 D17
Kilgrammie 67 C18
Kilgwrrwg Common 19 B30
Kilham Hum. 59 C46
Kilham Nor. 77 G34
Kilirvan Cottages 66 B12
Kilkerran Str. 67 C19
Kilkerran Str. 66 B13
Kilkhampton 6 D18
Killadam 64 C19
Killamarsh 51 D40
Killay 17 E22
Killchianaig 72 B12
Killean 72 F12
Killearn 74 B21
Killellan 66 B12
Killen Hgh. 84 D22
Killerby 62 E37
Killichonan 80 E21
Killichronan 79 F11
Killiecrankie 80 D25
Killilan 83 F15
Killimster 87 C29
Killin 80 G21
Killinallan 78 H4
Killinghall 57 D38
Killington 56 A32
Killington Lake Services 61 G31
Killingworth 71 F38
Killin Lodge 83 J21
Killinochonoch 72 A14
Killochyett 76 F30
Killundine 79 F11
Kilmacolm 73 D19
Kilmahog 80 K22
Kilmahumaig 72 A13
Kilmaluag 82 B10
Kilmany 81 H29
Kilmarie 82 H11
Kilmarnock 74 G20
Kilmartin 72 A14
Kilmaurs 74 F20
Kilmelford 79 J14
Kilmeny 78 H5
Kilmersdon 19 F32
Kilmeston 11 B41
Kilmichael Str. 66 A12
Kilmichael Str. 72 C15
Kilmichael Glassary 72 A14
Kilmichael of Inverlussa 72 B13
Kilmington Dev. 8 E28
Kilmington Wts. 9 A33
Kilmington Street 9 A33
Kilmorack 83 E20
Kilmore Hgh. 82 J12
Kilmore Str. 79 H14
Kilmory Hgh. 79 C11
Kilmory Hgh. 82 J9
Kilmory Str. 72 C13
Kilmory Castle 72 B14
Kilmuir Hgh. 84 B23
Kilmuir Hgh. 84 E22
Kilmuir Hgh. 82 B9
Kilmun 73 B17
Kilnave 78 H4
Kilndown 14 D53
Kiln Green 22 D44
Kilnhurst 51 C40
Kilninian 78 F9
Kilninver 79 H14
Kilnpit Hill 62 A36
Kilnsea 53 A50
Kilnsey 56 C35
Kilnwick 59 E45
Kilnwick Percy 58 E44
Kiloran 78 K10
Kilpatrick Str. 66 A14
Kilpeck 28 E30
Kilpheder 88 R3
Kilphedir 87 G25
Kilpin 58 G43
Kilpin Pike 58 G43
Kilrenny 81 K31
Kilsby 31 A41
Kilspindie 81 H28
Kilstay 64 E17
Kilsyth 74 C23
Kilton 63 E42
Kilvaxter 82 C9
Kilve 7 A27
Kilvington 42 A44
Kilwinning 73 F18
Kimberley Nfk. 44 E56
Kimberley Not. 41 A41
Kimblesworth 62 B38
Kimbolton Cbs. 32 B46
Kimbolton H.& W. 28 B31
Kimcote 41 G41
Kimmerghame House 77 E34
Kimmeridge 9 G35
Kimmerston 77 G35
Kimpton Ham. 21 G38
Kimpton Hfs. 32 G47
Kinbrace 87 E24
Kinbuck 80 K23
Kincaple 81 J30
Kincardine 84 A22
Kincardine O'Neil 81 A31
Kincardine-on-Forth 75 B25
Kinclaven 81 G27
Kincorth 85 J35
Kincraig 84 J24
Kindallachan 80 F25
Kindrummond 83 F21
Kineton Glo. 30 F36
Kineton War. 30 C39
Kinfauns 81 H27
Kingarth 72 E16
Kingcoed 19 A30
Kingham 30 F38
Kingholm Quay 68 F25
Kinghorn 75 B28
Kinglassie 75 A28
Kingledoors 69 A27
Kingoodie 81 G29
King's Acre 28 D30
Kingsand 4 E20
Kingsbarns 81 J31
Kingsbridge 5 F23
King's Bromley 40 D37
Kingsburgh 82 D9
Kingsbury 40 F38
Kingsbury Episcopi 8 B30
King's Caple 28 F31
Kingscavil 75 C26
Kingsclere 21 F41
King's Cliffe 42 F46
Kingscote 20 B34
Kingscross 66 A16
Kingsdon 8 B31
Kingsdown 15 C59
Kingseat 75 B27
Kingsey 22 A43
Kingsferry 25 E55
Kingsfold 12 A47
Kingsford 74 F20
Kingsgate 25 D59
Kingshall Street 34 B55
King's Heath 40 G36
King's Hill 40 F35
Kingshouse 80 H21
Kingshouse Hotel 79 E18
Kingskerswell 5 D24
Kingskettle 81 K29
Kingsland Dor. 8 E30
Kingsland Gwy. 46 D18
Kingsland H.& W. 28 B30
Kingsland Shr. 38 D30
Kings Langley 22 A46
Kingsley Che. 48 E31
Kingsley Ham. 11 A43
Kingsley Stf. 40 A36
Kingsley Green 12 A44
Kingsley Holt 40 A36
King's Lynn 44 D52
King's Meaburn 61 D32
Kingsmuir 81 F30
Kingsnorth 15 D56
King's Norton Lei. 41 E42
King's Norton W.M. 30 A36
King's Nympton 6 D22
King's Pyon 28 C30
Kings Ripton 33 A48
King's Somborne 10 A39
Kings Stanley 20 A34
King's Sutton 31 E41
Kingstag 9 C33
Kingstanding 40 F36
Kingsteignton 5 C24
Kingsterndale 50 E36
Kingsthorne 28 E31
Kingsthorpe 31 B43
Kingston Cbs. 33 C49
Kingston Dev. 5 F22
Kingston Dor. 9 D33
Kingston Dor. 9 G35
Kingston Grm. 84 C29
Kingston Ham. 10 D37
Kingston I.o.W. 11 F40
Kingston Kent 15 B58
Kingston Ltn. 76 B31
Kingston W.S. 12 D46
Kingston Bagpuize 21 B40
Kingston Blount 22 B43
Kingston Deverill 9 A34
Kingstone H.& W. 28 E30
Kingstone Som. 8 C29
Kingstone Stf. 40 C36
Kingston Lisle 21 C39
Kingston near Lewes 13 D49
Kingston Russell 8 E31
Kingston St. Mary 8 B28
Kingston Seymour 19 E29
Kingston upon Hull 59 G47
Kingston-upon-Thames 22 E47
Kingstown 60 A29
King's Walden 32 F47
Kingswear 5 E24
Kingswells 74 F20
Kings Weston 19 D31
Kingswinford 40 G34
Kingswood Avon 19 D32
Kingswood Bkh. 31 G42
Kingswood Glo. 20 B33
Kingswood Pow. 38 E28
Kingswood Sry. 23 F48
Kingswood War. 30 A37
Kingswood Common 28 C28
Kings Worthy 11 A40
Kingthorpe 52 E47
Kington H.& W. 29 C35
Kington H.& W. 28 C28
Kington Langley 20 D35
Kington Magna 9 B33
Kington St. Michael 20 D35
Kingussie 84 J23
Kingweston 8 A31
Kinharvie 68 G25
Kinkell 83 D21
Kinlet 39 G33
Kinloch Hgh. 86 E19
Kinloch Hgh. 82 H12
Kinloch Hgh. 82 J9
Kinloch Tay. 81 F27
Kinlochard 80 K20
Kinlochbervie 86 C18
Kinlocheil 79 C15
Kinlochewe 83 C16
Kinloch Hourn 83 J15
Kinloch Laggan 80 B21
Kinlochleven 79 D17
Kinloch Lodge 86 C21
Kinlochmoidart 79 C13
Kinlochmore 79 D17
Kinloch Rannoch 80 E22
Kinlochspelve 79 H12
Kinloss 84 C26
Kinmel Bay 47 D25
Kinmuck 85 H34
Kinnadie 85 E35
Kinnaird 81 H28
Kinnaird Castle 81 E32
Kinneff 81 C34
Kinnelhead 69 C26
Kinnerley 38 C29
Kinnersley H.& W. 28 D29
Kinnersley H.& W. 29 D34
Kinnersley Shr. 39 D32
Kinnerton 28 B28
Kinnesswood 81 K27
Kinninvie 62 D36
Kinoulton 41 B42
Kinross 81 K27
Kinrossie 81 G27
Kinsham 28 B29
Kinsley 51 A40
Kinson 10 E36
Kintbury 21 E39
Kintessack 84 C26
Kintillo 81 J27
Kintocher 85 J31
Kinton 28 A30

Kintore 85 H33
Kintour 78 K6
Kintra Str. 78 K4
Kintra Str. 78 H9
Kinuachdrach 72 A13
Kinveachy 84 H25
Kinver 40 G34
Kinwarton 30 C37
Kiplin 62 G38
Kippax 57 F40
Kippen 74 A22
Kippford 65 C24
Kippings Cross 23 G52
Kirbuster 89 E28
Kirby 63 F41
Kirby Bedon 45 E58
Kirby Bellars 42 D43
Kirby Cane 45 F59
Kirby Cross 35 F58
Kirby Grindalythe 59 C45
Kirby Hill N.Y. 57 C39
Kirby Hill N.Y. 62 F37
Kirby Knowle 57 A40
Kirby le Soken 35 F58
Kirby Misperton 58 B43
Kirby Muxloe 41 E41
Kirby Row 45 F59
Kirby Underdale 58 D44
Kirby Wiske 57 A39
Kirdford 12 B46
Kirivick 88 C7
Kirk 87 C28
Kirkabister She. 89 G40
Kirkabister She. 89 J40
Kirkandrews 65 D21
Kirkandrews upon Eden 60 A29
Kirkbampton 60 A29
Kirkbean 65 C25
Kirk Bramwith 51 A42
Kirkbride 60 A28
Kirkburn Bor. 75 G28
Kirkburn Hum. 59 D45
Kirkburton 50 A38
Kirkby Lcn. 52 C46
Kirkby Mer. 48 C30
Kirkby Fleetham 62 G38
Kirkby Green 52 G46
Kirkby in Ashfield 51 G41
Kirkby Industrial Estate 48 C30
Kirkby la Thorpe 42 A46
Kirkby Lonsdale 56 B32
Kirkby Malham 56 C34
Kirkby Mallory 41 E40
Kirkby Malzeard 57 B38
Kirkby Mills 58 A43
Kirkbymoorside 58 A42
Kirkby on Bain 53 F48
Kirkby Overblow 57 E39
Kirkby Stephen 61 F33
Kirkby Thore 61 D32
Kirkby Underwood 42 C46
Kirkby Wharfe 58 E41
Kirkcaldy 75 A28
Kirkcalla 67 F19
Kirkcambeck 70 G31
Kirkcolm 66 G16
Kirkconnel 68 B23
Kirkconnell D.& G. 65 C22
Kirkconnell D.& G. 68 G25
Kirkcowan 67 G19
Kirkcudbright 65 C22
Kirkdale D.& G. 65 C21
Kirkdale Mer. 48 C29
Kirkdean 75 F27
Kirk Deighton 57 D39
Kirk Ella 59 G46
Kirkfield 74 E22
Kirkfieldbank 74 F24
Kirkgunzeon 68 G24
Kirk Hallam 41 A40
Kirkham Lan. 55 F30
Kirkham N.Y. 58 C43
Kirkhamgate 57 G38
Kirkharle 71 E36
Kirkheaton Nor. 71 F36
Kirkheaton W.Y. 50 A37
Kirkhill D.& G. 69 D27
Kirkhill Hgh. 83 E21
Kirkhill Ltn. 75 D28
Kirkhope 69 A29
Kirkhouse 75 G29
Kirkibost 88 D7
Kirkinner 64 C20
Kirkintilloch 74 C22
Kirk Ireton 50 G38
Kirkland Cum. 61 C32
Kirkland Cum. 60 E26
Kirkland D.& G. 69 E26
Kirkland D.& G. 68 D24
Kirkland D.& G. 68 B23
Kirkland Guards 60 C27
Kirkland of Longcastle 64 D19
Kirk Langley 40 B38
Kirklauchlane 64 C16
Kirkleatham 63 D41
Kirklevington 62 F40
Kirkleyditch 49 E34
Kirklington Not. 51 G42
Kirklington N.Y. 57 A39
Kirklinton 69 G30
Kirkliston 75 C27
Kirkmabreck 64 C20
Kirkmaiden 64 E17
Kirk Merrington 62 C38
Kirk Michael I.o.M. 54 E25
Kirkmichael Str. 67 C19
Kirkmichael Tay. 80 D26
Kirkmichael Mains 69 E26
Kirkmuirhill 74 F23
Kirknewton Ltn. 75 D27
Kirknewton Nor. 70 A35
Kirkney 85 F31
Kirk of Shotts 74 D24

Kirkoswald Cum. 61 B31
Kirkoswald Str. 67 C18
Kirkpatrick 68 D25
Kirkpatrick Durham 68 F23
Kirkpatrick-Fleming 69 F28
Kirk Sandall 51 B42
Kirksanton 54 A27
Kirk Smeaton 51 A41
Kirkstall 57 F38
Kirkstile 69 D29
Kirkstone Pass Inn 60 F29
Kirkton Bor. 70 B31
Kirkton D.& G. 68 E25
Kirkton Fife 75 B28
Kirkton Grm. 85 G32
Kirkton Grm. 85 E32
Kirkton Grm. 85 H32
Kirkton Hgh. 83 E15
Kirkton Hgh. 87 J24
Kirkton Hgh. 83 G14
Kirkton Str. 68 A25
Kirkton Tay. 81 F30
Kirkton Tay. 81 B30
Kirkton Manor 75 G28
Kirkton of Auchterhouse 81 G29
Kirkton of Craig 81 E33
Kirkton of Culsalmond 85 F32
Kirkton of Durris 81 A33
Kirkton of Glenbuchat 84 H29
Kirkton of Glenisla 81 D28
Kirkton of Kingoldrum 81 E29
Kirkton of Largo 81 K30
Kirkton of Lethendy 81 F27
Kirkton of Logie Buchan 85 G35
Kirkton of Menmuir 81 D31
Kirkton of Skene 85 J34
Kirkton of Strathmartine 81 G29
Kirkton of Tealing 81 G30
Kirktown Grm. 85 D36
Kirktown Grm. 85 C35
Kirktown of Alvah 85 D32
Kirktown of Auchterless 85 E33
Kirktown of Bourtie 85 G34
Kirktown of Deskford 85 C31
Kirktown of Fetteresso 81 B34
Kirktown of Mortlach 84 F29
Kirktown of Rayne 85 G32
Kirktown of Slains 85 G36
Kirkwall 89 F30
Kirkwall Airport 89 G30
Kirkwhelpington 70 E35
Kirk Yetholm 70 A34
Kirmington 52 A47
Kirmond le Mire 52 C47
Kirn 73 C17
Kirriemuir 81 E29
Kirtlebridge 69 F28
Kirtleton 69 F28
Kirtling 33 C52
Kirtlington 31 G41
Kirtomy 87 B23
Kirton Lcn. 43 B49
Kirton Not. 51 F42
Kirton Sfk. 35 E58
Kirton End 43 A48
Kirton Holme 43 A48
Kirton in Lindsey 52 C45
Kirwaugh 64 C20
Kishorn 83 E14
Kislingbury 31 C42
Kittisford 7 C26
Kivernoll 28 E30
Kiveton Park 51 D40
Klibreck 86 E21
Knaith 52 D44
Knaphill 22 F45
Knapp Som. 8 B29
Knapp Tay. 81 G28
Knapp Hill 11 B40
Knapton Nfk. 45 B59
Knapton N.Y. 58 D41
Knapwell 33 B49
Knaresborough 57 D39
Knarsdale 61 A32
Knayton 57 A40
Knebworth 33 F48
Knedlington 58 G43
Kneep 88 D6
Kneesall 51 F43
Kneesworth 33 D49
Kneeton 42 A43
Knelston 17 F20
Knightcote 30 C40
Knighton Dev. 5 F21
Knighton Lei. 41 E42
Knighton Pow. 28 A28
Knighton Stf. 39 A33
Knighton Wts. 21 D38
Knighton on Teme 29 A32
Knightsford Bridge 29 C33
Knill 28 B28
Knipton 42 B44
Kniveton 50 G38
Knock Cum. 61 D32
Knock D.& G. 64 C15
Knock Grm. 85 D31
Knock Str. 79 G11
Knock W.I. 88 D10
Knockally 87 F27
Knockan 86 G18
Knockandhu 84 G28
Knockarthur 87 H23
Knockaughlie 68 D23
Knockbain 84 D22
Knockban 83 C18
Knockbrex 65 D21
Knock Castle 73 D17
Knockcoid 66 G16
Knockdee 87 B27
Knockdolian Castle 67 E17
Knockdow 73 C17
Knockdown 20 C34
Knockenkelly 66 A16
Knockentiber 73 G19

Knockglass 64 C16
Knockgray 67 D21
Knockholt Pound 23 F50
Knockie Lodge 83 H20
Knockin 38 C29
Knocklae 68 F22
Knocknaha 66 B12
Knocksharry 54 E25
Knockycoid 67 F18
Knodishall 35 B60
Knolls Green 49 E34
Knolton 38 B29
Knook 20 G35
Knossington 42 E44
Knott End 55 E29
Knotting 32 B46
Knottingley 58 G41
Knotty Green 22 B45
Knowe 67 F19
Knowehead 68 D22
Knowesgate 70 E35
Knoweside 67 B18
Knowle Avon 19 D32
Knowle Dev. 7 G26
Knowle Dev. 6 B20
Knowle Dev. 7 E23
Knowle W.M. 30 A37
Knowle Green Lan. 56 F32
Knowl Green Esx. 34 D53
Knowl Hill 22 D44
Knowlton 10 C36
Knowsley 48 C30
Knowstone 7 C24
Knucklas 28 A28
Knutsford 49 E33
Knutsford Services 49 E33
Knypersley 49 G34
Kuggar 2 G13
Kyleakin 82 G13
Kyle of Lochalsh 82 G13
Kylerhea 82 G13
Kylesku 86 E18
Kylesmorar 79 A14
Kyles Stockinish 88 H7
Kylestrome 86 E18
Kyre Magna 29 B32

L

Laceby 53 B48
Lacey Green 22 A44
Lach Dennis 49 E33
Lache 48 F29
Lackenby 63 E41
Lackford 34 A53
Lacock 20 E35
Ladbroke 31 C40
Laddingford 23 G52
Ladock 3 C14
Ladybank 81 J29
Ladydill 68 A25
Ladykirk 77 F38
Ladykirk House 77 F34
Ladysford 85 D34
Lag 68 E24
Lagavulin 78 K5
Lagg Str. 67 B18
Lagg Str. 66 A15
Laggan Grm. 84 F29
Laggan Hgh. 80 A22
Laggan Hgh. 79 A18
Laggan Str. 78 J4
Lagganmullan 65 C21
Laid 86 C20
Laide 86 J14
Laig 78 B10
Laigh Fenwick 74 F20
Laigh Glenmuir 68 A22
Laigh Kilmory 66 A15
Laighmuir 74 F20
Laindon 24 C52
Lair 83 E16
Lairg 86 H21
Laithes 61 C30
Lake 11 F41
Lakenheath 44 G53
Lakes End 43 F51
Lake Side 55 A29
Laleham 22 E46
Laleston 18 D24
Lamancha 75 E27
Lamarsh 34 E54
Lamb Corner 34 E56
Lambden 76 F33
Lamberhurst 13 A52
Lamberhurst Quarter 13 A52
Lamberton 77 E35
Lambley Nor. 61 A32
Lambley Not. 41 A42
Lambourn 21 D39
Lamellion 4 D18
Lamerton 4 C20
Lamesley 62 A38
Lamington 75 G25
Lamlash 72 G16
Lamloch 67 D21
Lamonby 61 C30
Lamorran 3 D14
Lampeter 26 D21
Lampeter Velfrey 16 C17
Lamphey 16 D16
Lamplugh 60 D26
Lamport 32 A45
Lamyatt 9 A32
Lanark 74 F24
Lancaster 55 C30
Lanchester 62 B37
Landbeach 33 B50
Land Cross 6 C20
Landerberry 85 J33
Landewednack 2 G13
Landford 10 C38

Landican 48 D28
Landkey Newland 6 B21
Landkey Town 6 B21
Landore 17 E22
Landrake 4 D19
Landulph 4 D20
Laneast 4 B18
Lane End Bkh. 22 B44
Lane End Cum. 60 G27
Lane End Kent 23 D51
Lane Ends Drm. 62 C37
Lane Ends G.M. 49 C35
Laneham 52 E44
Lane Head Dby. 50 E37
Lane Head Drm. 62 E37
Lanehead Drm. 61 B34
Lane Head G.M. 49 C32
Lanehead Nor. 70 E33
Laneshaw Bridge 56 E35
Langal 79 D13
Langar 42 B43
Langbank 73 C19
Langburnshiels 70 C31
Langcliffe 56 C34
Langdon Beck 61 C34
Langdon Hills 24 C52
Langenhoe 34 G56
Langford Bfd. 32 D47
Langford Dev. 7 E26
Langford Esx. 24 A54
Langford Not. 52 G44
Langford Oxf. 21 A38
Langford Budville 7 C27
Langford End 32 C47
Langham Esx. 34 E56
Langham Lei. 42 D44
Langham Nfk. 44 A56
Langham Sfk. 34 A55
Langhaugh 75 G28
Langho 56 F33
Langholm 69 E29
Langlee 70 B32
Langleeford 70 A35
Langley Che. 49 E35
Langley Esx. 33 E50
Langley Ham. 11 D40
Langley Hfs. 33 F48
Langley Kent 14 B54
Langley Nor. 70 G34
Langley War. 30 B37
Langley W.M. 40 G36
Langley Burrell 20 D35
Langley Marsh 7 C26
Langley Mill 41 A40
Langley Moor 62 B38
Langley Park 62 B38
Langold 51 D41
Langport 8 B30
Langrick 43 A48
Langridge 20 E33
Langrigg 60 B27
Langrish 11 B43
Langsett 50 B38
Langshaw 76 G31
Langstone 11 D43
Langthorne 62 G38
Langthorpe 57 C39
Langthwaite 62 F36
Langtoft Hum. 59 C46
Langtoft Lcn. 42 D47
Langton Drm. 62 E37
Langton Lcn. 53 F48
Langton Lcn. 53 E49
Langton N.Y. 58 C43
Langton by Wragby 52 E47
Langton Green Kent 13 A51
Langton Green Sfk. 35 A57
Langton Herring 9 F32
Langton Long Blandford 9 D34
Langton Matravers 9 G35
Langtree 6 D20
Langwathby 61 C31
Langwell House 87 F27
Langworth 52 E46
Lanivet 4 D16
Lanlivery 4 E16
Lanner 2 D13
Lanreath 4 E17
Lansallos 4 E17
Lansdown 20 E33
Lanton Bor. 70 A32
Lanton Nor. 77 G35
Lapford 7 E23
Laphroaig 78 K5
Lapley 40 D34
Lapworth 30 A37
Larachbeg 79 F12
Larach na Gaibhre 72 D13
Larbert 74 B24
Larg 67 F19
Largie 85 F32
Largiemore 72 B15
Largmore 67 E21
Largo Ward 81 K30
Largs 73 E18
Largybeg 66 A16
Largymore 66 A16
Larkfield 14 B53
Larkhall Avon 20 E33
Larkhall Str. 74 F23
Larkhill 20 G37
Larling 44 G55
Larriston 70 D31
Lartington 62 E37
Lasham 21 G42
Laskill 63 G41
Lassodie 75 A27
Lasswade 75 D29
Lastingham 63 G43
Lasynys 36 B21
Latchingdon 24 A54
Latchley 4 C20
Lathbury 32 D44

Landican...
Latheron 87 E27
Latheronwheel 87 E27
Latimer 22 B46
Latteridge 19 C32
Latton 20 B36
Laudale House 79 D13
Lauder 85 F31
Laugharne 17 C19
Laughterton 52 E44
Laughton E.S. 13 C51
Laughton Lcn. 52 C44
Laughton Lei. 41 G42
Laughton en le Morthen 51 D41
Launcells 6 E18
Launceston 6 G19
Launton 31 F42
Laurencekirk 81 C33
Laurieston Cen. 75 C25
Laurieston D.& G. 68 G22
Lavendon 32 C45
Lavenham 34 D55
Laverstock 10 A37
Laverstoke 21 G40
Laverton 57 B38
Law 74 E24
Lawers 80 G22
Lawford 34 E56
Lawhitton 6 G19
Lawkland 56 C33
Lawley 39 E32
Lawnhead 40 C34
Lawrenny 16 D16
Lawshall 34 C54
Lawton 28 C30
Laxay 88 E9
Laxdale 88 D10
Laxey 54 E26
Laxfield 35 A58
Laxfirth 89 H40
Laxford Bridge 86 D18
Laxo 89 F40
Laxton Hum. 58 G43
Laxton Nmp. 42 F45
Laxton Not. 51 F43
Laycock 57 E36
Layer Breton 34 G55
Layer-de-la-Haye 34 F55
Layer Marney 34 G55
Layham 34 D56
Laysters Pole 28 B31
Laytham 58 F43
Layton 55 F29
Lazenby 63 D41
Lazonby 61 C31
Lea Dby. 51 G39
Lea H.& W. 29 F32
Lea Lcn. 52 D44
Lea Sal. 38 E30
Lea Wts. 20 C35
Leadburn 75 E28
Leadenham 52 G45
Leaden Roding 33 G51
Leaderfoot 76 G31
Leadgate Cum. 61 B33
Leadgate Drm. 62 A37
Leadhills 68 B24
Leafield 30 G39
Leagrave 32 F46
Leahaugh 70 D31
Leake Common Side 53 G49
Lealands 13 C51
Lealholm 63 F43
Lealt Hgh. 82 C11
Lealt Str. 72 A12
Lea Marston 40 F38
Leamington Hastings 31 B40
Leamington Spa, Royal 30 B39
Leanach 72 A16
Leargybreck 78 H6
Leasgill 55 A30
Leasingham 42 A46
Leasingthorne 62 D38
Leatherhead 22 F47
Leatheringsett 44 B56
Leathley 57 E38
Leaths 68 G23
Leaton Shr. 39 D32
Leaton Shr. 38 D30
Lea Town 55 F30
Leaveland 15 B56
Leavening 58 C43
Leaves Green 23 E50
Lea Yeat 56 A33
Lebberston 59 A46
Lechlade 21 B38
Lechuary 72 A14
Leckford 10 A39
Leckfurin 87 C23
Leckgruinart 78 H4
Leckhampstead Bkh. 31 E43
Leckhampstead Brk. 21 D40
Leckhampton 29 G35
Leckie 83 C16
Leckmelm 86 J17
Leckwith 18 D27
Leconfield 59 D46
Ledaig 79 F16
Ledburn 32 F45
Ledbury 29 E33
Ledmore 86 G18
Ledsham 57 G40
Ledston 57 G40
Ledstone 57 G40
Lee Dev. 6 A20
Lee Lan. 55 D31
Lee Str. 78 H10
Leebotwood 38 F30
Lee Brockhurst 38 C31
Leece 54 C28
Leeds Kent 14 B54
Leeds W.Y. 57 F39
Leeds/Bradford Airport 57 E38
Leedstown 2 E12
Lee Green 49 F32

Lee Head 50 C36
Leek 49 G35
Leekbrook 49 G35
Leek Wootton 30 B38
Lee Mill Bridge 5 E21
Leeming N.Y. 57 A38
Leeming W.Y. 57 F36
Leeming Bar 62 G38
Lee-on-the-Solent 11 D41
Lees G.M. 49 B35
Lees W.Y. 57 F36
Lees Hill 70 G31
Leeswood 48 G28
Leftwich Green 49 E32
Legars 76 F33
Legbourne 53 D49
Legburthwaite 60 E29
Legerwood 76 F31
Legsby 52 D47
Leicester 41 E41
Leicester Forest East 41 E41
Leicester Forest East Services 41 E41
Leigh Dor. 9 D32
Leigh Glo. 29 F34
Leigh G.M. 49 B32
Leigh H.& W. 29 C33
Leigh Kent 23 G51
Leigh Shr. 38 E29
Leigh Sry. 23 G48
Leigh Wts. 20 B36
Leigh Delamere 20 D34
Leigh Delamere Services 20 D34
Leigh Sinton 29 C33
Leighton N.Y. 57 B37
Leighton Pow. 38 E28
Leighton Shr. 39 E32
Leighton Som. 20 G33
Leighton Bromswold 32 A47
Leighton Buzzard 32 F45
Leigh upon Mendip 19 G32
Leighwoods 19 D31
Leinthall Earls 28 B30
Leinthall Starkes 28 A30
Leintwardine 28 A30
Leire 41 F41
Leirinmore 86 B20
Leiston 35 B60
Leith 75 C28
Leitholm 76 F33
Lelant 2 E11
Lelley 59 F48
Lem Hill 29 A33
Lempitlaw 76 G33
Lemreway 88 F9
Lemsford 33 G48
Lenchwick 30 D36
Lendalfoot 67 D17
Lenham 14 B55
Lenham Heath 14 B55
Lenie 83 G21
Lennel 77 F34
Lennelhill 77 F34
Lennies 64 C20
Lennox Plunton 65 C22
Lennoxtown 74 C22
Lenton Lcn. 42 B46
Lenton Not. 41 B41
Lenwade 44 D56
Lenzie 74 C22
Leochel-Cushnie 85 H31
Leominster 28 C30
Leonard Stanley 20 A34
Leorin 78 K4
Lepe 11 E40
Lephin 82 E7
Lephinchapel 72 A15
Lephinmore 72 A15
Leppington 58 C43
Lepton 50 A38
Lerryn 4 E17
Lerwick 89 H40
Lerwick Airport (Tingwall) 89 H40
Lesbotten 89 K40
Lesbury 71 B38
Leslie Fife 81 K28
Leslie Grm. 85 G31
Lesmahagow 74 G24
Lesnewth 4 A17
Lessingham 45 C59
Lessonhall 60 B28
Leswalt 66 G16
Letchmore Heath 22 B47
Letchworth 33 E48
Letcombe Bassett 21 C39
Letcombe Regis 21 C39
Letham Fife 81 J29
Letham Tay. 81 F31
Lethanhill 67 B20
Lethem 70 C32
Lethen House 84 D25
Letterewe 83 B15
Letterfearn 83 G14
Letterfinlay 79 A18
Lettermore Hgh. 87 D22
Lettershaws 68 A25
Letterston 16 B15
Lettoch 84 F27
Letton H.& W. 28 D29
Letton H.& W. 28 A29
Letwell 51 D41
Leuchars 81 H30
Leurbost 88 E9
Leven Fife 81 K29
Leven Hum. 59 E47
Levencorroch 66 A16
Levens 55 A30
Levenwick 89 K40
Leverburgh 88 J6
Leverington 43 D50
Leverstock Green 22 A46

Leverton 43 A49
Leverton Outgate 43 A50
Le Villoque 3 E17
Levington 35 E58
Levisham 63 G44
Lew 21 A39
Lewannick 4 B18
Lewdown 6 G20
Lewes 13 C50
Lewiston 83 G21
Lewknor 22 B43
Lewtrenchard 6 G20
Lexden 34 F55
Leybourne 23 F52
Leyburn 62 G37
Leycett 39 A33
Ley Hill 22 A45
Leyland 55 G31
Leylodge 85 H33
Leys Castle 84 E22
Leysdown on Sea 25 D56
Leysmill 81 F32
Lezant 4 C19
Lhanbryde 84 C28
Libanus 27 F25
Libberton 75 F25
Liberton 75 D28
Lichfield 40 E37
Lickey End 29 A35
Licswm 47 E27
Liddesdale 79 E13
Liddington 21 C38
Lidgate 34 C53
Lidlington 32 E45
Lieurary 87 B26
Liff 81 G29
Lifton 6 G19
Liftondown 6 G19
Lighthorne 30 C39
Lightwater 22 E45
Lilbourne 31 A41
Lilburn Tower 71 A36
Lilleshall 39 D33
Lilley Bfd. 32 F47
Lilley Brk. 21 D40
Lilliesleaf 70 A31
Lillingstone Dayrell 31 E43
Lillingstone Lovell 31 D43
Lillington 30 B39
Limbrick 49 A32
Limbury 32 F46
Limekilnburn 74 E23
Limekilns 75 B26
Limington 8 B31
Limpenhoe 45 E59
Limpley Stoke 20 E33
Limpsfield 23 F50
Linby 51 G41
Linchmere 12 A44
Lincluden 68 F25
Lincoln 52 E45
Lindale 55 A30
Lindal in Furness 54 B28
Lindean 76 G30
Linden 71 D37
Lindenlane 71 D37
Lindertis 81 E29
Lindfield 13 B49
Lindford 12 A44
Lindley 50 A37
Lindley Green 57 E38
Lindores 81 J28
Lindow End 49 E34
Lindridge 29 B32
Lindsell 33 F52
Lindsey 34 D55
Lindsey Street 23 A50
Linefoot 60 C26
Linford 24 D52
Lingdale 63 E42
Lingen 28 B29
Lingfield 23 G49
Linglie 69 A30
Lingwood 45 E59
Linhope 69 C30
Liniclate 88 N3
Linicro 82 C9
Linkenholt 21 F39
Linkinhorne 4 C19
Linktown 75 A28
Linley 39 F32
Linlithgow 75 C25
Linlithgow Bridge 75 C25
Linshiels 70 C34
Linsidemore 86 J21
Linslade 32 F44
Linstead Parva 35 A59
Linstock 61 A30
Linthorpe 62 E40
Linthwaite 50 A37
Lintlaw 77 E34
Lintmill 85 C31
Linton Bor. 70 A33
Linton Cbs. 33 D51
Linton Dby. 40 D38
Linton H.& W. 29 F32
Linton Kent 14 B53
Linton N.Y. 56 C35
Linton W.Y. 57 E39
Linton upon Ouse 57 C40
Lintzford 62 A37
Linwood Lcn. 52 D47
Linwood Str. 74 D20
Lionel 88 A11
Liphook 12 A44
Liscard 48 C28
Liskeard 4 D18
L'Islet 3 E17
Liss 11 B43
Lissett 59 D47
Liss Forest 11 B43
Lissington 52 D47
Lisvane 18 C27
Litcham 44 D54

Litchborough 31 C42
Litchfield 21 F40
Litherland 48 C29
Litlington Cbs. 33 D49
Litlington E.S. 13 D51
Little Abington 33 D51
Little Addington 32 A45
Little Amwell 33 G49
Little Assynt 86 F17
Little Aston 40 E36
Little Ayre 89 H29
Little Ayton 63 F41
Little Baddow 24 A53
Little Badminton 20 C34
Little Ballinluig 80 E25
Little Bampton 60 A28
Little Barford 32 C47
Little Barningham 45 B57
Little Barrington 30 G38
Little Barrow 48 E30
Little Barugh 58 B43
Little Bavington 70 F35
Little Bealings 35 D58
Little Beck 63 F44
Little Bedwyn 21 E38
Little Bentley 35 F57
Little Berkhamstead 23 A48
Little Billing 31 B43
Little Blakenham 35 D57
Little Blencow 61 C30
Little Bookham 22 F47
Little Bourton 31 D40
Little Bowden 42 G43
Little Bradley 33 C52
Little Brampton 38 G29
Little Brechin 81 D31
Littlebredy 8 F31
Little Brickhill 32 E45
Little Brington 31 B42
Little Bromley 35 F57
Little Broughton 60 C26
Little Budworth 49 F32
Little Burstead 24 B52
Littlebury 33 E51
Littlebury Green 33 E50
Little Bytham 42 B47
Little Cairnbrock 66 G15
Little Carleton 67 E17
Little Carlton 53 D50
Little Casterton 42 D46
Little Cawthorpe 53 D49
Little Chalfont 22 B45
Little Chart 14 C55
Little Chesterford 33 D51
Little Cheverell 20 F35
Little Clacton 35 G57
Little Clifton 60 D26
Little Comberton 29 D35
Little Common 14 G53
Little Compton 30 E38
Little Cowarne 29 C32
Little Coxwell 21 B38
Little Crakehall 62 G38
Little Cressingham 44 E54
Little Crosby 48 B29
Little Dalby 42 D43
Littledean 29 G32
Little Dewchurch 28 E31
Little Downham 43 G51
Little Driffield 59 D46
Little Duchrae 68 G22
Little Dunham 44 D54
Little Dunkeld 80 F26
Little Dunmow 33 F52
Little Easton 33 F52
Little Eaton 41 A39
Little Ellingham 44 F56
Little End 23 A51
Little Eversden 33 C49
Little Fakenham 34 A55
Little Faringdon 21 A38
Little Fencote 62 G38
Little Fenton 58 F41
Littleferry 87 J24
Little Fransham 44 D55
Little Gaddesden 32 G45
Little Galdenoch 66 G15
Littlegill 68 A25
Little Glemham 35 C59
Little Gorsley 29 F32
Little Gransden 33 C48
Little Green 34 A56
Little Hadham 33 F50
Little Hale 42 A47
Little Hallingbury 33 G51
Littleham Dev. 6 C20
Littleham Dev. 7 G26
Little Hampden 22 A44
Littlehampton 12 D46
Little Harrowden 32 A44
Little Hay 40 E37
Little Hayfield 50 D36
Littlehempston 5 D24
Little Hereford 28 B31
Little Horkesley 34 E55
Little Horsted 13 C50
Little Horwood 31 E43
Little Houghton Nmp. 32 C44
Little Houghton S.Y. 51 B40
Little Hucklow 50 E37
Little Hulton 49 B33
Little Irchester 32 B45
Little Kelk 59 D46
Little Kimble 22 A44
Little Kingshill 22 B44
Little Langdale 60 F29
Little Langford 10 A36
Little Leigh 49 E32

Little Lever 49 B33
Little London E.S. 13 C51
Little London Ham. 21 F42
Little London Ham. 21 G39
Little London Lcn. 43 C50
Little London Lcn. 43 C48
Little London W.Y. 57 F38
Little Longstone 50 E37
Little Malvern 29 D33
Little Maplestead 34 E54
Little Marcle 29 E32
Little Marlow 22 C44
Little Massingham 44 C53
Little Melton 45 E57
Little Mill Gwe. 19 A29
Littlemill Grm. 81 A29
Littlemill Hgh. 84 E25
Littlemill Str. 67 B20
Little Milton 21 A42
Little Missenden 22 B45
Littlemore 21 A41
Little Moss 49 C35
Little Ness 38 C30
Little Neston 48 E28
Little Newcastle 16 B15
Little Newsham 62 E37
Little Oakley Esx. 35 F58
Little Oakley Nmp. 42 G44
Little Orton 60 A29
Little Ouseburn 57 C40
Littleover 41 B39
Little Paxton 32 B47
Little Petherick 3 A15
Little Plumpton 55 F29
Little Plumstead 45 D59
Little Ponton 42 B45
Littleport 43 G51
Little Raveley 43 G48
Little Ribston 57 D39
Little Richorn 65 C24
Little Rissington 30 G37
Little Rowsley 50 F38
Little Ryburgh 44 C55
Little Ryle 71 B36
Little Salkeld 61 C31
Little Sampford 33 E52
Little Saxham 34 B54
Little Scatwell 83 D19
Little Shelford 33 C50
Little Smeaton 51 A41
Little Snoring 44 B55
Little Sodbury 20 C33
Little Somborne 10 A39
Little Somerford 20 C35
Little Stainton 62 E39
Little Stanney 48 E30
Little Staughton 32 B47
Little Steeping 53 F50
Little Stoke 40 B35
Littlestone-on-Sea 15 E56
Little Stonham 35 B57
Little Stretton Lei. 41 E42
Little Stretton Shr. 38 F30
Little Strickland 61 E31
Little Stukeley 33 A48
Little Sutton 48 E29
Little Swinburne 70 F35
Little Sypland 65 C23
Little Tew 30 F39
Little Thetford 33 A51
Little Thirkleby 57 B40
Little Thornton 55 E29
Littlethorpe Lei. 41 F41
Littlethorpe N.Y. 57 C39
Little Thurlow 33 C52
Littleton Che. 48 F30
Littleton Ham. 11 A40
Littleton Drew 20 C34
Littleton upon Severn 19 B31
Little Torhouse 64 C19
Little Torrington 6 D20
Little Totham 34 G54
Little Town Cum. 60 D27
Littletown Drm. 62 B39
Little Town Lan. 56 F32
Little Urswick 54 B28
Little Wakering 25 C55
Little Walden 33 D51
Little Waldingfield 34 D55
Little Walsingham 44 B55
Little Waltham 34 G53
Little Washbourne 29 E35
Little Weighton 59 F45
Little Wenlock 39 E32
Little Whittington 70 G35
Littlewick Green 22 C44
Little Wilbraham 33 C51
Little Witley 29 B33
Little Wittenham 21 B41
Little Wolford 30 E38
Littleworth H.& W. 29 C34
Littleworth Oxf. 21 B39
Little Wratting 33 D52
Little Wymondley 33 F48
Little Wyrley 40 E36
Little Yeldham 34 E53
Litton Dby. 50 E37
Litton N.Y. 56 B35
Litton Som. 19 F31
Litton Cheney 8 E31
Liverpool 48 C29
Liverpool Airport 48 D30
Liversedge 57 G37
Liverton Cle. 63 E43
Liverton Dev. 5 C24
Liverton Street 14 B54
Livingston 75 D26
Livingston Village 75 D26
Lizard 2 G12
Laethliw 26 B20
Llaingoch 46 D18
Llaithddu 37 G26
Llanaber 37 D22
Llanaelhaearn 36 A19

Llanafan 27 A22
Llanafan-fechan 27 C25
Llanallgo 46 D21
Llanarmon Clw. 47 G27
Llanarmon Gwy. 36 B20
Llanarmon Dyffryn Ceiriog 38 B27
Llanarth Dyf. 26 C20
Llanarth Gwe. 28 G29
Llanarthney 17 B21
Llanasa 47 D27
Llanbabo 19 A29
Llanbadarn-fawr 37 G22
Llanbadarn-fynydd 28 A27
Llanbadarn-y-Garreg 28 D27
Llanbadoc 19 A29
Llanbadrig 46 C19
Llanbeder Gwe. 19 B29
Llanbedr Gwy. 36 C21
Llanbedr Pow. 28 D27
Llanbedr Pow. 28 F28
Llanbedr-Dyffryn Clwyd 47 G27
Llanbedrgoch 46 D21
Llanbedrog 36 B19
Llanbedr-y-cennin 47 F23
Llanberis 46 F21
Llanbister 28 A27
Llanblethian 18 D25
Llanboidy 17 B18
Llanbradach 18 B27
Llanbrynmair 37 E25
Llancarfan 18 D26
Llancayo 19 A29
Llancloudy 28 F30
Llancynfelyn 37 F22
Llandaf 18 D27
Llandanwg 36 C21
Llandarcy 18 B23
Llandawke 17 C18
Llanddaniel Fab 46 E21
Llanddarog 17 C21
Llanddeiniol 26 A21
Llanddeiniolen 46 F21
Llandderfel 37 B25
Llanddeusant Dyf. 27 F23
Llanddeusant Gwy. 46 D19
Llanddew 27 E26
Llanddewi 17 F20
Llanddewi-brefi 27 C22
Llanddewir Cwm 27 D26
Llanddewi Rhydderch 28 G29
Llanddoget 47 F24
Llanddona 46 E21
Llanddowror 17 C18
Llanddulas 47 E25
Llanddyfnan 46 E21
Llandecwyn 37 B22
Llandefaelog fach 27 E26
Llandefaelog-tre'r-graig 28 E27
Llandefalle 28 E27
Llandegai 46 E22
Llandegfan 46 E21
Llandegfedd 19 B29
Llandegla 47 G27
Llandegley 28 B27
Llandegwning 36 B18
Llandeilo 17 B22
Llandeilo-Abercywyn 17 C19
Llandeilo Graban 27 D26
Llandeilo'r Fan 27 E24
Llandeloy 16 B14
Llandenny 19 A30
Llandevenny 19 C30
Llandewi Velfrey 16 C17
Llandewi-Ystradenny 28 B27
Llandinabo 28 F31
Llandinam 37 G26
Llandissilio 16 B17
Llandogo 19 A31
Llandough 18 D27
Llandovery 27 E23
Llandow 18 D25
Llandre 37 G22
Llandrillo 37 B26
Llandrindod Wells 27 B26
Llandrinio 38 D28
Llandudno 47 D23
Llandudno Junction 47 E24
Llandwrog 46 G20
Llandybie 17 C22
Llandyfaelog 17 C20
Llandyfodwg 18 C25
Llandyfriog 26 D19
Llandyfrydog 46 D20
Llan-dygwydd 26 D18
Llandyrnog 47 F27
Llandysilio 38 D28
Llandysul Dyf. 26 D20
Llandysul Pow. 38 F27
Llanedeyrn 18 C27
Llanedy 17 C18
Llanegryn 37 E22
Llanegwad 17 B21
Llaneilian 46 C20
Llanelian-yn-Rhos 47 E24
Llanelidan 47 G27
Llanelieu 28 E27
Llanellen 28 G29
Llanelli 17 E20
Llanelltyd 37 D23
Llanelly 28 G28
Llanelwedd 27 C26
Llanenddwyn 36 C21
Llanengan 36 C18
Llanerchymedd 46 D20
Llanerfyl 37 E26
Llanfachraeth 46 D19
Llanfachreth 37 C23
Llanfaelog 46 E19
Llanfaelrhys 36 C18
Llanfaes Gwy. 46 E21
Llanfaes Pow. 27 F26
Llanfaethlu 46 D19
Llanfaglan 46 F20
Llanfair 36 C21
Llanfair Caereinion 38 E27
Llanfair Clydogau 27 C22

Llanfair-Dyffryn Clwyd 47 G27
Llanfairfechan 46 E22
Llanfairpwllgwyngyll 46 E21
Llanfair Talhaearn 47 E25
Llanfair-y-Cwmmwd 46 F20
Llanfairynghornwy 46 C19
Llanfair-yn-Neubwll 46 E19
Llanfallteg 17 B17
Llanfallteg West 16 C17
Llanfaredd 27 C26
Llanfarian 26 A21
Llanfechain 38 C27
Llanfechell 46 C19
Llanferres 47 F27
Llanfigael 46 D19
Llanfihangel Aberbythych 17 C21
Llanfihangel-ar-Arth 26 D20
Llanfihangel Glyn Myfyr 37 A25
Llanfihangel Gobion 19 A29
Llanfihangel Nant Bran 27 E25
Llanfihangel-nant-Melan 28 C27
Llanfihangel-Rhydithon 28 B27
Llanfihangel Rogiet 19 C30
Llanfihangel Tal-y-llyn 28 F27
Llanfihangel-uwch-Gwili 17 B20
Llanfihangel-y-Creuddyn 27 A22
Llanfihangel-yng-Ngwynfa 37 D26
Llanfihangel-y-pennant 36 A21
Llanfihangel-y-Pennant Gwy. 37 E22
Llanfihangel Ystrad 27 C22
Llanfihangel-y-traethau 36 B21
Llanfilo 28 E27
Llanfoist 28 G29
Llanfor 37 B25
Llanfrechfa 19 B29
Llanfrynach 27 F26
Llanfwrog Clw. 47 G27
Llanfwrog Gwy. 46 D19
Llanfyllin 38 D27
Llanfynydd Clw. 48 G28
Llanfynydd Dyf. 17 B21
Llanfyrnach 17 A18
Llangadfan 37 D26
Llangadog 27 F23
Llangadwaladr 46 F19
Llangaffo 46 F20
Llangain 17 C19
Llangammarch Wells 27 D25
Llangan 18 D25
Llangarron 28 F31
Llangasty Tal-y-llyn 28 F27
Llangathen 17 B21
Llangattock 28 G28
Llangattock Lingoed 28 F29
Llangedwyn 38 C27
Llangefni 46 E20
Llangeinor 18 C25
Llangeinwen 46 F20
Llangeitho 27 C22
Llangeler 17 A19
Llangelynin 36 E21
Llangendeirne 17 C20
Llan-gennech 17 D21
Llangennith 17 E20
Llangenny 28 G28
Llangernyw 47 F24
Llangian 36 C18
Llangibby 36 B19
Llangiwen 26 D21
Llanglydwen 16 B17
Llangoed 46 E22
Llangoedmor 26 D18
Llangollen 38 A28
Llangolman 16 B17
Llangors 28 F27
Llangorwen 37 G22
Llangovan 19 A30
Llangower 37 B25
Llangranncg 26 C19
Llangristiolus 46 E20
Llangrove 28 G31
Llangua 28 F29
Llangunllo 28 A28
Llangunnor 17 B20
Llangurig 37 G25
Llangwm Clw. 37 A25
Llangwm Dyf. 16 D15
Llangwm Gwe. 19 B30
Llangwm-isaf 19 A30
Llangwnnadl 36 B18
Llangwyfan 47 F27
Llangwyllog 46 E20
Llangwyryfon 27 A22
Llangybi Dyf. 27 C22
Llangybi Gwy. 36 A20
Llangyfelach 17 E22
Llangynhafal 47 F27
Llangynidr 28 G27
Llangynin 17 C18
Llangynog Dyf. 17 C19
Llangynog Pow. 37 C26
Llangynwyd 18 C24
Llanhamlach 27 F26
Llanharan 18 C26
Llanharry 18 C26
Llanhennock 19 B29
Llanhilleth 19 A28
Llanidloes 37 G25
Llaniestyn 36 B18
Llanigon 28 E28
Llanilar 27 A22
Llanilid 18 C25
Llanishen Gwe. 19 A30
Llanishen S.G. 18 C27
Llanllechid 46 F22
Llanllugan 37 E26
Llanllwch 17 C19
Llanllwchaiarn 38 F27
Llanllyfni 46 G20
Llanllywel 19 B29
Llanmadoc 17 E20
Llanmaes 18 D25
Llanmartin 19 C29
Llanmerewig 38 F27

Llanmiloe 17 D18
Llanmorlais 17 E21
Llannefydd 47 E25
Llannon 17 D21
Llannor 36 B19
Llanon 26 B20
Llanpumsaint 17 B20
Llanrhaeadr-ym-Mochnant 38 C27
Llanrhaiadr 47 F26
Llanrhidian 17 E20
Llanrhos 47 D23
Llanrhyddlad 46 D19
Llanrhystud 26 B21
Llanrian 16 A14
Llanrug 46 F21
Llanrumney 19 C28
Llanrwst 47 F23
Llansadurnen 17 C18
Llansadwrn Dyf. 17 A22
Llansadwrn Gwy. 46 E21
Llansaint 17 D19
Llansamlet 17 E22
Llansannan 47 F25
Llansantffraed 28 F27
Llansantffraed in Elvel 27 C26
Llansantffraid 26 B21
Llansantffraid Cwmdeuddwr 27 B25
Llansantffraid Glan Conwy 47 E24
Llansantffraid-ym-Mechain 38 C28
Llansawel 17 A22
Llansilin 38 C28
Llansoy 19 A30
Llanspyddid 27 F26
Llanstadwell 16 D15
Llansteffan 17 C19
Llanstephan 28 D27
Llantarnam 19 B29
Llanteg 16 C17
Llanthony 28 F28
Llantilio Crossenny 28 G29
Llantilio Pertholey 28 G29
Llantrisant Gwe. 19 B29
Llantrisant M.G. 18 C26
Llantrithyd 18 D26
Llantwit Fardre 18 C26
Llantwit Major 18 E25
Llanuwchllyn 37 B24
Llanvaches 19 B30
Llanvair Discoed 19 B30
Llanvair Waterdine 28 A28
Llanvapley 28 G29
Llanvetherine 28 G29
Llanveynoe 28 E29
Llanvihangel Crucorney 28 F29
Llanvihangel Pontymoel 19 A29
Llanvihangel Ystern-Llewern 28 G30
Llanwarne 28 F31
Llanwddyn 37 D26
Llanwenarth 28 G28
Llanwenog 26 D20
Llanwern Gwe. 19 C29
Llanwern Pow. 28 F27
Llanwinio 17 B18
Llanwnda Dyf. 16 A15
Llanwnda Gwy. 46 G20
Llanwnnen 26 D21
Llanwnog 37 F26
Llanwrda 27 E23
Llanwrin 37 E23
Llanwrthwl 28 B25
Llanwrtyd 27 D23
Llanwrtyd-Wells 27 D24
Llanwyddelan 37 E26
Llanyblodwel 38 C28
Llan-y-bri 17 C19
Llanybydder 26 D21
Llanycefn 16 B17
Llanychaer Bridge 16 A15
Llanycrwys 27 D22
Llanymawddwy 37 D25
Llanymynech 38 C28
Llanynghenedl 46 D19
Llanyre 27 B26
Llanystumdwy 36 B20
Llawhaden 16 C16
Llawnt 38 B28
Llawryglyn 37 F25
Llay 48 G29
Llechfaen 27 F26
Llechryd Dyf. 26 D18
Llechryd M.G. 18 A27
Lledrod 27 A22
Llidiadnenog 17 A21
Llidiardau 37 B24
Llithfaen 36 A19
Lloc 47 E27
Llong 48 F28
Llowes 28 D27
Llundain-fach 26 C21
Llwydcoed 18 A25
Llwydiarth 37 D26
Llwyncelyn 26 C20
Llwyndafydd 26 C19
Llwyngwril 36 E21
Llwyn-hendy 17 D21
Llwynmawr 38 B28
Llwyn-on 27 G26
Llwyn-Walter 17 B21
Llwyn-y-pia 18 B25
Llynclys 38 C28
Llysfaen 47 E24
Llyswen 28 E27
Llysworney 18 D25
Llys-y-frân 16 B16
Llywel 27 E24
Loanend 77 E35
Loanhead Ltn. 75 D27
Loans 73 G19
Loansdean 71 E37
Lochailort 79 B13
Lochaline 79 F12

Lochans 64 C16
Locharbriggs 68 E25
Lochassynt Lodge 86 F17
Lochawe 79 H17
Lochboisdale 88 R3
Lochbuie 79 H12
Lochcarron 83 E15
Loch Choire Lodge 87 E22
Lochdonhead 79 G13
Lochee 81 G29
Lochend D.& G. 65 C24
Lochend Fife 75 A27
Lochend Hgh. 87 B28
Lochend Hgh. 84 F22
Locheport 88 L4
Locherben 68 D25
Lochfoot 68 F24
Lochgair 72 A15
Lochgarthside 83 H21
Lochgelly 75 A27
Lochgilphead 72 B14
Lochgoilhead 79 K17
Loch Head 64 D19
Lochhill Grm. 84 C28
Lochhill Str. 68 B22
Lochinver 86 F16
Loch Loyal Lodge 87 D22
Lochmaben 69 E26
Lochmaddy 88 L5
Lochmore Cottage 87 D26
Lochmore Lodge 86 E18
Lochore 75 A27
Lochportain 88 K5
Lochranza 72 E15
Lochside Grm. 81 D33
Lochside Hgh. 87 E24
Lochside Hgh. 84 D24
Lochskipport 88 O4
Lochslin 84 C28
Lochstack Lodge 86 D18
Lochstrathy 87 D23
Lochton 67 E18
Lochuisge 79 E13
Lochwinnoch 73 E19
Lochwood 69 D26
Lockengate 4 D16
Lockerbie 69 E27
Lockeridge 20 E37
Lockerley 10 B38
Locking 19 F29
Lockington Hum. 59 E45
Lockington Lei. 41 C40
Locksbottom 23 E50
Lock's Heath 11 D41
Lockton 58 A44
Loddington Lei. 42 E43
Loddington Nmp. 32 A44
Loddiswell 5 F23
Loddon 45 F59
Lode 33 B51
Loders 8 E30
Lodsworth 12 B45
Lofthouse N.Y. 57 B36
Lofthouse W.Y. 57 G39
Loftus 63 E43
Logan 67 A21
Loganlea 75 D25
Loggerheads 39 B33
Logierait 80 E25
Login 16 B17
Lolworth 33 B49
Lonbain 82 D12
Londesborough 58 E44
London 23 C49
London Beach 14 D54
London Colney 22 A47
Londonderry N.Y. 57 A39
London (Gatwick) Airport 23 G48
London (Heathrow) Airport 22 D46
Londonthorpe 42 B45
Londubh 83 A14
Long Ashton 19 D31
Longbar 73 E19
Long Bennington 42 A44
Longbenton 71 G38
Longborough 30 F37
Long Bredy 8 E31
Longbridge War. 30 B38
Longbridge W.M. 30 A36
Longbridge Deverill 20 G34
Long Buckby 31 B42
Longburgh 60 A29
Longburton 9 C32
Long Clawson 42 C43
Longcliffe 50 G38
Long Compton 30 E38
Longcot 21 B38
Long Crendon 21 A42
Long Crichel 9 C35
Longcroft Cen. 74 C24
Longcroft Cum. 60 A28
Longcross 4 C20
Longden 38 E30
Longdon H.& W. 29 E34
Longdon Stf. 40 D36
Longdon upon Tern 39 D32
Longdown 7 F24
Longdowns 2 E13
Long Drax 58 G42
Long Duckmanton 51 E40
Long Eaton 41 B41
Longfield 24 E52
Longfield Hill 24 E52
Longford Dby. 40 B38
Longford G.L. 22 D46
Longford Glo. 29 F34
Longforgan 81 G29
Longformacus 76 E32
Longframlington 71 C37

Long Green 29 E34
Longham Dor. 10 E36
Longham Nfk. 44 D55
Long Hanborough 31 G40
Long Hermiston 75 D27
Longhirst 71 E38
Longhope 29 G32
Longhorsley 71 D37
Longhoughton 71 B38
Long Itchington 31 B40
Longlands 60 C28
Longlane Brk. 21 D41
Longlane Dby. 40 B38
Long Lawford 31 A40
Longley Green 29 C33
Load 8 B30
Longmanhill 85 C33
Long Marston Hfs. 32 G44
Long Marston N.Y. 58 D41
Long Marston War. 30 D37
Long Marton 61 D32
Long Melford 34 D54
Longmoor Camp 11 A43
Longmorn 84 D28
Long Newnton 20 B35
Longnewton Bor. 70 A31
Long Newton Cle. 62 E39
Longney 29 G33
Longniddry 76 C30
Longnor Shr. 38 E30
Longnor Stf. 50 F36
Longparish 21 G40
Long Preston 56 D34
Longridge Lan. 56 F32
Longridge Ltn. 75 D25
Longriggend 74 D24
Long Riston 59 E47
Long Rock 2 E10
Long Sandall 51 B42
Longsdon 49 G35
Longshaw 48 B31
Longside 85 E36
Longstanton 33 B49
Longstock 10 A39
Longstone 75 C28
Long Stowe 33 C49
Long Stratton 45 F57
Long Sutton Ham. 22 G43
Long Sutton Lcn. 43 C50
Long Sutton Som. 8 B30
Longthorpe 42 F47
Longton 55 G30
Longtown Cum. 69 G29
Longtown H.& W. 28 F29
Longville in the Dale 38 F31
Longwell Green 19 D32
Long Whatton 41 C40
Longwick 22 A43
Long Wittenham 21 B41
Longwitton 71 E36
Longwood Shr. 39 E32
Longworth 21 B39
Longyester 76 D31
Loose 14 B53
Loosley Row 22 A44
Lootcherbrae 85 D32
Lopcombe Corner 10 A38
Lopen 8 C30
Loppington 38 C30
Lorbottle 71 C36
Loscoe 41 A40
Lossiemouth 84 B28
Lostock Gralam 49 E32
Lostock Green 49 E32
Lostwithiel 4 D17
Lothbeg 87 G25
Lothersdale 56 E35
Lothmore 87 G25
Loudwater 22 B45
Loughborough 41 D41
Loughor 17 E21
Loughton Bkh. 32 E44
Loughton Esx. 23 B50
Lound Not. 51 D42
Lound Sfk. 45 F61
Louth Lcn. 53 D49
Loveacott 6 C21
Lovedean 11 C42
Lover 10 B38
Loversall 51 C41
Loves Green 24 A52
Lovesome Hill 62 G39
Lovington 8 A31
Low Ackworth 51 A40
Low Ardwell 64 D16
Low Auchenlarie 65 C21
Low Banks 65 D32
Low Baring 63 G43
Low Barlay 65 C21
Low Barlings 52 E46
Low Barugh 51 B39
Low Bentham 56 C32
Low Bolton 62 G36
Low Borrowbridge 61 F32
Low Bradfield 50 C38
Low Bradley 57 E36
Low Braithwaite 61 B30
Low Brunton 70 F35
Low Burnham 51 B43
Low Burton 57 A38
Lowca 60 D25
Low Catton 58 D43
Low Caythorpe 59 C47
Low Clanyard 64 E17
Low Coniscliffe 62 E38
Low Crosby 61 A30
Lowdham 41 A42
Low Eggborough 58 G41
Lowe Hill 49 G35
Low Ellington 57 A38
Lower Ashton 7 G24
Lower Assendon 22 C43
Lower Bayble 88 D11

Lower Beeding 13 B48
Lower Benefield 42 G45
Lower Berry Hill 28 G31
Lower Bockhampton 9 E33
Lower Boddington 31 C40
Lower Boscaswell 2 E9
Lower Bourne 22 G44
Lower Brailes 30 E39
Lower Broadheath 29 C34
Lower Bullingham 28 E31
Lower Burton 28 C30
Lower Caldecote 32 D47
Lower Cam 20 A33
Lower Chapel 27 E26
Lower Crossings 50 D36
Lower Cumberworth 50 B38
Lower Dalveen 68 C24
Lower Darwen 56 G32
Lower Dene 32 B46
Lower Drift 2 F10
Lower Dunsforth 57 C40
Lower Edenhope 38 G28
Lower Everleigh 20 F37
Lower Farringdon 11 A43
Lower Flass 56 D33
Lower Foxdale 54 F25
Lower Froyle 22 G43
Lower Gledfield 86 J21
Lower Godney 19 G30
Lower Green Kent 23 G52
Lower Green Nfk. 44 B55
Lower Halstow 24 E54
Lower Hardres 15 B57
Lower Harpton 28 B28
Lower Hawthwaite 54 A28
Lower Hempriggs 84 C27
Lower Heyford 31 F40
Lower Hordley 38 C29
Lower Killeyan 78 L4
Lower Kingswood 23 F48
Lower Kinnerton 48 F29
Lower Langford 19 E30
Lower Largo 81 K30
Lower Leck 56 B32
Lower Lybrook 28 G31
Lower Machen 19 C28
Lower Mayland 25 A55
Lower Nazeing 23 A49
Lower Penarth 18 D27
Lower Penn 40 F34
Lower Penrhuddlan 37 G26
Lower Peover 49 E33
Lower Quinton 30 D37
Lower Shelton 32 D45
Lower Shiplake 22 D43
Lower Shuckburgh 31 B40
Lower Slaughter 30 F37
Lower Smerby 66 H5
Lower Stanton St. Quintin 20 C35
Lower Stoke 24 D54
Lower Stony Bank 56 D33
Lower Street 14 F53
Lower Swell 30 F37
Lower Tadmarton 31 E40
Lower Tean 40 B36
Lower Thurlton 45 F60
Lower Town 16 A15
Lower Tysoe 30 D39
Lower Upham 11 C41
Lower Weare 19 F30
Lower Whitley 49 E32
Lower Winchendon 31 G43
Lower Woodford 10 A37
Lower Wyche 29 D33
Lowesby 42 E43
Lowestoft 45 F61
Loweswater 60 D27
Low Etherley 62 D37
Lowfield Heath 23 G48
Low Fremington 62 G36
Low Gate 70 G35
Lowgill 56 C32
Low Ham 8 A30
Low Hesket 61 B30
Low Hutton 58 C43
Lowick Nmp. 42 G45
Lowick Nor. 77 G36
Lowick Bridge 54 A28
Lowick Green 54 A28
Low Laithe 57 C37
Low Langdale End 63 G45
Low Leighton 50 D36
Low Limerigg 74 C24
Low Lorton 60 D27
Low Malzie 64 C19
Low Marishes 58 B44
Low Marnham 52 F44
Low Mill 63 G42
Low Moor 56 E33
Low Moorsley 62 B39
Lowna 63 G42
Low Newton by the Sea 71 A38
Low Row Cum. 60 C29
Low Row Cum. 70 G31
Low Row N.Y. 62 G35
Lowsonford 30 B37
Low Street 45 C59
Lowther 61 D31
Lowthorpe 59 C46
Lowton 49 C32
Low Town 71 D37
Low Valleyfield 75 B26
Low Wood 55 A29
Low Worsall 62 E39

Lucker 71 A37
Luckington 20 C34
Luckwell Bridge 7 B25
Lucton 28 B30
Ludborough 53 C48
Ludchurch 16 C17
Luddenden 57 G36
Luddenden Foot 57 G36
Luddesdown Hum. 52 A44
Luddington War. 30 C37
Ludford 28 A31
Ludford Magna 53 D48
Ludford Parva 52 D47
Ludgershall Bkh. 31 G42
Ludgershall Wts. 21 F38
Ludgvan 2 E11
Ludham 45 D59
Ludlow 28 A31
Ludwell 9 B35
Ludworth 62 B39
Luffincott 6 F19
Luffness 76 B30
Lugar 67 A21
Lugate 76 F30
Luggate Burn 76 C31
Luggiebank 74 C23
Lugton 74 E20
Lugwardine 28 D31
Luib 82 G11
Luib Hotel 80 H20
Lullington Dby. 40 D38
Lullington E.S. 13 D51
Lullington Som. 20 F33
Lulworth Camp 9 F34
Lumbutts 56 G35
Lumby 57 F40
Lumphanan 85 J31
Lumphinnans 75 A27
Lumsdaine 77 D34
Lumsden 85 G30
Lunan 81 E30
Lunanhead 81 E30
Luncarty 80 G26
Lund 59 E45
Lundie 81 H29
Lundin Links 81 K30
Lunna 89 F40
Lunning 89 F41
Lunsfords Cross 14 F53
Lunt 48 B29
Luntley 28 C29
Luppitt 7 E27
Lupton 55 A31
Lurgashall 12 B45
Lusby 53 F49
Lusragill 61 F32
Luskentyre 88 H6
Luss 73 A19
Lusta 82 D8
Lustleigh 7 G23
Luston 28 B30
Luthrie 81 H29
Luton Bfd. 32 F47
Luton Dev. 5 C25
Luton Kent 24 E53
Luton Airport 32 F47
Lutterworth 41 G41
Lutton Dev. 5 E21
Lutton Lcn. 43 C50
Lutton Nmp. 42 G47
Luxborough 7 B25
Luxulyan 4 E16
Lybster 87 E28
Lydbury North 38 G29
Lydd 15 E56
Lydd Airport 15 E56
Lydden 15 C58
Lyddington 42 F44
Lydd-on-Sea 15 E56
Lydeard St. Lawrence 7 B27
Lydford 6 G21
Lydford-on-Fosse 8 A31
Lydgate 56 G35
Lydham 38 F29
Lydiard Millicent 20 C36
Lydiard Tregoze 20 C37
Lydiate 48 B29
Lydlinch 9 C33
Lydney 19 B29
Lydstep 16 E16
Lye 40 G35
Lye Green 22 A45
Lylestone 76 E31
Lyme Regis 8 E29
Lyminge 15 C57
Lymington 10 E39
Lyminster 12 D46
Lymm 49 D32
Lymore 10 E38
Lympne 15 D57
Lympsham 19 F29
Lympstone 7 G25
Lynch 84 J23
Lyndhurst 10 D39
Lyndon 42 E45
Lyne 75 F28
Lyne Down 29 E32
Lyneham Wts. 20 D36
Lyneholmeford 70 F31
Lynemouth 71 D38
Lyne of Gorthleck 83 G21
Lyne of Skene 85 H33
Lyness 89 H29
Lyng Nfk. 44 D56
Lyng Som. 8 B29
Lynmouth 7 A23
Lynsted 25 E55
Lynton 7 A23
Lyonshall 28 C29
Lytchett Matravers 9 E35
Lytchett Minster 9 E35
Lyth 87 B28
Lytham 55 G29
Lytham St. Anne's 55 G29

Lythe 63 E44
Lythes 89 J30

M

Maaruig 88 G7
Mabe Burnthouse 2 E13
Mabie 68 F25
Mablethorpe 53 D51
Macclesfield 49 E35
Macclesfield Forest 49 E35
Macduff 85 C33
Macharioch 66 C13
Machen 19 C28
Machrie 72 G14
Machrihanish 66 A12
Machynlleth 37 E23
Mackworth 41 B39
Macmerry 76 C30
Maddaford 6 F21
Madderty 80 H25
Maddington 20 G36
Maddiston 75 C25
Madehurst 12 C45
Madeley Shr. 39 E33
Madeley Stf. 39 A33
Madeley Heath 39 A33
Madingley 33 B49
Madjeston 9 B34
Madley 28 E30
Madresfield 29 D34
Madron 2 E10
Maenaddwyn 46 D20
Maenclochog 16 B16
Maendy 18 D26
Maentwrog 37 A22
Maer 39 B33
Maerdy Clw. 37 A26
Maerdy Gwe. 28 F29
Maerdy M.G. 18 B25
Maesbrook 38 C28
Maeselwad 27 B23
Maeshafn 48 F28
Maesteg 18 B24
Maes Treylow 28 B28
Maes-y-cwmmer 18 B27
Maggieknockater 84 E29
Magham Down 13 C52
Maghull 48 B29
Magor 19 C30
Maiden Bradley 9 A34
Maidencombe 5 D25
Maidenhead 22 C44
Maiden Law 62 B37
Maiden Newton 8 E31
Maidens 67 C18
Maiden Wells 16 D15
Maidford 31 C42
Maids' Moreton 31 E43
Maidstone 14 B53
Maidwell 31 A43
Mail 89 K40
Mains of Bonskeid 80 D24
Mains of Craigmill 84 D26
Mains of Dalvey 84 F27
Mains of Idoch 85 E33
Mains of Towie 85 E33
Mains of Watten 87 C28
Mainsriddle 65 C26
Mainstone 38 G28
Maisemore 29 F34
Makerstoun 76 G32
Malborough 5 F23
Malden Rushett 22 E47
Maldon 24 A54
Malham 56 C34
Mallaig 79 A12
Mallaigvaig 79 A12
Malleny Mills 75 D27
Malltraeth 46 F20
Mallwyd 37 D24
Malmesbury 20 C35
Malpas Che. 38 A30
Malpas Cnw. 3 D14
Maltby Cle. 62 E40
Maltby S.Y. 51 C41
Maltby le Marsh 53 D50
Malton 58 B43
Malvern Link 29 D33
Malvern Wells 29 D33
Mambeg 73 A18
Mamble 29 A32
Mamhilad 19 A29
Manaccan 2 F13
Manafon 38 E27
Manaton 7 G23
Manby 53 D49
Mancetter 41 F39
Manchester 49 C34
Manchester Airport 49 D34
Mandally 83 J18
Manea 43 G50
Maneight 67 C21
Manfield 62 E38
Mangersta 88 D6
Mangotsfield 19 D32
Mankinholes 56 G35
Manley 48 E31
Manningford Abbots 20 F37
Manningford Bruce 20 F37
Manning's Heath 13 B48
Mannington 10 D36
Manningtree 35 E57
Mannofield 85 J35
Manorbier 16 E16
Manorbier Newton 16 D16
Manorneuk 74 A24
Mansell Gamage 28 D29
Mansell Lacy 28 D30
Manselton 17 E22
Mansfield Not. 51 F41
Mansfield Str. 68 B22

Mansfield Woodhouse 51 F41
Mansriggs 54 A28
Manston Dor. 9 C34
Manston Kent 25 E59
Manston W.Y. 57 F39
Manswood 9 D35
Manthorpe 42 B45
Manthorpe 42 D46
Manton Lei. 42 E44
Manton Wts. 20 E37
Manuden 33 F50
Maperton 9 B32
Maplebeck 51 F43
Maple Cross 22 B46
Mapledurham 21 D42
Mapledurwell 21 F42
Maplehurst 12 B47
Mapleton 40 A37
Mapperley Dby. 41 A40
Mapperley Not. 41 A41
Mapperton 8 E31
Mappleborough Green 30 B36
Mappleton 59 E48
Mappowder 9 D33
Maqueston 68 D23
Marazion 2 E11
Marbury 38 A31
March 43 F50
Marcham 21 B40
Marchamley 38 C31
Marchamley Wood 38 B31
Marchbankwood 69 D26
Marchburn 68 B22
Marchington 40 B37
Marchington Woodlands 40 C37
Marchmont House 76 F33
Marchwiel 38 A29
Marchwood 10 C39
Marcross 18 E25
Marden H.& W. 28 D31
Marden Kent 14 C53
Marden Wts. 20 F36
Marden Ash 23 A51
Marden Beech 14 C53
Mardy 28 G29
Marefield 42 E43
Mareham le Fen 53 F48
Mareham on the Hill 53 F48
Marehay 41 A39
Maresfield 13 B50
Marfleet 59 G47
Marford 48 G29
Margam 18 C23
Margaret Marsh 9 C34
Margaret Roding 33 G52
Margaretting 24 A52
Margate 25 D59
Margnaheglish 72 G16
Margrove Park 63 E42
Marham 44 D53
Marhamchurch 6 E18
Marholm 42 E47
Marian-glas 46 D21
Mariansleigh 7 C23
Marishader 82 C10
Maristow 4 D20
Marjoriebanks 69 E26
Mark Som. 19 G29
Mark Str. 56 F16
Markbeech 23 G50
Markby 53 E50
Mark Causeway 19 G29
Mark Cross 13 A51
Market Bosworth 41 E40
Market Deeping 42 D47
Market Drayton 39 B32
Market Harborough 42 G43
Market Lavington 20 F36
Market Overton 42 D44
Market Rasen 52 D47
Market Stainton 53 D48
Market Street 45 C58
Market Weighton 58 E44
Market Weston 34 A55
Markfield 41 E40
Markham 18 A27
Markham Clinton 51 E43
Markham Moor 51 E43
Markinch 81 K28
Markington 57 C38
Marksbury 19 E32
Marks Tey 34 F55
Markyate 32 G46
Marlborough 20 E37
Marldon 5 D24
Marlesford 35 C59
Marley Hill 62 A38
Marlingford 45 E57
Mar Lodge 80 B26
Marloes 16 D13
Marlow Bkh. 22 C44
Marlow Shr. 28 A29
Marlpit Hill 23 G50
Marnhull 9 C33
Marnoch 85 E31
Marple 49 D35
Marr 51 B41
Marrel 87 G26
Marrick 62 G36
Marrister 89 F41
Marros 17 D18
Marsden T.& W. 71 G40
Marsden W.Y. 50 A36
Marsett 56 A35
Marsh 8 C28
Marshams 45 C57
Marshaw 55 D31
Marsh Baldon 21 B41
Marshbrook 38 F30
Marsh Chapel 53 C49
Marshfield Avon 20 D33
Marshfield Gwe. 19 C28
Marshgate 4 A17

Marsh Gibbon

Marsh Gibbon 31 F42
Marsh Green 23 G50
Marsh Houses 55 D30
Marshlane 51 E40
Marshwood 8 E29
Marske 62 F37
Marske-by-the-Sea 63 D42
Marston *Che.* 49 E32
Marston *H.& W.* 28 C29
Marston *Lcn.* 42 A44
Marston *Oxf.* 21 A41
Marston *Stf.* 40 D34
Marston *Wts.* 20 F35
Marston Green 40 G37
Marston Magna 8 B31
Marston Meysey 20 B37
Marston Montgomery 40 B37
Marston Moretaine 32 D45
Marston on Dove 40 C38
Marston St. Lawrence 31 D41
Marston Stannett 28 C31
Marston Trussell 41 G42
Marstow 28 G31
Marsworth 32 G45
Marthall 49 E34
Martham 45 D60
Martin *Ham.* 10 C36
Martin *Lcn.* 52 F47
Martin Dales 52 F47
Martin Drove End 10 B36
Martinhoe 6 A22
Martinhoe Cross 6 A22
Martin Hussingtree 29 B34
Martinstown *Dor.* 9 F32
Martlesham 35 D58
Martletwy 16 C16
Martley 29 B33
Martock 8 C30
Marton *Che.* 49 F34
Marton *Cle.* 63 E41
Marton *Hum.* 59 F47
Marton *Lcn.* 52 D44
Marton *N.Y.* 58 A43
Marton *N.Y.* 57 C40
Marton *Shr.* 38 C30
Marton *Shr.* 38 E28
Marton *War.* 31 B40
Marton-le-Moor 57 B39
Martyr's Green 22 F46
Martyr Worthy 11 A41
Marwick 89 E28
Marwood 6 B21
Marybank 83 D20
Maryburgh 83 D21
Maryculter 81 A34
Marygold 77 E34
Maryhill *Grm.* 85 E34
Maryhill *Str.* 74 D21
Marykirk 81 D32
Marypark 84 F27
Maryport *Cum.* 60 C26
Maryport *D.& G.* 64 E17
Marystow 6 G20
Mary Tavy 5 C21
Maryton 81 E29
Marywell *Grm.* 81 A31
Marywell *Tay.* 81 F32
Masham 57 A38
Masongill 56 B32
Mastin Moor 51 E40
Mastrick 85 J35
Matching Green 33 G51
Matching Tye 33 G51
Matfen 71 F36
Matfield 23 G52
Mathafarn 37 E24
Mathern 19 B31
Mathon 29 D33
Mathry 16 A14
Matlask 45 B57
Matlock 51 F39
Matlock Bath 50 G38
Matterdale End 60 D29
Mattersey 51 D42
Mattersey Thorpe 51 D42
Mattingley 22 F43
Mattishall 44 D56
Mattishall Burgh 44 D56
Mauchline 67 A20
Maud 85 E35
Maughold 54 D27
Maulden 32 E46
Maulds Meaburn 61 E32
Maunby 57 A39
Maund Bryan 28 C31
Mavesyn Ridware 40 D36
Mavis Enderby 53 F49
Mawbray 60 B26
Mawdesley 48 A30
Mawdlam 18 C24
Mawgan 2 F13
Mawla 2 D13
Mawnan 2 F13
Mawnan Smith 2 F13
Maxey 42 E47
Maxstoke 40 G38
Maxton *Bor.* 70 A32
Maxton *Kent* 15 C59
Maxwellston 67 C18
Maxwelltown 68 F25
Maxwelton 68 E24
Maybole 67 C18
Mayfield *E.S.* 13 B51
Mayfield *Ltn.* 75 D29
Mayfield *Stf.* 40 A37
Mayford 22 F45
Maynard's Green 13 C51
Maypole 2 A11
Maypole Green 45 F60
Mayshiel 76 D32
Maywick 89 K39
Meadowfield 75 B28
Mead Vale 23 G48
Meal Bank 61 G31
Mealrigg 60 B27
Mealsgate 60 B28
Mearbeck 56 C34
Meare 19 G30
Meare Green 8 B29
Mearns 74 E21
Mears Ashby 32 B44
Measham 41 D39
Meathop 55 A30
Meavag 88 H7
Meavy 5 D21
Medbourne 42 F44
Meddon 6 D18
Meden Vale 51 F41
Medmenham 22 C44
Medomsley 62 A37
Medstead 11 A42
Meerbrook 49 F35
Meesden 33 E50
Meeth 6 E21
Meidrim 17 B18
Meifod 38 D27
Meigle 81 F28
Meikle Earnock 74 E23
Meikle Float 64 D16
Meikle Grenach 72 D16
Meikle Kilmory 72 D16
Meikleour 81 G27
Meikle Wartle 85 F33
Meikleyard 74 G21
Meillteyrn 36 B18
Meinciau 17 C20
Meir 40 A35
Meir Heath 40 A35
Melbost 88 D10
Melbost Borve 88 B10
Melbourn 33 D49
Melbourne *Dby.* 41 C39
Melbourne *Hum.* 58 E43
Melbourne *Str.* 75 F26
Melbury Abbas 9 B34
Melbury Bubb 8 D31
Melbury Osmond 8 D31
Melby 89 G37
Melchbourne 32 B46
Melcombe Bingham 9 D33
Melcombe Regis 9 G32
Meldon *Dev.* 6 F21
Meldon *Nor.* 71 E37
Meldon Park 71 E37
Meldreth 33 D49
Meldrum 74 A23
Melfort 79 J14
Melgarve 80 A20
Meliden 47 D26
Melinbyrhedyn 37 F24
Melincourt 18 A24
Melin-y-coed 47 F24
Melkington 77 F34
Melkinthorpe 61 D31
Melkridge 70 G33
Melksham 20 E35
Melksham Forest 20 E35
Melladalloch 72 C15
Mellerstain 76 G32
Melling *Lan.* 55 B31
Melling *Mer.* 48 B29
Melling Mount 48 B30
Mellis 35 A57
Mellon Charles 86 J14
Mellon Udrigle 86 J14
Mellor *G.M.* 49 D35
Mellor *Lan.* 56 F32
Mellor Brook 56 F32
Mells 20 G33
Melmerby 61 C32
Melmerby *N.Y.* 57 A36
Melmerby *N.Y.* 57 B39
Melplash 8 E30
Melrose 76 G31
Melsetter 89 J28
Melsonby 62 F37
Meltham 50 A36
Melton *Hum.* 59 G45
Melton *Sfk.* 35 C58
Melton Constable 44 B56
Melton Mowbray 42 D43
Melton Ross 52 A46
Melvaig 82 A13
Melverley 38 D29
Melvich 87 B24
Membury 8 D28
Membury Services 21 D39
Memsie 85 C35
Memus 81 E30
Menai Bridge 46 E21
Mendham 45 G58
Mendlesham 35 B57
Mendlesham Green 34 B56
Menheniot 4 D18
Mennock 68 C24
Menston 57 E37
Menstrie 74 A24
Mentmore 32 G45
Meoble 79 B13
Meole Brace 38 D30
Meonstoke 11 C42
Meopham 24 E52
Meopham Green 24 E52
Meopham Station 24 E52
Mepal 43 G50
Meppershall 32 E47
Mere *Che.* 49 D33
Mere *Wts.* 9 A34
Mere Brow 48 A30
Mere Clough 56 F34
Mere Green 29 B35
Mereworth 23 F52
Meriden 40 G38
Merkadale 82 F9
Merkland *D.& G.* 69 F28
Merkland *D.& G.* 68 F23
Merkland Lodge 86 F20
Merlin's Bridge 16 C15
Merrion 16 E15
Merriott 8 C30
Merrivale 5 C21
Merrow 22 F46
Merrymeet 4 D18
Mersham 15 D56
Merstham 23 F48
Merston 12 D44
Merthyr Cynog 27 E25
Merthyr Mawr 18 D24
Merthyr Tydfil 18 A26
Merthyr Vale 18 B26
Merton *Dev.* 6 D21
Merton *G.L.* 23 E48
Merton *Nfk.* 44 F55
Merton *Oxf.* 31 G41
Mervinslaw 70 B32
Meshaw 7 D23
Messing 34 G54
Messingham 52 B44
Metal Bridge 69 G29
Metfield 45 G58
Metheringham 52 F46
Methil 75 A29
Methley 57 G39
Methlick 85 F34
Methven 80 H26
Methwold 44 F53
Methwold Hythe 44 F53
Mettingham 45 F59
Mevagissey 4 F16
Mewith Head 56 C33
Mexborough 51 B40
Mey 89 K28
Meysey Hampton 20 A37
Miavaig 88 D6
Michaelchurch Escley 28 E29
Michaelchurch on Arrow 28 C28
Michaelstone-y-Vedw 19 C28
Michaelston-le-Pit 18 D27
Michaelstow 4 C16
Michael Wood Services 20 B33
Micheldever 11 A41
Micheldever Station 21 G41
Michelmersh 10 B39
Mickfield 35 B57
Micklebring 51 C41
Mickleby 63 E44
Mickleham 22 F47
Mickleover 41 B39
Micklethwaite 60 A28
Mickleton *Drm.* 62 D35
Mickleton *Glo.* 30 D37
Mickletown 57 G39
Mickley 57 B38
Mickley Square 71 G36
Mid Ardlaw 85 C35
Midbea 89 C30
Mid Beltie 85 J32
Mid Cairncross 81 C30
Mid Calder 75 D26
Middle Assendon 22 C43
Middle Aston 31 F40
Middle Barton 31 F40
Middlebie 69 F28
Middle Claydon 31 F43
Middlegill 69 C26
Middleham 57 A37
Middle Handley 51 E40
Middlehill 4 D18
Middlemarsh 9 D32
Middle Mill 16 B14
Middle Rasen 52 D46
Middlesbrough 62 E40
Middleshaw *Cum.* 55 A31
Middleshaw *D.& G.* 69 F27
Middlesknowes 70 B33
Middlesmoor 57 B36
Middlestone 62 C38
Middlestown 50 A38
Middleton *Cum.* 56 A32
Middleton *Dby.* 50 G38
Middleton *Dby.* 50 F37
Middleton *G.M.* 49 B34
Middleton *Ham.* 21 G40
Middleton *Lan.* 55 D30
Middleton *Ltn.* 75 E29
Middleton *Nfk.* 44 D52
Middleton *Nmp.* 42 F44
Middleton *Nor.* 71 E36
Middleton *Nor.* 77 G37
Middleton *N.Y.* 58 A43
Middleton *Sfk.* 35 B60
Middleton *Shr.* 28 A31
Middleton *Str.* 78 F5
Middleton *Tay.* 81 F27
Middleton *Tay.* 81 F31
Middleton *War.* 40 F37
Middleton *W.G.* 17 F20
Middleton *W.Y.* 57 G39
Middleton *W.Y.* 57 E37
Middleton Cheney 31 D40
Middleton in Teesdale 62 D35
Middleton-on-Sea 12 E45
Middleton on the Hill 28 B31
Middleton on the Wolds 59 E45
Middleton St. George 62 E39
Middleton Scriven 39 G32
Middleton Stoney 31 F41
Middleton Tyas 62 F38
Middle Town 2 A11
Middletown *Pow.* 38 D29
Middle Tysoe 30 D39
Middle Wallop 10 A38
Middlewich 49 F33
Middle Winterslow 10 A38
Middlewood 28 D28
Middle Woodford 10 A37
Middlezoy 8 A29
Middridge 62 D38
Midfield 86 B21
Midford 20 E33
Midgeholme 61 A32
Midgham 21 E41
Midgley 50 A38
Midgley 57 G36
Midhopestones 50 C38
Midhurst 12 B44
Mid Kelton 65 C23
Mid Lavant 12 D44
Midlem 70 A31
Midpark 72 E16
Mid Sannox 72 F16
Midsomer Norton 19 F32
Mid Thundergay 72 F14
Midtown *Hgh.* 86 B21
Midtown *Hgh.* 83 A14
Mid Yell 89 C41
Migvie 85 J30
Milborne Port 9 C32
Milborne St. Andrew 9 E34
Milborne Wick 9 B32
Milbourne 71 F37
Milburn 61 D32
Milbury Heath 19 B32
Milby 57 C40
Milcombe 31 E40
Mildenhall *Sfk.* 34 A53
Mildenhall *Wts.* 21 E38
Milebush *Kent* 14 C53
Mile End *Esx.* 34 F55
Mile End *Glo.* 28 G31
Mileham 44 D55
Mile Oak 13 D48
Milfield 77 G35
Milford *Dby.* 41 A39
Milford *Dev.* 6 C18
Milford *Nor.* 71 E37
Milford *Sry.* 22 G45
Milford *Stf.* 40 C35
Milford Haven 16 D15
Milford Heath 22 G45
Milford on Sea 10 E38
Milkieston 75 F28
Milkwall 19 A31
Milland 12 B44
Mill Bank 57 G36
Millbeck *Cum.* 60 F28
Millbeck *Cum.* 60 D28
Millbounds 89 D31
Millbreck 85 E35
Millbridge 22 G44
Millbrook *Bfd.* 32 E46
Millbrook *Cnw.* 4 E20
Millbrook *G.M.* 49 C35
Millbrook *Ham.* 10 C39
Mill Brow 49 D35
Millcombe 5 E24
Millden Lodge 81 C31
Milldens 81 E31
Millearn 80 J25
Mill End *Bkh.* 22 C43
Mill End *Cbs.* 43 G49
Millerhill 75 D29
Miller's Dale 50 E37
Millerston 74 D22
Mill Green *Esx.* 24 A52
Mill Green *Hfs.* 23 A48
Mill Green *W.M.* 40 E36
Millhalf 28 D28
Millhall 74 E21
Millhead 55 B30
Millheugh 74 E23
Mill Hill 23 B48
Millhouse *Cum.* 60 C29
Millhouse *Str.* 72 C15
Millhousebridge 69 E27
Millhouses *S.Y.* 51 D39
Millhouses *S.Y.* 51 B40
Millikenpark 74 D20
Millington 58 D44
Millisle *D.& G.* 64 D20
Millmeece 40 B34
Mill of Muiresk 85 E32
Millom 54 A27
Millport 73 E17
Millthorpe 51 E39
Millthrop 61 G32
Milltown *Dby.* 51 F39
Milltown *Dev.* 6 B21
Milltown *D.& G.* 69 F29
Milltown *Grm.* 85 H30
Milltown *Grm.* 85 E31
Milltown *Hgh.* 83 D19
Milltown of Aberdalgie 80 H26
Milltown of Auchindown 84 E29
Milltown of Campfield 85 J32
Milltown of Edinvillie 84 F28
Milnathort 81 K27
Milngavie 74 C21
Milnrow 49 A35
Milnsbridge 50 A37
Milnthorpe *Cum.* 55 A30
Milnthorpe *W.Y.* 51 A39
Milovaig 82 E7
Milrig 74 G21
Milson 29 A32
Milsted 14 B55
Milston 20 G37
Milton 81 F29
Milton *Avon* 19 E29
Milton *Cbs.* 33 B50
Milton *Cen.* 74 A20
Milton *Cen.* 80 K21
Milton *Cum.* 70 G31
Milton *Dby.* 41 C39
Milton *D.& G.* 68 E24
Milton *D.& G.* 64 C18
Milton *D.& G.* 68 F24
Milton *Dyf.* 16 D16
Milton *Grm.* 85 C31
Milton *Hgh.* 83 E18
Milton *Hgh.* 83 F20
Milton *Hgh.* 83 E21
Milton *Hgh.* 84 B23
Milton *Kent* 15 B57
Milton *Nmp.* 31 C43
Milton *Oxf.* 21 B40
Milton *Oxf.* 31 E40
Milton *Stf.* 49 G35
Milton *Str.* 67 C18
Milton *Str.* 73 D19
Milton *Str.* 74 C20
Milton Abbas 9 D34
Milton Abbot 4 C20
Milton Bryant 32 E45
Milton Clevedon 9 A32
Milton Combe 4 D20
Milton Cushnie 85 H31
Milton Damerel 6 D19
Miltonduff 84 D27
Milton Ernest 32 C46
Milton Green 48 G30
Milton Hill 21 B40
Miltonise 67 F17
Milton Keynes 32 E44
Milton Keynes Village 32 E44
Milton Lilbourne 20 E37
Milton of Auchinhove 85 J31
Milton of Auchriachan 84 H27
Milton of Balgonie 81 K29
Milton of Campsie 74 C22
Milton of Farr 84 F22
Milton of Lesmore 85 G30
Milton of Tullich 81 A29
Milton on Stour 9 B33
Milton Regis 25 E55
Milton under Wychwood 30 G38
Milverton 7 C27
Milwich 40 B35
Minard 72 A15
Minchinhampton 20 A34
Mindrum 77 G34
Mindrummill 77 G34
Minehead 7 A25
Minera 48 G28
Minety 20 B36
Minffordd *Gwy.* 37 D23
Minffordd *Gwy.* 37 B22
Mingarrypark 79 D12
Mingary 88 P3
Miningsby 53 F49
Minions 4 C18
Minishant 67 B19
Minllyn 37 D24
Minmore 84 G27
Minnigaff 67 G20
Minsca 69 E28
Minskip 57 C39
Minstead 10 C38
Minster *Kent* 25 E59
Minster *Kent* 25 D55
Minsteracres 62 A36
Minsterley 38 E29
Minster Lovell 30 G39
Minsterworth 29 G33
Minterne Magna 9 D32
Minting 52 E47
Mintlaw 85 E36
Minto 70 B31
Minto Cott 65 C22
Minton 38 F30
Mirehouse 60 E25
Mireland 87 B29
Mirfield 50 A38
Miserden 20 A35
Miskin *M.G.* 18 C26
Miskin *M.G.* 18 B26
Misson 51 C42
Misterton *Not.* 51 C43
Misterton *Som.* 8 D30
Mistley 35 E57
Mitcheldean 29 G32
Mitchell 3 C14
Mitchel Troy 28 G30
Mitton 40 D34
Mixbury 31 E42
Moaness 89 G28
Moat 68 A25
Mobberley *Che.* 49 E33
Mobberley *Stf.* 40 A36
Moccas 28 D29
Mochdre *Clw.* 47 E24
Mochdre *Pow.* 37 G26
Mochrum 64 D19
Mockbeggar 14 C53
Mockerkin 60 D26
Mockham Down Gate 6 B22
Modbury 5 E22
Moddershall 40 B35
Moelfre *Clw.* 38 C27
Moelfre *Gwy.* 46 D21
Moffat 69 C26
Mogerhanger 32 D47
Moira *Lei.* 41 D39
Molash 15 B56
Mol-chlach 82 H10
Mold 48 F28
Molehill Green 33 F51
Molescroft 59 E46
Molesden 71 E37
Molesworth 32 A46
Molland 7 C24
Mollington *Che.* 48 E29
Mollington *Oxf.* 31 D40
Mollinsburn 74 C23
Monar Lodge 83 E18
Monewden 35 C58
Moniaive 68 D23
Monifieth 81 G30
Monikie 81 G30
Monimail 81 J28
Monk Bretton 51 B39
Monk Fryston 58 G41
Monk Hesleden 62 C40
Monkhopton 39 F32
Monkland 28 C30
Monkleigh 6 C20
Monknash 18 D25
Monkokehampton 6 E21
Monkseaton 71 F39
Monks Eleigh 34 D55
Monks' Heath 49 E34
Monk Sherborne 21 F42
Monksilver 7 B26
Monks Kirby 41 G40
Monk Soham 35 B58
Monks Risborough 22 A44
Monkswood 19 A29
Monkton *Dev.* 7 E27
Monkton *Kent* 25 E58
Monkton *Str.* 67 A19
Monkton Combe 20 E33
Monkton Deverill 9 A34
Monkton Farleigh 20 E34
Monkton Wyld 8 E29
Monkwearmouth 62 A40
Monkwood 11 A42
Monmouth 28 G31
Monnington on Wye 28 D29
Monreith 64 D19
Montacute 8 C30
Montford 38 D30
Montford Bridge 38 D30
Montgarrie 85 H31
Montgarswood 67 A21
Montgomerie 67 A20
Montgomery 38 F28
Montgreenan 73 F19
Montrave 81 K29
Montrose 81 E33
Monxton 21 G39
Monyash 50 F37
Monymusk 85 H32
Monzie 80 H24
Moodiesburn 74 C22
Moorby 53 F48
Moor Cock 56 C32
Moorcock Inn 61 G33
Moor Crichel 9 D35
Moordown 10 E36
Moore 48 D31
Moorends 51 A42
Moorhampton 28 D29
Moor Head 55 E30
Moor House 77 D34
Moorhouse 60 A29
Moorland 8 A29
Moorlinch 8 A29
Moor Monkton 58 D41
Moor Row 60 E26
Moorsholm 63 E42
Moorside *G.M.* 49 B35
Moor Side *Lan.* 55 F30
Moor Side *Lcn.* 53 G48
Moortown *Ham.* 10 D37
Moortown *Lcn.* 52 C46
Morar 79 A12
Morborne 42 F47
Morchard Bishop 7 E23
Morcombelake 8 E29
Morcott 42 E45
Morda 38 C28
Morden *Dor.* 9 E35
Morden *G.L.* 23 E48
Mordiford 28 E31
Mordon 62 D39
More 38 F29
Morebath 7 C25
Morebattle 70 A33
Morecambe 55 C30
Moredon 20 C37
Morefield 86 J17
Moreland 75 A26
Moreleigh 5 E23
Morenish 80 G21
Moresby 60 D25
Moresby Parks 60 E25
Morestead 11 B41
Moreton *Dor.* 9 F34
Moreton *Esx.* 23 A51
Moreton *Mer.* 48 D28
Moreton *Oxf.* 21 A42
Moreton Corbet 38 C31
Moretonhampstead 7 G23
Moreton in Marsh 30 E38
Moreton Morrell 30 C39
Moreton on Lugg 28 D31
Moreton Pinkney 31 D41
Moreton Say 39 B32
Moreton Valence 29 G33
Morfa Bychan 36 B21
Morfa Nefyn 36 A18
Morgan's Vale 10 B37
Moriah 27 A22
Mork 19 A31
Morland 61 D31
Morley *Dby.* 41 A39
Morley *Drm.* 62 D37
Morley *W.Y.* 57 G38
Morley St. Botolph 44 E56
Morningside 74 E24
Morningthorpe 45 F58
Morpeth 71 E37
Morriston *Str.* 67 C18
Morriston *W.G.* 17 E22
Morston 44 A56
Mortehoe 6 A20
Morthen 51 D40
Mortimer 21 E42
Mortimer's Cross 28 B30
Mortimer West End 21 E42
Morton *Avon* 19 B32
Morton *Dby.* 51 F40
Morton *Lcn.* 42 C46
Morton *Lcn.* 52 C44
Morton *Not.* 51 G43
Morton *Sal.* 38 C28
Morton Bagot 30 B37
Morton-on-Swale 62 G39
Morvah 2 E9
Morval 4 E18
Morvich 83 G15
Morvich Lodge 87 H23
Morville 39 F32
Morwenstow 6 D18

Morwick Hall 71 C38
Mosborough 51 D40
Moscow *Cum.* 70 G32
Moscow *Str.* 74 F20
Mosedale 60 C29
Moselden Height 50 A36
Moseley 40 G36
Moss *Clw.* 48 G29
Moss *S.Y.* 51 A41
Mossat 85 H30
Moss Bank 48 C31
Mossblown 67 A20
Mossbank 89 E40
Mossburnford 70 B32
Mossdale *D.& G.* 68 F22
Mossdale *Str.* 67 C20
Mossend 74 D23
Mossknowe 69 G28
Mossley *Che.* 49 F34
Mossley *G.M.* 49 B35
Mossley Hill 48 D29
Mosspaul Inn 69 D30
Mosspeeble 69 D29
Mosstodloch 84 D29
Mossy Lea 48 A31
Mosterton 8 D30
Moston 49 B34
Mostyn 47 D27
Motcombe 9 B34
Motherby 61 D30
Motherwell 74 E23
Mottisfont 10 B39
Mottistone 11 F40
Mottram 49 C35
Mouldsworth 48 E31
Moulin 80 E25
Moulsecoomb 13 D49
Moulsford 21 C41
Moulsoe 32 D45
Moulton *Che.* 49 F32
Moulton *Lcn.* 43 C49
Moulton *Nmp.* 31 B43
Moulton *N.Y.* 62 F38
Moulton *Sfk.* 33 B52
Moulton Chapel 43 D48
Moulton St. Michael 45 F57
Moulton Seas End 43 C49
Mount 4 D17
Mountain Ash 18 B26
Mountain Cross 75 F27
Mountbenger 69 A29
Mountbengerhope 69 A29
Mountfield *E.S.* 14 E53
Mountgerald 83 C21
Mount Hawke 2 D13
Mountjoy *Cnw.* 3 B14
Mount Lothian 75 E28
Mountnessing 24 B52
Mounton 19 B31
Mount Pleasant *Bor.* 77 F34
Mount Pleasant *Sfk.* 35 A61
Mountsorrel 41 D41
Mountstuart 73 E17
Mount Tabor 57 G36
Mousehole 2 F10
Mouswald 69 F26
Mowbray Hill 57 A38
Mow Cop 49 G34
Mowhaugh 70 A34
Mowsley 41 G42
Mowtie 81 B34
Moy *Hgh.* 84 F23
Moy *Hgh.* 80 B20
Moy Hall 84 F23
Moylgrove 26 D17
Moy Lodge 80 B20
Muasdale 72 F12
Muchalls 81 A35
Much Birch 28 E31
Much Cowarne 29 D32
Much Dewchurch 28 E30
Muchelney 8 B30
Much Hadham 33 G50
Much Hoole 55 G30
Much Marcle 29 E32
Muchrachd 83 F18
Much Wenlock 39 E32
Mucklestone 39 B33
Muckletown 85 G31
Muckleycross 39 F32
Muckra 69 B28
Muckton 53 D49
Mudale 86 E21
Muddiford 6 B21
Muddles Green 13 C51
Mudeford 10 E37
Mudford 8 C31
Mugdock 74 C21
Mugeary 82 F10
Muggleswick 62 B36
Muie 87 H22
Muirdrum 81 B31
Muirhead *Str.* 74 D22
Muirhead *Tay.* 81 G29
Muirhouses 75 B26
Muirkirk 68 A22
Muirmill 74 B23
Muir of Fowlis 85 H31
Muir of Ord 83 D21
Muirshearlich 79 B17
Muirshiel 74 E21
Muirton of Ardblair 81 F27
Muker 61 G35
Mulbarton 45 E57
Mulben 84 D29
Mullacott Cross 6 A21
Mull Airport 79 F11
Mullion 2 G12
Mumby 53 E51
Munderfield Stocks 29 C32
Mundesley 45 B59

Mundford 44 F54
Mundham 45 F59
Mundon Hill 24 A54
Munerigie 83 J18
Mungasdale 86 J15
Mungoswells 76 C30
Mungrisdale 60 C29
Munlochy 83 D22
Munnoch 73 F18
Munslow 38 G31
Munslow Aston 38 G31
Murcott 31 G41
Murkle 87 B27
Murlaggan 79 A16
Murrayfield 75 C28
Murrow 43 E49
Mursley 32 F44
Murston 25 E55
Murthly 80 G26
Murton *Cum.* 61 D33
Murton *Drm.* 62 B39
Murton *Nor.* 77 F35
Murton *N.Y.* 58 D42
Musbury 8 E28
Musselburgh 75 C29
Muston *Lei.* 42 B44
Muston *N.Y.* 59 B46
Mustow Green 29 A34
Mutehill 65 D22
Mutford 45 G60
Muthill 80 J24
Mybster 87 C27
Myddfai 27 E23
Myddle 38 C30
Mydroilyn 26 C20
Mylor Bridge 3 E14
Mynachlog-ddu 16 A17
Mynydd-bâch 19 B30
Mynydd Isa 48 F28
Mynydd Llandegai 46 F22
Mynytho 36 B19
Mytchett 22 F44
Mytholm 56 G35
Mytholmroyd 57 G36
Mythop 55 F29
Myton-on-Swale 57 C40

N

Naburn 58 E41
Nackington 15 B57
Nacton 35 D58
Nadderwater 7 F24
Nafferton 59 D46
Nailbridge 29 G32
Nailsea 19 D30
Nailstone 41 E40
Nailsworth 20 B34
Nairn 84 D24
Nancegollan 2 E12
Nancledra 2 E10
Nanhoron 36 B18
Nannerch 47 F27
Nanpantan 41 D41
Nanpean 3 C15
Nanstallon 4 D16
Nant-ddû 27 G26
Nantgaredig 17 B20
Nantgarw 18 C27
Nantglyn 47 F26
Nantgwyn 27 A25
Nantile 46 G21
Nantmel 27 B26
Nantmor 37 A22
Nant Peris 46 G22
Nantwich 49 G32
Nant-y-Cafn 18 A24
Nant-y-caws 17 C20
Nant-y-dugoed 37 D25
Nantyffyllon 18 B24
Nantyglo 28 G27
Nant-y-moel 18 B25
Nant-y-pandy 46 E22
Naphill 22 B44
Nappa 56 D34
Napton on the Hill 31 B40
Narberth 16 C17
Narborough *Lei.* 41 F41
Narborough *Nfk.* 44 D53
Narthwaite 61 G33
Nasareth 46 G20
Naseby 31 A42
Nash *Bkh.* 31 E43
Nash *Gwe.* 19 C29
Nash *H.& W.* 28 B29
Nash *Shr.* 29 A32
Nassington 42 F46
Nasty 33 F49
Nateby *Cum.* 61 F33
Nateby *Lan.* 55 E30
Natland 55 A31
Naughton 34 D56
Naunton *Glo.* 30 F37
Naunton *H.& W.* 29 E34
Naunton Beauchamp 29 C35
Naust 83 A14
Navenby 52 G45
Navestock Side 23 B51
Navidale 87 G26
Nawton 58 A42
Nayland 34 E55
Nazeing 23 A50
Naze Park 35 F58
Neacroft 10 E37
Near Cotton 40 A36
Near Sawrey 60 G29
Neasham 62 E39
Neath 18 B23
Neath Abbey 18 B23
Neatishead 45 C59
Nebo *Dyf.* 26 B21
Nebo *Gwy.* 47 G24

Nebo *Gwy.* 46 C20
Nebo *Gwy.* 46 G20
Necton 44 D54
Nedd 86 E17
Nedging Tye 34 C56
Needham 45 G58
Needham Market 34 C56
Needingworth 33 A49
Needwood 40 C37
Neen Savage 29 A32
Neen Sollars 29 A32
Neenton 39 G32
Nefyn 36 A19
Neilston 74 E20
Neithrop 31 D40
Nelly Andrews Green 38 D28
Nelson *Lan.* 56 F34
Nelson *M.G.* 18 B27
Nemphlar 74 F24
Nempnett Thrubwell 19 E31
Nene Terrace 43 E48
Nenthall 51 B33
Nenthead 61 B33
Nenthorn 76 G32
Nercwys 48 F28
Nereabolls 78 J3
Nerston 74 E22
Nesbit 77 G35
Ness 48 E29
Nesscliff 38 D29
Neston *Che.* 48 E28
Neston *Wts.* 20 E34
Nether Alderley 49 E34
Netheravon 20 G37
Nether Blainslie 76 F31
Nether Brotherstone 76 E30
Nether Broughton 41 C42
Netherburn 74 F23
Nether Burrow 56 B32
Netherbury 8 E30
Netherby 69 F29
Nether Cassock 69 C28
Nether Cerne 9 E32
Nethercleuch 69 E27
Nether Compton 8 C31
Nether Dalgliesh 69 C28
Nether Dallachy 84 C29
Nether End 50 E38
Netherend 19 A31
Nether Exe 7 E25
Netherfield *E.S.* 14 F53
Netherfield *Not.* 41 A42
Netherhampton 10 B37
Nether Heyford 31 C42
Nether Hindhope 70 B33
Netherholm 74 F22
Nether Howcleugh 69 B26
Nether Kellet 55 C31
Nether Kinmundy 85 E36
Nether Langwith 51 E41
Netherlaw 65 D23
Netherley 81 A34
Nethermill 69 E26
Nether Monybuie 68 E23
Nether Padley 50 E38
Netherplace 74 E21
Nether Poppleton 58 D41
Netherseal 40 D38
Nethershield 67 A21
Nether Silton 62 G40
Nether Stowey 7 B27
Netherstreet 20 E35
Netherthird 67 B21
Netherthong 50 B37
Netherton *Cen.* 74 C21
Netherton *Che.* 48 E31
Netherton *Dev.* 5 C24
Netherton *H.& W.* 29 D35
Netherton *Mer.* 48 C29
Netherton *Nor.* 70 C35
Netherton *Nor.* 71 E38
Netherton *Tay.* 81 E31
Netherton *Tay.* 81 E27
Netherton *W.M.* 40 G35
Netherton *W.Y.* 50 A38
Netherton *W.Y.* 50 A37
Nethertown *Cum.* 60 F25
Nether Wallop 10 A39
Nether Wellwood 68 A22
Nether Whitacre 40 F38
Nether Whitecleuch 68 B24
Netherwitton 71 D37
Netherwood 68 A22
Netheryett 68 G24
Nethy Bridge 84 G26
Netley 11 D40
Netley Marsh 10 C39
Nettlebed 22 C43
Nettlecombe 7 B26
Nettleden 32 G46
Nettleham 52 E46
Nettlestead Green 23 F52
Nettlestone 11 E42
Nettlesworth 62 B38
Nettleton *Lcn.* 52 B47
Nettleton *Wts.* 20 D34
Netton 5 F21
Neuadd *Dyf.* 27 F23
Neuadd *Gwy.* 46 C19
Neuadd *Pow.* 27 G25
Neuadd *Pow.* 37 E26
Neuadd-fawr 28 F28
Nevendon 24 B53
Nevern 26 D16
New Abbey 68 G25
New Aberdour 85 C34
New Addington 23 E49
New Alresford 11 A41
New Alyth 81 F28
Newark *Cbs.* 43 E48
Newark *Ork.* 89 C33
Newark upon Trent 52 G44
Newarthill 74 E23
New Ash Green 24 E52

New Barn 24 E52
Newbattle 75 D29
New Belses 70 A31
New Bewick 71 B36
New Bilton 31 A40
Newbiggin *Cum.* 61 D30
Newbiggin *Cum.* 61 D32
Newbiggin *Cum.* 51 B31
Newbiggin *Drm.* 62 B37
Newbiggin *Drm.* 61 D35
Newbiggin *Nor.* 70 G35
Newbiggin *N.Y.* 56 A35
Newbiggin *N.Y.* 62 G35
Newbiggin by the Sea 71 E39
Newbigging *Bor.* 76 F31
Newbigging *Bor.* 69 A26
Newbigging *D.& G.* 69 D27
Newbigging *Ltn.* 75 D28
Newbigging *Str.* 75 F26
Newbigging *Tay.* 81 G30
Newbiggin on Lune 61 F33
New Bilton 31 A40
Newbold 51 E39
Newbold on Avon 31 A40
Newbold on Stour 30 D38
Newbold Pacey 30 C38
Newbold Verdon 41 E40
New Bolinbroke 53 G49
Newborough *Cbs.* 43 E48
Newborough *Gwy.* 46 F20
Newbottle 62 A39
Newbourn 35 D58
New Bradwell 32 D44
New Brampton 51 E39
New Brancepeth 62 B38
Newbridge *Cnw.* 2 E10
Newbridge *Cnw.* 4 D19
New Bridge *D.& G.* 68 F25
Newbridge *Gwe.* 19 B28
New Bridge *Hgh.* 87 B18
Newbridge *I.o.W.* 11 F40
Newbridge *Ltn.* 75 C27
Newbridge-on-Usk 19 B29
Newbridge on Wye 27 C26
New Brighton 48 C29
New Brinsley 51 G40
Newbrough 70 G34
Newburgh *Bor.* 69 B29
Newburgh *Fife* 81 J28
Newburgh *Grm.* 85 G35
Newburgh *Lan.* 48 A30
Newburn 71 G37
Newbury 21 E40
Newby 63 E41
Newby *Cum.* 61 A30
Newby *Cum.* 61 D31
Newby *N.Y.* 56 B33
Newby *N.Y.* 59 A46
Newby Bridge 55 A29
Newby Cote 56 B33
Newby Cross 60 A29
New Byth *Grm.* 85 D34
Newbyth *Ltn.* 76 C31
Newby Wiske 57 A39
New Cample 68 D24
Newcastle *Gwe.* 28 G30
Newcastle *Shr.* 38 G28
Newcastle Airport 71 F37
Newcastle Emlyn 26 D19
Newcastleton 69 E30
Newcastle under Lyme 49 A34
Newcastle upon Tyne 71 G38
New Channelkirk 76 E30
Newchapel *Glo.* 29 G32
New Chapel *Sry.* 23 G49
Newchapel *Stf.* 49 G34
Newchurch *Dyf.* 17 B19
Newchurch *Gwe.* 19 B30
Newchurch *I.o.W.* 11 F41
Newchurch *Kent* 15 D56
Newchurch *Lan.* 56 F34
Newchurch *Pow.* 28 C28
Newchurch *Stf.* 40 C37
New Clipstone 51 F41
New Costessey 45 D57
New Cowper 60 B27
New Coylton 67 B20
Newcraighall 75 C29
Newcross 27 A22
New Cumnock 58 B22
New Deer 85 E34
New Delaval 71 F39
New Delph 49 B35
New Denham 22 C46
New Earswick 58 D42
New Edlington 51 C41
New Elgin 84 C28
New End 30 C36
Newenden 14 E54
Newent 29 F33
Newerne 19 A32
New Farnley 57 F38
New Ferry 48 D29
Newfield *D.& G.* 68 G24
Newfield *Drm.* 62 A38
Newfield *Drm.* 62 B38
Newfound 21 F41
New Fryston 57 G40
Newgale 16 B14
Newgate 44 A56
Newgate Street 23 A49
Newgord 89 B41
New Grimsby 2 A10
Newhall *Bor.* 75 A39
Newhall *Che.* 39 A32
Newhall *Dby.* 40 C38
Newham 71 A37
New Hartley 71 F39
Newhaven *E.S.* 13 D50
Newhaven *Ltn.* 75 C28

Newhaven House 50 G37
New Hedges 16 D17
New Herrington 62 A39
Newhey 49 A35
New Holland 59 G46
Newholm 63 E44
New Horton Grange 71 F37
New Houghton *Dby.* 51 F40
New Houghton *Nfk.* 44 C53
Newhouse *Str.* 74 D23
Newhouse *Str.* 72 B15
Newhouses *Nor.* 71 E36
New Houses *N.Y.* 56 B34
New Hutton 61 G31
New Hythe 24 E53
Newick 13 B50
Newingreen 15 D57
Newington *Kent* 24 E54
Newington *Kent* 15 D57
Newington *Oxf.* 21 B42
Newington Bagpath 20 B34
New Inn *Dyf.* 17 A20
New Inn *Gwe.* 19 B29
New Inn *Gwe.* 19 A30
New Invention *Shr.* 28 A28
New Invention *W.M.* 40 E35
New Kelso 83 E15
Newkirk 85 J30
New Lanark 74 F24
Newland *Cum.* 55 B29
Newland *Glo.* 19 A31
Newland *H.& W.* 29 D33
Newland *N.Y.* 58 G42
Newland *Oxf.* 30 G39
Newlandrig 75 D29
Newlands *Bor.* 70 D31
Newlands *Cum.* 60 C29
Newlands *D.& G.* 68 E25
Newlands *Grm.* 84 D29
Newlands *Nor.* 62 A36
Newlands Corner 22 G46
Newlands of Geise 87 B26
New Langholm 69 E29
New Leake 53 G50
New Leeds 85 D35
New Longton 55 G31
New Luce 67 G17
Newlyn 2 F10
Newlyn East 3 C14
Newmachar 85 H34
New Mains 74 G24
Newmains 74 E24
Newmarket *Sfk.* 33 B52
Newmarket *W.I.* 88 D10
New Marske 63 D42
New Marton 38 B29
New Micklefield 57 F40
Newmill *Bor.* 69 B30
New Mill *Cum.* 60 F26
Newmill *Grm.* 85 E33
New Mill *W.Y.* 50 B37
Newmillerdam 51 A39
New Mills *Cnw.* 3 C14
New Mills *Dby.* 50 D36
Newmills *Fife* 75 B26
Newmills *Ltn.* 75 D27
New Mills *Pow.* 37 E26
Newmiln 81 G27
Newmilns 74 G21
New Milton 10 E38
New Mistley 35 E57
New Moat 16 B16
New Moor House 71 C36
Newnham *Glo.* 29 G32
Newnham *Ham.* 22 F43
Newnham *Hfs.* 33 E48
Newnham *H.& W.* 29 B32
Newnham *Kent* 14 B55
Newnham *Nmp.* 31 C41
New Ollerton 51 F42
New Oscott 40 E36
New Pitsligo 85 D34
New Polzeath 3 A15
Newport *Dev.* 6 B21
Newport *Dyf.* 26 D17
Newport *Esx.* 33 E51
Newport *Glo.* 19 B32
Newport *Gwe.* 19 C29
Newport *Hgh.* 87 F27
Newport *Hum.* 58 F44
Newport *I.o.W.* 11 F41
Newport *Nfk.* 45 D61
Newport *Shr.* 39 D33
Newport-on-Tay 81 H30
Newport Pagnell 32 D44
Newport Pagnell Services 32 D44
Newpound Common 12 B46
New Prestwick 67 A19
Newquay *Cnw.* 3 B14
New Quay *Dyf.* 26 B19
Newquay Airport 3 B14
New Rackheath 45 D58
New Radnor 28 B28
New Rent 61 C30
New Ridley 62 A36
New Romney 15 E56
New Rossington 51 C42
Newrow 75 B25
New Sauchie 74 A24
New Scone 81 H27
Newseat 85 F32
Newsham *Lan.* 55 F31
Newsham *N.Y.* 62 F37
Newsham *N.Y.* 57 A39
Newsholme *Hum.* 58 G43
Newsholme *Lan.* 56 D34
New Silksworth 62 A39
Newstead *Bor.* 76 G31
Newstead *Not.* 51 G41
Newthorpe 57 F40

Newton *Bor.* 70 A32
Newton *Cbs.* 33 D50
Newton *Cle.* 63 E41
Newton *Cum.* 54 B28
Newton *Dby.* 51 G40
Newton *D.& G.* 69 F28
Newton *D.& G.* 69 D27
Newton *Grm.* 84 C27
Newton *Ham.* 10 B38
Newton *Hgh.* 86 E18
Newton *Hgh.* 84 E23
Newton *H.& W.* 28 E29
Newton *H.& W.* 28 C31
Newton *Lan.* 55 F30
Newton *Lan.* 55 B31
Newton *Lcn.* 42 B46
Newton *Ltn.* 75 C26
Newton *M.G.* 18 D24
Newton *Nfk.* 44 D54
Newton *Nfk.* 43 D50
Newton *Nmp.* 42 G44
Newton *Nor.* 70 C35
Newton *Not.* 41 A42
Newton *N.Y.* 63 G44
Newton *Sfk.* 34 D55
Newton *Stf.* 40 C36
Newton *Str.* 75 G25
Newton *Str.* 74 D22
Newton *Str.* 72 A16
Newton *War.* 31 A41
Newton *W.G.* 17 F22
Newton Abbot 5 C24
Newtonairds 68 E24
Newton Arlosh 60 A28
Newton Aycliffe 62 D38
Newton Bewley 62 D40
Newton Blossomville 32 C45
Newton Bromshold 32 B45
Newton Burgoland 41 E39
Newton-by-the-Sea 71 A38
Newton by Toft 52 D46
Newton Ferrers 5 F21
Newton Flotman 45 F58
Newtongarry 85 F31
Newtongrange 75 D29
Newton Hall 71 G36
Newton Harcourt 41 F42
Newtonhill 81 A35
Newton House 68 B25
Newton Kyme 57 E40
Newton-le-Willows *Mer.* 48 C31
Newton-le-Willows *N.Y.* 57 A38
Newton Longville 32 E44
Newton Mearns 74 E21
Newtonmore 80 A23
Newton Morrell 62 F38
Newton on Ouse 58 C41
Newton-on-the-Moor 71 C37
Newton on Trent 52 E44
Newton Poppleford 7 G26
Newton Purcell 31 E42
Newton Regis 40 E38
Newton Reigny 61 C30
Newton St. Cyres 7 F24
Newton St. Faith 45 D58
Newton St. Loe 20 E33
Newton St. Petrock 6 D20
Newton Solney 40 C38
Newton Stewart 67 G20
Newton Tony 21 G38
Newton Tracey 6 C21
Newton upon Derwent 58 E43
Newton Valence 11 A43
Newtown *Brk.* 21 E40
Newtown *Cum.* 69 G30
Newtown *Cum.* 60 B26
Newtown *Cum.* 61 D31
Newtown *Dby.* 49 D35
Newtown *Dor.* 10 E36
New Town *E.S.* 13 B50
Newtown *Glo.* 29 E35
Newtown *Glo.* 19 A32
Newtown *Grm.* 84 C27
Newtown *Gwe.* 18 A27
Newtown *Gwe.* 19 A28
Newtown *Ham.* 10 B39
Newtown *Ham.* 11 C42
Newtown *Ham.* 10 C38
Newtown *Hgh.* 83 J19
Newtown *H.& W.* 29 D32
Newtown *I.o.M.* 54 F25
Newtown *I.o.W.* 11 E40
Newtown *Nor.* 71 A36
Newtown *Nor.* 77 G35
Newtown *Nor.* 71 C36
Newtown *Pow.* 38 F27
New Town *Str.* 73 E17
Newtown *Wts.* 9 B35
Newtown in St. Martin 2 F13
Newtown Linford 41 D41
Newtown St. Boswells 76 G31
New Tredegar 18 A27
New Trows 74 G24
New Tupton 51 F39
Newtyle 81 F28
New Ulva 72 B13
New Valley 88 D10
New Waltham 53 B48
New Whittington 51 E39
New Wimpole 33 C49
New York *Lcn.* 53 G48
New York *T.& W.* 71 G39
Neyland 16 D15
Nibley 19 A32
Nicholaston 17 F21
Nickie's Hill 70 G31
Nidd 57 C38
Niddry Rows 75 C26
Nigg *Grm.* 85 J35
Nigg *Hgh.* 84 B24

Nine Ashes 23 A51
Ninebanks 61 A33
Ninemile Bar 68 F24
Nine Mile Burn 75 E27
Ninfield 14 F53
Ningwood 11 F40
Nisbet 70 A32
Nisbet Hill 76 E33
Niton 11 G41
Nitshill 74 D21
Noak Hill 23 B51
Noblehouse 75 F27
Nobold 38 D30
Nocton 52 F46
Noke 31 G41
Nolton 16 C14
Nolton Haven 16 C14
No Mans Heath *Che.* 38 A31
No Man's Heath *War.* 40 E38
Nomansland *Dev.* 7 D24
Nomansland *Ham.* 10 C38
Noneley 38 C30
Nonington 15 B58
Nook *Cum.* 69 F30
Nook *Cum.* 55 A31
Norbreck 55 E29
Norbriggs 51 E40
Norbury *Dby.* 40 A37
Norbury *Shr.* 38 F29
Norbury *Stf.* 39 C33
Nordelph 43 E51
Norden 49 A34
Nordley 39 F32
Norham 77 F34
Norley 48 E31
Norleywood 10 E39
Normanby *Cle.* 63 E41
Normanby *Hum.* 52 A44
Normanby *N.Y.* 58 A43
Normanby-by-Spital 52 D46
Normanby le Wold 52 C47
Norman Cross 42 F47
Normandy 22 F45
Normans' Bay 13 D52
Normanton *Dby.* 41 B39
Normanton *Lcn.* 42 A45
Normanton *Lei.* 42 A44
Normanton *W.Y.* 57 G39
Normanton le Heath 41 D39
Normanton on Soar 41 C41
Normanton on the Wolds 41 B42
Normanton on Trent 51 F43
Northallerton 62 G39
Northam 6 C20
Northampton 31 B43
North and Middle Littleton 30 D36
North Anston 51 D41
North Aston 31 F40
Northaw 23 A48
North Baddesley 11 B40
North Ballachulish 79 D16
North Balloch 67 D19
North Barrow 9 B32
North Barsham 44 B55
North Benfleet 24 B53
North Berwick 76 B31
North Boarhunt 11 C42
North Boisdale 88 R3
Northborough 42 E47
Northbourne 15 B59
North Bovey 7 G23
North Bradley 20 F34
North Brentor 6 G20
North Brewham 9 A33
North Bridge 12 A45
North Buckland 6 A20
North Burlingham 45 D59
North Burton or Burton Fleming 59 B46
North Cadbury 9 B32
North Carlton *Lcn.* 52 E45
North Carlton *Not.* 51 D41
North Carrine 66 C12
North Cave 58 F44
North Cerney 20 A36
North Chailey 13 B49
Northchapel 12 B45
North Charlton 71 A37
North Cheriton 9 B32
Northchurch 22 A45
North Cliff *Hum.* 59 B48
North Cliffe *Hum.* 58 F44
North Clifton 52 E44
North Coates 53 B49
North Cockerington 53 C49
North Coker 8 C31
North Commonty 85 E34
Northcott Hamlet 6 F19
North Cove 45 G60
North Cowton 62 F38
North Crawley 32 D45
North Cray 23 D50
North Creake 44 B54
North Curry 8 B29
North Dalton 59 D45
North Deighton 57 D39
North Dell 88 A10
North Duffield 58 F42
North Elkington 53 C48
North Elmham 44 C55
North Elmsall 51 A40
North End *Avon* 19 E30
North End *Ham.* 21 E40
North End *Hum.* 59 F48
North End *Lcn.* 43 A48
North End *Mer.* 48 B29
North End *Nor.* 71 C37
Northend *War.* 30 C39
North End *W.S.* 12 D47
North Erradale 82 A13
North Fearns 82 F11
North Feorline 66 A15

North Ferriby 59 G45
Northfield *Bor.* 77 D35
Northfield *W.M.* 30 A36
North Finchley 23 B48
Northfleet 24 D52
North Frodingham 59 D46
North Galson 88 B10
North Gorley 10 C37
North Greenhill 70 F31
North Grimston 58 C44
North Hayling 11 D43
North Hazelrigg 77 G36
North Hill 4 C18
North Hinksey 21 A40
North Holmwood 22 G47
North Hourat 73 E18
North Huish 5 E23
North Hykeham 52 F45
Northiam 14 E54
Northill 32 D47
Northington 11 A41
North Johnston 16 C15
North Kelsey 52 B46
North Kessock 84 E22
North Killingholme 52 A47
North Kilvington 57 A40
North Kilworth 41 G42
North Kiscadale 66 A16
North Kyme 52 G47
North Lancing 12 D47
Northlands 53 G49
Northleach 30 G37
North Lees 57 B38
North Leigh 30 G39
Northleigh 7 F27
North Leverton with
  Habblesthorpe 51 D43
Northlew 6 F21
North Lopham 44 G56
North Luffenham 42 E45
North Marden 12 C44
North Marston 31 F43
North Middleton *Ltn.* 75 E29
North Middleton *Nor.* 71 A36
North Molton 7 B23
Northmoor 21 A40
Northmoor Green 8 A29
North Moreton 21 C41
Northmuir 81 E29
North Mundham 12 D44
North Muskham 51 F43
North Newbald 59 F45
North Newington 31 E40
North Newnton 20 F37
North Newton 8 A28
North Nibley 20 B33
North Ockendon 23 C51
Northolt 22 C47
Northop 48 F28
North Ormsby 53 C48
Northorpe 52 C44
North Otterington 57 A39
Northover 8 B31
North Owersby 52 C46
Northowram 57 G37
North Perrott 8 D30
North Petherton 8 A28
North Petherwin 4 B18
North Pickenham 44 E54
North Piddle 29 C35
North Poorton 8 E31
Northport 9 F35
North Queensferry 75 B27
North Rauceby 42 A46
Northrepps 45 B58
North Reston 53 D49
North Rigton 57 E38
North Rode 49 F34
North Ronaldsay Airport 89 B33
North Runcton 44 D52
North Sandwick 89 C41
North Scale 54 C27
North Scarle 52 F44
North Seaton Colliery 71 E38
North Shawbost 88 C8
North Shields 71 G39
North Shoebury 25 C55
North Shore 54 E28
North Skelton 63 E42
North Skirlaugh 59 F47
North Somercotes 53 C50
North Stainley 57 B38
North Stainmore 61 E34
North Stifford 24 C52
North Stoke *Avon* 20 E33
North Stoke *Oxf.* 21 C42
North Stoke *W.S.* 12 C46
North Street 15 B56
North Strome 83 F14
North Sunderland 77 G38
North Synton 69 A30
North Tamerton 6 F19
North Tawton 6 E22
North Third 74 B23
North Thoresby 53 C48
North Thundergay 72 F14
North Tidworth 21 G38
North Togston 71 C38
North Tolsta 88 C11
Northton 88 J5
North Tuddenham 44 D56
North Wallbottle 71 G37
North Walsham 45 B58
North Waltham 21 G41
North Warnborough 22 F43
North Watten 87 C28
Northway 29 E35
North Weald Bassett 23 A51
North Wheatley 51 D43
Northwich 49 E32
North Widcombe 19 F31
North Willingham 52 D47
North Wingfield 51 F40

North Witham 42 C45
Northwold 44 F53
Northwood *G.L.* 22 B46
Northwood *I.o.W.* 11 E40
Northwood *Shr.* 38 B30
Northwood Green 29 G33
North Wootton *Dor.* 9 C32
North Wootton *Nfk.* 44 C52
North Wootton *Som.* 19 G31
North Wraxall 20 D34
North Wroughton 20 C37
Norton *Che.* 48 D31
Norton *Cle.* 62 D40
Norton *Glo.* 29 F34
Norton *Gwe.* 28 F30
Norton *Hfs.* 33 E48
Norton *H.& W.* 30 D36
Norton *H.& W.* 29 C34
Norton *I.o.W.* 10 F39
Norton *Nmp.* 31 B42
Norton *Not.* 51 E41
Norton *N.Y.* 58 B43
Norton *Pow.* 28 B29
Norton *Sfk.* 34 B55
Norton *Shr.* 39 E33
Norton *S.Y.* 51 A41
Norton *W.G.* 17 F22
Norton *Wts.* 20 C34
Norton Bavant 20 G35
Norton Bridge 40 B34
Norton Canes 40 E36
Norton Canon 28 D29
Norton Disney 52 G44
Norton Fitzwarren 7 C27
Norton Green 10 F39
Norton Heath 24 A52
Norton in Hales 39 B33
Norton in the Moors 49 G34
Norton-le-Clay 57 B40
Norton Lindsey 30 B38
Norton Malreward 19 E31
Norton St. Philip 20 F33
Norton Subcourse 45 F60
Norton sub Hamdon 8 C30
Norwell 51 F43
Norwell Woodhouse 51 F43
Norwich 45 E58
Norwich Airport 45 D58
Norwick 89 A42
Norwood 51 D40
Norwoodside 43 F50
Noss Mayo 5 F21
Nosterfield 57 A38
Nosterfield End 33 D52
Nostie 83 G14
Note o' the Gate 70 C31
Notgrove 30 F37
Nottage 18 D24
Nottingham 41 A41
Notton 51 A39
Nounsley 34 G54
Noup 89 C30
Nox 38 D30
Nubbock 70 G34
Nuffield 21 C42
Nunburnholme 58 E44
Nuneaton 41 F39
Nuneham Courtenay 21 B41
Nun Monkton 58 D41
Nunney 20 G33
Nunnington 58 B42
Nunnykirk 71 D36
Nunthorpe 63 E41
Nunton 10 B37
Nunwick 57 B39
Nursling 10 C39
Nutbourne 12 C46
Nutbourne 11 D43
Nutfield 23 F49
Nuthall 41 A41
Nuthampstead 33 E50
Nuthurst 12 B47
Nutley *E.S.* 13 B50
Nutley *Ham.* 21 G42
Nyadd 74 A23
Nyetimber 12 E44
Nymet Rowland 7 E23
Nympsfield 20 A33
Nynehead 7 C27

O

Oadby 41 E42
Oakamoor 40 A36
Oakbank 75 D26
Oakdale 18 B27
Oake 7 C27
Oaken 40 E34
Oakenclough 55 E31
Oakenshaw *Drm.* 62 C37
Oakenshaw *W.Y.* 57 G37
Oakfield 19 B28
Oakford *Dev.* 7 C25
Oakford *Dyf.* 26 C20
Oakfordbridge 7 C25
Oakgrove 49 F35
Oakham 42 E44
Oakhanger 11 A43
Oakhill 19 G32
Oakington 33 B50
Oaklands *Dyf.* 17 C20
Oaklands *Hfs.* 33 G48
Oakle Street 29 E35
Oakley *Bfd.* 32 C46
Oakley *Bkh.* 31 G42
Oakley *Fife* 75 B26
Oakley *Ham.* 21 F41
Oakley *Sfk.* 35 A57
Oakley Green 22 D45
Oakridge Lynch 20 A35
Oaksey 20 B35

Oakthorpe 41 D39
Oaktree Hill 62 G39
Oakwood *Bor.* 69 A30
Oakwood *Nor.* 70 G35
Oakworth 57 F36
Oare *Brk.* 21 D41
Oare *Kent* 25 E56
Oare *Som.* 7 A23
Oare *Wts.* 20 E37
Oasby 42 B46
Oatfield 66 B12
Oathlaw 81 E30
Oban 79 H14
Oborne 9 C32
Occold 35 A57
Occumb 87 G26
Ochiltree 67 A21
Ochtermuthill 80 J24
Ochtertyre *Cen.* 74 A23
Ochtertyre *Tay.* 80 H24
Ochtrelure 64 C16
Ockbrook 41 B40
Ockham 22 F46
Ockle 79 C11
Ockley 12 A47
Ocle Pychard 28 D31
Odcombe 8 C30
Odd Down 20 E33
Oddingley 29 C35
Oddington *Glo.* 30 F38
Oddington *Oxf.* 31 G41
Oddsta 89 C41
Odell 32 C45
Odie 89 E32
Odiham 22 F43
Odsal Top 57 G37
Odstock 10 B37
Odstone 41 E39
Offchurch 30 B39
Offenham 30 D36
Offerton 62 A39
Offham 23 F52
Offord Cluny 33 B48
Offord D'Arcy 33 B48
Offwell 7 F27
Ogbourne Maizey 20 D37
Ogbourne St. Andrew 20 D37
Ogbourne St. George 20 D37
Ogden 57 F36
Ogle 57 F37
Ogmore 18 D24
Ogmore-by-Sea 18 D24
Ogmore Vale 18 B25
Ogwen Bank 46 F22
Okeford Fitzpaine 9 C34
Okehampton 6 F21
Old 31 A43
Old Aberdeen 85 J35
Old Alresford 11 A41
Old Belses 70 A31
Oldberrow 30 B37
Old Bewick 71 A36
Old Bolingbroke 53 F49
Oldborough 7 E23
Old Brampton 51 E39
Old Bridge of Urr 68 G23
Old Buckenham 44 F56
Old Burghclere 21 F40
Oldbury *Shr.* 39 F33
Oldbury *War.* 41 F39
Oldbury *W.M.* 40 G35
Oldbury Naite 19 B32
Oldbury upon Severn 19 B32
Old Byland 58 A41
Old Cambus 77 D34
Old Cassop 62 C38
Old Clee 53 B48
Old Cleeve 7 A26
Old Clipstone 51 F42
Old Colwyn 47 E24
Oldcotes 51 D41
Old Dailly 67 D18
Old Dalby 41 C42
Old Deer 85 E35
Old Edlington 51 C41
Oldfield 29 B34
Old Fletton 42 F47
Oldford 20 F33
Old Glossop 50 C36
Old Goole 58 G43
Old Gore 29 F32
Old Grimsby 2 A10
Old Hall 87 C28
Oldham 49 B35
Oldhamstocks 76 C33
Old Heath 34 F56
Old Howford 75 G29
Old Hunstanton 44 A52
Oldhurst 33 A48
Old Hutton 55 A31
Old Kilpatrick 74 C20
Old Knebworth 33 F48
Oldland 19 D32
Old Laxey 54 E26
Old Leake 53 G50
Old Malton 58 B43
Old Micklefield 57 F40
Old Milverton 30 B38
Old Monkland 74 D23
Old Newton 34 B56
Old Passage 19 C31
Old Radnor 28 C28
Old Rayne 85 G32
Old Romney 15 E56
Old Scone 81 H27
Old Somerby 42 B45
Old Sodbury 20 C33
Old Spital 61 E35
Oldstead 58 A41
Old Stratford 31 D43
Old Swan 48 C30

Old Tebay 61 F32
Old Town *Cnw.* 2 A11
Old Town *Cum.* 55 A31
Old Town *Nor.* 70 D34
Old Tupton 51 F39
Old Warden 32 D47
Old Windsor 22 D45
Old Wives Lees 15 B56
Old Woking 22 F46
Olgrinmore 87 C26
Oliver's Battery 11 B40
Ollaberry 89 D39
Ollach 82 F11
Ollerton *Che.* 49 E33
Ollerton *Not.* 51 F42
Ollerton *Shr.* 39 C32
Olmarch 27 C22
Olmstead End 33 D52
Olney *Bkh.* 32 C44
Olrig House 87 B27
Olton 40 G37
Olveston 19 C32
Ombersley 29 B34
Ompton 51 F42
Once Brewed 70 G33
Onchan 54 F26
Onecote 50 G36
Onibury 28 A30
Onich 79 D16
Onllwyn 27 G24
Onneley 39 A33
Onthank 74 F20
Openwoodgate 41 A39
Opinan 82 B13
Opinan 86 J14
Orange Lane 76 F33
Orbliston 84 D29
Orby 53 F50
Orcadia 73 D17
Orchard *D.& G.* 69 D27
Orchard *Str.* 73 B17
Orchard Portman 8 B28
Orcheston 20 G36
Orcop 28 F30
Ord 82 H12
Ordhead 85 H32
Ordie 85 J30
Ordiequish 84 D29
Ordsall 51 E43
Oreston 5 E21
Orford 35 C60
Orlestone 15 D56
Orleton *H.& W.* 28 B30
Orleton *H.& W.* 29 B32
Orlingbury 32 A44
Ormesby 63 E41
Ormesby St. Margaret 45 D60
Ormesby St. Michael 45 D60
Ormiclate 88 O3
Ormidale 72 B16
Ormiston 76 D30
Ormiston Mains 76 D30
Ormsaigmore 78 D10
Ormsary 72 C13
Ormskirk 48 B29
Orosay 88 F9
Orphir 89 G29
Orpington 23 E50
Orrell 48 B31
Orrisdale 54 D25
Orsett 24 C52
Orston 42 A43
Orthwaite 60 E38
Orton 61 F32
Orton Longueville 42 F47
Orton on the Hill 41 E39
Orton Waterville 42 F47
Orwell 33 C49
Osbaldeston 56 F32
Osbaldwick 58 D42
Osbaston 41 E40
Osbournby 42 B46
Oscroft 48 F31
Osgathorpe 41 D40
Osgodby *Lcn.* 52 C46
Osgodby *N.Y.* 59 A46
Osgodby *N.Y.* 58 F42
Oskaig 82 F11
Oskamull 78 F10
Osmaston 40 A37
Osmington 9 F33
Osmondwall 89 J29
Osmotherley 62 G40
Osnaburgh 81 J30
Ospringe 25 E56
Ossett 57 G38
Ossington 51 F43
Ostend 25 B55
Oswaldkirk 58 B42
Oswaldtwistle 56 G33
Oswestry 38 C29
Otford 23 F51
Otham 14 B53
Othery 8 A29
Otley *Sfk.* 35 C58
Otley *W.Y.* 57 E38
Otterbourne 11 B40
Otterburn *Nor.* 70 D34
Otterburn *N.Y.* 56 D34
Otterburn Camp 70 D34
Otter Ferry 72 B15
Otterham 4 A17
Otterhampton 19 G28
Ottershaw 22 E46
Otterswick 89 D41
Otterton 7 F26
Ottery St. Mary 7 F27
Ottinge 15 C57
Ottringham 59 G48

Oughterby 60 A28
Oughtershaw 56 A34
Oughterside 60 C27
Oughtibridge 51 C39
Oulston 58 B41
Oulton *Cum.* 60 A28
Oulton *Nfk.* 45 C57
Oulton *Sfk.* 45 F61
Oulton *Stf.* 40 B35
Oulton *W.Y.* 57 G39
Oulton Broad 45 F61
Oulton Street 45 C57
Oundle 42 G46
Ousby 61 C32
Ousdale 87 G26
Ousden 34 C53
Ousefleet 58 G44
Ouston *Drm.* 62 A38
Ouston *Nor.* 61 A33
Outchester 77 G37
Outer Hope 5 F22
Out Gate 60 G29
Outhgill 61 F33
Outlane 50 A36
Out Rawcliffe 55 E29
Outwell 43 E51
Outwood *Sry.* 23 G49
Outwood *W.Y.* 57 G39
Ovenden 57 G36
Over 33 A49
Overbister 89 C32
Overbury 29 E35
Overcombe 9 F32
Over Compton 8 C31
Over Fingland 68 C25
Over Haddon 50 F38
Over Hazelfield 65 D23
Over Hulton 49 B32
Over Kellet 55 C31
Over Kiddington 31 F40
Over Norton 30 F39
Overpool 48 E29
Overscaig Hotel 86 F20
Overseal 40 D38
Over Silton 62 G40
Oversley Green 30 C36
Overstone 32 B44
Over Stowey 7 B27
Overstrand 45 A58
Overthorpe 31 D40
Overton *Che.* 48 E31
Overton *Clw.* 38 A29
Overton *D.& G.* 68 G25
Overton *Ham.* 21 G41
Overton *Lan.* 55 D30
Overton *N.Y.* 58 D41
Overton *Shr.* 28 A31
Overton *W.G.* 17 F20
Overton *W.Y.* 50 A38
Overton Bridge 38 A29
Overtown 74 E24
Over Wallop 10 A38
Over Whitacre 40 F38
Over Whitton 70 F33
Overy Staithe 44 A54
Oving *Bkh.* 31 F43
Oving *W.S.* 12 D45
Ovingdean 13 D49
Ovingham 71 G36
Ovington *Drm.* 62 E37
Ovington *Ham.* 11 A41
Ovington *Nfk.* 44 E55
Ovington *Nor.* 71 G36
Ower *Ham.* 10 C39
Owermoigne 9 F33
Owler Bar 50 E38
Owlerton 51 C39
Owlpen 20 B33
Owlswick 22 A43
Owmby 52 B46
Owmby-by-Spital 52 D46
Owslebury 11 B41
Owston *Lei.* 42 E43
Owston *S.Y.* 51 A41
Owston Ferry 52 B42
Owstwick 59 F48
Owthorne 59 G49
Owthorpe 41 B42
Oxborough 44 E53
Oxcombe 53 E49
Oxen End 33 F52
Oxenholme 61 G31
Oxenhope 57 F36
Oxen Park 55 A29
Oxenton 29 E35
Oxenwood 21 F39
Oxford 21 A40
Oxford Cross 6 A20
Oxhey 22 B47
Oxhill 30 D39
Oxley Green 34 G55
Oxnam 70 B33
Oxshott 22 E47
Oxspring 50 B38
Oxted 23 F49
Oxton *Bor.* 76 E30
Oxton *Not.* 51 G42
Oxton *N.Y.* 58 E41
Oxwich 17 F20
Oykel Bridge 86 H19
Oyne 85 G32

P

Packington 41 D39
Padanaram 81 E30
Padbury 31 E43
Paddlesworth 15 C57
Paddock 50 A37
Paddockhole 69 E28
Paddock Wood 23 G52

Padeswood 48 F28
Padfield 50 C36
Padgate 49 D32
Padiham 56 F33
Padside 57 D37
Padstow 3 A15
Padworth 21 E42
Paganhill 20 A34
Page Bank 62 C38
Pagham 12 E44
Paglesham 25 B55
Paignton 5 D25
Pailton 41 G40
Painscastle 28 D27
Painshawfield 71 G36
Painsthorpe 58 D44
Painswick 20 A34
Paisley 74 D20
Pakefield 45 F61
Pakenham 34 B55
Palacerigg 74 C23
Pale 37 B25
Paley Street 22 D44
Palgowan 67 E19
Palgrave 35 A57
Palnackie 65 C24
Palnure 67 G20
Palterton 51 F40
Pamber End 21 F42
Pamber Green 21 F42
Pamber Heath 21 E42
Pamphill 9 D35
Pampisford 33 D50
Panborough 19 G30
Panbride 81 G31
Pandy Clw. 38 B27
Pandy Gwe. 28 F29
Pandy Gwy. 37 E22
Pandy Tudur 47 F24
Panfield 34 F53
Pangbourne 21 D42
Pannal 57 D39
Pannanich 81 A29
Pant 38 C28
Pant-glâs 36 A20
Panton 52 E47
Pant-y-dŵr 27 A25
Pantymenyn 16 B17
Pant-y-mwyn 47 F27
Pant-y-Wacco 47 E27
Papa Westray Airport 89 B30
Papcastle 60 C27
Papil 89 J39
Papple 76 C31
Papplewick 51 G41
Papworth Everard 33 B48
Papworth St. Agnes 33 B48
Par 4 E16
Parbold 48 A30
Parbrook 8 A31
Parc 37 B24
Parcllyn 26 C18
Pardshaw 60 D26
Parham 35 B59
Parish Holm 68 A23
Park D.& G. 68 D25
Park Grm. 81 A33
Parkdargue 85 E32
Parkend Glo. 19 A32
Parkend Nor. 70 F34
Park End Str. 66 E16
Parker's Green 23 G52
Parkeston 35 E58
Parkgate Che. 48 E28
Parkgate 49 E33
Park Gate Ham. 11 D41
Parkham 6 C19
Parkhead 61 B31
Parkhouse 19 A30
Parkhurst 11 E40
Parkmill 17 F21
Parkneuk 81 C33
Parkstone 10 E36
Park Street 12 A47
Park Village 70 G32
Parley Green 10 E36
Parracombe 6 A22
Parrog 16 A16
Parsonby 60 C27
Parson Drove 43 E49
Partick 74 D21
Partney 53 F50
Partington 49 C33
Parton Cum. 60 A28
Parton Cum. 60 E25
Parton D.& G. 68 G22
Parton Glo. 29 F34
Partridge Green 12 C47
Parwich 50 G37
Paston Street 45 B59
Patcham 13 D49
Patching 12 D46
Patchway 19 C32
Pateley Bridge 57 C37
Pathead Str. 68 B22
Pathhead Fife 75 A28
Pathhead Grm. 81 D33
Pathhead Ltn. 75 D29
Path of Condie 80 J26
Patna 67 B20
Patney 20 F36
Patrick 54 E24
Patrick Brompton 62 G38
Patrington 59 G49
Patrixbourne 15 B57
Patterdale 60 E29
Pattingham 40 F34
Pattishall 31 C42
Paul 2 F10
Paulerspury 31 D43
Paull 59 G47
Paulton 19 F32
Pauperhaugh 71 D37

Pave Lane 39 D33
Pavenham 32 C45
Pawlett 19 G28
Pawston 77 G34
Paxford 30 E37
Paxton 77 E35
Payhembury 7 E26
Payne's Hall 33 G49
Paynter's Lane End 2 D12
Paythorne 56 D34
Peacehaven 13 D50
Peacemarsh 9 B34
Peak Dale 50 E36
Peak Forest 50 E37
Peakirk 42 E47
Pean Hill 25 E57
Peasedown St. John 20 F33
Peasemore 21 D40
Peasenhall 35 B59
Pease Pottage 13 A48
Peaslake 22 G46
Peasmarsh 14 E54
Peaston 76 D30
Peathill 85 C35
Peatling Magna 41 F41
Peatling Parva 41 G41
Peaton 38 G31
Pebble Coombe 23 F48
Pebmarsh 34 E54
Pebworth 30 D37
Pecket Well 56 G35
Peckforton 48 G31
Peckleton 41 E40
Pedair-ffordd 38 C27
Pedmore 40 G35
Pedwell 8 A30
Peebles 75 F28
Peel Bor. 76 G30
Peel I.o.M. 54 E24
Pegswood 71 E38
Pegwell 25 E59
Peinchorran 82 F11
Peinlich 82 D10
Pelcomb Cross 16 C15
Peldon 34 G55
Pelsall 40 E36
Pelton 42 A38
Pelutho 60 B27
Pelynt 4 E18
Pemberton 48 B31
Pembrey 17 D20
Pembridge 28 C29
Pembroke 16 D15
Pembroke Dock 16 D15
Pembury 23 G52
Penallt 19 A31
Penally 16 E17
Penare 3 D15
Penarth 18 D27
Penbontrhydybeddau 37 G22
Penbryn 26 C18
Pencader 17 A20
Pencarreg 26 D21
Pencelli 27 F26
Penclawdd 17 E21
Pen-coed 18 C25
Pencombe 29 C32
Pencraig H.& W. 28 F31
Pencraig Pow. 37 C26
Pendeen 2 E9
Penderyn 18 A25
Pendine 17 D18
Pendlebury 49 B33
Pendleton 56 F33
Pendock 29 E33
Pendoggett 4 C16
Pendoylan 18 D26
Penegoes 37 E23
Penffordd 16 B16
Pengam 18 B27
Pengenffordd 28 E27
Pen-groes oped 19 A29
Penhale 2 G12
Penhale 2 C13
Penhalvean 2 E13
Penhelig 37 F22
Penhill 20 C37
Penhow 19 B30
Penhurst 13 C52
Penicuik 75 D28
Peniculu 82 E10
Peniel 47 F26
Penifiler 82 E10
Peninver 66 A13
Penisa'r waun 46 F21
Penistone 50 B38
Penketh 48 D31
Penkill 67 D18
Penkridge 40 D35
Penley 38 A30
Penllech 36 B18
Penllergaer 17 E22
Penllyn 18 D25
Penmachno 47 G23
Penmaen 17 F21
Penmaenan 47 E23
Penmaenmawr 47 E23
Penmaenpool 37 D22
Penmark 18 E26
Penmon 46 D22
Penmorfa 36 A21
Penmynydd 46 E21
Penn 22 B45
Pennal 37 E23
Pennan 85 C34
Pennance 2 D13
Pennant Dyf. 26 B21
Pennant Pow. 37 F24
Pennard 17 F21
Pennersaughs 69 F28
Pennington Cum. 54 B27
Pennington Ham. 10 E39
Penn Street 22 B45

Pennsylvania 20 D33
Penny Bridge 55 A29
Pennyghael 79 H11
Pennyglen 67 B18
Pennygown 79 F12
Pennymoor 7 D24
Penparc Dyf. 26 D18
Penparc Dyf. 16 A14
Pen-parcau 36 G21
Penpelleni 19 A29
Penpont Cnw. 4 C16
Penpont D. & G. 68 D24
Penpont Pow. 27 F25
Penrhiw 26 D18
Penrhiwceiber 18 B26
Penrhiwllan 26 D19
Penrhiwpal 26 D19
Penrhos Berw. 28 G30
Penrhos Gwy. 36 B19
Penrhos Pow. 27 G24
Penrhos Lligwy 46 D20
Penrhyn 46 C19
Penrhyn Bay 47 D24
Penrhyncoch 37 G22
Penrhyndeudraeth 37 B22
Penrhyn-side 47 D24
Penrice 17 F20
Penrioch 72 F14
Penrith 61 C31
Penrose 3 A14
Penruddock 61 D30
Penryn 2 E13
Pensarn Clw. 47 E25
Pensarn Dyf. 17 C20
Pensax 29 B33
Pensby 48 D28
Penselwood 9 A33
Pensford 19 E32
Penshaw 62 A39
Penshurst 23 G51
Pensilva 4 C18
Penston 76 C30
Pentewan 4 F16
Penthryn-fawr 38 D28
Pentir 46 F21
Pentire 2 B13
Pentlepoir 16 D17
Pentlow 34 D54
Pentney 44 D53
Penton Mewsey 21 G39
Pentraeth 46 E21
Pentre Clw. 47 F26
Pentre M.G. 18 B25
Pentre Pow. 38 F28
Pentre Pow. 38 G27
Pentre Pow. 28 F27
Pentre Bach Clw. 48 E28
Pentrebach Dyf. 27 E24
Pentrebâch M.G. 18 A26
Pentre-bach Pow. 27 E25
Pentre Berw 46 E20
Pentre-bont 47 G23
Pentre-bwlch 38 A27
Pentre-celyn 47 G27
Pentre-cwrt 17 A19
Pentre Dolau Honddu 27 D25
Pentredwr 38 A28
Pentredwr 17 E22
Pentrefelin Gwy. 36 B21
Pentrefelin Gwy. 46 C20
Pentre Ffwrndan 48 E28
Pentrefoelas 47 G24
Pentre-galar 16 A17
Pentregat 26 C19
Pentre Gwynfryn 36 C21
Pentre Halkyn 48 E28
Pentrehyling 38 F28
Pentre Isaf 47 F24
Pentre-llwyn-llwyd 27 C25
Pentre-llyn 27 A22
Pentre piod 37 B24
Pentre'rfelin Clw. 38 C27
Pentre'r-felin Pow. 27 E25
Pentre-tafarn-y-fedw 47 F24
Pentre ty gwyn 27 E24
Pentre-Uchaf 47 E27
Pentrich 51 G39
Pentridge 10 C36
Pentwyn 9 C28
Pentyrch 18 C27
Penwithick 4 E16
Penwortham 55 G31
Penybanc 17 B22
Pen-y-bont Clw. 38 C28
Pen-y-bont Dyf. 17 B19
Pen-y-bont Pow. 37 D26
Penybont Pow. 28 B27
Pen-y-bont-fawr 37 C26
Pen-y-bryn 26 D17
Penycae Clw. 38 A28
Pen-y-Cae Pow. 27 G24
Pen-y-coedcae 18 C26
Penycwm 16 B14
Pen-y-fai 18 C24
Pen-y-ffordd 48 F29
Pen-y-fforest 28 D27
Pen-y-garn 37 G22
Penygarnedd 38 C27
Pen-y-Gop 37 A25
Pen-y-graig 18 B25
Penygroes Dyf. 17 C21
Penygroes Gwy. 46 G20
Pen-y-Gwryd Hotel 46 G22
Pen-y-pass 46 G22
Pen-y-Heolgerrig 18 A26
Penysarn 46 C20
Peny-stryt 48 G28
Pen-y-waun 27 E24
Penywaun 18 A25
Penzance 2 E10
Penzance Heliport 2 E10
Peopleton 29 C35
Peper Harow 22 G45
Peplow 39 C32

Pepper Arden 62 F38
Percyhorner 85 C35
Perham Down Camp 21 G38
Perranarworthal 2 E13
Perranporth 2 C13
Perranuthnoe 2 F11
Perranwell Station 2 E13
Perranzabuloe 2 C13
Perry Barr 40 F36
Pershore 29 D35
Pertenhall 32 B46
Perth 81 H27
Perton 40 F34
Peterborough 42 E47
Peterchurch 28 E29
Peterculter 85 J34
Peterhead 85 E37
Peterlee 62 B40
Petersfield 11 B43
Peters Marland 6 D20
Peterstone Wentlloge 19 D28
Peterston super-Ely 18 D26
Peterstow 28 F31
Peter Tavy 5 C21
Petham 15 B57
Petrockstow 6 E21
Pett 14 F54
Pettaugh 35 C57
Petteridge 23 F52
Pettinain 75 F25
Pettistree 35 C59
Petton 7 C26
Petts Wood 23 D50
Pettycur 75 B28
Pettymuick 85 G35
Petworth 12 B45
Pevensey 13 D52
Pevensey Bay 13 D52
Pewsey 20 E37
Philiphaugh 69 A30
Philipstoun 75 C26
Philleigh 3 E14
Phocle Green 29 F32
Phoenix Green 22 F43
Pica 60 D26
Pickburn 51 B41
Pickering 58 A43
Picket Post 10 D37
Pickford 40 G38
Pickhill 57 A39
Picklescott 38 F30
Pickmere 49 E32
Pickwell Dev. 6 A20
Pickwell Lei. 42 D43
Pickworth Lcn. 42 B46
Pickworth Lei. 42 D45
Picton Che. 48 E30
Picton N.Y. 62 F40
Piddinghoe 13 D50
Piddington Nmp. 32 C44
Piddington Oxf. 31 G42
Piddlehinton 9 E33
Piddletrenthide 9 E33
Pidley 33 A49
Pie Corner 29 B32
Piercebridge 62 E38
Pierowall 89 C30
Piet's Nest 70 C31
Pigdon 71 E37
Pikehall 50 G37
Pilgrims Hatch 23 B51
Pilham 52 C44
Pill 19 D31
Pillaton 4 D19
Pillerton Hersey 30 D39
Pillerton Priors 30 D38
Pilleth 28 B28
Pilley 51 B39
Pilling 55 E30
Pilling Lane 55 E29
Pillowell 19 A32
Pilning 19 C31
Pilsdon 8 E31
Pilsley Dby. 50 E38
Pilsley Dby. 51 F40
Pilton Dev. 6 B21
Pilton Lei. 42 E45
Pilton Nmp. 42 G46
Pilton Som. 19 G31
Pimperne 9 D35
Pinchbeck 43 C48
Pinchbeck Bars 42 C47
Pinchbeck West 43 C48
Pinfold 48 A29
Pinhoe 7 F25
Pinley 30 A39
Pinminnoch 67 D17
Pinmore 67 D18
Pinner 22 C47
Pinvin 29 D35
Pinwherry 67 E17
Pinxton 51 G40
Pipe and Lyde 28 D31
Pipe Gate 39 A33
Piperhill 84 D24
Pipers Pool 4 B18
Pipewell 42 G44
Pirbright 22 F45
Pirnmill 72 F14
Pirton Hfs. 32 E47
Pirton H.& W. 29 D34
Pishill 22 B43
Pistyll 36 A19
Pitagowan 80 D24
Pitcaple 85 G33
Pitchcombe 20 A34
Pitchcott 31 F43
Pitchford 38 E31
Pitch Green 22 A43
Pitch Place 22 F45
Pitchroy 84 F27
Pitcombe 9 A32
Pitcox 76 C32
Pitcur 81 G28

Pitlessie 81 J29
Pitlochry 80 E25
Pitmedden 85 G34
Pitminster 8 C28
Pitney 8 B30
Pitscottie 81 J30
Pitsea 24 C53
Pitsford 31 B43
Pitstone Green 32 G45
Pitt 11 B40
Pittendreich 84 C27
Pittentrail 87 H23
Pittenweem 81 K31
Pittington 62 B39
Pitton 10 A38
Pity Me 62 B38
Pityoulish 84 H25
Pixley 29 E32
Plaidy 85 D33
Plains 74 D23
Plaistow 12 A46
Plaitford 10 C38
Plas Isaf 47 F25
Plas Madoc 38 A28
Plas Newydd 38 A28
Platt 23 F52
Platt Bridge 49 B32
Plawsworth 62 B38
Plaxtol 23 F52
Playden 14 E55
Playford 35 D58
Playing Place 3 D14
Playley Green 29 E33
Plealey 38 E30
Plean 74 B24
Pleasington 56 G32
Pleasley 51 F41
Plenmeller 70 G33
Pleshey 33 G52
Plockton 83 F14
Plowden 38 G29
Ploxgreen 38 E29
Pluckley 14 C55
Pluckley Station 14 C55
Plumbland 60 C27
Plumgarths 61 G30
Plumley 49 E33
Plumpton Cum. 61 C30
Plumpton E.S. 13 C49
Plumpton Green 13 C49
Plumpton Head 61 C31
Plumstead G.L. 23 D50
Plumstead Nfk. 45 B57
Plumtree 41 B42
Plungar 42 B43
Plwmp 26 C19
Plym Bridge 5 E21
Plymouth 4 E20
Plymouth Airport 5 D21
Plympton 5 E21
Plymstock 5 E21
Plymtree 7 E26
Pockley 58 A42
Pocklington 58 E44
Pode Hole 43 C48
Podimore 8 B31
Podington 32 B45
Pointon 42 B47
Pokesdown 10 E37
Polbae 67 F18
Polbain 86 G15
Polbathic 4 E19
Polbeth 75 D26
Polebrook 42 G46
Polegate 13 D51
Polesworth 40 E38
Polglass 86 H16
Polgooth 3 C15
Polgown 68 C23
Poling 12 D46
Poling Corner 12 D46
Polkerris 4 E16
Pollington 51 A42
Polloch 79 D13
Pollokshaws 74 D21
Polmaddie 67 E21
Polmassick 3 D15
Polmont 75 C25
Polnood 69 A27
Polnessan 67 B20
Polperro 4 E18
Polruan 4 E17
Polsham 19 G31
Polstead 34 E55
Poltimore 7 F25
Polton 75 D28
Polwarth 76 F33
Polyphant 4 B18
Polzeath 3 A15
Pomathorn 75 E28
Pondersbridge 43 F48
Ponders End 23 B49
Ponsanooth 2 E13
Ponsworthy 5 C22
Pont Aber Glaslyn 36 A21
Pontamman 17 C22
Pontantwn 17 C20
Pontardawe 18 A23
Pontarddulais 17 D21
Pont ar Hydfer 27 F24
Pontarllechau 27 F23
Pontarsais 17 B20
Pontblyddyn 48 F28
Pont Crugnant 37 F24
Pont Cyfyng 47 G23
Pont-Cysllte 38 A28
Pont Dolgarrog 47 F23
Pontefract 57 G40
Ponteland 71 F37
Pont-erwyd 37 G23
Pontesbury 38 E30
Pontesford 38 E30

Pontfadog 38 B28
Pontfaen Dyf. 16 A16
Pont-faen Pow. 27 E25
Pontfaen Shr. 38 B28
Pont Gihirych 27 F24
Ponthenry 17 D20
Ponthir 19 B29
Ponthirwaun 26 D18
Pontllanfraith 18 B27
Pontlliw 17 D22
Pontlottyn 18 A27
Pontlyfni 46 G20
Pont Nedd Fechan 18 A25
Pontnewydd Gwe. 19 B28
Pontnewynydd 19 A28
Pont Pen-y-benglog 46 F22
Pontrhydfendigaid 27 B23
Pontrilas 28 F29
Pont Rhyd-y-cyff 18 C24
Pont-rhyd-y-fen 18 B23
Pontrhydygroes 27 A23
Pontrobert 38 D27
Ponts Green 13 C52
Pontshaen 26 D20
Pontshill 29 F32
Pontsticill 27 G26
Pont Walby 18 A24
Pontwely 26 D20
Pontyates 17 D20
Pontyberem 17 C21
Pontybodkin 48 G28
Ponty-clun 18 C26
Ponty-cymmer 18 B25
Pontyglazier 16 A17
Pont-y-gwaith 18 B26
Pontymister 19 B28
Pont-y-pant 47 G23
Pontypool 19 A28
Pontypridd 18 C26
Pont-y-rhyl 18 C25
Pontysgawryd 38 D27
Pontywaun 19 B28
Pooksgreen 10 C39
Pool Cnw. 2 D12
Pool W.Y. 57 E38
Poole 10 E36
Poole Keynes 20 B35
Poolewe 83 A14
Pooley Bridge 61 D30
Poolhill 29 F33
Pool of Muckart 80 K25
Pool Quay 38 D28
Pool Street 34 E53
Popeswood 22 D44
Popham 21 G41
Porchfield 11 E40
Porin 83 D19
Poringland 45 E58
Porkellis 2 E12
Porlock 7 A24
Porlock Weir 7 A24
Portachoillan 72 E13
Port Appin 79 F15
Port Askaig 78 H5
Portavadie 72 D15
Port Bannatyne 72 D16
Portbury 19 D30
Port Carlisle 69 G28
Port Charlotte 78 J3
Portchester 11 D42
Port Clarence 62 D40
Port Dinorwic 46 F21
Port Driseach 72 C15
Port Ellen 78 K5
Port Elphinstone 85 G33
Portencross 73 F17
Portend 80 K21
Port Erin 54 G24
Port Erroll 85 F36
Portessie 85 C30
Port e Vullen 54 D27
Port-Eynon 17 F20
Portfield Gate 16 C15
Portgate 6 G20
Port Glasgow 73 C19
Portgordon 84 C29
Portgower 87 G26
Porth Cnw. 3 B14
Porth M.G. 18 B26
Porthallow 2 F13
Porthcawl 18 D23
Porthcothan 3 A14
Porthcurno 2 F9
Port Henderson 82 B13
Porth-gain 16 A14
Porthkerry 18 E26
Porthleven 2 F12
Porthmadog 36 B21
Porth Mellin 2 G12
Porthmeor 2 E10
Porth Navas 2 F13
Porthoustock 3 F14
Porthscatho 3 E14
Porthtowan 2 D12
Porthyrhyd Dyf. 27 E23
Porthyrhyd Dyf. 17 C21
Portincaple 73 A18
Portinnisherrich 79 J15
Portinscale 60 D28
Port Isaac 3 A15
Portishead 19 D30
Portknockie 85 C30
Port Lamont 72 D16
Portlethen 81 A35
Portloe 3 E15
Port Logan 64 D16
Portmahomack 84 A25
Port Mary 65 D23
Portmeirion 36 B21
Port Mor 78 C10
Portmore 10 E39
Port Mulgrave 63 E43
Portnacroish 79 F15
Portnaguran 88 D11

Portnahaven 78 K3
Portnalong 82 F9
Portnaluchaig 79 B12
Portnancon 86 B20
Portnellan 80 H20
Portobello Ltn. 75 C29
Portobello W.M. 40 F35
Port of Menteith 80 K21
Port of Ness 88 A11
Porton 10 A37
Portpatrick 64 C15
Portquin 3 A15
Port Ramsay 79 F14
Portreath 2 D12
Portree 82 E10
Port St. Mary 54 G24
Port Seton 76 C30
Portskerra 87 B24
Portskewett 19 C30
Portslade-by-Sea 13 D48
Portslogan 64 C15
Portsmouth Ham. 11 E42
Portsmouth Lan. 56 G34
Port Soderick 54 F25
Portsoy 85 C31
Port Sunlight 48 D29
Port Talbot 18 C23
Portway H.& W. 28 D30
Portway War. 30 A36
Port Wemyss 78 K3
Port William 64 D19
Portwrinkle 4 E19
Portyerrock 64 E20
Posenhall 39 E32
Poslingford 34 D53
Postbridge 5 C22
Postcombe 22 B43
Postling 15 D57
Postwick 45 E58
Poteath 73 E17
Potsgrove 32 E45
Potten End 22 A46
Potterhanworth 52 F46
Potterhanworth Booths 52 F46
Potter Heigham 45 D60
Potterne 20 F35
Potterne Wick 20 F35
Potters Bar 23 A48
Potter's Cross 40 G34
Potterspury 31 D43
Potter Street 23 A50
Potto 62 F40
Potton 33 D48
Pottrow 44 C53
Pott Shrigley 49 D35
Poughill Cnw. 6 E18
Poughill Dev. 7 E24
Poulner 10 D37
Poulshot 20 F35
Poulton 20 A36
Poulton-le-Fylde 55 E29
Pound Green 13 B51
Pound Hill 13 A48
Poundland 67 E17
Poundon 31 F42
Poundsgate 5 C23
Poundstock 4 A17
Powburn 71 B36
Powderham 7 G25
Powerstock 8 E31
Powfoot 69 G27
Pow Hill 62 A36
Powick 29 C34
Powler's Piece 6 D19
Powmill 75 A26
Poxwell 9 F33
Poyle 22 D46
Poynings 13 C48
Poyntington 9 B32
Poynton 49 D35
Poys Street 35 A59
Praa Sands 2 F11
Pratt's Bottom 23 E50
Praze-an-Beeble 2 E12
Prees 38 B31
Preesall 55 E29
Preesall Park 55 E29
Prees Green 38 B31
Prenderguest 77 E35
Prendwick 71 B36
Pren-gwyn 26 D20
Prenteg 36 A21
Prenton 48 D29
Prescot Mer. 48 C30
Prescott Shr. 38 C30
Prescott Shr. 39 G32
Presley 84 D26
Pressen 77 G34
Prestatyn 47 D26
Prestbury Che. 49 E35
Prestbury Glo. 29 F35
Presteigne 28 B29
Presthope 38 F31
Prestleigh 9 A32
Prestolee 49 B33
Preston Bor. 76 E33
Preston Dor. 9 F33
Preston Glo. 20 A36
Preston Hfs. 32 F47
Preston Hum. 59 F47
Preston H.& W. 28 E32
Preston Kent 25 E56
Preston Kent 25 E58
Preston Lan. 55 G31
Preston Lei. 42 E44
Preston Ltn. 76 C31
Preston Ltn. 75 C29
Preston Nor. 71 A37
Preston Sfk. 34 C55
Preston Wts. 20 D36
Preston Wts. 21 D38
Preston Bissett 31 F42
Preston Brook 48 D31

Preston Candover 21 G42
Preston Capes 31 C41
Preston Cross 29 E32
Preston Green 30 B37
Preston Gubbals 38 D30
Preston Hall 75 D29
Prestonmill 65 C25
Preston on Stour 30 D38
Preston on the Hill 48 D31
Preston on Wye 28 D29
Prestonpans 75 C29
Preston under Scar 62 G36
Preston upon the Weald Moors 39 D32
Preston Wynne 28 D31
Prestwich 49 B34
Prestwick Str. 67 A19
Prestwick T.& W. 71 F37
Prestwick Airport 67 A19
Prestwold 41 C41
Prestwood 22 A44
Price Town 18 B25
Prickwillow 43 G51
Priddy 19 F31
Priestcliffe 50 E37
Priesthaugh 69 C30
Priest Hill 56 F32
Priest Hutton 55 B31
Priestweston 38 F28
Primethorpe 41 F41
Primrosehill 76 E33
Primsidemill 70 A34
Princes Risborough 22 A44
Princethorpe 31 A40
Princetown 5 C21
Prinsted 11 D43
Priors Hardwick 31 C40
Priors Marston 31 C40
Priston 19 E32
Prittlewell 24 C54
Probus 3 D14
Prospect 60 B27
Providence Green 57 D40
Prudhoe 71 G37
Ptarmigan Lodge 80 K19
Puckeridge 33 F49
Puckington 8 C29
Pucklechurch 20 D33
Puddinglake 49 E33
Puddington Che. 48 E29
Puddington Dev. 7 D24
Puddletown 9 E33
Pudleston 28 B31
Pudsey 57 F38
Pulborough 12 C46
Pulford 48 G29
Pulham 9 D33
Pulham Market 45 G57
Pulham St. Mary 45 G58
Pulloxhill 32 E46
Pulverbatch 38 E30
Pumpherston 75 D26
Pumpsaint 27 D22
Puncheston 16 A16
Puncknowle 8 F31
Punnett's Town 13 B52
Purbrook 11 D42
Purewell 10 E37
Purfleet 23 D51
Puriton 19 G29
Purleigh 24 A54
Purley 23 E49
Purley-on-Thames 21 D42
Purse Caundle 9 C32
Purslow 38 G29
Purton Glo. 19 A32
Purton Wts. 20 C36
Purton Stoke 20 B36
Purvishaugh 76 G32
Pury End 31 D43
Pusey 21 B39
Putley 29 E32
Puttenham Hfs. 32 G44
Puttenham Sry. 22 G45
Puxton 19 E30
Pwll 17 D20
Pwllcrochan 16 D15
Pwll-glâs 47 G27
Pwllheli 36 B19
Pwllmeyric 19 B31
Pwll Trap 17 C18
Pwll-y-cwm 28 G30
Pyecombe 13 C48
Pye Corner 33 G50
Pye Green 40 D35
Pyle 18 C24
Pylle 9 A32
Pymore 43 G50
Pyrford 22 F46
Pyrgad 28 G27
Pyrton 21 B41
Pytchley 32 A44
Pyworthy 6 E19

Q

Quabbs 38 G28
Quadring 43 B48
Quainton 31 F43
Quarley 21 G38
Quarndon 41 A39
Quarnford 49 F35
Quarrier's Village 73 D19
Quarrington 42 A46
Quarrington Hill 62 C39
Quarrywood 84 C27
Quarter Str. 73 D17
Quarter Str. 74 E23
Quatford 39 F33
Quatt 39 G33

Quebec 62 B37
Quedgeley 29 G34
Queen Adelaide 43 G51
Queenborough 25 D55
Queen Camel 8 B31
Queen Charlton 19 E32
Queensferry Clw. 48 F29
Queensferry Ltn. 75 C27
Queen's Head 38 C29
Queenzieburn 74 C22
Quendale 89 L39
Quendon 33 E51
Quenington 20 A37
Queniborough 41 D42
Quethiock 4 D19
Quidenham 44 G56
Quidhampton 10 A37
Quina Brook 38 B31
Quine's Hill 54 F26
Quinhill 72 E13
Quinton 31 C43
Quinton 40 G35
Quintrell Downs 3 B14
Quixwood 76 D33
Quoig 80 H24
Quorndon 41 D41
Quothquan 75 G25
Quoyloo 89 E28

R

Raby 48 E29
Rachan Mill 75 G27
Rachub 46 F22
Rackenford 7 D24
Racks 69 F26
Rackwick Ork. 89 B30
Rackwick Ork. 89 H28
Radcliffe G.M. 49 B33
Radcliffe Nor. 71 C38
Radcliffe on Trent 41 B42
Radcot 21 B38
Raddery House 84 D23
Radford Semele 30 B39
Radipole 9 F32
Radlett 22 A47
Radley 21 B41
Radstock 19 F32
Radstone 31 D41
Radway 30 D39
Radway Green 49 G33
Radwell 32 C46
Radwinter 33 E52
Radyr 18 C27
Raechester 70 E35
Raecleuch 69 B26
Rafford 84 D26
Ragdale 41 D42
Raglan 19 A30
Ragnall 52 E44
Rahane 73 B18
Rainford 48 B30
Rainham Esx. 23 C51
Rainham Kent 24 E54
Rainhill 48 C30
Rainhill Stoops 48 C31
Rainow 49 E35
Rainton 57 B39
Rainworth 51 G41
Raisbeck 61 F32
Rait 81 H28
Raithby 53 D49
Raithby 53 F49
Rake 12 B44
Raleigh's Cross Inn 7 B26
Ramasaig 82 E7
Rame 4 F20
Rame 2 E13
Rampisham 8 D31
Rampside 54 C28
Rampton Cbs. 33 B50
Rampton Not. 51 E43
Ramsbottom 49 A34
Ramsbury 21 D38
Ramscraigs 87 J23
Ramsdean 11 B43
Ramsdell 21 F41
Ramsden 30 G39
Ramsden Bellhouse 24 B53
Ramsden Heath 24 B53
Ramsey Cbs. 43 G48
Ramsey Esx. 35 E58
Ramsey I.o.M. 54 D27
Ramsey Forty Foot 43 G49
Ramsey St. Mary's 43 G48
Ramsgate 25 E59
Ramsgate Street 44 B56
Ramsgill 57 B37
Ramshaw 62 B35
Ramshope 70 C33
Ramshorn 40 A36
Ramsley 6 F22
Ramsnest Common 12 A45
Ranby 51 D42
Rand 52 E47
Randwick 20 A34
Rangeworthy 19 C32
Rankinston 67 B20
Rannoch School 80 E21
Rannoch Station 80 E20
Ranskill 51 D42
Ranton 40 C34
Ranworth 45 D59
Rapness 89 C31
Rascarrel 65 D23
Rash 56 A32
Raskelf 57 B40
Rassau 28 G27
Rastrick 57 G37
Ratagan 83 G15
Ratby 41 E41
Ratcliffe Culey 41 F39

Ratcliffe on Soar 41 C40
Ratcliffe on the Wreak 41 D42
Rathen 85 C35
Rathillet 81 H29
Rathmell 56 D34
Ratho 75 C27
Rathven 85 C30
Ratley 30 D39
Ratlinghope 38 F30
Rattar 89 K28
Rattery 5 D23
Rattlesden 34 C55
Rattray 81 F27
Raughton 60 B29
Raughton Head 60 B29
Raunds 32 A45
Ravenfield 51 C40
Ravenglass 60 G26
Raveningham 45 F59
Ravenscar 63 F45
Ravensdale 54 D26
Ravensden 32 C46
Ravenshead 51 G41
Ravensmoor 49 G32
Ravensthorpe Nmp. 31 A42
Ravensthorpe W.Y. 57 G38
Ravenstone Bkh. 32 C44
Ravenstone Lei. 41 D40
Ravenstonedale 61 F33
Ravenstruther 75 F25
Ravensworth 62 F37
Raw 63 F45
Rawcliffe Hum. 58 G42
Rawcliffe N.Y. 58 D41
Rawcliffe Bridge 58 G42
Rawdon 57 F38
Rawmarsh 51 C40
Rawnsley 40 D36
Rawreth 24 B53
Rawridge 8 D28
Rawtenstall 56 G34
Rawthey Bridge 61 G33
Rawyards 74 D23
Raydon 34 E56
Raydon 34 E56
Raylees 70 D35
Rayleigh 24 B54
Rayne 34 F53
Rayners Lane 22 C47
Reach 33 B51
Read 56 F33
Reading 22 D43
Reading Street Kent 14 D55
Reading Street Kent 25 E59
Reagill 61 E32
Rearquhar 87 J23
Rearsby 41 D42
Reaveley 71 B36
Reawick 89 H39
Reay 87 B25
Reculver 25 E58
Redberth 16 D16
Redbourn 52 B45
Redbourne 52 B45
Redbridge G.L. 23 C50
Redbridge Ham. 10 C39
Redbrook Clw. 38 A31
Redbrook Glo. 19 A30
Redburn Hgh. 83 C21
Redburn Hgh. 84 E25
Redburn Nor. 70 G33
Redcar 63 D42
Redcastle 84 D22
Redding 75 C25
Reddish 49 C34
Redditch 30 B36
Rede 34 C54
Redenham 60 C27
Redenhall 45 G58
Redesdale Camp 70 D34
Redesmouth 70 E34
Redford Tay. 81 F31
Redford W.S. 12 B44
Redfordgreen 69 B29
Redgorton 80 H26
Redgrave 34 A56
Redhill Avon 19 E30
Redhill Sry. 23 F48
Redhill Heliport 23 G49
Red House 38 E29
Redisham 45 G60
Redland 19 D31
Redlingfield 35 A57
Red Lodge 33 A52
Redlynch Som. 9 A33
Redlynch Wts. 10 B38
Redmain 60 C27
Redmarley D'Abitot 29 E33
Redmarshall 62 D39
Redmile 42 B43
Redmire 62 G36
Redmoor 4 D16
Rednal 38 C29
Redpath 76 G31
Redpoint 82 C13
Red Roses 17 C18
Red Row 71 D38
Redruth 2 D12
Red Street 49 G34
Redwick Avon 19 C31
Redwick Gwe. 19 C30
Redworth 62 D38
Reed 33 E49
Reedham 45 E60
Reedness 58 G43
Reeds Holme 56 G34
Reepham Lcn. 52 E46
Reepham Nfk. 44 C56
Reeth 62 G36
Regaby 54 D26
Reiff 86 G15
Reigate 23 F48
Reighton 59 B47
Reiss 87 C29
Relubbus 2 E11
Relugas 84 E25
Remenham 22 C43
Remenham Hill 22 C43

Remenham Hill 22 C43
Rempstone 41 C41
Rendcomb 20 A36
Rendham 35 B59
Renfrew 74 D20
Renhold 32 C46
Renishaw 51 E40
Rennington 71 B38
Renton 73 C19
Renwick 61 B31
Repton 41 C39
Reraig 83 G14
Rescobie 81 E31
Resipole 79 D13
Resolis 84 C22
Resolven 18 A24
Restalrig 75 C28
Reston 77 D34
Reswallie 81 E31
Retford, East 51 D43
Retire 4 D16
Rettendon 24 B53
Rettendon Place 24 B53
Revesby 53 F49
Rewe 7 F25
Reydon 35 A60
Reymerston 44 E56
Reynalton 16 D16
Reynoldston 17 E20
Rezare 4 C19
Rhadyr 19 A29
Rhagatt 37 A26
Rhandirmwyn 27 D23
Rhayader 27 B25
Rhemore 79 E11
Rhenigidale 88 G8
Rhewl 38 A27
Rhewl Clw. 38 B28
Rhewl Gwy. 46 F21
Rhicarn 86 F16
Rhiconich 86 C18
Rhicullen 84 B22
Rhidorroch House 86 J17
Rhigos 18 A25
Rhiwbryfdir 37 A22
Rhiwderin 19 C28
Rhiwlas Clw. 38 B28
Rhiwlas Gwy. 46 F21
Rhodes 49 B34
Rhodesia 51 E41
Rhondda 18 B25
Rhonehouse 65 C23
Rhoose 18 E26
Rhôs Dyf. 17 A19
Rhos W.G. 18 A23
Rhoscolyn 46 E18
Rhoscrowther 16 D15
Rhosdylluan 37 C24
Rhosesmor 48 F28
Rhosfawr 46 D20
Rhosgadfan 46 G21
Rhosgoch 28 D27
Rhos-hill 26 D17
Rhoshirwaun 36 C17
Rhoslan 36 A20
Rhoslefain 36 E21
Rhosllanerchrugog 38 A28
Rhosmeirch 46 E20
Rhosneigr 46 E19
Rhosnesni 48 G29
Rhos-on-Sea 47 D24
Rhossili 17 F20
Rhosson 16 B13
Rhostryfan 46 G20
Rhostyllen 38 A29
Rhosybol 46 D19
Rhos-y-garth 27 A22
Rhos-y-gwaliau 37 B25
Rhos-y-llan 36 B18
Rhu Str. 72 D14
Rhu Str. 73 B18
Rhuallt 47 E26
Rhubodach 72 C16
Rhuddall Heath 48 F31
Rhuddlan 47 E26
Rhude Cross 6 E18
Rhue 86 J16
Rhulen 28 D27
Rhunahaorine 72 F13
Rhydargaeau 17 B20
Rhydcymerau 17 A21
Rhydd 29 D33
Rhyd-ddu 46 G21
Rhydding 18 A23
Rhydfro 18 A23
Rhydlanfair 47 G24
Rhydlewis 26 D19
Rhydlios 36 B17
Rhyd-lydan 47 G24
Rhydowen 26 D20
Rhydspence 28 D28
Rhydtalog 48 G28
Rhyd-uchaf 37 B25
Rhydwyn 46 D19
Rhyd-y-ceirw 48 G28
Rhŷd-y-clafdy 36 B19
Rhydycroesau 38 B28
Rhydyfelin 18 C26
Rhyd-y-felin 26 A21
Rhyd-y-groes 38 E28
Rhyd-y-meirch 19 A29
Rhŷd-y-sarn 37 A22
Rhyl 47 D26
Rhymney 18 A27
Rhynd 81 H27
Rhynie Grm. 85 G30
Rhynie Hgh. 84 B24
Ribbesford 29 A33
Ribble Head 56 B33
Ribbleton 55 F31
Ribby 55 F29

Ribchester 56 F32
Ribigill 86 C21
Riby 52 B47
Riby Cross Roads 52 B47
Riccall 58 F42
Riccarton 74 G20
Richards Castle 28 A30
Richborough Port 25 E59
Richings Park 22 C46
Richmond 62 F37
Richmond Hill 54 F25
Richmond upon Thames 22 D47
Rickarton 81 B34
Rickerby 61 A30
Rickford 19 F30
Rickinghall 34 A56
Rickling 33 E51
Rickling Green 33 E51
Rickmansworth 22 B46
Riddell 70 A31
Riddings Cum. 69 F30
Riddings Dby. 51 G40
Riddings N.Y. 57 D36
Riddlecombe 6 D22
Riddlehamhope 61 B35
Riddlesden 57 E36
Ridge 23 A48
Ridgebourne 27 B26
Ridgehill Avon 19 E31
Ridge Lane 40 F38
Ridgewell 34 D53
Ridgewood 13 C50
Ridgmont 32 E45
Riding Mill 71 G36
Ridley 70 G33
Ridley Green 48 G31
Ridlington Lei. 42 E44
Ridlington Nfk. 45 B59
Ridsdale 70 E35
Riechip 80 F26
Rievaulx 58 A41
Rig 68 B23
Rigg 69 G28
Riggend 74 C23
Righoul 84 D24
Rigside 74 G24
Riley Green 56 G32
Rilla Mill 4 C18
Rillington 58 B44
Rimington 56 E34
Rimpton 9 B32
Rimsdale 87 D23
Rimswell 59 G49
Ringford 65 C22
Ringland 45 D57
Ringles Cross 13 B50
Ringmer 13 C50
Ringmore 5 F22
Ringmore 5 F22
Ringsfield 45 G60
Ringshall 32 G45
Ringstead Nfk. 44 A53
Ringstead Nmp. 32 A45
Ringwood 10 D37
Ringwould 15 C59
Ripe 13 C51
Ripley Dby. 51 G39
Ripley N.Y. 57 C38
Ripley Sry. 22 F46
Ripon 57 B39
Rippingale 42 C46
Ripple H.& W. 29 E34
Ripple Kent 15 B59
Ripponden 50 A36
Risabus 78 L4
Risby 34 B53
Risca 19 B28
Rise 59 E47
Risegate 43 B48
Riseholme 52 E45
Riseley Bfd. 32 B46
Riseley Brk. 22 E43
Rishangles 35 B57
Rishton 56 F33
Rishworth 50 A36
Rising Bridge 56 G33
Rising Sun Inn 10 E38
Risley 49 C32
Rispond 86 B20
Rivenhall End 34 G54
River 12 B45
Riverhead 23 F51
Rivington 49 A32
Roade 31 C43
Roadhead 70 F31
Roadside Hgh. 87 B27
Roadside Str. 67 B21
Roadside of Kinneff 81 C34
Roadwater 7 B26
Road Weedon 31 C42
Roag 82 E8
Roa Island 54 C28
Roath 18 D27
Roberton Bor. 69 B30
Roberton Str. 68 A25
Robertsbridge 14 C53
Robertstown 57 G37
Robeston Wathen 16 C16
Robin Hood Dby. 50 E38
Robin Hood W.Y. 57 G39
Robin Hood's Bay 63 F45
Robin's Brae 89 L39
Roborough Dev. 6 D21
Roborough Dev. 5 D21
Rob Roy's House 79 J17
Roby 48 C30
Rocester 40 B37
Roch 16 B14
Rochdale 49 A34
Roche 3 B15
Rochester Kent 24 D53
Rochester Nor. 70 D34
Rochford 24 B54
Rock Cnw. 3 A15

Scawby

Rock H.& W. 29 A33
Rock Nor. 71 B38
Rock W.S. 12 C47
Rockbeare 7 F26
Rockbourne 10 C37
Rockcliffe Cum. 69 G29
Rockcliffe D.& G. 65 C24
Rock Ferry 48 D29
Rockfield Gwe. 28 G30
Rockfield Hgh. 84 A25
Rockhampton 19 B32
Rockhill Sal. 28 A28
Rockingham 42 F44
Rockland All Saints 44 F55
Rockland St. Mary 45 E59
Rockland St. Peter 44 F55
Rockley 20 D37
Rockwell Green 7 C27
Rodbourne 20 C35
Rodbridge Corner 34 D54
Roddam 71 B36
Rode 20 F34
Rode Heath Che. 49 G34
Rodeheath Che. 49 F34
Rodel 88 J6
Roden 38 D31
Rodford 20 C33
Rodhuish 7 B26
Rodington 38 D31
Rodley 57 F38
Rodmarton 20 B35
Rodmell 13 D50
Rodmersham 25 E55
Rodney Stoke 19 G30
Rodsley 40 A38
Rodwell 9 G32
Roecliffe 57 C39
Roe Green 23 A48
Roesound 89 F39
Roewen 47 E23
Roffey 12 A47
Rogart 87 H23
Rogate 12 B44
Rogerstone 19 C28
Rogiet 19 C30
Roker 62 A40
Rollesby 45 D60
Rolleston Lei. 42 E43
Rolleston Not. 51 G43
Rolleston Stf. 40 C38
Rollestone 20 G36
Rolston 59 E48
Rolvenden 14 D54
Rolvenden Layne 14 D54
Romaldkirk 62 D35
Romanby 62 G39
Romannobridge 75 F27
Romansleigh 7 C23
Romford Dor. 10 D36
Romford Esx. 23 C51
Romiley 49 C35
Romsey 10 B39
Romsley H.& W. 40 G35
Romsley Shr. 39 G33
Ronachan 72 E13
Rookhope 61 B35
Rookley 11 F41
Rooks Bridge 19 F29
Roos Hum. 59 F48
Roose 54 C28
Roosecote 54 C28
Rootpark 75 E25
Ropley 11 A42
Ropley Dean 11 A42
Ropsley 42 B45
Rora 85 D36
Rorrington 38 E29
Rose 2 C13
Roseacre 55 F30
Rose Ash 7 C23
Rosebank 74 F24
Rosebery 75 E29
Rosebrough 71 A37
Rosebush 16 B16
Rosedale Abbey 63 G43
Roseden 71 A36
Rosehall 86 H20
Rosehaugh House 84 D22
Rosehearty 85 C35
Rosehill 39 B32
Rosemarket 16 D15
Rosemarkie 84 D23
Rosemary Lane 7 D27
Rosemount Str. 67 A19
Rosemount Tay. 81 F27
Rosewell 75 D28
Roseworthy 2 E12
Rosgill 61 E31
Roshven 79 C13
Roskhill 82 E8
Rosley 60 B29
Roslin 75 D28
Rosliston 40 D38
Rosneath 73 B18
Ross D.& G. 65 D22
Ross Nor. 77 G37
Rossett 48 G29
Rossington 51 C42
Rossland 74 C20
Ross-on-Wye 29 F32
Roster 87 D28
Rostherne 49 D33
Rosthwaite 60 E28
Rosyth 75 B27
Rothbury 71 C36
Rotherby 41 D42
Rotherfield 13 B51
Rotherfield Greys 22 C43
Rotherfield Peppard 22 C43
Rotherham 51 C40
Rothersthorpe 31 C43
Rothersthorpe Services 31 C43
Rotherwick 22 F43
Rothes 84 E28
Rothesay 72 D16
Rothienorman 85 F33
Rothiesholm 89 E32
Rothley Lei. 41 D41
Rothley Nor. 71 E36
Rothwell Lcn. 52 C47
Rothwell Nmp. 42 G44
Rothwell W.Y. 57 G39
Rottal 81 D29
Rottingdean 13 D49
Rottington 60 E25
Rougham 44 C54
Rougham Green 34 B55
Roughburn 80 B19
Rough Close 40 B35
Rough Common 15 B57
Roughlee 56 E34
Roughley 40 F37
Roughsike 70 F31
Roughton Lcn. 53 F48
Roughton Nfk. 45 B58
Roughton Shr. 39 F33
Roundhay 57 F39
Roundstonefoot 69 C27
Roundway 20 E36
Rousdon 8 E28
Rousham Gap 31 F40
Rous Lench 30 C36
Routenburn 73 D17
Routh 59 E46
Row Cnw. 4 C16
Row Cum. 55 A30
Rowanburn 69 F30
Rowanston 67 C19
Rowardennan Hotel 73 A19
Rowarth 50 D36
Rowchester House 76 F33
Rowde 20 E35
Rowfoot 70 G32
Rowhedge 34 F56
Rowington 30 B38
Rowland 50 E38
Rowland's Castle 11 C43
Rowland's Gill 62 A37
Rowledge 22 G44
Rowley 62 B36
Rowley Regis 40 G35
Rowlstone 28 F29
Rowly 22 G46
Rowner 11 D41
Rownhams 10 C39
Rownhams Services 10 C39
Rowrah 60 E26
Rowsham 32 G44
Rowsley 50 F38
Rowstock 21 C40
Rowston 52 G46
Rowton Che. 48 F30
Rowton Shr. 38 D29
Rowton Shr. 39 C32
Row Town 22 E46
Roxburgh 76 G32
Roxby 52 A45
Roxby Cle. 63 E43
Roxton 32 C47
Roxwell 24 A52
Royal Leamington Spa 30 B39
Royal Oak Drm. 62 D38
Royal Oak Lan. 48 B30
Royal Tunbridge Wells 13 A52
Roybridge 79 B18
Roydon Esx. 33 G50
Roydon Nfk. 44 C53
Roydon Nfk. 44 G56
Roydon Hamlet 23 A50
Royston Hfs. 33 D49
Royston S.Y. 51 A39
Royton 49 B35
Rozel 3 F18
Ruabon 38 A29
Ruan High Lanes 3 D15
Ruan Lanihorne 3 D14
Ruan Minor 2 G13
Ruardean 29 G32
Rubery 29 A35
Ruckcroft 61 B31
Ruckinge 15 D56
Ruckland 53 E49
Ruddington 41 B41
Rudford 29 F33
Rudgeway 19 C32
Rudgwick 12 A46
Rudheath Woods 49 E32
Rudley Green 24 A54
Rudry 18 C27
Rudston 59 C46
Rudyard 49 G35
Rufford 48 A30
Rufforth 58 D41
Ruffside 62 A35
Rugby 31 A41
Rugeley 40 D36
Ruishton 8 B28
Ruislip 22 C46
Rumblingbridge 75 A26
Rumburgh 45 G59
Rumford Cen. 75 C25
Rumford Cnw. 3 A14
Rumney 19 D28
Rumwell 7 C27
Runcorn 48 D31
Runcton Holme 44 E52
Rundlestone 5 C21
Runhall 44 E56
Runham 45 D60
Runsell Green 24 A53
Runswick 63 E44
Runtaleave 81 D28
Runwell 24 B53
Ruscombe 22 D43
Rushall H.& W. 29 E32
Rushall Nfk. 45 G57
Rushall W.M. 40 E36
Rushall Wts. 20 F37
Rushbrooke 34 B54
Rushbury 38 F31
Rushden Hfs. 33 E49
Rushden Nmp. 32 B45
Rushford 44 G55
Rushlake Green 13 C52
Rushmere 45 G60
Rushmere St. Andrew 35 D58
Rushmoor 22 G44
Rushock 29 A34
Rusholme 49 C34
Rushton 42 G44
Rushton Spencer 49 F35
Rushwick 29 C34
Rushyford 62 D38
Ruskie 80 K22
Ruskington 52 G46
Rusko 65 C21
Rusland 55 A29
Rusper 13 A48
Ruspidge 29 G32
Russell's Water 22 C43
Rustington 12 D46
Ruston 59 A45
Ruston Parva 59 C46
Ruswarp 63 F44
Rutherend 74 F22
Rutherford 76 G32
Rutherglen 74 D21
Ruthernbridge 4 D16
Ruthin 47 G27
Ruthven Bor. 77 F34
Ruthven Grm. 85 E31
Ruthven Hgh. 80 A23
Ruthven Tay. 81 F28
Ruthwell 69 G26
Ruyton-XI-Towns 38 C29
Ryal 71 F36
Ryarsh 24 E52
Rydal 60 F29
Ryde 11 E42
Rydon 6 E19
Rye 14 E55
Rye Foreign 14 E55
Rye Harbour 14 F55
Ryehill 68 C23
Ryemuir 69 E26
Ryhall 42 D46
Ryhill Hum. 59 G48
Ryhill W.Y. 51 A39
Ryhope 62 A40
Rylstone 56 D35
Ryme Intrinseca 8 C31
Ryther 58 F41
Ryton Shr. 39 E33
Ryton T.& W. 71 G37
Ryton-on-Dunsmore 30 A39

S

Sabden 56 F33
Sacombe 33 G49
Sacriston 62 B38
Sadberge 62 E39
Saddell 72 G13
Saddington 41 F42
Saddle Bow 44 D52
Saddleworth 50 B36
Sadgill 61 F30
Saffron Walden 33 E51
Sageston 16 D16
Saham Toney 44 E55
Saighton 48 F30
St. Abbs 77 D35
St. Agnes Cnw. 2 C13
St. Agnes Ltn. 76 D32
St. Albans 22 A47
St. Allen 3 C14
St. Andrews 81 J31
St. Andrews Major 18 D27
St. Anne 3 D17
St. Annes 55 G29
St. Ann's 69 D26
St. Ann's Chapel 4 C20
St. Anthony 2 F13
St. Arvans 19 B31
St. Asaph 47 E26
St. Athan 18 E26
St. Aubin 3 G17
St. Austell 4 E16
St. Bees 60 E25
St. Blazey 4 E16
St. Blazey Gate 4 E16
St. Boswells 76 G31
St. Brelade 3 G17
St. Breock 3 A15
St. Breward 4 C16
St. Briavels 19 A31
St. Brides 16 C14
St. Bride's Major 18 D24
St. Bride's super-Ely 18 D26
St. Brides Wentllooge 19 C28
St. Budeaux 4 E20
Saintbury 30 E37
St. Buryan 2 F10
St. Catherines 79 K17
St. Clears 17 C18
St. Cleer 4 D18
St. Clement Cnw. 3 D14
St. Clement Jer. 3 G18
St. Clether 4 B18
St. Colmac 72 D16
St. Columb Major 3 B15
St. Columb Minor 3 B14
St. Columb Road 3 C15
St. Combs 85 C36
St. Cross South Elmham 45 G58
St. Cyrus 81 D33
St. David's Dyf. 16 B13
St. Davids Fife 75 B27
St. David's Tay. 80 H25
St. Day 2 D13
St. Decumans 7 A26
St. Dennis 3 C15
St. Dogmaels 26 D17
St. Dominick 4 D19
St. Donats 18 E25
St. Endellion 3 A15
St. Enoder 3 C14
St. Erme 3 C14
St. Erney 4 E19
St. Erth 2 E11
St. Erth Praze 2 E11
St. Eval 3 B14
St. Ewe 3 D15
St. Fagans 18 D27
St. Fergus 85 D36
St. Fillans 80 H22
St. Florence 16 D16
St. Gennys 4 A17
St. George Clw. 47 E25
St. Georges Avon 19 E29
St. George's S.G. 18 D26
St. Germains 76 C30
St. Germans 4 E19
St. Giles in the Wood 6 D21
St. Giles on the Heath 6 F19
St. Harmon 27 A25
St. Helena 45 D57
St. Helen Auckland 62 D37
St. Helens E.S. 14 F54
St. Helens I.o.W. 11 F42
St. Helens Mer. 48 C31
St. Helier G.L. 23 E48
St. Helier Jer. 3 G17
St. Hilary Cnw. 2 E11
St. Hilary S.G. 18 D26
St. Ippollitts 32 F47
St. Ishmael's 16 D14
St. Issey 3 A15
St. Ive 4 D19
St. Ives Cbs. 33 A49
St. Ives Cnw. 2 D11
St. Ives Dor. 10 D37
St. James South Elmham 45 G59
St. Joan à Gores Cross 20 F36
St. John Cnw. 4 E20
St. John Jer. 3 F17
St. John's 54 E25
St. John's Chapel Dev. 6 C21
St. John's Chapel Drm. 61 C34
St. John's Highway 43 D51
St. John's Town of Dalry 68 E22
St. Judes 54 D26
St. Just Cnw. 2 E9
St. Just Cnw. 3 E14
St. Just Lane 3 E14
St. Katherines 85 F33
St. Keverne 2 F13
St. Kew 4 C16
St. Kew Highway 4 C16
St. Keyne 4 D18
St. Lawrence Esx. 25 A55
St. Lawrence I.o.W. 11 G41
St. Leonards Bkh. 22 A45
St. Leonards Dor. 10 D37
St. Leonards E.S. 14 G53
St. Levan 2 F9
St. Lythan's 18 D27
St. Mabyn 4 C16
St. Margarets Hfs. 33 G49
St. Margarets H.& W. 28 E29
St. Margaret's at Cliffe 15 C59
St. Margaret's Hope 89 H30
St. Margaret South Elmham 45 G59
St. Mark's 54 F25
St. Martin Cnw. 2 F13
St. Martin Cnw. 4 E18
St. Martin Gny. 3 E17
St. Martin Jer. 3 G18
St. Martins Shr. 38 B29
St. Martins Tay. 81 G27
St. Mary 3 F17
St. Mary Bourne 21 F40
St. Mary Church 18 D25
St. Mary Cray 23 E50
St. Mary Hill 18 D25
St. Mary in the Marsh 15 E56
St. Mary's 89 G30
St. Mary's Bay 15 E56
St. Mary's Hoo 24 D54
St. Mawes 3 E14
St. Mawgan 3 B14
St. Mellion 4 D19
St. Mellons 19 C28
St. Merryn 3 A14
St. Mewan 3 C15
St. Michael Caerhays 3 D15
St. Michael Penkevil 3 D14
St. Michaels H.& W. 28 B31
St. Michaels Kent 14 D54
St. Michael's on Wyre 55 E30
St. Minver 3 A15
St. Monans 81 K31
St. Neot 4 D17
St. Neots 32 B47
St. Nicholas Dyf. 16 A15
St. Nicholas S.G. 18 D26
St. Nicholas at Wade 25 E58
St. Ninians 74 A24
St. Osyth 35 G57
St. Ouen's Church 3 G17
St. Owen's Cross 28 F31
St. Pauls Cray 23 E50
St. Paul's Walden 32 F47
St. Peter Port 3 E17
St. Peters 25 E59
St. Peter's Church 3 G17
St. Pinnock 4 D17
St. Quivox 67 A19
St. Sampson 3 E17
St. Saviour Gny. 3 E16
St. Saviour Jer. 3 G18
St. Stephen 3 C15
St. Stephen's Cnw. 4 E20
St. Stephens Cnw. 6 G19
St. Stephens Hfs. 22 A47
St. Teath 4 B16
St. Tudy 4 C16
St. Twynnells 16 E15
St. Veep 4 E17
St. Vigeans 81 F32
St. Wenn 3 B15
St. Weonards 28 F30
Salcombe 5 G23
Salcombe Regis 7 G27
Salcott 34 G55
Sale 49 C33
Saleby 53 E50
Salehurst 14 E53
Salem Dyf. 17 B22
Salem Dyf. 37 G22
Salem Gwy. 46 G21
Salen Hgh. 79 D12
Salen Str. 79 F11
Salesbury 56 F32
Salford Bfd. 32 E45
Salford G.M. 49 C34
Salford Oxf. 30 F38
Salford Priors 30 C36
Salfords 23 G48
Salhouse 45 D59
Saline 75 A26
Salisbury 10 A37
Sall 45 C57
Sallachy Hgh. 83 F15
Sallachy Hgh. 86 H21
Salmonby 53 E49
Salperton 30 F36
Salsburgh 74 D24
Salt 40 C35
Salta 60 B26
Saltaire 57 F37
Saltash 4 E20
Saltburn 84 C23
Saltburn-by-the-Sea 63 D42
Saltby 42 C44
Saltcoats 73 F18
Saltdean 13 D49
Salterforth 56 E34
Saltergate 63 G44
Salter's Brook Bridge 50 C37
Salter's Lode 43 E51
Salterswall 49 F32
Saltfleet 53 C50
Saltfleetby St. Clements 53 C50
Saltfleetby St. Peter 53 D50
Saltford 19 E32
Salthouse 44 A56
Saltmarshe 58 G43
Saltney 48 F29
Salton 58 B43
Saltwick 71 F37
Saltwood 15 D57
Salvington 12 D47
Salwarpe 29 B34
Salwayash 8 E30
Sambourne 30 B36
Sambrook 39 C33
Samlesbury 55 F31
Sampford Arundel 7 D27
Sampford Brett 7 A26
Sampford Courtenay 6 E22
Sampford Peverell 7 D26
Sampford Spiney 5 C21
Sampool Bridge 55 A30
Samuelston 76 C30
Sanahole 72 A16
Sanaigmore 78 H3
Sancreed 2 F10
Sancton 58 F44
Sandaig 82 J13
Sanday Airport 89 C32
Sandbach 49 F33
Sandbach Services 49 F33
Sandbank 73 B17
Sandbanks 10 F36
Sandend 85 C31
Sanderstead 23 E49
Sandford Avon 19 F30
Sandford Cum. 61 E33
Sandford Dev. 7 E24
Sandford Dor. 9 F35
Sandford I.o.W. 11 F41
Sandford Shr. 38 B31
Sandford Str. 74 F23
Sandford-on-Thames 21 A41
Sandford Orcas 9 B32
Sandford St. Martin 31 F40
Sandgarth 89 F31
Sandgate 15 D58
Sandgreen 65 C21
Sandhaven 85 C35
Sandhead 64 D16
Sandhills 12 A45
Sandhoe 70 G35
Sandholm Bor. 69 E30
Sandholme Hum. 58 F44
Sandhurst Brk. 22 E44
Sandhurst Glo. 29 F34
Sandhurst Kent 14 E54
Sand Hutton N.Y. 58 D42
Sandhutton N.Y. 57 A39
Sandiacre 41 B40
Sandilands 53 D51
Sandiway 49 E32
Sandleheath 10 C37
Sandleigh 21 A40
Sandness 89 G37
Sandon Esx. 24 A53
Sandon Hfs. 33 E49
Sandon Stf. 40 C35
Sandown 11 F42
Sandplace 4 E18
Sandquoy 89 C33
Sandridge 32 G47
Sandringham 44 C53
Sandsend 63 E44
Sand Side 54 A28
Sandsound 89 H39
Sandtoft 51 B43
Sandway 14 B54
Sandwell 40 F35
Sandwich 15 B59
Sandwick Cum. 61 E30
Sandwick She. 89 K40
Sandwick W.I. 88 D10
Sandwith 60 E25
Sandy Bfd. 32 D47
Sandy Dyf. 17 D20
Sandybrow 48 F31
Sandycroft 48 F29
Sandyford D.& G. 69 D28
Sandyford Str. 67 A19
Sandygate Dev. 5 C24
Sandygate I.o.M. 54 D26
Sandyhills 65 C24
Sandylane Stf. 39 B33
Sandy Lane Wts. 20 E35
Sandy Lane W.Y. 57 F37
Sandypark 7 G23
Sandyway Cross 7 B23
Sanquhar 68 C23
Santon Bridge 60 F27
Santon Downham 44 G54
Sapcote 41 F40
Sapiston 34 A55
Sapperton Glo. 20 A35
Sapperton Lcn. 42 B46
Saracen's Head 43 C49
Sarclet 87 D29
Sardis 16 D15
Sarisbury 11 D41
Sarn Gwy. 36 B18
Sarn M.G. 18 C25
Sarn Pow. 38 F28
Sarn Pow. 37 F25
Sarnau Dyf. 26 C19
Sarnau Pow. 38 D28
Sarnau Pow. 27 E26
Sarn-bâch 36 C19
Sarnesfield 28 C29
Saron Clw. 47 F26
Saron Dyf. 17 A19
Saron Gwy. 46 F21
Sarratt 22 B46
Sarre 25 E58
Satley 62 B37
Satterleigh 6 C22
Satterthwaite 60 G29
Sauchen 85 H33
Sauchieburn House 74 B23
Saughall 48 E29
Saughtree 70 D31
Saul 20 A33
Saundby 51 D43
Saundersfoot 16 D17
Saunderton 22 A43
Saunton 6 B20
Sausthorpe 53 F49
Saval 86 H21
Sawbridgeworth 33 G51
Sawdon 59 A45
Sawley Dby. 41 B40
Sawley Lan. 56 E33
Sawley N.Y. 57 C38
Sawston 33 D50
Sawtry 42 G47
Saxby Lcn. 52 D46
Saxby Lei. 42 C44
Saxby All Saints 52 A45
Saxelby 42 C43
Saxilby 52 E44
Saxlingham 44 B56
Saxlingham Green 45 F58
Saxlingham Nethergate 45 F58
Saxmundham 35 B59
Saxondale 41 A42
Saxon Street 33 C52
Saxtead 35 B58
Saxtead Green 35 B58
Saxthorpe 45 B57
Saxton 57 F40
Sayers Common 13 C48
Scackleton 58 B42
Scaftworth 51 C42
Scagglethorpe 58 B44
Scalasaig 78 K10
Scalby Hum. 58 G44
Scalby N.Y. 63 G46
Scaldwell 31 A43
Scaleby 69 G30
Scalebyhill 69 G30
Scale Houses 61 B31
Scales Cum. 54 B28
Scales Cum. 60 D29
Scales Lan. 55 F30
Scalford 42 C43
Scaling 63 E43
Scalloway 89 J40
Scalpsie 72 E16
Scamblesby 53 E48
Scamodale 79 C14
Scampston 58 B44
Scampton 52 E45
Scaniport 84 E22
Scapa 89 G30
Scar 89 C32
Scarastavore 88 H6
Scarborough 59 A46
Scarcliffe 51 F40
Scarcroft 57 E39
Scardroy 83 D18
Scargill 62 E36
Scarinish 78 F6
Scarisbrick 48 A29
Scarning 44 D55
Scarrington 42 A43
Scarth Hill 48 B30
Scartho 53 B48
Scatsta Airport 89 E39
Scaur 65 C24
Scawby 52 B45

Scawby Brook 52 B45
Scawton 58 A41
Scaynes Hill 13 B49
Scethrog 28 F27
Scholar Green 49 G34
Scholes W.Y. 50 B37
Scholes W.Y. 57 G37
Scholes W.Y. 57 F39
Schoolgreen 22 E43
Scleddau 16 A15
Scole 35 A57
Scopwick 52 G46
Scoraig 86 J16
Scorborough 59 E46
Scorrier 2 D13
Scorriton 5 D23
Scorton Lan. 55 E30
Scorton N.Y. 62 F38
Sco Ruston 45 C58
Scotby 61 A30
Scotch Corner 62 F38
Scotforth 55 D30
Scothern 52 E46
Scotlandwell 81 K27
Scotsdike 69 F29
Scotston 80 F25
Scotstoun 74 D21
Scotstown Hgh. 79 D14
Scottas 82 J13
Scotter 52 B44
Scotterthorpe 52 B44
Scotton Lcn. 52 C44
Scotton N.Y. 62 G37
Scotton N.Y. 57 D39
Scoughall 76 B32
Scoulton 44 E55
Scourie 86 D17
Scousburgh 89 L39
Scouthead 49 B35
Scrabster 89 K27
Scrafield 53 F49
Scrainwood 70 C35
Scraptoft 41 E42
Scratby 45 D61
Scratchwood Services 22 B47
Scrayingham 58 D42
Scredington 42 A46
Scremby 53 F50
Scremerston 77 F36
Screveton 42 A43
Scrivelsby 53 F48
Scriven 57 D39
Scroggs 69 E27
Scronkey 55 E30
Scrooby 51 C42
Scropton 40 B37
Scruton 62 G38
Sculcoates 59 F47
Sculthorpe 44 B54
Scunthorpe 52 B44
Seaborough 8 D30
Seacliff 76 B32
Seacombe 48 C29
Seacroft 53 F51
Seafield Ltn. 75 D26
Seafield Str. 67 A19
Seaford 13 E50
Seaforth 48 C29
Seagrave 41 D42
Seaham 62 B40
Seahouses 77 G38
Seal 23 F51
Sealand 48 F29
Seale 22 G44
Seamer N.Y. 62 E40
Seamer N.Y. 59 A46
Seamill 73 F17
Sea Palling 45 C60
Searby 52 B46
Seasalter 25 E56
Seascale 60 F26
Seathwaite 60 E28
Seathwaite 60 G28
Seatoller 60 E28
Seaton Cnw. 4 E19
Seaton Cum. 60 C26
Seaton Dev. 8 E28
Seaton Hum. 59 E47
Seaton Lei. 42 F45
Seaton Burn 71 F38
Seaton Carew 63 D41
Seaton Delaval 71 F39
Seaton Ross 58 E43
Seaton Sluice 71 F39
Seatown 8 E30
Seave Green 63 F41
Sea View 11 E42
Seaville 60 A27
Seavington St. Michael 8 C30
Seawick Sands 35 G57
Sebastopol 19 B28
Sebergham 60 B29
Seckington 40 E38
Sedbergh 61 G32
Sedbury 19 B31
Sedbusk 61 G32
Sedgeberrow 30 E36
Sedgebrook 42 B44
Sedgefield 62 D39
Sedgeford 44 B53
Sedgehill 9 B34
Sedgley 40 F35
Sedgwick 55 A31
Sedlescombe 14 F53
Sedlescombe Street 14 F53
Seend 20 E35
Seend Cleeve 20 E35
Seer Green 22 B45
Seething 45 F59
Sefton 48 B29

Seghill 71 F38
Seighford 40 C34
Seisdon 40 F34
Selattyn 38 B28
Selborne 11 A43
Selby 58 F42
Selham 12 B45
Selkirk 69 A30
Sellafield 60 F26
Sellafirth 89 C41
Sellindge 15 D56
Selling 15 B56
Sellick 32 E47
Selly Oak 40 G36
Selmeston 13 D51
Selsdon 23 E49
Selsey 12 E44
Selsfield Common 13 A49
Selside 56 B33
Selsted 15 C58
Selworthy 7 A25
Semblister 89 G39
Semer 34 D56
Semington 20 E34
Semley 9 B34
Send 22 F46
Sendmarsh Inn 22 F46
Senghenydd 18 B27
Sennen 2 F9
Sennen Cove 2 F9
Sennybridge 27 F25
Sessay 57 B40
Setchey 44 D52
Seton Mains 76 C30
Setter She. 89 H41
Setter She. 89 G39
Settiscarth 89 F29
Settle 56 C34
Settrington 58 B44
Seven Bridges 20 B37
Sevenhampton 21 B38
Sevenoaks 23 F51
Sevenoaks Weald 23 F51
Seven Sisters 18 A24
Seven Springs 29 G35
Severn Beach 19 C31
Severn Stoke 29 D34
Sevington 15 C56
Sewards End 33 E51
Sewerby 59 C48
Seworgan 2 E13
Sewstern 42 C44
Shabbington 21 A42
Shackerstone 41 E39
Shackleford 22 G45
Shader 88 B9
Shadforth 62 B39
Shadingfield 45 G60
Shadoxhurst 14 D55
Shadwell Nfk. 44 G55
Shadwell W.Y. 57 F39
Shaftesbury 9 B34
Shafton 51 A39
Shalbourne 21 E39
Shalcombe 10 F39
Shalden 21 G42
Shaldon 5 C25
Shalfleet 11 F40
Shalford Esx. 34 F53
Shalford Sry. 22 G46
Shalmsford Street 15 B57
Shalstone 31 E42
Shalunt 72 C16
Shamley Green 22 G46
Shandon 73 B18
Shandwick 84 B24
Shangton 42 F43
Shankend 70 C31
Shanklin 11 F42
Shannochie 66 A15
Shap 61 E31
Shapwick Dor. 9 D35
Shapwick Som. 8 A30
Shardlow 41 B40
Shareshill 40 E35
Sharlston 51 A39
Sharnal Street 24 D53
Sharnbrook 32 B45
Sharnford 41 F40
Sharow 57 B39
Sharpenhoe 32 E46
Sharperton 70 C35
Sharpness 19 A32
Sharpthorne 13 A49
Sharrington 44 B56
Shatterford 39 G33
Shaugh Prior 5 D21
Shavington 49 G33
Shaw Brk. 21 E40
Shaw G.M. 49 B35
Shaw Wts. 20 E34
Shawbost 88 C8
Shawbury 38 C31
Shawell 41 G41
Shawford 11 B40
Shawforth 56 G34
Shawhead 68 F24
Shaw Mills 57 C38
Shaw Paddock 61 G33
Shawton 74 F22
Shawtonhill 74 F22
Shawwood 67 A21
Shearington 69 G26
Shearsby 41 F42
Shebbear 6 E20
Shebdon 39 C33
Shebster 87 B26
Sheddens 74 E21
Shedfield 11 C41
Sheen 50 F37
Sheephouse 28 D28
Sheep Park 64 C19
Sheepscombe 29 G34
Sheepstor 5 D21

Sheepwash Dev. 6 E20
Sheepwash Nor. 71 E38
Sheepway 19 D30
Sheepy Magna 41 E39
Sheepy Parva 41 E39
Sheering 33 G51
Sheerness 25 D55
Sheet 11 B43
Sheffield 51 D39
Sheffield Green 13 B50
Shefford 32 E47
Shefford Woodlands 21 D39
Sheigra 86 B17
Sheilhall 65 C23
Sheinton 39 E32
Shelderton 28 A30
Sheldon Dby. 50 F37
Sheldon Dev. 7 E27
Sheldon W.M. 40 G37
Sheldwich 15 B56
Shelf 57 G37
Shelfanger 45 G57
Shelfield 40 E36
Shelford 41 A42
Shelley Esx. 23 A51
Shelley W.Y. 50 A38
Shelley Far Bank 50 A37
Shellingford 21 B39
Shellow Bowells 23 A51
Shelsley Beauchamp 29 B33
Shelsley Walsh 29 B33
Shelton Bfd. 32 B46
Shelton Nfk. 45 F58
Shelton Not. 42 A43
Shelton Shr. 38 D30
Shelve 38 F29
Shenfield 24 B52
Shenington 30 D39
Shenley 22 A47
Shenley Brook End 32 E44
Shenley Church End 32 E44
Shennanton 67 G19
Shenstone 40 E37
Shenton 41 E39
Shenval 84 G28
Shenvault 84 E26
Shepeau Stow 43 D49
Sheperdine 19 B32
Shephall 33 F48
Shepherdswell 15 C58
Shepley 50 B37
Shepperton 22 E46
Shepreth 33 D49
Shepshed 41 D40
Shepton Beauchamp 8 C30
Shepton Mallet 19 G32
Shepton Montague 9 A32
Sheraton 62 C40
Sherborne Dor. 9 C32
Sherborne Glo. 30 G37
Sherborne St. John 21 F42
Sherbourne 30 B38
Sherburn Drm. 62 B39
Sherburn N.Y. 59 B45
Sherburn Hill 62 B39
Sherburn in Elmet 57 F40
Shere 22 G46
Shereford 44 C54
Sherfield English 10 B38
Sherfield on Loddon 21 F42
Sherford 5 F23
Sheriffhales 39 D33
Sheringham 45 A57
Sherington 32 D44
Shernborne 44 B53
Sherrington 9 A35
Sherston 20 C34
Sherston Parva or Pinkney 20 C34
Sheshader 88 D11
Shettleston 74 D22
Shevington 48 B31
Shevington Moor 48 A31
Sheviock 4 E19
Shide 11 F41
Shiel 68 F22
Shiel Bridge 83 H15
Shieldaig 83 D14
Shieldaig Lodge Hotel 83 B14
Shieldhill 74 C24
Shielfoot 79 D12
Shifnal 39 E33
Shilbottle 71 C37
Shildon 62 D38
Shillahill 69 E27
Shillingford Dev. 7 C25
Shillingford Oxf. 21 B41
Shillingford St. George 7 G25
Shillingstone 9 C34
Shillington 32 E47
Shillmoor 70 C34
Shilton Oxf. 21 A38
Shilton War. 41 G40
Shimpling 45 G57
Shimpling Street 34 C54
Shincliffe 62 B38
Shiney Row 62 A39
Shinfield 22 E43
Shinness 86 G21
Shipbourne 23 F51
Shipdham 44 E55
Shipham 19 F30
Shiplake 22 D43
Shipley Nor. 71 B37
Shipley Shr. 40 F34
Shipley W.S. 12 B47
Shipley W.Y. 57 F39
Shipleybridge 23 G49
Shipmeadow 45 F59
Shippon 21 B40
Shipston on Stour 30 D38
Shipton Glo. 30 G36

Shipton N.Y. 58 D41
Shipton Sal. 38 F31
Shipton Bellinger 21 G38
Shipton Gorge 8 E30
Shipton Green 12 D44
Shipton Moyne 20 C34
Shipton-on-Cherwell 31 G40
Shipton under Wychwood 30 G38
Shiptonthorpe 58 E44
Shirburn 22 B43
Shirebrook 51 F41
Shiregreen 51 C39
Shirehampton 19 D31
Shiremoor 71 F39
Shirenewton 19 B30
Shire Oak 40 E36
Shireoaks 51 D41
Shirland 51 G39
Shirley Dby. 40 A38
Shirley G.L. 23 E49
Shirley Ham. 10 C39
Shirley W.M. 30 A37
Shirl Heath 28 B30
Shirmers 68 F22
Shirrell Heath 11 C41
Shirwell 6 B21
Shiskine 66 A15
Shobdon 28 B29
Shobrooke 7 E24
Shocklach 38 A30
Shoeburyness 25 C55
Sholden 15 B59
Shoot Cnw. 6 D18
Shop Cnw. 3 A14
Shopford 70 F31
Shop Street 35 B58
Shoreham 23 E51
Shoreham-by-Sea 13 D48
Shoresdean 77 F35
Shoreswood 77 F35
Shorne 24 D52
Shorne Ridgeway 24 D52
Shortacombe 6 G21
Short Ferry 52 E46
Shortgate 13 C50
Short Heath W.M. 40 F36
Short Heath W.M. 40 E35
Shortlanesend 3 D14
Shortlees 74 G20
Shorwell 11 F40
Shoscombe 20 F33
Shotatton 38 C29
Shotesham 45 F58
Shotley 35 E58
Shotley Bridge 62 A36
Shotley Gate 35 E58
Shotley Street 35 E58
Shottenden 15 B56
Shottermill 12 A44
Shotteswell 31 D40
Shottisham 35 D59
Shottlegate 41 A39
Shotton Clw. 48 F29
Shotton Drm. 62 C40
Shotton Nor. 70 A34
Shotton Nor. 71 F38
Shotton Colliery 62 B39
Shotts 74 D24
Shotwick 48 E29
Shouldham 44 E52
Shouldham Thorpe 44 E52
Shrawardine 38 D30
Shrawley 29 B34
Shrewley 30 B38
Shrewsbury 38 D31
Shrewton 20 G36
Shripney 12 D45
Shrivenham 21 C38
Shropham 44 F55
Shroton 9 C34
Shrub End 34 F55
Shucknall 28 D31
Shudy Camps 33 D52
Shulishader 88 D11
Shurdington 29 G35
Shurlock Row 22 D44
Shustoke 40 F38
Shute 8 E28
Shutford 30 D39
Shutlanger 31 D43
Shuttington 40 E38
Shuttlewood 51 E40
Sibbaldbie 69 E27
Sibbertoft 41 G42
Sibdon Carwood 38 G30
Sibford Ferris 30 E39
Sibford Gower 30 E39
Sible Hedingham 34 E53
Sibsey 53 G49
Sibson 41 E39
Sibster 87 C29
Sibthorpe 42 A43
Sicklesmere 34 B54
Sicklinghall 57 E39
Sid 7 G27
Sidbury Dev. 7 F27
Sidbury Shr. 39 G32
Sidcot 19 F30
Sidcup 23 D50
Siddal 57 G37
Siddick 60 C25
Siddington Che. 49 E34
Siddington Glo. 20 B36
Sidestrand 45 B58
Sidford 7 F27
Sidinish 88 L4
Sidlesham 12 E44
Sidlowbridge 23 G48
Sidmouth 7 G27
Siefton 38 G30
Sigginston 18 D25
Sigglesthorne 59 E47
Signet 30 G38
Silchester 21 E42

Sileby 41 D42
Silecroft 54 A27
Silfield 45 F57
Silian 26 C21
Silkstone 50 B38
Silkstone Common 50 B38
Silk Willoughby 42 A46
Silloans 70 C34
Silloth 60 A27
Silpho 63 G45
Silsden 57 E36
Silsoe 32 E46
Silton 9 B33
Silverburn I.o.M. 54 F25
Silverburn Ltn. 75 E28
Silverdale Lan. 55 B30
Silverdale Stf. 40 A34
Silver End Bfd. 32 D46
Silver End Esx. 34 F54
Silver Hill 14 F53
Silverstone 31 D42
Silverton 7 E25
Silvington 39 G32
Simonburn 70 F34
Simonsbath 7 B23
Simonstone 56 F33
Simprim 77 F34
Sinclairston 67 B20
Sinclairtown 75 A28
Sinderby 57 A39
Sinderhope 61 A34
Singdean 70 C31
Singleton Lan. 55 F29
Singleton W.S. 12 C44
Singlie 69 A29
Singrett 48 G29
Sinnahard 85 H30
Sinnington 58 A43
Sinton Green 29 B34
Sionside 77 G36
Sissinghurst 14 D53
Siston 19 D32
Sithney 2 F12
Sittingbourne 25 E55
Six Ashes 39 G33
Six Bells 19 A28
Sixhills Lcn. 52 D47
Six Hills Lei. 41 C42
Six Mile Bottom 33 C51
Sixmile Cottages 15 C57
Sixpenny Handley 9 C35
Sizewell 35 B60
Skaill Ork. 89 G31
Skaill Ork. 89 F28
Skares 67 B21
Skarfskerry 89 K28
Skateraw 76 C33
Skaw 89 F41
Skeabost 82 E10
Skeeby 62 F37
Skeffling 53 A49
Skeffington 42 E43
Skegby 51 F41
Skegness 53 F51
Skelbo 87 J23
Skelbrooke 51 A41
Skeldon Mills 67 B19
Skelfhill 69 C30
Skellingthorpe 52 E45
Skellister 89 G40
Skellow 51 A41
Skelmanthorpe 50 A38
Skelmersdale 48 B30
Skelmorlie 73 D17
Skelpick 87 C23
Skelton Cle. 63 E42
Skelton Cum. 61 C30
Skelton Hum. 58 G43
Skelton N.Y. 58 D41
Skelton N.Y. 57 C39
Skelton Green 63 E42
Skelwick 89 C30
Skelwith Bridge 60 F29
Skendleby 53 E50
Skenfrith 28 F30
Skerne 59 D46
Skerray 87 B22
Skerton 55 C30
Sketty 17 E22
Skewen 18 B23
Skidby 59 F46
Skigersta 88 A11
Skilgate 7 C25
Skillington 42 C45
Skinburness 60 A27
Skinningrove 63 E43
Skipness 72 E15
Skipsea 59 D47
Skipsea Brough 59 D47
Skipton 56 D35
Skipton-on-Swale 57 B39
Skipwith 58 F42
Skirbeck 43 A49
Skirethorns 56 C35
Skirling 75 G26
Skirpenbeck 58 D43
Skirwith Cum. 61 C32
Skirwith N.Y. 56 B33
Skirza 87 B29
Skullomie 87 B22
Skye (Broadford) Airport 82 G12
Skye of Curr 84 G25
Slack 56 G35
Slackhall 50 D36
Slackhead 85 C30
Slad 20 A34
Slade Dev. 6 A21
Slaggyford 61 A32
Slaidburn 56 D33
Slaithwaite 50 A36
Slaley 62 A35
Slamannan 74 C24
Slapton 32 F45
Slapton Dev. 5 F24

Slapton Nmp. 31 D42
Slaugham 13 B48
Slaughterbridge 4 B17
Slaughterford 20 D34
Slawston 42 F43
Sleaford Ham. 12 A44
Sleaford Lcn. 42 A46
Sleagill 61 E31
Sleap 39 D32
Sleapford 39 D32
Sledmere 59 C45
Sleight 9 E35
Sleights 63 F44
Slepe 9 E35
Slickly 87 B28
Sliddery 66 A15
Sligachan Hotel 82 F10
Sligrachan 73 A17
Slimbridge 20 A33
Slindon Stf. 40 B34
Slindon W.S. 12 D45
Slinfold 12 A47
Slingsby 58 B42
Slip End Bfd. 33 E48
Slip End Bfd. 32 G46
Slipton 32 A45
Slitting Mill 40 D36
Slochd 84 G24
Slochnacraig 81 D27
Slockavullin 72 A14
Slogarie 68 G22
Sloothby 53 E50
Slough 22 C45
Sluggan 84 G24
Slumbay 83 F14
Slyne 55 C30
Smailholm 76 G32
Smaithwaite 60 E29
Smallburgh 45 C59
Smallburn 68 A22
Small Dole 13 C48
Smalley 41 A40
Smallfield 23 G49
Small Heath 40 G37
Smallholm 69 F26
Small Hythe 14 D54
Smallridge 8 D28
Smallwood 49 F34
Smallworth 44 G56
Smarden 14 C54
Smeale 54 C26
Smeeth 15 D56
Smeeton Westerby 41 F42
Smethwick 40 G36
Smirisary 79 C12
Smirton 66 E16
Smisby 41 D39
Smithfield 69 G30
Smith's Green 33 F51
Smithton 84 E23
Smockington 41 F40
Snailbeach 38 E29
Snailwell 33 B52
Snainton 59 A45
Snaith 58 G42
Snape N.Y. 57 A38
Snape Sfk. 35 C59
Snarestone 41 E39
Snargate 14 E55
Snave 15 D56
Snead 38 F29
Sneaton 63 F44
Sneaton Thorpe 63 F45
Snelland 52 D46
Snelston 40 A37
Snetterton 44 F55
Snettisham 44 B52
Snig's End 29 F33
Snitter 71 C36
Snitterby 52 C45
Snitterfield 30 C38
Snodland 24 E53
Snowshill 30 E37
Snydale 57 G39
Soar Dev. 5 G23
Soar Dyf. 17 B22
Soar Pow. 27 E25
Soberton 11 C42
Soberton Heath 11 C42
Softlaw East Mains 76 G33
Soham 33 A51
Soldon Cross 6 D19
Sole Street 24 E52
Solihull 30 A37
Sollas 88 K3
Sollers Hope 29 E32
Sollom 48 A30
Solsgirth 75 A25
Solva 16 B14
Solwaybank 69 F29
Somerby Lcn. 52 B46
Somerby Lei. 42 D43
Somercotes 51 G40
Somerley 12 E44
Somerleyton 45 F60
Somersby 53 E49
Somersham Cbs. 33 A49
Somersham Sfk. 34 D56
Somerton Oxf. 31 F41
Somerton Sfk. 34 C54
Somerton Som. 8 B30
Sompting 12 D47
Sonning 22 D43
Sonning Common 22 C43
Sonning Eye 22 D43
Sookholme 51 F41
Sopley 10 E37
Sopworth 20 C34
Sorbie 64 D20
Sorbietrees 69 E30
Sordale 87 B27
Sorisdale 78 D8
Sorn 67 A21

Sornhill 74 G21
Sortat 87 B28
Sotby 53 E48
Sotterley 45 G60
Soulbury 32 F44
Soulby 61 E33
Souldern 31 E41
Souldrop 32 B45
Sound *Che.* 39 A32
Sound *She.* 89 H40
Sourhope 70 B34
Sourin 89 D30
Sourton 6 F21
Soutergate 54 A28
South Acre 44 D54
Southall 22 C47
South Allington 5 G23
South Alloa 74 A24
Southam *Glo.* 29 F35
Southam *War.* 31 B40
South Ambersham 12 B45
Southampton 11 C40
Southampton Airport 11 C40
South Anston 51 D41
South Barrow 8 B31
South Benfleet 24 C54
South Bersted 12 D45
South Boisdale 88 R3
Southborough 23 G51
Southbourne *Dor.* 10 E37
Southbourne *W.S.* 11 D43
South Brent 5 D22
South Brewham 9 A33
South Broomhill 71 D38
Southburgh 44 E56
Southburn 59 D45
South Cadbury 9 B32
South Camphill 73 E18
South Carlton 52 E45
South Carrine 66 C12
South Cave 59 F45
South Cerney 20 B36
South Chard 8 D29
South Charlton 71 B37
South Cheriton 9 B32
South Church 62 D38
South Cliffe 58 F44
South Clifton 52 E44
South Cockerington 53 D49
South Common 13 C49
South Cornelly 18 C24
South Cove 45 G60
South Creake 44 B54
South Crosland 50 A37
South Croxton 41 D42
South Dalton 59 E45
South Darenth 23 E51
Southdean 70 C32
South Dell 88 A10
Southease 13 D50
South Elkington 53 D48
South Elmsall 51 A40
Southend 66 B12
Southend Airport 24 C54
Southend-on-Sea 24 C54
Southerndown 18 D24
Southerness 65 C25
South Erradale 82 B13
Southery 44 F52
South Fawley 21 C39
South Feorline 66 A14
South Ferriby 59 G45
Southfleet 24 D52
South Galson 88 B10
South Garrochty 72 E16
Southgate *Dyf.* 26 A21
Southgate *G.L.* 23 B48
Southgate *Nfk.* 45 C57
Southgate *W.G.* 17 F21
South Godstone 23 G49
South Gorley 10 C37
South Green 24 B52
South-haa 89 D39
South Hall 72 C16
South Hanningfield 24 B53
South Harting 11 C43
South Hayling 11 E43
South Hazelrigg 77 G36
South Heath 22 A45
South Heighton 13 D50
South Hetton 62 B39
South Hiendley 51 A39
South Hill 4 C19
South Hinksey 21 A41
South Hole 6 C18
South Holmwood 22 G47
South Hornchurch 23 C51
South Hourat 73 E18
South Huish 5 F22
South Hykeham 52 F45
South Hylton 62 A39
Southill 32 D47
Southington 21 G41
South Kelsey 52 C46
South Killingholme 52 A47
South Kilvington 57 A40
South Kilworth 41 G42
South Kirkby 51 A40
South Kirkton 85 J33
South Kiscadale 66 A16
South Kyme 42 A47
South Lancing 12 D47
Southleigh *Dev.* 8 E28
South Leigh *Oxf.* 21 A39
South Leverton 51 D43
South Limmerhaugh 68 A22
South Littleton 30 D36
South Lopham 44 G56
South Luffenham 42 E45
South Marston 20 C37
South Merstham 23 F48
South Middleton 70 A35
South Milford 57 F40

South Milton 5 F22
South Mimms 23 A48
Southminster 25 A55
South Molton 7 C23
South Moreton 21 C41
South Mundham 12 D44
South Muskham 51 G43
South Newbald 59 F45
South Newington 31 E40
South Newton 10 A36
South Normanton 51 G40
South Nutfield 23 G49
South Ockendon 23 C51
Southoe 32 B47
Southolt 35 B57
South Ormsby 53 E49
Southorpe 42 E46
South Otterington 57 A39
South Owersby 52 C46
Southowram 57 G37
South Oxhey 22 B47
South Perrott 8 D30
South Petherton 8 C30
South Petherwin 6 G19
South Pickenham 44 E54
South Pool 5 F23
Southport *Mer.* 48 A29
South Port *Str.* 79 H16
South Ra;uceby 42 A46
South Raynham 44 C54
Southrepps 45 B58
South Reston 53 D50
Southrey 52 F47
Southrop 20 A37
Southrope 21 G42
South Runcton 44 E52
South Scarle 52 F44
Southsea 11 E42
South Shawbost 88 C8
South Shields 71 G39
South Shore 54 F28
South Skirlaugh 59 F47
South Somercotes 53 C50
South Stainley 57 C39
South Stoke *Avon* 20 E33
South Stoke *Oxf.* 21 C42
South Stoke *W.S.* 12 C46
South Tarbrax 75 E26
South Tawton 6 F22
South Thoresby 53 E50
South Thundergay 72 F14
South Tidworth 21 G38
South Town *Ham.* 11 A42
Southtown *Nfk.* 45 E61
Southtown *Ork.* 89 H30
Southwaite *Cum.* 61 B30
Southwaite *Cum.* 61 F33
Southwaite Services 61 B30
South Walsham 45 D59
South Warnborough 22 G43
Southwater 12 B47
Southway 4 D20
South Weald 23 B51
Southwell *Dor.* 9 G32
Southwell *Not.* 51 G43
South Weston 22 B43
South Wheatley 51 D43
Southwick *Ham.* 11 D42
Southwick *Nmp.* 42 F46
Southwick *T.&W.* 62 A39
Southwick *Wts.* 20 F34
South Wigston 41 F41
South Willingham 52 D47
South Wingate 62 C40
South Wingfield 51 G39
South Witham 42 D45
Southwold 35 A61
South Wonston 11 A40
South Woodham Ferrers 24 B54
South Wootton 44 C52
South Wraxall 20 E34
South Zeal 6 F22
Soutra Mains 76 E30
Soval Lodge 88 E9
Sowerby *N.Y.* 57 A40
Sowerby *W.Y.* 57 G36
Sowerby Bridge 57 G36
Sowerby Row 60 C29
Sowton 7 F25
Spacey Houses 57 D39
Spadeadam 70 F31
Spalding 43 C48
Spaldington 58 F43
Spaldwick 32 A47
Spalford 52 F44
Spanby 42 B46
Sparham 44 D56
Spark Bridge 55 A29
Sparkford 9 B32
Sparkhill 40 G36
Sparkwell 5 E21
Sparrowpit 50 D36
Sparrow's Green 13 A52
Sparsholt *Ham.* 11 A40
Sparsholt *Oxf.* 21 C39
Spartylea 61 B34
Spaunton 58 A43
Spaxton 8 A28
Spean Bridge 79 B18
Spearywell 10 B39
Speen *Bkh.* 22 A44
Speen *Brk.* 21 E40
Speeton 59 B47
Speke 48 D30
Speldhurst 23 G51
Spellbrook 33 G50
Spelsbury 30 F39
Spencers Wood 22 E43
Spennithorne 57 A37
Spennymoor 62 C38
Spetchley 29 C34
Spetisbury 9 D35
Spey Bay 84 C29
Spey Bridge 80 A23

Spiggie 89 L39
Spilsby 53 F50
Spindlestone 77 G37
Spinningdale 84 A22
Spion Kop 72 D14
Spital 87 C27
Spitalburn 81 B32
Spitalhaugh 75 F27
Spital in the Street 52 C45
Spittal *D.& G.* 64 C19
Spittal *D.& G.* 67 G20
Spittal *Dyf.* 16 B15
Spittal *Hum.* 58 D43
Spittal *Ltn.* 76 C30
Spittal *Nor.* 77 E36
Spittalfield 81 F27
Spittal of Glenmuick 81 B29
Spittal of Glenshee 81 C27
Spixworth 45 D58
Spofforth 57 D39
Spondon 41 B40
Spooner Row 44 F56
Sporle 44 D54
Sportsman's Arms 47 G25
Spott 76 C32
Spottiswood 76 F32
Spratton 31 A43
Spreakley 22 G44
Spreyton 7 F22
Spridlington 52 D46
Springburn 74 D22
Springfield *D.& G.* 69 G29
Springfield *Esx.* 24 A53
Springfield *Fife* 81 J29
Springfield *Grm.* 84 D26
Springholm 68 G24
Springside 73 G19
Springthorpe 52 D44
Springwell 62 A38
Sproatley 59 F47
Sproston Green 49 F33
Sprotbrough 51 B41
Sproughton 35 D57
Sprouston 76 G33
Sprowston 45 D58
Sproxton *Lei.* 42 C44
Sproxton *N.Y.* 58 A42
Spurstow 48 G31
Sronlairig Lodge 83 J21
Stableford 40 B34
Stackpole 16 E15
Stacksteads 56 G34
Staddiscombe 5 E21
Stadhampton 21 B42
Staffield 61 B31
Staffin 82 C10
Stafford 40 C35
Stafford Park 39 E33
Stagebank 76 E30
Stagsden 32 D45
Stagshaw Bank 70 G35
Stainburn *Cum.* 60 D26
Stainburn *N.Y.* 57 E38
Stainby 42 C45
Staincross 51 A39
Staindrop 62 D37
Staines 22 D46
Stainfield 52 E47
Stainforth *N.Y.* 56 C34
Stainforth *S.Y.* 51 A42
Staining 55 F29
Stainland 50 A36
Stainsacre 63 F45
Stainton *Cle.* 62 E40
Stainton *Cum.* 55 A31
Stainton *Cum.* 61 D30
Stainton *Drm.* 62 E36
Stainton *N.Y.* 62 G37
Stainton *S.Y.* 51 C41
Stainton by Langworth 52 E46
Staintondale 63 G45
Stainton le Vale 52 C47
Stair *Cum.* 60 D28
Stair *Str.* 67 A20
Staithes 63 E43
Stakeford 71 E38
Stake Pool 55 E30
Stalbridge 9 C33
Stalham 45 C59
Stalham Green 45 C59
Stalisfield Green 14 B55
Stallingborough 53 A48
Stalling Busk 56 A35
Stalmine 55 E29
Stalybridge 49 C35
Stambourne 34 E53
Stamford *Lcn.* 42 E46
Stamford *Nor.* 71 B38
Stamford Bridge 58 D43
Stamfordham 71 F36
Stanborough 33 G48
Stanbridge 32 F45
Stanbrook 29 D34
Stanbury 57 F36
Stand 74 D22
Standburn 75 C25
Standeford 40 E35
Standford 12 A44
Standish *Glo.* 20 A33
Standish *G.M.* 48 B31
Standlake 21 A39
Standon *Ham.* 11 B40
Standon *Hfs.* 33 F49
Standon *Stf.* 40 B34
Standwell Green 35 A57
Stane 74 E23
Stanecastle 73 G19
Stanfield 44 C55
Stanford *Bkh.* 32 D47
Stanford *Kent* 15 D57
Stanford Bishop 29 C32
Stanford Bridge 29 B33
Stanford Dingley 21 D41

Stanford in the Vale 21 B39
Stanford le Hope 24 C52
Stanford on Avon 31 A41
Stanford on Soar 41 C41
Stanford on Teme 29 B33
Stanford Rivers 23 A51
Stanghow 63 E42
Stanground 43 F48
Stanhoe 44 B54
Stanhope *Bor.* 69 A27
Stanhope *Drm.* 62 C35
Stanion 42 G45
Stanley *Dby.* 41 A40
Stanley *Drm.* 62 A37
Stanley *Stf.* 49 G35
Stanley *Tay.* 81 G27
Stanley *W.Y.* 57 G39
Stanley Common 41 A40
Stanley Hill 29 D32
Stanlow 48 E30
Stanmer 13 D49
Stanmore *Brk.* 21 D40
Stanmore *G.L.* 22 B47
Stannersburn 70 E33
Stannington *Nor.* 71 F38
Stannington *S.Y.* 51 D39
Stansbatch 28 B29
Stansfield 34 C53
Stanshope 40 A37
Stanstead 34 C54
Stanstead Abbots 33 G49
Stanstead Street 34 D54
Stansted 24 E52
Stansted Airport 33 F51
Stansted Mountfitchet 33 F51
Stanton *Glo.* 30 E36
Stanton *Sfk.* 34 A55
Stanton *Stf.* 40 A37
Stanton by Bridge 41 C39
Stanton by Dale 41 B40
Stanton Drew 19 E31
Stanton Fitzwarren 20 B37
Stanton Harcourt 21 A40
Stanton Hill 51 F40
Stanton-in-Peak 50 F38
Stanton Lacy 28 A30
Stanton Long 38 F31
Stanton on the Wolds 41 B42
Stanton Prior 19 E32
Stanton St. Bernard 20 E36
Stanton St. John 21 A41
Stanton St. Quintin 20 C35
Stanton Street 34 B55
Stanton under Bardon 41 D40
Stanton upon Hine Heath 38 C31
Stanwardine in the Fields 38 C30
Stanway *Esx.* 34 F55
Stanway *Glo.* 30 E36
Stanwell 22 D46
Stanwick 32 A45
Stanwix 40 A29
Stape 63 G43
Stapeley 39 A32
Stapenhill 40 C38
Staple 15 B58
Staple Cross 14 E53
Staplefield 13 B48
Staple Fitzpaine 8 C28
Stapleford *Cbs.* 33 C50
Stapleford *Dby.* 41 B40
Stapleford *Hfs.* 33 G49
Stapleford *Lcn.* 52 G44
Stapleford *Wts.* 10 A36
Stapleford Abbotts 23 B51
Staplegrove 8 B28
Staplehurst 14 C53
Stapleton *H.&W.* 28 B29
Stapleton *Lei.* 41 F40
Stapleton *N.Y.* 62 E38
Stapleton *Shr.* 38 E30
Stapleton *Som.* 8 B30
Staplow 29 D32
Star *Dyf.* 17 A18
Star *Str.* 74 G24
Starbeck 57 D39
Starbotton 56 B35
Starcross 7 C25
Starkholmes 51 G39
Starling's Green 33 E50
Starston 45 G58
Startforth 62 E36
Startley 20 C35
Statham 49 D32
Stathern 42 B43
Station Town 62 C40
Staughton Green 32 B47
Staughton Highway 32 B47
Staunton *Glo.* 28 G31
Staunton *Glo.* 29 F33
Staunton in the Vale 42 A44
Staunton on Arrow 28 B29
Staunton on Wye 28 D29
Staveley *Cum.* 55 A29
Staveley *Cum.* 61 G30
Staveley *Dby.* 51 E40
Staveley *N.Y.* 57 C39
Staverton *Dev.* 5 D23
Staverton *Glo.* 29 F34
Staverton *Nmp.* 31 B41
Staverton *Wts.* 20 E34
Staverton Bridge 29 F34
Stawell 8 A29
Stawley 7 C26
Staxigoe 87 C29
Staxton 59 B46
Staylittle *Dyf.* 37 F22
Staylittle *Pow.* 37 F24
Staynall 55 E29
Staythorpe 51 G43
Stebbing 33 F52
Stechford 40 G37
Stedham 12 B44
Steel 61 A35
Steele Road 70 D31

Steen's Bridge 28 C31
Steep 11 B43
Steeple *Dor.* 9 F35
Steeple *Esx.* 25 A55
Steeple Ashton 20 F35
Steeple Aston 31 F40
Steeple Barton 31 F40
Steeple Bumpstead 33 D52
Steeple Claydon 31 F42
Steeple Gidding 42 G47
Steeple Langford 10 A36
Steeple Morden 33 D48
Steeton 57 E36
Stein 82 D8
Stella 71 G37
Stelling Minnis 15 C57
Stenalees 4 E16
Stenhousemuir 74 B24
Stenness 89 E38
Stenscholl 82 C10
Stenson 41 B39
Stenton 76 C32
Stepaside *Dyf.* 16 D17
Steppingley 32 E46
Stepps 74 D22
Sternfield 35 B59
Stert 20 F36
Stetchworth 33 C52
Stevenage 33 F48
Stevenston 73 F18
Steventon *Ham.* 21 G41
Steventon *Oxf.* 21 B40
Stevington 32 C45
Stewartby 32 D46
Stewarton *Str.* 66 C12
Stewarton *Str.* 74 F20
Stewkley 32 F44
Stewponey 40 G34
Steyning 12 C47
Steynton 16 D15
Stibb 6 D18
Stibbard 44 C55
Stibb Cross 6 D20
Stibb Green 21 E38
Stibbington 42 F46
Stichill 76 G33
Stickford 53 F49
Sticker 3 C15
Stickford 53 F49
Sticklepath 6 F22
Stickney 53 G49
Stiffkey 44 A55
Stifford 23 C51
Stile Bridge 14 C53
Stilligarry 88 O3
Stillingfleet 58 E41
Stillington *Cle.* 62 D39
Stillington *N.Y.* 58 C41
Stilton 42 G47
Stinchcombe 20 B33
Stinsford 9 E33
Stirchley 39 E33
Stirling 74 A24
Stisted 34 F54
Stithians 2 E13
Stivichall 30 A39
Stixwould 52 F47
Stoak 48 E30
Stobo 75 G27
Stobs Camp 70 C31
Stoborough 9 F35
Stobs Camp 70 C31
Stock 24 B52
Stockbridge 10 A39
Stockbury 24 E54
Stockcross 21 E40
Stockerston 42 F44
Stockholm 69 D26
Stockiemuir 74 B20
Stockingford 41 F39
Stocking Pelham 33 F50
Stockland 8 D28
Stockland Bristol 19 G28
Stockleigh English 7 E24
Stockleigh Pomeroy 7 E24
Stocklinch 8 C29
Stockport 49 C35
Stocksbridge 50 C38
Stocksfield 71 G36
Stockton *H.&W.* 28 B31
Stockton *Nfk.* 45 F59
Stockton *Shr.* 39 F33
Stockton *War.* 31 B40
Stockton Cross 28 B31
Stockton Heath 49 D32
Stockton on Tees 62 E40
Stockton on Teme 29 B33
Stockton on the Forest 58 D42
Stockwood 8 D31
Stodmarsh 25 E58
Stody 44 B56
Stoer 86 F16
Stoford *Som.* 8 C31
Stoford *Wts.* 10 A36
Stogumber 7 B26
Stogursey 19 G28
Stoke *Dev.* 6 C18
Stoke *Ham.* 21 F40
Stoke *Ham.* 11 D43
Stoke *Kent* 24 D54
Stoke *W.M.* 30 A39
Stoke Abbott 8 D30
Stoke Albany 42 G44
Stoke Ash 35 A57
Stoke Bardolph 41 A42
Stoke Bliss 29 B32
Stoke Bruerne 31 C43
Stoke-by-Clare 34 D53
Stoke-by-Nayland 34 E55
Stoke Canon 7 F25
Stoke Charity 11 A40
Stoke Climsland 4 C19
Stoke D'Abernon 22 F47
Stoke Doyle 42 G46
Stoke Dry 42 F44
Stoke Edith 29 D32

Stoke Ferry 44 E53
Stoke Fleming 5 F24
Stoke Gabriel 5 E24
Stoke Gifford 19 C32
Stoke Golding 41 F39
Stoke Goldington 32 D44
Stokeham 51 E43
Stoke Hammond 32 F44
Stoke Holy Cross 45 E58
Stokeinteignhead 5 C25
Stoke Lacy 29 D32
Stoke Lyne 31 F41
Stoke Mandeville 32 G44
Stokenchurch 22 B43
Stokenham 5 F24
Stoke on Trent 40 A34
Stoke Orchard 29 F35
Stoke Poges 22 C45
Stoke Prior *H.& W.* 29 B35
Stoke Prior *H.& W.* 28 C31
Stoke Rivers 6 B22
Stoke Rochford 42 C45
Stoke Row 21 C42
Stoke St. Gregory 8 B29
Stoke St. Mary 8 B28
Stoke St. Michael 19 G32
Stoke St. Milborough 38 G31
Stokesay 38 G30
Stokesby 45 D60
Stokesley 63 F41
Stoke sub Hamdon 8 C30
Stoke Talmage 21 B42
Stoke Trister 9 B33
Stoke upon Tern 39 C32
Stoke Wake 9 D33
Stondon Massey 23 A51
Stone *Bkh.* 31 G43
Stone *Glo.* 19 B32
Stone *H.& W.* 29 A34
Stone *Kent* 14 E55
Stone *Kent* 23 D51
Stone *Stf.* 40 B35
Stone Allerton 19 F30
Ston Easton 19 F32
Stonebridge 40 G38
Stonebroom 51 G40
Stone Cross *E.S.* 13 D52
Stone Cross *Kent* 15 D56
Stone Cross *Kent* 13 A51
Stonecrouch 14 D53
Stoneferry 59 F47
Stonefield Castle 72 C14
Stonegarthside 69 F30
Stonegate 13 B52
Stonegrave 58 B42
Stonehaugh 70 F33
Stonehaven 81 B34
Stone House *Cum.* 56 A33
Stonehouse *D.& G.* 68 G24
Stonehouse *Glo.* 20 A34
Stonehouse *Str.* 74 F23
Stoneleigh 30 A39
Stonesby 42 C44
Stonesfield 30 G39
Stone's Green 35 F57
Stone Street 45 G59
Stonestreet Green 15 D56
Stonethwaite 60 E28
Stoneybridge 88 O3
Stoneyburn 75 D25
Stoney Cross 10 C38
Stoneykirk 64 C16
Stoney Middleton 50 E38
Stoney Stanton 41 F40
Stoney Stoke 9 A33
Stoney Stratton 9 A32
Stoney Stretton 38 E29
Stoneywood *Cen.* 74 B23
Stoneywood *Grm.* 85 H34
Stonham Aspal 35 C57
Stonnall 40 E36
Stonor 22 C43
Stonton Wyville 42 F43
Stonybreck 89 C37
Stony Cross 29 D33
Stony Stratford 31 D43
Stoodleigh 7 D25
Stopham 12 C46
Stopsley 32 F47
Storeton 48 D29
Storey Arms 27 F25
Storiths 57 D36
Stornoway 88 D10
Stornoway Airport 88 D10
Storrington 12 C46
Storth 55 A30
Storwood 58 E43
Stotfold 33 E48
Stottesdon 39 G32
Stoughton *Lei.* 41 E42
Stoughton *Sry.* 22 F45
Stoughton *W.S.* 12 C44
Stoul 79 A13
Stoulton 29 D35
Stourbridge 40 G34
Stourpaine 9 D34
Stourport 29 A33
Stour Provost 9 B33
Stour Row 9 B34
Stourton *Stf.* 40 G34
Stourton *War.* 30 E38
Stourton *Wts.* 9 A33
Stourton *W.Y.* 57 F39
Stourton Caundle 9 C33
Stoven 45 G60
Stow *Bor.* 76 F30
Stow *Lcn.* 52 D44
Stow Bardolph 44 E52
Stow Bedon 44 F55
Stowbridge 44 E52
Stow cum Quy 33 B51
Stowe *Shr.* 28 A29
Stowe *Stf.* 40 C36

Stowey 19 F31
Stowford Dev. 7 G27
Stowford Dev. 6 G20
Stowlangtoft 34 B55
Stow Longa 32 A47
Stow Maries 24 A54
Stowmarket 34 C56
Stow-on-the-Wold 30 F37
Stowting 15 C57
Stowupland 34 B56
Straad 72 D16
Strachan 81 A32
Strachur 79 K16
Stradbroke 35 A58
Stradishall 34 C53
Stradsett 44 E52
Stragglethorpe 52 G45
Strahanna 68 D22
Straid Str. 67 D17
Straith 68 E24
Straiton Ltn. 75 D28
Straiton Str. 67 C19
Straloch 80 D26
Stramshall 40 B36
Strands 60 F27
Stranfasket 67 E21
Strang 54 F26
Stranraer 66 G16
Strata Florida 27 B23
Stratfield Mortimer 21 E42
Stratfield Saye 21 E42
Stratfield Turgis 21 E42
Stratford St. Andrew 35 B59
Stratford St. Mary 34 A56
Stratford sub Castle 10 A37
Stratford Tony 10 B36
Stratford-upon-Avon 30 C37
Strath 87 C28
Strathan Hgh. 79 A15
Strathan Hgh. 86 F16
Strathaven 74 F22
Strathblane 74 C21
Strathbran Lodge 83 C18
Strathcarron 83 E15
Strathcoil 79 G12
Strathdon 84 H29
Strathkanaird 86 H17
Strathkinness 81 J30
Strathmiglo 81 J28
Strathmore Lodge 87 D27
Strathpeffer 83 D20
Strathrannoch 83 B19
Strathvaich Lodge 83 B19
Strathy 87 B24
Strathyre 80 J21
Stratton Cnw. 6 E18
Stratton Dor. 9 E32
Stratton Glo. 20 A36
Stratton Audley 31 F42
Stratton St. Margaret 20 C37
Stratton St. Michael 45 F58
Stratton Strawless 45 C58
Streat 13 C49
Streatley Bfd. 32 F46
Streatley Brk. 21 C41
Street 8 A30
Street Dinas 38 B29
Street End Kent 15 B57
Street End W.S. 12 E44
Streethay 40 D37
Street Houses 58 E41
Streetly 40 F36
Street on the Fosse 9 A32
Strefford 38 D30
Strelley 41 A41
Strensall 58 C42
Strensall Camp 58 D42
Strensham Services 29 D35
Strete 5 F24
Stretford 49 C34
Stretford Court 28 C30
Strethall 33 D50
Stretham 33 A51
Stretton Che. 48 G30
Stretton Che. 49 D32
Stretton Dby. 51 F39
Stretton Lei. 42 D45
Stretton Stf. 40 C38
Stretton Stf. 40 D34
Stretton Grandison 29 D32
Stretton-on-Dunsmore 31 A40
Stretton on Fosse 30 E38
Stretton Sugwas 28 D30
Stretton under Fosse 41 G40
Strichen 85 D35
Stringston 7 A27
Strixton 32 B45
Stroan 67 F19
Stroanfreggan 79 C16
Stroat 19 B31
Strollamus 82 G12
Stromeferry 83 F14
Stromness 89 F28
Stronachlachar 80 J19
Stronachullin Lodge 72 C14
Stronchullin 73 B17
Strond 88 J6
Strone Hgh. 79 B17
Strone Hgh. 83 G21
Strone Str. 73 A18
Strone Str. 73 B17
Stronechrubie 86 G18
Stronenaba 79 B18
Strongchreggan 79 C16
Stronmilchan 79 H17
Stronphadruig Lo. 80 C23
Stronsay Airport 89 E32
Strontian 79 D14
Strood 24 D53
Strood Green 12 B46
Stroud Glo. 20 A34
Stroud Ham. 11 B43

Stroud Green 20 A34
Stroxton 42 B45
Strubby 53 D50
Strumore 88 L5
Strumpshaw 45 E59
Struy 83 E19
Stuartfield 85 E35
Stubbington 11 D41
Stubbins 49 A33
Stublick 70 G34
Stubton 42 A44
Stuckbeg 73 A18
Stuckton 10 C37
Studdon 61 A34
Studfold Cum. 61 G33
Studfold N.Y. 56 B34
Studham 32 G46
Studland 10 F36
Studley War. 30 B36
Studley Wts. 20 D35
Studley Roger 57 B38
Stump Cross Esx. 33 D51
Stump Cross N.Y. 57 C36
Stuntney 33 A51
Stunts Green 13 C52
Sturmer 34 D53
Sturminster Marshall 9 D35
Sturminster Newton 9 C33
Sturry 25 E57
Sturton Hum. 52 B45
Sturton Lcn. 52 D44
Sturton le Steeple 51 D43
Stuston 35 A57
Stutton N.Y. 57 E40
Stutton Sfk. 35 E57
Styal 49 D34
Styrrup 51 C42
Suckley 29 C33
Sudborough 42 G45
Sudbourne 35 C60
Sudbrook Gwe. 19 C31
Sudbrook Lcn. 42 A45
Sudbrooke Lcn. 52 E46
Sudbury Dby. 40 B37
Sudbury G.L. 22 C47
Sudbury Sfk. 34 D54
Suffield Nfk. 45 B58
Suffield N.Y. 63 G45
Sugnall 39 B33
Suie 67 E19
Sulby 54 D26
Sulgrave 31 D41
Sulham 21 D42
Sulhamstead 21 E42
Sullington 12 C47
Sullom 89 E39
Sullom Voe (Oil Terminal) 89 E39
Sully 8 E27
Sumburgh 89 L40
Sumburgh Airport 89 L40
Summer Bridge 57 C38
Summercourt 3 C14
Summerfield 29 A34
Summerford Keynes 20 B36
Summerhouse 62 E38
Summerseat 49 A33
Summertown 21 A41
Summit 49 A35
Sunadale 72 F14
Sunbury 22 E46
Sundaywell 68 E24
Sunderland Bor. 76 G30
Sunderland Cum. 60 C27
Sunderland T.& W. 62 A39
Sunderland Bridge 62 C38
Sundhope 69 A29
Sundon 32 F46
Sundon Park 32 F46
Sundridge 23 F50
Sunk Island 53 A48
Sunlaws 70 A33
Sunningdale 22 E45
Sunninghill 22 E45
Sunningwell 21 A40
Sunniside 62 C37
Sunny Bank 60 G28
Sunnylaw 74 A23
Surbiton 22 E47
Surfleet 43 C48
Surfleet Seas End 43 C48
Surlingham 45 E59
Sustead 45 B57
Susworth 52 B44
Sutcombe 6 D19
Sutterby 53 E49
Sutterton 43 B48
Sutton Bfd. 33 D48
Sutton Cbs. 42 F46
Sutton Cbs. 33 A50
Sutton Che. 48 E31
Sutton Dyf. 16 C15
Sutton G.L. 23 E48
Sutton Kent 15 C59
Sutton Nfk. 45 D57
Sutton Not. 51 D42
Sutton Not. 42 B43
Sutton N.Y. 57 E36
Sutton Sfk. 35 D59
Sutton Shr. 39 B32
Sutton Shr. 38 D31
Sutton Stf. 39 C33
Sutton S.Y. 51 A41
Sutton W.S. 12 C45
Sutton-at-Hone 23 D51
Sutton Bassett 42 F43
Sutton Benger 20 D35
Sutton Bonington 41 C41
Sutton Bridge 43 C50
Sutton Cheney 41 E40
Sutton Coldfield 40 F37
Sutton Courtenay 21 B41
Sutton Hill 39 E33
Sutton Howgrave 57 B39
Sutton in Ashfield 51 G41

Sutton Lane Ends 49 E35
Sutton Leach 48 C31
Sutton le Marsh 53 D51
Sutton Maddock 39 E33
Sutton Mallet 8 A29
Sutton Mandeville 9 B35
Sutton Montis 9 B32
Sutton-on-Hull 59 F47
Sutton on Sea 53 D51
Sutton on the Forest 58 C41
Sutton on the Hill 40 B38
Sutton on Trent 51 F43
Sutton St. Edmund 43 D49
Sutton St. James 43 D49
Sutton St. Nicholas 28 D31
Sutton Scotney 11 A40
Sutton under Brailes 30 E39
Sutton-under-Whitestonecliffe 57 A40
Sutton upon Derwent 58 E43
Sutton Valence 14 C54
Sutton Veny 20 G34
Sutton Waldron 9 C34
Swaby 53 E49
Swadlincote 40 C38
Swaffham 44 E54
Swaffham Bulbeck 33 B51
Swaffham Prior 33 B51
Swafield 45 B58
Swainby 62 F40
Swainshill 28 D30
Swainsthorpe 45 E58
Swainswick 20 E33
Swalcliffe 30 E39
Swalecliffe 25 E57
Swallow 52 B47
Swallow Beck 52 F45
Swallowcliffe 9 B35
Swallowfield 22 E43
Swallownest 51 D40
Swalwell 71 G38
Swanage 10 G36
Swanbourne 32 F44
Swanbridge 18 E27
Swanland 59 G45
Swanley 23 E51
Swanley Village 23 E51
Swanmore 11 C41
Swannington Lei. 41 D40
Swannington Nfk. 45 D57
Swanscombe 24 D52
Swansea 17 E22
Swansea Airport 17 E21
Swan Street 34 B53
Swanton Abbot 45 C58
Swanton Morley 44 D56
Swanton Novers 44 B56
Swanwick Dby. 51 G40
Swanwick Ham. 11 D41
Swarby 42 A46
Swardeston 45 E58
Swarkestone 41 C39
Swarland 71 C37
Swarland Estate 71 C37
Swarraton 11 A41
Swaton 42 B47
Swavesey 33 B49
Sway 10 E38
Swayfield 42 C45
Swaythling 11 C40
Swaythorpe 59 C46
Sweetshouse 4 D16
Sweffling 35 B59
Swepstone 41 D39
Swerford 30 E39
Swettenham 49 F34
Swffryd 19 B28
Swilland 35 C57
Swillbrook 55 F30
Swillington 57 F39
Swimbridge 6 B22
Swinden 56 D34
Swinderby 52 F44
Swindon Glo. 29 F35
Swindon Nor. 70 D35
Swindon Stf. 40 F34
Swindon Wts. 20 C37
Swine 59 F47
Swinefleet 58 G43
Swineshead Bfd. 32 B46
Swineshead Lcn. 43 A48
Swineshead Bridge 43 A48
Swiney 87 E28
Swinford Lei. 31 A41
Swingfield 15 C58
Swingfield Minnis 15 C58
Swinhoe 71 A38
Swinhope 53 C48
Swinithwaite 57 A36
Swinnie 70 B32
Swinstead 42 C46
Swinton Bor. 77 F34
Swinton G.M. 49 B33
Swinton N.Y. 57 B38
Swinton N.Y. 58 B43
Swinton S.Y. 51 C40
Swintonmill 77 F34
Swithland 41 D41
Swordale Hgh. 83 C21
Swordale W.I. 88 D10
Swordland 79 A13
Swordly 87 B23
Sworton Heath 49 D32
Swyddffynnon 27 B22
Swynnerton 40 B34
Swyre 8 F31
Sychdyn 48 F28
Sychnant 27 A25
Sydenham 22 A43
Sydenham Damerel 4 C20
Syderstone 44 B54
Sydling St. Nicholas 9 E32
Sydmonton 21 F40

Syerston 42 A43
Sykehouse 51 A42
Sykes 56 D32
Symbister 89 F41
Symington Str. 73 G19
Symington Str. 75 G25
Symonds Yat 28 G31
Symondsbury 8 E30
Synton 69 A30
Syre 87 D22
Syresham 31 D42
Syston Lcn. 42 A45
Syston Lei. 41 D42
Sywell 32 B44

T

Tackley 31 F40
Tacolneston 45 F57
Tadcaster 57 E40
Taddington 50 E37
Tadley 21 E42
Tadlow 33 D48
Tadmarton 30 E39
Tadworth 23 F48
Tafarnaubach 28 G27
Tafarn-y-Gelyn 47 F27
Taff's Well 18 C27
Tafolwern 37 E24
Tai'r Bull 27 F25
Tairlaw 67 D19
Tai'r-ysgol 17 E22
Takeley 33 F51
Takeley Street 33 F51
Talachddu 27 E26
Talacre 47 D27
Talardd 37 C24
Talaton 7 F26
Talbenny 16 C14
Talbot Green 18 C26
Talerddig 37 E25
Talgarreg 26 C20
Talgarth Gwy. 37 F22
Talgarth Pow. 28 E27
Taliesin 37 F22
Talisker 82 F9
Talke 49 G34
Talkin 61 A31
Talladale 83 B15
Talla Linnfoots 69 A27
Tallarn Green 38 A30
Tallentire 60 C27
Talley 17 A22
Tallington 42 E46
Talmine 86 B21
Talnotry 67 F20
Talog 17 B19
Talsarn 26 C21
Talsarnau 37 B22
Talskiddy 3 B15
Talwrn 47 E26
Talybont Dyf. 37 G22
Tal-y-bont Gwy. 36 C21
Tal-y-bont Gwy. 47 F23
Tal-y-bont Gwy. 46 E22
Talybont Pow. 28 F27
Tal-y-cafn 47 E23
Tal-y-llyn 37 E23
Talysarn 46 E22
Tamerton Foliot 4 D20
Tamworth 40 E38
Tandridge 23 F49
Tanfield 62 A37
Tanfield Lea 62 A37
Tangley 21 F39
Tangmere 12 D45
Tan Hill 61 F34
Tankersley 51 C39
Tan-lan 37 A22
Tannach 87 D29
Tannachie 81 B33
Tannadice 81 E30
Tannington 35 B58
Tansley 51 G39
Tansor 42 F46
Tantobie 62 A37
Tanton 62 E40
Tanworth 30 A37
Tan-y-bwlch 37 A22
Tan-y-graig 36 B19
Tangyrisiau 37 A22
Tan-y-groes 26 D18
Tan-y-Pistyll 37 C26
Taplow 22 C45
Tarbert Str. 72 E12
Tarbert Str. 72 B12
Tarbert Str. 72 D14
Tarbert W.I. 88 H7
Tarbet Hgh. 86 D17
Tarbet Hgh. 79 A13
Tarbet Str. 80 K19
Tarbolton 67 A20
Tarbrax 75 E26
Tardebigge 29 B35
Tardy Gate 55 G31
Tarfside 81 C30
Tarland 85 J30
Tarleton 55 G30
Tarlton 20 B35
Tarnbrook 55 D31
Tarporley 48 F31
Tarrant Gunville 9 C35
Tarrant Hinton 9 C35
Tarrant Keyneston 9 D35
Tarrant Monkton 9 D35
Tarrant Rushton 9 D35
Tarring-Neville 13 D50
Tarrington 29 D32
Tarrnacraig 72 G15
Tarrona 69 E29
Tarr Steps 7 B24

Tarskavaig 82 H11
Tarves 85 F34
Tarvie 83 D20
Tarvin 48 F30
Tasburgh 45 F57
Tasley 39 F33
Tatenhill 40 C38
Tathwell 53 D49
Tatsfield 23 F50
Tattenhall 48 G30
Tatterford 44 C54
Tattersett 44 B54
Tattershall 53 G48
Tattershall Bridge 52 G47
Tattershall Thorpe 53 G48
Tattingstone 35 E57
Tatworth 8 D29
Taunton 8 B28
Taunton Deane Services 7 C27
Taverham 45 D57
Tavernspite 16 C17
Tavistock 4 C20
Taw Green 6 F22
Tawstock 6 B21
Taxal 50 E36
Tayburn 74 F21
Tayinloan 72 F12
Taynish 72 B13
Taynton Glo. 29 F33
Taynton Oxf. 30 G38
Taynuilt 79 G16
Tayport 81 H30
Tayvallich 72 B13
Tealby 52 C47
Team Valley 62 A38
Teangue 82 J12
Tebay 61 F32
Tebay West Services 61 F31
Tebworth 32 F45
Tedburn St. Mary 7 F24
Teddington G.L. 22 D47
Teddington Glo. 29 E35
Tedstone Delamere 29 C32
Tedstone Wafre 29 C32
Teesport 63 D41
Tees-side Airport 62 E39
Teeton 31 A43
Teffont Evias 9 A35
Teffont Magna 9 A35
Tegryn 17 A18
Teigh 42 D44
Teigngrace 5 C24
Teignmouth 5 C25
Teindside 69 C30
Telford 39 E32
Tellisford 20 F34
Telscombe 13 D50
Temon 70 G32
Templand 69 E26
Temple Cnw. 4 C17
Temple Ltn. 75 E29
Temple Balsall 30 A38
Temple Bar 26 C21
Temple Cloud 19 F32
Templecombe 9 B33
Temple Ewell 15 C58
Temple Grafton 30 C37
Temple Guiting 30 F36
Temple Hirst 58 G42
Temple Normanton 51 F40
Temple Sowerby 61 D32
Templeton Dev. 7 D24
Templeton Dyf. 16 C17
Templeton Bridge 7 D24
Templetown Drm. 62 B36
Tempsford 32 C47
Tenbury Wells 28 B31
Tenby 16 D17
Tendring 35 F57
Ten Mile Bank 44 F52
Tenterden 14 D54
Tepper Moor 70 F34
Terally 64 D17
Terling 34 G53
Ternhill 39 B32
Terregles Banks 68 F25
Terrick 22 A44
Terriers 22 B44
Terrington 58 B42
Terrington St. Clement 43 C51
Terrington St. John 43 D51
Teston 14 B53
Testwood 10 C39
Tetbury 20 B34
Tetbury Upton 20 B34
Tetchill 38 B29
Tetcott 6 F19
Tetford 53 E49
Tetney 53 B49
Tetsworth 21 A42
Tettenhall 40 E34
Tettenhall Wood 40 F34
Teversal 51 F40
Teversham 33 C50
Teviothead 69 C30
Tewin 33 G48
Tewkesbury 29 E34
Teynham 25 E55
Thakeham 12 C47
Thame 22 A43
Thames Haven 24 C53
Thamesmead 23 C50
Thaneston 81 C32
Thanington 15 B57
Thankerton 75 G25
Tharston 45 F57
Thatcham 21 E41
Thaxted 33 E52
Theakston 57 A40
Thealby 52 A44
Theale Brk. 21 D42
Theale Som. 19 G30
Thearne 59 F46
Theberton 35 B60

The Broad 28 B30
The Bryn 19 A29
The Bustard 20 G36
The Chart 23 F50
The City 22 B43
The Cleaver 28 F31
The Common 10 A38
The Craig's 86 J20
The Cronk 54 D25
The Den 73 E19
The Downs Glo. 20 A35
The Flatt 70 F31
The Folly 28 B30
The Forstal 14 C54
The Fouralls 39 B32
The Green 54 A27
The Heath Sfk. 35 E57
The Heath Stf. 40 B36
The Hill 54 A27
The Leacon 14 D55
The Lee 22 A45
The Lhen 54 D26
Thelnetham 34 A56
The Lodge 73 A17
Thelwall 49 D32
Themelthorpe 44 C56
The Milton 80 H23
The Moor 14 E53
The Mumbles 17 F22
Thenford 31 D41
The Pound 28 A27
Therfield 33 E49
The Rink 76 G30
The Roe 47 E26
The Sands 22 G44
The Shoe 20 D34
The Stocks 14 E55
Thetford 44 G54
Theydon Bois 23 B50
Thimbleby Lcn. 53 E48
Thimbleby N.Y. 62 F40
Thingwall 48 D28
Thirkleby 57 B40
Thirlby 57 A40
Thirlestane 76 F31
Thirlspot 60 E29
Thirn 57 A38
Thirsk 57 A40
Thirtleby 59 F47
Thistleton Lan. 55 F30
Thistleton Lei. 42 D45
Thistley Green 33 A52
Thixendale 58 C44
Thockrington 70 F35
Tholomas Drove 43 E49
Tholthorpe 57 C40
Thomas Close 61 B30
Thompson 44 F55
Thomshill 84 D28
Thonock 52 C44
Thoralby 56 A35
Thoresway 52 C47
Thorganby Lcn. 53 C48
Thorganby N.Y. 58 E42
Thorgill 63 G43
Thorington Street 34 E56
Thorlby 56 D35
Thorley Hfs. 33 G50
Thorley I.o.W. 10 F39
Thorley Street Ham. 10 F39
Thorley Street Hfs. 33 G50
Thormanby 57 B40
Thornaby on Tees 62 E40
Thornage 44 B56
Thornborough Bkh. 31 E43
Thornborough N.Y. 57 B38
Thornbury Avon 19 B32
Thornbury Dev. 6 E19
Thornbury H.& W. 29 C32
Thornbury W.Y. 57 F38
Thornby 31 A42
Thorncombe 8 D29
Thorndon 35 B57
Thorne 51 A42
Thorner 57 E39
Thorne St. Margaret 7 C26
Thorney Cbs. 43 E48
Thorney Not. 52 E44
Thorney Hill 10 E37
Thorney Toll 43 E49
Thornfalcon 8 B28
Thornford 9 C32
Thorngrafton 70 G33
Thorngrove 8 A29
Thorngumbald 59 G48
Thornham 44 A53
Thornham Magna 35 A57
Thornham Parva 35 A57
Thornhaugh 42 E46
Thornhill Cen. 74 A22
Thornhill Cum. 60 F26
Thornhill Dby. 50 D37
Thornhill D.& G. 68 D24
Thornhill M.G. 18 C27
Thornhill W.Y. 50 A38
Thornholme 59 C47
Thornley Drm. 62 C37
Thornley Drm. 62 C39
Thornley Gate 61 A34
Thornliebank 74 E21
Thorns 34 C53
Thornset 50 D36
Thornthwaite Cum. 60 D29
Thornthwaite N.Y. 57 D37
Thornton Bkh. 31 E43
Thornton Dyf. 16 D15
Thornton Fife 75 A28
Thornton Hum. 58 E43
Thornton Lan. 55 E29
Thornton Lcn. 53 F48
Thornton Lei. 41 E40

Thornton *Mer.* 48 B29
Thornton *W.Y.* 57 F36
Thornton Curtis 52 A46
Thornton Dale 58 A44
Thornton Hough 48 D29
Thornton-in-Craven 56 E35
Thornton in Lonsdale 56 B32
Thornton-le-Beans 62 G39
Thornton-le-Clay 58 C42
Thornton le Moor 52 C46
Thornton-le-Moor 57 A39
Thornton le Moors 48 E30
Thornton le Street 57 A40
Thorntonloch 76 C33
Thorntonpark 77 F35
Thornton Rust 56 A35
Thornton Steward 57 A37
Thornton Watlass 57 A38
Thornwood Common 23 A50
Thoroton 42 A43
Thorp Arch 57 E40
Thorpe *Dby.* 50 G37
Thorpe *Lcn.* 53 D50
Thorpe *Not.* 51 G43
Thorpe *N.Y.* 57 C36
Thorpe *Sry.* 22 E46
Thorpe Abbotts 45 G57
Thorpe Arnold 42 C43
Thorpe Audlin 51 A40
Thorpe Bassett 58 B44
Thorpe Bay 25 C55
Thorpe by Water 42 F44
Thorpe Constantine 40 E38
Thorpe End Garden Village 45 D58
Thorpe Green 34 C55
Thorpe Hesley 51 C39
Thorpe in Balne 51 A41
Thorpe Langton 42 F43
Thorpe le Soken 35 F57
Thorpe le Street 58 E44
Thorpe Malsor 32 A44
Thorpe Mandeville 31 D41
Thorpe Market 45 B58
Thorpeness 35 B60
Thorpe on the Hill 57 G39
Thorpe on the Hill 52 F45
Thorpe St. Andrew 45 E58
Thorpe St. Peter 53 F50
Thorpe Salvin 51 D41
Thorpe Satchville 42 D43
Thorpe Thewles 62 D39
Thorpe Waterville 42 G46
Thorpe Willoughby 58 F41
Thorrington 34 F56
Thorverton 7 E25
Thrandeston 35 A57
Thrapston 32 A45
Threapland 56 C35
Threapwood 38 A30
Three Bridges 13 A48
Three Burrows 2 D13
Three Chimneys 14 D54
Three Cocks 28 E27
Three Crosses 17 E21
Three Gates 29 B32
Three Holes 43 E51
Threekingham 42 B46
Threeleg Cross 13 A52
Three Legged Cross 10 D36
Threemile Cross 22 E43
Threemilestone 2 D13
Three Pots Inn 41 F40
Threepwood 76 F31
Threlkeld 60 D29
Threshfield 56 C35
Thrimby 61 D31
Thringarth 61 D35
Thringstone 41 D40
Thrintoft 62 G39
Thriplow 33 D50
Throckenholt 43 E49
Throcking 33 E49
Throckley 71 G37
Throckmorton 29 D35
Throes 33 F52
Throphill 71 E37
Thropton 71 C36
Throwleigh 6 F22
Thrumpton 41 B41
Thrumster 87 D29
Thrunton 71 B36
Thrupp *Glo.* 20 A34
Thrupp *Oxf.* 31 G40
Thrushelton 6 G20
Thrussington 41 D42
Thruxton *Ham.* 21 G38
Thruxton *H.& W.* 28 E30
Thrybergh 51 C40
Thundersley 24 C53
Thurcaston 41 D41
Thurcroft 51 D40
Thurgarton *Nfk.* 45 B57
Thurgarton *Not.* 41 A42
Thurgoland 50 B38
Thurlaston *Lei.* 41 F41
Thurlaston *War.* 31 A40
Thurlby *Lcn.* 52 F45
Thurlby *Lcn.* 42 D46
Thurleigh 32 C46
Thurlestone 5 F22
Thurloxton 8 A28
Thurlstone 50 B38
Thurlton 45 F60
Thurmaston 41 E42
Thurnby 41 E42
Thurne 45 D60
Thurnham 14 B54
Thurning 42 G46
Thurnscoe 51 B40
Thursby 60 B29
Thursford 44 B55
Thursford Green 44 B55

Thursley 12 A45
Thurso 87 B27
Thurstaston 48 D28
Thurston 34 B55
Thurstonfield 60 A29
Thurstonland 50 A37
Thurton 45 E59
Thuxton 44 E56
Thwaite *N.Y.* 61 G34
Thwaite *Sfk.* 35 B57
Thwaite Head 60 G29
Thwaite St. Mary 45 F59
Thwaites Brow 57 E36
Thwing 59 C46
Tibbermore 80 H26
Tibberton *Glo.* 29 F33
Tibberton *H.& W.* 29 C35
Tibberton *Shr.* 39 C32
Tibbie Shiels Inn 69 A28
Tibenham 45 F57
Tibshelf 51 F40
Tibthorpe 59 D45
Ticehurst 13 A52
Tichborne 11 A41
Tickencote 42 E45
Tickenham 19 D30
Tickhill 51 C41
Ticklerton 38 F30
Ticknall 41 C39
Tickton 59 E46
Tidcombe 21 F38
Tiddington *Oxf.* 21 A42
Tiddington *War.* 30 C38
Tidebrook 13 B52
Tideford 4 D19
Tidenham 19 B31
Tideswell 50 E37
Tidmarsh 21 D42
Tidmington 30 E38
Tidpit 10 C36
Tiers Cross 16 C15
Tiffield 31 C42
Tigerton 81 D31
Tighnabruaich 72 C15
Tilbrook 32 B46
Tilbury 24 D52
Tilehurst 21 D42
Tilford 22 G44
Tillathrowie 85 F30
Tilley 38 C31
Tillicoultry 75 A25
Tillingham 25 A55
Tillington 12 B45
Tillmouth Park 77 F34
Tillybardine 81 C30
Tillyfourie 85 H32
Tilmanstone 15 B59
Tiln 51 D43
Tilney All Saints 43 D51
Tilney High End 43 D51
Tilney St. Lawrence 43 D51
Tilshead 20 G36
Tilstock 38 B31
Tilston 48 G30
Tilstone Fearnall 48 F31
Tilsworth 32 F45
Tilton on the Hill 42 E43
Tiltups End 20 B34
Timberland 52 G47
Timbersbrook 49 F34
Timberscombe 7 A25
Timble 57 D37
Timsbury *Avon* 19 F32
Timsbury *Ham.* 10 B39
Timsgarry 88 D6
Tincleton 9 E33
Tindale 61 A32
Tingewick 31 E42
Tingley 57 G38
Tingrith 32 E46
Tingwall 89 E30
Tinhay 6 G19
Tinnis 69 A29
Tinsley Green 13 A48
Tintagel 4 B16
Tintern Parva 19 A31
Tintinhull 8 C30
Tintwistle 50 C36
Tinwell 42 E46
Tiptoe 10 E38
Tipton 40 F35
Tipton St. John's 7 F26
Tiptree 34 G54
Tirabad 27 D24
Tiree Airport 78 F6
Tiretigan 72 D13
Tirley 29 F34
Tirril 61 D31
Tirymynach 38 D28
Tisbury 9 B35
Tissington 50 G37
Titchberry 6 A21
Titchfield 11 D41
Titchmarsh 42 G46
Titchwell 44 A53
Tithby 41 B42
Titley 28 B29
Titsey 23 F50
Tittensor 40 B34
Tittleshall 44 C54
Tiverton *Che.* 48 F31
Tiverton *Dev.* 7 D25
Tivetshall St. Margaret 45 G57
Tivetshall St. Mary 45 G57
Tividale 40 F35
Tixall 40 C35
Tixover 42 E45
Toab *Ork.* 89 G31
Toab *She.* 89 L39
Tobermory 79 E11
Toberonochy 79 K13
Tobson 88 D7
Tockenham 20 D36
Tockholes 56 G32

Tockington 19 C32
Tockwith 57 D40
Todber 9 B34
Todding 28 A30
Toddington *Bfd.* 32 F46
Toddington *Glo.* 30 E36
Toddington Services 32 F46
Todenham 30 E38
Todhills 69 G29
Todmorden 56 G35
Todwick 51 D40
Toft *Cbs.* 33 C49
Toft *Che.* 49 E33
Toft *Lcn.* 42 D46
Toft *She.* 89 E40
Toft Hill 62 D37
Toft Monks 45 F60
Toft next Newton 52 D46
Toftrees 44 C54
Tofts 87 B29
Toftwood Common 44 D55
Togston 71 C38
Tokavaig 82 H12
Tolsta Chaolais 88 D7
Tolvah 80 A24
Tolworth 22 E47
Tomatin 84 G24
Tombrake 74 A21
Tombreck 84 F22
Tomcrasky 83 H18
Tomdoun 83 J17
Tomess 79 B17
Tomich *Hgh.* 83 E21
Tomich *Hgh.* 84 B23
Tomich *Hgh.* 83 G19
Tomintoul 84 H27
Tomnavoulin 84 G28
Tomsléibhe 79 G12
Tonbridge 23 G52
Tondu 18 C24
Tonfanau 36 E21
Tong *Shr.* 39 E33
Tong *W.I.* 88 D10
Tong *W.Y.* 57 F38
Tonge 41 C40
Tongham 22 G44
Tongland 65 C22
Tong Street 57 G37
Tongue 86 C21
Tongwynlais 18 C27
Tonna 18 B23
Ton Pentre 18 B25
Ton-reg 18 C26
Tonwell 33 G49
Tonypandy 18 B26
Tonyrefail 18 C26
Toot Baldon 21 A41
Toot Hill *Esx.* 23 A51
Toothill *Wts.* 20 C37
Topcliffe 57 B40
Topcroft 45 F58
Topcroft Street 45 F58
Top of Hebers 49 B34
Toppesfield 34 E53
Topsham 7 G25
Torbay 5 D25
Torbeg *Grm.* 81 A29
Torbeg *Str.* 66 A14
Torboll 87 J23
Torbryan 5 D24
Torcross 5 F24
Tore 84 D22
Torhousemuir 64 C19
Torinturk 72 D14
Torksey 52 E44
Torlum 88 M3
Torlundy 79 C17
Tormarton 20 D33
Tormisdale 78 J3
Tormore 72 G14
Tornagrain 84 E23
Tornahaish 84 J28
Tornapress 83 E14
Tornaveen 85 J32
Torness 83 G21
Torosay Castle 79 G13
Torpenhow 60 C28
Torphichen 75 C25
Torphins 85 J32
Torpoint 4 E20
Torquay 5 D25
Torquhan 76 F30
Torrance 74 C22
Torridon 83 D15
Torrin 82 G11
Torrisdale 87 B22
Torrisholme 55 C30
Torroble 86 H21
Torry 85 J35
Torryburn 75 B26
Torteval 3 F16
Torthorwald 69 F26
Tortington 12 D46
Torton 29 A34
Tortworth 20 B33
Torvaig 82 E10
Torver 60 G28
Torwood 74 B24
Torwoodlee 76 G30
Torworth 51 D42
Toscaig 82 F13

Toseland 33 B48
Tosside 56 D33
Tostock 34 B55
Totaig 82 D8
Totarol 88 D7
Totegan 87 B24
Totland 10 F39
Totley 51 D39
Totnes 5 D24
Toton 41 B40
Totscore 82 C9
Tottenhill 44 D52
Totteridge 23 B48
Totternhoe 32 F45
Tottington 49 A33
Totton 10 C39
Touchen-end 22 D44
Toward 73 D17
Toward Quay 73 D17
Towcester 31 D42
Towednack 2 E10
Towersey 22 A43
Towie 85 H30
Towiemore 84 E29
Tow Law 62 C37
Town End *Cbs.* 43 F50
Town End *Cum.* 55 A30
Town Green 48 B30
Town Head 61 F30
Townhead *D.& G.* 69 E26
Townhead *D.& G.* 65 D22
Townhead *Ltn.* 76 D31
Townhead *Str.* 74 G24
Townhead of Greenlaw 68 G23
Townhill 75 B27
Town Of Lowton 49 C32
Townshend 2 E11
Town Street 44 G53
Town Yetholm 70 A34
Towthorpe 58 D42
Towton 57 F40
Towyn 47 E25
Toynton All Saints 53 F49
Toynton St. Peter 53 F50
Trabboch 67 A20
Tradespark 84 D24
Trallong 27 F25
Tranent 76 C30
Tranmere 48 D29
Trantlebeg 87 C24
Trantlemore 87 C24
Trapp 17 C22
Traprain 76 C31
Traquair 75 G29
Travellers' Inn 47 E27
Traveller's Rest 32 G45
Trawden 56 F35
Trawscoed 27 A22
Trawsfynydd 37 B23
Trealaw 18 B26
Treales 55 F30
Trearddur Bay 46 E18
Trebanog 18 B26
Trebanos 18 A23
Trebartha 4 C18
Trebetherick 3 A15
Treborough 7 B26
Trebudannon 3 B14
Trebullett 4 C19
Treburley 4 C19
Treburvaugh 28 B28
Trebyan 4 D16
Trecastle 27 F24
Trecwn 16 A15
Trecynon 18 A25
Tredegar 18 A27
Tredington *Glo.* 29 F35
Tredington *War.* 30 D38
Tredinnick 4 E18
Tredrissi 26 D16
Treen 2 F9
Treeton 51 D40
Trefasser 16 A14
Trefdraeth 46 E20
Trefecca 28 E27
Trefechan 18 A26
Trefeglwys 37 F25
Treffgarne 16 B15
Treffgarne Owen 16 B14
Trefforest 18 C26
Trefilan 26 C21
Treflach 38 C28
Trefonen 38 C28
Trefor 46 D19
Trefriw 37 F22
Tregadillett 4 B18
Tregaian 46 E20
Tregare 28 G28
Tregaron 27 C22
Tregarth 46 F22
Tregeare 4 B18
Tregeiriog 38 B27
Tregele 46 C19
Tregeseal 2 E9
Tregonetha 3 B15
Tregony 3 D15
Tregurrian 3 A14
Tregynon 37 F26
Trehafod 18 B26
Treharris 18 B26
Tre-Herbert *Dyf.* 26 D21
Treherbert *M.G.* 18 B25
Trekenner 4 C19
Trelawnyd 47 E26
Trelech 17 A18
Trelights 3 A15
Trelill 4 C16
Trelleck 19 A31
Trelleck Grange 19 A30
Trelogan 47 D27

Tremadog 36 A21
Tremaine 4 B18
Tremar 4 D18
Trematon 4 D19
Tremeirchion 47 E26
Trenance 3 B14
Trench 38 B29
Trenear 2 E12
Treneglos 4 B18
Trent 8 C31
Trentham 40 A34
Trentishoe 6 A22
Trent Vale 40 A34
Treoes 18 D25
Treorchy 18 B25
Trer-ddôl 37 F22
Trerule Foot 4 E19
Trescott 40 F34
Tresillian 3 D14
Treskinnick Cross 4 A18
Tresmeer 4 B18
Tresparrett 4 A17
Tresparrett Posts 4 A17
Tressait 80 D24
Tresta *She.* 89 G39
Tresta *She.* 89 C42
Treswell 51 E43
Tretio 16 B13
Tretire 28 F31
Tretower 28 F27
Treuddyn 48 G28
Trevalga 4 A16
Trevarrack 2 E10
Trevarrick 3 D15
Trevaughan *Dyf.* 17 C18
Trevaughan *Dyf.* 17 B20
Treveighan 4 B16
Trevellas 2 C13
Trevelmond 4 D18
Trevine 16 A14
Treviscoe 3 C15
Trevone 3 A14
Trevor 36 A19
Tre-walkin 28 E27
Trewarmett 4 B16
Trewellard 2 E9
Trewen 4 B18
Trewern 38 D28
Trewidland 4 D18
Trewithian 3 E14
Trewoofe 2 F10
Trewornan 3 A15
Treyford 12 C44
Triangle 57 G36
Trickett's Cross 10 D36
Trimdon 62 C39
Trimdon Colliery 62 C39
Trimdon Grange 62 C39
Trimingham 45 B58
Trimley St. Martin 35 E58
Trimley St. Mary 35 E58
Trimsaran 17 D20
Trinafour 80 D23
Tring 32 G45
Tring Wharf 32 G45
Trinity *Jer.* 3 F18
Trinity *Tay.* 81 D32
Trislaig 79 C16
Trispen 3 C14
Tritlington 71 D38
Trochry 80 F25
Troed-rhiw-dalar 27 C25
Troedyraur 26 D19
Troed-yr-harn 27 E26
Troedyrhiw 18 A26
Trondavoe 89 E39
Troon *Cnw.* 2 E12
Troon *Str.* 73 G19
Troqueer 68 F25
Troston 34 A54
Trottiscliffe 24 E52
Trotton 12 B44
Troutal 60 G28
Troutbeck *Cum.* 61 F30
Troutbeck *Cum.* 60 D29
Troutbeck Bridge 60 F29
Trowbridge 20 F34
Trowell 41 A40
Trowell Services 41 A40
Trow Green 19 A31
Trows 76 G32
Trowse Newton 45 E58
Trudoxhill 20 G33
Trull 8 B28
Trumpet 29 E32
Trumpington 33 C50
Trunch 45 B58
Truro 3 D14
Trusham 7 G24
Trusley 40 B38
Trusthorpe 53 D51
Trysull 40 F34
Tubney 21 B40
Tuckenhay 5 D24
Tuckingmill 2 D12
Tuddenham *Sfk.* 34 A53
Tuddenham *Sfk.* 35 D57
Tudeley 23 G52
Tudhoe 62 C38
Tudweiliog 36 B18
Tufton *Dyf.* 16 B16
Tufton *Ham.* 21 G40
Tugby 42 E43
Tugford 38 G31
Tughall 71 A38
Tuirnaig 83 A14
Tullibody 74 A24
Tullich *Hgh.* 84 B24
Tullich *Str.* 79 J16
Tullich Muir 84 B23
Tulliemet 80 E25
Tulloch 87 J22
Tullochgorm 72 A15

Tulloch Station 80 B19
Tullynessle 85 H31
Tumble 17 C21
Tumby 53 G48
Tumby Woodside 53 G48
Tummel Bridge 80 E23
Tunbridge Wells, Royal 13 A52
Tundergarth Mains 69 E27
Tunstall *Hum.* 59 F49
Tunstall *Kent* 24 E54
Tunstall *Lan.* 56 B32
Tunstall *N.Y.* 62 G38
Tunstall *Sfk.* 35 C59
Tunstall *Stf.* 49 G34
Tunstall *T.& W.* 62 A39
Tunworth 21 G42
Tupsley 28 D31
Turkdean 30 G37
Tur Langton 42 F43
Turn 49 A34
Turnastone 28 E29
Turnberry 67 C18
Turnditch 40 A38
Turner's Hill 13 A49
Turners Puddle 9 E34
Turnford 23 A49
Turnhouse 75 C27
Turnworth 9 D34
Turriff 85 E33
Turvey 32 C45
Turville 22 B43
Turweston 31 E42
Tushielaw 69 B29
Tushingham cum Grindley 38 A31
Tutbury 40 C38
Tutnall 29 A35
Tutshill 19 B31
Tuttington 45 C58
Tuxford 51 E43
Twatt *Ork.* 89 E28
Twatt *She.* 89 G39
Twechar 74 C23
Tweedhope Foot 69 B26
Tweedmouth 77 E36
Tweedshaws 69 B26
Tweedsmuir 69 A27
Twemlow Green 49 F33
Twenty 42 C47
Twickenham 22 D47
Twigworth 29 F34
Twineham 13 B48
Twitchen 7 B23
Two Bridges 5 C22
Two Dales 50 F38
Two Mills 48 E29
Two Pots 6 A21
Twycross 41 E39
Twyford *Bkh.* 31 F42
Twyford *Brk.* 22 D43
Twyford *Ham.* 11 B40
Twyford *Lei.* 42 D43
Twyford *Nfk.* 44 C56
Twyn-carno 18 A27
Twynholm 65 C22
Twyning 29 E34
Twyning Green 29 E34
Twynllanan 27 F23
Twyn-y-Sheriff 19 A30
Twywell 32 A45
Tyberton 28 E29
Tycroes 17 C22
Tycrwyn 38 D27
Tydd Gote 43 D50
Tydd St. Giles 43 D50
Tydd St. Mary 43 D50
Tye Common 24 B52
Ty-hen 36 B17
Tyldesley 49 B32
Tyler Hill 25 E57
Tylers Green 22 B45
Tylorstown 18 B26
Tylwch 37 G25
Ty-nant *Clw.* 37 A25
Ty-nant *Gwy.* 37 C25
Tyndrum 80 G18
Tynegreen 70 G35
Tynehead 75 E29
Tynemouth 71 G39
Tynewydd *M.G.* 18 B25
Ty-newydd *Pow.* 37 E26
Tyninghame 76 C32
Tynribbie 79 F15
Tynron 68 D24
Tyn-y-Cwm 37 G24
Tyn-y-ffordd 27 A23
Tyn-y-ffridd 38 B27
Tynygongl 46 D21
Tynygraig 27 B22
Ty'n-y-groes 47 E23
Ty'nyswydd 27 B22
Tyringham 32 D44
Tythegston 18 D24
Tytherington *Avon* 19 C32
Tytherington *Che.* 49 E35
Tytherington *Wts.* 20 B35
Tytherleigh *Avon* 8 D29
Tywardreath 4 E16
Tywardreath Highway 4 E16
Tywyn *Gwy.* 36 E21
Tywyn *Gwy.* 47 E23

U

Uachdar 88 M3
Ubbeston Green 35 A59
Ubley 19 F31
Uckerby 62 F38
Uckfield 13 B50
Uckington 29 F35
Uddingston 74 D22
Uddington 74 G24
Udimore 14 F54

Udny Green 85 G34
Udstonhead 74 F23
Uffculme 7 D26
Uffington Lcn. 42 E46
Uffington Oxf. 21 C39
Uffington Shr. 38 D31
Ufford Cbs. 42 E46
Ufford Sfk. 35 C59
Ufton 30 B39
Ufton Nervet 21 E42
Ugadale 66 A13
Ugborough 5 E22
Ugglebarnby 63 F44
Ugley 33 F51
Ugthorpe 63 E43
Uig Hgh. 82 C9
Uig Str. 73 B17
Ulbster 87 D29
Ulceby Hum. 52 A47
Ulceby Lcn. 53 E50
Ulceby Cross 53 E50
Ulceby Skitter 52 A47
Ulcombe 14 C54
Uldale 60 C28
Uley 20 B33
Ulgham 71 D38
Ullapool 86 J17
Ullenhall 30 B37
Ulleskelf 58 E41
Ullesthorpe 41 G41
Ulley 51 D40
Ullingswick 29 D32
Ullinish 82 F9
Ullock 60 D26
Ulpha 60 G27
Ulrome 59 D47
Ulsta 89 D40
Ulverston 54 B28
Ulwell 10 F36
Ulzieside 68 C23
Umberleigh 6 C22
Unapool 86 E18
Uncleby 58 D44
Underbarrow 61 G30
Under Burnmouth 69 E30
Underhills 67 A20
Underwood 51 G40
Undy 19 C30
Union Mills 54 F26
Unst Airport 89 B42
Unstone 51 E39
Unsworth 49 B34
Unthank Cum. 61 C30
Unthank Cum. 61 B32
Unthank D.& G. 69 D29
Unthank End 61 C30
Upavon 20 F37
Up Cerne 9 D32
Upchurch 24 E54
Upcott 6 E21
Up Exe 7 E25
Uphall 75 C26
Uphall Station 75 D26
Upham 11 B41
Up Hatherley 29 F35
Uphill 19 F29
Upholland 48 B31
Uplawmoor 74 E20
Upleadon 29 F33
Upleatham 63 E42
Uploders 8 E31
Uplowman 7 D26
Uplyme 8 E29
Upminster 23 C51
Up Nately 22 F43
Upottery 8 D28
Upper Ardchronie 84 A22
Upper Arley 39 G33
Upper Barr 67 G20
Upper Basildon 21 D41
Upper Bayble 88 D11
Upper Beeding 13 C48
Upper Bentley 29 B35
Upper Boddington 31 C40
Upper Borth 37 G22
Upper Bourne 22 G44
Upper Brailes 30 E39
Upper Broughton 41 C42
Upper Bucklebury 21 E41
Upperby 61 A30
Upper Caldecote 32 D47
Upper Chapel 27 D26
Upper Chute 21 F39
Upper Clatford 21 G39
Upper Clynnog 36 A20
Upper Coll 88 D10
Upper College 38 B31
Upper Craigenbay 67 F21
Upper Cumberworth 50 B38
Upper Dean 32 B46
Upper Denby 50 B38
Upper Denton 70 G32
Upper Dicker 13 C51
Upper Dovercourt 35 E58
Upper Druimfin 79 E11
Upper Elkstone 50 G36
Upper Godney 19 G30
Upper Gravenhurst 32 E47
Upper Green Brk. 21 E39
Upper Green Esx. 33 E50
Upper Hale 22 G44
Upper Halliford 22 E46
Upper Halling 24 E52
Upper Hambleton 42 E45
Upper Helmsley 58 D42
Upper Heyford Nmp. 31 C42
Upper Heyford Oxf. 31 F40
Upper Hill 28 C30
Upper Hopton 50 A37
Upper Hulme 50 F36
Upper Inglesham 21 B38
Upper Killay 17 E21
Upper Kirby 35 F58

Upper Kirton 73 E17
Upper Knockando 84 E27
Upper Lambourn 21 C39
Upper Langwith 51 F41
Upper Leigh 40 B36
Upper Longdon 40 D36
Upper Lybster 87 E28
Upper Lydbrook 29 G32
Uppermill 49 B35
Upper Minety 20 B36
Upper Mitton 29 A34
Upper Moor Side 57 F38
Upper Mumbie 69 E28
Upper Penrhuddlan 37 G26
Upper Poppleton 58 D41
Upper Rochford 29 B32
Upper Rusko 67 G21
Upper Sanday 89 G31
Upper Sapey 29 B32
Upper Scoulag 73 E16
Upper Seagry 20 C35
Upper Shelton 32 D45
Upper Sheringham 45 A57
Upper Skelmorlie 73 D17
Upper Slaughter 30 F37
Upper Somborne 10 A39
Upper Soudley 29 G32
Upper Stondon 32 E47
Upper Stowe 31 C42
Upper Street 45 D59
Upper Strensham 29 E34
Upper Sundon 32 F46
Upper Swell 30 F37
Upper Tasburgh 45 F58
Upper Tean 40 B36
Upperthong 50 B37
Upper Thurnham 55 D30
Upperton 12 B45
Uppertown 89 H30
Upper Tysoe 30 D39
Upper Weedon 31 C42
Upper Winchendon 31 G43
Upper Woodford 10 A37
Upper Wraxall 20 D34
Upper Wyche 29 D33
Uppingham 42 E44
Uppington 39 E32
Upsall 57 A40
Upshire 23 A50
Upstreet 25 E58
Upton Cbs. 32 A47
Upton Che. 48 F30
Upton Cnw. 6 E17
Upton Dev. 5 F22
Upton Dor. 9 E35
Upton Ham. 21 F39
Upton Ham. 10 C39
Upton Lcn. 52 D44
Upton Mer. 48 D28
Upton Nfk. 45 D59
Upton Nmp. 31 B43
Upton Not. 51 G43
Upton Not. 51 E43
Upton Oxf. 21 C41
Upton Som. 7 C25
Upton W.Y. 51 A40
Upton Bishop 29 F32
Upton Cheyney 19 D32
Upton Cressett 39 F32
Upton Cross 4 C18
Upton Grey 22 G43
Upton Hellions 7 E24
Upton Lovell 20 G35
Upton Magna 38 D31
Upton Noble 9 A33
Upton Pyne 7 E25
Upton St. Leonards 29 G34
Upton Scudamore 20 G34
Upton Snodsbury 29 C35
Upton upon Severn 29 D34
Upton Warren 29 B35
Upwaltham 12 C45
Upware 33 A51
Upwell 43 E50
Upwey 9 F32
Upwood 43 G48
Urafirth 89 E39
Urchfont 20 F36
Urgha Beag 88 H7
Urlay Nook 62 E40
Urmston 49 C33
Urquhart 84 C28
Urra 63 F41
Ushaw Moor 62 B38
Usk 19 A29
Usselby 52 C46
Usworth 62 A39
Utley 57 E36
Utterby 53 C49
Uttoxeter 40 B36
Uwchmynydd 36 C17
Uxbridge 22 C46
Uyeasound 89 B41
Uzmaston 16 C15

V

Valley 46 E18
Valleyfield 65 C22
Valley Truckle 4 B16
Valsgarth 89 A42
Valtos 88 D6
Van 37 G25
Vange 24 C53
Varteg Hill 19 A28
Vatten 82 E8
Vaul 78 F6
Vaynor 27 A26
Veensgarth 89 H40
Velindre Dyf. 17 A19
Velindre Dyf. 16 A17

Velindre Pow. 28 E27
Venn 5 F22
Vennington 38 D29
Venn Ottery 7 F26
Ventnor 11 G41
Vernham Dean 21 F39
Vernon Arms Inn 29 B35
Verwig 26 D17
Verwood 10 D36
Veryan 3 E15
Vickerstown 54 C27
Victoria Cnw. 3 B15
Victoria Gwe. 18 A27
Vidlin 89 F40
Viewlaw 71 D37
Viewly Hill 62 C37
Vigo Village 24 E52
Vinehall Street 14 E53
Vine's Cross 13 C51
Virginia Water 22 E46
Virginstow 6 F19
Voe 89 F40
Vowchurch 28 E29
Voy 89 F28

W

Wackerfield 62 D37
Wacton 45 F57
Wadborough 29 D34
Waddesdon 31 G43
Waddingham 52 C45
Waddington Lan. 56 E33
Waddington Lcn. 52 F45
Wadebridge 3 A15
Wadeford 8 C29
Wadenhoe 42 G46
Wadesmill 33 G49
Wadhurst 13 A52
Wadshelf 51 E39
Wadsley Bridge 51 C39
Wadworth 51 C41
Waen Clw. 48 F28
Waen Clw. 47 F27
Waen Shr. 38 C28
Waenoleu 38 C27
Wag 87 F26
Wainfleet All Saints 53 G50
Waingroves 41 A40
Wainhouse Corner 4 A17
Wainstalls 57 G36
Waitby 61 F33
Wakefield 57 G39
Wakerley 42 F45
Wakes Colne 34 F54
Walberswick 35 A60
Walberton 12 D45
Walbottle 71 G37
Walcot Lcn. 52 G47
Walcot Lcn. 42 B46
Walcot Shr. 38 D31
Walcote 41 G41
Walcott Green 45 G57
Walcott 45 B59
Walden Stubbs 51 A41
Walderslade 24 E53
Walderton 11 C43
Waldridge 62 B38
Waldringfield 35 D58
Waldron 13 C51
Wales 51 D40
Walesby Lcn. 52 C47
Walesby Not. 51 E42
Walford H.& W. 28 F31
Walford H.& W. 28 A29
Walford Som. 8 B28
Walford Heath 38 C30
Walgherton 39 A32
Walgrave 32 A44
Walhampton 10 E39
Walkden 49 B33
Walker 71 G38
Walker Barn 49 E35
Walkerburn 75 G29
Walker Fold 56 E32
Walkeringham 51 C43
Walkerith 51 C43
Walkern 33 F48
Walkford 10 E38
Walkhampton 5 D21
Walkington 59 F45
Walk Mill 56 G34
Wall Cnw. 2 E12
Wall Nor. 70 G35
Wall Stf. 40 E36
Wallaceton 68 E24
Wallacetown 67 C18
Wallasey 48 C28
Wall Heath 40 F34
Wallingford 21 C42
Wallington G.L. 23 E48
Wallington Hfs. 33 E48
Walliswood 12 A47
Walls 89 H38
Wallsend 71 G39
Wall under Heywood 38 F31
Wallyford 75 C29
Walmer 15 B59
Walmer Bridge 55 G30
Walmersley 49 A34
Walmley 40 F37
Walpole 35 A59
Walpole Highway 43 D51
Walpole St. Andrew 43 D51
Walpole St. Peter 43 D51
Walsall 40 F36
Walsall Wood 40 E36
Walsden 56 G35
Walsgrave on Sowe 41 G39
Walsham Le Willows 34 A56
Walshaw 49 A33
Walshford 57 D40

Walsoken 43 D50
Walston 75 F26
Walsworth 32 E47
Walterstone 28 F29
Waltham Hum. 53 B48
Waltham Kent 15 C57
Waltham Abbey 23 A49
Waltham Chase 11 C41
Waltham Cross 23 B49
Waltham Forest 23 B49
Waltham on the Wolds 42 C44
Waltham St. Lawrence 22 D44
Walton Bkh. 32 G44
Walton Bkh. 32 E44
Walton Cbs. 42 E47
Walton Cum. 70 G31
Walton Dby. 51 F39
Walton Lei. 41 G41
Walton Pow. 28 B28
Walton Sfk. 35 E58
Walton Som. 8 A30
Walton Stf. 40 B35
Walton W.Y. 51 A39
Walton Cardiff 29 E35
Walton East 16 B16
Walton in Gordano 19 D30
Walton-le-Dale 55 G31
Walton on Thames 22 E47
Walton-on-the-Hill Mer. 48 C29
Walton on the Hill Sry. 23 F48
Walton on the Hill Stf. 40 C35
Walton-on-the-Naze 35 F58
Walton on the Wolds 41 C41
Walton Park 68 F23
Walton Superior 48 D31
Walton upon Trent 40 D38
Walton West 16 C14
Walwen 48 E28
Walwick 70 F35
Walworth 62 E38
Walwyn's Castle 16 C14
Wambrook 8 D28
Wamphraygate 69 D27
Wampool 60 B28
Wanborough Sry. 22 G45
Wanborough Wts. 21 C38
Wandel 68 A25
Wandon 71 A36
Wandsworth 23 E48
Wangford Hum. 59 D46
Wangford 35 A60
Wanlip 41 D42
Wanlockhead 68 B24
Wannock 13 D50
Wansford Hum. 59 D46
Wansford Nmp. 42 F46
Wanstead 23 B49
Wanstrow 20 G33
Wantage 21 C40
Wapley 19 D32
Wappenbury 30 B39
Wappenham 31 D42
Warblebank 60 B28
Warbleton 13 C52
Warborough 21 B42
Warboys 43 G49
Warbstow 4 A18
Warburton 49 D32
Warcop 61 E33
Warden Kent 25 D56
Warden Nor. 70 G35
Wardgate 40 A38
Wardington 31 D40
Wardle Che. 49 G32
Wardle G.M. 49 A35
Wardley 42 E44
Wardlow 50 E37
Wardlow Mire 50 E37
Ware 33 G49
Wareham 9 F35
Warehorne 14 D55
Warenford 71 A37
Waren Mill 77 G37
Warenton 71 A37
Wareside 33 G49
Waresley Cbs. 33 C48
Waresley H.& W. 29 A34
Warfield 22 D44
Wargate 43 B48
Wargrave 22 D43
Warham 44 A55
Wark Nor. 77 G34
Wark Nor. 70 F34
Warkleigh 6 C22
Warkton 42 G44
Warkworth 71 C38
Warlaby 62 G39
Warleggan 4 D17
Warley 40 G36
Warlingham 23 F49
Warmanbie 69 G27
Warmfield 57 G39
Warmingham 49 F33
Warmington Nmp. 42 F46
Warmington War. 31 D40
Warminster 20 G34
Warminster Common 20 G34
Warmley 19 D32
Warmsworth 51 B41
Warmwell 9 F33
Warndon 29 C34
Warnford 11 B42
Warnham 12 A47
Warren Che. 49 E34
Warren Dyf. 16 E15
Warren House Inn 6 G22
Warren Street 14 B55
Warreners House 71 E37
Warrington Bkh. 32 C44
Warrington Che. 48 D31
Warsash 11 D40
Warslow 50 G36
Warsop 51 F41
Warsop Vale 51 F41

Warter 58 D44
Warthill 58 D42
Wartling 13 D52
Wartnaby 42 C43
Warton Lan. 55 G30
Warton Lan. 55 B31
Warton Nor. 71 C36
Warton War. 40 E38
Warwick War. 30 B38
Warwick Bridge 61 A30
Wasbister 89 D30
Wasdale Head 60 F27
Washaway 4 D16
Washbourne 5 E23
Wash Common 21 E40
Washfield 7 D25
Washfold 62 F36
Washford 7 A26
Washford Pyne 7 D24
Washingborough 52 E46
Washington T.& W. 62 A39
Washington W.S. 12 C47
Washington Birtley Services 62 A38
Washmere Green 34 D55
Washwood Heath 40 G37
Waskerley 62 B36
Wasperton 30 C38
Wass 58 B41
Watcarrick 69 D28
Watchet 7 A26
Watchfield 21 B38
Watchgate 61 G31
Watendlath 60 E28
Waterbeach 33 B50
Waterbeck 69 F28
Watercombe 9 F33
Waterden 44 B54
Water End 32 G46
Waterfall 50 G36
Waterfoot Cum. 61 D30
Waterfoot Str. 74 E21
Waterford Hfs. 33 G49
Water Fulford 58 E42
Waterhead Cum. 60 F29
Waterhead Str. 74 G22
Waterheads 75 E28
Waterhouses Drm. 62 B37
Waterhouses Stf. 40 A36
Wateringbury 23 F52
Wateringhouse 89 H29
Waterlane 20 A35
Waterloo H.& W. 29 E35
Waterloo Mer. 48 C29
Waterloo Nfk. 45 D58
Waterloo Str. 74 E24
Waterloo Tay. 80 G26
Waterloo Cross 7 D26
Waterlooville 11 D42
Water Lumb 56 G34
Watermeetings 68 B25
Watermillock 61 D30
Water Newton 42 F47
Water Orton 40 F37
Waterperry 21 A42
Waterrow 7 C26
Watersfield 12 C46
Waterside Bkh. 22 A45
Waterside Cum. 60 B28
Waterside D.& G. 69 F27
Waterside Str. 74 C22
Waterside Str. 67 C20
Waterside Str. 74 F20
Waterstock 21 A42
Waterston 16 D15
Water Stratford 31 E42
Waters Upton 39 D32
Water Yeat 54 A28
Watford Hfs. 22 B46
Watford Nmp. 31 B42
Watford Gap Nmp. 31 B41
Watford Gap Stf. 40 E37
Watford Gap Services 31 B42
Wath N.Y. 57 C37
Wath N.Y. 57 B39
Wath Brow 60 E26
Watherston 76 F30
Wath upon Dearne 51 B40
Watlington Nfk. 44 D52
Watlington Oxf. 21 B42
Watnall Chaworth 41 A41
Watten 87 C28
Wattisfield 34 A56
Wattisham 34 C56
Wattlesborough 38 D29
Watton Hum. 59 E46
Watton Nfk. 44 E55
Watton-at-Stone 33 G49
Wattston 75 C23
Wattstown 18 B26
Waunarlwydd 17 E22
Waunfawr 46 G21
Waunlwyd 18 A27
Wavendon 32 E45
Waverbridge 60 B28
Waverton Che. 48 F30
Waverton Cum. 60 B28
Wawne 59 F46
Waxham 45 C60
Waxholme 59 G49
Wayfield 24 E53
Warningcamp 12 D46
Warninglid 13 B48
Wayford 8 D30
Wayoh Fold 49 A33
Waytown 8 E30
Way Village 7 D24
Wealdstone 22 C47
Weare 19 F30
Weare Giffard 6 C20
Wearhead 61 C34
Wearne 8 B30
Weasenham All Saints 44 C54
Weasenham St. Peter 44 C54
Weathercote 56 B33

Weaverham 49 E32
Weaverthorpe 59 B45
Wedderlie 76 E32
Weddington 41 F39
Wedhampton 20 F36
Wedmore 19 G30
Wednesbury 40 F35
Wednesfield 40 E35
Weedon 32 G44
Weedon Bec 31 C42
Weedon Lois 31 D42
Weeford 40 E37
Week 7 D23
Weekley 42 G44
Week St. Mary 4 A18
Weel 59 F46
Weeley 35 F57
Weeley Heath 35 F57
Weem 80 E24
Weens House 70 B31
Weeping Cross 40 C35
Weeting 44 G53
Weeton Lan. 55 F29
Weeton W.Y. 57 E38
Weisdale 89 H39
Welborne 44 D56
Welbourn 52 G45
Welburn 58 C43
Welbury 62 F39
Welby 42 B45
Welches Dam 43 G50
Welcombe 6 D18
Weldon 42 F45
Weldon Bridge 71 D37
Welford Brk. 21 D40
Welford Nmp. 41 G42
Welford-on-Avon 30 C37
Welham 42 F43
Welhamgreen 23 A48
Well 57 A38
Welland 29 E33
Welldale 69 G27
Well End 22 C44
Wellesbourne 30 C38
Well Hill 23 E51
Welling 23 D50
Wellingborough 32 B44
Wellingham 44 C54
Wellingore 52 G45
Wellington Cum. 60 F26
Wellington H.& W. 28 D30
Wellington Shr. 39 D32
Wellington Som. 7 C27
Wellington Heath 29 D33
Wellington Marsh 28 D31
Wellow Avon 20 F33
Wellow I.o.W. 10 F39
Wellow Not. 51 F42
Wells 19 G31
Wells-next-the-Sea 44 A55
Wells of Ythan 85 F32
Wellwood 75 B26
Welney 43 F51
Welshampton 38 B30
Welsh Bicknor 28 G31
Welsh Hook 16 B15
Welsh Harp 38 E28
Welsh Newton 28 G30
Welshpool 38 E28
Welsh St. Donat's 18 D26
Welson 28 C28
Welton Cum. 60 B29
Welton Hum. 59 G45
Welton Lcn. 52 E46
Welton Nmp. 31 B41
Welton Nor. 71 G36
Welton le Marsh 53 F50
Welton le Wold 53 D48
Welwick 59 G49
Welwyn 33 G48
Welwyn Garden City 33 G48
Wem 38 C31
Wembdon 8 A28
Wembury 5 F21
Wembworthy 6 E22
Wemyss Bay 73 D17
Wenallt 37 C24
Wendens Ambo 33 E51
Wendlebury 31 G41
Wendling 44 D55
Wendover 22 A44
Wendron 2 E12
Wendy 33 D49
Wenhaston 35 A60
Wennington Cbs. 33 A48
Wennington Esx. 23 C51
Wennington Lan. 56 C32
Wensley Dby. 50 F38
Wensley N.Y. 57 A36
Wentbridge 51 A40
Wentnor 38 F29
Wentworth Cbs. 33 A50
Wentworth S.Y. 51 C39
Wenvoe 18 D27
Weobley 28 C30
Weobley Marsh 28 C30
Wereham 44 E52
Wern Pow. 28 G27
Wern Sal. 38 B28
Werneth-Low 49 C35
Wern-gron 37 C22
Werrington Dev. 6 G19
Werrington Nmp. 42 E47
Werrington Stf. 40 A35
Wervin 48 E30
Wescott Barton 31 F40
Wessington 51 G39
West Aberthaw 18 E26
West Acre 44 D53
West Adderbury 31 E40
West Allerdean 77 F35
West Alvington 5 F23
West Anstey 7 C24
West Ashby 53 E48

West Ashling 12 D44
West Ashton 20 F34
West Ayton 59 A45
West Bagborough 7 B27
West Barkwith 52 D47
West Barnby 63 E44
West Barns 76 C32
West Barsham 44 B55
West Bay 8 E30
West Beckham 45 B57
West Belsay 71 F36
Westbere 25 E57
West Bergholt 34 F55
West Bexington 8 F31
West Bilney 44 D53
West Blatchington 13 D48
Westborough 42 A44
Westbourne Sfk. 35 D57
Westbourne W.S. 11 D43
West Bradenham 44 E55
West Bradford 56 E33
West Bradley 8 A31
West Bretton 50 A38
West Bridgford 41 B42
West Bromwich 40 F36
Westbrook 28 D28
West Buckland Dev. 6 B22
West Buckland Som. 7 C27
West Burrafirth 89 G38
West Burton N.Y. 57 A36
West Burton W.S. 12 C46
Westbury Bkh. 31 E42
Westbury Sal. 38 E29
Westbury Wts. 20 F34
Westbury Leigh 20 F34
Westbury-on-Severn 29 G33
Westbury on Trym 19 D31
Westbury-sub-Mendip 19 G30
West Butsfield 62 B37
West Butterwick 52 B44
Westby 55 F29
West Byfleet 22 E46
West Calder 75 D26
West Camel 8 B31
West Carbeth 74 C21
West Cauldcoats 74 F22
West Challow 21 C39
West Charleton 5 F23
West Chelborough 8 D31
West Chevington 71 D38
West Chiltington 12 C46
West Chisenbury 20 F37
West Clandon 22 F46
Westcliff Esx. 24 C54
Westcliff I.o.W. 11 G41
West Cliffe 15 C59
West Clyth 87 E28
West Coker 8 C31
Westcombe 9 A32
Westcote 30 F38
Westcott Bkh. 31 G43
Westcott Dev. 7 E26
Westcott Sry. 22 G47
West Cottingwith 58 E42
West Cowick 58 G42
West Cranmore 19 G32
West Cross 17 F22
West Culvennan 67 G18
West Curthwaite 60 B29
Westdean 13 E51
West Dean W.S. 12 C44
West Dean Wts. 10 B38
West Deeping 42 E47
West Derby 48 C30
West Dereham 44 E52
West Ditchburn 71 A37
West Down 6 A21
Westdowns 4 B16
West Drayton G.L. 22 D46
West Drayton Not. 51 E43
West Edington 71 E37
West Ella 59 G46
West End Avon 19 E30
West End Gwy. 36 B19
West End Ham. 11 C40
West End Hum. 59 F45
West End Hum. 59 C46
West End Sry. 22 E45
West End Str. 75 F25
Wester Causewayend 75 D26
Westerdale Hgh. 87 C27
Westerdale N.Y. 63 F42
Westerfield 35 D57
Westergate 12 D45
Westerham 23 F50
Westerham Hill 23 F50
Wester Happrew 75 F27
Westerhope 71 G38
Westerleigh 19 D32
Western Bank 60 B28
Wester Parkgate 69 E26
Wester Pencaitland 76 D30
Wester Teaninich 84 C22
Westerton 62 C38
Westertown 75 E25
West Fallodon 71 A37
West Farleigh 14 B53
West Felton 38 C29
Westfield Cum. 60 D25
Westfield E.S. 14 F54
Westfield Hgh. 87 B26
Westfield Ltn. 75 D25
Westfield Moor 14 F54
West Firle 13 E51
Westgate Drm. 61 C35
Westgate Hum. 51 B43
Westgate Nfk. 44 A55
Westgate-on-Sea 25 D59
West Gerinish 88 N3
West Grafton 21 E38
West Grimstead 10 B38

West Grinstead 12 B47
West Haddlesey 58 G41
West Haddon 31 A42
West Hagbourne 21 C41
West Hagley 40 G35
West Hall 70 G31
West Hallam 41 A40
West Halton 59 G45
Westham Dor. 9 G32
Westham E.S. 13 D52
West Hanney 21 B40
West Hanningfield 24 A53
West Hardwick 51 A40
West Harptree 19 F31
West Harton 71 G39
West Hatch 8 B28
Westhay 19 G30
Westhead 48 B30
West Heath G.L. 23 D50
West Heath Ham. 22 F44
West Heath W.M. 30 A36
West Helmsdale 87 G26
West Hendred 21 C40
West Heslerton 59 B45
Westhide 28 D31
West Hill Avon 19 D30
West Hill Dev. 7 F26
Westhill Gra. 85 J34
West Hoathly 13 A49
West Holme 9 F34
Westhope 28 C30
West Horndon 24 C52
Westhorpe Lcn. 43 B48
Westhorpe Sfk. 34 B56
West Horrington 19 G31
West Horsley 22 F46
West Horton 77 G36
West Hougham 15 C58
Westhoughton 49 B32
Westhouse 56 B32
West Howe 10 E36
West Humble 22 F47
West Huntspill 19 G29
West Hyde 22 B46
West Ilsley 21 C40
West Itchenor 11 D43
West Keal 53 F49
West Kennett 20 E37
West Kilbride 73 F18
West Kingsdown 23 E51
West Kington 20 D34
West Kirby 48 D28
West Knighton 9 F33
West Knoyle 9 A34
West Kyloe 77 G36
West Langdon 15 C59
West Langwell 87 H22
West Lavington W.S. 12 B44
West Lavington Wts. 20 F36
West Layton 62 F37
West Leake 41 C41
West Learmouth 77 G34
West Lees 62 F40
Westleigh Dev. 6 C20
Westleigh Dev. 7 D26
Westleigh G.M. 49 B32
Westleton 35 B60
West Lexham 44 D54
Westley 34 B54
Westley Waterless 33 C52
West Lilling 58 C42
Westling 89 B41
Westlington 31 G43
West Linton 75 E27
Westlinton 69 G29
West Littleton 20 D33
West Longridge 77 F35
West Looe 4 E18
West Lulworth 9 F34
West Lutton 59 C45
West Lydford 8 A31
West Lyng 8 B29
West Lynn 44 C52
West Mains 77 F36
West Malling 23 F52
West Malvern 29 D33
West Marden 11 C43
Westmarsh 25 E58
West Marton 56 D34
West Meon 11 B42
West Meon Hut 11 B42
West Mersea 34 G56
Westmeston 13 C49
Westmill 33 F49
West Milton 8 E30
West Minster 25 D55
West Monkton 8 B28
West Moors 10 D36
West Morden 9 E35
Westmuir 81 E29
Westness 89 E29
Westnewton Cum. 60 B27
West Newton Hum. 59 F47
West Newton Nfk. 44 C52
Westnewton Nor. 70 A35
Weston Avon 20 E33
Weston Brk. 21 D40
Weston Che. 48 D31
Weston Che. 49 G33
Weston Dor. 9 G32
Weston Hfs. 33 E48
Weston Lcn. 43 C48
Weston Nmp. 31 D41
Weston Not. 51 F43
Weston N.Y. 57 E37
Weston Shr. 39 F32
Weston Shr. 28 A29
Weston Shr. 38 C31
Westonbirt 20 C34
Weston by Welland 42 F43
Weston Colville 33 C52
Weston Coyney 40 A35
Weston Favell 32 B44

Weston Heath 39 D33
Westoning 32 E46
Weston in Gordano 19 D30
Weston Jones 39 C33
Weston Longville 45 D57
Weston-on-Avon 30 C37
Weston on the Green 31 G41
Weston Patrick 21 G42
Weston Rhyn 38 B28
Weston Subedge 30 D37
Weston-super-Mare 19 E28
Weston Turville 32 G44
Weston under Lizard 40 D34
Weston under Penyard 29 F32
Weston under Wetherley 30 B39
Weston Underwood Bkh. 32 C44
Weston Underwood Dby. 40 A38
Weston upon Trent Stf. 41 C40
Weston upon Trent Stf. 40 C35
Westonzoyland 8 A29
West Orchard 9 C34
West Overton 20 E37
Westow 58 C43
West Parley 10 E36
West Peckham 23 F52
West Pelton 62 A38
West Pennard 8 A31
West Pentire 2 B13
West Perry 32 B47
Westport Str. 66 A12
West Putford 6 D19
West Quantoxhead 7 A27
Westquarter 75 C25
West Rainton 62 B39
West Rasen 52 D46
Westray Airport 89 B30
West Raynham 44 C54
West Retford 51 D42
Westrigg 75 D25
West Rounton 62 F40
West Row 33 A52
West Rudham 44 C54
West Runton 45 A57
Westruther 76 F32
Westry 43 F49
West Saltoun 76 D30
West Sandwick 89 D40
West Scrafton 57 A36
West Somerton 45 C60
West Stafford 9 F33
West Stockwith 51 C43
West Stoke 12 D44
West Stonesdale 61 F34
West Stour 9 B33
West Stourmouth 25 E58
West Stow 34 A54
West Tanfield 57 B38
West Taphouse 4 D17
West Tarbert 72 D14
West Thirston 71 D37
West Thorney 11 D43
West Thurrock 23 D51
West Tilbury 24 D52
West Tisted 11 B42
West Tofts Nfk. 44 F54
West Tofts Tay. 81 G27
West Torrington 52 D47
West Town Avon 19 E30
West Town Ham. 11 E43
West Town H.& W. 28 B30
West Tytherley 10 A38
West Walton 43 D50
West Walton Highway 43 D50
Westward Ho 6 C20
Westwell Kent 14 C55
Westwell Oxf. 21 A38
Westwell Leacon 14 C55
West Wellow 10 C38
West Wemyss 75 A29
Westwick 33 B50
West Wickham Cbs. 33 D52
West Wickham G.L. 23 E49
West Williamston 16 D16
West Winch 44 D52
West Wittering 11 E43
West Witton 57 A36
Westwood 20 F34
West Woodburn 70 E34
West Woodhay 21 E39
Westwoodside 51 C43
West Worldham 11 A43
West Worlington 7 D23
West Wratting 33 C52
West Wycombe 22 B44
West Yell 89 D40
Wetheral 61 A30
Wetherby 57 E40
Wetherden 34 B56
Wetheringsett 35 B57
Wethersfield 34 E53
Wethersta 89 F39
Wetherup Street 35 B57
Wetley Rocks 40 A35
Wettenhall 49 F32
Wetton 50 G37
Wetwang 59 D45
Wetwood 39 B33
Wexcombe 21 F38
Weybourne 45 A57
Weybread 45 G58
Weybridge 22 E46
Weycroft 8 D29
Weydale 87 B27
Weyhill 21 F39
Weymouth 9 G33
Whaddon Bkh. 32 E44
Whaddon Cbs. 33 D49
Whaddon Glo. 29 G34
Whaddon Wts. 10 B37
Whaddon Gap 33 D49
Whaley Bridge 50 D36
Whaley Thorns 51 E41
Whalley 56 F33

Whalley Range 49 C34
Whalsay Airport 89 F41
Whalton 71 E37
Whaness 89 G28
Whaplode 43 C49
Whaplode Drove 43 D49
Whaplode St. Catherine 43 C49
Wharfe 56 C33
Wharles 51 F30
Wharmley 70 G34
Wharncliffe Side 50 C38
Wharram le Street 58 C44
Wharton Che. 49 F32
Wharton H.& W. 28 C31
Whashton 62 F37
Whasset 53 A31
Whatcote 30 D39
Whateley 40 F38
Whatfield 34 D56
Whatley 20 G33
Whatlington 14 F53
Whatstandwell 51 G39
Whatton 43 B43
Whauphill 64 D19
Whaw 62 F35
Wheatacre 45 F60
Wheatenhurst 20 A33
Wheathampstead 32 G47
Wheatley 21 A41
Wheatley Hill 62 C39
Wheatley Lane 56 F34
Wheaton Aston 40 D34
Wheddon Cross 7 B25
Wheel 6 A21
Wheelerstreet 22 G45
Wheelock 49 G33
Wheelton 56 G32
Wheen 81 C29
Wheldrake 58 E42
Whelford 20 B37
Whelpo 60 C29
Whelpside 75 D27
Whenby 58 C42
Whepstead 34 C54
Wherstead 35 D57
Wherwell 21 G39
Wheston 50 E37
Whetley Cross 8 D30
Whetsted 23 G52
Whetstone 41 F41
Whicham 54 A27
Whichford 30 E39
Whiddon Down 6 F22
Whigstreet 81 F30
Whilton 31 B42
Whim 75 E28
Whimble 7 F26
Whimpwell Green 45 C59
Whinburgh 44 E56
Whin Lane End 55 E29
Whinnyfold 85 F31
Whinnyhill D.& G. 68 G25
Whinny Hill Not. 51 F41
Whippingham 11 E41
Whipsnade 32 G46
Whipton 7 F25
Whisby 52 F45
Whisgills 89 N3
Whissendine 42 D44
Whissonsett 44 C55
Whistley Green 22 D43
Whiston Mer. 48 C30
Whiston Nmp. 32 B44
Whiston Stf. 40 D34
Whiston Stf. 40 A36
Whiston S.Y. 51 C40
Whiston Cross 29 E33
Whitbeck 54 A27
Whitbourne 29 C33
Whitbourne Ford 29 C33
Whitburn Ltn. 75 D25
Whitburn T.& W. 71 G40
Whitby Che. 48 E30
Whitby N.Y. 63 E44
Whitbyheath 48 E29
Whitchester 71 G36
Whitchurch Avon 19 E32
Whitchurch Bkh. 32 F44
Whitchurch Dev. 4 C20
Whitchurch Dyf. 16 B14
Whitchurch Ham. 21 G40
Whitchurch H.& W. 28 G31
Whitchurch Oxf. 21 D42
Whitchurch S.G. 18 C27
Whitchurch Shr. 38 A31
Whitchurch Canonicorum 8 E29
Whitcombe 9 F33
Whitcott Keysett 38 G28
Whitebrook 19 A31
Whiteburn 76 F31
Whitecairn 64 C18
Whitecairns 85 H35
Whitecastle 75 F26
Whitecraig 75 D29
Whitecroft 29 F27
Whitecrook 64 C17
Whitecross Cen. 75 C25
Whitecross Cnw. 2 E11
Whitefield 49 B33
Whitegate Che. 49 F32
Whitehall Ork. 89 E32
Whitehaven 60 E25
Whitehill 11 A43
Whitehills 85 G32
Whitehouse Grm. 85 H32
Whitehouse Str. 72 D14
Whitekirk 76 B31
White Lackington 9 E33
Whitelackington 8 C29
White Ladies Aston 29 C35
Whitelaw Bor. 77 E34
Whitelaw Str. 74 F22
Whitelee 70 C33

Whitelees 73 G19
Whiteley Bank 11 F41
Whiteley Green 49 E35
Whiteleys 64 C16
Whiteley Village 22 E46
White Mill 17 B20
Whitemire 84 D25
Whitemore 49 F34
Whiteness 89 H39
White Notley 34 G53
Whiteparish 10 B38
White Pit 53 E49
White Post 14 B54
Whiterashes 85 G34
White Roding 33 G51
Whiteshill 20 A34
Whitesmith 13 C51
Whitestaunton 8 C28
Whitestone Dev. 7 F24
Whitestone Str. 72 G13
White Stone H.& W. 28 D31
Whitestone Str. 72 G13
White Waltham 22 D44
Whiteway 29 G35
Whitewell 56 E32
Whitewreath 84 D28
Whitfield Avon 19 B32
Whitfield Kent 15 C59
Whitfield Nmp. 31 E42
Whitfield Nor. 61 A33
Whitford Clw. 47 E27
Whitford Dev. 8 E28
Whitgift 58 G44
Whitgreave 40 C34
Withorn 64 D20
Whiting Bay 66 A16
Whitington 44 F53
Whitland 17 C18
Whitlaw Bor. 76 F30
Whitlaw Bor. 70 B31
Whitley Brk. 22 D43
Whitley N.Y. 58 G41
Whitley Bay 71 F39
Whitley Bridge 58 G41
Whitley Chapel 61 A35
Whitley Row 23 F51
Whitminster 20 A33
Whitmore 40 A34
Whitnash 30 B39
Whitney 28 D28
Whitrigg Cum. 60 A28
Whitrigg Cum. 60 C28
Whitropefoot 70 D31
Whitsbury 10 C37
Whitsome 77 E34
Whitsomehill 77 F34
Whitson 19 C29
Whitstable 25 E56
Whitstone 4 A18
Whittingham 71 B36
Whittingslow 38 G30
Whittington Dby. 51 E39
Whittington Glo. 30 F36
Whittington H.& W. 29 C34
Whittington Lan. 55 B31
Whittington Shr. 38 B29
Whittington Stf. 40 E37
Whittington Stf. 40 G34
Whittlebury 31 D42
Whittle-le-Woods 55 G31
Whittlesey 43 F48
Whittlesford 33 D50
Whittlieburn 73 D18
Whitton Bor. 70 A33
Whitton Cle. 62 D39
Whitton Hum. 58 G44
Whitton Nor. 71 C36
Whitton Pow. 28 B28
Whitton Sfk. 35 D57
Whitton Shr. 28 A31
Whittonditch 21 D38
Whittonstall 62 A36
Whitway 21 F40
Whitwell Dby. 51 E41
Whitwell Hfs. 32 F47
Whitwell I.o.W. 11 G41
Whitwell Lei. 42 E45
Whitwell N.Y. 62 G38
Whitwell-on-the-Hill 58 C43
Whitwick 41 D40
Whitwood 57 G40
Whitworth 49 A34
Whixall 38 B31
Whixley 57 D40
Whorlton Drm. 62 E37
Whorlton N.Y. 62 F40
Whygate 70 F33
Whyle 28 B31
Wibsey 57 F37
Wibtoft 41 G40
Wichenford 29 B33
Wichling 14 B55
Wick Avon 20 D33
Wick Hgh. 87 C29
Wick H.& W. 29 D35
Wick M.G. 18 D25
Wick W.S. 12 D46
Wick Airport 87 C29
Wicken Cbs. 33 A51
Wicken Nmp. 31 E43
Wicken Bonhunt 33 E51
Wickenby 52 D46
Wickersley 51 C40
Wickford 24 B53
Wickham Brk. 21 D39
Wickham Ham. 11 C41
Wickham Bishops 34 G54
Wickhambreux 15 B58
Wickhambrook 34 C53
Wickhamford 30 D36
Wickham Heath 21 E40
Wickham Market 35 C59
Wickhampton 45 E60
Wickham St. Paul's 34 E54
Wickham Skeith 34 B56

Wickham Street Sfk. 34 C53
Wickham Street Sfk. 34 A56
Wick Hill 22 E44
Wicklewood 44 E56
Wickmere 45 B57
Wick St. Lawrence 19 E29
Wickwar 20 C33
Widcombe 8 C28
Widdington 33 E51
Widdrington 71 D38
Widdrington Station 71 D38
Widecombe in the Moor 5 C23
Widegates 4 E18
Widemouth 6 E17
Wide Open 71 F38
Widford Esx. 24 A52
Widford Hfs. 33 G50
Widmerpool 41 C42
Widnes 48 D31
Widworthy 8 E28
Wield 11 A42
Wigan 48 B31
Wiggaton 7 E26
Wiggenhall St. Germans 43 D51
Wiggenhall St. Mary Magdalen 43 D51
Wiggenhall St. Mary the Virgin 43 D51
Wiggenhall St. Peter 44 D52
Wigginton Hfs. 32 G45
Wigginton N.Y. 58 D41
Wigginton Oxf. 30 E39
Wigginton Stf. 40 E38
Wigglesworth 56 D34
Wiggonby 60 A28
Wiggonholt 12 C46
Wighill 57 E40
Wighton 44 A55
Wigmore H.& W. 28 B30
Wigmore Kent 24 E54
Wigsley 52 E44
Wigsthorpe 42 G46
Wigston 41 F42
Wigtoft 43 B48
Wigton 60 B28
Wigtown 64 C20
Wike 57 E39
Wilbarston 42 G44
Wilberfoss 58 D43
Wilburton 33 A50
Wilby Nmp. 32 B44
Wilby N.Y. 35 A58
Wilcot 20 E37
Wilcott 38 D29
Wildboarclough 49 F35
Wilden 32 C46
Wildmanbridge 74 E24
Wildsworth 52 C44
Wileysike House 70 F32
Wilford 41 B41
Wilkesley 39 A32
Wilkhaven 84 A25
Wilkieston 75 D27
Wilkin's Green 22 A47
Willand 7 D26
Willaston Che. 48 E29
Willaston Che. 49 G32
Willen 32 D44
Willenhall H.& W. 28 E48
Willerby Hum. 59 F46
Willerby N.Y. 59 B46
Willersey 30 E37
Willersley 28 D29
Willesborough 15 C56
Willesborough Lees 15 C56
Willesley 20 C34
Willey Shr. 39 F32
Willey War. 41 G40
Williamscot 31 D40
Willian 33 E48
Willingale Doe 23 A51
Willingcott 6 A20
Willingdon 13 D51
Willingham Cbs. 33 A50
Willingham Lcn. 52 D44
Willington Bfd. 32 D47
Willington Dby. 40 C38
Willington Drm. 62 C37
Willington T.& W. 71 G39
Willington War. 30 E38
Willington Corner 48 F31
Willitoft 58 F43
Williton 7 A26
Willoughby Lcn. 53 E50
Willoughby War. 31 B41
Willoughby on the Wolds 41 C42
Willoughby Waterleys 41 F41
Willoughton 52 C45
Willows Green 34 G53
Wilmcote 30 C37
Wilmington Dev. 8 D28
Wilmington E.S. 13 D51
Wilmington Kent 23 D51
Wilmslow 49 D34
Wilnecote 40 E38
Wilpshire 56 F32
Wilsden 57 F36
Wilsford Lcn. 42 A46
Wilsford Wts. 10 A37
Wilsford Wts. 20 F36
Wilsill 57 C37
Wilsley Green 14 D53
Wilsley Pound 14 D53
Wilsontown 75 E25
Wilstead 32 D46
Wilstone 32 G45
Wilton Bor. 69 B30
Wilton Cle. 63 E41
Wilton Cum. 60 E26
Wilton H.& W. 28 F31
Wilton N.Y. 58 A44
Wilton Wts. 10 A36
Wilton Wts. 21 E38
Wilverley Post 10 D38
Wimbish 33 E51

Wimbish Green

Wimbish Green 33 E52
Wimblebury 40 D36
Wimblington 43 F50
Wimborne Minster 9 D35
Wimborne St. Giles 10 C36
Wimbotsham 44 E52
Wimpstone 30 D38
Wincanton 9 B33
Winceby 53 F49
Winchburgh 75 C26
Winchcombe 30 F36
Winchelsea 14 F55
Winchelsea Beach 14 F55
Winchester 11 A40
Winchet Hill 14 C53
Winchfield 22 F43
Wincle 49 F35
Wincobank 51 C39
Windermere 61 G30
Winderton 30 D39
Windle Hill 48 E29
Windlesham 22 E45
Windley 41 A39
Windmill 50 E37
Windmill Hill *E.S.* 13 C52
Windmill Hill *Som.* 8 C29
Windrush 30 G37
Windsor *Brk.* 22 D45
Windsor *Cum.* 60 F27
Windygates 81 K29
Windy Yet 74 E20
Winestead 59 G48
Winewall 56 F35
Winfarthing 45 G57
Winford 19 E31
Winforton 28 D28
Winfrith Newburgh 9 F34
Wing *Bkh.* 32 F44
Wing *Lei.* 42 E44
Wingate 62 C39
Wingates *G.M.* 49 B32
Wingates *Nor.* 71 D37
Wingerworth 51 F39
Wingfield 53 A58
Wingham 15 B58
Wingmore 15 C57
Wingrave 32 G44
Winkburn 51 G43
Winkfield 22 D45
Winkfield Row 22 D44
Winkfield Street 22 D45
Winkhill 50 G36
Winkleigh 6 E22
Winksley 57 B38
Winkton 10 E37
Winlaton Mill 71 G37
Winmarleigh 55 E30
Winnall 28 E30
Winnersh 22 D43
Winnington 49 E32
Winscombe 19 F30
Winsford *Che.* 49 F32
Winsford *Som.* 7 B25
Winsham 8 D29
Winshill 40 C38
Winsh-wen 17 E22
Winskill 61 C31
Winslade 21 G42
Winsley 20 E34
Winslow 31 F43
Winson 20 A36
Winsor 10 C39
Winster *Cum.* 61 G30
Winster *Dby.* 50 F38
Winston *Drm.* 62 E37
Winston *Sfk.* 35 B57
Winstone 20 A35
Winterborne Clenston 9 D34
Winterborne Herringston 9 F32
Winterborne Houghton 9 D34
Winterborne Kingston 9 E34
Winterborne Monkton 9 F32
Winterborne Stoke 20 D35
Winterborne Strickland 9 D34
Winterborne Whitechurch 9 D34
Winterborne Zelston 9 E34
Winterbourne *Avon* 19 C32
Winterbourne *Brk.* 21 D40
Winterbourne Abbas 9 E32
Winterbourne Bassett 20 D36
Winterbourne Earls 10 A37
Winterbourne Gunner 10 A37
Winterbourne Monkton 20 D36
Winterbourne Steepleton 9 F32
Winterburn 56 D35
Wintercleuch 68 C25
Winteringham 59 G45
Winterley 49 G33
Wintersett 51 A39
Winterslow 10 A38
Winterton 52 A45
Winterton-on-Sea 45 D60
Winthorpe 52 G44
Winton *Cum.* 61 E33
Winton *Dor.* 10 E36
Winton *N.Y.* 62 G40
Wintour's Leap 19 B31

Wintringham 58 B44
Winwick *Cbs.* 42 G47
Winwick *Che.* 49 C32
Winwick *Nmp.* 31 A42
Wirksworth 50 G38
Wirswall 38 A31
Wisbech 43 E50
Wisbech St. Mary 43 E50
Wisborough Green 12 B46
Wiseton 51 D43
Wishaw *Str.* 74 E23
Wishaw *War.* 40 F37
Wisley 22 F46
Wispington 53 E48
Wissett 35 A59
Wistanstow 38 G30
Wistaston 49 G32
Wistaston Green 49 G32
Wiston *Dyf.* 16 C16
Wiston *Str.* 75 G25
Wistow *Cbs.* 43 G48
Wistow *N.Y.* 58 F41
Wiswell 56 F33
Witcham 43 G50
Witchampton 9 D35
Witchford 33 A51
Witham 34 G54
Witham Friary 20 G33
Witham on the Hill 42 D46
Witherenden 13 B52
Witheridge 7 D24
Witherley 41 F39
Withern 53 D50
Withernsea 59 G49
Withernwick 59 E47
Withersdale Street 45 G58
Withersfield 33 D52
Witherslack 55 A30
Withiel 3 B15
Withington *Che.* 49 F34
Withington *Glo.* 30 G36
Withington *G.M.* 49 C34
Withington *H.& W.* 28 D31
Withington *Shr.* 38 D31
Withington Green 49 E34
Withleigh 7 D25
Withnell 56 G32
Withybrook 41 G40
Withycombe 7 A26
Withycombe Raleigh 7 G26
Withyham 13 A50
Withypool 7 B24
Witley 12 A45
Witnesham 35 C57
Witney 30 G39
Wittering 42 E46
Wittersham 14 E55
Witton 81 C31
Witton Gilbert 62 B38
Witton le Wear 62 C37
Witton Park 62 C37
Wiveliscombe 7 C26
Wivelsfield 13 B49
Wivelsfield Green 13 B49
Wivenhoe 34 F56
Wivenhoe Cross 34 F56
Wiveton 44 A56
Wix 35 F57
Wixford 30 C36
Wixoe 34 D53
Woburn 32 E45
Woburn Sands 32 E45
Woking 22 F46
Wokingham 22 E44
Wolborough 5 C24
Woldingham 23 F49
Wold Newton *Hum.* 53 C48
Wold Newton *Hum.* 59 B46
Wolf Cleugh 61 B34
Wolfclyde 75 G26
Wolferton 44 C52
Wolfhill *Tay.* 81 G27
Wolf Hills 61 A33
Wolf's Castle 16 B15
Wolfsdale 16 B15
Woll 69 A30
Wollaston *Nmp.* 32 B45
Wollaston *Shr.* 38 D29
Wollaston *Stf.* 40 G34
Wollaton 41 B41
Wollerton 39 B32
Wolsingham 62 C36
Wolstanton 40 A34
Wolston 31 A40
Wolvercote 21 A40
Wolverhampton 40 F34
Wolverley 29 A34
Wolverton *Bkh.* 32 D44
Wolverton *Ham.* 21 F41
Wolverton *War.* 30 D38
Wolvesnewton 19 B30
Wolvey 41 G40
Wolviston 62 D40
Wombleton 58 A42
Wombourne 40 F34
Wombwell 51 B39
Womenswold 15 B58

Womersley 51 A41
Wonastow 28 G30
Wonersh 22 G46
Wonston 11 A40
Wooburn 22 C45
Wooburn Green 22 C45
Woodale 57 B36
Woodall Services 51 D40
Woodbank 48 E29
Woodbastwick 45 D59
Woodbeck 51 E43
Woodborough *Not.* 41 A42
Woodborough *Wts.* 20 E37
Woodbridge 35 D58
Woodbury 7 G26
Woodbury Salterton 7 G26
Woodchester 20 A34
Woodchurch *Kent* 14 D55
Woodchurch *Mer.* 48 D28
Woodcombe 7 A25
Woodcote 21 C42
Woodcott 21 F40
Woodcroft 19 B31
Wood Dalling 44 C56
Woodditton 33 C52
Woodeaton 31 G41
Woodend *Cum.* 60 E26
Wood End *Hfs.* 33 F49
Woodend *Ltn.* 75 C26
Woodend *Ltn.* 75 D25
Woodend *Nmp.* 31 D42
Wood End *War.* 30 A37
Wood Enderby 53 F48
Woodfalls 10 B37
Woodfields 56 F32
Woodford *G.L.* 23 B50
Woodford *Glo.* 19 B32
Woodford *G.M.* 49 D34
Woodford *Nmp.* 32 A45
Woodford Bridge 6 D19
Woodford Halse 31 C41
Woodgreen 10 C37
Woodhall *Ltn.* 76 C32
Woodhall *N.Y.* 62 G35
Woodhall Spa 52 F47
Woodham *Drm.* 62 D38
Woodham *Sry.* 22 E46
Woodham Ferrers 24 B53
Woodham Mortimer 24 A54
Woodham Walter 24 A54
Woodhaven 81 H30
Woodhead *Grm.* 85 F33
Woodhead *Grm.* 81 C32
Woodhill 39 G33
Woodhorn 71 E38
Woodhorn Demesne 71 E39
Woodhouse *Lei.* 41 D41
Woodhouse *S.Y.* 51 D40
Woodhouse Eaves 41 D41
Woodhouselees 69 F29
Woodhouse Mill 51 D40
Woodhouses *Che.* 48 E31
Woodhouses *G.M.* 49 B35
Woodhurst 33 A49
Woodingdean 13 D49
Woodland *Dev.* 5 D23
Woodland *Drm.* 62 D36
Woodland *Str.* 67 D17
Woodlands *D.& G.* 69 F26
Woodlands *Dor.* 10 D36
Woodlands *Ham.* 10 C39
Woodlands *S.Y.* 51 B41
Woodlands Park 22 D44
Wood Lane 38 B30
Woodleigh 5 F23
Woodlesford 57 G39
Woodley *Brk.* 22 D43
Woodley *G.M.* 49 C35
Woodmancote *Glo.* 29 F35
Woodmancote *Glo.* 20 A36
Woodmancote *W.S.* 13 C48
Woodmancott 21 G41
Woodmansey 59 F46
Woodmoor 38 E28
Woodnesborough 15 B59
Woodnewton 42 F46
Wood Norton 44 C56
Woodpark 70 F34
Woodplumpton 55 F30
Woodrising 44 E55
Woodseats 51 D39
Woodseaves 40 C34
Woodsetts 51 D41
Woodsford 9 E33
Woodside *Brk.* 22 D45
Woodside *D.& G.* 69 F26
Woodside *Grm.* 85 J35
Woodside *Tay.* 81 G27
Woodstock 31 G40
Woodstock Slop 16 B16
Wood Street 22 F45
Woodton 45 F58
Woodville 41 D39
Woodwalton 43 G48
Woodwick 89 E29
Woodyates 10 C36
Woofferton 28 B31

Wookey 19 G31
Wookey Hole 19 G31
Wool 9 F34
Woolacombe 6 A20
Woolaston 19 B31
Woolavington 19 G29
Woolbeding 12 B44
Wooler 70 A35
Woolfardisworthy 7 E24
Woolfardisworthy 6 C19
Woolfords Cottages 75 E26
Woolhampton 21 E41
Woolhope 29 E32
Woolland 9 D33
Woolley *Cbs.* 32 A47
Woolley *W.Y.* 51 A39
Woolmere Green 29 B35
Woolmer Green 33 G48
Woolpack 14 D54
Woolpit 34 B55
Woolscott 31 A42
Woolsthorpe *Lcn.* 42 C45
Woolsthorpe *Lcn.* 42 B44
Woolston *Che.* 49 D32
Woolston *Ham.* 11 C40
Woolstone 21 C38
Woolston Green 5 D23
Woolton 48 D30
Woolton Hill 21 E40
Woolverstone 35 E57
Woolverton 20 F33
Woolwich 23 D50
Woonton 28 C29
Wooperton 71 B36
Wooplaw 76 F30
Woore 39 A33
Wootton *Bfd.* 32 D46
Wootton *Hum.* 52 A46
Wootton *Kent* 15 C58
Wootton *Nmp.* 31 C43
Wootton *Oxf.* 31 G40
Wootton *Oxf.* 21 A40
Wootton *Stf.* 40 C34
Wootton *Stf.* 40 A37
Wootton Bassett 20 C36
Wootton Bridge 11 F41
Wootton Courtnay 7 A25
Wootton Fitzpaine 8 E29
Wootton Green 32 D45
Wootton Rivers 20 E37
Wootton St. Lawrence 21 F41
Wootton Wawen 30 B37
Worcester 29 C34
Wordsley 40 G34
Worfield 39 F33
Workington 60 D25
Worksop 51 E41
Worlaby 52 A46
World's End *Brk.* 21 D40
Worlds End *Ham.* 11 C42
Worle 19 E29
Worleston 49 G32
Worlingham 45 F60
Worlington 33 A52
Worlingworth 35 B58
Wormald Green 57 C39
Wormbridge *H.& W.* 28 E30
Wormbridge *Shr.* 39 D32
Wormegay 44 D52
Wormelow Tump 28 E30
Wormerlaw 76 F33
Wormhill 50 E37
Wormiehills 81 F32
Worminghford 34 E55
Worminghall 21 A42
Wormington 30 E36
Wormiston 75 F28
Wormit 81 H29
Wormleighton 31 C40
Wormley *Hfs.* 23 A49
Wormley *Sry.* 12 A45
Wormshill 14 B54
Wormsley 28 D30
Worplesdon 22 F45
Worrall 51 C39
Worsbrough 51 B39
Worsley 49 B33
Worstead 45 C59
Worsted Lodge 33 C51
Worsthorne 56 F34
Worston 56 E33
Worth *Kent* 15 B59
Worth *W.S.* 13 A49
Wortham 34 A56
Worthen 38 E29
Worthenbury 38 A30
Worthing *Nfk.* 44 D55
Worthing *W.S.* 12 D47
Worthington 41 C40
Worth Matravers 9 G35
Worting 21 F41
Wortley *Glo.* 20 B33
Wortley *S.Y.* 51 C39
Wortley *W.Y.* 57 F38

Worton *N.Y.* 56 A35
Worton *Wts.* 20 F35
Wortwell 45 G58
Wotton 22 G47
Wotton under Edge 20 B33
Wotton Underwood 31 G42
Woughton on the Green 32 E44
Wouldham 24 E53
Wrabness 35 E57
Wrafton 6 B20
Wragby *Lcn.* 52 E47
Wragby *W.Y.* 51 A40
Wramplingham 45 E57
Wrangaton 5 E22
Wrangle 53 G50
Wrangle Lowgate 53 G50
Wrantage 8 B29
Wrawby 52 B46
Wraxall 19 D30
Wray 56 C32
Wray Barton 7 G23
Wraysbury 22 D46
Wrayton 56 B32
Wrea Green 55 F29
Wreay 61 B30
Wrecclesham 22 G44
Wrekenton 62 A38
Wrelton 58 A43
Wrenbury 38 A31
Wreningham 45 F57
Wrentham 45 G60
Wrenthorpe 57 G39
Wressle 58 F43
Wrestlingworth 33 D48
Wretton 44 F52
Wrexham 48 G29
Wrexham Trading Estate 38 A29
Wribbenhall 29 A33
Wrightington Bar 48 A31
Wrinehill 39 A33
Wrington 19 E30
Writtle 24 A52
Wrockwardine 39 D32
Wroot 51 B43
Wrotham 23 F52
Wrotham Heath 23 F52
Wroughton 20 C37
Wroxall *I.o.W.* 11 F41
Wroxall *War.* 30 A38
Wroxeter 38 E31
Wroxham 45 D59
Wroxton 31 D40
Wyberton 43 A49
Wyboston 32 C47
Wybunbury 39 A32
Wychbold 29 B35
Wych Cross 13 A50
Wychnor 40 D37
Wyck Rissington 30 F37
Wycliffe 62 E37
Wyddial 33 E49
Wye 15 C56
Wyke 57 G37
Wykeham 59 A45
Wyke Marsh 9 B33
Wyken 41 G39
Wyke Regis 9 G32
Wykey 38 C29
Wylam 71 G37
Wylde Green 40 F37
Wylfa 46 C19
Wyllie 18 B27
Wylye 10 A36
Wymeswold 41 C42
Wymington 32 B45
Wymondham *Lei.* 42 D44
Wymondham *Nfk.* 45 E57
Wynford Eagle 8 E31
Wyre Piddle 29 D35
Wysall 41 C42
Wythall 40 A36
Wytham 21 A40
Wythburn 60 E29
Wythenshawe 49 D34
Wyton *Cbs.* 33 A48
Wyton *Hum.* 59 F47
Wyverstone 34 B56
Wyvis Lodge 83 B20

Y

Yaddlethorpe 52 B44
Yafforth 62 G39
Yair House 76 G30
Yalding 14 B53
Yanworth 30 G36
Yapham 58 D43
Yapton 12 D45
Yarburgh 53 C49
Yarcombe 8 D28
Yardley 40 G37
Yardley Gobion 31 D43
Yardley Hastings 32 C44
Yarkhill 29 D32

Yarlet Hall 40 C35
Yarlington 9 B32
Yarlsber 56 B33
Yarm 62 E40
Yarmouth 10 F39
Yarnacott 6 B22
Yarnbrook 20 F34
Yarnfield 40 B34
Yarnscombe 6 C21
Yarnton 31 G40
Yarpole 28 B30
Yarrow 69 A29
Yarrow Feus 69 A29
Yarwell 42 F46
Yate 20 C33
Yatesbury 20 D36
Yattendon 21 D41
Yatton *Avon* 19 E30
Yatton *H.& W.* 29 C32
Yatton *H.& W.* 28 B30
Yatton Keynell 20 D34
Yaverland 11 F42
Yaxham 44 D56
Yaxley *Cbs.* 42 F47
Yaxley *Sfk.* 35 A57
Yazor 28 D30
Yeading 22 C47
Yeadon 57 E38
Yealand Conyers 55 B31
Yealand Redmayne 55 B30
Yealmpton 5 E21
Yearby 63 D41
Yearsley 58 B41
Yeaton 38 D30
Yeaveley 40 A37
Yeavering 70 A35
Yedingham 58 B44
Yelling 33 B48
Yelvertoft 31 A41
Yelverton 5 D21
Yenston 9 B33
Yeoford 7 F23
Yeolmbridge 6 G19
Yeovil 8 C31
Yeovil Marsh 8 C31
Yeovilton 8 B31
Yerbeston 16 D16
Yesnaby 89 F28
Yetminster 8 C31
Yett 74 E23
Yettington 7 G26
Yetts of Muckart 80 K26
Y-Ffôr 36 B20
y-Ffrith 47 D26
Yielden 32 B46
Yieldshields 74 E24
Yiewsley 22 C46
Ynysboeth 18 B26
Ynysddu 18 B27
Ynysgyffylog 37 D22
Ynyshir 18 B26
Ynys Tachwedd 37 F22
Ynystawe 17 D22
Ynys-wen 18 B25
Ynysybwl 18 B26
Yockenthwaite 56 B35
Yockleton 38 D30
Yokefleet 58 G44
Yoker 74 D21
Yonder Bognie 85 E31
York 58 D41
Yorkletts 25 E56
Yorkley 19 A32
York Town 22 E44
Youlgreave 50 F38
Youlthorpe 58 D43
Youlton 57 C40
Young's End 34 G53
Yoxall 40 D37
Yoxford 35 B59
Y-Rhiw 36 C18
Ysbyty-Ifan 37 A24
Ysbyty Ystwyth 27 A23
Ysceifiog 47 E27
Ysgubor-y-coed 37 F22
Yspbty Cynfyn 27 A23
Ystalyfera 18 A23
Ystrad 18 B25
Ystradfellte 27 G25
Ystradffin 27 D23
Ystradgynlais 27 G23
Ystrad Meurig 27 B23
Ystradmynach 18 B27
Ystradowen 18 D26
Ythanbank 85 F35
Ythsie 85 F34

Z

Zeal Monachorum 7 E23
Zeals 9 A33
Zelah 3 C14
Zennor 2 E10

INDEX TO PLACE NAMES IN IRELAND

Aasleagh 92 B3
Abbey 93 C6
Abbeydorney 90 B3
Abbeyleix 94 B8
Achill Sound 92 B3
Aclare 92 A5
Adamstown 94 C9
Adare 91 A5
Adrigole 90 C3
Aghabullogue 91 C5
Aghada 92 B4
Aghagower 92 B4
Aghalee 97 B10
Aghanloo 96 A9
Aghavannagh 94 B10
Aghaville 90 C4
Aghern 91 B6
Aghleam 92 A2
Aghnacliff 93 B7
Aghnagar Br. 90 C2
Agivey 97 A9
Aglish 91 B7
Ahafona 90 A3
Ahakista 90 C3
Ahascragh 93 C6
Aghoghill 97 B10
Aldergrove 97 B10
Allen 94 A9
Allenwood 94 A9
Allihies 90 C2
An Cóbh *see Cobh*
An Muileann gCearr *see Mullingar*
An Nás *see Naas*
An tAonach *see Nenagh*
An tinbhear Mór *see Arklow*
Annacotty 91 A5
Annagassan 95 C10
Annagry 96 A6
Annalong 95 B11
Annascaul 90 B2
Annestown 91 C6
Annsborough 95 B11
Antrim 97 B10
Araglin 91 B6
Ardagh 90 B4
Ardara 96 B6
Ardattin 94 B9
Ardcath 95 C10
Ardee 95 C9
Ardfert 90 B3
Ardfinnan 91 B7
Ardglass 95 B11
Ardgroom 90 C3
Ardmore 91 C7
Ardnacrusha 91 A5
Ardpatrick 91 B5
Ardrahan 92 C5
Ardscull 94 A9
Ardstraw 96 B8
Arklow 94 B10
Arless 94 B8
Armagh 95 B9
Armoy 97 A10
Arthurstown 94 C9
Articlave 97 A9
Artigarvan 96 B8
Arva 93 B7
Ashbourne 95 C10
Ashford 94 A10
Ashford 90 B4
Askeaton 90 A5
Athboy 93 B9
Athea 90 B4
Athenry 93 C5
Athleague 93 B6
Athlone 93 C7
Athy 94 B9
Attymon 93 C5
Augher 96 C8
Aughnacloy 96 C9
Aughrim 93 C6
Aughrim 92 C5
Aughrim 94 B10
Avoca 94 B10

B
Baile Átha Luain *see Athlone*
Bailieborough 93 B9
Balbriggan 95 C10
Balintober 92 B4
Balla 92 B4
Ballaghaderreen 93 B5
Balleyliffen 96 A8
Ballickmoyler 94 B8
Ballina 91 B5
Ballina 92 A4
Ballinaboy 92 C2
Ballinafad 92 C6
Ballinagh 93 B8
Ballinagore 93 C8
Ballinakill 94 B8
Ballinalack 93 B8
Ballinalee 93 B7
Ballinamallard 96 C7
Ballinamona 91 B5
Ballinamore 96 C7
Ballinamult 91 B7
Ballinascarthy 91 C5
Ballinasloe 93 C6
Ballincollig 91 C5
Ballincrea 94 C8
Ballindine 92 B5
Ballineen 90 C5
Ballingarry 91 A7
Ballingarry 91 B5
Ballingeary 90 C4
Ballingurteen 90 C4
Ballinhassig 91 C5
Ballinlough 93 B5
Ballinrobe 92 B4
Ballinskelligs 90 C2
Ballinspittle 91 C5
Ballintober 93 B6
Ballintoy 97 A10
Ballintra 96 B6
Ballinure 91 A7
Ballisodare 96 C5
Ballivor 93 C9
Ballon 94 B9

Ballyagran 91 B5
Ballybay 96 C9
Ballybofey 96 B7
Ballyboghil 95 C10
Ballybogy 97 A9
Ballybrack 90 C2
Ballybrack 94 A10
Ballybrittas 93 C8
Ballybrophy 93 D7
Ballybunion 90 A3
Ballycahill 91 A7
Ballycallan 94 B8
Ballycanew 94 B10
Ballycarry 97 B11
Ballycastle 92 A4
Ballycastle 97 A10
Ballyclare 97 B11
Ballyclough 91 B5
Ballyconneely 92 C2
Ballyconnell 96 C7
Ballycotton 91 C6
Ballycroy 92 A3
Ballycumber 93 C7
Ballydangan 93 C6
Ballydavid 93 C6
Ballydehob 90 C4
Ballydesmond 90 B4
Ballydonegan 90 C2
Ballyduff 90 B3
Ballyduff 91 B6
Ballyfarnan 96 C6
Ballyferriter 90 B2
Ballyfin 93 C8
Ballyforan 93 C6
Ballygalley 97 B11
Ballygar 93 B6
Ballygawley 96 C8
Ballyglass 93 B5
Ballygowan 95 B11
Ballyhack 94 C9
Ballyhahill 90 A4
Ballyhaise 96 C8
Ballyhalbert 95 B12
Ballyhale 94 C8
Ballyhaunis 92 B5
Ballyhean 92 B4
Ballyheige 90 B3
Ballyhillin 96 A8
Ballyhooly 91 B6
Ballyjamesduff 93 B8
Ballykeeran 93 C7
Ballykelly 96 A8
Ballyknock 91 B6
Ballylanders 91 B6
Ballylaneen 94 C8
Ballylinan 94 B9
Ballylongford 90 A4
Ballymacarberry 91 B7
Ballymack 94 B8
Ballymacmangue 91 B7
Ballymacoda 91 C7
Ballymagorry 96 B8
Ballymahon 93 B7
Ballymakeery 90 C4
Ballymartin 95 B11
Ballymena 97 B10
Ballymoe 93 B6
Ballymoney 96 B8
Ballymoney 97 A9
Ballymore 93 C7
Ballymore Eustace 94 A9
Ballymote 96 C5
Ballymoyle 94 B10
Ballymurphy 94 B9
Ballymurry 93 B6
Ballynabolla 94 C9
Ballynacally 90 A4
Ballynacargy 93 B7
Ballynacelligott 90 B3
Ballynahinch 92 C3
Ballynahinch 95 B11
Ballyneety 90 A5
Ballynockan 94 A10
Ballynonty 91 A7
Ballynure 97 B11
Ballyporeen 91 B6
Ballyragget 94 B8
Ballyroan 94 B8
Ballyronan 97 B9
Ballytore 94 A9
Ballyvaughan 92 C4
Ballyvoy 97 A10
Ballywalter 97 B12
Ballyward 95 B10
Ballywilliam 94 C9
Balnamore 97 A9
Balrath 95 C10
Baltimore 90 D4
Baltinglass 94 B9
Baltray 95 C10
Banagher 93 C7
Banbridge 95 B11
Bandon 91 C5
Bangor 97 B11
Bangor Erris 92 A3
Bansha 91 B6
Banteer 91 B5
Bantry 90 C4
Barefield 90 A5
Barna 92 C4
Barnatra 92 A3
Barraduff 90 B4
Bawnboy 96 C7
Béal Átha na Sluaighe *see Ballinasloe*
Béal an Átha *see Ballina*
Bealaclugga 92 C4
Bealalaw Br. 90 C3
Beaufort 90 B3
Belclare 92 B5
Belclare 92 C5
Belcoo 96 C7
Belderrig 92 A3
Belfast 97 B11
Belgooly 91 C6
Bellaghy 97 B9
Bellahy 92 B5

Bellanagare 93 B6
Bellanaleck 96 C7
Bellavary 92 B4
Belleek 96 C6
Belleek 95 B10
Belmullet 92 A3
Beltra 96 C5
Beltra 92 B4
Belturbet 96 C8
Benburb 95 B9
Bennettsbridge 94 B8
Beragh 96 B8
Bessbrook 95 B10
Bettystown 95 C10
Binghamstown 92 A2
Birdhill 91 A6
Birr 93 C7
Blacklion 96 C7
Blackrock 95 C10
Blackwater 95 B9
Blackwater 94 C10
Blanchardstown 94 A10
Blarney 91 C5
Blessington 94 A9
Blue Ball 93 C7
Blueford 90 B4
Bodyke 93 D5
Boherbue 90 B4
Bohola 92 B4
Borris 94 B9
Borris-in-Ossory 93 D7
Borrisokane 93 A6
Borrisoleigh 91 A7
Boviel 97 B9
Boyle 93 B6
Bracknagh 93 C8
Brandon 90 B2
Bray 94 A10
Bré *see Bray*
Brideswell 93 C6
Bridgend 96 A8
Bridgetown 94 C9
Brittas 94 A10
Brittas Bay 94 B10
Broadford 91 A5
Broadford 90 B5
Brookeborough 96 C8
Broomfield 95 B9
Brosna 90 B4
Broughshane 97 B10
Bruff 91 B5
Bruree 91 B5
Bullaun 93 C5
Bunbeg 96 A6
Buncrana 96 A8
Bunclody 94 B9
Bundoran 96 C6
Bunmahon 94 C8
Bunnahowen 92 A3
Bunnanadden 96 C5
Bunnyconnellan 92 A4
Burnfoot 96 A8
Burren 92 C4
Burtonport 96 B6
Bushmills 97 A9
Butler's Bridge 96 C8
Butlerstown 91 C5
Buttevant 91 B5

C
Caherconlish 91 A6
Caherdaniel 90 C2
Cahir 91 B7
Cahirciveen 90 C2
Caisléan an Bharraigh *see Castlebar*
Caledon 95 B9
Callan 94 B8
Caltra 93 C6
Camaross 94 C9
Camolin 94 B10
Camp 90 B3
Campile 94 C9
Cappamore 91 A6
Cappawhite 91 A6
Cappoquin 91 B7
Carbury 94 A9
Carlanstown 95 C9
Carlingford 95 B10
Carlow 94 B9
Carna 92 C3
Carnagh 95 B9
Carndonagh 96 A8
Carnduff 97 A10
Carnew 94 B10
Carney 94 C9
Carnlough 97 B11
Carragh 94 A9
Carraig na Siúire *see Carrick-on-Suir*
Carraroe 92 C3
Carrick 96 B5
Carrick 94 C9
Carrick-on-Shannon 93 B6
Carrick-on-Suir 94 C8
Carrickbeg 94 C8
Carrickboy 93 B7
Carrickfergus 97 B11
Carrickmacross 95 C9
Carrickmore 96 B8
Carrig 93 C7
Carrigaholt 90 A3
Carrigaline 91 C6
Carrigallen 93 B7
Carriganimmy 90 C4
Carrigans 96 B8
Carrigart 96 A7
Carrigtohill 91 C6
Carrowkeel 96 A8
Carryduff 97 B11
Cashel 91 A7
Castlebar 92 B4
Castlebellingham 95 C10
Castleblakeney 93 C6
Castleblayney 95 B9
Castlebridge 94 C10
Castlecaulfield 97 B9
Castlecomer 94 B8

Castleconnell 91 A6
Castlecor 91 B5
Castledawson 97 B9
Castlederg 96 B7
Castledermot 94 B9
Castleellis 94 C10
Castlefinn 96 B7
Castlegregory 90 B2
Castleisland 90 B4
Castlemaine 90 B3
Castlemartyr 91 C6
Castleplunket 93 B6
Castlepollard 93 B8
Castlerea 93 B6
Castlerock 97 A9
Castleroe 97 A9
Castletown 93 C8
Castletown 93 D8
Castletown Bere 90 C3
Castletownroche 91 B6
Castletownshend 90 C4
Castlewellan 95 B11
Causeway 90 B3
Cavan 96 C8
Cavanagarven 96 C9
Ceanannus Mór 93 B9
Ceatharlach *see Carlow*
Celbridge 94 A9
Charlemont 95 B9
Charlestown 92 B5
Cheekpoint 94 C9
Churchtown 94 C9
Churchtown 94 C10
Cill Airne *see Killarney*
Cill Chainnigh *see Kilkenny*
Cill Mhantáin *see Wicklow*
Clady 96 B7
Clady 97 B9
Clanabogan 96 B8
Clane 94 A9
Clara 93 C7
Clarecastle 90 A5
Clareen 93 C7
Claregalway 92 C5
Claremorris 92 B5
Clarinbridge 92 C5
Clashmore 91 B7
Claudy 96 B8
Clifden 92 C2
Cliffoney 96 C6
Clogh 94 B8
Clogh 94 B10
Cloghan 96 B7
Cloghan 93 B8
Cloghan 93 C7
Clogheen 91 B6
Clogheen 91 B7
Clogher 96 C8
Clogherhead 95 C10
Cloghy 95 B12
Clohamon 94 B9
Clonakilty 91 C5
Clonard 93 B8
Clonaslee 93 C7
Clonbern 93 B5
Clonbullogue 93 C8
Clonbur 92 B4
Clondalkin 94 A10
Clonea 94 C8
Clonee 94 A10
Clonegal 94 B9
Clones 94 C8
Clonfert 93 C6
Clonmany 96 A8
Clonmel 91 B7
Clonmellon 93 B8
Clonmore 94 B9
Clonmore 91 A7
Clonoulty 91 A7
Clonroche 94 C9
Clontarf 94 A10
Clontibret 95 B9
Clonygowan 93 C8
Cloonacool 96 B5
Cloonbannin 90 B4
Cloone 93 B7
Cloonfad 92 B5
Cloonkeen 92 B5
Cloonlara 91 A5
Clough 95 B11
Clough Mills 97 A10
Cloughjordan 93 D6
Cloyne 91 C6
Cluain Meala *see Clonmel*
Coachford 91 C5
Coagh 97 B9
Coalisland 97 B9
Cobh 91 C6
Coleraine 97 A9
Collaney 96 C5
Collon 95 C10
Collooney 96 C5
Collorus 90 C3
Comber 97 B11
Cong 92 B4
Conlig 97 B11
Connor 97 B10
Convoy 96 B7
Cookstown 97 B9
Coolbawn 93 D6
Coole 93 B8
Coolgreany 94 B10
Coolmore 96 B6
Coolock 94 A10
Cooraclare 90 A4
Cootehill 96 C8
Coppeen 90 C5
Cork 91 C6
Corkey 97 A10
Cornafulla 93 C7
Cornamona 92 B4
Corofin 92 D4
Costello 92 C3
Courtmacsherry 91 C5
Courtown Harbour 94 B10
Craanford 94 B10
Craig 96 B8

Craigavad 97 B11
Craigavon 95 B10
Cratloe 91 A5
Craughwell 92 C5
Crawfordsburn 97 B11
Creegh 90 A4
Creeslough 96 A7
Creggan 96 B8
Creggs 93 B6
Crinkill 93 C7
Croagh 91 A5
Crockets Town 92 A4
Cromane 90 B3
Crooked Wood 93 B8
Crookhaven 90 D3
Crookstown 91 C5
Croom 91 A5
Cross 92 B4
Crossbarry 91 C5
Crossdoney 93 B8
Crossgar 95 B11
Crosshaven 91 C6
Crosskeys 93 C8
Crossmaglen 95 B9
Crossmolina 92 A4
Crossnakiel 93 B8
Crumlin 97 B10
Crusheen 92 D5
Culdaff 96 A8
Cullahill 91 A8
Cullaville 95 B9
Culleens 92 A4
Cullybackey 97 B10
Cullyhanna 95 B9
Culmore 96 A8
Cummer 92 C5
Curracloe 94 C10
Curragh 94 A9
Curraglass 91 B6
Curry 92 B5
Cushendall 97 A10
Cushendun 97 A10
Cushina 93 C8

D
Daingean 93 C8
Dalkey 94 A10
Dalystown 93 C6
Darby's Br. 90 B2
Darkley 95 B9
Darragh 90 A4
Delgany 94 A10
Delvin 93 B8
Dernacreeve 96 C7
Derrybeg 96 A6
Derrybrian 93 C5
Derrygonnelly 96 C7
Derrylin 96 C7
Derrymore 90 B3
Derrynawilt 96 C8
Derryrush 92 C3
Derrytrasna 95 B10
Dervock 97 A10
Desertmartin 97 B9
Dingle 90 B2
Doagh 97 B10
Dolla 91 A6
Donabate 95 D10
Donadea 94 A9
Donagh 96 C8
Donaghadee 97 B11
Donaghcloney 95 B10
Donaghmore 97 B9
Donaghmore 91 A7
Donard 94 A9
Donegal 96 B6
Doneraile 91 B5
Donohill 91 A6
Doochary 96 B6
Doon 91 A6
Doonbeg 90 A3
Douglas 91 C6
Douglas Bridge 96 B8
Downpatrick 95 B11
Dowra 96 C6
Drangan 91 A7
Draperstown 97 B9
Drimoleague 90 C4
Drinagh 90 C4
Dripsey 91 C5
Drogheda 95 C10
Droichead Átha *see Drogheda*
Droichead Nua 94 A9
Dromahair 96 C6
Dromard 96 C5
Dromard 95 B10
Dromin 95 C10
Dromina 91 B5
Dromiskin 95 C10
Drommahane 91 B5
Dromod 93 B7
Dromore 96 B8
Dromore 95 B10
Dromore West 96 C5
Drum 96 C8
Drumahoe 96 B8
Drumaness 95 B11
Drumbilla 95 B10
Drumcard 96 C7
Drumcliff 96 C5
Drumcollogher 91 B5
Drumcondra 94 A10
Drumconrath 95 C9
Drumfree 96 A8
Drumkeeran 96 C6
Drumlish 93 B7
Drumquin 96 B8
Drumshanbo 96 C6
Drumsna 93 B6
Duagh 90 B4
Dublin 94 A10
Dugort 92 A2
Duleek 95 C10
Dun Dealgan *see Dundalk*

Dún Garbhán *see Dungarvan*
Dún Laoghaire 94 A10
Dunboyne 95 D10
Duncannon 94 C9
Duncannon Br. 90 B4
Duncormick 94 C9
Dundalk 95 C10
Dundalk 95 B11
Dundonald 97 B11
Dundonnell 93 C6
Dundrum 95 B11
Dundrum 91 A6
Dundrum 94 A10
Dunfanaghy 96 A7
Dungannon 97 B9
Dungarvan 94 B8
Dungarvan 91 B7
Dungiven 96 B9
Dungloe 96 B6
Dungourney 91 C6
Dunkerrin 93 D7
Dunkineely 96 B6
Dunkitt 94 C8
Dunlavin 94 A9
Dunleer 95 C10
Dunloy 97 A10
Dunmanway 90 C4
Dunmore 92 B5
Dunmore East 94 C9
Dunmurry 97 B11
Dunnamanagh 96 B8
Dunnamore 96 B9
Dunquin 90 B2
Dunshaughlin 95 C9
Durlas *see Thurles*
Durrow 94 B8
Durrus 90 C3
Dyan 95 B9
Dysart 94 A9

E
Easky 92 A5
Edenderry 93 C8
Ederney 96 B7
Edgeworthstown 93 B7
Eglinton 96 A8
Elphin 93 B6
Elton 91 B6
Emly 91 B6
Emmoo 93 B6
Emyvale 96 C9
Enfield 94 A9
Ennis 90 A5
Enniscorthy 94 B9
Enniskean 91 C5
Enniskerry 94 A10
Enniskillen 96 C7
Ennistymon 92 D4
Eochaill *see Youghal*
Errill 91 A7
Eyeries 90 C3
Eyrecourt 93 C6

F
Fahan 96 A8
Falcarragh 96 A6
Farranfore 90 B3
Feakle 93 D5
Fedamore 91 A5
Feeny 96 B8
Fenagh 96 C7
Fenagh 94 B9
Fenit 90 B3
Ferbane 93 C7
Fermoy 91 B6
Ferns 94 B9
Ferrybank 94 B10
Fethard 94 C9
Fethard 91 B7
Fiddown 94 C8
Finnea 93 B8
Fintona 96 C8
Fintown 96 B6
Finuge 90 B3
Fivemiletown 96 C8
Flagmount 93 D5
Fontstown 94 A9
Ford 94 B10
Forkhill 95 B10
Foxford 92 B4
Foygh 93 B7
Foynes 90 A4
Freemount 91 B5
Frenchpark 93 B6
Freshford 94 B8
Furraleigh 91 B8

G
Gaillimh *see Galway*
Galbally 91 B6
Galmoy 91 A7
Galros 93 C7
Galway 92 C4
Garlowcross 95 C9
Garrison 96 C6
Garristown 95 C10
Garvagh 97 B9
Garvagh 93 B7
Garvaghy 96 C8
Gaybrook 93 C8
Geashill 93 C8
Gerahies 90 C3
Gilford 95 B10
Glandore 90 C4
Glanmire 91 C6
Glanworth 91 B6
Glarryford 97 B10
Glashabeg 90 B2
Glaslough 96 C9
Glassan 93 C7
Glenamaddy 93 B5
Glenamoy 92 A3
Glenariff 97 A10
Glenarm 97 B11
Glenavy 97 B10
Glenbeigh 90 B3
Glencolumbkille 96 B5
Glencullen 94 A10
Glenealy 94 B10
Gleneely 96 A8

Glenfarne 96 C7
Glengarriff 90 C3
Glengavlen 96 C7
Glenmore Kilkeny 94 C8
Glennagevlagh 92 B3
Glenties 96 B6
Glenville 91 B6
Glin 90 A4
Glinsk 92 C3
Gloghane 90 B2
Glounthaune 91 C6
Glynn 97 B11
Glynn 94 C9
Golden 91 B7
Goleen 90 D3
Goresbridge 94 B9
Gorey 94 B10
Gormanston 95 C10
Gort 92 C5
Gortahork 96 A6
Gorteen 93 C5
Gorteen 91 B7
Gorteeny 93 C6
Gortin 96 B8
Gowran 94 B8
Gracehill 97 B10
Graiguenamanagh 94 B9
Graigue 94 B9
Granard 93 B8
Grange 96 C5
Grange 95 C10
Grange 94 B8
Grange 91 C7
Grangebellow 95 C10
Grangeford 94 B9
Greencastle 96 A9
Greencastle 96 B8
Greencastle 95 B10
Greenisland 97 B11
Greenore 95 B10
Greyabbey 97 B11
Greystones 94 A10
Groomsport 97 B11
Gurteen 93 B6
Gweedore 96 A6
Gweesalia 92 A3
H
Hacketstown 94 B9
Halltown 95 C9
Hamiltonsbawn 95 B9
Headford 92 C4
Helen's Bay 97 B11
Herbertstown 91 A6
Hillsborough 95 B10
Hilltown 95 B10
Hollyford 91 A6
Hollymount 92 B4
Hollywood 94 A9
Holycross 91 A7
Holywood 97 B11
Horseleap 93 C7
Horseleap Cross Roads 93 C5
Hospital 91 B6
Howth 94 A10
Hurler's Cross 91 A5
I
Inagh 92 D4
Inch 94 B10
Inch 90 B3
Inchigeelagh 90 C4
Inis Córthaidh see Enniscorthy
Inis see Ennis
Inistioge 94 C8
Inniscrone 92 A4
Innishannon 91 C5
Inniskeen 95 B9
Inver 96 B6
Inverin 92 C4
Irvinestown 96 C7
J
Jamestown 93 B6
Johnstown 91 A7
Johnstown Bridge 94 A9
Jonesborough 95 B10
Julianstown 95 C10
K
Kanturk 91 B5
Keadue 96 C6
Keady 95 B9
Kealkill 90 C4
Keel 92 B2
Keenagh 93 B7
Kells 97 B10
Kells 94 B8
Kenmare 90 C3
Kerrykeel 96 A7
Kesh 96 B7
Kilargue 96 C6
Kilbaha 90 A3
Kilbeggan 93 C8
Kilbehenny 91 B6
Kilberry 95 C9
Kilberry 93 C8
Kilbride 95 D10
Kilbride 94 B10
Kilbrittain 91 C5
Kilcar 96 B5
Kilchreest 93 C5
Kilcock 94 A9
Kilcolgan 92 C5
Kilconnell 93 C6
Kilconny 96 C8
Kilcoole 94 A10
Kilcormac 93 C7
Kilcrohane 90 C3
Kilcullen 94 A9
Kildalkey 93 B9
Kildare 94 A9
Kildavin 94 B9
Kildavin 94 B9
Kildorrey 91 B6
Kildress 97 B9
Kildysart 90 A4
Kilfenora 92 D4
Kilfinane 91 B6
Kilgarvan 90 C4

Kilgowan 94 A9
Kilkea 94 B9
Kilkee 90 A3
Kilkeel 95 B11
Kilkenny 94 B8
Kilkerrin 93 B5
Kilkieran 92 C3
Kilkinlea 90 B4
Kill 94 A9
Kill 94 C8
Killadeas 96 C7
Killadoon 92 B3
Killala 92 A4
Killann 94 B9
Killarney 90 B3
Killateeaun 92 B4
Killavullen 91 B5
Killeigh 93 C8
Killen 96 B7
Killena 94 B10
Killenaule 91 A7
Killerig 94 B9
Killeshandra 96 C7
Killeter 96 B7
Killimer 90 A4
Killimor 93 C6
Killinaboy 92 D4
Killinchy 95 B11
Killinick 94 C10
Killough 95 B11
Killurin 94 C9
Killybegs 96 B6
Killyclougher 96 B8
Killygordon 96 B7
Killylea 95 B9
Killyleagh 95 B11
Kilmacanogue 94 A10
Kilmacrennan 96 A7
Kilmaganny 94 C8
Kilmaine 92 B4
Kilmaley 90 A4
Kilmallock 91 B5
Kilmanagh 94 B8
Kilmeague 94 A9
Kilmeedy 91 B5
Kilmihill 90 A4
Kilmona 91 C5
Kilmore Quay 94 C9
Kilmurry 91 A5
Kilmurry McMahon 90 A4
Kilnaleck 93 B8
Kilrane 94 C10
Kilrea 97 B9
Kilreekill 93 C6
Kilronan 92 C3
Kilross 91 B6
Kilrush 90 A4
Kilsaran 95 C10
Kilsheelan 91 B7
Kiltartan 92 C5
Kiltealy 94 B9
Kilteel 94 B10
Kiltimagh 92 B5
Kiltoom 93 C6
Kiltormer 93 C6
Kiltulla 93 C5
Kiltyclogher 96 C6
Kilwaughter 97 B11
Kilworth 91 B6
Kingscourt 95 C9
Kinlough 96 C6
Kinnegad 93 C8
Kinnitty 93 C7
Kinsale 91 C5
Kinsalebeg 91 C7
Kinvara 92 C5
Kirkcubbin 95 B11
Kiltegan 94 B9
Knightstown 90 C2
Knock 92 B5
Knock 90 A4
Knockananna 94 B10
Knockanarrigan 94 B9
Knockanevin 91 B6
Knockbrandon 94 B10
Knockbrett 91 A7
Knockcroghery 93 B6
Knocklong 93 B6
Knockmore 92 A4
Knocknaboul 90 B4
Knocknagashel 90 B4
Knocknagree 90 B4
Knocknalina 92 A3
Knocktopher 94 C8
L
Labasheeda 90 A4
Lack 96 B7
Lagavara 97 A10
Laghey 96 B6
Laghtgeorge 92 C5
Lahardane 92 A4
Lahinch 92 D4
Lanesborough 93 B7
Laragh 94 A10
Larne 97 B11
Lauragh 90 C3
Laurencetown 93 C6
Lawrencetown 95 B10
Leap 90 C4
Leckaun 96 C6
Leecarrow 93 B6
Leenane 92 B3
Leitrim 96 C6
Leixlip 94 A10
Lemybrien 91 B7
Letterbreen 96 C7
Letterfrack 92 B3
Letterkenny 96 B7
Lettermacaward 96 B6

Lettermullan 92 C3
Lifford 96 B8
Limavady 96 A9
Limerick 91 A5
Lisacul 93 B5
Lisbellaw 96 C7
Lisburn 97 B10
Liscarney 92 B3
Liscarroll 91 B5
Liscolman 97 A10
Lisdoonvarna 92 C4
Lismore 91 B7
Lisnakill 94 C8
Lisnarrick 96 C7
Lisnaskea 96 C8
Lispole 90 B2
Lisryan 93 B8
Lissatinnig Br. 90 C3
Lissycasey 90 A4
Listerlin 94 C8
Listowel 90 B4
Littleton 91 A7
Lixnaw 90 B3
Loch Garman see Wexford
Loch Gowna 93 B7
Loghill 90 A4
Londonderry 96 A8
Longford 93 B7
Loughbrickland 95 B10
Loughgall 95 B9
Loughglinn 93 B5
Loughlinisland 95 B11
Loughlinstown 94 A10
Loughrea 93 C5
Louisburgh 92 B3
Louth 95 C9
Lower Ballinderry 97 B10
Lucan 94 A10
Lukeswell 94 C8
Lurgan 95 B10
Lusk 95 C10
Lyracrumpane 90 B4
M
Maam 92 B3
Maam Cross 92 C3
Maas 96 B6
Macosquin 97 A9
Macroom 90 C5
Maghera 97 B9
Magherafelt 97 B9
Magheralin 95 B10
Magheramason 96 B8
Maghery 97 B9
Magilligan 96 A8
Maguiresbridge 96 C8
Mahoonagh 90 B4
Mala see Mallow
Malahide 95 D10
Malin 96 A8
Malin More 96 B5
Mallow 91 B5
Manorcunningham 96 B7
Manorhamilton 96 C6
Manulla 92 B4
Markethill 95 B9
Maynooth 94 A9
Mayo 92 B4
Mayobridge 95 B10
Meentullynagarn 96 B6
Meigh 95 B10
Middletown 95 B9
Midleton 91 C6
Mile House 94 B9
Milestone 91 A6
Milford 96 A7
Milford 96 B9
Milford 91 B5
Millbrook 93 B8
Millisle 97 B11
Millstreet 90 B4
Millstreet 91 B7
Milltown 96 C8
Milltown 95 B10
Milltown 92 B5
Milltown 94 A9
Milltown 90 B2
Milltown 90 B3
Milltown Malbay 92 D4
Minane Br. 91 C6
Mine Head 91 C7
Mitchelstown 91 B6
Moate 93 C7
Mohil 93 B7
Mohill 94 B8
Moira 95 B10
Monaghan 96 C9
Monasterevan 93 C8
Moneygall 91 A5
Moneymore 97 B9
Moneyneany 97 B9
Moneyreagh 97 B11
Monivea 93 C5
Montpelier 91 A6
Mooncoin 94 C8
Moone 94 B9
Moorfields 97 B10
Morley's Br. 90 C4
Moss-side 97 A10
Mossley 97 B11
Mount Bellew 93 C6
Mount Hamilton 96 B8
Mount Norris 95 B10
Mount Nugent 93 B8
Mount Talbot 93 B6
Mountcharles 96 B6
Mountjoy 96 B8
Mountmellick 93 C8
Mountrath 93 C8
Mountshannon 93 D6
Moville 96 A8
Moy 95 B9
Moyard 92 B2
Moyasta 90 A3
Moycullen 92 C4
Moyett 93 B8

Moygashel 95 B9
Moygawnagh 92 A4
Moylough 93 C5
Moynalty 93 B9
Moyne 93 B7
Moyvalley 94 A9
Moyvore 93 B7
Moyvoughly 93 C7
Muckross 90 B4
Muff 96 A8
Muine Bheag 94 B9
Muineachán see Monaghan
Mullagh 93 B9
Mullagh 90 A4
Mullaghmore 96 C6
Mullaghroe 93 B6
Mullan 96 C7
Mullany's Cross 96 C5
Mullinahone 91 A7
Mullinavat 94 C8
Mullingar 93 B8
Mulrany 92 B3
Mungret 91 A5
Murrogh 92 C4
Myshall 94 B9
N
Naas 94 A9
Narin 96 B6
Naul 95 C10
Navan 95 C9
Neale 92 B4
Nenagh 91 A6
New Birmingham 91 A7
New Buildings 96 B8
New Inn 93 C8
New Inn Tiperary 91 B7
New Kildimo 91 A5
New Ross 94 C9
Newbliss 96 C8
Newbridge 93 B6
Newbridge 90 A5
Newbridge see Droichhead Nua
Newcastle 94 A10
Newcastle 91 B7
Newcastle 95 B11
Newcastle West 90 B4
Newgrange 95 C10
Newmarket 91 B5
Newmarket 94 C8
Newmarket-on-Fergus 91 A5
Newport 92 B3
Newport 91 A6
Newport Trench 97 B9
Newry 95 B11
Newtown 94 C9
Newtown 91 B6
Newtown Cromwellin 97 B10
Newtownabbey 97 B11
Newtownards 97 B11
Newtownbutler 96 C8
Newtowncunningham 96 B7
Newtownforbes 93 B7
Newtowngore 96 C7
Newtownhamilton 95 B9
Newtownmountkennedy 94 A10
Newtownstewart 96 B8
Ninemilehouse 91 B8
Nobber 95 C9
Nohoval 91 C6
North Ring 91 C5
Nurney 94 A9
Nutt's Corner 97 B10
O
O'Briensbridge 91 A5
Old Leighlin 94 B8
Oldcastle 93 B8
Oldtown 95 C10
Omagh 96 B8
Omeath 95 B10
Oola 91 A6
Oran 93 B6
Oranmore 92 C5
Oristown 95 C9
Oughterard 92 C4
Oulart 94 B10
Ovens 91 C5
Owenbeg 92 A5
Oylgate 94 C9
P
Pallas Green 91 A6
Pallaskenry 91 A5
Palmerston 94 A10
Park 96 B8
Parknasilla 92 C3
Partry 92 B4
Passage East 94 C9
Passage West 91 C6
Patrickswell 91 A5
Pettigoe 96 B7
Piltown 94 C8
Plumbridge 96 B8
Pomeroy 96 B9
Pontoon 92 B4
Port Láirge see Waterford
Portacloy 92 A3
Portadown 95 B11
Portaferry 95 B11
Portarlington 93 C8
Portavogie 95 B12
Portballintrae 97 A9
Portglenone 97 B10
Portland 95 D6
Portlaoise 93 C8
Portland 95 D6
Portlaw 94 C8
Portlurin 92 A3
Portmagee 90 C2
Portmarnock 95 D10
Portmuck 97 B11
Portnoo 96 B6
Portrane 95 D10
Portroe 91 A6
Portrush 97 A9
Portsalon 96 A7
Portstewart 97 A9
Portumna 93 C6
Poulgorm Br. 90 C4

Power's Cross 93 C6
Poyntz Pass 95 B10
Prosperous 94 A9
Puckane 93 D6
Q
Quin 91 A5
R
Ramelton 96 A7
Randalstown 97 B10
Raphoe 96 B7
Rasharkin 97 B10
Rath 93 C7
Rathangan 94 A9
Rathconrath 93 B7
Rathcoole 94 A9
Rathcormac 91 B6
Rathdangan 94 B9
Rathdowney 91 A7
Rathdrum 94 B10
Rathfarnham 94 A10
Rathfriland 95 B10
Rathgormuck 91 B7
Rathkeale 91 A5
Rathkeevin 91 B7
Rathlackan 92 A4
Rathlee 92 A4
Rathluirc 91 B5
Rathmolyon 95 D9
Rathmore 90 B4
Rathmullen 96 A7
Rathnew 94 B10
Rathnure 94 C9
Rathowen 93 B7
Rathvilly 94 B9
Ratoath 95 C10
Reanagowan 91 B7
Rear Cross 91 A6
Recess 92 C3
Redcross 94 B10
Redhills 96 C8
Rhode 93 C8
Richhill 95 B9
Ring 91 B7
Ringaskiddy 91 C6
Ringsend 97 B11
Riverstown 96 C6
Riverstown 91 C6
Robertstown 94 A9
Rochfortbridge 93 C8
Rockchapel 90 B4
Rockcorry 96 C8
Rockhill 91 B5
Rooksy 93 B7
Rosapenna 96 A7
Rosbeg 95 B5
Rosbercon 94 C9
Roscommon 93 B6
Roscrea 93 D7
Rosegreen 91 B7
Rosenallis 93 C8
Rosmuck 92 C3
Ross Carbery 90 C4
Rosscahill 92 C4
Rossduff 94 C8
Rosses Point 96 C5
Rossinver 96 C6
Rosslare 94 C10
Rosslare Harbour 94 C10
Rosslea 96 C8
Rossnowlagh 96 B6
Rostellan 91 C6
Rostrevor 95 B10
Roundstone 92 C3
Roundwood 94 A10
Rush 95 C10
S
Saggart 94 A10
Saintfield 95 B11
St. Johnston 96 B8
Saliahig 90 C2
Sallins 94 A9
Salthill 92 C4
Saul 95 B11
Scarriff 93 D5
Scartaglen 90 B4
Scarva 95 B10
Scotch Corner 97 C9
Scotstown 96 C8
Scramoge 93 B6
Screeb 92 C3
Screggan 93 C7
Scribbagh 96 C6
Seapatrick 95 B10
Shanacrane 90 C4
Shanagarry 91 C6
Shanagolden 90 A4
Shanavogh 90 A4
Shannon 91 A5
Shannonbridge 93 C6
Shantonagh 95 B9
Shanvus 96 C6
Sharavogue 95 D10
Shercock 93 B9
Shillelagh 94 B9
Shinrone 93 D7
Shrigley 95 B11
Shrule 92 B4
Silvermines 91 A6
Sion Mills 96 B8
Six Road Ends 97 B11
Sixmilebridge 91 A5
Sixmilecross 96 B8
Skerries 95 C10
Skibbereen 90 C4
Slane 95 C9
Sligeach see Sligo
Sligo 96 C6
Smithborough 96 C8
Snave Br. 90 C4
Sneem 90 C3
Spa 96 B7
Spiddle 92 C4
Spink 94 B9
Srah 92 B4
Stamullen 95 C10

Stewartstown 97 B9
Stillorgan 94 A10
Stoneyford 94 B8
Strabane 96 B8
Stradbally 93 C8
Stradbally 90 B2
Stradbally 91 B8
Stradone 93 B8
Straffan 94 A9
Strandhill 96 C5
Strandhill 96 C5
Strangford 95 B11
Stranocum 97 A10
Stranorlar 96 B7
Stratford 94 B9
Strokestown 93 B6
Summerhill 95 D9
Swan 94 B8
Swanlinbar 96 C7
Swatragh 97 B9
Swinford 92 B5
Swords 95 D10
T
Taghmon 94 C9
Tallaght 94 A10
Tallanstown 95 C9
Tallow 91 B6
Tallowbridge 91 B7
Tamney 96 A7
Tandragee 95 B10
Tang 93 B7
Tarbert 90 A4
Tassagh 95 B9
Templeboy 96 C5
Templederry 96 C5
Templemore 91 A7
Templenoe 90 C3
Templepatrick 97 B10
Templetuohy 91 A7
Tempo 96 C8
Terenure 94 A10
Termonfeckin 95 C10
Terryglass 93 C6
The Harrow 94 B10
The Loup 97 B9
The Sheddings 97 B10
Thomastown 94 B8
Thurles 91 A7
Timahoe 94 A9
Timahoe 94 B8
Timoleague 91 C5
Timolin 94 B9
Tinahely 94 B10
Tipperary 91 B6
Tober 93 C7
Tobermore 97 B9
Toberscanavan 96 C6
Togher 95 C10
Togher 93 C7
Togher 90 C4
Tomgraney 93 D5
Toombeola 92 C3
Toomebridge 97 B10
Toomevara 91 A6
Toormore 90 C3
Tower 91 C5
Trá Lí see Tralee
Trá Mhór see Tramore
Tralee 90 B3
Tramore 94 C8
Trillick 96 C8
Trim 95 C9
Trory 96 C7
Tuam 92 B5
Tubbercurry 96 C5
Tulach Mhór see Tullamore
Tulla 91 A5
Tullamore 93 C8
Tullaroan 94 B8
Tullow 94 B9
Tully 96 C7
Tully 96 C8
Tullyallen 95 C10
Tullyhogue 97 B9
Tulsk 93 B6
Twomileborris 91 A7
Tydavnet 96 C8
Tyholland 97 C9
Tyrrellspass 93 C8
U
Union Hall 90 C4
Upper Ballinderry 97 B10
Upperchurch 91 A6
Upperlands 97 B9
Urlingford 91 A7
V
Valleymount 94 A9
Ventry 90 B2
Vicarstown 93 C8
Villierstown 91 B7
Virginia 93 B8
W
Waringstown 95 B10
Warrenpoint 95 B10
Waterford 94 C8
Watergrasshill 91 B6
Waterside 96 B8
Waterville 90 C2
Wattlebridge 96 C8
Wellington Br. 94 C9
Westport 92 B3
Westport Quay 92 B3
Wexford 94 C10
Whitecross 95 B10
Whitegate 91 C6
Whitehall 94 B8
Whitehead 97 B11
Whitehouse 97 B11
Wicklow 94 B10
Wilkinstown 95 C9
Windgap 94 C8
Windmill Cross 94 A9
Woodenbridge 94 B10
Woodford 93 C6
Woodtown 95 C9
Y
Youghal 91 C7